The Handbook of Interior Design

The Handbook
of Interior Design

Edited by

Jo Ann Asher Thompson and
Nancy H. Blossom

WILEY Blackwell

This edition first published 2015
© 2015 John Wiley & Sons, Ltd

Registered Office
John Wiley & Sons Ltd, The Atrium, Southern Gate, Chichester, West Sussex, PO19 8SQ, UK

Editorial Offices
350 Main Street, Malden, MA 02148-5020, USA
9600 Garsington Road, Oxford, OX4 2DQ, UK
The Atrium, Southern Gate, Chichester, West Sussex, PO19 8SQ, UK

For details of our global editorial offices, for customer services, and for information about how to apply for permission to reuse the copyright material in this book please see our website at www.wiley.com/wiley-blackwell.

The right of Jo Ann Asher Thompson and Nancy H. Blossom to be identified as the authors of the editorial material in this work has been asserted in accordance with the UK Copyright, Designs and Patents Act 1988.

Library of Congress Cataloging-in-Publication Data
The handbook of interior design / edited by Jo Ann Asher Thompson and Nancy H. Blossom.
    pages cm
   Summary: "The Handbook of Interior Design offers a compilation of current ways of thinking that inform the discipline of interior design" – Provided by publisher.
   Includes bibliographical references and index.
   ISBN 978-1-4443-3628-3 (hardback)
  1. Interior architecture.   2. Interior architecture–Philosophy.   3. Interior decoration.   4. Interior decoration–Philosophy.   I. Thompson, Jo Ann Asher, 1948– editor.   II. Blossom, Nancy H., editor.
NA2850.H365 2014
729–dc23

                   2014018382

A catalogue record for this book is available from the British Library.

Cover image: Photo of Tietgenkollegiet, Ørestad Nord, near Copenhagen, Denmark. Interior design by Aggebo & Henriksen. Photo © OLE AKHØJ

Set in 10.5/13 pt MinionPro by Toppan Best-set Premedia Limited

1   2015

Contents

Notes on Contributors   viii

Preface   xv

Introduction: The Shaping of Interior Design   1

SECTION I   EXPLORATIONS OF THE HISTORY OF INTERIOR DESIGN   9

1 An Overview of Phenomenology for the Design Disciplines   11
David Wang

2 Dorothy Draper and the American Housewife: A Study of Class Values and Success   29
John C. Turpin

3 The Political Interior   46
Mary Anne Beecher

4 Taylorizing the Modern Interior: Counter-Origins   58
Ronn M. Daniel

5 Bringing the Past In: Narrative Inquiry and the Preservation of Historic Interiors   70
Erin Cunningham

SECTION II   PERSPECTIVES ON THE PRACTICE OF INTERIOR DESIGN   95

6 Aesthetic Coding in Interior Design   97
Mads Nygaard Folkmann

Contents

7 Toward a Creative Ecology of Workplace Design 112
Margaret Portillo and Jason Meneely

8 Designing Emotional Connection into the Workplace: A Story
of Authentic Leadership 128
Sheila Danko

9 Exploring the Schism: Toward an Empathetic Language 148
Shauna Corry Hernandez

10 Ways of Knowing in Design: A Position on the Culture of Interior
Design Practice 171
Janice Barnes

11 Sustainable Life-Span Design: A New Model 186
Amber Joplin

12 Frameworks for Decision-Making in Design for the Aging 212
Halime Demirkan

13 Designing More Successful Social Spaces: Lessons Learned from a
Continuing Care Retirement Community Study 226
Nichole M. Campbell

14 Developing a Person-Centric Design Philosophy 246
Jill Pable

15 In Support of Contemporary Identity: The Modern Palestinian
Home 260
May Sayrafi

16 Creativity in Interior Design: Cross-Cultural Practitioners'
Reviews of Entry-Level Portfolios 273
Siriporn Kobnithikulwong

17 Human Responses to Water Elements in Interior Environments:
A Culture and Gender Comparison 293
Gwo Fang Lin

18 Concerns with Daylight and Health Outcomes 310
Michael D. Kroelinger

19 Healthy Interiors for the Visually Impaired 327
Dak Kopec

20 Interior People Places: The Impact of the Built Environment on
the Third Place Experience 347
Dana Vaux

21 Places in the Virtual and Physical Continuum: Examining the
    Impact of Virtual Behaviors on Place Attributes of Wireless
    Coffee Shops   366
    Newton D'Souza and Yu Fong Lin

22 The Relationship between Historic Preservation and Sustainability
    in Interior Design   382
    Lisa Tucker

23 Forging Empathetic Connections to Create Compatible Designs
    in Historic Buildings   393
    Jessica Goldsmith

**SECTION III   CONSIDERATIONS OF EDUCATION IN
INTERIOR DESIGN**   **415**

24 The Phenomenological Contribution to Interior Design
    Education and Research: Place, Environmental Embodiment,
    and Architectural Sustenance   417
    David Seamon

25 Testing a Culture-Based Design Pedagogy: A Case Study   432
    Abimbola O. Asojo

26 Connecting the Scholarship of Teaching and Learning to the
    Discipline of Interior Design   446
    Isil Oygur and Bryan D. Orthel

27 Engaging Voices within a Dynamic Problem-Based Learning
    Context   465
    Tiiu Poldma

28 Aesthetic Theory and Interior Design Pedagogy   478
    Ji Young Cho and Benyamin Schwarz

29 Interior Design Teaching and Learning in Elementary and
    Secondary Education (K-12)   497
    Stephanie A. Clemons

30 Community-Building through Interior Design Education   516
    Patrick Lucas

31 A Reflective Journey in Teaching Interior Design: The Virtual
    Studio   524
    Kathleen Gibson

Index   **538**

Notes on Contributors

Abimbola O. Asojo, PhD, Associate Professor of Interior Design, University of Minnesota, studied in the US, the UK, and Nigeria. Her research includes cross-cultural design issues, African architecture, computing and design, lighting design, and global design issues. She has published in *the Journal of Interior Design*, *Traditional Dwellings and Settlements Review*, *Designing for the 21st Century* journal, and the *Journal of Design Communication*.

Janice Barnes, PhD, is the Global Discipline Leader, Principal, Planning+Strategies for the design firm Perkins+Will. With nearly twenty-five years of experience in design practice and research, the focus of Janice's work is on work practices. By bringing practical experience together with empirical research, Janice recognizes the critical aspects of business processes and links these to appropriate organizational responses.

Mary Anne Beecher, PhD, heads the Department of Design at the Ohio State University. She holds a doctoral degree in American studies (with an emphasis in material culture studies) from the University of Iowa, and interior design degrees from Iowa State University. Her research explores the evolution of interior space in the 20th century through the influence of design and culture. She has taught in the United States and Canada.

Nichole M. Campbell, PhD, is an Assistant Professor in Department of Interior Design at the University of Florida. She holds degrees from the University of Wisconsin-Madison, Illinois State University, and DePauw University. Her teaching foci are environment and behavior theory and interior design studio. Current research interests are on the design and construction of buildings that optimize health and wellness, with a particular emphasis on elderly inhabitants and supportive social interaction through the built environment.

Ji Young Cho, PhD, Leed-AP, is an Assistant Professor at the Interior Design Program in the College of Architecture and Environmental Design, Kent State University. She received her PhD in architectural studies from the University of Missouri, Columbia, and Bachelor's and Master's degrees in architecture from the Pusan National University in South Korea. Her research interests include pedagogy of design education, design cognition and process, and environment–behavior relations. As a designer for 10 years, she has completed more than 50 projects in South Korea. In 2008 one of her projects received first place in the Interior Design Educators Council Creative Scholarship category.

Stephanie A. Clemons, PhD, is Professor and Coordinator of the Interior Design Program at Colorado State University. She holds degrees from Colorado State University, Utah State University, and Michigan State University, and is certified by the National Council of Interior Design Qualifications (NCIDQ) as a professional interior designer. Her research interests are K-12 linkages with interior design, third places, and sense of self and place. She has served in several leadership roles including president of the Interior Design Educators Council and president of the American Society of Interior Designers.

Shauna Corry Hernandez, PhD, is an Associate Professor and Chair of the Interior Design Program at the University of Idaho. She received her PhD and MA from Washington State University and has taught at the University of Idaho and North Dakota State University where she served as Interior Design and Facility Management Program Coordinator. She has been with the University of Idaho since 2001, and enjoys teaching history of interiors and design studios. Her research focuses on universal design, social justice issues, and cultural responsibility in design. She has been recognized for her prowess in the classroom as the recipient of the Alumni Awards of Excellence for mentorship and the Hoffman Teaching Excellence Award.

Erin Cunningham, PhD, is an Assistant Professor in the Interior Architecture Program at the University of Oregon. She holds degrees from the University of Florida, the University of Manitoba, and the University of Victoria. Her research focuses on the history and preservation of 19th- and 20th-century interior spaces. Her research interests include social settlement houses, vernacular architecture, and public housing interiors. Erin's current work also explores the development of a social welfare focus in the interior design profession, and the application of narrative methodology to the study of historic spaces. In both her research and teaching, Erin explores interior space from a socio-historical perspective, concentrating on issues of race, gender, and class. She has presented on her research at conferences and the Vernacular Architecture Forum, and recently published " 'Renovating an Industry': The Expanding Role of Interior Design in Times of Recession" in *Interiors: Design, Architecture, Culture.*

Ronn M. Daniel, M.Arch., is the Interior Design Program Coordinator at James Madison University in Harrisburg, Virginia, where he teaches design theory, design history, and interior design studios. His research explores the intersections between interior space, technological modernization, and social and ideological change in the 20th century.

Sheila Danko, Professor and Chair of the Department of Design and Environmental Analysis at Cornell University, has a multi-disciplinary design background with training in architecture, industrial, graphic, and interior design. Professor Danko has received the honor of being named a J. Thomas Clark Professor of Entrepreneurship for her research entitled *Values-Led Entrepreneurship by Design*.

Halime Demirkan holds a PhD from the Middle East Technical University in computer-aided architectural design and now serves and the Chairperson and Associate Dean of the Department of Interior Architecture and Environmental Design at Bilkent University, one of Turkey's leading research universities. She is an industrial engineer and experienced as an instructor at the Middle East Technical University and as a researcher at the Scientific and Technical Council of Turkey. Her current research and teaching include design education, universal design, and ergonomics.

Newton D'Souza is a Professor in the Department of Architectural Studies at the University of Missouri, Columbia where he teaches design studio, environment behavior, and design research. He holds a PhD from the University of Wisconsin-Milwaukee and has an academic and practice background as an architect and design researcher in the US, Singapore, and India. Over the past 10 years, intrigued by his own experience as an architect, he has conducted research in design process, learning environments, creativity research, and the use of new media in design education. His current work includes research in the potential of virtual reality for design education and the use of multiple intelligences among architectural designers.

Jessica Goldsmith holds a PhD in design, construction, and planning from the University of Florida. She is an Assistant Professor at Radford University in Valdosta, Georgia, and is certified by the National Council for Interior Design Certification (NCIDQ) as a professional interior designer. Her research focus is on student learning and historic preservation.

Mads Nygaard Folkmann is an Associate Professor in the field of design studies and design culture in the Department of Design and Communication at the University of Southern Denmark. His research interests are design culture, aesthetics, and symbolism in design. His work has been published in Danish and English in journals such as *Design Issues* and *Design and Culture*.

Kathleen Gibson is an Associate Professor of Interior Design at Cornell University. She is also the Director of Undergraduate Studies for the Department of Design and Environmental Analysis. Her research focuses on computer-aided design (CAD) where she investigates the effect of digital media on creativity, studio processes, and decision-making. Gibson practices interior design and has achieved national publication and award recognition for her work.

Amber Joplin, D. Des., completed her doctoral degree at the Interdisciplinary Design Institute at Washington State University. Prior to completing her degree she assisted in the WSU GIS and Simulation Lab and participated in research on pedestrian accessibility and public transportation modeling. Her dissertation research involves developing, and testing with GIS, a matrix for sustainable aging that includes individual, social, material support and natural systems.

Siriporn Kobnithikulwong, PhD, serves as Department Chair and Head of the Interior Design Master's Program for the Department of Interior Architecture at the Thammsat University, Thailand. Thammsat is the second-oldest institution of higher education and known as one of the most prestigious universities in Thailand. She holds a Bachelor of Architecture degree in interior architecture from Chulalongkorn University in Bangkok and a Master's of Interior Design from the University of Florida. She was the recipient of an international student academic award for her doctoral work at the University of Florida.

Dak Kopec, PhD, holds a doctorate in environmental psychology with a concentration in perception and design and two Master's degrees, one in architecture and another in community psychology. He is currently an Assistant Professor at Radford University, and has served twice as a visiting lecturer at Virginia Commonwealth University in Doha Qatar and visiting professor at the University of Hawaii in the Schools of Architecture and Medicine. He is the author of several journal articles and three books: *Environmental Psychology for Design*; *Health, Sustainability and the Built Environment*; and *Evidence-Based Design: A Process for Research and Writing*.

Michael D. Kroelinger, PhD, is a Professor at the Herberger Institute for Design and the Arts at Arizona State University, Tempe. He has lectured extensively on various aspects of the built environment and has conducted research projects that evaluate how buildings perform and how they should be designed. He maintains relationships with universities throughout the world and is a frequent lecturer on architectural lighting and daylighting. Kroelinger is a registered architect in Arizona and is also lighting certified by the National Council on Qualifications for the Lighting Professions. Michael received a PhD from the University of Tennessee, an M.Arch. from the University of Arizona, a Master's degree from the University of Tennessee, and a Bachelor's degree from the University of Alabama.

Gwo Fang (Max) Lin, PhD, is a full-time instructor on the Interior Design Program at the International Academy of Design & Technology (IADT) in Seattle. His varied career includes higher education, interior design, construction, commercial and residential property management, and business development. Dr. Lin graduated from Washington State University with a PhD in the individual interdisciplinary doctoral program with study focus in the field of interior design. Through his professional practice in interior design he had developed knowledge and experience in green building practice and holds a LEED Accredited Professional credential. He is also a National Council for Interior Design Qualification (NCIDQ) certificate holder. Following six years of high-end residential interior design experience, he followed his passion in interior design and founded GC Design Group. He continues building his professional experience through his design practice and teaching design.

Patrick Lucas, PhD, serves as the Director of the School of Interiors at the University of Kentucky College of Design. He holds a PhD in American studies from Michigan State University; he is the author of numerous articles and has presented his work at conferences around the world. His work includes the development of a manuscript entitled "Athens on the Frontier: Grecian Style in the Valley of the West, 1820–1860." His current research focuses on Greensboro, North Carolina, architect Edward Lowenstein and his mid-20th-century design aesthetic. While at the University of North Carolina he was the recipient of the Board of Governors Excellence in Teaching Award, recognizing his community-engaged approach to design and his commitment to quality education.

Yu Fong Lin holds an interior design graduate degree from the University of Houston and is a graphic design undergraduate degree from the Chung Yuan University. He has many years of experience in the graphic design and interior design industries. He is interested in visual effects in interior spaces, product design, and human behavior. His current research is focused on using virtual reality technology to explore human behavior and perception in virtual environments, specifically in relation to lighting design and purchasing behavior. Other research interests include the exploration of how cultural differences and environmental stimuli influence consumers' visual perception and cognition in retail stores.

Jason Meneely, PhD, is an Associate Professor in the Department of Interior Design at Florida State University. Prior to joining the department he served as a Research Associate in the department of Design and Environmental Analysis at Cornell University. His research examines strategies for enhancing creative performance in individuals, teams, and organizations. He also examines the use of technology to support creative problem-solving and is leading an effort to integrate digital sketching in design education. His work has been published in the *Creativity Research Journal* and the *Journal of Interior Design*, and he has received awards at international conferences.

Bryan D. Orthel, PhD, is an Assistant Professor of Interior Design at Kansas State University. His research interests focus on preservation actions associated with communal perceptions of history and the scholarship of teaching and learning for design. His scholarship examines how people understand and use history in their lives and living environments. Other research interests include the pedagogy of design, design thinking, and creativity. In his teaching and scholarship he attempts to merge pragmatic, everyday issues with creative problem-solving.

Isil Oygur, PhD, is an Assistant Professor of Industrial Design at Bahçeşehir University. She holds a PhD from Washington State University and a Master of Science degree from Istanbul Technical University. Her research interests include qualitative user research and user-centered design, with a specific focus on ethnography and contextual differences in the application of user-research methods.

Jill Pable, PhD, is an Associate Professor in the Department of Interior Design at Florida State University and an NCIDQ-certified interior designer. She served as national president of the Interior Design Educators Council in 2009–2010 and is the author of *Sketching Interiors at the Speed of Thought* and co-author, with Catherine Ankerson, of *Interior Design: Strategies for Teaching and Learning*.

Tiiu Poldma, PhD, is a Professor at the University of Montreal. Currently she serves as Vice Dean of Graduate Studies at the Faculty of Environmental Design and coordinates the baccalaureate interior design program at the School of Industrial Design. Her research and design expertise includes work in the commercial and residential sectors and creating interiors with a particular interest in how light, color, and design elements impact interior spaces.

Margaret Portillo, PhD, Professor and Chair of the Interior Design Department, University of Florida, is the author of *Color Planning for Interiors: An Integrative Approach to Color*. Her research program focuses on design thinking and creativity, particularly emphasizing workplace environments. Portillo lead the FIDER Research Council (now known as CIDA) and currently serves as editor-in-chief for the *Journal of Interior Design*.

May Sayrafi is a member of faculty in the Architecture Department at Birzeit University, Palestine. Her research interests include home environments, cultural and historical preservation, and human behavior in the built environment. She was a Fulbright scholar at Washington State University and received an Award of Excellence from the Interior Design Educators Council in 2010.

Benyamin Schwarz, PhD, is a Professor in the Department of Architectural Studies at the University of Missouri. In 2011 he was named one of the top 25 professors and education leaders in the US by DesignIntelligence magazine. He received his Bachelor's degree in architecture and urban planning from Technion, the Institute of Technology of Israel, and his PhD in architecture, with an emphasis on environmental gerontology, from the University of Michigan. He has designed numerous buildings and facilities for the elderly in Israel and in the US. Dr. Schwarz has been the editor of the *Journal of Housing for the Elderly* since 2000.

David Seamon, PhD, is a Professor of Architecture at Kansas State University. His interests focus on a phenomenological approach to place, architecture, environmental experience, and environmental design as place-making. Selected books that he has authored include *Dwelling, Seeing, and Designing: Toward a Phenomenological Ecology* and *Goethe's Way of Science: A Phenomenology of Nature*, edited with physicist Arthur Zajonc.

Lisa Tucker, PhD, is an Associate Professor and Chair of the Interior Design Program at Virginia Tech. She is a practicing interior designer and architect with a BS in architecture, a Master's in architectural history, a Certificate of Historic Preservation from the University of Virginia, and a PhD in architectural studies from the University of Missouri-Columbia. In 2013 she was the recipient of the university's Alumni Award for Excellence in Teaching. Her research and professional work focuses on the relationship between historic preservation and sustainability.

John C. Turpin, PhD, is Dean of the School of Art and Design and Professor of Interior Design at High Point University. His scholarship on the history of the interior design profession focuses on the early decorators. His work has been published in numerous design journals such as the *Journal of Interior Design* and the *Journal of Cultural Research in Art Education*. He is currently a co-editor of *Interiors: Design, Architecture, Culture*.

Dana Vaux is an Assistant Professor of Interior Design at the University of Nebraska-Kearney. Her research focuses on the cultural qualities that generate an ethos of place. Through this research, she hopes to identify universal characteristics of "place" that transcend physical localities, and thereby to derive a general theory of common characteristics.

David Wang, PhD, is Professor of Architecture at Washington State University. He teaches courses in architectural theory, architectural ethics and practice, and East/West philosophies of architecture and aesthetics. He is co-author of *Architectural Research Methods*, and over the years has lectured widely in the US, Scandinavia, and China on design research.

Preface

This compilation of essays is shaped by our long-held view that there is not a single way to think about interior design. Rather, the body of knowledge that has accumulated over the relatively brief history of the discipline reflects the multiple philosophies, theories, and perspectives that shape this knowledge. The intent is to explore this multiplicity through diverse voices, challenging readers to consider how this diversity shapes interior design.

In putting together this work, we invited worldwide participation to ensure a broad spectrum of contributors. Each author's experiences, academic training, cultural background, and understanding of both the discipline and the profession of interior design shape each essay. Similarly, these are what shape a collective perception of how the discipline is understood, how it is taught, and how it is practiced.

Some essays in this collection present issues that are well known. These issues are revisited with new information or through new voices. Others present new ways of thinking and framing ideas about interior design. Each chapter offers any reader, student, instructor, or practicing designer an in-depth discussion of a topic with theoretical base, exploration, and explanation. Each chapter demonstrates the way the author thinks about interior design. As a group the essays, although limited by the scope of a single volume, portray the complexity and reality found in the field.

With this in mind, we invite you to pay careful attention to how these scholars approach research questions, argue positions, or seek to apply knowledge. We encourage you to use this volume as a means to explore and to challenge your own way of thinking about interior design.

Introduction: The Shaping of Interior Design

"We see design reflected in countless artifacts with which we furnish and sustain our environment...But what shapes design?" (Galle 2002). Galle effectively answers this question in subsequent writings, suggesting that there is a direct connection between an individual's understanding of design and the way, for instance, she practices. An interior designer who views design as a creative artistic endeavor will emphasize an interior's uniqueness, embellishing and decorating its surfaces. An interior designer, who views design as a problem-solving effort seeks highly functional and efficient space solutions. The way designers conceive the nature and purpose of design affects their practice (Galle 2011).

Then what shapes the way designers conceive the nature of design? It is commonly understood that these conceptions and ideas are shaped by the culture and time in which individuals have been educated, trained, and worked, as well as by the institutional and corporate structures and practices that surround them. In the 21st century, these conceptions reflect complex issues that defy the historic intuitive nature of early decorators, craftsmen, and artisans.

The debate over what shapes interior design has too often been characterized as a struggle between practitioners and academics. This struggle is most apparent between the concepts of applied and abstract knowledge and the pursuit of research. If one is in the academy, particularly in research universities, the term is understood to be the pursuit of new knowledge through empirical means. If one is engaged in the practice of interior design, it is likely that research is understood to be the search for information, for example, product specifications, or anthropometric data, to be applied to an existing problem in a design project. This definition is also often used in the studio classroom. Many times these two definitions of research are

The Handbook of Interior Design, First Edition. Edited by Jo Ann Asher Thompson and Nancy H. Blossom.
© 2015 John Wiley & Sons, Ltd. Published 2015 by John Wiley & Sons, Ltd.

perceived to be in conflict. Information is practical and applicable; new knowledge is impractical and abstract. In fact, each is mutually supportive. Both shape interior design.

A gap in the discipline exists because collectively we have not sought to fully understand and appreciate the reciprocity of the linkages between the generation of knowledge and the application of knowledge. If the way a designer approaches design in practice is dependent on a personal conception, then a shared appreciation of this abstract knowledge of design is essential. Likewise, if the way a design researcher approaches the generation of new knowledge is dependent on a personal conception of design, then a practical understanding of design application is essential.

In an effort to establish common ground, an understanding of several key terms is necessary. In the context of this book, a framework is a set of ideas or facts that provide support for an argument, a concept, or an idea. When an author draws from multiple disciplines or philosophies to build a position, a critical framework guides the reader through the discussion of the author's ideas. Some scholars present the framework clearly as a component of the discussion. Others use the literature to build a framework and leave it to the reader to identify the components and tie them together. For example, Newton D'Souza and Yu Fong Lin rely on the literature in their essay, "Places in the Virtual and Physical Continuum: Examining the Impact of Virtual Behaviors on Place Attributes of Wireless Coffee Shops," drawing heavily from scholarship in environment and behavior to support their argument that there is a virtual–physical continuum. In another example, Siriporn Kobnithikulwong uses the literature to frame her research question in her essay, "Creativity in Interior Design: Cross-Cultural Practitioners' Reviews of Entry-Level Portfolios," returning to the literature later to tie together conclusions about cross-cultural creativity.

Although the term "methodology" is generally understood, some variations in meaning and interpretation often occur among disciplines. Methodology is the theoretical underpinning for understanding the "best practices" that can be applied to a specific inquiry or case. In his essay, "Human Responses to Water Elements in Interior Environments: A Culture and Gender Comparison," Gwo Fang Lin uses a formal statistical model to guide the research question and support his findings. Patrick Lucas, on the other hand, supports his argument using a more informal, case-study approach in the essay "Community-Building through Interior Design Education." Nichole Campbell's essay, "Designing More Successful Social Spaces: Lessons Learned from a Continuing Care Retirement Community Study," uses a series of "What" questions – established through logical reasoning – as the basis for investigation.

Establishing a methodology is key to the ultimate understanding and interpretation of a study, especially in the cases of inter- or multi-disciplinary studies. These theoretical underpinnings inform the development of and approach to a research question, and can also be seen as essential to a practicing designer's approach to a design project. Ji Young Cho and Benyamin Schwarz, in their essay "Aesthetic Theory and Interior Design Pedagogy," offer insights into the idea of "schema." Their essay clearly articulates how certain behaviors and preconceived ideas influence the way students and faculty interact in design studios. Schema is defined as an organized pattern of behavior or a mental structure of preconceived ideas that influence design academics and practitioners.

No discussion of key terms can be complete without consideration of the term "theory." This term is often used, many times rather indiscriminately and casually, to explain nearly every phenomenon that exists in the world today. Thus, to avoid confusion, it is important to clarify that theory is defined simply as a "body of knowledge." Each author whose work is included in the *Handbook of Interior Design* relies upon a body of knowledge and specific theoretical and methodological orientations in order to explore the rich and complex schema that shape interior design. For example, Tiiu Poldma relies heavily upon the body of knowledge from the domains of education and aesthetic theory to frame the discussion in "Engaging Voices within a Dynamic Problem-Based Learning Context," and Dana Vaux draws upon theories of "place" in the essay "Interior People Places: The Impact of the Built Environment on the Third Place Experience."

The sections of the handbook are intended to loosely organize the chapters without confining the way each is interpreted or understood. While there is wide representation of schema in each section of the handbook, there are also chapters that share a flow of ideas or a mutual philosophy across the different sections. Take for example three essays, one by David Wang, another by Mads Folkmann, and the third by David Seamon. Each is found in a different section of the handbook. Yet each author is a devotee of phenomenology. In "An Overview of Phenomenology for the Design Disciplines," Wang suggests that disciplines such as interior design regularly deal with phenomenological factors, yet lack a foundational understanding of the history of the epistemology. He first situates phenomenology in a historical philosophical lineage, and then establishes ways that it relates to the design literature. Danish scholar Mads Nygaard Folkmann continues a phenomenological discussion in his essay "Aesthetic Coding in Interior Design" by examining three modern cases: Verner Panton's *Visiona II*, Louise Campbell's front office for the Danish Ministry of Culture, and the Tietgen Dormitory in Copenhagen. David Seamon also posits a phenomenological approach to place, architecture, environmental experience, and environmental design as place-making. Focusing on the three themes of "place," "environmental embodiment," and "architectural sustenance," his essay uses cases from his university classrooms to demonstrate how he leads students to understand both the underpinning and the application of phenomenology in design education. Although each essay falls into a different organizational section of the handbook, each shares the common foundation of phenomenological theory.

Theoretical positions evolve over years of narrower design studies. Take for example the essay by John Turpin, "Dorothy Draper and the American Housewife: A Study of Class Values and Success." Turpin's explorations of the history of interior design in America concentrate on the work of Draper, the New York designer who pioneered the development of interior design and decor in commercial settings.

Turpin focuses on the impoverishing effects of patriarchal trends in art and design criticism by highlighting the neglected contributions of Draper and other talented women who enriched the practice and aesthetic of interior design. His work is well grounded in feminist theory. This new essay, however, takes a fresh approach. Still looking closely at Draper and her place in interior design history, Turpin uses contemporary theories from the domains of marketing and advertising (Reynolds & Olson 2001) to interpret the success that Dorothy Draper had in appealing to the market of the American middle-class housewife. An evolution in theoretical position is evident in Turpin's new framework for interpreting the value systems of the upper class (Draper) and the emerging middle class (house-wives) of the mid-20th century. Further, this same framework might be reconsidered and applied to values of contemporary consumers in the interior design market of the 21st century. While Turpin's topic is quite narrow, the application of his thinking is quite broad.

Similarly, in "Reflective Journey in Teaching Interior Design: The Virtual Studio," Kathleen Gibson offers a thoughtful overview of 20 years of teaching in the classroom. The journey she shares encompasses a full range of instructional exploration and innovation alongside empirical and epistemological research. Using computer technology and virtual interiors as her vehicle, she reflects on her continuing search for effective teaching methodologies that will move interior design education and practice forward. This essay validates Oygur and Orthel's argument for the need to document the scholarship of teaching and learning in "Connecting the Scholarship of Teaching and Learning to the Discipline of Interior Design." Professor Gibson's journey serves as evidence of the contribution such studies can make to the body of knowledge in the discipline of interior design.

A schema that is broadly shared among interior design scholars is that the interior frames experiences and provides a structure within which these experiences can develop. At a micro scale, "Developing a Person-Centric Design Philosophy," by Jill Pable, demonstrates how this belief impacts the author's personal advocacy in design. Grounding her position in the literature of the social sciences, Pable encourages a "person-centric" framework in interior design research and practice. She offers her personal journey in forming such a philosophy and suggests that when a designer develops one's own philosophy it may well be found outside of traditional design knowledge – as it was in her case. Using examples from her practice and research experience in design for the disadvantaged, Pable demonstrates how her philosophy underpins all of her work and provides balance to the full spectrum of human experience that designers must consider.

A poignant personal experience was the inspiration for Shauna Corry Hernandez' research study presented in the essay "Exploring the Schism: Toward an Empathetic Language," where she explores the apparent schism between users who are disabled and designers and managers of the built environment. Recognizing that even though it is federally mandated that all buildings must meet accessibility codes in the US, a large segment of the population remains excluded from using them, her essay, grounded in empirical research, posits the development of an empathetic language for inclusive design that is understood by all members of the design community.

In the essay "Forging Empathetic Connections to Create Compatible Designs in Historic Buildings," Jessica Goldsmith also advocates for an empathetic language to inform designers. However, in contrast to the personal impetus that is embedded in Corry's work, Goldsmith places her emphasis on the historic structure itself and the need to recognize the specific challenges that designers must address when dealing with the adaptive reuse of significant interior spaces. Lisa Tucker supports Goldsmith's argument and advances the discussion by recognizing the significance of adaptive reuse of buildings as an imperative of sustainability, in "The Relationship between Historic Preservation and Sustainability in Interior Design."

The power of the interior to shape emotion is acknowledged by Sheila Danko in the essay, "Designing Emotional Connection into the Workplace: A Story of Authentic Leadership." Using narrative inquiry as her methodology, Professor Danko constructs a narrative, "A Sense of Purpose," from interviews transcribed verbatim and analyzed for emergent themes. The narrative examines how artifacts, aesthetics, and symbols communicate the meaningfulness of work as well as enhance people's emotional connection to the workplace. Erin Cunningham also frames her essay in narrative theory. In "Bringing the Past In: Narrative Inquiry and the Preservation of Historic Interiors," she proposes a new research approach to piece together disparate points of view. This study moves beyond appearance and design form to examine the experiences and relationships represented in historic spaces.

May Sayrafi frames a discussion of identity represented by the cultural, social, and political aspects that shape a home in the essay "Contemporary Identity: The Modern Palestinian Home." Grounding her work in the historic roots of Palestine, Sayrafi examines the different dimensions that shape the interior spaces of a modern Palestinian home. Using the emergent themes from the study, Sayrafi interprets a distinct character for the Palestinian home and uses it to develop design strategies that are responsive to the current modes of living and the shared values of contemporary Palestinians. Likewise, Abimbola Asojo's essay on the development of a cultural framework for interior design education acknowledges the importance of cultural influence on interior spaces. In "Testing a Culture-Based Design Pedagogy: A Case Study," she discusses studio design projects purposefully structured to raise the cultural awareness of students. Using this very focused examination as a base, she applies the results to a more broadly reaching pedagogical argument.

The creation of healthy, sustainable, and dynamic interior environments is a recurring focus of many scholars and practitioners of interior design, and this theme informs many of the essays throughout the book. In the essay "Concerns with Daylight and Health Outcomes," Michael Kroelinger argues through a review of the literature that environmental attributes, such as the presence of daylight in an interior, enhance the human experience of buildings and spaces – while at the same time supporting a sustainable environment. In his essay, Kroelinger identifies key issues that impact healthful interiors in relation to daylight and provides research examples from across a variety of disciplines to demonstrate why daylight is instrumental in supporting human health. Through these examples, Kroelinger supports his point of view that future research is critical to the continued evolution of what constitutes a healthful interior space.

Using a case-study approach Dak Kopec examines problems associated with the aging population of the United States and the impact having to care for an elderly relative has on a family in his essay "Healthy Interiors for the Visually Impaired." Scholar Halime Demirkan focuses her essay on the conceptual design phase of the design process when designing interiors for maturing adults. The aim of her essay "Frameworks for Decision-Making in Design for Aging," is to develop an epistemological and methodological approach that permits designers to capture, describe, prioritize, act on, and evaluate alternative design solutions for the elderly and adults with a physical disability or visual impairment. Demirkan situates her research on maturing populations within the context of how methods and knowledge are linked within the cognitive strategies of the design process.

Several of the contributing authors suggest new frameworks for thinking about concepts of interior design. Many of these theories represent multi-disciplinary approaches to thinking and knowing. In her essay "Sustainable Life-Span Design: A New Model," Amber Joplin argues that most existing built environments do not serve the needs of our rapidly aging population in a manner sustainable for individuals, society, or the environment. In support of her argument Joplin presents the results of an extensive multi-disciplinary literature review of Western practices in environments for the aging and suggests that there is a gap in the current scholarship in this area. To demonstrate her emergent theory, Joplin presents models from design, education, gerontology, and economics that have been integrated by means of comparative tables to identify significant issues that she proposes must be considered in the design of sustainable life-span design.

Margaret Portillo and Jason Meneely also acknowledge components of systems theory in their study of creativity in the contemporary work environment. In the essay "Toward a Creative Ecology of Workplace Design," the researchers identify a need for a new model for interior design, inspired by ecological concepts, that acknowledges the creative workplace as an interrelated system of dynamic, complex, and varied human–space interactions sustaining individuals, groups, and organizations. Sharing insights from a multi-methods study exploring job satisfaction, climate for creativity, worker characteristics, and the physical workplace, Portillo and Meneely draw conclusions about ways to cultivate a creative ecology in the workplace and raise questions for additional thought and study.

"The Political Interior," by Mary Anne Beecher, and Janice Barnes' "Ways of Knowing: A Position on the Culture of Interior Design Practice" offer discussions of economy, power, and responsibility as it is reflected in the actual practice of interior design from a historical and contemporary perspective, while Ronn Daniel offers an alternative understanding of interior design as a profession in "Taylorizing the Modern Interior: Counter-Origins," based on the ideas of theorist Fredrick Taylor. Moving away from themes of culture or emotive qualities of the interior,

Daniel looks at the origins of scientific office management to demonstrate the roots of functional space planning in contemporary interior design.

Clearly the contributors to *The Handbook of Interior Design* are highly influenced by a mental structure of preconceived ideas representing some or many aspects of the world. Each scholar relies on this broad understanding to shape an approach to scholarship, practice, and inquiry in interior design. There is a variance of scale among the many chapters, again influenced by each author's point of view, tenure in practice, or research and disciplinary grounding. Some writings stem from specific narrow questions while others look at more macro issues of the discipline. It is possible that viewpoints in some essays contradict or challenge those of another. All demonstrate the richness that can be found in challenging the theoretical and practical realities of the field of interior design.

What shapes interior design? We leave it to the reader to explore these chapters, consider the ideas presented there, accepting some rejecting others, and finally to shape a personal answer to that question.

References

Galle, P. 2002. "Philosophy of design: an editorial introduction," *Design Studies*, 23(3): 211–218.

Galle, P. 2011. "Foundational and instrumental design theory," *Design Issues*, 27(4): 81–94.

Reynolds, T. and Olson, J. 2001. *Understanding Consumer Decision Making: The Means-End Approach to Marketing and Advertising Strategy*. Mahwah, NJ: Lawrence Erlbaum.

Section I

Explorations of the History Of Interior Design

1

An Overview of Phenomenology for the Design Disciplines

David Wang

Introduction

The word phenomenology is used often in design circles, but accessible definitions of the term are harder to come by. This is unfortunate because disciplines such as interior design, architecture, landscape architecture, and product design regularly deal with phenomenological factors. These include how users respond to light and color, to tactility, to climate, or to user preferences. Other related factors include way-finding, sense of belonging, and cultural differences in how space and place are experienced. Such a wide variety of factors is one challenge to a concise definition of the word. Another reason is that "phenomenology" is a technical term with a rich history in Western philosophy, one which those of us trained in the design disciplines may not have had systematic access to.

This essay situates phenomenology in its historical-philosophical lineage and, in light of this, identifies ways it applies to design. The history makes clear how, by the mid-19th century, phenomenology had split into two conceptual threads – what is called here individual phenomenology and corporate phenomenology – both remaining relevant for design theory and practice. Interspersed throughout this section of the essay are sections headed "applications to design." These are numbered progressively, each relating to the aspect of phenomenology being explained. After the historical introduction, a "map of phenomenology" is provided (Figure 1.1), identifying four regions in the phenomenological literature related to the design disciplines. The conclusion summarizes current trends in design theory and practice, underlining their connections to phenomenological principles.

The Handbook of Interior Design, First Edition. Edited by Jo Ann Asher Thompson and Nancy H. Blossom.

Phenomenology: A Brief History

The Greek word *phanesthai*, which means "(to be) about to reveal itself," is the root for our word phenomenology. *Phanesthai* is in the Greek middle voice, denoting the subject acting upon itself. This middle voice is different from the active voice, in which the subject acts upon another entity, or the passive voice, in which the subject is acted upon by another entity (Heidegger 1962: 51). Putting these two elements together, we have *phanesthai* as the self-revealing, or the self-coming-into-light, of an object, independent of external causes. It is from this root that phenomenological inquiry emphasizes immediate experience. Immediate experience refers to experience that cannot be captured by sentences, equations, photographs, even social conventions; all of these are second-hand derivatives of the initial self-revealing reality.

This self-revealing aspect is historically important because phenomenological inquiry arose as a reaction against Enlightenment biases in general, and scientific method in particular. The Enlightenment outlook celebrated measurability, that is, a thing is not knowable unless and until it can be empirically defined, its height and width and depth all captured by fixed propositions. Measurability was the spirit behind René Descartes' prescriptions for scientific knowledge, patterned after the unchanging nature of geometry, accessible only by the reasoning mind (Descartes [1637] 1980).[1] In such an ideological climate, not only physical phenomena but even inquiries into beauty were driven by a scientific agenda. For example, on the Continent, Alexander Baumgarten (1714–1762) held that feelings for the beautiful were "confused" until they can be scientifically ascertained (Baumgarten [1739] 1970).[2] As well, in England, John Locke (1632–1704) divided between an object's primary qualities (those that can be measured: "solidity, extension…number") versus its secondary qualities (those that "in truth are nothing in the objects themselves": colors, sounds, tastes) (Locke [1690] 1994: 71). So in Locke's very influential view, factors usually associated with immediate experience – colors, sounds, tastes – were not essential to the objects they just happen to be attached to.

It was against this scientific mindset that Edmund Husserl (1859–1938) first embarked on a journey that led to phenomenological inquiry. Husserl was initially a psychologist, but he soon felt the limits of the field, noticing that its empirical methods were unable to delve deep enough in accessing original (read: immediate) experience – the "things themselves" (Lauer 1965: 10). Thus began another hallmark focus of phenomenological inquiry: getting to being itself as the starting point of inquiry.

This emphasis on being is strongest in the thought of Martin Heidegger (1889–1976) who was a student of Husserl's early in his career; they parted ways later. Heidegger contributed some of the most well-known technical terms to phenomenology studies, one of which is "being-in-the-world." Being-in-the-world does not designate two things, that is, a being (1) that is in the world (2). Instead, the entire term denotes a single reality: being-in-the-world (1). And so Heidegger sometimes calls this single and immediate reality "thrown-ness": at every instant, one is simply thrown into his or her context; one has no control over the immediate reality of that immediate reality (Heidegger 1962: 174). To further take away from contingent human factors in this or that immediate reality, Heidegger uses the word *Dasein*, which simply means there-being, or being-there, to describe this immediate one-ness of being-in-the-world. Here is the first opportunity to consider how this applies to design.

Application to design #1. Graphically capturing subjective feelings

Early in her career, Clare Cooper Marcus investigated residents' subjective attitudes about their home environments. She found that the conventional tools of qualitative research – interviews, for instance – were not sufficient in accessing her subjects' inmost feelings. They merely produced reports of, that is, only secondary access to, those feelings. She then came upon Heidegger's phenomenology; here is her reaction in her own words:

> I attempted to approach this material via what philosopher Martin Heidegger called "pre-logical thought." This is not "illogical" or "irrational," but rather a mode of approaching being-in-the-world that permeated early Greek thinkers at a time before the categorization of our world into mind and matter, cause and effect, in-here and out-there had gripped...the Western mind. I firmly believe that a deeper level of person/environment interaction can be approached only by means of a...process that...eliminates observer and object. (Cooper Marcus 1995: 10–11)

Cooper Marcus operationalized this insight by asking her subjects to sketch their feelings about their homes, thereby circumventing the need for propositional descriptions. How successful she was can be debated, but it is clear that she had developed a tactic for design inquiry rooted in phenomenology theory.

The takeaway in Cooper Marcus' innovation is the idea that clients – or perhaps all persons without formal design education – can better report their own attitudes about environments when not asked to express those attitudes propositionally. In this regard, Charles Moore's approach in designing St. Matthew's Church in Los Angeles deserves mention (Pressman 1995: 59–65). The congregation was noted for being a contentious group. Over four months, Moore held design charrettes with the parishioners to arrive upon a consensus.

Exercises included participants arranging found objects (Fruit Loops, cellophane, scissors and paper, even parsley) into different configurations which later informed the design. Another exercise had participants projecting their wishes onto various graphic configurations, and so on. In the end, 87% of the congregation approved of the design (Groat and Wang 2002).[3] The phenomenological component in this approach is high because, like the Cooper Marcus example, the designers were able to harvest intuitive (read: immediate) data previous to that data being framed into a propositional design program. This is an example of a design process capturing the "thrown-ness" of the realities experienced by clients.

To return to our history of phenomenology: so far, note that the emphasis is upon immediate individual subjective experience. Let us call this individual phenomenology. There are many examples in the literature focusing on individual phenomenology. For a single (and short) primary source describing phenomenology in this sense, the Introduction to Maurice Merleau-Ponty's *Phenomenology of Perception* is recommended (Merleau-Ponty [1945] 1995). For a sustained applied study, Gaston Bachelard's *The Poetics of Space* is a good source (Bachelard [1958] 1994). Yi-fu Tuan's *Sense and Place: The Perspective of Experience* is another work; this is one of the many that concern "sense of place" from the standpoint of individual phenomenology. There is also Steen Eiler Rasmussen's *Experiencing Architecture*, which addresses immediate engagement of the individual senses with the materiality of built environments. More recently, this is also the focus of Juhani Pallasmaa's *Eyes of the Skin: Architecture and the Senses*. From Husserl to Pallasmaa, the main focus here is upon *Dasein's* individual immediate experiences.

Application to design #2. Rich, thick, tactility and sensuality in design

Almost always, when designers invoke "phenomenology," what they have in mind is the power of design to enhance immediate individual phenomenological experiences. Examples are projects like Fay Jones' Thorncrown Chapel, the mysteriously magical church built of wood lattices, sitting in the woods of Arkansas, or Steven Holl's St. Ignatius Chapel in Seattle, with its glowing but shadowy interiors colored by different shades of glass. These projects possess significant phenomenological value because of their ability to stimulate heightened sensual engagement. These two projects are particularly relevant for interior design studies in that they illustrate different approaches to the idea of "interior." In Thorncrown Chapel, the lattice-like treatment of the building skin results in inclusion of the surrounding woods as part of the interior experience. Put another way, the building almost seems to disappear into the interiority of the nature that surrounds it, a particularly fitting strategy for a chapel design.

Holl's project takes the opposite approach, segregating the interior from the outside by opaque walls, only to allow light to filter inside in controlled ways, heightening the richness and sensuality of the interior experience. This treatment of light for sacred space has a long tradition behind it – from Reims to Ronchamp. At any rate, heightening individual subjective experience – termed here rich, thick, tactility and sensuality in design – is a well-established translation of philosophical phenomenology into design practice. Further, it can be applied to defining regional characteristics in design, as outlined below.

Application to design #3. Critical regionalism

In a recent student exercise in theory-building, one team produced a poster entitled "Northwest Style is not Northwest Style Without Cedar."[4] The theory posited the categories of color, acoustics, aroma, feel, and the native American tradition, as captured in the use of cedar in design that is characteristic of the United States Pacific Northwest region. This approach follows suit with Kenneth Frampton's theory of critical regionalism, one that promotes faithfulness in design to a region's geographical and cultural history, sensitivity to that region's climate and light, and retention of its tactile attributes (Frampton 1983). Heightening a region's tactile offerings in design, Frampton argues, increases the "boundedness" of a locale; what Heidegger calls dwelling (Heidegger 1951a). This principle is exemplified in the student poster, which cites how the use of cedar in a modernist interior from the 1930s (in a design by the firm of Belluschi & Yeon) gave the project a distinct regional flavor even when the overall project was done in the more abstract (and location-less) lines and planes of the International Style.

Where did this emphasis on the pleasurable aesthetic aspects of individual phenomenology come from? It came largely from Christian Norberg-Schulz, whose work is probably the most influential in applying Heidegger's phenomenology to design theory overall (e.g., Norberg-Schulz 1980). But Norberg-Schulz's handling of Heidegger is not without Norberg-Schulz's added overlays. In brief: Heidegger's technical terms – again: being-in-the-world, thrown-ness, *Dasein*, etc. – do not inherently entail pleasurable aesthetic experience. In fact, in *Being and Time*, Heidegger spends some time addressing *Dasein*'s discomforts (Heidegger 1962: 120). Heidegger's term for *Dasein*'s discomfort is *unheimlich*, or not-at-home-ness (many of Cooper Marcus' subjects, for instance, did not report happy phenomenological ties with their homes; Norberg-Schulz's approach would be at more of a loss in explaining this category of experience). Also, in Heidegger, phenomenological experience is usually blind to locale per se.[5] Consider: the very notion of "thrown-ness" means one cannot determine ahead of time where one is thrown. For Heidegger, the thrown-ness of being-in-the-world is operative whether one is in Prague or Peoria, whether in London or Lubbock. But in his theory "towards" a phenomenology of architecture, Norberg-Schulz almost exclusively considers uplifting and aesthetically pleasurable experiences of places largely indexed to the empirical attributes of those places. This is why Norberg-Schulz features Prague in his *Towards a Phenomenology of Architecture* – and why Peoria, for instance, would be much less of an example for his agenda.

Prague is richer historically, thicker in social-cultural depth, and as a result of these and other factors, tactilely and sensually more stimulating. But by the time Heidegger's phenomenology was translated by Norberg-Schulz for architectural theory, rich, thick, pleasurable aesthetic experiences of built environments became the major value of "phenomenology" for designers. The key here is not to critique

Norberg-Schulz for lack of faithfulness in applying Heidegger's principles to design; the key is to recognize that this is what "phenomenology" has come to mean for many in the design disciplines.

But phenomenology has another thread. For example: when we say an object's design conforms to "the spirit of the times," we are dealing with corporate phenomenology. Corporate phenomenology deals with (1) the movement and (2) the character of periods of cultural time as they affect design praxis, design experience, and design styles. In this thread of phenomenology, individual experiences are less in view; the focus is upon the cultural corporate whole. And to understand why this is corporate phenomenology, note that the zeitgeist of a cultural period has all the features of immediate individual phenomenology: it moves immediately (in the sense that it is always already in motion, without any one person "at the controls," as it were); and as it moves it self-reveals in material culture as the "shapes" of that culture. It is also easy to think of the spirit of the times as having its own ontology, or being, independent of the beings of individual persons (although it comprises them).

Individual as well as corporate phenomenology both issue from a preoccupation with consciousness, which began in the late 18th century and continued into the nineteenth. As philosophy shifted from theologically based derivations of knowledge to more humanistic ones, theories of knowledge became less dependent upon revelation, and more dependent upon theories of mind, and as we already noted, upon scientific deductions. Immanuel Kant's (1724–1804) theory of consciousness is the headwaters for both these threads of phenomenology. This is not the place for an overview of Kant's "critical philosophy."[6] Suffice it to say that Kant held to the unity of consciousness as the enabling basis for any true knowledge to be possible. The Husserl–Heidegger thread – that is, individual phenomenology – built on this by emphasizing the unity of consciousness and its surroundings for individual persons (again: being-in-the-world is one, not two, entities). This unified the Cartesian split between what an individual thinks (*res cogitans*) and what is out there (*res extensa*).

In contrast, G. W. F. Hegel (1770–1831) took Kant's theory of consciousness and asked this question: What if all individual consciousnesses were put together? After all, isn't the entirety of cultural interactions just such an integration? Hegel took this corporate consciousness of culture and used it to explain such things as shifts in aesthetic styles: from primitive to Egyptian to Greek art, for example (Hegel [1817] 2004). The emphasis is upon the block characteristics of entire cultures as they move through time; the art and architecture these cultures leave behind are the "shapes" of those cultures.[7] Heinrich Wölfflin's classic work *Renaissance and Baroque* stands as an enduring example of Hegelian corporate phenomenology applied to design-historical analysis. While most histories of design focus on the characteristics of periods of design, Wölfflin's is one of the few works that addresses cultural factors influencing shifts of style between periods, specifically, the shift from Renaissance to Baroque (Wölfflin [1888] 1968). In comparison to the Renaissance, the Baroque, perhaps in response to the Counter-Reformation, was more dynamic, more scenographic; it emphasized mass over line, illusions of space versus clearly articulated surfaces; illusions of movement over Renaissance symmetry, and so on (Wolfflin [1888] 1968: 30–31, 73–88). The Wolfflin–Hegelian approach to explaining changes in design styles has not been followed much in the design literature, and this is to the detriment of this literature. For instance, such an approach can explicate much in the way of how block cultural percolations worked in bringing about the recent shifts from modernist to postmodernism to deconstruction to cyber-influenced design. The design literature awaits such a study.

Application to design #4. Online participatory design communities

The advent of the internet has increased opportunities to express the "block characteristics of entire cultures" in design terms. Here are some examples. Threadless.com, an online retailer of T-shirts, operates what Pisano and Verganti call an "innovation mall":

> By operating an innovation mall where 600,000 members submit proposals for about 800 new designs weekly, Threadless gets a steady flow of unusual and singular ideas. (Mall members and visitors to the website vote on the designs, but the Threadless staff makes the final decision on which ones to produce and rewards their creators. (Pisano and Verganti 2008)[8]

Another of the authors' examples is Alessi:

> Alessi, an Italian company famous for the postmodern design of its home products, bet that postmodern architecture would be a fruitful domain for generating interesting product ideas and that it could find the best people in that field to work with. It invited 200-plus collaborators from that domain to propose product designs. (Pisano and Verganti 2008: 80)

Made possible by the internet, these approaches are unprecedented in "taking the temperature" of a community's aesthetic preferences. In this sense they are examples of corporate phenomenology as expressed in design processes.

Application to design #5. Design ethnography

A related way design process captures corporate phenomenology is the increasing use of design ethnography. Borrowed from anthropology, ethnography involves living with a community of people for a sustained period of time to obtain on-the-ground information about their cultural ways. Salvador, Bell, and Anderson used this approach by spending several weeks in northern Italy to obtain first-hand information about residential lifestyles in that region. They learned that kitchens to their informants are what living rooms are in American residences: places of family gathering. Other findings: in northern Italy there is no such thing as "take out"; much of the food comes via family networks in the region; paper plates and plastic ware are non-existent; water is never drunk out of bottles (out of glasses instead), while coffee is always served in porcelain cups (Salvador, Bell, and Anderson 1999). This is information about "block" cultural characteristics that is difficult to capture by the usual client meetings that result in a written program – which, again, on phenomenological terms, would be second-hand information. Regrettably, the authors didn't itemize the design decisions derived from their ethnographic work. But this task was assigned to graduate design students in a research methods class; one student phrased the exercise as going from common facts to artifacts. Their suggestions: a centralized kitchen interior with a large centralized table (*la tavola è la vita* – "the table is life"); cushy seating for long meals; a prominent but accessible place to display silverware and china; use of local materials and local labor. These are programmatic cues derived from "taking the temperature" of a specific corporate phenomenology.

Application to design #6. History research linking design to cultural trends

Knowing changes in cultural attitudes over stretches of history may be helpful in designing new environments for a particular region. One example is the work of the Green Architecture Research Center, based at the Xi'an Institute of Architecture and Technology in Xi'an, China. Since the early 1990s, the GARC has been instrumental in designing and building new residences in rural communities in a sensitive critical regionalist manner across China: from new sustainable cave dwellings in north central China, to rammed-earth dwellings in southern China, to solar-powered residences for rural Tibetans outside of Lhasa. (For critical regionalism, see reference to Kenneth Frampton in Application #3 above.) In the case of the cave dwellings, the GARC identified five stages in the history of cave structures. First, 2,000 years ago the cave dwellings were no more than holes dug into mountainsides. But second, as cave culture progressed, newer caves were given masonry fronts to signify economic progress. In the third stage, the dwellings semi-detached from mountainsides to become lean-to structures, this for both economic reasons as well as advancements in construction know-how. Fourth, more or less fully detached structures were nevertheless still called *yaodong* (caves) because of the historical significance of the cultural form. These stages were enough to inform the GARC to evolve a fifth stage: fully detached "cave" structures, two stories high, built using green principles (e.g., better ventilation, local materials, sod roofs for heat, etc.). The process was ethnographic in that the designs were evolved on site, with local users able to reject any designs they found to not conform to cultural tradition – for example, the signature semi-circular cave opening was a necessary carry-over from past stages. The point is that knowledge of the cultural evolution of built forms through history – that is, knowledge of the corporate phenomenology behind those forms – was essential in deriving acceptable new designs for the local population.

Application to design #7. Corporate expression in design

More will be said about this in the conclusion; suffice it to say here that computer technology provides new ways to enact Hegel's thesis (and Wolfflin's application of his thesis) that a culture's corporate *Geist* (spirit) can leave empirical shapes of itself in art forms. We get a sense of this in Facebook's ability to track "Gross National Happiness" by compiling happy and sad words used by its users at any point in time. This index measured corporate sadness when Michael Jackson died, but great happiness when Barack Obama was elected.[9] As we will see, this technology can be harnessed to measure corporate phenomenology in design terms.

A Map of Phenomenology for the Design Disciplines

Provided in Figure 1.1 is a map of phenomenology, locating four regions in which phenomenological research and/or design can be located (a version of this map was first published in Wang and Wagner 2007). These four regions are: (1) Individual Phenomenology; (2) Phenomenology of History and Culture; (3) Phenomenology of Design Production; and (4) Phenomenology and Metaphysics.

Given what has been covered earlier in this essay, regions labeled Individual Phenomenology and Phenomenology of History and Culture (lower left and lower right, respectively) should be clear. At the individual pole are placed many of the names already cited. At the history and culture pole, similarly, we see Hegel and Wolfflin. But note where the Pisano and Verganti example is located (see Application #4); also note where the GARC-*yaodong* cave-dwelling project is located (see Application #6). These are located on the diagonal connecting Phenomenology of History and Culture with the Phenomenology of Design Production (upper left pole). This underlines the following: aside from locating the various regions, this map is useful in providing sliding scales to situate various examples of design activity onto the overall geography of phenomenological inquiry.

It is notable that, despite much literature on "design thinking" (e.g., Nigel Cross et al.), design process – that is, the processes through which designs are created – is not often explicitly connected to the phenomenology literature. This map does so, at the upper left region, which also includes the sliding scales that lead up to it, both vertically and diagonally. The creative processes by which designs come into being are indeed high in phenomenological characteristics. Peter Rowe, in his *Design Thinking*, documents the multiple schematic iterations design teams go through to give birth to a finished design concept (Rowe 1988). These iterations are *in situ*, on the spot, which is to say, immediate. Similarly, Wang and Keen directly adapted

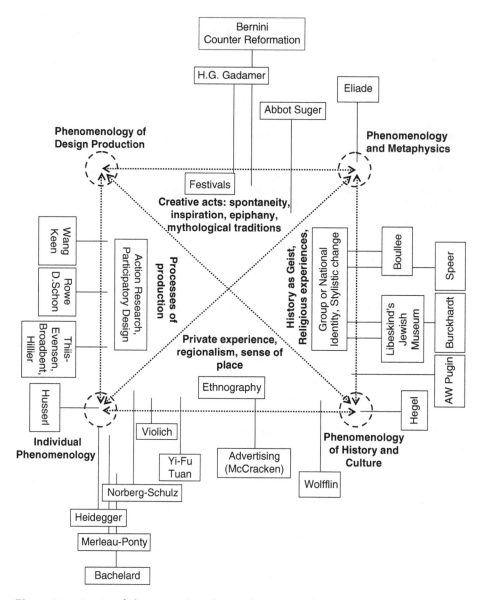

Figure 1.1 A map of phenomenology for the design disciplines. © 2007 David Wang and Sarah Wagner.

Husserl's theory of the productions of consciousness to the iterative stages of the design of a house (Wang and Keen 2001).

In elevating immediate experience, and because of its engagement with being as such, it is easy for phenomenology to segue into religious themes. This is the fourth region of the map, at the upper right, labeled Phenomenology and Metaphysics. Note that this region can also connect to Individual Phenomenology (the diagonal link). Thus we come full circle back to works such as Holl's St. Ignatius Chapel, or

Jones' Thorncrown Chapel. These were cited as having high individual phenomenological value because of their rich, thick tactility and sensuality (Application #2). But by having such attributes, they also create what Mircea Eliade terms "sacred space." Eliade posits that inhabitation itself – as in an inhabited world – requires a process of separating from (or an ordering of) chaotic space (Eliade 1959: 21–65). In this regard all designed, articulated spaces possess an element of the sacred; or at least they should. An example from history would be Abbot Suger's renovations to St. Denis in the 12th century, which marked the beginning of the Gothic period of cathedral construction. Motivated by the Platonic tradition, Suger sought to transform the existing structure into one filled with "wonderful and uninterrupted light...pervading the interior with beauty" (Suger 1946b: 101) and "[urging] us onward from the material to the immaterial" (Suger 1946a: 75).

Finally, note the headings in each of the pie-shaped quadrants of the map. Ethnography is the quadrant bridging Individual Phenomenology with Phenomenology of History and Culture. Here can be situated such design research as Salvador et al.'s ethnographic study of the design for Italian kitchens. Group or National Identity is the quadrant between Phenomenology of History and Culture and Phenomenology and Metaphysics. Throughout design history, group identity has been invoked to justify design actions. One recent example is Daniel Libeskind's rationale that the use of zinc panels in his Jewish Museum in Berlin is "very Berlin-like" (Libeskind 1995: 40). Inspiration/creative acts bridge the gap between Phenomenology and Metaphysics and Phenomenology of Design Production in that often the acts of creativity appeal to spiritual inspiration. Finally, Action Research bridges between Individual Phenomenology and Phenomenology of Design Production. This quadrant approaches design creativity more empirically, seeking to document the design process usually by protocols and/or other measurable means. Included here are also some forms of participatory design.

In sum, phenomenological inquiry takes facets of human experience largely ignored by "scientific method" and makes them material for rigorous study. Perhaps more importantly, it provides a philosophical basis upon which to situate many factors encountered in the design disciplines daily: immediate experience in response to environmental designs; understanding creative processes; aesthetic and sacred dimensions of space and place. These are all resonant with *phanesthai*. The map provided can be used as a tool to clarify the various regions of how *phanesthai* has been harnessed in service to design. It is also helpful for conceptualizing future efforts in design and research from a phenomenological point of view.

Conclusion: Connections between Phenomenology and Current Trends in Design

Principles of phenomenology as outlined above relate to quite a few current trends in design theory and practice. Much of this has been enabled by computer technology. By way of conclusion, then, the following trends are noted: (a) erasure between theory and praxis; (b) architectural versioning; (c) dynamic tectonics; (d) participatory design; (e) "sense of place" research; and (f) sustainable design.

Erasure between theory and praxis

The ability of computer technology to execute millions of computations per second opens new possibilities to express phenomenological principles in the design realm. Representations in both 2D (computer modeling software) and 3D (rapid prototyping) of design concepts can be produced very quickly, so much so that the time gap between what the designer thinks (theory) and what he or she does (practice) is significantly reduced. Theorist Michael Speaks calls this thinking-as-doing, and regards it as a new kind of "design intelligence" that can be "tested, redesigned, and retested quickly, cheaply, and under conditions that closely approximate reality" (Speaks 2005). This trend resonates with phenomenology's emphasis upon immediacy of experience, as well as the notion that *phanesthai* is the self-revelation of an object – in this case, as a design concept comes into being.

"Versioning"

Perhaps a more powerful example of self-revelation and spontaneous expression – although at present it remains quite abstract – is the notion of design as "versioning." Because of the computational power of the computer, a building can be thought of as a series, rather than as a fixed object. As every generation of design theory has in some way looked to nature for justification, versioning theory argues that nature itself is not static; it is rather "a continuous evolution of form" (Rocker 2011). Hence designed environments should follow suit. The most well-known theorist working in this trend is Greg Lynn. His Embryological House is not a single structure, but "a series of one-of-a-kind houses that are customized for individual clients." Lynn argues that this is design that engages with "contemporary issues of variation, customization and continuity" (Rocker 2011: 8–9). Note how Lynn's point goes directly to phenomenology of history and culture, to wit, that design needs to express the cultural zeitgeist of its times. Again, versioning (and its related concept "folding" – which refers to computation-based power to produce multiple versions of a design rather than one) is more experimental than practical.[10] But with no end in sight for what cyberpower can bring, it is relevant to note this trend in design thinking as a shift away from objects, and towards to processes, or series, that can accommodate (or reflect) ever-quickening pace of change in culture at large. This relates to dynamic tectonics.

Dynamic tectonics

For the city of Dubai, architect David Fisher has proposed a skyscraper with floors that rotate independent of each other, resulting in a constantly undulating form in the skyline.[11] In the city of Doetinchem in the Netherlands, a structure (called D-Tower) measures the emotions of the city's residents and changes color in response.[12] That these projects forge new ways to capture "immediate" connections between users and built forms should be self-evident; the key here is to link these examples to *phanesthai*, that is, to phenomenology as expressed in designed objects. The attraction here is the bridge these projects provide between heightened individual phenomenological experience – in the sense of rich, thick, tactility and sensuality (see Application #2) – with visual-sensual expressions of corporate phenomenology (see Application #7). The D-tower reflects the "block" emotions of a community of people in empirical ways that, prior to computer technology, were unheard of. And a skyscraper with 80 individually rotating floors raises provocative links to the corporate participation of the residents interiorly (without the control of any one resident) as well as the visual participation of the entire community exteriorly, as the tower shifts and sways like an enormous plant blowing in the wind. This leads to "participatory design" and phenomenology.

Participatory design, harnessed phenomenologically

The example given earlier of Charles Moore's participatory process in the design of St. Matthew's Church was probably not driven by phenomenological principles; it was simply a tactic to win over a group of parishioners with hands-on engagement in the design process. But "participatory design" itself offers significant connections to corporate phenomenology; and this is a connection that has not been addressed much in the current design literature. The D-Tower is an example of "participatory design" with enormous phenomenological implications. But in this sense of user-engagement, there is no reason why something quite technical – like "smart" or "intelligent" building design in which heating and lighting systems respond (immediately) to occupant behavior – cannot be included in the domain of participatory design in a phenomenological sense.[13] The operational question designers must ask is this: how can subjective preferences of clients or users, as a block, be captured real-time in design? Answering this question innovatively almost certainly ensures cutting-edge design solutions.

"Sense of community" research

Robert Putnam is well known for showing that social capital, defined as "connections among individuals...social networks and the norms of reciprocity and trustworthiness that arise from them" (Putnam 2000: 19), has significantly decreased in American culture since the 1980s. In the design literature, the assumption is that physical design alone can more or less counter this trend. Here is Elizabeth Plater-Zyberk, designer of New Urbanist communities such as Seaside, Florida, and The Kentlands near Washington DC: "By providing a full range of housing types and workplaces…the bonds of an authentic community are formed…By promoting suitable civic buildings, democratic initiatives are encouraged and the organic evolution of society is secured" (quoted in Boles 1989). On this view, just by arranging certain building typologies into certain figure-ground patterns will result in "authentic community," regardless of the individual histories of that community's occupants. We can call this the "if-we-build-it-they-will-come" fallacy. Another of Putnam's books, one less well known, suggests a different story. In *Better Together: Restoring the American Community*, Putnam and his co-authors present 12 case studies showing how "sense of community" was achieved not by physical design, but rather by community action, led by visionary individuals (Putnam, Feldstein, and Cohen 2004). Here again, a correct grasp of corporate phenomenological theory on the part of designers might result in more attention paid to people rather than to physical design. It calls for a more targeted interdisciplinary mix of design know-how with social science research (e.g., active engagement with neighborhood groups, interviews, history research, etc.).

Sustainable design

William McDonough's Hanover Principles for sustainable design are as follows: (1) insist on the rights of humanity and nature to coexist; (2) recognize interdependence; (3) respect relationships between spirit and matter; (4) Accept responsibility for the consequences of design; (5) create safe objects of long-term value; (6) eliminate the concept of waste; (7) rely on natural energy flows; (8) understand the limitations of design; and (9) seek constant improvement by the sharing of knowledge (McDonough 2008). The principles can be subsumed in this definition of sustainable design: sustainable design entails blending human habitation into the cycles of nature as they unfold in succession, with the least disruption possible. Framed in this way, it becomes clear just how much the sustainable design agenda is congruous with the phenomenological outlook: the emphasis upon self-unfolding, for instance, or the return to a pre-dichotomous way of understanding human experience and nature as a single unity – that is, as being-in-the-world. It is to view design not as something that is done to nature, which would be, to return to our very first point, an active-voice approach to design. But design would also not be a passive reality. Sustainable design encourages design with a middle-voice attitude – much in the middle-voice spirit of *phanesthai* – so that the processes of nature can continue to emerge immediately and organically on their own, with the least disruption from human impositions.

Again, for most designers, "phenomenology" is usually limited in meaning to the design of stimulating environments that heighten aesthetic pleasure. Hopefully this essay has shown that, if the philosophical sources of phenomenology can be grasped, phenomenology can be applied to a much larger scope of design endeavors.

Acknowledgments

The work and/or intellectual contributions of the following graduate students are present in this chapter, in alphabetical order: Maryam Afshar, Kyle Davis, Julia Day, Jonathan Follett, Jennifer Hohlbein, Isil Oygur, Mason Shaffer, Dana Vaux, Paul Yoon, Richard Xu.

Notes

1 "Scientific method" can be traced to Descartes' four-step method to certain knowledge in Section 2 of his *Discourse on Method*, written in 1637: (1) accept nothing as true until it is clear and distinct to the mind; (2) divide each "difficulty" into its component parts; (3) find a hierarchy of logic, going from the simplest propositions to the more complex; (4) make sure that nothing related to the analysis has been omitted. Descartes [1637] 1980: 41.

2 Alexander Baumgarten was the Enlightenment thinker who initiated aesthetics – the study of the beautiful, or of *taste* – as a distinct line of philosophical inquiry. Baumgarten's use of the word *aesthetica* appears in his first major work, *Metaphysica*, in 1739. Even though Baumgarten explicitly used this word to designate the realm of sense, as opposed to the realm of cognitive (or theoretical) knowledge, the emphasis was upon the idea of sensuous *knowing*. In other words, it is still central to Baumgarten's way of thinking that study of aesthetics be a systematic scientific discipline. Hence, in his day it was customary to assign theoretical knowledge to a "higher cognitive faculty" while the realm of *aisthesis* was assigned to a "lower cognitive faculty." And the "ideas" related to this lower faculty were "confused," or "unclear" ideas. See Barnouw 1993: 75–82.

3 This example is further addressed in Groat and Wang 2002: 119–121: "Design in Relation to Research."

4 Jennifer Hohlbein, Kyle Davis, Jon Follett, and Paul Yoon, "Northwest Style Is Not Northwest Style Without Cedar." Student final project in Arch 525 / ID 530 Architectural Theory, Washington State University, December 2010.

5 One might disagree with this by invoking Heidegger's famous treatment of the bridge in "Building Dwelling Thinking": it is the bridge that "gathers" the site and makes it a locale. The entire essay, it can be argued, is a refutation that Heidegger's phenomenology is blind to locale. But this goes right to the heart of the Heidegger/Norberg-Schulz difference. Heidegger's baseline treatment of his phenomenological terms (*Dasein*, thrownness, etc.) precedes his usage of those terms for analyses of certain topics such as building and dwelling, or works of art, in "The Origin of the Work of Art" (1951b). The terms themselves, perhaps as best defined in *Being and Time*, do not *necessarily* entail the pleasurable affections that come with dwelling, or with appreciating works of art. In this sense, Heidegger's technical terms are well established philosophically before they are used for analyses of empirical engagements. Perhaps put another way, the ontology his terms describe does not depend upon particular empirical engagements. Norberg-Schulz reverses this order: empirical features are what they are – the "fascination" of Prague, the "grandiosity" of Rome, etc. – in order that phenomenological

dwelling can be achieved. For the bridge reference, see Heidegger 1951a: 356. This edition also includes "The Origin of the Work of Art."

6   For an accessible overview of Kant's critical system, see Scruton 1983.

7   Hegel's philosophy does recognize individuals, but these are rare individuals who embody the *Geist* (spirit) of the times, and who thus can usher in, for an entire culture, the "shape" of what that culture is to be. Hegel called these "world-historical individuals." And even though his attention was upon political figures (Napoleon, for instance), certainly the theory of world-historical individuals can be applied to major artists who shift the course of art history (e.g., Michelangelo, Stravinsky, Frank Lloyd Wright, etc.). See Hegel 1953: 34–43.

8   Pisano and Verganti 2008: 78–86. References to Treadless.com are on pp. 81–82.

9   Facebook measuring the mood in the US, http://www.physorg.com/news174057519.html (accessed October 22, 2010).

10 It has been pointed out that "versioning" derives from non-Cartesian theories of space. But as much as versioning insists on a building as a series (rather than as an object), it still exists in physical context as (largely) a fixed reality: "there is a highly positive feedback between our Euclidean intuition and the experimental behavior of physical space" (Kinayoglu 2007: 18–19). The citation is from Poincaré, *La Science l'hypothèse* (Paris, 1902). http://etd.lib.metu.edu.tr/upload/12608818/index.pdf. Accessed May 18, 2011.

11 Dynamic Architecture. http://www.dynamicarchitecture.net/revolution/index.php?section=2. Accessed May 18, 2011.

12 For how this works, see http://www.d-toren.nl/site/read.htm. Accessed May 18, 2011.

13 Although these are not from a phenomenological perspective (which is the point made above: they *can* be from such a standpoint). Here are three examples of intelligent building research: Cole and Brown 2009; Janda 2009: 9–14; Mahdavi 2009.

References

Bachelard, G. [1958] 1994. *The Poetics of Space*, trans. John Stilgoe. Boston: Beacon Press.

Barnouw, J. 1993. "The beginnings of 'aesthetics' and the Leibnizian conception of sensation," in P. Mattick Jr (ed.), *Eighteenth-Century Aesthetics and the Reconstruction of Art*. Cambridge: Cambridge University Press, pp. 52–95.

Baumgarten, A. [1739] 1970. *Aesthetica*. Hildesheim and New York: Georg Olms.

Boles, D. 1989. "Reordering the suburbs," *Progressive Architecture* 5: 78–91.

Cole, R. J. and Brown, Z. 2009. "Reconciling human and automated intelligence in the provision of occupant comfort," *Intelligent Buildings International* 1: 39–55.

Cooper Marcus, C. 1995. *House as a Mirror of Self*. Berkeley, CA: Conari Press.

Cross, N. 2011. *Design Thinking*. Oxford: Berg.

Descartes, R. [1637] 1980. *Discourse on Method*, trans. F. E. Sutcliffe. Harmondsworth: Penguin Books.

Dynamic Architecture. http://www.dynamicarchitecture.net/revolution/index.php?section=2. Accessed May 18, 2011.

Eliade, M. 1959. *The Sacred and the Profane*, trans. W. Trask. New York: Harcourt Brace Jovanovich.

Facebook. 2010. *Measuring the Mood in the US*. http://www.physorg.com/news174057519.html. Accessed October 22, 2011.

Frampton, K. 1983. "Towards a critical regionalism: six points for an architecture of resistance," in H. Foster (ed.), *Postmodern Culture*. London: Pluto Press.

Groat, L. and Wang, D. 2002. *Architectural Research Methods*. New York: John Wiley.

Hegel, G. W. F. [1817] 2004. *Introductory Lectures on Aesthetics*, trans. Bernard Bosanquet. New York: Penguin.

Hegel, G. W. F. 1953. *Reason in History*, trans. Robert S. Hartman. New York: Liberal Arts Press.

Heidegger, M. 1951a. "Building dwelling thinking," in D. F. Krell (ed.), *Basic Writings*. New York: HarperCollins, pp. 347–363.

Heidegger, M. 1951b. "The origin of the work of art," in D. F. Krell (ed.), *Basic Writings*. New York: HarperCollins, pp. 129–212.

Heidegger, M. 1962. *Being and Time*, trans. John Macquarrie and Edward Robinson. New York: Harper & Row.

Janda, K. 2009. "Buildings don't use energy: people do," in *Proceedings of the Passive and Low Energy Architecture Conference 2009 - Architecture, Energy and the Occupant's Perspective*. Quebec City: Presses de Laval, pp. 9–14.

Kinayoglu, G. 2007. "A Reconsideration of the Concept of Architecture Space in the Virtual Realm." Master's thesis, Middle East Technical University, Graduate School of Natural and Applied Sciences.

Lauer, Q. 1965. "Introduction," in E. Husserl, *Phenomenology and the Crisis of Philosophy*. New York: Harper Torchbooks.

Libeskind, D. 1995. *1995 Raoul Wallenberg Lecture*. Ann Arbor: University of Michigan.

Locke, J. [1690] 1994. *An Essay Concerning Human Understanding*. London: J. M. Dent.

Mahdavi, A. 2009. "Patterns and implications of user control actions in buildings," *Indoor and Built Environment* 18(5): 440–446.

McDonough, W. 2008. "The Hanover principles," in H. F. Mallgrave and C. Contandriopoulos (eds.), *Architectural Theory*, vol. 2, Malden, MA: Blackwell Publishing, pp. 584–585.

Merleau-Ponty, M. [1945] 1995. *Phenomenology of Perception, 1945*, trans. Colin Smith. London and New York: Routledge.

Norberg-Schulz, C. 1980. *Towards a Phenomenology of Architecture*. New York: Rizzoli.

Pallasmaa, J. [1996] 2012. *Eyes of the Skin: Architecture and the Senses*. Oxford: John Wiley & Sons.

Pisano, G. P. and Verganti, R. 2008. "Which kind of collaboration is right for you?," *Harvard Business Review* December: 78–86.

Pressman, A. 1995. *The Fountainheadache: The Politics of Architect–Client Relations*. New York: John Wiley.

Putnam, R. 2000. *Bowling Alone*. New York: Simon & Schuster.

Putnam, R., and Feldstein, L. M., with Cohen, D. 2004. *Better Together: Restoring the American Community*. New York: Simon & Schuster.

Rasmussen, S. E. [1959] 2000. *Experiencing Architecture*. Cambridge, MA: MIT Press.

Rocker, I. M. 2008. "Versioning: architecture as series?", in K. Terzidis (ed.), *Proceedings of the First International Conference on Critical Digital: "What Matter(s)?"* April 18–19, 2008, Harvard University Graduate School of Design. Cambridge, MA: Harvard University, pp. 157–169.

Rowe, P. 1988. *Design Thinking*. Cambridge, MA: MIT Press.

Salvador, T., Bell, G., and Anderson, K. 1999. "Design ethnography," *Design Management Journal*: 35–41.

Scruton, R. 1983. *Kant*. Oxford and New York: Oxford University Press.

Speaks, M. 2005. "After theory," *Architectural Record* 193(6): 72–75.

Suger. 1946a. "De Administratione, XXXIV," in *Abbot Suger on the Abbey Church of St. Denis and its Art Treasures*, trans. E. Panofsky. Princeton: Princeton University Press.

Suger. 1946b. "De Consecratione IV," in *Abbot Suger on the Abbey Church of St. Denis and its Art Treasures*, trans. E. Panofsky. Princeton: Princeton University Press.

Wang, D. and Wagner, S. 2007. "A map of phenomenology for the design disciplines," *Environmental and Architectural Phenomenology Newsletter* 18(3): 10–15.

Wang, D. and Keen, J. 2001. "Intentionality and the production of architectural design(s): an application of Section 37 of Husserl's ideas," *Environmental and Architectural Phenomenology Newsletter* 12(3): 12–15.

Wolfflin, H. [1888] 1968. *Renaissance and Baroque*, trans. Kathrin Simon. Ithaca, NY: Cornell University Press.

Tuan, Yi-fu [1977] 2001. *Sense and Place: The Perspective of Experience*, Minneapolis: University of Minnesota Press.

2

Dorothy Draper and the American Housewife: A Study of Class Values and Success

John C. Turpin

Introduction

Between 1930 and 1960 Americans regard interior decorator[1] Dorothy Draper (1889 – 1969) as a pioneer in the area of commercial design, induct her into numerous Halls of Fame, identify her as Woman of the Year (1948), and recognize her name as the most familiar in the business in 1960.[2] What is particularly provocative about this list is the diversity of the constituencies who recognize her achievements. Her clients, successful businessmen, identify her as an early expert in commercial design; her peers within the design professions elect her into the Halls of Fame; the business community recognizes her as Woman of the Year, and a public poll yields her name as the most recognizable by the masses.

Of all the groups, the latter is the most unexpected. Many of the first and second generation of lady decorators built a client base from members of their same class (Blossom and Turpin 2008). Draper is different. While she uses her social connections to great advantage, she consciously pursues the middle class throughout her career through advice books and columns, and the design of public interiors. Without a formal education in decoration or design, Draper relies on her socially perceived position as an upper-class woman of "taste," which she fashions into a viable, marketable commodity. She uses this commodity as entrée into the world of advice literature and never relinquishes it. However, the mere act of writing cannot sustain her career; the public must validate the value of her product through consumption.

According to Reynolds and Olson, this sustained act of consumption implies that consumer values underscore each purchase (Reynolds and Olson 2001). If true, then

The Handbook of Interior Design, First Edition. Edited by Jo Ann Asher Thompson and Nancy H. Blossom.

how did Draper, an upper-class, Edwardian debutante raised in a gated community, understand the values of the middle-class American housewife? This essay explores the relationship between Dorothy Draper and the American middle-class housewife in an attempt to understand how these two value systems successfully converge between 1925 and 1950.

Literature Review

The literature addressing the relationship between decorators and their individual clients, and decorators and consumers, differs significantly. The vast majority of the scholarship regarding the historical figures in the interior design profession relies on the celebrity status of the decorator. During the first decade of the 21st century a flourish of biographies were published on "celebrity" decorators, Elsie de Wolfe, Francis Elkins, Dorothy Draper, Van Day Truex, and Albert Hadley – each as the topic of their own book (Lewis 2001, 2005; Salny 2005; Sparke 2005; Varney and Shaw 2006). Although most of the texts rely on the celebrity lifestyle of the individual decorators in order to entice readership, the titles demonstrate a desire to lay claim to some aspect of history. Albert Hadley is "America's preeminent interior designer," while Dorothy Draper is "America's most fabulous decorator." Van Day Truex defines "20th century taste and style," and de Wolfe is responsible for the birth of "modern interior decoration."

While the texts must be recognized for the compilation and presentation of archival material, most of them lack a scholarly analysis of the designer's work or contributions to the profession or society at large; Sparke's work is the exception. Voyeuristic details of their idiosyncratic lives or those of their famous clients produce a fascinating, albeit myopic view, of upper-class American society – particularly that of the designer and the client. While each of these texts has benefited from surveys of women in design, progress toward a critical understanding of these women and their relationship to society remains slow.

Studies or articles attempting to explore the relationship between interior designers and the consumer (masses) are difficult to find. Perhaps the most significant text at this point is Penny Sparke's, *As Long As It's Pink: The Sexual Politics of Taste*, that analyzes the relationship between gender, taste, and consumption during the 20th century (Sparke 1995). Taste is a distinguishing component of this study in that Sparke believes that society relegated taste to the feminine sphere where it became the primary means through which women negotiated the private, alternative face of modernity that touched and transformed their lives. This is based on taste's ability to communicate complex messages about values, aspirations, beliefs, and identities. The text addresses the topic broadly and does not pursue in depth the manner in which any given designer engaged the female consumer – but that was not the purpose of the book. Sparke does, however, reveal the authority of the female consumer in the marketplace as a powerful force.

Texts such as those previously mentioned encourage a much broader review of the literature regarding women interior decorators/designers. A 2007 study analyzes the content of the existing literature – surveys, monographs, case studies – focused on women's roles in the developing profession of interior design. The intent is to understand the degree to which women influenced the historical narrative and the manner in which they were discussed. The study uncovers five distinct concepts – gender, taste, consumerism, identity, and modernism – that demonstrate great value in understanding the female designer's experiences with and contributions to society (Turpin 2007). The findings respond to the fact that many decorators were women who used their taste as a commodity to sell products or services to American housewives seeking opportunities for self-expression during a century defined by modernism. Despite the studies about decorators, one concept rarely comes into the conversation: the idea of understanding "success."

Even though success is not explicitly discussed in much of the literature, many authors imply a decorator's success when they use terms like trendsetter or tastemaker. Without further exploration, the resulting conclusion suggests that decorators do nothing but follow the capricious whims of the consumer. This devalues the female consumer, suggesting that she is nothing but a shopper, when in fact her purchases are an attempt to express her values, aspirations, beliefs, and identities – and the decorator who is responsible for making "pretty things." The only author to propose a more substantive argument for a decorator's success is Penny Sparke in "The Domestic Interior and the Construction of Self: The New York Homes of Elsie de Wolfe" (Sparke 2004):

> [Elsie de Wolfe's] success as a professional decorator undoubtedly stemmed from her ability to focus on those aspects of her persona with which other women could identify. Her enhanced characterization of her own femininity, her social aspirations and her ambivalent sense of her own nationality, proved to be those with which many of the female members of the emergent elite of American society were also preoccupied and which they sought to express through their domestic interiors.

Sparke's statement implies that success is based on some sort of shared value system between the designer and the consumer. De Wolfe, like many of her peers, works predominantly with a clientele (female socialites) from her own class. The shared value system lubricates the design process as decisions by both the designer and the client grew from similar cultural roots often grounded in class and gender.

Draper, however, chooses a much different professional career path. She quickly abandons residential design for the wealthy and focuses her efforts on large-scale public commissions – apartment buildings, restaurants, retail spaces – frequented by a much larger range of Americans; she also strategically begins writing advice books and columns. Even though her primary clients are wealthy businessmen, the end-user represents individuals from numerous classes. In a 1957 interview with

Edward R. Murrow, Draper laments the experience of commuters. "Think of those poor commuters who die young just because they go on such uncomfortable trains."

Carleton Varney, current president of Draper & Company and a past employee of Draper's, states, "To Dorothy, public space represent[s] a place for people to come and feel elevated in the presence of great beauty, where the senses could look and feel and absorb the meaning of a quality life" (Varney (1988). Draper manifests this belief by reinterpreting aristocratic European designs for middle-class consumption in public spaces, such as retail stores and restaurants. Perhaps more importantly, she also incorporates this approach in her advice books. An analysis of her door designs, as found in *Decorating Is Fun!*, brings to light Draper's interest in offering the middle class diluted versions of doors in a number of high styles (Renaissance, baroque, neoclassical) at an affordable price (Turpin 2000).

The literature review reveals a clear move toward understanding women's participation in the public sphere of business as consumers and service providers; however, understanding their success remains virtually unexplored. Sparke indicates a relationship between the designer and the consumer – underscored by shared values. In her case study, the designer, de Wolfe, and the consumer, her wealthy clients, come from the same class. De Wolfe designs within a framework grounded in her own class experiences for individuals in similar situations.

However, Draper, a member of the elite class, connects with the middle class – a group whose value system is quite different than her own. Research focusing on consumer behavior can help articulate the relationship between those who make products or offer services and those who consume them.

Theoretical Framework

Consumer behavior has become a widely studied field since the 1960s.[3] Researchers address gender, race, and class in an attempt to understand the choices consumers make. One general conclusion is that individual values are almost always at the core of the process.

Reynolds and Olson (2001) make this evident in their Means-End Theory (MET) for marketing and advertising strategy. The authors rely on cognitive psychology to craft a model that depends on relationships between three separate elements: the attributes of a product (means), the consequences for the consumer based on those attributes, and the personal values (ends) reinforced by those consequences (see Figure 2.1).

Reynolds and Olson break down each of the categories for further exploration. For example, attributes can be represented by form or style. Consequences are either tangible or emotional. Anticipated values are higher-order feelings or life goals. As can be seen in Figure 2.1, the reliance on consumer values in the processes of evaluating products is underscored. If consequences are negative and do not support values, then the product is not accepted. However, if the consumer perceives the

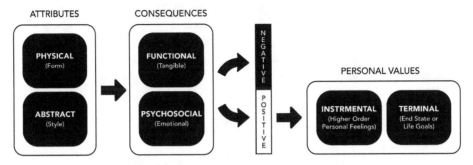

Figure 2.1 Diagram of Reynolds and Olson's Means-End Theory. Graphic by Jeremy Bolton.

consequences as being positive, then it is understood that it supported a portion of their belief system. This clearly implies that the "product," and by extension the designer, is successful. Reynolds and Olson's paradigm can easily be applied to Draper and reinforces the five concepts (gender, taste, consumerism, identity, and modernism) motivating so much of the research involving women and interior design, which essentially uncovered a critical relationship between females on both sides of a business transaction focused on products and services for the domestic environment.

Draper is responsible for both the physical form and the style of her "products," in this case, a finished interior or her advice in a written text. The consumer then evaluates the product to determine consequences. In order for an interior to be viewed as positive, it must first be functional. If a consumer cannot sit at a table comfortably or use a sink because it is too high, then a space fails immediately as the consumer is frustrated. The psychosocial aspect of consequences relative to design might relate to an aesthetic response where the consumer is most likely to be moved emotionally. Purchasing a home follows this process. If a home is well designed and is therefore functional and aesthetically pleasing, then the consumer finds value in living a comfortable life. These choices reflect their taste, as well as a much deeper series of personal values.

The primary intent of the Reynolds and Olson model is to demonstrate how and why consumers purchase a product, which encourages the design of product based on data regarding consumer behavior, leading to profit in production and sales. However, I suggest that the model has the potential to uncover critical relationships between the values of the designer and the consumer if it is considered in a different context. In this context the attributes of a product are a reflection of Draper's values rather than a simple means to an end (profit) driven by fashion or fad. To test this model, statements by Draper are carefully analyzed and cross-referenced with critical aspects of her life experiences. Class and gender play a role as these concepts form crucial experiences defined by pre-existing social constructs.

The following discussion focuses on two values of particular importance to the middle class during the first half of the 20th century: progress toward a better life and happiness via psychological comfort. Draper's products are then evaluated, based on the Reynolds and Olson model, to see if her values resonate with the consumer in order to articulate at least one means of understanding success.

Draper and the Middle Class

Progress toward a better way of life

During the middle of the 19th century, the middle class glorifies economic independence as a means of attaining stability, continuity, and domesticity (Davis 2001). Maintaining the status quo ensures that they will not lose their newfound position in society that was granted by the effects of the Industrial Revolution. By the turn of the century, stability is not enough. With the increase of wealth in the United States as a result of the Reconstruction era, many members of the middle class vault into the upper class with tremendous speed and pecuniary force. The class they leave behind grows envious of their lifestyle and no longer settles for stability. They desire orderly progress. "The root assumption [is] that progress [is] an inspired and irrevocable law" (Baritz 1989). The middle class views their ascension to the elite levels of society as inevitable, given enough time, at least for some of them.[4] In the meantime, they prepare for the "inevitable" by acting, behaving, and living like their social superiors to the point that their financial means will allow. Without any direct knowledge of how to do this, they search for advice; and who better than the "grandes dames" of taste, the women of the upper class, to come to their aid?

Decorating Is Fun!, Draper's first publication in 1939, joins a growing list of interior decoration books that includes works by Edith Wharton, Elsie de Wolfe, and Emily Post.[5] Books on decoration fall into three general categories. The first category focuses more on the study of interior decoration. Books such as Edith Wharton and Ogden Codman's *The Decoration of Houses* (1897), Joy Wheeler Dow's *The Book of a Hundred Houses* (1906), and Gladys Miller's *Decoratively Speaking* (1939) concentrate on historical styles and architectural details for upper-class homes.

The other extreme is the do-it-yourself books. Emily Burbank's *Be Your Own Decorator* (1922) rarely addresses historical periods and, instead, focuses readers on how to use the current inventory in their home to enhance their space. The "do-it-yourself" concept is a prime consideration and many of the tasks require that the occupants complete the labor.

The third category includes books that negotiate the middle of the spectrum. Authors target the middle class by providing some information on historic styles and budgets. The one trait that often defines this group is the severity of the "dos" and "don'ts." Unlike the more scholarly approach in the first category and the lack of criticism in the second, these authors speak of good taste and employ it as their validation for good decoration.

Emily Post's *The Personality of a House: The Blue Book of Home Design and Decoration* (1930) sets the standard for this category. These books count on the insecurities of middle-class women who question their own taste. Amidst the popularity of decorating books, Draper offers her approach that integrates traits of the second and third categories. She excludes historical styles from the discussion, considers the significance of budget, and, most importantly, communicates in a tone as if she were speaking to her best friend over tea.

Draper begins by demystifying the art of decoration by asking her readers "Have you ever considered how much pure stuff and nonsense surrounds this subject of interior decoration?" She continues by stating "almost everyone believes that there is something deep and mysterious about it or that you have to know all sorts of complicated details about periods before you can lift a finger" (Draper 1939). Having put her readers' apprehensions to rest, Draper delivers her stylistic approach to decoration that is underscored by her values. A discussion of her advice (the products) becomes the first data for the theoretical framework according to Reynolds and Olson: the attributes.

In *Decorating Is Fun!* Draper provides design advice for each room in the house. We will look at the dining room and bedroom, in part because the images she provides allow us to "see" the physical and abstract attributes (form and style, respectively). Figure 2.2 depicts a romantic table set for four. The forms suggest that the furnishings are derivative of high-style pieces, but with some modern adjustments. The chairs reference the Victorian era with heavy tufting and Queen Anne legs, although Draper has painted them white. The stiff backs imply a need for good posture while in the company of others. Layers of window treatments boast swags, jabots, and ruffles framing an expanse of glass that might suggest a country view. While the floral wallpaper offers an air of formality, the polka dot tablecloth is playful and informal. Four tall, elegant candles frame an equal number of white vases filled with red tulips to give the illusion of a magnificent centerpiece. The styling of the vignette harks back to elaborate table settings experienced by the wealthy. The table is meticulously set with the appropriate plateware, silverware, and glassware. The table appears full, as if guests will be sitting down to a luxurious seven-course meal.

Draper's design of a bedroom for the Hampshire House (shown in Figure 2.3) follows a similar formula. Two four-post tester beds with colorful floral valances and modest side panels are the focal point of this relatively intimate bedroom in a Manhattan apartment building. The Chinese-inspired fretwork on the headboard hints at the exotic or the imported. A skirted vanity table and oversized chair and ottoman in the same textile as the bed's accouterments welcome the inhabitants as if secluded in a far-off countryside estate. A promise of that view is hidden behind the layers of textiles, trimmed in tassels. The bold pink and white striped wallpaper visually extends the verticality of the room.

Draper's design choices (as evidenced by the attributes) in *Decorating Is Fun!* support her values. She clearly draws upon her past experiences as a wealthy member of Tuxedo Park society to inform her aesthetic stylings. Recognizing the importance of a beautiful surrounding, Draper re-creates these pseudo-historic, high-style

Figure 2.2 Table set from the five-and-ten-cent store (Draper 1939: 190). Reproduced by permission of Dorothy Draper & Company, Inc.

Figure 2.3 Bedroom (Draper 1939: 166). Reproduced by permission of Dorothy Draper & Company, Inc.

spaces on a middle-class budget. Her intent is to elevate the quality of life by transporting the users psychologically from the city to the country or at least allowing them to experience the joys of living the good life. Draper communicates the importance of her surroundings in the dedication of *Decorating Is Fun!*

To
My Mother and Father
Susan and Paul
Tuckerman
The best amateur planners I know, who after more than fifty
years of married life, secretly long to build still another house
and to whom plans and decorations
are an unending fascination, delight and
challenge, this little book is dedicated with
love,
gratitude and admiration.

Draper is referring to the fifth house in Tuxedo Park which the Tuckermans would inhabit. The legacy of the Tuckerman homes is significant to the community of Tuxedo Park and Dorothy. These surroundings underpin her knowledge of, and appreciation for, grand interiors.

Once Draper's advice book hit the bookshelves, consumers review the material for its functional and psychosocial consequences, the next phase of the model. Functionally, the spaces are successful as a place to eat and a place to sleep. As a piece of literature (design advice in written form), the functional (tangible) consequences of the books prove beneficial in educating women on how to create an aesthetically pleasing space on a modest budget.

Acutely aware of her audience, Draper provides strategies for the middle-class housewife to decorate in a manner reminiscent of the upper class. The various components of the dining room come from the five-and-ten-cent store. Draper educates the reader on how "to substitute good taste for money in such a way that charm will not suffer in the least" (Draper 1939). In the bedroom, Draper's use of white paint on the bed frames is quite ingenious; it nullifies the social judgment of the type of wood used in the furniture. The simple lines of the beds read as modern interpretations as opposed to an inexpensive, traditional frame. In both cases, inexpensive furnishings create a high-style appearance. Overstuffed seating, robust floral textiles, and historically referenced details in furnishings belie the perception of a middle-class income.

At the psychosocial (emotional) level middle-class housewives evaluate Draper's advice under the auspices of a general desire to emulate the upper class as a reflection of steady progress toward a better way of life (Bledstein and Johnston 2001). Although the home becomes an opportunity for women to express their identities, it also continues to be a manifestation of the husband's success. The care and decoration of the house communicates the success of the woman at fulfilling her socially constructed role as a "model housewife." Furthermore, Draper's advice is particularly successful at empowering women who felt as if they had "no taste." She made clear the point that all women have the ability to make a lovely home. The countless scenarios Draper presents in her text for each room type challenge the idea of a specific fashion or fad that the reader has to follow. Consequently, a middle-class housewife's emotional response to the text is a validation of their good taste and their success as housewives – both of which address their psychosocial needs.

The positive reaction to the consequences supports the middle-class housewives' personal values, the final analysis in the model. They experience higher-order personal feelings of financial independence and progress as manifested by their ability to decorate their homes with such style and elegance. End states or life goals reflect their desire to emulate the upper class and "live the good life" – at least within the reality of their means.

Here, the values of Draper and the consumer merge. Draper knows the value of living in beautiful spaces that elevate the individual; one might say that, in this instance, she embraces the views of the Aesthetic Movement. The aesthetes believe that "the character of the environment sets a standard for the individual to live by. Beautiful surroundings…can instill within each person a corresponding beauty of demeanor, thought, and deed" (Brandt 1989). Draper experiences this at first hand. Middle-class housewives seek the same experience as a reflection of their desire toward steady progress, and the eventual goal of "living the good life."

Happiness

The first half of the 20th century is a difficult time for Americans. World War I derails any notion of a peaceful century. The fight is external and at an unimaginable scale. The Great Depression seems a punishment for the debauchery and loose living of the 1920s, while World War II demonstrates that conflicts could actually get worse. During these three decades the American people yearn for distractions.[6] They need an escape from worrying about how to feed the family or whether or not a telegram will arrive telling of the loss of a husband, father, or son on the battlefield. They value happiness in the form of psychological comfort, which comes in the need of escapist experiences.

The desire for escapism or fantasy is manifested in many aspects of daily life. The most obvious is the explosive popularity of movies. The relatively new medium becomes the "space of supreme illusion" during the 1920s and 1930s (Fischer 1942). The antics of Charlie Chaplin (1889–1977), the sultry romances of Rudolph Valentino (1895–1926) and the unforgettable screen performances of Greta Garbo (1905–1990) sweep audiences away from their own lives and insert them into someone else's that is more intriguing and exciting.

According to some historians, movies become more escapist during the 1940s because of the psychological stress of the war (Weibel 1977). Walt Disney's (1901–1966) *Snow White* (1937), *Pinocchio* (1940), *Fantasia* (1940), *Dumbo* (1941), and

Figure 2.4 The Mirror Room at Kerr's department store in Oklahoma City, Oklahoma (1941). Reproduced by permission of Dorothy Draper & Company, Inc.

Bambi (1942) effectively provide escapist afternoons considering they were always some of the highest-grossing films of the year. Americans lose themselves in romantic stories with inevitable happy endings.

Other cultural experiences reflect the American appetite for escapism. Department stores appeal to fantasies of escape and luxury by providing customers with atmospheres of pleasure and comfort (Leach 1993). Window displays delight the eye and the employees place each customer on a pedestal while being served. The department store is particularly meaningful to the female consumer, where feminine taste is indulged and dreams and realities mingle seamlessly (Sparke 1995). Draper's design of the women's floor at Kerr's department store (1941) in Oklahoma City, the next subject up for analysis, blends movie and shopping experiences. The Mirror Room (shown in Figure 2.4) transforms into a glamorous stage that mimics the elegance of the black and white movies for American women seeking distraction from the physical and psychological pressures of everyday life.

The attributes of the interior include a predominantly gray and white palette with a lemon yellow accent. Draper announces the space with a bold sign befitting a theater's marquee. Its shape is a blend of baroque vigor and modern minimalism. Draper frames the opening much like a proscenium, making the experience of entering the dressing room quite grand. Floor-to-ceiling drapes support the theatrics of the space with large spotlight-like lighting fixtures above. Four wall mirrors framed in Draper's neo-baroque scrollwork act as focal points for the space and yet define the single most significant location in the room – the center, which is hidden by the mirrored column.

Dorothy Draper's design choices are a reflection of her love of romanticism as defined by her childhood experiences in Tuxedo Park. The idyllic setting with its tree-canopied roads, rolling hills, and clear lakes created an exquisite backdrop to the architectural marvels that dot the landscape and a vivid setting for a young child's imagination. Herbert Claiborne Pell (1884–1961) recalls a great deal of freedom as a child in "Life in Tuxedo Park." Children roam free because of the absence of the automobile and an 8-foot-tall barbed wire fence that circles the community. "Modern" games such as kite-flying, marbles, or tag are not options in Tuxedo. The children, instead, exercise their imagination in an untarnished landscape dotted with villas, palazzos, cottages, and chateaus on gracious plots of land trimmed in indigenous foliage. Pell remembers afternoons wandering through the woods "doing that which at the moment seemed good to us" (Pell 1973). Many times this includes an exploration of the forests with the intent of discovering hidden silver mines or perhaps playing Indians. Dorothy participates in such activities; in fact, her mother dresses her in boy's clothes when these occasions arise.[7] However, even amongst such beautiful surroundings, Draper recalls wanting to escape from Tuxedo Park because of the endless rules of etiquette that accompany membership in the upper class. She too seeks psychological comfort. Draper knows the value of escapism and fantasy and carries it forward into her adult life and professional career.

The Mirror Room acts as both a place to escape and a place to fantasize. The modern geometry coated in shades of gray provokes memories of the silver screen, which often features scenes of high fashion. Draper, who was raised as an Edwardian debutante, participates in the romance of fashion as is evident from the exquisite dress and wrap that she dons for her 1957 interview with Edward R. Murrow. When she moves through her apartment, the location of the interview, it is as if she is waltzing – another favored pastime according to her youngest daughter, Penelope. Draper's choice in clothing, however, lacks the modern style popular at the time. Her outfit boasts traditional floral motifs and a crinoline undergarment to add fullness. Draper's performance for the camera is an accurate reflection of the woman who uses clothing as a romantic form of escape. Similar to her own attire, Draper's Mirror Room showcases her romantic style with neo-baroque scrollwork and lemon yellow chairs.

For the female customer, the Mirror Room functions as both stage and runway (tangible consequences). Women enjoy the theatrics of exiting the private dressing room into the common area in a new garb. Each garment allows the customer to engage in playacting – in front of an intimate audience no less – and be transported into a world of luxury beyond the drudgery, bills, and monotony of daily life defined by the circumstances of World War II. The customer takes center stage and all eyes are on her. She spins in the new dress trying to catch a glimpse of her new costume at all angles in one of the many reflective surfaces.

The mirrors, the most powerful objects in the space, play a major role in inducing the effect. They have the power to "draw customers into a narcissistic maze of self-reflection, creating an environment in which they might interact with the goods in the most intimate and personal way" (Leach 1993). Such hypnotic experiences are nothing short of a harmless drug that counteracts the reality of the female house-wife's current circumstances. Many become depressed and seek help, as indicated by an increase in the formation of support groups across the nation (Campbell 1984).

One should not overlook the most conspicuous of the mirrors in the space: the central column. Of all the mirrors, this one has a unique purpose. It prevents the unwanted, judgmental eye of the male gaze. Draper locates the column right in front of the prime location where a female customer would go to access views of herself in all of the mirrors. This offers the women an added layer of psychological comfort as she denies uninvited parties the opportunity to scrutinize her new clothes, her playacting, or even her self. This brief escape is crucial as women stress over the safety of their loved ones overseas and are burdened with the respon-sibility of maintaining the illusion that life continues as normal even though they now assume the stressful roles of both mother and father. The emotional conse-quence of using the Mirror Room is one of relief, happiness, control, and security – all crucial element of psychological comfort.

The incorporation of fantasy and escape makes Draper's interiors a welcome relief for all – lower, middle, and upper class. During the stressful years of both world wars and the Depression, people value comfort and distraction as a means to reaching the end goal of happiness. Consumers seek out places of retreat – like the cinema and retail stores – in order to alleviate the overwhelming stress of their lives. Draper offers individual spaces embedded with emotion. She imbues her style with romanticism as seen in the baroque scrollwork and intensely optimistic colors like lemon yellow. Draper's design approach allows female consumers to live in a state of happiness; one that is carefree and controllable.

Conclusion

By the end of her career, Draper writes articles for *House & Garden*, publishes two advice books (*Decorating Is Fun!*, 1939; *Entertaining Is Fun*, 1941), authors an advice column for newspaper mogul William Randolph Hearst, and is appointed director of *Good Housekeeping*'s "Studio for Living" (November 1941–December 1945). Simultaneously, Draper wins high-profile design commissions that the public can enjoy. Time and again, the attributes (form and style) of Draper's products (written or interiors) are positively evaluated by female consumers (the target market) for functional (physical) and psychosocial (emotional) consequences, thus providing support of their personal values either through higher-order personal feelings or life goals. According to Reynolds and Olson's Means-End Theory, the middle-class housewife's acceptance of Draper's products supports her desire for steady progress and happiness. Perhaps more importantly, however, this study brings to light one way in which Draper's success as a businesswoman might be explained beyond financial success and the elusive criterion of being named a trendsetter or tastemaker.

The results of this study also offer an opportunity to analyze the work of the decorator. Sparke reminds us that women utilize their taste as a means of negotiating modernity. In this case, the women are both the producer and the consumer, the decorator and the housewife. Draper's products are as much an expression of her values, aspirations, beliefs, and identity as they are of those of the consumer. Her romantic tendencies underscore the creation and consumption of her products. In the words of her daughter, "she just love[s] romance…[and] adore[s] romantic things."[8] Draper masterfully wields bright colors, large floral patterns, and pseudo-historical references (in text or form) to help the middle class emulate their social superiors on a modest budget, which supports the possibility of the American Dream, and yet offers them happiness by escaping to places in which they can retreat from the harsh realities of the 20th century.

Draper wants the same things. While her desire for beautiful spaces unsurprisingly originates from her own childhood experiences in Tuxedo Park, she also seeks happiness. After 19 years of marriage, Draper finds herself divorced in 1931 and living temporarily in a one-bedroom apartment with Penelope and the family dog, who share the bunk beds while Draper sleeps on the couch. After she settles into single life – a difficult task for an upper-class woman in her forties – Draper's son goes to war. Despite her upper-class status, Draper experiences the first half of the 20th century in a very similar fashion as the American housewife. Romanticism is a means for these women to cope with the challenges of modern life.

Most of the early interior decorators work within their own social circle. Elsie de Wolfe, Sister Parish, and Nancy McClelland are just a few examples. They each create reputations based on services provided to members of their own social class. Draper, however, taps into the values of the middle class – both intentionally and accidentally. Her strategy is quite effective. In essence, Draper courts the middle class by offering free decorating advice that empowers them as individuals, then when a business tycoon asks her to design a retail store, restaurant, or hotel, Draper's fan base is just lying in wait to see their mentor's latest work. This yields high returns on the businessman's investment, the criterion by which he evaluates Draper's success. Combined with her business acumen, Draper's romantic – and decidedly feminine – approach to design allows her to become one of the most recognizable and successful names in the industry.

Notes

1   For the purposes of this study, Dorothy Draper is referred to as a decorator. While her career starts in decoration, she quickly moves toward larger, more complex design problems in the public realm, in which the scope of the project warrants the term interior

designer as now defined by the profession. However, Draper dispenses decorating advice in her publications for the middle class, and their understanding of Draper as a professional during her career is very likely as a decorator.

2 According to Carleton Varney, the Center for Research in Marketing completed a survey revealing Draper was more familiar to American housewives than industrial designer Russell Wright (1904–1976), furniture designer and decorator Paul McCobb (1917–1969), architect and furniture/industrial designer George Nelson (1908–1986), and architect and furniture designer T. H. Robsjohn-Gibbings (1905–1976) – all leading men in the various fields of design. See Varney 2006: 27.

3 The scholarship on consumer behavior takes root in the 1960s and continues to develop addressing issues of race, gender, and class. See Nicosia 1966; Markin 1974; Pitts and Woodside 1984; Costa 1994; Danzinger 2005.

4 Baritz notes that the middle class believed that life would continue to improve and that the "present was less desirable than the future." The middle class demonstrated their ambitions of wealth through their emulative behavior of the upper class. See Baritz 1989: 80. See also Davis 2001.

5 Betty Dickson Thornley (b. 1885) was the ghostwriter for *Decorating Is Fun!*

6 "The people are seeking to escape from themselves," concluded a writer in *Advertising and Selling* in 1926. "They want to live in a more exciting world." This quote reveals that even during the 1920s Americans want to engage in a life of escapism and fantasy, albeit for different reasons other than the Depression and war. See Marchand 1985: xvii.

7 In 2006, the author had the privilege to interview Penelope Buchanan (1923–2010), the youngest of Dorothy Draper's three children. The detail of Draper being dressed in male clothes as a child comes from this interview (Penelope Minturn Draper Buchanan, Gates Mills, Ohio, March 2006.)

8 Penelope also stated that her mother frequented the theater and movies with a couple of very close friends. Personal interview with Penelope Buchanan at her home in Gates Mills, Ohio, March 2006.

References

Baritz, L. 1989. *The Good Life: The Meaning of Success for the American Middle Class*. New York: Alfred A. Knopf.

Bledstein, Burton J. and Johnston, R. D., eds. 2001. *The Middling Sorts: Exploration in the History of the American Middle Class*. New York: Routledge.

Blossom, N. and Turpin, J. C. 2008. "Risk as a window to agency: a case study of three decorators," *Journal of Interior Design* 34(1): 1–13.

Brandt, B. 1989, October. "In quest of usefulness and beauty: changing interpretations of the Arts and Crafts ideal. Part II: the Aesthetic Movement," *Designers West* 36(13): 166–168.

Burbank, E. 1922. *Be Your Own Decorator*. New York: Dodd, Mead.

Campbell, D. 1984. *Women at War with America*. Cambridge, MA: Harvard University Press.

Costa, J. 1994. *Gender and Consumer Behavior*. Thousand Oaks: Sage Publications.

Danzinger, P. 2005. *Let Them Eat Cake: Marketing Luxury to the Masses – As Well As the Classes*. Chicago: Dearborn Trade Publication.

Davis, C. 2001. "The corporate reconstruction of middle-class manhood," in B. J. Bledstein and R. D. Johnston (eds.), *The Middling Sorts: Exploration in the History of the American Middle Class*. New York: Routledge, pp. 201–216.

"Draper in Oklahoma," 1944, April. *Interiors* 50.

Draper, D. 1939. *Decorating Is Fun!* New York: Doubleday, Doran.

Draper, D. 1941. *Entertaining Is Fun*. New York: Doubleday, Doran.

Fischer, B. E. S. 1942, October 28. "Dorothy Draper, designer, ties up her hotel decoration all in one package," *Christian Science Monitor* C10.

Leach, W. 1993. *Land of Desire: Merchants, Power, and the Rise of a New American Culture*. New York: Pantheon Books.

Lewis, A. 2001. *Van Day Truex: The Man Who Defined Twentieth Century Taste and Style*. New York: Viking Studio.

Lewis, A. 2005. *Albert Hadley: The Story of America's Preeminent Interior Designer*. New York: Rizzoli.

Marchand, R. 1985. *Advertising the American Dream: Making Way for Modernity, 1920–1940*. Berkeley: University of California Press.

Markin, R. 1974. *Consumer Behavior: A Cognitive Orientation*. New York: Macmillan.

Miller, G. 1939. *Decoratively Speaking: The Essentials and Principles of Interior Decoration*. New York: Doubleday, Doran.

Murrow, E. R. 1957, May. "Interview with Dorothy Draper," in *Person to Person with Edward R. Murrow*. New York: CBS, vide ocassette.

Nicosia, F. 1966. *Consumer Decision Processes; Marketing and Advertising Implications*. Englewood Cliffs, NJ: Prentice Hall.

Pell, H. C. 1973, March 12. "Life in Tuxedo Park," transcript of the Columbia University Oral History Program presented to the Tuxedo Park Library.

Pitts, R. and Woodside, A. 1984. *Personal Values and Consumer Psychology*. Lexington, MA: Lexington Books.

Post, E. 1930. *The Personality of a House: The Blue Book of Home Design and Decoration*. New York: Funk & Wagnall's.

Reynolds, T. and Olson, J. 2001. *Understanding Consumer Decision Making: The Means-End Approach to Marketing and Advertising Strategy*. Mahwah, NJ: L. Erlbaum.

Salny, S. 2005. *Francis Elkins: Interior Design*. New York: W. W. Norton.

Sparke, P. 1995. *As Long As It's Pink: The Sexual Politics of Taste*. London: HarperCollins.

Sparke, P. 2004. "The domestic interior and the construction of self: the New York homes of Elsie de Wolfe," in S. McKellar and P. Sparke (eds.), *Interior Design and Identity*. Manchester: Manchester University Press, pp. 72–91

Sparke, P. 2005. *Elsie de Wolfe: The Birth of Modern Interior Decoration*. New York: Acanthus Press.

Turpin, J. 2000. "The doors of Dorothy Draper: vestiges of Victorian manners with a middle class sensibility," *Form: The Journal of Architecture, Design & Material Culture* 1(1): 8–15; http://digitalcommons.unl.edu/archinform/.

Turpin, J. 2007. "The history of women in interior design: a review of literature," *Journal of Interior Design* 33(1): 1–16.

Varney, C. 1988. *The Draper Touch*. New York: Prentice Hall.

Varney, C. and Shaw, D. 2006. *In the Pink: Dorothy Draper, America's Most Fabulous Decorator*. New York: Pointed Leaf Press.

Weibel, K. 1977. *Mirror, Mirror: Images of Women Reflected in Popular Culture*. Garden City, NY: Anchor Books.

Wharton, E. and Codman, O. 1897. *The Decoration of Houses*. New York: Charles Scribner's Sons.

Wheeler, J. 1906. *The Book of a Hundred Houses: A Collection of Pictures, Plans and Suggestions for Householders*. New York: Duffield.

3

The Political Interior

Mary Anne Beecher

The study of the political is, by its very nature, a study of power relationships. This is certainly true of electoral politics, with its partisan allegiances and inherent hierarchies. It is also true, however, of the everyday politics that frame most encounters in the workplace, the academy, and all types of social interactions, including familial relationships. An exploration of the political interior should therefore include an interrogation of the meaning of "everyday" interior spaces and their ability to communicate cultural and design values on many levels.

I believe that it is the ubiquitous interiors of the everyday environment that are best positioned to illustrate the political potential of space to express and influence these power relationships. Using the example of an often overlooked model for promoting design to the "masses" in what I will argue are early modern interior design practices, I will attempt to articulate here that designed interior spaces that take a stand can be found in the most surprising places, and that when designers of interior spaces act aggressively to make a difference in the quality of the built environment for all people, there is much to be gained on both sides of the equation.

The term "political" is broad and can be applied to many concepts related to the built environment. For the purposes of this essay, it is intended to describe the process of advocating for an identifiable point of view; of rejecting neutrality; and of acknowledging the role of a larger external system or context in determining the meaning of something – in this case, a designed space and its influence on the experience of its occupants. For the purposes of this essay, I will also rely on another political concept – that of "grass roots" or local actions – to empower the participants in the design process through the sharing of knowledge.

The Handbook of Interior Design, First Edition. Edited by Jo Ann Asher Thompson and Nancy H. Blossom.

The interior – and the domestic interior in particular – is the dwelling place for our bodies, and as such, it is also the aspect of the built environment with which people have the most intimate psychological relationship. It is therefore the most logical site for strategic political interventions that can really make a difference in people's lives. Gaston Bachelard described our connection to our domestic interiors as well as their ability to represent what matters most to us when he noted that "our house is our corner of the world" (Bachelard 1964). It is because of its ability to serve as a microcosm of all that our life experience is, that the house and its rooms become an ideal site for examining design's political potential.

The association of interior design with the domestic realm has historical roots in North America because of the fact that the earliest acknowledged professional interior designers most often dealt with the production of residential space. These earliest practitioners focused on creating atmospheres that supported the personal, functional, and aesthetic requirements of their clients (Sparke 2008).

While architecture, graphic design, and industrial design in the modern era often enjoyed the privileged position of addressing an anonymous and all-encompassing "public" through their practice, the work of interior designers seems (rightly or wrongly) understood as a more intimate, more particular, and ultimately more personal pursuit. Perhaps this is because, even as the profession makes efforts to promote a more technical identity for itself today, it also continues to emphasize its responsiveness to clients' needs and desires through the educational and practice-based principles it promotes. The educational objectives required for professional accreditation in North America, for instance, reinforce interior design's people- or client-centered perspective by requiring that students develop an understanding of "human factors," and suggesting that they generate "creative solutions that support human behavior" (CIDA 2011). Likewise, professional organizations such as ASID (the American Society of Interior Designers) reinforce these values by describing the process used by professionals to produce designs as "a systematic and coordinated methodology" that integrates research and knowledge into the creative process, "whereby the needs and resources of the client are satisfied to produce an interior space that fulfills the project goals" (ASID 2011).

Guidelines such as these result in the public's ongoing perception that interior design is a service-based practice. Interior designers, by implication, may therefore feel that there is a lack of any sense of agency with regard to their ability to shape the built environment in particular, intentional ways. The political potential of interior design is located, at least in part, in these intentions that surpass the framework of identified project requirements, no matter how elaborate or mundane the project.

What I hope to suggest in this essay is that by consciously acknowledging the political nature of even the most common designed interior spaces, we can appreciate the potential significance of the complex relationships that impact their production and use, thereby advancing interior designers' ability to make a difference in the physical environment and in the lives of the people who experience it.

The theoretical perspective used to frame this discussion merges feminist theory and material culture theory. Feminist theory celebrates the articulation of the significance of everyday engagements. Its literature has long-proclaimed the perspective that "the personal is political" (Hanisch [1970] 2000). Writers like radical feminist Carol Hanisch fought to bring an awareness of the detrimental impact that accepting specific hierarchical social structures such as patriarchy has on a society to new audiences, beginning in the 1960s. First published in 1970, Hanisch's specific argument that the personal experiences of individuals within a group are valid sources of information from which to draw culturally based conclusions and upon which to base connections within and beyond the group continues to resonate with persons who find themselves lacking an equal voice in society today.

I find that much of what is written about the nature of interior space and the state of the interior design profession resonates with the themes of historic feminist literature – especially those works that pertain to issues of power, inequity, and the value of work traditionally done by women. Cheryl Buckley's early work on the history of women in design encouraged the re-evaluation of how the constant presence of a patriarchal system has shaped cultural perceptions of the value of designs of all kinds, based, in part, on the gender of who created it, who desired it, who consumed it, and who defined it as significant (Buckley 1986). Designers who criticize the ways in which contemporary interior design is perceived similarly invoke the influence of oppressive paradigms such as having to work within a culture that routinely assigns credit for all architectural production to architects and that fails to comprehend the level of technical expertise that interior designers contribute to the integrated design process (Ankerson and Gabb 2010).

Readings of interiors and their contents as material evidence of cultural values also provide a link between feminist criticism and the built environment. The association of interior space itself with a female identity and the subsequent secondary status assigned it within the built environment because of this connection also echo cries for the recognition of the inequities with which women have been forced to operate historically. Historian Beverly Gordon established the historic conceptualization of interior spaces as analogous with the female gendered body with its inherent container – the womb – and she further posited that a cultural understanding of interior space as "lesser" than exterior space can be attributed to the inevitability of its association with the feminine. It is, perhaps, the femaleness of interiors that provides an explanation for why interior spaces are nearly always the first part of a building to be simplified or eliminated when budgets for new buildings get tightened (Gordon 1996).

In terms of interpreting practice and addressing the dominance of the interior design profession by women, authors such as Lucinda Havenhand have presented compelling arguments for rethinking the typically accepted hierarchy of the design disciplines that subjugates works by women and design that is private or domestic in terms of setting to a lesser tier of significance (Havenhand 2004). In addition to Cheryl Buckley, Pat Kirkham and John Turpin have both argued for the credibility and value of women's contributions to the production of designed interior space. Both have provided detailed biographical documentation as evidence to support their position (Buckley 1986; Kirkham [1939] 2000; Turpin 2007). The need for equal participation and respect for each design discipline's contributions to the design process resounds in works that critique the relegation of interior design to decisions made "after the fact" in the production of designs for new buildings (Havenhand 2004).

Although it is important to credit the contribution of feminist theory to the construction of a political role for interior space within modern culture, this is not an essay about gender issues in relation to interior design per se. Instead, it is a discussion of the ways in which a historical effort to democratize the design of the interior might serve as a model for advocating for the importance of the interior's influence on human experience today and therefore, how the political interior can become a site for arguing the necessity of bringing good design to the everyday built environment. This investigation into how a specific segment of the American public was made aware of modern approaches to the design of interiors in North America illustrates the ability of interior space to express layers of political perspectives. This study also has implications for contemporary practice as it provides a model for a democratic approach to design that engenders a sense of agency on the part of all persons who are responsible for the creation of improved spaces.

Politicized Roots

It is generally agreed that interior design as the professional endeavor we recognize today did not exist prior to the 20th century. Early efforts to design interior spaces were typically linked to architectural and structural practices or were exercises in the decoration of surfaces with little consideration given to the relationship between aesthetics and spatial arrangement or quality. With the dawn of the 20th century, however, the idea that the size and shape of spaces and their configuration within a building could have a significant impact on the quality of the lives of their occupants began to emerge, and an audience hungry for modernity began to seek information about how better spaces could be attained.

Instruction for how to design interiors took several forms in the early 20th century, and each subscribed to a different philosophical perspective on design practice. These divergent roots of contemporary interior design practice each yielded its own set of politically potent ways of impacting the nature of modern interior spaces. Because clients most often desired artistic input into the decoration of their homes, early interior design professionals primarily concerned themselves with the treatment of surfaces and the provision of furniture. These early practitioners usually had little or no formal training and relied on their inherent "good taste," both of which identities were evidenced by their knowledge of the principles of design and their access to expensive goods and wealthy clients. Treated as artistic expressions, the interiors produced within the context of modern art movements enjoyed a position of avant-gardism by challenging norms of how space could be defined and occupied. The interiors created as a result of these efforts also served as forceful symbols of one's awareness of culture and the arts and participation in inevitable power hierarchies.

The specialized study of art also became part of early formal design education, but more in terms of the execution of "principles." Frank Alvah Parsons established a leading program at the New York School of Art in 1904 that first formalized an educational approach to the principles of interior design that were directly derived from previously established principles of art, but extended beyond visual considerations. Parsons also penned *Interior Decoration, Its Principles and Practice*, a text that became a primer on the fundamentals of interior design practice and the body of knowledge that provided a foundation for interior design in the first half of the 20th century (Parsons 1920).

The study of applied art merged with domestic science within the context of home economics and served as the primary mode of education for the majority of American women interested in studying the design and use of interior space until the mid-20th century in America. As early as the 1920s, most large land-grant colleges and universities in the US provided a version of "applied art" study that promoted facilitating more efficient domestic processes while creating aesthetically improved domestic environments in most types of American homes. In this same era, parallel efforts to broaden home economics study to include design education emerged in Canada.

These programs created design-oriented graduates with the skills to make informed choices about the layout of their houses, the interior finish materials used to create the backdrop for their modern families, and an ability to select well-constructed and high-quality furnishings. They also generated a population of informed potential design consumers who were savvy about soliciting the services of professional designers to meet their interior design needs. When the interior design of non-residential spaces emerged as a viable career option, these programs expanded their study beyond the domestic environment to address the design properties of other types of spaces.

What is often unacknowledged is that in addition to educating university students to become both designers and consumers of design, American land-grant universities promoted the principles of interior design practice to members of the middle and working classes through publicly accessible information provided by "extension programs." First established in 1914 with the passage of the Smith–Lever Act, extension programs provided a mechanism for bringing the expertise of researchers to the masses. Experts who taught or conducted research about design-related issues and their impact on domestic spaces across the US provided content for publications and public presentations that were made to women who craved knowledge about how to plan the interior spaces of their homes. Universities such as Cornell in New York State, Wisconsin, and Iowa State pioneered strategies for teaching interior design principles "in the field" to the general public so that improvements to layouts, to the quality of work and storage areas, and to the appearance of domestic spaces could be accomplished in everyday houses – often at minimal expense. They also spearheaded product and equipment studies that encouraged the critical consideration of the design of domestic products and their performance criteria (Bix 2002).

Interiors at the Grass Roots

The interior spaces that emerged as a result of the types of educational efforts embraced by early design educators portray the ways in which modern design principles could be employed in unexpected ways to affect improvements in a range of public and private environments. As a case to demonstrate the embedded political nature of designed interior space, I will describe and interpret one unassuming Depression era kitchen from the State of New York, where work done by home economics faculty at Cornell University pioneered the promotion of modern design principles to the general public in the early 20th century.

Prior to its improvement in 1934, the Epps' kitchen in Ulster County, New York lacked light and order, and its occupants could not take full advantage of the space it occupied. Missing built-in cabinetry (which was not unusual at that time), its furnishings were mismatched and crowded into one corner of a large room. Documentary snapshots of the kitchen's original condition show a tall, portable, manufactured cabinet looming darkly to one side of the sink while a shelf-like counter on the other side tilted precariously to aid its drainage. The ability of this counter to serve as a work surface for many kitchen activities appears to be undermined by the angle at which it rests. The door to a closet, visible on the right-hand side of the photograph, would inevitably bump into an adjacent oil stove each time it was opened, and a table cut through the middle of the space, closing off the work zone from the rest of the kitchen area.

Mrs. Epps, the primary occupant of the kitchen, may have recognized the less than perfect conditions of her work space because she participated in the "Reading Course for Farmer's Wives," originating at Cornell. This program was begun in 1900 by Martha Van Rensselaer as a precursor to the distribution of knowledge about design and home management through the extension services of many universities. Between 1900 and 1913, Van Rensselaer produced publications for Cornell that circulated at a rate of approximately five per year. She personally researched the initial topics, wrote copy, produced drawings and diagrams for process-oriented topics, and mailed the bulletins. Between 1901 and 1917, the circulation of Cornell's published bulletins grew from 2,000 to more than 75,000 per year (Percival 1957).

Van Rensselaer also responded personally to many of her readers. It is in acts such as this that the potency of grassroots design is most obviously revealed. Both the bulletins and the personal letters Van Rensselaer penned touched recipients such as May Abbuhl of Greene, New York, who described her appreciation for the expert's personal attention in a letter dated September 22, 1907. Abbuhl wrote that she found the bulletins "suggestive, inspiring and helpful," and that she received and treasured them among her "choicest literature" (Abbuhl 1907). Her description of her feelings about the publications conveyed her belief that they provided a kind of personal conduit between her and the domestic experts at Cornell (and Van Rensselaer in particular) as well as her recognition of the presence of a kind of implied social code. "When I think of all the important things you [Van Rensselaer] have on your hands," she wrote, "and of all the interesting, attractive, and worthy friends you have, I am astonished and worried, too, to have you send me your papers. Wouldn't it be wiser," she added, "to cut out the unessential and unimportant folk and things?" (Abbuhl 1907).

One of the purposes of the extension service was, of course, to eliminate such perceived boundaries and to increase access to knowledge and improved living circumstances for persons not formally affiliated with advanced education. It became important for programs like the one at Cornell, therefore, to reduce the perception of experts "telling" people what they should do and to encourage its participants to learn to help each other.

As interest in the reading course grew, Van Rensselaer encouraged the formation of study clubs to spark group discussion of the issues raised in the bulletins. She traveled frequently around the state to facilitate club meetings in grange halls, farmers' institutes, and private farmhouses. With such efforts, Van Rensselaer, and eventually her staff, worked to establish a culture of participatory design reform among the rural women of New York, who gradually began to see themselves as authorities on the topic.

As a probable participant in a group that shared design and home management advice provided by the experts at Cornell, Mrs. Epps contacted a local home demonstration agent in the early 1930s to request a "kitchen conference" to help rectify the design challenges of her workplace. Meeting directly in the Rare and Manuscript Collection, Cornell University itself, a gathering of neighbors and a home demonstration leader assessed the current conditions of her kitchen, took photographs and made drawings, and ultimately proposed strategies for making improvements using design advice provided by the extension program at Cornell.

Encouraged to undertake several steps to make her kitchen more modern and efficient, Mrs. Epps painted the manufactured cabinet white and moved it away from the sink. She placed matching open shelves hung on the wall on either side of the sink and had level counters constructed to its right and left to be used as work surfaces. The area below these counters became storage for a range of larger items, and compartments were built that were tailored to each item. The storage areas on the wall could be completely open or closed off from view with inexpensive covers such as tightly fitting roller shades and simple home-sewn curtains. Because Mrs. Epps was tall, she was able to incorporate shelves all the way up the kitchen walls to the ceiling.

By removing the door to the closet and replacing it with a curtain, Mrs. Epps resolved the conflict with the oil stove and the supplies and equipment stored there could be more easily seen and used. Photographs of the improved Epps kitchen prominently feature her electric lighting and plumbed sink, patterned linoleum flooring, and the smooth white painted surfaces of the plaster walls and wood-paneled ceiling. The use of these modern materials and systems gave her a brightly lit workplace that could be easily washed, while still avoiding an unpleasant feeling of sterility. The photographs also show the inclusion of a metal cart to be used to easily transport supplies across the large room and a well-lit "planning center" (in the form of a "remodeled" older desk) where Mrs. Epps could conduct her domestic business like a modern manager.

The cost of transforming this kitchen would have been insignificant because of the continued use of some of the modified furniture and cabinetry and the reuse of lumber for shelving and counter tops. The reliance on minimalism in the form of narrow, open shelves that discouraged clutter and over-stacking also contributed to the cost-effectiveness and the room's modernity.

The home demonstration agent who reviewed Mrs. Epps' kitchen improvements in a follow-up to the original conference praised her flexibility, her ingenuity, and her ability to serve as an expert, adding in her report that "Mrs. Epps will always think of better ways to do things and will change the situation to make these improvements possible" (New York State Federation of Home Bureaus Records 1939). This point is critical to our understanding of the kitchen as a political space, as it demonstrates the influence of the interactive design process on both the spaces and the people who used them. By giving the participants concrete situations to consider, the "kitchen conferences" transformed the ways that women viewed their environments, helping them to see the spaces as malleable. It also provided them with a sense of agency to literally affect architectural space, sometimes taking up tools to create new shelves or to raise work surfaces themselves. By encouraging women to gather in each other's homes to evaluate the deficits of their own workplaces and to understand general strategies for making the needed improvements to the spaces, future designers and design consumers learned to constructively evaluate each other's circumstances and to effect change and improvement.

These customized corrections took many forms. Ergonomic adjustments could be accomplished by propping up cabinets and tables or shortening their legs so that healthy standing and seated work positions could be established. Additions could be made to storage spaces easily and at little or no cost by using scrap and surplus materials to subdivide existing cabinetry. The use of older portable kitchen cabinets in new configurations also proved to be one of the least costly and most popular modifications made to at least one-quarter of the hundreds of rural kitchens documented by the faculty at Cornell.

Significant Constituencies

If the political interior is the interior that asserts its ability to make a difference, then the designed, yet humble, kitchen interiors of Depression era New York farmhouses serve well to illustrate the unexpected potential of interiors to assert their significance within the built environment and in the lives of the numerous persons who were affiliated with them. This focus on the everyday environment remains a useful reminder that, like the underestimated profession that is interior design, our expectations of where meaningful design resides deserve to be challenged.

My research on the history of the interior design profession reveals that while a portion of its foundation rests in modern architectural production, it is also grounded on the rise of the applied arts, informed consumerism, and the study of efficiency and product development within the arena of home economics. The proliferation of 20th-century advice literature and shelter magazines correlates with this influence of design on the modern everyday environment.

The obvious constituent groups to have been directly affected by the act of designing everyday modern interiors such as the kitchen spaces described here are the extension experts and home demonstration agents who led the design instruction efforts and cultivated interest in the program(s) that promoted improving the interior environments and the knowledge base of the farm women who served as their "students." Yet an analysis of the circumstances that surrounded their production demonstrates that the influence of these humble spaces reaches well beyond the persons who were directly connected to them.

Because extension experts employed by universities stood with their feet in both public and private arenas, they found themselves in a position to exert their influence in more than one direction. As educators, they brought their promotion of the importance of modernization to an audience that lacked the information, confidence, and financial resources to make radical changes to their physical surroundings. By guiding women through critical and analytical processes, experts encouraged the development of design expertise in the general populace. By encouraging women to have conversations about how to see opportunities to make improvements, they helped cultivate networks of trust and community that countered the sense of isolation so often associated with rural living in the early 20th century.

At the same time, as participants in a system of higher education, extension experts utilized their so-called "free" system of support and education for the public at large to solidify a demand for their research and service activities, thereby demonstrating a need for their work to the administrators of land-grant institutions. Often looked down upon as an applied science by academic colleagues in more traditional fields of science and the humanities, the beneficial practical knowledge produced by home economists focused on the so-called household arts (whose proponents, like interior designers, were nearly always female) and helped the research produced in what historian Laura Shapiro once described as a "shamelessly irrelevant academic ghetto" seem relevant to taxpayers and voters (Shapiro 1986).

Steady increases in student enrolment and an infusion of research findings into popular literature can both be interpreted, at least in part, as evidence of a growing interest in and appreciation of the benefits of good design. At the same time, many historians of the home economics movement have criticized the early participants for working within the patriarchal academy, making it possible for university administrators to avoid having to deal with challenging the status quo of resource allocation and traditionally gendered fields of study.

The female "students" on farms and in small towns who benefited from the dissemination of design knowledge can be understood as having felt a different kind of politicized influence. These women often entered into dynamic relationships with the home economists and demonstration agents who touched their lives and reduced their self-perceptions of feeling uneducated and, as May Abbuhl described herself, unimportant. After learning about the potential for employing modern design principles to improve the living conditions of their families, however, many expressed a satisfying sense of resourcefulness, empowerment, and a healthy connection to their neighbors and community. The collegial process used to generate ideas for improving the designs of kitchens in New York State, for instance, created a shared sense of investment in the improvements made to the houses of individuals. At the same time, the frugality employed by their extension teachers helped these thrifty and conservation-minded women celebrate the value of reusing materials and furnishings to create more efficient and aesthetically pleasing environments at minimal cost. That the end result did not exactly match the pictures of modern kitchens portrayed in magazines of the same period did not matter as much as the pride amateur designers took in doing more with less.

Young women who literally became students by pursuing higher education in this time period also stood to benefit from the cultivation of a study area that merged domestic topics with scientific methods. The hands-on learning methods employed in applied art programs that eventually became the study of interior design as we know it today gained valuable critical thinking and problem-solving skills that served them well in a range of private and professional pursuits. Many who studied the "household arts" in the first half of the 20th century applied what they learned as informed consumers and successful homemakers. For those with professional aspirations, however, growth in the graduate programs that expanded the knowledge base of the disciplines contained within home economics provided increased opportunities to assist in research projects, to generate publications, and ultimately, to teach subsequent generations.

Professional designers who emerged into practice via other conduits such as the study of the fine arts or architecture also stood to gain from the creation of more informed design consumers. An expanding middle class that increasingly understood the difference between good and bad design and expressed a growing demand for a modern designed environment created a platform for the acknowledgment, and ultimately the acceptance, of an interior design profession that provided services as well as goods in both the residential and the commercial realms (and ultimately others).

Manufacturers were not neutral players in the generation of the public's interest in modern design either. By working with researchers who tested new devices and materials, manufacturers could incorporate the latest ergonomic and consumer behavior research when developing and promoting their products. By making their products available for testing or incorporation into classroom and lab spaces, manufacturers also raised the brand awareness of potential future buyers of their goods.

The collective professional effort to improve the Epps kitchen and perhaps thousands of other everyday interior spaces like it in the 1930s may seem quite distant from today's interior design practice in both time and the literal nature of the work. I believe, however, that contemporary interior design practices can derive lessons from this case. By interpreting the layers of the potentially political interactions that operated simultaneously to produce an improved and *designed* interior environment where one did not previously exist, the possibility of the interior itself to reshape the lives of its occupants, to impact the allocation of resources – both natural and synthetic – becomes apparent. Ultimately, it suggests the ways in which the invocation of power impacts the nature of the built environment today and in the future.

First, if the principles that drive interior design as a method of creating architectural space are ever to reach a broad-based audience, professional interior designers need to eliminate the lingering perception that interior design is an exclusive service for the rich. This requires interior designers to continually and publicly prioritize the relationship between the nature of space and the activities it supports rather than its physical appearance. Like the efficiency experts whose research informed the layout of kitchens to support the type of work that actually needed to be done there, today's designers need to clearly articulate their ability to affect the quality of the actions that take place in the spaces they design.

Secondly, interior designers should consider how to focus on the development of models of practice that reach built environments that need the kind of improvement that interior designers are most able to provide. By taking their expertise into the field rather than waiting for "clients" to come to them, design experts such as the women who helped Mrs. Epps can empower their constituents to make their own decisions and to help each other. It is collaborative efforts such as this that hold the possibility of reaching out to the broadest range of environments on a global scale.

Thirdly, interior designers are very good at understanding people and the design approach that will most benefit them. Mrs. Epps did not have the means to eliminate her old kitchen and invest in a manufactured replacement. Her ability to construct vernacular solutions that evoked modernity through their smooth surfaces and clean white paint met the criteria for improvement held by the experts and they valued and promoted results such as hers to others in need of help. By letting go of the often unreachable standards of perfection touted in magazines and the works of "high-style" designers, occupants of these "real" interior spaces could feel pride in and satisfaction with the results of their remodeling efforts.

Finally, in order to maximize the political potential of designed interiors, practicing professionals and educators need to increase the accessibility of their knowledge so that a more informed base of design consumers can be created, putting the focus back on the quality of the user's experiences instead of on aesthetics. The grassroots-level interventions described here are just one model for how the media, design researchers, and practicing professionals can coordinate their efforts to encourage the development of interior spaces that take a stand.

References

Abbuhl, M. 1907, September. *Letter to Martha Van Rensselaer. Division of Rare and Manuscript Collections.* Cornell University, Ithaca, NY.

ASID (American Society of Interior Design). 2011. www.asid.org/ASID.

Ankerson, K. and Gabb, B. 2010. "Benefits of interior design for all," in C. S. Martin and D. Guerin (eds.), *The State of the Interior Design Profession.* New York: Fairchild Books, pp. 584–585.

Bachelard, G. 1964. *The Poetics of Space.* Boston: Beacon Press.

Bix, A. 2002. "Equipped for life: gendered technical training and consumerism in home economics, 1920–1980," *Technology and Culture* 43: 728–754.

Buckley, C. 1986. "Made in patriarchy: toward a feminist analysis of women and design," *Design Issues* 3: 3–14.

CIDA (Council for Interior Design Accreditation). 2011 Professional Standards. http://accredit-id.org/wp-content/uploads/Policy/Professional%20Standards%202011.pdf. Accessed April 30, 2014.

Gordon, B. 1996. "Women's domestic body: the conceptual conflation of women and interiors in the industrial age," *Winterthur Portfolio* 31: 281–301.

Hanisch, C. [1970] 2000. "The personal is political," in B. Crow (ed.), *Radical Feminism: A Documentary Reader.* New York: New York University Press, pp. 113–116.

Havenhand, L. 2004. "A view from the margin: interior design," *Design Issues* 20: 33.

Kirkham, P. [1939] 2000. *Women Designers in the USA.* New Haven: Yale University Press.

New York State Federation of Home Bureaus Records. 1915–1991. Collection Number 23-17-853. Division of Rare and Manuscript Collections, Cornell University.

Parsons, F. A. 1920. *Interior Decoration, Its Principles and Practice.* Garden City: Doubleday.

Percival, C. M. 1957. *Martha Van Rensselaer.* Ithaca, NY: Cornell University Press.

Shapiro, L. 1986. *Perfection Salad: Women and Cooking at the Turn of the Century.* New York: Farrar, Straus & Giroux.

Sparke, P. 2008. *The Modern Interior.* London: Reaktion Books.

Turpin, J. 2007. "The history of women in interior design: a review of literature," *Journal of Interior Design* 33: 1–15. doi: 10.1111/j.1939-1668.2007.tb00418.x

4

Taylorizing the Modern Interior: Counter-Origins

Ronn M. Daniel

Introduction

In her profound book *The Modern Interior* historian Penny Sparke proposes a revisionist definition of the modern interior:

> [The modern interior,] which was formed and developed between the middle years of the nineteenth and twentieth centuries, went beyond style and encompassed many more inside spaces than those contained within the home...The visual languages through which it was expressed could range from Louis Quinze to Streamlined Moderne. The modern interior addressed in this study can be understood, therefore, in a very general sense, as the *inside location of people's experiences of, and negotiations with, modern life*. (Sparke 2008; emphasis added)

With Sparke's expanded definition in mind, our understanding of the 20th-century origins of the interior design profession broadens. In particular, this essay will discuss the earliest designers of American corporate office interiors, a group of men who called themselves "scientific office managers." They were disciples of the turn-of-the-century industrial theorist Frederick Winslow Taylor, and they practiced a nascent form of interior design. They drew and analyzed floor plans, designed lighting schemes, promoted indoor air-filtration and conditioning, and designed furniture and specialized equipment. Their work was a comprehensive attempt to form and mediate the collision between intimate human environments, a vital new architectural typology, and the emerging social and cultural realities of industrial modernity. Borrowing the language of French historian Michel

The Handbook of Interior Design, First Edition. Edited by Jo Ann Asher Thompson and Nancy H. Blossom.

Foucault, the scientific office managers were visionary theorists of the emerging disciplinary society.

Scientific (Office) Management

The interior space of an early 20th-century American corporate office was the mechanical/architectural heart of an enormous paper-processing machine. Its employees would arrive to the office building riding streetcars and carriages on fixed iron rails; they were hoisted high into the sky inside mechanical conveyors hanging from braided steel cables in open vertical shafts. The office's rhythms were regulated with a clockwork precision: to enter, workers were obliged to present a paper card into a mechanical clock, stamping the exact moment of arrival.

At precisely 8:00 a.m. every morning, a light would flash high upon a wall, a bell would ring, and the workday would commence. For female clerks this typically meant seating oneself before a mechanical printing machine – a typewriter – ears connected by tubes to a rotating wax-cylinder audio recording machine. There might be as many as 200 or even 300 women in each room. As the workers typed, each depression of the printing machine's buttons would be logged on a mechanical counter and scored in keystrokes per minute. Every 20 minutes it was time for a set of printed documents to advance. The typed papers would be loaded onto conveyor belts, sent overhead in a wire basket, fired by pneumatic tube, or gathered up by a brigade of scurrying office boys.[1]

In the early 20th century it was still a novel idea that human work could (and should) be organized as mechanically and precisely as the gears of a machine. This so-called "scientific management" of labor was invented by Frederick Winslow Taylor.[2] Taylor was an American engineer who developed his ideas by closely studying the actions of laborers and machinists in the Midvale Steel Works in Philadelphia over a period of years in the 1880s. By minutely documenting each task step by step, measuring with rulers and stopwatches, and then experimenting with alternative tool and processes, Taylor convincingly demonstrated that an outside "expert" could determine the single most efficient way a worker might accomplish a given task. In this way, Taylor invented a new paradigm of industrial organization. He "imagined a machine in which the mechanical and human parts were virtually indistinguishable" (Hughes 2004). Taylor rationalized and optimized each work task, and each worker, seeking to eliminate every superfluous movement, unnecessary step, and wasted material. He substituted the mechanical repetition of the automaton for the holistic labor of the craftsman: "In the past, the man has been first; in the future the system must be first." (Taylor 1911). Scientific management, or "Taylorism" as it also came to be known, has been called the most important American contribution to Western thought since the *Federalist Papers* (Braverman 1975).

Taylor's ideology of scientific management legitimated the central role of managerial planning experts. In matters of business, industry, government, and agriculture – even in the domestic management of households – carefully trained specialists could maximize output by rationalizing tasks, materials, and tools.[3] Maximized output meant efficiency, and efficiency was believed to be the engine of profit and progress. The "scientific" expert would become the warden of organizational knowledge and technical expertise. He would take complete control of the work process, regulating every activity. "All possible brain work should be removed from the shop and centered in the planning or laying-out department" (Taylor 1903), thereby "specify[ing] not only what is to be done, but how it is to be done and the exact time allowed for doing it" (Taylor 1911). A lifetime of accumulated experience and instinct, once held by the shop foreman (or homemaker, scrivener, or farmer), was displaced by the scientific manager, wielding the iron-clad "rules, laws, and formulae" necessary in order to "plan ahead" (Taylor 1911). Taylor's technocracy was a revolutionary idea masquerading as self-evident truism, and it spread quickly throughout the industrialized world. By 1913, only two years after its English publication, *The Principles of Scientific Management* had been translated into Russian, French, German, Dutch, Swedish, Russian, Italian, Spanish, and Japanese (Hughes 2004).

Although Taylor conceived of his work as a broadly applicable "set of principles," his specific studies focused on the factory floor and industrial yard. It was left for his followers to extend the model into other realms. For the specific case of "scientific office management," one journal was particularly influential: *System* (later *System: The Magazine of Business*), published by the Shaw-Walker Company in Muskegon, Michigan from 1900 to 1927. In addition, I have identified four published manuals from that time period: Lee Galloway, *Office Management* (1919); William Henry Leffingwell, *Scientific Office Management* (1917); Carl Copeland Parsons, *Business Administration: The Principles of Business Organization and System* (1909); and John William Schulze, *The American Office: Its Organization, Management, and Records* (1913). Each author was a self-proclaimed disciple of Frederick W. Taylor. These four men, as well as the editors at *System*, conceived of the corporate office – that administrative beehive of book-keepers, office boys, salesmen, typists, and file clerks – as essentially a giant paperwork factory. Just as the efficiency of an ironworks factory could be increased by the rationalization of its tools and procedures, so too could the office interior. Spatial environments could be optimized, workers better trained, office tools perfected, procedures rationalized, and waste eliminated. In an age of emerging continent-scale, and even global-scale, industrial processes, "a comparatively small force of highly specialized employees under the direction of a few experts" (Galloway 1919) could be organized so as to direct and manage the disparate activities of thousands.

The Railroads have made it possible for a manufacturer to places his goods at a low cost in any part of the country; and with favorable conditions, he can undersell a rival at the gate of the latter's plant. Then comes the test of organization and system. Each firm must count the cost, must eliminate all waste, must secure the benefits of large-scale production, must buy cheap, produce economically, route scientifically and market its product without waste. Other things equal, the victory comes to the best organization. (Parsons 1909)

The most profitable corporation, and thereby the most successful one, would be "scientifically" organized as a paperwork factory, designed and overseen by a team of elite Taylorist scientific office managers.

Counter-Origins

While the need for administrative oversight is as ancient as the oldest cities, the notion that administrative work required a separate and distinct architectural space – an office building – is surprisingly recent (Gatter 1982: 14). The earliest modern examples date from the middle decades of the 19th century.[4] By the 1870s large multi-story office buildings could be found in US urban centers, although these were typically organized as honeycombs of small-scale commercial suites, each just a handful of rooms. It was only in the late 1880s and the 1890s, following the establishment of the modern corporation, that anything resembling the contemporary open-plan office building appears. It was into this context that the scientific office managers emerged. Their work – drawings, diagrams, custom furniture designs, equipment designs, annotated photographs, graphs, charts, etc. – can be understood as rudimentary attempts to develop design principles for this emerging new form of interior space.[5] They concerned themselves with a very familiar list of questions: they investigated space planning, furniture design, lighting, health and wellness in interior environments, interior equipment, casework, ergonomics, color, and acoustics. Aligning this list alongside our contemporary definitions and standards, it is clear that the scientific office managers quite comprehensively practiced an early form of interior design.[6]

The first place to begin to evaluate the scientific office managers as proto-interior designers is to note their reliance on the drawing and analysis of floor plans.

They worked extensively towards the rationalization of adjacencies and work "flow" through the office. One common technique was to overlay a diagram mapping the flow of clerical documents through the office on top of the existing (unsatisfactory) floor plan. This diagram would invariably demonstrate the chaotic, non-sequential relationship between spatial organization and work tasks, highlighting what the Taylorists named "waste motion." "If letters weighed ten pounds apiece, probably a correct routing would quickly enough be found. But because they usually weigh but an ounce or so, failures to attain a direct routing are often observed. It takes nearly as much time, however, to carry one ounce one hundred feet as to carry ten pounds" (Leffingwell 1917b). The key to eliminating waste motion was the redesign of floor plans. Furniture, partitions, and equipment would be reorganized so as to maximize efficiency and streamline the flow of paperwork. The goal was explicit: "there should be no doubling back in the progress of work through the office" (Schulze 1913).

The notion that paperwork should "flow" through the office was often taken to its logical extreme. The literature includes examples of early 20th-century office interiors that were planned around a network of moving conveyor belts, analogous to the moving assembly lines developed by Henry Ford in his factories. The belts would pass alongside each clerk, who would collect and return papers onto the moving line. In other offices where either the architectural geometry or work sequences were not conducive to such an absolute linearity, paper might move from clerk to clerk inside bundles of pneumatic vacuum tubes or inside suspended metal gondola-baskets hanging from overhead circulating cables (American Pneumatic Service Company 1912). In all of these examples, the office was designed as a "set of channels through which work should circulate direct, clean, even, rapid" (Murphy 1914).

The concept of minimizing waste motion was not, however, limited to the movement of paper. Take for example this remarkable passable written by W. H. Leffingwell in 1917:

> Drinking water is a necessity in every office. . . . Too often fountains are placed in out of the way corners and other inaccessible places. The average person should drink water at least five or six times a day. If each of one hundred clerks in an office were compelled to walk fifty feet to, and fifty feet from, the fountain, five times a day, each one would walk five hundred feet a day. Multiplied by one hundred clerks the distance traveled would be fifty thousand feet, or nearly ten miles. Multiplied by three hundred working days, the clerks would be walking three thousand miles for water in a year. (1917c: 10–11)

In spite of the fact that a healthy, well-hydrated clerk was more likely to be an efficient worker, the seconds required to walk the 50 feet for a drink at the fountain was time not spent pressing buttons, recording dictation, or filing documents; to Leffingwell's calculus, those precious lost seconds were the consequence of faulty architectural planning.

As fundamental as the battle against waste motion was, the Taylorist office theorists also concerned themselves more broadly with the full scope of space-planning questions. They designed efficient egress pathways ("Desks should be placed in pairs, with an aisle on each side of the pair, so that a clerk can leave his desk without disturbing anyone" (Leffingwell 1917c); they advocated integration between plan and structural system; they drew bubble diagrams to study adjacency requirements (Van Deventer 1909); and they discussed degrees of "public-ness" and "private-ness" within the office suite (Stanger 1911). They were concerned with spatial "compactness" and the intensive, efficient utilization of leased floor space (Anonymous 1909). In short, for the Taylorist office theorists, the design of the office floor plan was paramount; "The selection and arrangement of the men and equipment in the space available is. . . second to no other [problem] in the office" (Schulze 1913).

Complementing the scientific office managers' design work in plan was their attention to furniture, casework, and interior equipment. The analogy with Taylor's pioneering industrial studies was direct: just as the proper configuration of a coal shovel proved vital for the efficient loading of steam engines, so too the intelligent design of a worker's desk was essential for efficient clerical function.

> The desk is the most used piece of furniture in the office. The office employee is at it constantly. The highest type of working efficiency in a desk is obtained when the desk itself is so constructed and so arranged that it does not in the slightest degree interfere with the progress of a person's work, but, on the other hand, aids in every possible way. (Schulze 1913)

As to the design of the desk, a "sanitary" one, lifted on slender legs, was strongly preferred over the older designs; traditional bureaus that descended all the way to the floor were believed to harbor "dust or dirt [that] can accumulate without being seen" (Schulze 1913). Even more problematic were the traditional patent-cabinet or roll-top desks. Those desks had been designed for the clerks of the pre-corporate era – enclosed, self-sufficient work-stations filled with numerous cubbies, enclosures, slots, and drawers to contain his hand-copied papers and ledger books.[7] In the corporate Taylorist age, however, these enclosed desks began to look like vaults, dangerous traps into which important papers might fall, slipping out of the paperwork channel and becoming lost and abandoned. The sanitary desk – with its clean, flat surface on which all vital papers remained visible – afforded no sanctuaries into which renegade papers might slip.

If any drawers were permitted below the smooth desktop, they were few and exactingly regulated. Rigid inventories were written to specify exactly which items were permitted, and in what quantities and locations:

> The equipment of the office manager's desk calls for a calendar, ink eradicator, ink eraser, pencil eraser, three penholders, out desk basket, in desk basket, ink-well, mucilage pot, pen tray, two glass cups, waste basket, ruler, scissors, and two paper-weights. His supply equipment includes: various blank forms, desk blotter, six hand blotters, clips of various sizes and kinds, fasteners, pasters, pins, rubber bands, washers, lead pencils, pens, engraved letter paper, second sheets, envelopes of prescribed sizes, scratch pads and memorandum pad. Twice a week, at times when there will be least interference, an office boy goes through the desks of the whole establishment and replenishes supplies. To guide him he has the list allotted for every class of desk, showing the minimum and maximum quantity of each article. He keeps between these two figures. (Wooley 1911)

To discourage non-compliance, the Taylorists recommended that managers inspect the drawers randomly and frequently.[8]

To customize standard desks for specific work tasks, the scientific managers recommended, and often designed, numerous supplementary mechanisms and modifications. The literature records numerous examples: sliding leaves, drop panels, inset file tubs, retractable typewriter platforms, desk-mounted storage cubbies, custom drawer configurations, foot-pedal controls, ergonomic footrests, etc. Ergonomic studies, often performed using photography in front of gridded walls, confirmed the efficacy of the configuration. Often complementing the modified desks was customized interior casework, such as storage cabinets and bookshelves. Matched with the modified desks and casework were carefully considered task and executive chairs:

> The same principles of selection and standardization should be applied to office chairs. An employee does his best work when he is submitted to the least discomfort. Upholstered chairs are not comfortable for any length of time, nor are straight wooden seats. For ordinary use the wooden saddle seat has been pronounced by office furniture men to be considerably more restful than any other kind of seat, with the exception of the more expensive cane seats. Cane seats are still less fatiguing, but are objectionable for general use because of their poor wearing qualities. For executives the cane seat covered with perforated leather is suggested. They allow plenty of ventilation, are attractive in appearance and do not shine the clothes. The backs of chairs should be formed of spindles rather than of solid wood or upholstery, to allow ample ventilation. For stenographers and typists special chairs have been designed composed of wooden saddle seats with adjustable spring backs. They can be adjusted to fit the height and convenience of the persons using them. All office chairs should be of the revolving kind to avoid the waste effort incurred in moving chairs back and forth when it is necessary to rise or change the position. (Schulze 1913)

Working together the desk, cabinets, and task chair comprised a productive ensemble, designed as "equipment that will enable the worker to perform operations with the fewest motions" (Leffingwell 1917a).

Although the scientific office managers did most of their work through floor plans and interior equipment, the scope of their practices was broad and comprehensive; they managed to address nearly every contemporary interior design concern. For example they were early advocates for the introduction of filtered and conditioned ventilation into building interiors (Koon 1913). They also studied interior illumination requirements and recommended both natural light and artificial light solutions (Estep 1912). To combat fatigue caused by excessive sitting and repetitive motion, they promoted office-wide, periodic callisthenic breaks. They proposed design solutions against interior noise pollution. They even speculated about the health effects of interior color (Leffingwell 1917c). Considered in total, the Taylorist office theorists systematically employed a comprehensive set of interior design techniques to give form and coherence to the new forms of interior space in the corporate office.

"Negotiations with Modern Life"

The Taylorist office theorists endeavored the perfect system, a human-machine assembly flawless in every part and function. They specified the quantity of paperclips in a manager's drawer, the optimal angle between a typist's forearm and torso, the foot-candles required on an accountant's ledger, and the maximum permitted number of steps to the water fountain. They aimed to regulate space to the quarter of an inch and time to the fraction of a second. Masquerading as simple technicians of efficient capitalism, they were ideological visionaries, designers of the emerging technocratic order. Before their eyes danced the intoxicating, utopian dream of an orderly factory, creating orderly men leading to an orderly world (McLeod 1983).

As the French historian and theorist Michel Foucault reminds us, it has not only been the philosophers who dreamed of a perfect modern world:

> there was also a military dream of society; its fundamental reference was not to the state of nature, but to the meticulously subordinated cogs of a machine, not to the primal social contract, but to permanent coercions, not to fundamental rights, but to indefinitely progressive forms of training. (Foucault 1978)

This is what Foucault named "the disciplinary society." With its emphasis on productivity and efficiency, with its mechanisms of control and regulation, and through its techniques of visibility and positive conditioning, Foucault argued that the disciplinary society was the paradigmatic and deterministic form of political, economic, and cultural organization in the modern world. He described that world as constructed so as to better order, arrange, reproduce, and amplify:

> architecture that is no longer built simply to be seen (as with the ostentation of palaces), or to observe the external space (cf. the geometry of fortresses), but to permit an internal, articulated and detailed control – to render visible those who are inside it; in more general terms, an architecture that would operate to transform individuals: to act on those it shelters, to provide a hold on their conduct, to carry the effects of power right to them, to make it possible to know them, to alter them. (Foucault 1978)

Foucault's writings help us to understand that, rather than just the amusing, mad scribblings of self-important micromanagers, scientific office management must be understood as the material enactment of a profound political philosophy. Hiding behind the "scientific" counting of footsteps and the weighing of papers by the ounce, behind human bodies measured and graphed for ergonomic fitness, behind gridded and redrawn floor plans, was a utopian vision of a minutely regulated, productive, technocratic clockwork society. Undoubtedly that vision was motivated by the image of a marching columns of soldiers, each young body disciplined into correct and proper form, calibrated for the projection of maximum power and effect. Clerical workers were soldiers, managers commanders, and corporate offices battlegrounds:

> It is a good plan, when laying out a new office … to cut small squares of cardboard or paper of various colors, each color representing a department. The squares, approximately cut to scale, can be arranged on a large sheet of paper on which the floor plan is drawn, just as a general would position his troops on a map showing the field of battle. (Schultze 1913)

In Foucault's disciplinary society power is not the arbitrary hand of authority exercised from above; rather, it is distributed as a network of constructive "micro-power." It constitutes; it organizes, arranges, quantifies, corrects, and amplifies. Schoolchildren at their desks, patients in their beds, factory workers on the assembly-line, all are measured and aligned with the precision of soldiers marching in formation. Each typist sits at her desk, facing forward, working to a steady beat, efficient and rational.

The Taylorists aspired towards a perfected system, regimented in every detail and perfectly calibrated in all its motions. They permitted no space for informal improvisation, nor did they consider any idea of design as a balanced negotiation between conflicting interests and competing powers.[9] As the office theorists argued repeatedly, there really was just "one best way" (Brandeis 1911), before which all other inferior and inefficient configurations must be judged inadequate.

That judgment would be performed by an elite group of professional and progressive experts (male of course), best suited by class, breeding, and education to determine what needed to be done.[10] They would offer the definitive assessment of how space, equipment, and work should be organized, so as to best conform to the mechanical requirements of a totalizing system, calibrated in every motion and systematized in every detail. In this sense, the standardization so apparent in their designs – the identical desks in rows by the hundreds, the identical white blouses, the optimized task chairs, the runs of rectilinear filing cabinets, even the invention of carbon paper duplicates and unornamented white plaster walls – was more than just the material expression of a conformist sensibility. It was more than an aesthetic ideal, although it was certainly that.[11] It was more than simply the expression of military hierarchy and order, although it was that too.[12] Rather, the absolute standardization of the early 20th century corporate office must be seen as the material and organizational expression of Taylor's "disciplinary" philosophy. The idea that a cadre of professional experts using rigorous scientific (or pseudo-scientific) analysis could solve social and economic problems through empirical means was a theory that reached deeply into the history of 20th-century design. It was of course the fundamental axiom of functionalism, and in that, a key tenet of 20th-century modernism. It is no surprise at all to learn that Le Corbusier himself was an enthusiastic Taylorist: "All is organized; all is clear and purified... Taylorism is not a question of anything more than exploiting intelligently scientific discoveries. Instinct, groping, and empiricism are replaced by scientific principles of analysis, organization, and classification" (Jeanneret and Ozenfant 1918). And it remains today a powerful and resonant contemporary ideal, now perhaps best known as "evidence-based design."

Excavating the long-forgotten careers of the Taylorist office theorists can provide a new lens for thinking about the history of interior design in the 20th century. When we acknowledge their manuals as a nascent form of interior design practice, we discover an overlooked history that locates the design of interior space at the center of the some of most important questions of modern life, not least of which was the theorization of the most important new architectural typology of the 20th century. Men like Leffingwell, Schulze, Galloway, and Parsons (and the editors of *System*) explicitly set out to mediate the collisions between new forms of interior space, new types of industrial organization, new mechanical technologies, and rapidly shifting cultural patterns. They were inadvertent visionaries masquerading as pragmatic technicians, designers who recognized the potential for interior design to engage with some of the most complex questions of their day. In the crude instrumentalism of their work, they may remind us of that which the decorative flourishes of their interior decorator contemporaries have at times tended to obscure: interior design has always been the spatial negotiation of modern life.

Acknowledgments

Research for this project was supported by the James Madison University Program of Grants for Faculty Educational Leaves.

Notes

1 This description of turn-of-the-century office practices is an amalgamation of historical material found in several accounts, including Chase 1910; Davies 1982; Delgado 1979; Fine 1990; Kwolek-Folland 1994; Schlereth 1992; and Yates 1989.

2 Taylor published his definitive text – *The Principles of Scientific Management* – in 1911, more than a decade after his ideas had become widely known. Influential discussions of his work can be found in Braverman 1975; Hughes 2004; and Kanigel 1997.

3 Taylor considered his methods applicable to "every sphere of life, in the management of our homes, farms, of the business of our tradesmen, of our churches, or our governmental departments" (1911: 8).

4 Exact chronologies for the development of the early office buildings have been difficult to determine. Architectural historian Nikolaus Pevsner (1976: 213–224) cites freestanding insurance buildings as early as the 1820s in London. American critic George Hill in his essay "Office Building" (1901–1902: 11–18) dates their beginning in the United Sates from 1858. Economic historian Alfred Chandler (1988) adds the essential contextual fact that the modern corporation dates only from the early 1880s.

5 This account of scientific office management theory is a compilation of material from five primary sources: Galloway 1919; Leffingwell 1917c; Parsons 1909; Schulze 1913; and the influential business journal *System* (later *System: The Magazine of Business*) 1902–1919.

6 The NCIDQ 2004 definition is considered authoritative, and has been endorsed by CIDA, ASID, and IIDA.

7 The most famous example of the Patent cabinet was the Wooton Desk (c.1870–1884), manufactured in Indiana by the Wooton Desk Manufacturing Company. One version of the Wooton Desk contained 102 distinct cubbies.

8 "the general rule is that the top left hand drawer is used for current unfinished work; the lower left hand drawer is used for towels and personal articles; there is no center drawer in most of the desks. The top right hand drawer is filled with convenient sized

compartments for lead pencils, erasers, rubber bands, pins, clips, letter heads and enve-
lopes....Periodical inspections are made, and it is insisted upon that the drawers be
used in the manner instructed" (Schulze 1913: 64).

9   A position upheld with great vigor and clarity by the influential mid-20th-century
     design critic Colin Rowe in his books *The Mathematics of the Ideal Villa* (Rowe 1976)
     and *Collage City* (Rowe and Koetter 1978).

10   In a telling passage in *Principles of Scientific Management*, Taylor describes his selection
     of a workman on whom he will conduct studies. The man is named Schmidt, and in a
     section of imagined dialogues Taylor mocks both Schmidt's German accent and his
     apparent stupidity (1911: 44–46).

11   "Although this office is arranged in a fairly effective manner, it does not look well, and
     cannot be efficient throughout because of the lack of standardized equipment" (Leffin-
     gwell 1917c: 135; emphasis added).

12   "As you know, one of the cardinal principles of the military type of management is that
     every man in the organization shall receive his orders directly through the one superior
     officer who is over him. The general superintendent of the works transmits his orders
     on tickets or written cardboards through the various officers to the workmen in the
     same way that orders through a general in command of a division are transmitted"
     (Giedion 1948: 99, quoting F. W. Taylor).

References

American Pneumatic Service Company. 1912. *The Story of a Service Idea: A History of the
     Origin and Development of the American Pneumatic Service Company.* Boston: The
     Company.

Anonymous. 1909. "Battlefields of business," *System* 508–511.

Brandeis, L. 1911. *Evidence Taken by the Interstate Commerce Commission in the Matter of
     Proposed Advances in Freight Rates of Carriers: Briefs of Council, August to December,
     1910.* Volume 8. Washington: Government Printing Office.

Braverman, H. 1975. *Labor and Monopoly Capital: The Degradation of Work in the Twentieth
     Century.* New York: Monthly Review Press.

Chandler, A. D. 1988. "The beginnings of 'big business' in American industry," in T. K.
     McCraw (ed.), *The Essential Alfred Chandler: Essays Toward a Historical Theory of Big
     Business.* Boston: Harvard Business School Press, pp. 47–73.

Chase, F N. 1910. *Women Stenographers.* Portland, ME: Southworth Printing Company.

Davies, M. W. 1982. *Woman's Place is at the Typewriter: Office Work and Office Workers,
     1870–1930.* Philadelphia: Temple University Press

Delgado, A. 1979. *The Enormous File: A Social History of the Office.* London: John Murray.

Estep, H. L. 1912. "How to light the office," *System* 145–155.

Fine, L. M. 1990. *The Souls of the Skyscraper: Female Clerical Workers in Chicago, 1870–1930.*
     Philadelphia: Temple University Press.

Foucault, M. 1978. *Discipline and Punish: The Birth of the Prison*, trans. A. Sheridan. New
     York: Pantheon Books.

Galloway, L. 1919. *Office Management: Its Principles and Practice, Covering Organization,
     Arrangement, and Operation with Special Consideration of the Employment, Training,
     and Payment of Office Workers.* New York: Ronald Press.

Gatter, L. S. 1982. "The Office: An Analysis of the Evolution of a Workplace," M.Arch. thesis, Massachusetts Institute of Technology.

Giedion, S. 1948. *Mechanization Takes Command: A Contribution to Anonymous History*. New York: Oxford University Press.

Hill, G. 1901–1902. "Office building," in R. Sturgis (ed.), *A Dictionary of Architecture and Building: Biographical, Historical and Descriptive*. New York: Macmillan.

Hughes, T. P. 2004. *American Genesis: A Century of Invention and Technological Enthusiasm, 1870–1970*. Chicago: University of Chicago Press.

Jeanneret, C.-É. (Le Corbusier) and Ozenfant, A. 1918. "Après le Cubism," *Commentaires* (November 15): 11.

Kanigel, R. 1997. *The One Best Way: Frederick Winslow Taylor and the Enigma of Efficiency*. Boston: MIT Press.

Koon, S. G. 1913. "Fresh air and your payroll," *System* 297–304.

Kwolek-Folland, A. 1994. *Engendering Business: Men and Women in the Corporate Office, 1870–1930*. Baltimore. Johns Hopkins University Press.

Leffingwell, W. H. 1917a. "What scientific management did for my office," *System* 68–74.

Leffingwell, W. H. 1917b. "41 Ways to save time in an office," *System* 139–147.

Leffingwell, W. H. 1917c. *Scientific Office Management. A report on the Results of the Applications of the Taylor System of Scientific Management to Offices Supplemented with a Discussion of How To Obtain the Most Important of These Results*. Chicago and New York: A.W Shaw.

McLeod, M. 1983. "Architecture or revolution: Taylorism, technocracy, and social change," *Art Journal* 43(2): 132–147.

Murphy, C. D. 1914 "Less office routine," *System* 490–498.

NCIDQ (National Council of Interior Design Qualifications). 2004. "Definition of interior design." http://www.ncidq.org/AboutUs/AboutInteriorDesign/DefinitionofInterior Design.aspx. Accessed May 20, 2014.

Parsons, C. C. 1909. *Business Administration: The Principles of Business Organization and System, and the Actual Methods of Business Operation and Management*. Chicago: The System Company.

Pevsner, N. 1976. *A History of Building Types*. Princeton, NJ: Princeton University Press.

Rowe, C. 1976. *The Mathematics of the Ideal Villa and Other Essays*. Boston: MIT Press.

Rowe, C. and Koetter, F. 1978. *Collage City*. Boston: MIT Press.

Schlereth, T. J. 1992. *Cultural History and Material Culture: Everyday Life, Landscapes, Museums*. Charlottesville: University Press of Virginia.

Schulze, J. W. 1913. *The American Office: Its Organization, Management and Records*. New York: Key Publishing Company.

Sparke, P. 2008. *The Modern Interior*. London: Reaktion Books.

Stanger, W. A. 1911. "How to arrange the office," *System* 371–377.

Taylor, F. W. 1903. *Shop Management*. New York: American Society of Mechanical Engineers.

Taylor, F. W. 1911. *The Principles of Scientific Management*. New York: Harper & Brothers.

Van Deventer, J. H. 1909. "Mapping office routine," *System* 76–78.

Wooley, E. M. 1911. "Efficiency methods applied to your desk," *System* 124–132.

Yates, J. 1989. *Control Through Communication: The Rise of System in American Management*. Baltimore: Johns Hopkins University Press.

5

Bringing the Past In: Narrative Inquiry and the Preservation of Historic Interiors

Erin Cunningham

Introduction

This essay proposes narrative research as a vehicle for capturing critical tension points in the development of historic interiors. The research presented is part of a larger ongoing research project that looks at the role of narrative in the preservation, restoration, and interpretation of the Hull House and Henry Street settlement houses.[1] Preservation efforts rarely go beyond the exterior surface of buildings, leaving historically significant interiors particularly vulnerable to changing conceptions of significance. However, the significance of a site is often located in the actions that took place within the walls of these buildings. This study moves beyond appearance and design form to examine the experiences and relationships to which they gave space and context. Key to understanding these experiences and relationships is acknowledging the multiple voices that were involved in negotiating each site's significance. Examining diverse stakeholder narratives brings to life the values, beliefs, and emotionality surrounding a protected site. It takes us beyond simply chronicling preservation efforts and allows for the examination of deeper meanings that arise from the built environment, bringing forward stories and experiences of those who shaped historic spaces, which might otherwise be lost in the mechanics of physical preservation efforts.

Narrative inquiry focuses on the "scholarship of stories" (Portillo 2000). Academics from a diverse group of fields, including history, psychology, sociology, education, and law, have found narrative inquiry's focus on human experience and meaning-making valuable. An interesting body of literature has also emerged that couples narrative research with an analysis of the interior environment. Scholars

The Handbook of Interior Design, First Edition. Edited by Jo Ann Asher Thompson and Nancy H. Blossom.

have applied it to interior design as a theoretical orientation, as a way in which to examine design processes, and as a tool for enhancing design analysis and communication (Danko, Portillo, and Meneely 2006; Ganoe 1999; Portillo and Dohr 2000; Smith 2001). One promising avenue for design research that has not been explored, however, is the use of narrative inquiry as a tool for analyzing historic interiors. To bridge this gap, I propose that narrative inquiry offers a vehicle for capturing primary tension points in the development of historic interiors.

This essay comprises three sections. The first section explores narrative research, its application in multiple fields, and the insight it provides into historical events and places. The second section outlines my methodological approach, which is an amalgam of case-study methodology and narrative inquiry. The third section contains an in-depth analysis of a single critical juncture in the preservation of the Hull House Settlement to illustrate an application of narrative inquiry. Exploration of this juncture involves the presentation of a series of stakeholder narratives which illustrate different viewpoints about the significance of this site at a particular time in its history. The intent is to demonstrate how the Hull House Settlement and its preservation project traverse varied, intersecting narratives, and to provide a richer interpretation of the interior environment at this historic site.

Narrative Research: Why Do Stories Matter?

As a methodology and type of research writing, narrative inquiry is attractive for its ability to bring forward marginalized voices and provide a more nuanced understanding of historical events. It is also attractive for its ability to capture how people experience and make sense of the built environment. This study's approach is shaped by narrative studies that deal with similar subject matter, stakeholders, and sources. These studies come from multiple fields, including law, history, and interior design. In legal studies, scholars have utilized narrative to challenge the idea of objectivity that infuses legal writing and decisions. Legal scholar Richard Delgado asserts that narratives help question "presuppositions," or a dominant "mindset," which may influence a legal decision (Delgado 1989). Using the example of a racially fraught court case, he explores how stories "build consensus" and how, in turn, "counterstories" can help challenge this consensus.

Specifically, Delgado explores a series of stories that develop around a university's decision not to hire an African American professor. In response, the professor files a discrimination lawsuit against the university. Delgado presents and examines a series of narratives that describe this "race-tinged event." First, Delgado outlines the stock narrative, which he constructs around the hiring committee's explanation of why the professor did not get the job despite his qualifications and the obvious need for more minority representation on the staff. Delgado then uses a number of counternarratives, created by what he calls "outgroups," to illustrate what the stock story "includes and leaves out and how it perpetuates one version of social reality rather than another." These narratives include the narrative of the African American professor and a student activist protestor. Delgado's paper is compelling for its use of multiple narratives and voices to provide a more in-depth, nuanced understanding of a particular event as well as for illustrating how stories can allow us to "see the world through others' eyes." His research highlights the ability of narratives to capture subjective experience and interpretation. Delgado's use of narrative speaks to this study, which examines Hull House through the multiple perspectives of the settlement's founders, residents, and communities.

Drawing disparate pieces of information together into a coherent narrative is common in the field of history. Traditionally, histories were written in narrative form. These narratives were sweeping, multi-volume works, which documented the political history of different nations or societies over a large span of time. Monographic or scientific history, "technical, specialized analyses of particular events or problems in the past," succeeded narrative history in the early 20th century as the predominant historic form (Wood 2008). By the late 20th century, a renewed interest in the narrative form emerged. However, this was not a return of the grand narrative of traditional histories. Instead, historians began to explore the use of narrative as an experimental form of historical writing that provided a new way to access the past and different voices from the past (Goodman 1998).

An excellent example of a more current use of narrative in historical studies is James Goodman's book *Stories of Scottsboro*. Similar to Delgado, Goodman uses multiple narratives to explore a single event, the Scottsboro trials (Goodman 1994). In 1931, nine African American youth, ranging in age from 13 to 19, were accused of raping two white women in Scottsboro, Alabama. An all-white jury convicted and sentenced to death eight of the defendants. Numerous civil rights groups and political organizations appealed the ruling and the case was tied up in state and federal courts for nearly two decades. Each chapter of Goodman's book narrates the events surrounding the trials from the point of view of a different historic actor, including the views of the black defendants, the women they were accused of raping, the National Association for the Advancement of Colored People, and the white Alabamans, among others. Goodman argues, like Delgado, that readers "cannot fully understand that conflict, or any other, without trying to understand it from many different points of view."

Presented in the third person, the narrative chapters in Goodman's book are based on archival sources, including trial manuscripts, newspaper accounts, and legal decisions.[2] The use of narrative in *Stories of Scottsboro* enables readers to see the story from several different perspectives. Like Delgado, Goodman's focus is on people, the quality of their experience as well as their interpretation of events. He invites us to see historical events through the eyes of those involved, rather than as a researcher. Shifting between different stakeholder narratives allows Goodman to explore how various groups can construe a historical event differently. Narrative analysis, as illustrated in Delgado's and Goodman's studies, provides not only a methodology for exploring events, whether historical or not, but also a way of presenting research. Both authors draw on the narrative form to offer new insight into their research fields. By focusing on stakeholders and their experiences, narrative allows the authors to humanize contemporary and historical events.

Narrative inquiry also offers a flexible approach for the study of interior design and the interior environment. A great deal of the literature that links the interior design field to narrative inquiry focuses on the structure of narratives. Interior design scholars have linked narrative structure to the principles and elements of design as well as the creative process. And they have used it to construct narratives and to distill information from interview narratives (Danko, Portillo, and Meneely 2006; Ganoe 1999; Portillo and Dohr 2000). The findings of these studies point to the ability of narrative inquiry to aid designers in understanding how people physically and mentally experience and inhabit space, which in turn enables designers to create more people-centered spaces and designs. This research, which examines how people experience space, reveals how narrative inquiry might be used to produce, inhabit, and interpret space.

Joy Dohr and Margaret Portillo have published extensively on the application of narrative inquiry in design research and practice. In *Design Thinking for Interiors*, they advocate that "narrative methods as part of a multiple-methods research strategy" can provide insight into the multi-faceted nature of the interior environment (Dohr and Portillo 2011). They outline four narrative types utilized in interior design research: anecdote narratives; initiating narratives; visual narratives; and research narratives. All of these narrative types help to uncover "the experience of interiors and their meaning and value." An anecdote narrative illuminates a single, subjective perspective – that of the storyteller. An initiating narrative, which is also highly subjective, goes beyond "sharing information" and is used to introduce or inform a study and help "formulate" research questions. A visual narrative involves telling a story through images, while a research narrative looks to answer research questions. Although a research narrative also aims to capture subjective experience, it is based on multiple academic sources and is "triangulated," "verifiable," and "authoritative." Dohr and Portillo's idea of research narratives is particularly compelling for this study, which looks to use the subjective experience captured in narratives as a "lens" into the "objective reality" of preservation (Dohr and Portillo 2011).

Narrative inquiry has not made significant inroads into the preservation field, even though the idea of narrative is fundamental to the preservation process. Historic preservation and the process of landmark designation are excellent subjects for narrative inquiry research.

Principally this facility has to do with the American system of designation, which requires that the historic significance of a site be determined before a site receives heritage designation. In order to establish significance, the nominator must construct a persuasive narrative around a historic site or structure detailing its historic importance and value to contemporary society. The historic nomination forms provide these stories and help to mold the meaning of historic sites and structures

(Green 1998). The story told by the site's official designation strongly mediates the way the past is approached at historic sites.

But the statement of significance in the designation application does not represent the complete story of historic sites. The story of a historic site does not begin or end with its designation. Historic sites are reproduced countless times as they are occupied and consumed. Consequently, many different narratives surround the interpretation of these sites. In the case of the Hull House and Henry Street settlements, their preservation and interpretation represents an ongoing arbitration between public and professional narratives. These intermingled stories continue to redefine the significance of these historic sites.

Preservationist Ned Kaufman highlights the importance of stories to the understanding of historic sites. "One of the ways people express feelings about places" Kaufman asserts, "is by telling stories" (Kaufman 2009). Accordingly, he challenges preservationists to pay attention to stories and to examine them "for what they reveal about people and places." When "people frame their thoughts in narratives," he continues, "they reach into realms of feeling and value that the profession's scientific or evaluative methods do not capture." Kaufman highlights historic sites as both the "embodiment" and the "container" of stories. The ability of narrative inquiry to address the built environment, access historical perspectives, and engage archival sources makes it a valuable tool for this study of historic interiors.

This Inquiry's Methodological Approach

This research employs multiple methods. Case-study methodology provides the framework for an examination of historic interiors within their larger context and over a period of time. The two cases explored are the Hull House Settlement in Chicago and the Henry Street Settlement in New York City. Social settlement houses provide a good vehicle for the study of the preservation of historic interiors. They are complex historic sites that have evolved over many years and have accommodated many different actors. Since the inception of the settlement house movement, its social goals have been intimately tied to the physical structures of its settlement houses. And, with its settlement houses, the movement has focused on interiors and their impact on the character and experiences of their neighbors.[3] Rather than charting the entire history of these settlement houses, these cases examine critical junctures in the history of these two sites. Critical junctures refer to key moments, or turning points, in the history of these two settlement houses where the meaning of these sites was renegotiated or contested.[4] Preservationist Daniel Bluestone asserts, "people invent and reinvent meaning, value and devalue and value again their buildings" (Bluestone 1999/2000). The Hull House and Henry Street settlements were subject to a similar process of reinvention and renewal at critical moments and junctures in their pasts. These critical junctures were established by an initial reading of archival sources to isolate key moments in the negotiation over meaning in the history of these two settlements.

Although the overarching research framework for this project is the case-study structure, narrative inquiry methods shape the approach to the sources within each case. Exploration of each critical juncture involves the presentation of a series of stakeholder narratives, which illustrate different viewpoints about the significance of these two sites at a particular time in the settlements' history. This approach involved an initial reading of these archival sources to isolate critical junctures in the negotiation over meaning in the history of these two settlements. Once these junctures were established, additional investigation isolated a variety of perspectives revolving around each critical juncture. Out of these data a series of stakeholder narratives was constructed. An analysis of these narratives explores how certain viewpoints came to dominate the interpretation of each site.

In some cases the stakeholder is an individual such as Jane Addams, while in other cases the stakeholder represents a group, like the Harrison-Halsted Community Group. The purpose of these narratives is to capture the subjective "voice" of these diverse stakeholders. Archival sources were read carefully, compelling passages were marked, and these passages were forged together to create a coherent narrative.[5] The forging of the narratives was an iterative process involving multiple drafts to ensure that the narratives captured the language, wording, and emotional tenor of the stakeholder. Within the narratives shifts between my, the narrator's, voice and the stakeholder's voice are carefully indicated with the use of quotation marks. And around these narratives, I provide context, explanation and transitions.[6]

Within this study each narrative is explored as an individual story as well as compared to other stories to determine interaction and intersections. Significantly, utilizing narrative inquiry methodology enables this study to move beyond an architectural analysis of historic interior spaces and, instead, capture the relationships that the interior spaces of the Hull House and Henry Street settlements represented. Through exploring the various narratives that surround these historic sites, this study exposes the human context that informed, and continues to inform, their presentation and interpretation.

The narratives presented within this study are consistent with Dohr and Portillo's classification of a research narrative. They look to answer research questions, such as "How have individual personalities and community values manifested themselves in the interior spaces of these two settlement houses?" or "How did the figure of Jane Addams come to be the ascendant narrative in the significance and interpretation of the Hull Houses site?" Notably, the story, or narrative, created is not an "objective" account of an event, but rather a detailed look into the subjective experience of an individual or group of people. As a result, the researcher has to establish credibility concerning the "accuracy of the data and the plausibility of the plot" (Polkinghorne 1995). The "accuracy of the data" is established through the use of triangulation where the what, when, and how of the narrative is corroborated by collecting evidence through multiple methods. The "plausibility of the plot" rests on the "explanatory power and plausibility" of the story. One of the ways narrative researchers achieve validation of their constructs is by emic verification – having the interviewee read the finished narrative for accuracy. This is not possible with narratives based on archival sources. Validity has to be established in a different manner. Where possible these narratives use direct quotes from the archival sources.

Additionally, this study uses triangulation of sources to establish narrative validity. Individual narratives are validated through the use of corroborative evidence collected from multiple sources. Sources for these narratives include personal correspondence, board minute meetings, settlement studies, fundraising information, and newspaper articles. From such diversity of records may be drawn an account of the process by which first reformers and later preservationists made decisions regarding the manner in which these sites would be maintained and interpreted. These extensive records allow for an examination of alternative community narratives, which offer further insight into the negotiation of significance at the Hull House and Henry Street settlements.

By demonstrating narrative inquiry as a way in which to enhance understanding of historic preservation and historic interiors, this study contributes to the body of knowledge on narrative research. Like Delgado and Goodman, it suggests that we cannot fully understand critical historical junctures without first examining these junctures from multiple points of view. And like Portillo, Dohr, and Kaufman it uses narrative inquiry as a way to access the stories and experience embodied in the built environment. Accordingly, this study seeks to determine how different voices have shaped the Hull House and Henry Street sites. By emphasizing the experiences and relationships that are continually played out in the built environment, the narrative approach of this project allows for a new perspective on these familiar spaces. It allows for the possibility that "architecture and space" can be "multi-voiced" and "multi-faceted" and, through doing so, provides a more fluid explanation of the preservation process and its contribution to the study of the past (Llewellyn 2003).

Critical Juncture: Hull House Preservation

The critical juncture explored below examines the preservation of Chicago's historic Hull House Settlement. In 1889 social reformer Jane Addams founded the Hull House Settlement in a run-down Italianate Victorian mansion located in the Halsted neighborhood. The community had a large immigrant population, which she hoped to direct her activities towards. By making their homes among the poor, predominantly immigrant, urban dwellers, reformers like Addams sought to bridge the social, economic, and cultural divide between the wealthy upper classes and the working classes. The Hull House Settlement provided a communal living environment for middle-class reformers as well as services for the surrounding immigrant neighborhood, such as daycare services, English classes, and cooking and sewing classes (Carson 1990; Davis 1984; Haar 2002a; McGerr 2003; Spain 2001; Wright 1980).

Careful deliberation went into the selection and placement of furniture within Hull House. At the time of the founding of Hull House the middle-class home was undergoing a transformation. The overstuffed rooms, wall-to-wall carpeting, heavy draperies, papered walls, and ornate furniture that marked Gilded Age interiors were being thrown over in favor of polished wood floors, painted walls, simple wood furniture and window treatments, and "open, flexible spaces" (Cohen 2004). This change in aesthetics was tied to education and social developments, such as the emerging home economics field, new theories that germs were transmitted through air and dirt, and the Progressive reform emphasis on the environment and its influence on character formation. At Hull House, Jane Addams created a model interior that she hoped her immigrant neighbors would replicate. By the 1910s Hull House had grown into a 13-building complex that enveloped the original building, and covered half a city block. It contained a theater, a kindergarten, a nursery, a music school, an art gallery and a public gymnasium. The Chicago architecture firm Pond & Pond, which was influenced by the Prairie school of architecture, designed these additions. Hull House retained these proportions until 1961 when the Harrison-Halsted neighborhood became the site of the new University of Illinois campus in Chicago.

Orientation

In 1967, Jane Addams' Hull House Museum opened on the new University of Illinois campus in Chicago. Designed to commemorate Hull House founder Jane Addams, the museum encompassed two structures, a mansion originally built in 1856 and a brick dining hall built in 1906. The museum was constructed from the remnants of the historic Hull House Settlement, which six years earlier, in 1961, had spanned an entire city block. At this time the Hull House mansion was the cornerstone of a complex containing 12 other structures (Peter Fish Studios, n.d.).

Between 1961 and 1967 a number of competing groups, including the University of Illinois, its students, the Harrison-Halsted neighborhood, and the Hull House Settlement, shaped the reconstitution of the Hull House Settlement into a museum. The conflict began when the city of Chicago offered the settlement's Harrison-Halsted neighborhood, roughly 130 acres, as the site for the new University of Illinois campus in 1960.[7] If the university accepted this site, the majority of the Halsted neighborhood, including the Hull House Settlement, would be torn down. Members of the local community and the Hull House Settlement mobilized almost immediately against the proposed campus, initiating a protest to save Hull House and the Halsted neighborhood that would garner national attention. From April 14 to April 17, 1961, the city council Planning and Housing Committee held an intensive three-day public hearing on the proposed location of the University of Illinois campus at the Harrison-Halsted site. Interested parties from the university, the Hull House Settlement, and the Halsted neighborhood spoke on behalf of their various interests. Following the debate, on May 11, 1961, the city council voted to approve the Harrison-Halsted site for the new University of Illinois at Chicago campus.[8] Four prominent stakeholder narratives emerged around the proposed demolition of Hull House: these included the Hull House residents, the university, the Harrison-Halsted neighborhood, and the students.

Hull House narrative: "Jane Addams slept here"

Russell Ballard, head resident of Hull House from 1943 to 1962, represented the voice of the Hull House residents at the public hearing. He spoke against the demolition of the settlement and its neighborhood.

On April 13, 1961 Russell Ballard addressed the Planning Commission on behalf of the Hull House Settlement. Since the announcement of the Harrison-Halsted site in February, Ballard had actively campaigned against the proposed demolition of the Hull House Settlement and the neighborhood that surrounded it. "There's something here of real value," he had stated to a *Chicago Daily News* reporter in February, "We don't tear down Lincoln's home." He elaborated, "The name of Jane Addams and her work are known throughout the world," and although Hull House was not her birthplace it was a "birthplace of another kind." The "good will generated by Jane Addams still abides in the rooms and corridors of the physical setting where she labored to improve the lot of her neglected neighbors. She still lives and her spirit is reflected in the continuing service today" (*Chicago Daily News* 1961a). Ballard's concern extended beyond the boundaries of the Hull House Settlement structure to include the neighborhood it served. And, when he gave his statement to the Planning and Housing Committee he affirmed, "those of us who live and work at Hull-House are supporting our neighbors in their protest." With regard to the proposed demolition of the Hull House Settlement for a new university for the "greater good" of the community, Ballard asked, "Who can judge what is the 'greater good'?" He outlined that the American Institute of Architects' Committee on Preservation of Historic Buildings had voted to preserve Hull House as "perhaps Chicago's most important historic structure." And, referencing a letter from the Amalgamated Clothing Workers of America as well as Senator Paul H. Douglas, Ballard outlined that this opinion was widely shared. "Yes, a national protest is mounting," he concluded, "and the multitude of friends of Hull House are not going to be satisfied with a bronze plaque mounted on a brand new modern building, reading 'Jane Addams Slept here' " (Ballard 1961).

University narrative: "The end of a makeshift education"[9]

The university defended the choice of the Halsted neighborhood at the public hearing. The following narrative captures the university's position.

Between April 13 and April 17 a number of university officials appeared before the city's Planning and Housing Committee to be questioned concerning their choice of the Harrison-Halsted site as the new campus for the University of Illinois. For around 30 years, the university's Board of Trustees had negotiated with the city of Chicago for an urban-based campus for the University of Illinois. Negotiations escalated in 1958 when Mayor Daley announced his plan to redevelop Chicago. Key to his plans was finding a new campus for the University of Illinois. This was welcome news for the university, which housed its Chicago students in a temporary campus in the industrial Navy Pier area of Chicago. This site was noisy, run-down, and no longer had the capacity to meet the needs of a growing student body. And, the need to address this "overtaxed" site ahead of the incoming influx of postwar babies was pertinent (*Chicago Daily News* 1961b). The university had already petitioned the city for the use of four different sites: a golf course near North Riverside, Megis field on Northerly Island, a south loop railway site, and Garfield Park. The first two sites were unavailable, the railway site could not be developed in time for the university's fall 1964 opening deadline, and Garfield Park, which was the university's preferred site, posed time-consuming legal issues, such as "reversion clauses" in donated tracts that complicated the acquisition of this site. As an alternative site the city proposed the Harrison-Halsted neighborhood on June 28, 1960 ("Time Line" n.d.). Eager to begin building, and conscious of the "plus factors of availability [and] accessibility," the university agreed upon this site. The "flat and now treeless neighborhood," was not the type of setting that the university had envisioned building its new campus in. "It hurt us to give up the natural beauties of Garfield Park and start from scratch," Charles Havens, director of the university's physical plant had reported to the *Chicago Daily News* in February, but this area can become "a campus the people of Chicago can be proud of" (*Chicago Daily News* 1961c).

Community narrative: "A neighborhood will change"[10]

Although many people spoke on behalf of the Halsted community over the three-day hearings, the majority of the community members stood on the sidelines while their fate was debated. The next narrative spotlights the reaction of Halsted community members to the city council's decision in favor of the university at the conclusion of the three-day hearing.

Over the course of three days, the Harrison-Halsted community group had listened patiently to arguments for and against the Harrison-Halsted site.[11] There was a great deal at stake for these community members. If the council voted in favor of the Harrison-Halsted site these Chicago residents faced the loss of their community and their homes. "They are taking away our heritage," one concerned resident had stated (Mabley 1961). "The rich always take from the poor," asserted another (*Chicago Daily Tribune* 1961a). On April 18, the Chicago city council approved the demolition of the Harrison-Halsted neighborhood and the Hull House Settlement to make way for the new University of Illinois' Chicago campus. Incensed Halsted community members paid a visit to City Hall. A three-member committee of Halsted area residents met with Mayor Daley to request that another site be found for the university while 40 more neighborhood residents waited patiently in the lobby of City Hall. The meeting with Daley was a disappointment; he reaffirmed the city's and the university's decision to use the Harrison-Halsted site.

Faced with Daley's intransigence, the community group representatives reported to the gathering in the lobby: "There is no use trying to see him again, He just simply isn't going to satisfy us" (*Chicago Daily News* 1961c). As the group began to leave City Hall they encountered a crowd of students demonstrating in support of the mayor's decision. Facing the possibility of losing their homes and relocation, the community group found the students' counter-picketing offensive. When the "mothers" began to object to the signs, some students "pushed the women around" (Scala, n.d.). This angered the neighborhood residents, who asked themselves what right this "bunch of dumb kids" had to "fight [for the site] anyway? they won't even be in the campus! By the time that thing is built – they'll be gone" (Scala, n.d.).

Student narrative: " 'Big hurrah' from navy pier"[12]

The students at the University of Illinois' Navy Pier site also had no official voice at the public hearing, but at the conclusion of the hearing they rallied in support of the council's decision, providing an alternative prospective to the protests of the Halsted community.

Many students were excited about securing a permanent site for the university. Over the past few years "many tempting locations" had been "paraded before" them and "in succession each one" had been "overruled." When city officials finally announced their approval of the Halsted site, a group of students assembled at City Hall to demonstrate their "approval and support." Upon entering City Hall, they encountered a group of "irate citizens" protesting the Halsted location. This group of "screaming, crying, hysterical women converged" on the students (Harbinson 1961). They "pushed and jostled" the students, and at one point a "student's sign was ripped out of his hands and torn up" (*Chicago Daily News* 1961c). The "mob" yelled "Youse kids ain't educated," exclaiming that they were "selfish for taking their homes from them" (Harbinson 1961). Some students scoffed at the "horde"'s claims to a neighborhood, pointing out that anyone who took a "tour through the Harrison-Halsted neighborhood" could see that it was only a "slum district." The women's calls to save Hull House generated a more mixed response. Some students felt that Hull House should be maintained as a "library" or a "shrine" to Jane Addams (Fleming 1961). Others felt that the calls to save Hull House were "nonsense" and "Addams would have been sorry to hear that the U. of I. site was denied for the umpteenth time just to save her old recreation house" (*Chicago Daily News* 1961d). All the students agreed that the university needed a "new site" and needed it "NOW" (*Per Illini* 1961). The scuffle ended when the students were ushered into Mayor Daley's office, where they were reassured that Daley "would not deviate in selection of the site and that the university would be built despite differences of opinion"

(*Chicago Daily News* 1961c). Although none of the current students would "benefit from the new university" they felt that their fight for the campus was not for themselves "but for the entire city of Chicago – including the Harrison-Halsted women, whose own children will receive the benefits" (Harbinson 1961).

Afterwards

The struggle over the Hull House complex and the Harrison-Halsted neighborhood was divisive, and these narratives reflect the level of emotion invested in these sites. For the university, and many of the students, the settlement represented a symbol of a bygone era and an impediment to progress, while the Hull House residents and the Harrison-Halsted community group felt that the settlement represented the heart of the Halsted community and had for several decades. Each stakeholder had a legitimate claim on the site and spaces of Hull House. These included: the expansion of a public university; the maintenance of a venerable neighborhood institution; and the protection of a culturally rich and diverse neighborhood. From these negotiations, however, the university's voice, and those of its students, emerged dominant. And, as illustrated below, the reconstitution of the interiors of Hull House was predominantly shaped by the university. When it won its claim to the Halsted site, the university restaged the interiors of the Hull House mansion to reflect its own vision of Hull House, substituting office furniture with sideboards and grounding the meaning of the site in the historical figure of Addams. The process of demolition and restoration transformed the meaning of the Hull House institution and the Hull House interiors. The interiors, as museum spaces, no longer served to anchor the settlement in its neighborhood. And the settlement, without its architecture, was no longer a neighborhood institution.

By 1963 the majority of the Harrison-Halsted site was demolished and its residents relocated. Hull House's services were dispersed around the city and all but two of its buildings demolished. Under mounting public pressure the university agreed to preserve the original Hull House mansion and the settlement's dining hall as a museum commemorating Jane Addams.[13] The community's response to this proposal was unenthusiastic. Russell Ballard did not think the preservation went far enough; "the meaning of historic Hull House is incorporated not in the Hull-mansion alone, but in the cluster of buildings which symbolize the community of people who helped to establish America's social conscience" ("Save the Hull House" 1961). Jesse Binford, a resident of the Hull House settlement since 1905 and representative of the Harrison-Halsted community group, stated that she would rather see the entire Hull House "demolished" than turned into a museum and incorporated into the university. She stated, "We'll never get the university trustees to understand what we're fighting for, and we'll never understand the power politics that is trying to take our community away from us" (*Chicago American* 1961). For Binford, the settlement structures became meaningless once they were divested of their public service and neighborhood functions.

Despite community misgivings, the university restored the Hull House mansion to what was believed to be its appearance as a mid-Victorian brick mansion. Architect Walter Netsch, who headed the design of the new campus, claimed to be behind the choice to return the Hull House Mansion to its 1856 appearance. "I decided that the idea of Jane Addams should go back to the farmhouse she lived in," Netsch asserted in a 1995 interview. He also claimed to be behind the university's choice to save the dining hall building "because that was the building that Frank Lloyd Wright first gave his famous speech on *The Art and Craft of the Machine, in 1901*" (Netsch 1995).

To oversee the exterior restoration of these two buildings the university hired the architecture firm Frazier, Raferty, Orr, and Fairbank. They based their restoration of the mansion on an 1896 painting of the Hull House mansion, which creatively reconstructed what the house might have looked like in its original state. In this painting, the Hull House mansion is depicted with a rooftop cupola, a veranda that extends around the building, and a hipped roof.

To return it to this state, the architects removed a third floor from the mansion, which was added in the early 20th century, constructed a hipped roof and rooftop cupola as well as a veranda that extended around the house, and resurfaced the mansion in brick.[14] In order to fit the dining hall into the small amount of space allotted to the Hull House structures, the architects relocated it 200 feet northwest of its original site and rotated it to face north and south. The stucco and brick dining hall was placed on a new concrete foundation and resurfaced entirely with brick. The architects restored the interior of the dining hall, where Hull House residents traditionally shared meals and entertained guests, to its 1910s–1920s appearance. Large wood tables and bentwood chairs filled the space, whose main purpose in the museum complex was as a conference center. The first floor of the Hull House mansion housed the museum's main exhibition space, while its second floor became the Preston Bradley Library, which housed archival material pertaining to Jane Addams and the Hull House Settlement. Notably, the university's stakeholder voice was amplified, as the dining room became a conference center for the university and the second floor of the mansion a library.

The university took charge of the interior restoration of the mansion, forming a subcommittee on memorabilia to oversee the work (Hull House Committee, October 27). Chaired by Mark Hale, director of the University of Illinois' newly formed Jane Addams' School of Social Work, the members of the subcommittee all worked for the University of Illinois, and consisted of Allen S. Weller, dean of Fine and Applied Arts. Frazer G. Poole, director of the University of Illinois Undergraduate Library, Leonard Currie, dean of the College of Art and Architecture, and Robert B. Downs, dean of Library Administration (Hull House Committee, 1964). Other organizations helped the committee with its restoration efforts, including the Museum of Science and Industry, the Chicago Historical Society, and the Faculty Wives Club.[15] As evident in the composition of the subcommittee on memorabilia, and its affiliates, the former Hull House residents as well as community stakeholders were sidelined in interior restoration decisions.

The decision to restore the exterior of the Hull House mansion to its 1856 appearance created a "dilemma" for the interior restoration. When Jane Addams "took possession of the House in 1889," the subcommittee on memorabilia outlined, "it was already a slum dwelling" ("Conclusions," n.d.). The committee deemed that the building's "most significant time" was Addams' first 20 years at Hull House, 1889–1910, and this should be reflected in the restoration. However, the committee felt that this was "unfortunately an ugly period in furnishings ('mission oak,' hanging lights, etc.)" and did not match the restored 1856 appearance of the mansion. The solution was to restore the Hull House's period interiors to represent the 1840–1860 era, which the members rationalized, would allow them to showcase Hull House's "good" antiques and "express" Addams' original intent of "gracious, cultured hospitality" (p. 5). Moreover, this "feeling of a home," they determined was representative of the Hull House Settlement throughout its evolution.

Before restoration the mansion's double parlors and reception room were a "hodgepodge" of furniture with no "specific style"; mission style chairs stood next to a Victorian sleigh sofa, while Tiffany pendant lamps graced each room. After restoration the double parlors were staged as mid-19th-century period interiors ("Jane Addams' Hull House" 1967). To restore the parlor on the southeast of the mansion to a mid-19th-century appearance, the committee stripped wallpaper from the walls, placed a replica Persian rug on the rooms' newly polished wood floors, and added a bookcase desk from the 1880s. A custom-made electric chandelier was also added to the room to allude to the house's original gas lighting (see Figure 5.1).

In the parlor on the southwest of the mansion, which was previously used as the settlement's library, the turn-of-the-20th-century bookcases were stripped away and replaced with a period sideboard. A replica Persian rug was added and the Tiffany style pendant lamp was removed and replaced with another custom chandelier (see Figure 5.2).

Mrs. James Ward Throne's "American Rooms" exhibit at the Art Institute of Chicago inspired the restoration and staging of these two parlors. The committee felt that two examples of 19th-century parlors were particularly appropriate to their restoration efforts, the New York Parlor and the Georgia Double Parlor. Both these parlors represented the 1850s era ("Conclusions," n.d.). With their wall-to-wall carpeting, ornate furniture, and heavy draperies these interiors characterized Gilded Age interiors much more than the Progressive-style interiors that Addams established when she originally furnished the Hull House mansion. But, to justify its decision to stage these parlors as mid-19th-century interiors, the committee referenced Addams' statement in *Twenty Years at Hull House*, "We were careful to keep it in character with the fine old residence" (Addams 1911).

What was previously the reception room to the north of the building became the museum's main exhibit space. This transformation involved stripping the room down to its bare bones. The wood paneling, from the turn of the 20th century, was removed and the other woodwork was painted over. Display cases were added that housed photographs and maps associated with the Hull House and Jane Addams (see Figure 5.3).

Figure 5.1   Southeast parlor before and after restoration. Images by author.

Finally, with the restoration, the Octagon Room to the far south of the mansion, previously used as an office space for head resident Russell Ballard, was converted into a memorial room for Jane Addams. The room's furnishings, as well as the pictures of Addams and other famous Hull House residents which had covered the walls, were stripped away and a bust of Addams was placed on a pedestal in the center of the room (see Figure 5.4).

In 1965 the restored settlement structures were designated a National Historic Landmark.[16] In keeping with the university's Restoration Committee, the nomination form established the period of significance for the Hull House Settlement to be

Figure 5.2   Southwest parlor before and after restoration. Images by author.

that of Jane Addams' occupancy, from 1889 to 1935.[17] The nomination form outlined that although "the ethnic neighborhood and the nineteenth century structures, which crowded around it, and were the setting for the settlement house, have
all been removed and replaced with towering university structures," and although
"the architectural character of Hull-House is a contradiction" with the exterior and
interior of the house restored to different periods, the Hull House mansion was still
worthy of preservation as an example of one of the first and best known settlement
houses.[18]

An *Architectural Forum* article, published in 1965, described the restored Hull
House mansion, which "pops up at the east edge of the [campus] site," as a "gesture
to the losing side, and a substantial delay to the university's timetable" (Dixon 1965).

Figure 5.3   Reception room before and after restoration. Images by author.

In 1967 this "gesture to the losing side" opened as a museum. A bronze plaque was placed on the front of the newly restored Hull House mansion. It did not read "Jane Addams slept here," as Russell Ballard had feared (Ballard 1961). But, it was not far off. Instead the plaque read, "Jane Addams Hull House has been designated as a registered National Historic Landmark under the provisions of the Historic Sites Act of August 21, 1935. This site possesses exceptional value in commemorating or illustrating the history of the United States" ("Restored Hull House" 1967). By focusing solely on Jane Addams, the national designation form reflected the university's interpretation of Hull House and its interior restoration efforts. The Hull House narrative, and that of its neighbors, was further downplayed.

Figure 5.4 Octagon Room before and after restoration. Images by author.

When noted reporter and author Studs Terkel interviewed her in 1967 about the demolition of the Hull House Settlement, Florence Scala, one of the leaders of the Harrison-Halsted community group, stated:

All that was soft and beautiful was destroyed. You saw no meaning in anything anymore. There's a college campus on the site now. It will perform a needed function in our life.

Yet there is nothing quite beautiful about the thing. They'll plant trees there, sure, but it's walled off from the community. You can't get in. The kids, the students, will have to make a big effort to leave the campus and walk down the streets of the areas. Another kind of walling off. (Scala 1967)

As Scala explained so eloquently, the voice of the community was marginalized in the interpretation and physical restoration of the Hull House Settlement. Notably, in its efforts to commemorate Jane Addams, the university unwittingly wrote the community out of the preserved interiors of the Hull House structures. The university's Restoration Committee cleared the reception room, which had been cluttered full of furniture to accommodate visiting neighbors. And it turned the second floor of Hull House, where previously neighborhood children had dressed for their drama productions, into a library (*Chicagoan* 1967). The Octagon Room, which had once displayed the pictures of many of Hull House's famous residents, now held only Jane Addams' bust. As well, the restoration bypassed the Progressive style showcased in the original Hull House interiors, one of the chief influences exercised by the settlement, in favor of purely Victorian-style interiors. Although the original Hull House interiors showcased domestic characteristics, they were also a laboratory for social and political reform. The Hull House Settlement was both a service institution and a home to its residents.

The restoration of these interiors to a purely domestic space overlooked this past. Ironically, in the efforts to commemorate Addams, the restoration also largely wrote her out of the space with a physical restoration that commemorated an era that pre-dated both Addams and the Halsted neighborhood she served.

Conclusion

People change the space they live in. As illustrated in this critical juncture of the Hull House Settlement, people make decisions about the interiors of spaces, and these decisions reflect broader social, historical, cultural and political dimensions. Importantly, the preservation of Hull House marked a critical juncture in the history of this space. Multiple stakeholder narratives around this critical juncture in Hull House's history emphasize the meaning, values, and emotions that were invested in this protected site. And they help shed light on the reconstitution of the Hull House interiors at this crucial moment in the site's history.

The critical juncture analyzed in this essay is vital to the conception of the Hull House Settlement as a preserved space. It highlights a moment of plurality in the history of this site, where multiple voices emerged that conflicted with, or else complemented, one another. Using narrative methods to capture the voices that mark these critical moments provides a lens onto the ways in which historical actors constituted their environments at key points in history. The transformation of the Hull House Settlement into a museum was a dramatic transition. The Italianate Victorian mansion that emerged from this process stood out against the modern architecture of the university's campus, while the mansion's interiors showcased a type of domestic environment that had no connection to the Hull House Settlement. Battles at critical junctures, like the preservation of Hull House, are concretized in their interiors, and examining these interiors helps to provide perspective on "other, less visible issues" (Cooper Marcus 2006). Just as interiors can provide an important lens onto broader social, political, and historical trends, exploring this larger environment through narrative can provide an important perspective on the changes people make to their interior environments.

Importantly, this project establishes historic interiors as a significant area of study and proposes a model for studying these interiors. This model has two central elements: organizing interior space conceptually by critical junctures, or moments of transition, and examining the narratives of the people that were connected to these sites at these critical junctures. Importantly, it provides a method for capturing voices in a changing environment. Narrative takes us beyond chronicling preservation efforts and allows us to examine the deeper understandings and multiple meanings that arise from the built environment, bringing forward stories and experiences of those who shaped historic spaces.

This study transforms space into an analytical tool for studying historical phenomena. However, the model it proposes has relevance to design practice today. It encourages designers to examine the ways in which people construct interiors in response to their surrounding environments. It provides a way to read interior architecture as a site of multiple, sometimes, contested meanings. And it draws the focus of designers beyond the interior layout of rooms to assess material culture as a powerful statement of social, political, and cultural values.

Notes

1   Settlement houses were established at the turn of the 20th century as part of a larger Progressive era reform initiative called the settlement house movement. A unique type of social reform in turn-of-20th-century America, this movement represented the efforts of middle-class women and men to improve the lives of urban poor by encouraging social contact between the classes. To facilitate this contact, these middle-class women and men established homes for themselves, called settlement houses, in poor, urban neighborhoods, dominated by immigrants.

2   Goodman supplies only a preface, with no written introduction or conclusion. As such, his analysis is not separated from the narratives, but instead rises almost inductively from the presentation of the stories, particularly in his choice of stories, themes, and context. See: Goodman 1994: xii–xiii.

3   Both Hull House and Henry Street were among the first settlements to be founded in the United States. The founders of the Hull House and Henry Street settlements, Jane Addams and Lillian Wald respectively, were women whose work in settlements, as well as related reform efforts, gave them national prominence. And their handiwork, the Hull House Settlement and the Henry Street Settlement, are the only two settlement houses to receive National Landmark Designation. Finally, both settlement houses are well archived. Each case is based extensively on archival sources, which includes government documents, letters, meeting minutes, diaries and so forth. The archives utilized include: the University of Minnesota's Henry Street Settlement Records, Henry Street Oral History Project and the Helen Hall Papers; New York Public Library's Lillian Wald Papers; Columbia's Visiting Nurse Service of New York Records; the University of Illinois at Chicago's Special Collections, which house the Jane Addams Memorial

Collection, including the Hull House Collection as well as the Hull House Oral History Collection, the Louise de Koven Bowen Papers and the University Archives; Smith College's Ellen Gates Starr papers and the Jane Addams Papers.

4   Critical junctures were determined by a detailed examination of available primary and secondary sources. They were chosen for several reasons. First, at these moments in time preservationists, reformers, and community members had to define the significance of these sites in order for these institutions to move forward. Second, they reflect parallels in each site's history. Finally, these junctures were chosen because they mark moments when debate over the meaning of the Hull House and Henry Street settlements materialized in their interior environments.

5   To inform the construction of these narratives, this study pulls from Irving Seidman's use of "storied vignettes." Seidman advocates the use of "storied vignettes" as a way of communicating what a researcher has learned from in-depth interviews. He develops these vignettes through a process of cutting, pasting, and synthesizing transcribed interviews. Basically, Seidman reads through a transcript, marks "compelling" passages as important, cuts and pastes these passages together, rereads the synthesized interview and then crafts a vignette out of the remaining passages. Where possible, the narrative is in the interviewee's own words. Seidman recognizes that some transitions will have to be in the narrator's voice, but he asserts that these instances should be clearly marked within the narrative in order to avoid confusion. See Seidman 1998.

6   This is similar to an approach employed by Margaret Portillo and Joy Dohr. In their study on creativity and workplace design, the voice of the researcher is clear in relation to the presented narrative, providing context and explanation and marking transitions from one user perspective to another. See Portillo and Dohr 2000.

7   The city had designated the Harrison-Halsted site a land clearance site in 1959. The Hull House Settlement endorsed this designation as a way in which to generate funding and initiative for neighborhood revitalization. Among these initiatives a new Catholic church and school were constructed for $600,000. See Haar 2002b: 154.

8   See *Chicago Daily Tribune* 1961b; Avery 1961; Schreiber 1961; *Chicago Daily Tribune* 1961d and 1961c.

9   See "A neighborhood will change and so will a way of education," n.d., University Archives, Box 8, Folder 89, University of Illinois at Chicago Special Collections.

10 See ibid.

11 The Harrison-Halsted community group was mostly composed of women. Many of the neighborhood men worked for the city and feared repercussions if they joined the protests.

12 See Fleming 1961.

13 Hundreds of letters protesting the impending destruction of the Hull House Settlement were sent to Mayor Daley, Dr. David Henry, president of the University of Illinois, and Chicago area newspapers.

14 Based on photographic and documentary evidence, this painting and the architect's restoration were historically incorrect. The roof of the mansion was likely cross-gabled, the cupola may never have existed, and it is unclear if the veranda ever extended around the entire house. See Michael 2003.

15 The Faculty Wife Club took charge of obtaining "authentic furnishings for the Hull House Mansion." See Flynn (chairman of the Hull House Committee), "Letter

to President Henry," University Library Archives, Box 2, Folder 25/26, University of Illinois at Chicago Special Collections.

16 In 1974, these remaining Hull House buildings also received landmark designation from the City of Chicago.

17 The National Park Service utilizes thematic guidelines in determining and organizing national landmarks. The thematic heading that the Hull House was categorized under was "Social and Humanitarian Movements" with the subheading of "Poverty Relief and Urban and Social Reform."

18 "Jane Addams' Hull House," National Register Nomination Form, 1964. Note: this National Landmark Designation did not come with any protection from alteration or demolition. On April 23, 1970, Chicago's Landmark Commission also voted unanimously to give the Hull House mansion landmark status. The University of Illinois challenged this designation. University officials testified to the Commission that "the University must preserve the right to use the land on which Hull House stands for future expansion of Circle campus." Bowing to the university, in a precedent-setting move, the Landmark Commission voted to give the Hull House mansion National Landmark Designation in name only – the landmarking did not include a "mandatory ban on demolition." In response to this decision, one Landmark Commission member stated "Hull House is a bastardized reconstruction to begin with, except for its Dining Hall." See Gapp 1974.

References

"A neighborhood will change and so will a way of education." n.d. University Archives, Box 8, Folder 89. University of Illinois at Chicago Special Collections.

Addams, J. 1911. *Twenty Years at Hull House*. New York: Macmillan.

Avery, S. 1961, April 13. "Plan final fight over U. of I. site," *Chicago Tribune*, p. W1.

Ballard, Russell. 1961, April 13. "Statement of Russell W. Ballard to the Committee on Housing & Planning," Russell Ballard Papers, Box 2, Folder 20. University of Illinois, Chicago.

Bluestone, D. 1999/2000. "Academics in Tennis Shoes: Historic Preservation and the Academy," *Journal of Architectural Historians* 58: 300–307.

Carson, M. 1990. *Settlement Folk: Social Thought and the American Settlement Movement 1885–1930*. Chicago: University of Chicago Press.

Chicago American. 1961, July. "Miss Binford raps Hull House loss," *Chicago American*.

Chicago Daily News. 1961a, February 4. "Standing in the way of land clearance: progress threatens Hull House," *CDN*.

Chicago Daily News. 1961b, February 10. "UI selects Halsted site," *CDN*, p. 14A.

Chicago Daily News. 1961c, February 11. "U. of I. aides promise beautiful campus here," *CDN*.

Chicago Daily News. 1961d, March. "Letters to the editors: the great site fight goes on and on," *CDN*.

Chicago Daily Tribune. 1961a, April 1. "Angry women sit in Daley's office 3 hrs," *CDT*, p. 1.

Chicago Daily Tribune. 1961b, April 13. "Council group opens U.I. site hearing today," *CDT*, p. D7.

Chicago Daily Tribune. 1961c, April 20. "U.I. Decision Stands After New Disorders," *CDT*, p. 3.

Chicago Daily Tribune. 1961d, May 11. "Council OKs W. side U. of I. Site, 41 to 3," *CDT*, p. 3.

Chicagoan. 1967, June. "Hull Mansion – historic treasure on campus," *The Chicagoan*, p. 3.

Cohen, L. 2004. "Embellishing a life of labor: an interpretation of the material culture of American working-class homes, 1885–1915," *Journal of American Culture* 3: 754.

"Conclusions: uses and furnishings of Hull House." n.d. Hull House Museum Archival Records, Box 8, Preservation of Hull House Folder. University of Illinois at Chicago Special Collections.

Cooper Marcus, C. 2006. *House as a Mirror of Self: Exploring the Deeper Meaning of Home.* Lake Worth, FL: Nicholas-Hays.

Danko, S., Portillo, M., and Meneely, J. 2006. "Humanizing design through narrative inquiry," *Journal of Interior Design* 31: 10–28.

Davis, A. 1984. *Spearheads for Reform: The Social Settlements and the Progressive Movement, 1890–1914.* New Brunswick, NJ: Rutgers University Press.

Delgado, R. 1989. "Storytelling for oppositionists and others: a plea for narrative," *Michigan Law Review* 87: 2411–2441.

Dixon, J. M. 1965. "Campus City Chicago," *Architectural Forum* 123: 27.

Dohr, J. and Portillo, M. 2011. *Design Thinking for Interiors: Inquiry, Experience, Impact.* New Jersey: John Wiley.

Fleming, H. 1961, February 10. "UI selects Halsted site," *Chicago Daily News*, p. C6.

Flynn, C. E. "Letter to President Henry," University Library Archives, Box 2, Folder 25/26. University of Illinois at Chicago Special Collections.

Ganoe, C. 1999. "Design as narrative: a theory of inhabiting interior space," *Journal of Interior Design* 25: 1–15.

Gapp, Paul. 1974, April 7. "Decision raises questions," *Chicago Tribune*, p. 40.

Goodman, J. 1994. *Stories of Scottsboro.* New York: Vintage Books.

Goodman, J. 1998. "For the Love of Stories reviews," *American History* 26: 255–274.

Green, H. 1998. "The social construction of historical significance," in M. Tomlin (ed.), *Preservation of What, for Whom?* Ithaca, NY: National Council of Preservation Education, pp. 85–94.

Haar, S. 2002a. "At home in public: the Hull House settlement and the study of the city," in A. Bingaman, L. Sanders, and R. Zorach (eds.), *Embodied Utopias: Gender, Social Change, and the Modern Metropolis.* London: Routledge, pp. 99–115.

Haar, S. 2002b. "Location, location, location: gender and the archaeology of urban settlement," *Journal of Architectural Education* 55: 150–160.

Harbinson, D. 1961, April 23. "From Navy Pier," *Chicago Sunday Tribune*, p. CB.

"Hull House Committee. Minutes of meeting in Illini Center." n.y., October 27. University Library Archives, Box 2, Folder 25/26. University of Illinois at Chicago Special Collections.

"Hull House Committee. Sub-committee on Memorabilia. Minutes of meeting in Urbana." 1964, December 4. University Library Archives, Box 2, Folder 25/26. University of Illinois at Chicago Special Collections.

"Jane Addams' Hull House." 1967. University Archives, Box 57. University of Illinois at Chicago Special Collections.

Kaufman, N. 2009. *Place, Race, and Story: Essays on the Past and Future of Historic Preservation.* New York: Routledge.

Llewellyn, Mark. 2003. "Polyvocalism and the public: 'doing' a critical historical geography of architecture," *Area* 35: 264–270.

Mabley, J. 1961. "City's little people were sold out," *Daily News*.

McGerr, M. 2003. *A Fierce Discontent: The Rise and Fall of the Progressive Movement in America*. Oxford: Oxford University Press.

Michael, V. 2003. "Recovering the layout of the Hull House Complex, scholarly essay and image gallery," *Urban Experience in Chicago: Hull House and its Neighborhoods, 1889–1963*. http://tigger.uic.edu/htbin/cgiwrap/bin/urbanexp/main.cgi?file=new/show_doc_search.ptt&doc=834. Accessed May 1, 2014.

National Register of Historic Places. 1964. "Jane Addams' Hull House. National Register Nomination Form," http://pdfhost.focus.nps.gov/docs/NHLS/Text/66000315.pdf. Accessed May 1, 2014.

Netsch, W. 1995. *Oral History Interview with Betty J. Blum*. Chicago: Art Institute of Chicago.

Per Illini. 1961, March 27. "Same old story," *Per Illini*.

Peter Fish Studios. n.d. "Photographs of Hull House interiors," Hull House Museum Archival Records, Box 8, Preservation of Hull House Folder.

Polkinghorne, D. E. 1995. "Narrative configuration in qualitative analysis," In J. Amos Hatch and R. Wisniewski (eds.), *Life History and Narrative*. London: Routledge, pp. 5–23.

Portillo, M. 2000. "Narrative inquiry," *Journal of Interior Design* 26: iv.

Portillo, M. and Dohr, J. 2000. "Creativity and narrative in Eva Maddox Associates: design beyond space," *Journal of Interior Design* 26: 41–57.

"Restored Hull House makes June debut: Plaque." 1967, June. *Events to Recall Jane Addams' Legacy*, 1.

"Save the Hull House committee statement." 1961, June 12. Hull House Collection, Box 9, Folder 51. University of Illinois at Chicago Special Collections.

Scala, F. n.d. "Oral history interview with Robert H. Young," Florence Scala Collection, Box 1, Folder 10. University of Illinois at Chicago Special Collections.

Scala, F. 1967. "Oral history interview by Studs Terkel," in S. Terkel (ed.), *Division Street: America*. New York: Pantheon Books.

Schreiber, E. 1961, April. "Council unit nears vote on campus site," *Chicago Daily Tribune*, p. 18.

Seidman, I. 1998. *Interviewing as Qualitative Research: A Guide for Researchers in Education and the Social Sciences*, 2nd edn. New York: Teachers College Press.

Smith, D. 2001. "Interior architecture as a storied life: narrative-research and the built environment," *IDEA* 1(2): 1–5.

Spain, D. 2001. *How Women Saved the City*. Minneapolis: University of Minnesota Press.

"Time line of the University's choice of the Harrison-Halsted site." n.d. Hull House Collection, Box 9, Folder 51. University of Illinois at Chicago Special Collections.

Wood, G. 2008. *The Purpose of the Past: Reflections on the Uses of History*. New York: Penguin Press.

Wright, G. 1980. *Moralism and the Model Home: Domestic Architecture and Cultural Conflict in Chicago, 1873–1913*. Chicago: University of Chicago Press.

Section II

Perspectives on the Practice of Interior Design

6

Aesthetic Coding in Interior Design

Mads Nygaard Folkmann

How do places affect the way they are perceived? Of course, everybody has a singular and unique way of perceiving and experiencing places. On the other hand, experiences are never coincidental in the sense that each individual entirely and arbitrarily determines how experiences turn out; the place frames experience and provides a structure for it to develop within. In this sense, each time we perceive and experience places, or practically anything, we actualize the dialectics of subject and object. Thus, it is exactly at the intersection of subjective perception and objective matter that cognition and meaning evolve and come into being for the individual.

When discussing the experience of places in regard to interior design, it may be worthwhile to focus on the side of the object, that is, how design can contribute to the constitution of places and thus, ultimately, to the promotion of certain kinds of experiences of places. Thus, using interior design devices means seeking to shape the conditions of experience. The aim of this essay is to demonstrate and discuss how strategies of interior design contribute to an interior as a place.

The essay has two main sections. The first discusses theoretical matters of experience, understanding, and aesthetic coding in design. Further, this platform is discussed in terms of interior design and the practice of designing interiors by asking how means of interior design can be used to encode, transform, and organize structures of meaning in a way that creates localized places. Consequently, the second section of the essay focuses on an analysis of three exemplary cases of interior designs (all of Danish provenance) that discuss central concepts and demonstrate the defining of places through processes of creating meaning by means of interior design. The cases are Verner Panton's *Visiona II* (1970), Louise Campbell's front office for the Danish Ministry of Culture (2006), and the Tietgen Dormitory in Copenhagen (2008).

Theoretical Outline: Ambience and Understanding

Seen in the context of experience, it is interesting to examine not only how we experience the interior, but also how design creates and stages experience. Thus, the point is both to illustrate how design is perceived, is experienced, and is decoded and to investigate how design creates and encodes in the phase of designing.

Entrance into a discussion of experience is provided by a look at the theoretical construct of phenomenology, which focuses on the conditions of experience. The term "phenomenology" refers to the theory, *logos*, of that which shows itself, *phainomenon*. In comparison to epistemology, phenomenology focuses not only on how we know, but also on what is experienced. Essentially based on a dichotomy of subject and object, phenomenology addresses phenomena as they appear to the human subject.

According to the early 20th-century German philosopher Edmund Husserl, the founder of phenomenology, our way to phenomena goes through our experience of them. However, in his search for the being of phenomena (the world of objects) he is led back to investigate the formation of the structures in consciousness that provide the conditions for meaning to come into being. Thus, consciousness always directs itself towards something, and thus the appearance of this something is determined. In this sense, what is of interest is not so much the specific objects, but rather their way of appearing in relation to consciousness. In the later phenomenology of Maurice Merleau-Ponty, however, the actual world of objects gains in importance, because the emphasis is on the interdependence of the experiencing subject and the experienced world (Merleau-Ponty 1964).

What is interesting about interior design in this connection is that – with its many means of defining surroundings and spaces and their surfaces, textures, and colors – it is an important tool for designating the specific ways that the world of objects appears. Observing and sensing the modern world through its tactile and visual surfaces, we can note how these affect and structure our experience in particular ways; there are huge differences between, for example, experiencing the world through the formal structures of functionalistic design or through Verner Panton's experimental, psychedelic room-scapes as in *Visiona II*.

In like manner, in the book *What Things Do*, the philosopher Peter-Paul Verbeek, with influence from Actor-Network Theory, investigates the "thinking from the perspective of things" in relation to subjects and labels it "post-phenomenological" (Verbeek 2005). His point is that humans act and perceive through artifacts, which thus have a fundamental mediating role. This brings the relation of subject and object beyond the traditional phenomenological focus on the conditions of experience in the subjects; the acknowledgment of the role of actual "things" shifts the focus to the objects and their role in conditioning experience: "Things...mediate how human beings are present in their world and how the world is present to them; they shape both subjectivity and objectivity" (Verbeek 2005).

While phenomenology sees this from the perspective of consciousness, the starting point for a post-phenomenological reflection is the being of things and the fact that things are entities with a presence in the world. Consequently, one aspect of post-phenomenological reflection is an attempt to deconstruct the dichotomy of subject and object in experience and thus not accept human subjectivity as the only origin of the structure of experience.

A phenomenology of design, from the perspective of post-phenomenological reflection, can be developed in an investigation of how design mediates the structures of experience. Thus, design can be seen as a "the creative act that consists in conceiving experiences to be lived by the help of forms" (Vial 2010). Accordingly, I believe that it is important to focus on the specific character of the designed objects and interiors – how they produce meaning and condition experience – and to use this reflection as a framework for understanding the interaction of human subjects and design.

A contribution to this kind of investigation can be found in the concept of aesthetic coding in design, as I have discussed elsewhere (Folkmann 2010). Thus, aesthetic coding in design can be seen to have two aspects with different implications. First, it is connected with the phenomenologically informed reflection of how designed interiors appeal to experience; that is, how interiors and objects can attract attention and relate to the sensory apparatus of perception. This unfolds in the concept of ambience as it is understood especially by the German philosopher Gernot Böhme. A similar understanding of ambience has also been acknowledged in relation to interior design by Jean Baudrillard (Baudrillard 1968). Second , the specificity of aesthetic coding relates to how design stages meaning in a more abstract-conceptual sense and relates to its "content" of meaning; that is, whether the design appears to be a transparent medium for its ideational content, or whether it points, auto-reflectively, to itself as a carrier of meaning. Accordingly, design can establish a specific relation between its physical manifestation and its idea, which may demand or even command a specific order of alignment or mode of understanding. Thus, this dimension of aesthetic coding has interpretive implications.

These two aspects – the kind of sensual appeal of design and its challenges to understanding – are particularly relevant in relation to interior design, as interior design has the capacity to create a totality in (the perception of) place; at best, interior design can evoke a high aesthetic effect of ambience, because it is capable of creating and encapsulating a highly calculated environment, while at the same time, in an extension of the sensual effects, building on and challenging the way we meet and understand our surroundings.

Evoking and intensifying ambience

It belongs to the field of common knowledge that places can have a specific atmosphere that we can sense as soon as we enter; we often perceive ambience on a level preceding conscious recognition. This effect of ambience is both fleeting, as it is hard to grasp, and powerful, as it determines our experience of the place, the mood we are put in and thus our further engagement with the place – and possibly also the way we meet and engage with the people in it.

On this point, Böhme's philosophical-phenomenological concept of ambience, *Atmosphäre*, can be helpful in an attempt to analyze how things, situations, and surroundings appeal to us. Böhme's basic interest is with the conditions of perception, and he defines ambience as a kind of relationship between subject and object. Ambience is always experienced by a subject, but it is also the objective result of an effect evoked by a specific constellation of things (Böhme 1995). Thus, to Böhme the ambience resides in the space between subject and object, as expressed in this central quote:

> Obviously, ambiences are neither conditions of the subject, nor characteristics of the object. Still, however, they are only experienced in the actual perception of a subject and are co-constituted in their being, their character, through the subjectivity of the perceiver. And even though they are not characteristics of the objects, they are obviously produced through the characteristics and interplay of objects. That is, ambiences are something between subject and object. (Böhme 2001)

As a "first reality of perception," ambience is experienced as a coherent unit, and this is also how it expresses itself. It encompasses all aspects of sensory impressions (visual, haptic, auditory, olfactory, and gustatory). Böhme also discusses the classical understanding of "synaesthesia," as a concept that resides in ambience. Böhme is, however, especially interested in the power of color, which is, of course, very important in interior design but not the only important factor. Consequently, Böhme states that ambience can not only be experienced, but also created in the context of "aesthetic work," the intentional effort to give surroundings, things, and people certain qualities that let them appear as special with a power of appeal to be perceived in a certain (controlled) way (Böhme 1995). His understanding of aesthetic work is influenced by the concepts of experience society (Schulze 2005) and experience economy (Pine and Gilmore 1999), which demonstrate how the aesthetic calculation of forms, objects, and interiors is an inherent part of contemporary culture.

Thus, design can be conceived with a high degree of "aestheticism" and construed to be perceived "aesthetically" (Kyndrup 2008), and by virtue of this coding it can relate to societal, cultural, and social contexts. Importantly, aesthetic coding not only relates to sensually charged surfaces, but also to functions (cf. Steinbrenner 2010), an important feature of design. Likewise, interiors cannot be conceived without their basic ability to encompass people and nurture their needs and purposes with the place in question.

To take a more "post-phenomenological" perspective in investigating the promotion of experience on behalf of the object character of interior design, we might focus on the various sensual means that interior design can employ and use for

actual staging ambience. These include color, texture, materials, geometrical proportions and scaling, employment and interplay of form, and the relation of these
aspects to the function of the place. Further, the interior can evoke an intensification
of the ambience.

The intensification of ambience is often deliberately achieved and a part of the
interior designer's aesthetic strategy. Likewise, it occurs in the kind of interior
design that seeks to attract attention and, in this way, to both engage the users or
the audience in the process of creating ambience and reflectively point to itself as a
place of meaning creation. An example of this would be a project at the Kolding
School of Design where the student Signe Fink countered the prevalent Nordic
tradition of minimalism with its white, clean interiors (a style that generally goes
unnoticed as an aesthetic strategy because of its habitual and ubiquitous presence)
and instead aimed for "maximalism" with surfaces in strong colors and the use of
textures as textiles and fur.[1]

To use a philosophical term, in the words of the philosopher Martin Seel, the
intensification of ambience enables and evokes an "aesthetic perception," *ästhetische
Wahrnehmung*, that not only invests itself in the immediate appearance of the
world, as the world is given to us as "a momentary and simultaneous abundance of
appearance," but also promotes the appearance of a "pure present" that is otherwise
inaccessible to ordinary perception (cf. Seel 2007).

To Seel, then, aesthetic perception is a matter of looking in a certain intentional
way that involves "attention to the play of appearances." The given objects or surroundings remain the same, but they are seen with an enhanced sense of the
presence of the situation. However, this aspect of sensual perception originates in
and is encouraged by a design that can point reflectively to itself and by stimulating
a more intense "looking" provoke this kind of "aesthetic perception," as if the design
intends to be perceived with an enhanced sense of presence. Thus, the design can
reflectively point to itself as a locus of this process; a place of maximalism
can perform not only as a space of sensual ambience, but also as a reflective space
of meaning-enabling, which questions how space is perceived.

Enabling and challenging understanding

Apart from the sensual aspect, encoding aesthetic meaning in interior design has to
do with issues of meaning and understanding. The encoded meaning can appeal
to a linear process of understanding where meaning is immediately apprehended,
or it may demonstrate a resistance to understanding. Thus, the interior may present
itself as a riddle, or, rather, it may contain various degrees of riddles or features (in
the form of sensually communicating details such as fur on the walls, and/or abstract
idea content) that almost defy comprehension.

As a discipline, hermeneutics frames processes of understanding (*hermeneuein*
means to interpret) based on the assumption that we can never end the process of
attributing and constructing new meaning as we strive for understanding. Thus, acts

of interpretation and understanding are always dynamic processes; parts are always relating to an ongoing construction of a whole (Gadamer 1960), and every process of understanding implies the flipside of non-understanding, whereby a plurality of meanings is acknowledged (cf. Hörisch 1998).

In this context, hermeneutical devices deal with the access to understanding (and with the denial of understanding) in interior design as well as with the aesthetic coding of this access or denial in interior design. This is indeed a question regarding the relation of the design to its content of meaning. In addition, this level of aesthetic coding not only deals with the specific content (what the intended meaning of a specific design might be on a conceptual level; its idea) but also with the question of its "rhetoric," how the meaning is staged, and how the design reflects this meaning through its actual presence and unfolding in a physical setting by means of sensual aspects of form, materials, color, etc. Thus, what is the "meaning" (if it can be stated), how is it conveyed, and through which means? How does the design present itself to our understanding? As easily comprehended or as something that resists comprehension?

In relation to this point, a central aspect of hermeneutically informed aesthetic coding in design is how a "surplus of meaning" can be contained in interior design and, thus, how this is reflected in the actual design. In the tradition of aesthetic theory, a central topic has been how aesthetic objects can contain something "more," an extra quality or value that exceeds functional relevancy. In aesthetic theory, attempts have been made to conceptualize how aesthetic objects (primarily works of art) can represent or contain something that is otherwise unrepresentable or incomprehensible and thus goes beyond understanding. In this role, the aesthetic object operates as a medium for an otherwise ungraspable surplus of meaning.

Thus, for the German philosopher Theodor W. Adorno, works of art (his topic) can be the locus of a *Herstellung des Mehr* whereby the works of art "let themselves be actualized as appearances of expression; they are not only the otherness of the empirical: everything in them turns into otherness" (Adorno 1970). Paradoxically, this "otherness" is conveyed by, and at the same time separated from, the structure of the work of art.

If we extend the reflection from the domain of art, this means that all aesthetic media can contain a function that disturbs linear communication, lets the aesthetic medium appear as an object with a high degree of "aestheticism," takes communication in new direction, or tries to challenge understanding and perhaps break with existing paradigms of understanding.

Applying the consequences of this to the domain of human perception, Martin Seel states that art (his topic), in "bringing forward otherwise unrepresentable circumstances," has to do with "ways of human commitment in the real or the unreal, in conditions of the world in the past, the present, or the future. Ways of *meeting the world* [*Weltbegegnung*] are put forward, whereby ways of *meeting the meeting of the world* [*Arten der Begegnung mit Weltbegegnung*] will be possible" (Seel 2000 [his italics]). As a consequence, understanding aesthetic media is not a goal-oriented process, but "more about an otherwise impossible meeting with otherwise impossible possibilities of perceiving ourselves" (Seel 2007).

Thus, aspects of non-understanding or incomprehensibility in aesthetic media engage us in a new understanding; prisms for understanding, new ways of meeting the world and, reflectively, of meeting this meeting, are engaged, which in turn enables new patterns of perceiving and understanding. In its ability to encompass all aspects of a place, interior design can be particularly effective as a medium for meeting the world in new and/or reflective ways, thus evoking new kinds of experience and experiencing. Interior design can function as schemes for a new kind of perception and understanding that transcends everyday perception. In turn, this can enable a new kind of seeing.

Following Roger Scruton, this kind of seeing through an aesthetic medium is a controlled "seeing as" that focuses on specific aspects of seeing, consciously reflects this seeing, and points to an "unasserted thought" that is otherwise impossible outside the medium of art (Scruton 1974). Scruton claims that "the "unasserted" nature of "seeing as" dictates the structure of aesthetic experience. Aesthetic media can be employed to grasp aspects of meaning that are otherwise difficult to handle.

Importantly, this process must be related to the sensual presence of the aesthetic medium. In this way, aesthetic theory has emphasized the importance of pointing to the constitutive and formative role of the whole in aesthetic media, while maintaining the singular aspect of the aesthetic experience of the work (Bubner 1989). Thus, aesthetic experience can be seen as a process that starts in a sensual experience and which, in turn, leads to the "search for the totality in the detail" (Bubner 1989).

A noteworthy point in this context is that the whole and the abstract play a constitutive role for aesthetic objects, as their wider implication of meaning lies exactly in the abstract-conceptual constructions of the aesthetic work, while the specificity of the aesthetic creation lies in the extension and implication of the singularity of the aesthetic creation. The concentration of meaning is constructed from the bottom up with a base in sensual matter. It all starts in the actual design.

Aspects of Interior Design

As a medium of meaning, interior design activates specific settings of meaning. To be more precise, the design employs a dual process of transforming and organizing meaning, and thus each design creates a specific framework of meaning that takes off from given means and thus alters existing patterns of, for example, ambience and understanding, and arranges these according to new patterns. Thus, all design is always linked to the past (e.g., in historically given conditions) while also throwing up new structures of meaning.

In this section, I will propose a framework for considering aspects in analyzing and conceiving aesthetic coding in interior design. The framework is based on the theoretical outline of (1) sensual appeal and (2) challenges to understanding, and

Table 6.1 Aspects of aesthetic coding in interior design

Aesthetic coding	Exploring the nature of "places"	Principles of organization	Strategies of integration
Appeal to the senses: evoking ambience	Ambience: – Intensification vs. – Transparence	– Orientation, identification vs. – Disorientation	Scaling: span from details to totality
Appeal to understanding: content of meaning/idea/symbolic-connotative affordance	Reflection of meaning: – Low reflection (immanence) vs. – High reflection (surplus of meaning, unasserted thoughts)	Functional and symbolic meaning: – Integration (seamless communication) vs. – Friction (pointing in new directions of understanding)	

will be explored through the three cases. Hence, the concrete examples are employed to explain and widen the concepts. The framework points to three central aspects of (1) experimental setting and exploration of "place," (2) principles of organization, and (3) integration of elements into a unity and, further, describes how these unfold in dichotomies that point in different directions of creating the interior as place (See Table 6.1). The three cases are described in succession to clarify aspects of each, with each of the cases containing all these elements.

Exploring the nature of place

Many of Verner Panton's interior designs can be regarded as examples of an explorative and reflective investigation of principles of interior design. He works intensely with the intensification of ambience. His designs explore the sensual impact and range of basic constituents of ambience such as strong colors, the use of organic and geometrical forms in combination, and the role of the surface and the texture and fabric of materials; they also explore the possibilities of materials that were new in Panton's time (e.g., new types of plastic). Thus, many of his designs can be regarded as an act of isolating what a place is, what the various devices of interior design can be used for, and how a place signifies. They are laboratories of the possibilities of interior design.

The exhibition project *Visiona II* (1970) is an illustrative example. Created in collaboration with the German chemical company Bayer to demonstrate the use of Dralon, an acrylic fiber material, the project is an early example of advertising and branding a product through the staging of events (cf. Engholm 2006).

Visiona II was a complex of different spaces that used red or green colors, displayed surfaces in hard plastic bubbles or organic, fuzzy carpets, and employed

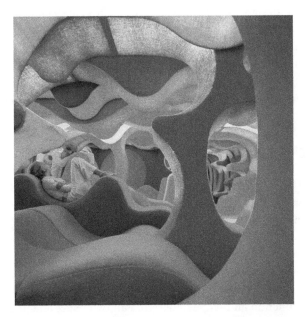

Figure 6.1　*Visiona II*, exhibition project, 1970. Design: Verner Panton. Photo: Panton Design.

lighting made of plastic in the shape of mushrooms or as suspended, silvery, glittering metallic elements with a fluctuating, almost hypnotic effect (see the contemporary commercial movies on youtube.com). Of special interest is the 48 m^2 interior space with organically shaped modules in brightly colored textiles (see Figure 6.1).

Each module forms an unbroken, organic line around floor, walls and ceiling without angles; in their combination, they create a space full of variety and of possible (upholstered) sitting or lying positions. As an exhibition project, *Visiona II* can be hard to experience today, although it is occasionally presented in retrospective exhibitions of Panton's design; mostly, however, these displays do not include the sound effects and intoxicating odors that were also part of the original concept. Thus, the project was meant to have a massive appeal to all the senses.

In this sense, *Visiona II* represents an intensification of ambience, thus appealing to an "aesthetic perception," to follow Martin Seel, and, consequently, resulting in an enhanced "attention to the play of appearances" and a heightened sense of the place as place. The opposite would be to create a mode of transparency where the design does not attract attention to itself and its process of creating place.

Further, Panton's design challenges understanding. It creates a space not only of basic functions (sitting, lying, etc., even as the functionality of such a space can be questioned) but also of encoded meaning that aims at being decoded. In its modular structures of color, organic shapes, possible functions, and encapsulating space, *Visiona II* uses given means (and the brand new one of Dralon) in a new combination; the design of *Visiona II* is based on given elements, but evokes a transformation of meaning that points to a new dimension and organization of meaning by asserting an "unassertive thought" that it is possible to live, be in spaces, and have visions in new ways.

In this way, Panton's design engages reflectively in the production of symbolic meaning, that is, it affords meaning in a certain direction regarding cultural connotations. Thus, on the level of symbolic-connotative affordance, in its conception and execution, it contains, as does all design, a value taxonomy that relates to culture; through its level of symbolic meaning the design is intended to produce an impact or an effect on the way in which people comprehend and engage in culture (Folkmann 2011).

Thus, Panton's design is highly reflective in affording a new model for life by proposing a new order of experiencing, meeting, and understanding the world. It does this by constituting the interior as a place of meaning; to tighten the argument, this task can only be performed comprehensively by the all-encompassing means of interior design. Panton's design performs and executes the utopian potential of this idea, and, vice versa, challenges the notions of design; that is to say, our understanding of the function and scope of design. Panton creates an encapsulating place that also acts out a radical idea of the potential of design for framing our experience, cognition, and understanding of the world.

Exploring principles of organization

Interior design is central for organizing places and, in this act, providing structures of orientation (in order to let us find our way around) and a sense of identity and identification (that we know where we are). In her interior design for the $102\,m^2$ antechamber to the receptionist's office in the Danish Ministry of Culture (2006), the designer Louise Campbell has made the explication of organization the guiding principle in the creation of the sense of place. Situated in a protected historical building, the challenge of the design task was to preserve the existing room while creating an open office environment; the Minister should be able to open his or her door to speak to anyone, and the office should balance between signaling a busy passage to the Minister's office (not a part of the project and, thus, still kept in an old-fashioned style with wood panels) and giving employees an undisturbed work space.

The solution, developed in collaboration with textile designer Anne Fabricius Møller and product designer Marianne Britt Jørgensen, stresses the different functions in the office by separating them in booths with steel frames with a designated color to each booth (see Figure 6.2).

Thus, each function has been symbolically attributed to a color: (1) the area of the photocopier of the office is gray in reference to mechanical functions; (2) the area of the two personal assistants, the so-called "calendar girls," is pink, a soft color

Figure 6.2 Antechamber to the minister's office, Danish Ministry of Culture (2006). Design: Louise Campbell. Photo: Simon Ladefoged.

that signals service (to modify this cliché, the pink booth contains a boxing ball conceived to let the "calendar girls" get rid of their accumulated aggression); (3) the area of the Minister's secretaries is dark red, as they are mentally often in the red zone; (4) the neutral beige is assigned to the head of the office, who has to be in balance and keep the office operating smoothly; and (5) the cool light blue area belongs to the employees who have to coordinate with other offices in the Ministry: they have to maintain calm and keep things in perspective. In each booth, all fixtures are (ideally) made in the same color; the table and the Eames chairs are specially manufactured, and the carpets' textiles are dyed. All booths have curtains toward the hallway and the windows but not toward the other booths; the principle is that employees should be able to work undisturbed by visitors, but not by each other.

With this use of color zones to identify different sections of the room, the interior design encourages an aesthetic perception while also challenging understanding. On the one hand, the design identifies different functions that can be instantly decoded through the color scheme. Seen from a functional perspective, it should be possible seamlessly to decode the system without even noticing the design devices; the design should operate as a transparent medium for an encoded meaning. But on the other hand, the design attracts attention and points to its own presence and construction of organization in the space of the room (clearly marked by the booths that are added to the existing room, that is, originally non-integrated matter, foreign to the room). Further, decoding the meaning of the colors is not straightforward, and so the design challenges understanding. It offers friction to the otherwise seamless communication of its meaning.

A notable feature of Campbell's design – which is a basic feature of much interior design – is that it integrates its functional elements within its sensual, aesthetic expression; the sensual appearance, through the colors, supports the functional aspect of the office, and, vice versa, the functionalities of the booths give relevance to the use of colors. Thus, as mutually intertwined, the function and the use of color are equally integrated in the symbolic communication of the design. This can be regarded as a design-specific feature; on the level of symbolic communication and experience, design, in contrast to art, can consciously include and employ functional aspects (Misselhorn 2010). In essence, the functional aspect of the design is not to be separated from the layer of symbolic meaning in the design, but contributes fundamentally to it. The question, then, is how each individual design uses this as an asset in its communication and making meaning as a place.

Campbell's design states implicitly, but with emphasis, that there can be no decoding of the meaning of the functions outside the layer of symbolic meaning evoked by the use of colors; thus, her design not only reflects that the visitor has to engage in a process of understanding in order to comprehend the space; she also lets the design evoke a friction of function and symbolic meaning. This friction may not, however, point in the direction of an abyss of all meaning and understanding, but rather to the fundamental aspect of the principles of organization that must engage in functional as well as symbolic elements: how places can be created as seamless structures of immediate orientation, or how they can point, through means of friction and in a display of their construction of orientation, implicitly to their own limits and thus to the user's ability to comprehend. This is a consideration for all interior design in its construction of meaning. Thus, the point, beyond Campbell's design, is that interior designs can work and play with this effect of demonstrating their own principles of organization and the access to them through functional and symbolic coding.

Exploring principles of integration

The Tietgen Dormitory in Copenhagen is not a commonplace interior design project but an example of an early integration of interior design in an architectural building process. The interior designers, Julie Henriksen and Mathilde Aggebo, were included early in the sketching phase by the architectural firm Lundgaard and Tranberg, as the architects intended a building with a sensual and tactile outside as well as inside appearance (see Figure 6.3).

The result, inaugurated in 2008, is a circular building with a rhythmical sequence of small cubes that pop out from the surface of the building and, importantly in

Figure 6.3   The Tietgen Dormitory in Copenhagen (2008). Interior design: Julie Henriksen and Mathilde Aggebo. Architects: Lundgaard & Tranberg. Photo: Ole Akhøj.

this context, with variation in different textures (hard vs. soft, rough vs. smooth, open vs. closed, use of grooves and fractures, etc.), use of amplified graphics, and specks of strong colors on mailboxes and washing machines. Thus, devices of interior design, i.e. the use of textures, the use of ornamental graphics, and the choice and use of colors, have contributed to the setting of the meeting with the place and to the creation of an ambience that leads to sensual and social well-being (cf. Graabæk 2009).

The Tietgen Dormitory is a characteristic building and has been acknowledged as such in Denmark, where in 2010 in the newspaper *Politiken* elected it as the most beautiful and outstanding building of the decade (cf. also the celebration of the building in the special issue of the architectural journal *Arkitektur DK*, 2007). Again, the building is a piece of self-reflective design; not only does it create ambience, it also points to this act of creating meaning through the direct appealing setting; this stands in comparison to more anonymous designs which also, in their own right, communicate ambience, but more discreetly and less reflectively.

Another notable feature in this building is the different scales of the elements, which contribute to the creation of ambience. These range from the overall architectural design of the form and proportion of the building, where, for example, the circular structure of the building surrounds an inner yard, to the arrangement, organization, and detailing of both interiors and exteriors. Then, as the architects originally made room for interior design, the perspective can be reversed, and interior design can be seen as the overall comprehensive approach to the appearance of the architectural design in the creation and promotion of ambience, also in the building's exterior.

Thus, the integrative approach of the Tietgen Dormitory has resulted in an upscaling of principles of interior design, which not only provides good arguments for the importance of interior design, but also demonstrates how marked characteristics in a sensual appeal can be used to enhance and reflect ambience. Hermeneutically, the Tietgen Dormitory shows that not only does the "search for the totality" originate "in the detail" (to repeat Bubner), but also that the detail promotes the totality of the design.

Regarding the aspect of understanding, the marked ambience can potentially take the comprehension of the building in new directions. When we meet a place with special characteristics, we become aware that we are meeting a place and can begin to question its setting and the way it stages meaning, its content and possible surplus of meaning, and, further, the symbolic-connotative affording of meaning.

In my view, the Tietgen Dormitory does not contain the kind of chasm in functional and symbolic meaning that is found in Campbell's design; the functional and the symbolic levels of meaning support each other. With a broader application, the Tietgen Dormitory indicates that the comprehension of the design can be incorporated within the formal and sensual structures of the design. Thus, an integrative approach to interior design can produce an ambience that in turn promotes a surplus of symbolic meaning and, vice versa, this surplus of meaning can be contained within the design as part of the ambience such that we meet new ways of encountering the world through the building.

Conclusion

The three cases and the theoretical outline above cannot, of course, be exhaustive for all interior design, but they can be informative about the making of localized places with devices of interior design on the level of the construction of the sensual appeal of ambience and the transformation and (re)organization of meaning. Through a clarification of these aspects of aesthetic coding, reactively in analysis or proactively in a design process, it may be possible to heighten awareness of them in interior design. In dealing with meaning creation on the level of place and physical surroundings, interior design will be ever more important – and, for this reason, it can prove productive to try to see what is going on not only on the surface but also beneath it.

Note

1   I thank Helle Graabæk for making me aware of this project.

References

Adorno, T. W. 1970. *Ästhetische Theorie* [Aesthetic Theory]. Frankfurt am Main: Suhrkamp.

Arkitektur DK. 2007. Volume 7. Copenhagen: Arkitektens Forlag.

Baudrillard, J. 1968. *Le système des objets* [The System of Objects]. Paris: Gallimard.

Böhme, G. 1995. *Atmosphäre. Essays zur neuen Ästhetik* [Essays on the New Aesthetics]. Frankfurt am Main: Suhrkamp.

Böhme, G. 2001. *Aisthetik. Vorlesungen über Ästhetik als allgemeine Wahrnehmungslehre* [Lectures on Aesthetics as Common Theory of Perception]. Munich: Wilhelm Fink.

Bubner, R. 1989. *Ästhetische Erfahrung* [Aesthetic Experience]. Frankfurt am Main: Suhrkamp.

Engholm, I. 2006. *Verner Panton*. Copenhagen: Aschehoug.

Folkmann, M. N. 2007. *Louise Campbell*. Copenhagen: Aschehoug.

Folkmann, M. N. 2010. "Evaluating aesthetics in design: a phenomenological approach," *Design Issues* 26(1): 40–53.

Folkmann, M. N. 2011. "Encoding symbolism: immateriality and possibility in design," *Design and Culture* 3(1): 51–74.

Gadamer, H. 1960. *Wahrheit und Methode* [Truth and Method]. Tübingen: Mohr Siebeck.

Graabæk, H. 2009. "Atmosfæren, Tietgenkollegiet og tekstildesigneren" [The Ambience, the Tietgen Dormitory, and the Textile Designer]. Master's thesis. Copenhagen: Danish Centre for Design Research.

Hörisch, J. 1998. *Die Wut des Verstehens* [The Rage of Understanding]. Frankfurt am Main: Suhrkamp.

Kyndrup, M. 2008. *Den æstetiske relation* [The Aesthetic Relation]. Copenhagen: Gyldendal.

Merleau-Ponty, M. 1964. *Le visible et l'invisible* [The Visible and the Invisible]. Paris: Gallimard.

Misselhorn, C. 2010. "Die symbolische Dimension der ästhetischen Erfahrung von Kunst und Design" [The symbolic dimension of the aesthetic experience of art and design], in J. Steinbrenner and J. Nida-Rümelin (eds.), *Ästhetische Werte und Design* [Aesthetic Values and Design]. Ostfildern: Hatje Cantz, pp. 75–96.

Pine, B. J. and Gilmore, J. H. 1999. *The Experience Economy*. Boston: Harvard University Press.

Schulze, G. 2005. *Die Erlebnisgesellschaft: Kultursoziologie der Gegenwart* [The Experience Society: The Contemporary Sociology of Culture]. Frankfurt am Main: Campus.

Scruton, R. 1974. *Art and Imagination: A Study of the Philosophy of Mind*. London: Methuen.

Seel, M. 2000. *Ästhetik des Erscheinens* [Aesthetics of Appearance]. Munich: Hanser.

Seel, M. 2007. *Die Macht der Erscheinung* [The Power of Appearance]. Frankfurt am Main: Suhrkamp.

Steinbrenner, J. 2010. "Wann ist Design? Design zwischen Funktion und Kunst" [When is design? Design between function and art], in J. Steinbrenner and J. Nida-Rümelin (eds.), *Ästhetische Werte und Design* [Aesthetic Values and Design]. Ostfildern: Hatje Cantz, pp. 11–29.

Verbeek, P. 2005. *What Things Do: Philosophical Reflections on Technology, Agency, and Design*. University Park: Pennsylvania State University Press.

Vial, Stéphane. 2010 *Court traité du design* [Short Treatise on Design]. Paris: PUF.

7

Toward a Creative Ecology of Workplace Design

Margaret Portillo and Jason Meneely

Introduction

In a single day, we sometimes work in what may be considered traditional offices, but increasingly find ourselves working in cars, airplanes, coffee shops, and at home. Some work happens in solitude while other tasks get done face to face or transpire virtually. This essay recognizes the evolving ecology of workplace design. How does a contemporary work environment shape our work and, more importantly, influence innovation? Conversely how does the way we think, engage, challenge, and build consensus impact the workplace? The complex relationships between people and place can no longer be explained in positivistic terms of stimulus and response. Rather, we see the need for a new model, inspired by ecological concepts, that acknowledges the creative workplace as an interrelated system of dynamic, complex, and varied human–space interactions sustaining individuals, groups, and organizations.

In this essay, we introduce an ecological model that speaks to conditions for creativity as well as recognizing obstacles preventing innovation from occurring. Importantly, this ecologically based model applies to work occurring across diverse habitats; from dedicated workspaces to temporary bivouacs, from on-site hubs to off-site refuges, from physical workspaces to virtual ones. Across environments, a goal remains the same: optimize individual and team performance while strategically strengthening the organization. Creativity penetrates a range of workplace attitudes, motivations, behaviors, and outcomes. The ecological model presented in this chapter fosters an increased understanding of adaptations and innovations in workplace design. We begin by discussing one example of the evolving workplace

The Handbook of Interior Design, First Edition. Edited by Jo Ann Asher Thompson and Nancy H. Blossom.

influenced by technology, new work processes, and expectations; in this case, comparing knowledge transfer and technology-based workplaces to mid-century precedents.

The discussion next turns to the need for adaptability in the individual and across groups defining a work environment. We then proceed to share insights from a multi-methods study exploring job satisfaction, climate for creativity, worker characteristics, and the physical workplace. The essay concludes by drawing conclusions about ways to cultivate a creative ecology in the workplace and raises questions for additional thought and study.

The Evolving Workplace

Both focused adaptations and paradigm-shifting breakthroughs contribute to novel and appropriate workplace designs. For example, in some sectors play is now explicitly integrated into the seriousness of work. Understanding the evolution of fun in the work environment offers insights into ecological strategies for a changing the workplace: adapting to new ideas of work, diversifying physical workspaces, and maximizing creative energy exchange.

The origins of this trend can be traced to Silicon Valley in the late 1980s and 1990s, where a spirit of entrepreneurship coupled with rapidly accelerating technological and work process shifts produced the dot-com era. West coast start-ups formed by entrepreneurial upstarts began forming a new type of work culture that grew rampantly, declined sharply, but nevertheless has had staying power and influence in the workplace today (Van Meel and Vos 2001).

Spending significantly more time at work than home, the typical dot-com employee not only began dressing more casually in the workplace but began morphing their offices into work-play spaces, replete with ping-pong tables, golf greens, dartboards, basketball hoops, and fully stocked break rooms. With a radical break from modernist workplace ideals, these dot-com settings often incorporated found signature pieces into their interior spaces, marking their individuality and aspirations to change the world. For example, founder of IDEO, David Kelly, frequently made it a point during his tours of the firm to comment on the full-scale DC-3 plane wing suspended from the ceiling.

Symbolizing one of the most precedent-setting aircraft ever invented, the "Douglas," in no uncertain terms drew a parallel with one of the most innovative aircraft ever invented to a level of innovation sought after by IDEO in designing products, services, spaces, and interactive experiences. Yet if a wing of a DC-3 became a commonplace fixture in knowledge-transfer workplaces, its symbolic poignancy would be greatly reduced. Creativity exists in context.

Likewise this essay does not offer a one-size-fits-all prescriptive approach to the creative workplace. Design does not (and cannot) substitute for indecisive leadership, defective products, inefficient processes, micromanagement, or failure to adapt to a changing marketplace. What good design can do, however, is support the evolving workplace ecology and even sometimes provide strategies to adapt to a changing world.

Again, creativity demands comparison. It cannot be judged without informed precedent. In the past, a mid-century ideal of the workplace offered elegant high-rise offices, manifested in glass, steel, and granite, designed to impress. The first perception of classic international-style work settings, for example, was one of a well-appointed lobby, containing a symmetrically organized grouping of Mies' Barcelona or Le Corbusier's Piet L2 chairs in an architectural enveloped in a beautifully proportioned space containing a truth-to-materials palette of glass, metal, exotic words and stone. This office form represented the epitome of modernist good taste (Van Meel and Vos 2001). Here the presence of an expansive corner executive office with a sprawling mahogany desk was not questioned. Transcending local vernacular or even the organizational identity of the corporate client, this approach to workplace design spoke volumes to success, power, and hierarchy.

In contrast to this mid-century prototype, "a fun in the workplace" approach centers on anti-establishment, unconventional and iconoclastic spaces where social hierarchy has been somewhat flattened and status is only given to good ideas. Both orientations create a shared identity and sense of purpose; one draws strength as establishment while the other celebrates the anti-establishment. Commitment to excellence may well be the same across approaches, but the physical and social manifestation of the organization is quite different. Play aligns with an explicit fostering of creativity, even willingness to experiment and fail, at times, placing a premium on challenging conformity and existing norms.

While the historical roots of the workplace were aligned with a commitment to production, efficiency, and appropriateness, we see play in the workplace not as a replacement for the seriousness of work but as a vital counterpoint that pits novelty against appropriateness – two key ingredients for innovation. As Gardner noted, "creativity is best described as the human capacity to regularly solve problems or to fashion products in a domain, in a way that is initially novel, but ultimately acceptable in a culture" (Gardner 1989). We are not advocating frivolous play; rather, we are talking about serious play or challenging fun where novelty and acceptance collide.

While the heyday of the dot-com era clearly is past, the approach to fun in the workplace is still alive and well. In 2010 *Fortune* magazine ranked Google as one of the best places to work (Tkaczyk 2010). This workplace campus, affectionately dubbed the Googleplex, speaks volumes to a new form of corporate culture. At Google, first impressions note a chaotic vibrancy of lava lamps contrasting with a grand piano in a space where search queries are prominently projected on the walls. Where long hours are coupled with intense performance, demands to best the competition are expected. So how do Google staff decompress? Throughout the Googleplex, employees can enjoy workout spaces filled with weights and rowing machines, and after the workout they can schedule an in-house massage. Long hours spent at work prompt the use of on-site washers and dryers to catch up on laundry. Others refocus by playing in the video arcade or challenging co-workers to a game of foosball or ping-pong. So how does this new emphasis on fun in the workplace relate to creativity?

Adaptability: The Push and Pull of the Creative Individual

Early research into the creative person was primarily focused on identifying the characteristics of highly regarded eminent creators – creativity with a big "C." However, a trajectory of contemporary research has emerged which examines everyday creativity – creativity with a small "c." A primary assumption of this perspective is that creativity is a self-actualized ability achievable by all humankind, rather than a God-given trait (Davis 2008). While personal traits do play a crucial role in creative performance, self-actualized creativity relies on identifying and overcoming personal and environmental roadblocks to creative behavior, as noted by Cohen and Ambrose:

> External transformation involves sensitivity to a context as well as awareness of the limitations of a field and the desire to work hard to transform it....Internal transformation involves sensitivity to one's self and the openness and willingness to modify one's present ways of thinking in order to construct a unique point of view. (Cohen and Ambrose 1999)

Psychological inquiries into the characteristics of creative people have identified numerous traits that comprise the creative personality. They include a willingness to fail and take risks, high energy levels, attraction to complexity and ambiguity, independence, openness to change, and a sense of humor (Barron 1963; Barron and Harrington 1981; Cohen and Ambrose 1999; Domino 1970; Eysenck 1993; James and Asmus 2001; Mackinnon 1965; Plucker and Renzulli 1999; Sternberg and Lubart 1995).

Taken as a whole these traits describe a person who is poised to be adaptable. Expanding on these adaptive characteristics Csikszentmihalyi's study of over 90 eminent creators identified several bipolar or paradoxical traits, including a capacity to be: smart yet naive, playful yet disciplined, imaginative yet realistic, humble yet proud, masculine yet feminine, rebellious yet conservative, passionate yet objective (Csikszentmihalyi 1996). Similarly, in research examining personality correlates of eminently creative individuals Mackinnon found that creative male architects displayed increased levels of self-awareness, openness to emotions, and intuition which typically represent a more female orientation (Mackinnon 1962). Mackinnon concluded, "It would appear that the creative person has the capacity to tolerate the tension that strong opposing values create in him, and in his creative striving he effects some reconciliation of them" (Mackinnon 1962, 1970).

Adaptability as a correlate of the creative person also emerged in a study conducted by the authors that examined relationships between cognitive styles and creative performance in a sample of beginning design students (Meneely and

Portillo 2005). As a whole, the sample displayed a right-brained thinking style indicating a preference for big-picture issues and generative thinking. However, those students whose projects were judged to be more creative, by an expert panel of judges, also displayed an additional preference for a left-brained thinking style. These findings suggest that creative performance was linked to flexibility of thinking. While creativity originates from the individual, it is more than individual traits or characteristics; it involves social-psychological dimensions, diversity, and context in the case of interior design (Portillo and Dohr 2000).

Diversity: Maximizing the Interpersonal Side of Creativity

While creative individuals typically display adaptable personality traits, highly creative teams often comprise diverse individuals with varied backgrounds, mindsets, and behaviors. Some scholars observed that the creative capacity of individual team members does not matter as much as finding the right combination of individuals. Leonard and Straus advocated for working with people who think differently to diversify ideation and reduce team entrenchment (Leonard and Straus 1997). Similarly Herrmann, as well as Basadur and Head, argued for assembling cognitively balanced or "whole-brained" teams where flexibility among thinking styles ensure that problems are examined from multiple perspectives (Basadur and Head 2001; Herrmann 1989). Ultimately, diversified teams increase the potential problem-solving space for developing creative solutions by expanding the gamut of behaviors, thoughts, and experiences beyond a sole creator.

Creative solutions challenge the status quo; therefore, a team that constructively leverages interpersonal conflict during problem-solving will often outperform a team that easily agrees. In fact, Schweiger and Sandberg found that teams who employed dialectical inquiry and devil's advocacy outperformed teams who employed a more consensual approach (Schweiger and Sandberg 1989a, 1989b). While devil's advocacy provides a counterpoint to a single idea or assumption, dialectical inquiry involves two or more people who hold differing views, yet desire to come to some resolution or find a higher truth through a dynamic process of exchange or reason (Schweiger, Sandberg, and Ragan 1986). Leonard and Strauss termed this process "creative abrasion," where the friction of opposing ideas can be transformed into a force for innovation.

While the potential for creative abrasion increases with team diversity, people with different backgrounds, disciplines, and mindsets often have a hard time understanding one another. According to Leonard and Strauss, "If abrasion is not managed into creativity, it will constrict the constructive impulses of individuals and organizations alike. Rightly harnessed, the energy released by the intersection of different thought processes will propel innovation" (Leonard and Strauss 1997). In a creative ecology, tension – a healthy antagonism – creates a culture in which to innovate. The creative ecology thrives on diversity across individuals, teams, and physical spaces within an organization.

While many companies already understand the benefits of interdisciplinary problem-solving, it is important to realize that team diversity can also span cultural and generational divides. One emerging interpersonal tension involves the rise of the millennial generation into the workforce. Perhaps the by-product of a rapidly advancing society, the exponential rate of social and technological change appears to have increased the generational divide between Boomers, Gen Xers, and Millennials.

Although many contend that the generational divide threatens to disturb workplace interactions (Hill 2002; Jacobson 2007; Myers and Sadaghiani 2010), we argue that intergenerational diversity can be tapped as a potential resource for fostering creativity in the workplace. BrainStore, a Swiss consulting company, intentionally crosses these intergenerational divides by inviting local teenagers to join creative workshops with seasoned client company executives. In an interview with Muioi, BrainStore founder Nadja Schnetzler stated, "One of the ideas behind the company was to blend the professionalism of experts with the unbridled enthusiasm of kids" (Muioi 2000).

Interestingly, Csikszentmihalyi identified that highly creative individuals across fields typically exhibited apparently paradoxical traits in their personalities such as being both disciplined and playful; having an expert knowledge base and also remaining naive, drawing upon both masculine and feminine characteristics (Csikszentmihalyi 1996). Yet the individual worker, no matter how creative, does not operate in a vacuum. Gifford maintains that to understand human behavior in the workplace requires an understanding of worker characteristics, management style, and physical work setting (Gifford 2002). Likewise, multiple dimensions come into play in defining creativity. Evidence for the coexistence of paradoxical traits has been found in highly skilled designers (Portillo and Dohr 2000).

Interrelated: Framing Creativity from an Ecological Perspective

The phenomenon of creativity transpires as a complex system of relationships among people, their environment, their processes and products. We choose an ecological model to frame creativity since it allows us to examine its contributing components without isolating them from their broader interrelated context. In other words the whole is greater than the sum of its parts.

While scholarly research into the phenomenon of creativity has increased over the last 50 years, earlier studies tended to focus on parts and how they connect for immediate creative performance. For example, early psychological studies on creativity focused on correlating certain personality traits, such as risk-taking ability, to creative performance. However, social psychologists later challenged this orientation with convincing arguments, showing how the social environment could destroy creative potential of the individual, citing cases where children are raised in overly corrective environments or where employees work in overly hierarchical offices (Amabile 1992, 1996).

It follows that individual creativity is necessary, but not sufficient for creative performance in the workplace. This truth is recognized by our ecological model that frames creativity as an open system adapting over time. Physicists studying how matter and energy flow within complex systems developed a theory of dissipative structures, which are open systems that maintain themselves in a dynamic or chaotic state, yet remain structurally stable over time despite flow and change in the components which make up the system (Prigogine and Nicolis 1977). In other words, the system, despite being chaotic, remains self-organizing. As Fritjof Capra noted:

> The dynamics of these dissipative structures specifically include the spontaneous emergence of new forms of order. When the flow of energy increases, the system may encounter a point of instability, known as a "bifurcation point" at which it can branch off into an entirely new state where new structures and new forms of order may emerge. This spontaneous emergence of order at critical points of instability is one of the most important concepts of the new understanding of life. It is technically known as self-organization and is often referred to simply as "emergence." It has been recognized as the dynamic origin of development, learning and evolution. In other words, creativity – the generation of new forms – is a key property of all living systems. And since emergence is an integral part of the dynamics of open systems, we reach the important conclusion that open systems develop and evolve. Life constantly reaches out into novelty. (Fritjof Capra 2002)

Likewise the workplace offers a dynamic model. We define a creative ecology as an interrelated system of dependencies which supports the movement of creative energy through a given habitat, ultimately resulting in the adaptation of the entire system. Just as nature depends on biodiversity for ecological health, so too do creative ecologies. In nature biodiversity enables energy – usually food energy – to be transferred and transported rather than consumed by the system. Similarly a creative ecology depends on the diversity of its organisms (people with diverse skills and thinking styles), the diversity of its habitats (diverse environments, disciplines, and domains), and the diversity of its processes (risk-taking yet safe-keeping, playful yet judgmental) to keep creative energy moving through the system.

Figure 7.1 illustrates the interaction between individuals, teams, and organizations. The model recognizes creativity as adapting over time in a system which can grow, stabilize, or stagnate. The model embraces diversity and paradox as key elements to fueling creative growth. Within this model, the act of creativity draws on the iterative phases of preparation, incubation, illumination, and verification defined in classic work by Graham Wallis. Person in concert with process contributes to the development and maturation of the system. Finally, the model recognizes creative press and product as tangible outcomes of creativity. The model can be useful across a range of domains, organizations, and settings.

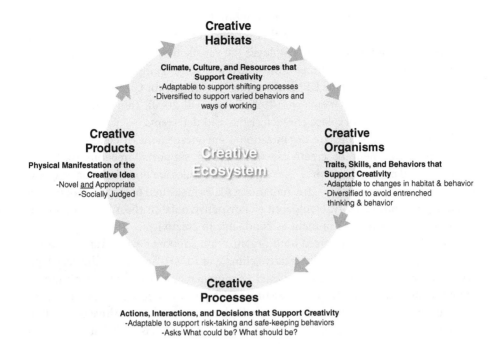

Creative Habitats

Climate, Culture, and Resources that Support Creativity
-Adaptable to support shifting processes
-Diversified to support varied behaviors and ways of working

Creative Products

Physical Manifestation of the Creative Idea
-Novel <u>and</u> Appropriate
-Socially Judged

Creative Ecosystem

Creative Organisms

Traits, Skills, and Behaviors that Support Creativity
-Adaptable to changes in habitat & behavior
-Diversified to avoid entrenched thinking & behavior

Creative Processes

Actions, Interactions, and Decisions that Support Creativity
-Adaptable to support risk-taking and safe-keeping behaviors
-Asks What could be? What should be?

Figure 7.1

Lessons for a Creative Ecology

The research study on creativity and the workplace offers insights into new ways of working and offers a model of creative ecology. This study, headed by Alexandra Miller, focused on the workplace and employed mixed methods research to explore the relationship between job satisfaction, climate for creativity, and workplace design (Miller 2005). The research approach facilitated holistic assessment and the forming of patterns emerging from quantitative and qualitative data (Miller and Portillo 2006). PUSH, the workplace under study, offered insights into how an award-winning advertising agency optimizes innovation. Offering a creative ecology of workplace design for study, PUSH explicitly positioned "fun" as a core organizational value (arguably creating a much-needed foil to toil).

Some early researchers investigating the manifestations of fun work environments, Robert C. Ford and his colleagues, defined this phenomenon as "A fun work environment intentionally encourages initiatives and supports a variety of enjoyable and pleasurable activities that positively impact the attitude and productivity of individuals and groups" (Ford, McLaughlin, and Newstrom 2003). The model of fun in the workplace showed that job satisfaction was significantly higher than average for the 31 participating employees of the 42 PUSH employees at the time of the data collection.

This study empirically tested the assumption that employees who perceive work as fun are more satisfied on the job that those counterparts who do not share this attitude. In addition to assessing employee job satisfaction with the 18-item standardized Job in General instrument, the study also gauged employee perceptions of workplace creativity with the KEYS: Assessing the Climate for Creativity Instrument (Amabile, Burnside, and Gryskiewicz 1999; Balzer et al. 2000). This 78-item measure tapped into creative workplace characteristics and deterrents.

The positive sub-scales are organizational encouragement of creativity; supervisory encouragement of creativity; work group supports; freedom; sufficient resources; and challenging work. The negative sub-scales are organizational impediments and workload pressure. The remaining scales measured perceptions of overall creativity and productivity. Compared to normative data on the KEYS, employees perceived their work environment as conducive to creativity.

Interestingly, they recognized both organization support for innovation and the apparent lack of obstacles in the creative climate at PUSH. Scoring in the very high category were the scales: organizational encouragement, (lack of) organizational impediments, (lack of) workload pressure, and supervisory encouragement. All the scales of the instrument ranged from very high to moderate. A positive correlation between job satisfaction and a perceived creative climate was found at PUSH. Yet some differences emerged between departments and employee groups.

When considering PUSH's success in the field of advertising, the overall employee perception of creativity appeared somewhat lower than expected. Investigating this finding in greater detail was quite interesting. Specifically, those in creative departments actually scored very high in terms of their own perceived creativity; however, those working in business areas viewed the overall climate for creativity in more moderate terms. Within a creative ecology, differences emerge between perceptions of individual employees and in their collective work groups. That is, employees likely vary in their perceptions of the workplace. Even within a "creative" organization, this finding showed that some employees perceived themselves and their organization as significantly more creative than others working within the same domain.

Yet the case has been made that any type of work offers the possibility for innovation whether the task involves design or accounting. Expanding employee thinking about their own ability to problem-solve innovatively might even be more important in an organization that contains what might be commonly perceived as "creative" and "non-creative" work groups. However, the workforce as a whole viewed PUSH as supporting a creative climate integrating employee characteristics, a defined management orientation, and physical work. Not only does this study offer insights into the phenomenon of fun in the workplace, it also illustrates key characteristics of a creative ecology of the workplace.

Layering on the quantitative foundation of the study, site observations and employee interviews created a multi-layered representation of a dynamic workplace – brought to life through the construction of a narrative capturing a memorable instance of how fun fuels creativity at PUSH. This narrative, documented through the eyes of a manager orchestrating a high-stakes client pitch, described a process of intensive brainstorming, experimentation, and the transformation of the foyer and conference room to create the right ambience to ensure successful conditions for a significant client meeting.

On a day-to-day basis, employees work long hours and engage in serious fun. For example, it would not be uncommon to see a stress ball war break out between the cubicles. The overscaled "PUSH" buzzer over the entrance to the firm invites comparison to a humungous doorbell inviting clients to come play. The overlarge circular green "PUSH" buzzer symbolizes go, advance, fresh, currency. Their website entreats you to "push here". The primary entrance to the firm is a revolving door; not selected for novelty's sake but to reinforce the concept that you always "push, never pull." Playful design gestures continue in the foyer, open office plan, and conference room, where whimsical, biomorphic lighting fixtures and quirky furniture details continue the narrative. The intent of the saturated hues of the cubicles further underscores the feeling of fun.

However, some employees shared their concerns about the saturated yellows in the small cubicle. While the intense palette contributed to the feeling of vibrancy in the larger, shared spaces, the coloration did not appear as universally liked in the more private, focused cubicles. While some private offices surrounded the perimeter, most of these either did not have doors or had open doors, increasing a sense of connection.

The break space offers a place to gather, celebrate, and toast successes. Interestingly, all the employees interviewed for the study of PUSH commented on how the organization used the physical environment to share its passion and potential for client engagement. For example, for one client pitch, the conference room was laid in sod. For a major newspaper account, the main reception desk was transformed into a newspaper kiosk, prominently featuring the client's newspaper along with magazines, candies, and other items found at a newsstand. A freshly rolled newspaper was laid at the doormat outside the primary interior doors and the conference room was literally wallpapered with newspapers published by the potential client. The sense of intensity, creativity, and fun appeared to be infectious as the client signed on PUSH, Inc. by delivering a "one-off" newspaper mock-up with the headline "PUSH wins Sentinel account!"

Over time the relative success of the PUSH, of course, depends on many market and economic factors. Further, as an organization like PUSH evolves and changes over time, so too will the meaning of fun be translated into a design vocabulary.

Another study, with insights on a creative ecology of workplace, was conducted through on-site research at the DreamWorks Campus in Glendale, California (Portillo and Dohr 2000). At the time of the study, precedent dictated that the world-class animation studio typically had open office spaces, with pops of intense color, almost as though the animators themselves were being drawn into a cartoon. Yet to recruit top talent away from competing studios, the DreamWorks management and the design team, including Steven Ehrlich Architects and Gensler and Associates, decided on a different tack: create individual office spaces for the animators (known as artists in the industry). A private office with a view to a beautifully landscaped atrium celebrated each artist as a highly skilled professional.

In this workplace, the color and materials palette was not intensely saturated, but consisted of neutral shades, subtle and varied in texture. The creation of fun and whimsical animation films does not have to occur within a cartoon-like work environment. (Some artists found that type of environment patronizing.)

Yet by all accounts, DreamWorks was a fun workplace. Fun and discipline coexisted on the campus. The campus itself was landscaped with mature plantings and had a prominent central water feature with a stream that wound its way through the grounds. The artists observed during the study readily congregated at the pond on the campus. Stories abounded of artists and employees getting wet whenever possible, having fun, for example, through events such as nocturnal Koi releases. A sense of fun also permeated individual offices bursting with images, words, toys, lights, and craziness. Here the interior designers and architects made a conscious decision to hold back on "the design" by giving the artists a neutral architectural canvas to define their space in idiosyncratic and personal ways. By allowing the employee to personally contribute to the visual manifestation of the organization and its cultural values we see that "fun" can translate into a colorful work environment that does not have to be prescriptive and literal.

Lessons for designers extend beyond hue, value, and chrome to communicating a cohesive message where common areas make space for serious fun, directed and focused on a very serious bottom-line issue. Some clients may not care to engage with such unorthodox organizations. Some individuals may not want to work in a "fun" environment. A delicate balance between serious work and fun also must be maintained. Yet benefits may well outweigh the concerns in many instances (Meyer 1999). While this study showed much promise, more research is needed to flesh out the provocative findings emerging from Alexandra Miller's study (Miller 2005).

In their book *The Blue Ocean Strategy*, W. Chan Kim and Renee Mauborgne describe cases of companies redefining their market and, thus, make way for significant innovation (Kim and Mauborgne 2005). For example, they laud Cirque du Soleil for creating an entirely new market space. At a certain point in time, organizational leadership, market readiness, and economic conditions came into alignment, making way for great success – whether or not this leadership and innovation will continue into the future is not known.

This is also similar to studying and understanding the creative workplace. The passage of time and precedent are necessary to know in the final analysis what innovations prove to be lasting and what simply become passing trends. Adaptation, once again, is required to stay limber and competitive.

As designers turn their attention to addressing creativity in the workplace we present three fundamental lessons to facilitate the emergence of a healthy creative ecology. These lessons embody the evolving role of workplace design, to nurture and support adaptable and self-regulating systems while energizing creativity through the use of paradoxical and diverse spaces. These lessons also embody a new role for the designers, letting the workplace emerge from within the ecological system rather than from the prescription of the design team. To ensure a healthy ecology we argue that creative workplace design must support adaptability and diversity among people, processes, and place at all levels to effectively support the exchange of creative energy.

Lesson #1. Design for support not control

Creativity in the workplace is anything but a closed prescriptive system. Creative systems emerge, shift, evolve, and die over time. Further, true innovation and impact can only be judged against precedent and with the passage of time. A company or organization lauded today for its innovation may not be as well recognized later; conversely an individual, collaborative, or system may be ahead of their time and may not even receive recognition within their lifetime.

Systems must be allowed to become self-regulating, attempts to over control – through design – can become detrimental and limiting to the natural evolution of the habitat. Interior designers would be best served not to design prescriptively. Forming productive partnerships with clients and stakeholders creates the foundations for design satisfaction and greater longevity. In a certain sense, it is the sustainable thing to do. For example, PUSH laid sod in their conference room for a client meeting; nighttime Koi releases helped define the culture at DreamWorks. The ecological model encourages us to design for process, not prestige.

In a certain respect, systems unfold organically. They resist design but emerge as a byproduct of process, management style, culture, and unpredictable economic and social factors. At times, designers can take a back seat to allow people and organizations to influence and shape their creative habitats. Meaning and a shared sense of identity are at risk when design becomes too prescriptive. For example, if a designer had laid astro-turf and papered the walls in the conference room at PUSH or if a designer thought a DC-3 wing would be a funky add-on to IDEO's workspace, the system would be robbed of inherent meaning and creative energy. Maturation of an organization or system must rise from within.

Does this suggest developing strategies to design malleable spaces to encourage diversity and participatory design engagement?

Lesson #2. Design for system-wide diversity

We present a model for the creative workplace that is both establishment and anti-establishment (see Figure 7.2). This model brings fun into the workplace as a counterpoint to the already established traditions of serious work – rooted in mid-century ideals. While we support bringing play in the workplace we also recognize that too much play becomes counterproductive, just as too much seriousness inhibits

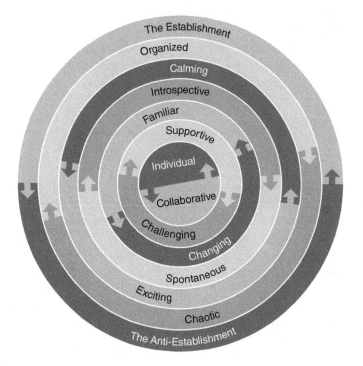

Figure 7.2

innovation. Adaptation is key to fostering the balance between novelty and appropriateness.

The root of the ecological model is based, in part, on a study done by Meneely. In this research Meneely surveyed 201 students in fine arts, architecture, interior design, and building construction to describe characteristics of their ideal creative environment. A content analysis revealed seemingly contradictorily yet creatively charged dimensions of such environments including: (1) individual and collaborative, (2) challenging and supportive, (3) familiar and changing, (4) introspective or planned and spontaneous, (5) calming and exciting, (6) chaotic and organized.

These exploratory findings suggest that perceptions of the creative environment appear more paradoxical and complex than universal. For example, some students felt they could be most creative working alone, while others felt they could be more creative working collaboratively. A third cohort felt that they needed to interlace both solo and collaborative venues to maximize their problem-solving. Some students also mentioned that they needed a supportive environment to be creative, while others mentioned that they preferred a more competitive environment where their ideas are challenged and questioned.

By providing paradoxical spaces at work, people, despite their diversity, can find their preferred ecological niche to support performance and, hopefully, job satisfaction.

While Figure 7.2 has ramifications for physical workspaces, we see applications for this model as offering utility in other design sectors.

Lesson #3. There is no creative panacea

Designing a creative ecology is not a destination, it is a process. We apologize to readers who were looking for a prescriptive set of guidelines to design creative space; this model does not lend itself to off-the-shelf solutions. Creativity is steeped in context and we maintain that what work in one venue might well not necessarily work in another. Also, today's markets impose rapid demands for organizations to continuously evolve, limiting the shelf-life of the "perfect" solution. In this chapter we have argued for an ecological workplace to support adaptability at all levels of the organization. This calls for the thoughtful intersection of leadership and design.

This process suggests a new role for the workplace designer. No longer will interior designers be able to hand over the keys and say, "Voilà. Here is your new space." Ideally, an ongoing relationship and commitment must be fostered, where the designer becomes one keystone species of many, one stakeholder in a complex, interwoven, and evolving creative habitat of workplace.

References

Amabile, T. 1992. "Social environments that kill creativity," in S. S. Gryskiewicz and D. A. Hills (eds.), *Reading in Innovation*. Greensboro, NC: Center for Creative Leadership.

Amabile, T. 1996. *Creativity in Context*. Boulder, CO: Westview Press.

Amabile, T., Burnside, R. and Gryskiewicz, S. 1999. *User's Manual for Keys Assessing the Climate for Creativity: A Survey from the Center of Creative Leadership*. Greensboro, NC: Center for Creative Leadership.

Balzer, W. K., Kihm, J. A., Smith, P. C., Irwin, J. L., Bachiochi, P. D., Robie, C., et al. 2000. "Users' manual for the job descriptive index (jdi; 1997 version) and the job in general scales," in J. M. Stanton and C. D. Crossley (eds.), *Electronic Resources for the jdi and jig*. Bowling Green, OH: Bowling Green State University.

Barron, F. 1963. *Creativity and Psychological Health*. New York: Van Nostrand.

Barron, F. and Harrington, D. 1981. "Creativity, intelligence, and personality," in M. Rosenzweig and L. Porter (eds.), *Annual Review of Psychology*. Palo Alto, CA: Annual Reviews, vol. 32, pp. 439–476.

Basadur, M. and Head, M. 2001. "Team performance and satisfaction: a link to cognitive style within a process framework," *Journal of Creative Behavior* 35(4): 227–248.

Capra, F. 2002. *The Hidden Connections: Integrating the Biological, Cognitive, and Social Dimensions of Life into a Science of Sustainability*. New York: Doubleday.

Chan Kim, W. and Mauborgne, R. 2005. *Blue Ocean Strategy: How to Create Uncontested Market Space and Make Competition Irrelevant*. Boston: Harvard Business School Publishing Corporation.

Cohen, L. and Ambrose, D. 1999. "Adaptation and creativity," in M. A. Runco and M. R. Pritzker (eds.), *Encyclopedia of Creativity*. New York: Academic Press.

Csikszentmihalyi, M. 1996. *Creativity: Flow and the Psychology of Discovery and Invention*. New York: HarperCollins.

Davis, G. A. 2008. *Creativity Is Forever* (5th ed.). Dubuque, IA: Kendall Hunt.

Domino, G. 1970. "Identification of potentially creative persons from the adjective check list," *Journal of Consulting and Clinical Psychology* 35: 48–51.

Eysenck, H. 1993. "Creativity and personality: suggestions for a theory," *Psychological Inquiry* 4(3): 147–178.

Ford, R. C., McLaughlin, F., and Newstrom, J. 2003. "Questions and answers about fun at work," *Human Resource Planning* 26(4): 18–33.

Gardner, H. 1989. *To Open Minds*. New York: Basic.

Gifford, R. 2002. *Environmental Psychology: Principles and Practice*. Colville, WA: Optimal Books.

Herrmann, N. 1989. *The Creative Brain* (2nd ed.). Kingsport, TN: Quebecor Printing Book Group.

Hill, R. P. 2002. "Managing across generations in the 21st century: important lessons from the ivory trenches," *Journal of Management Inquiry* 11(1): 60–66.

Jacobson, W. S. 2007. "Two's company, three's a crowd, and four's a lot to manage: supervising in today's intergenerational workplace," *Popular Government* (Fall): 18–23.

James, K. and Asmus, C. 2001. "Personality, cognitive skills, and creativity in different life domains," *Creativity Research Journal* 12(2): 149–159.

Leonard, D. and Straus, S. 1997. "Putting your company's whole brain to work," *Harvard Business Review* 75(4): 110–123.

Mackinnon, D. 1962. "The nature and nurture of creative talent," *American Psychologist* 17: 484–495.

Mackinnon, D. 1965. "Personality and the realization of creative potential," *American Psychologist* 20: 273–281.

Mackinnon, D. 1970. "The personality correlates of creativity: a study of American architects," in P. Vernon (ed.), *Creativity*. Harmondsworth: Penguin Books, pp. 289–311.

Meneely, J. 2008. "Constructing a climate for creativity: perceptual differences of the creative work environment." Unpublished Funded Research Study. University of Florida.

Meneely, J. and Portillo, M. 2005. "The adaptable mind in design: relating personality, cognitive style, and creative performance," *Creativity Research Journal* 17(2&3): 155–166.

Meyer, H. 1999. "Fun for everyone," *Journal of Business Strategy* 20(2): 13–17.

Miller, A. M. 2005. "Fun in the Workplace: Toward an Environment-Behavior Framework Relating Office Design, Employee Creativity, and Job Satisfaction." Master's thesis. University of Florida, Gainesville.

Miller, A. and Portillo, M. 2006. *Creative Work and Play in a Workspace Designed for Fun*. Paper presented at the Interior Design Educators Council Annual Conference, Scottsdale, AZ.

Muoio, A. March 2000. "Great ideas in aisle 9," *Fast Company* 33.

Myers, K. and Sadaghiani, K. 2010. "Millennials in the workplace: a communication perspective on millennials' organizational relationships and performance," *Journal of Business and Psychology* 25: 225–238.

Plucker, J. A. and Renzulli, J. S. 1999. "Psychometric approaches to the study of human creativity," in R. J. Sternberg (ed.), *Handbook of Creativity*. Cambridge: Cambridge University Press.

Portillo, M. and Dohr, J. 2000. "Creativity and narrative in Eva Maddox Associates: design beyond space," *Journal of Interior Design* 26(2): 41–57.

Prigogine, I. and Nicolis, G. 1977. *Self-Organization in Nonequilibrium Systems: From Dissipative Structures to Order through Fluctuations*. New York: Wiley.

Schweiger, D. M. and Sandberg, W. R. 1989a. "Experiential effects of dialectical inquiry, devil's advocacy and consensus approaches to strategic decision making," *Academy of Management Journal* 32(4): 745–772.

Schweiger, D. M. and Sandberg, W. R. 1989b. "The utilization of individual capabilities in group approaches to strategic decision-making," *Strategic Management Journal* 10: 31.

Schweiger, D. M., Sandberg, W. R. and Ragan, J. W. 1986. "Group approaches for improving strategic decision making: a comparative analysis of dialectical inquiry, devil's advocacy, and consensus," *The Academy of Management Journal* 29(1): 51–71.

Sternberg, R. and Lubart, T. 1995. *Defying the Crowd: Cultivating Creativity in a Culture of Conformity*. New York: The Free Press.

Tkaczyk, C. August 16, 2010. "100 best companies," *Fortune Magazine* 162.

Van Meel, J. and Vos, P. 2001. "Funky offices: reflections on office design in the new economy," *Journal of Corporate Real Estate* 3(4): 322–334.

8

Designing Emotional Connection into the Workplace: A Story of Authentic Leadership

Sheila Danko

Introduction

Meaning and emotional connection are fundamental to creative work. As expressed by Margaret Wheatley in her book, *Finding Our Way: Leadership for an Uncertain Time.*

> Every change, every burst of creativity, begins with the identification of a problem or opportunity that somebody finds meaningful. As soon as people become interested in an issue, their creativity is engaged. If we want people to be innovative, leaders must engage them in meaningful issues. (Wheatley 2005)

In a recent review of 21st-century literature on creativity, two findings stand out for leaders and designers: first that the only consistent predictor of creative performance is intrinsic motivation, and second, that the social environment at work can influence creative thinking. "People are most creative when they are motivated primarily by the interest, enjoyment, satisfaction, and challenge of the work itself – i.e., by intrinsic motivation" state Hennessey and Amabile (2010). Why? Because intrinsic motivation, they argue, ensures that people are more likely to fully engage their cognitive abilities and exhibit the perseverance needed to innovate.

Put another way, the interests and issues people value create a "passion of purpose" that motivates them to work harder at creative problem-solving. Intrinsic motivation then can be thought of as the bridge connecting our rational, intellectual self to our emotional, values-driven self. "Values play a significant role in creative behavior," confirms Runco, and they are not only manifested as interests, motives and

The Handbook of Interior Design, First Edition. Edited by Jo Ann Asher Thompson and Nancy H. Blossom.
© 2015 John Wiley & Sons, Ltd. Published 2015 by John Wiley & Sons, Ltd.

commitments, but also impact self-direction and self-transcendence (Runco 2007). This developmental influence of values on one's individual life course and personal growth is also important to organizational development and growth. The challenge facing leaders is to find ways to connect a person's individual values and motivations to the larger organizational values and mission.

One solution may be through design of the workplace. Traditionally, leaders and designers have focused on how the social environment influences creativity through the choreography of work processes and team communications which support behaviors that promote creative thinking. But this chapter seeks to explore an alternate focus: how might design help people increase their commitment to work? Traditionally, leaders do this in two very important ways: first, by helping people develop a greater values consciousness related to their work, i.e., an awareness of the values that spark their interests and motivations; and second, by communicating the meaningfulness of work, i.e., the impact of the work on broader societal issues. If design is to be a tool for leaders to increase commitment to work, it needs to support more than work process and team dynamics; it also needs to communicate the meaningfulness and social purpose of work by forging connections to the personal values of individuals. But how?

This study explores answers to that question. Through narrative inquiry, the emotional connections between individual values and motivations are linked to workplace design and ultimately authentic leadership style and practice. At the centerpiece of this chapter is a true story of how one VP-level leader communicated her personal values and motivation for work through her office design. Entitled *A Sense of Purpose*, the story evidences how artifacts, aesthetics, and symbols foster emotional connections to work for both leader and follower. Through the story we come to understand how values, meaning-making, and motivations can be embodied in the physical environment, used as a reflective tool, and transferred from leader to follower. Through this narrative of authentic leadership by design we develop insight into the following questions:

- How can the design of the workplace (artifacts, aesthetics and symbols) mediate emotional connection?
- How do individual values and motivations become shared organizational values and motivations?
- How can leaders use design to foster greater self-awareness, relational transparency, and internalized moral perspective both for themselves and their followers?

Emotion, Meaning, and Motivation at Work

Several areas of scholarship inform this inquiry. First, research on the emotional organization emphasizes the importance of managing emotions in the workplace and, in particular, the need to focus on positive emotions and their possible influences across the organization. Second, scholarship on artifacts, aesthetics, and symbolism reveals a mediating role of the designed environment in communicating the meaning and purpose of work. Lastly, the emerging concept of authentic leadership provides a framework for understanding how passion of purpose is transferred between leader and follower, giving insight into how individual values evolve into organizational values. All three scholarly arenas are evidenced in the narrative, *A Sense of Purpose*.

The Emotional Organization: Linking Emotion and Values to Positive Engagement

During the past decade theories of organizational management and development have shifted away from an emphasis on analytical issues to include emotional issues as well. Once thought to be germane only to individual performance, emotions at work are now being recognized as the turnkey to understanding broader issues of organizational change and transformation.

> Organizations change or stagnate because of the emotions that energize or freeze people. All organizations are emotional arenas where feelings shape events, and events shape feelings. Emotions are not an optional extra, or incidental to "real" work. They are part of the warp and weft of work experiences and practices. (Fineman 2003)

Understanding emotions helps us to understand how social structures, norms, and values of an organization are shaped. Emotions both characterize and inform work processes and are deeply woven into the way roles are enacted and learned, power is exercised, trust is held, commitment formed, and decisions made (Fineman 2003). Fineman goes on to later argue that to understand the emotional organization necessitates a shift from the traditional within the individual focus to exploring how emotions operate across the organization, i.e. the social and relational context of emotion at work (Fineman 2008).

Understanding the nature of emotions is the first step to designing emotional connection into the workplace. "Emotions are direct responses to events, issues, relationships and objects that are important to people" (Frijda 1988; Lazarus 1991 in Smollan and Sayers 2009). Emotions are short, target-centered, and intense reactions linked to something specific, and as such are distinguishable from moods, which are often longer-lasting and more diffuse (Gooty, Connelly, Griffith, and Gupta 2010). More important for this research is the fact that emotions are considered temporary state affects, as opposed to stable trait affects like values and motivations. This is an important distinction because it clarifies that values underpin people's emotional reactions. People's personal value priorities not only trigger temporary emotional responses but also guide their long-term worldviews, their attitudes, and their decisions to behave and act in a certain way (Rohan 2000). It is this attitudinal and behavioral influence of values that links emotions to motivations.

While both positive and negative emotions influence organizational effectiveness, a preponderance of the research to date has focused on negative emotions, resulting in a call for scholarship that examines positive and proactive emotions in organizations (Quick and Quick 2004; Roberts 2006). Positive organizational scholarship (POS), as it has come to be known, is "the study of that which is positive, flourishing, and life giving in organizations" (Cameron and Caza 2004). POS is concerned primarily with the study of positive outcomes, proactive processes, and stable, long-term attributes of organizations and their members (Wright and Quick 2009). POS is also concerned with dynamic change processes as a result of individual attitudes and behaviors, especially those that contribute to societal good and self-transcendent values (Wright and Quick 2009). By analyzing a case of proactive emotional engagement in an organization and presenting it in storied form, this research links leadership actions to design interventions through an ongoing, dynamic sequence of interpersonal events and expands the scope of positive organizational scholarship.

> We recommend continuing to build bridges across proactivity research in the different domains...as well as going further to draw stronger links between proactivity and related fields such as entrepreneurship, innovation, and stress management. We also encourage researchers to continue to compare proactive behaviors to more passive forms of work behavior (e.g., Griffin et al 2007). (Parker, Bindl, and Strauss 2010)

By examining the intersections between the domains of design and leadership, we can learn to manage emotions across organizations more effectively through the design of physical settings.

Artifacts, Aesthetics, and Symbolism: Linking Workplace Design to Emotions and Meaning-Making

While the research on emotions in the workplace is rich (Brotheridge and Lee 2008; Elfenbein 2007; Fisher 2010) there is a void in the literature about the impact of workplace design on employee emotions (Elsbach and Pratt 2007). "Recent organizational research on the relationship between the properties of physical settings and the experience of mood and emotions has been slim with very little accumulated knowledge" (Brief and Weiss 2002). Yet understanding how design impacts perceptions, interactions, and emotions over time is important to leaders who want to use it as a leadership tool. In one study where multiple stakeholders were interviewed about the artifacts within a large public transportation organization, researchers demonstrated that emotion toward artifacts blends into emotion toward the organization (Rafaeli and Vilnai-Yavetz 2004). In their book *Artifacts and Organizations: Beyond Mere Symbolism*, Rafaeli and Pratt argue that a triad of influences in physical settings – artifacts, aesthetics, and symbols – work in concert to impact management, collective identity, and communications strategies in the organizational environment. Together they create a holistic understanding of how the physical setting impacts employee emotions through behavioral (artifacts), sensory (aesthetic), and cognitive (symbolic) interactions (Rafaeli and Pratt 2006).

Linking workplace design to emotional connection should be holistic in perspective and process-oriented if it is to inform our understanding of design as a tool for leadership. Research shows that mediation objects play three roles: as carriers of controversies, of compromises, and of prescriptions (Hussenot and Missonier 2010). In other words, objects can provoke dialogue, create shared meaning, and direct behaviors. "Rather than a static analysis, human–object interaction needs to be understood and observed through a process analysis, taking into account the evolution of objects and interactions" (Hussenot and Missonier 2010). By using narrative method, this research contributes to a process-oriented understanding of how meaning and motivation is influenced by people interacting with the physical environment. By creating a storied understanding of how artifacts, aesthetics, and symbols are presented and interpreted over time within an organization, this research evidences an important interplay between leaders and followers – the dynamic, emotional process of meaning-making within organizations.

A primary role of leaders in organizations involves "sensegiving" (communicating meaning) within organizations. "Sensegiving-for-others is the process of disseminating new understandings to audiences to influence their sensemaking-for-self" (Gioia and Chittipeddi 1991). Research by Maitlis examined formal structures leaders might use to create sensegiving, such as meetings, reports proposals, etc., but not the more passive measures such as aesthetics and symbolism (Maitlis 2005). Maitlis notes that previous research has focused largely on who the people engaged in sensegiving are and what strategies they are using, but "we know little about the conditions associated with sensegiving in organizations – where, when, or why it occurs, despite the fundamental nature of these issues" (Maitlis and Lawrence 2007).

Though office design is composed of static elements, it has a dynamic influence on stakeholders and the organization by creating a physical narrative that underpins (or undermines) authentic emotions and work processes. "Narrative construction as sensemaking is a collective social process that includes cognitive dissonance, conflict, and negotiation" (Albolafia 2010). This essay builds on both Maitlis' and Albolafia's work by exploring issues of dissonance, conflict, and negotiation through the meanings embodied in symbolic objects and documenting through narrative how design enables a process of sensegiving and sensemaking in support of authentic leadership.

Authentic Leadership: Linking Individual Values to Organizational Values

Authentic leadership is an emerging concept grounded in positive organizational scholarship and transformational leadership theory (Avolio, Gardner, Walumbwa, Luthans, and May 2003; Avolio and Gardner 2005). It is characterized by several distinguishing qualities including self-awareness, relational transparency, an internalized moral perspective, and balanced information-processing (Walumbwa, Avolio, Gardner, Wernsing, and Peterson 2008). Self-awareness refers to knowing who you are and the values of importance to you. "Authenticity can be defined as owning one's personal experiences, be they thoughts, emotions, needs, preferences, beliefs, or processes captured by the injunction to know oneself" (Harter 2003; Walumbwa et al. 2008).

The second distinguishing quality, relational transparency, refers to a willingness to share true inner emotions and vulnerabilities in an effort to maintain open, honest communications and interactions. Authentic leaders also work to develop an internalized moral perspective, a moral compass that aligns actions with beliefs, particularly in the face of conflicting pressures. Lastly, authenticity is associated with even-handed consideration of multiple information sources. The narrative, *Sense of Purpose*, focuses on the first three characteristics.

Over the past several years, authentic leadership has also come to be defined as a pattern of leader behavior that promotes a positive psychological and ethical climate with a particular concern for fostering positive self-development (Walumbwa et al. 2008). Rather than training leaders not to express their emotions, leaders would benefit from better training in *how* to express their emotions effectively. This may help leaders develop greater comfort with expressing genuine emotions and avoid the temptation toward surface acting. "Mastering the basic skills behind genuine emotional expression and deep acting may make the workplace more productive and enjoyable for both leaders and followers" (Humphrey, Pollack, and Hawver 2008), particularly when the emotional expression helps individuals identify values of importance and reframe how they can achieve them through their work. Reframing or frame-breaking, for the purposes of this work, refers to a values shift or realignment between the individual and the organization. Through the presentation of a contradictory or nontraditional frame of reference, leaders help others develop self-awareness, shifting their perceptions of their ability to impact their work and society.

Values alignment between the individual and the organization is critical to organizational success because conflicting values affect an individual's engagement, motivation, and passion for work – all of which have been linked to reduced turnover, absenteeism, enhanced job performance, and work satisfaction as well as overall psychological well-being (Meyer and Maltin 2010; Meyer, Becker, and Vandenberghe 2004; Rubino, Luksyte, Perry, and Volpone 2009). The absence of values alignment has been linked to emotional exhaustion and burnout (Humphrey et al. 2008; Rubino et al. 2009). People who find work intrinsically rewarding tend to regard work as a calling, an expression of oneself (Peterson, Walumbwa, Byron, and Myrowitz 2009) and are likely to exhibit a host of positive effects that some research links to innovation and creativity (George and Zhou 2007; Hennessey and Amabile 2010; Rubino et al. 2009).

Leadership traits, behaviors, and influences are intertwined with followership emotions, interaction patterns, and relationships and therefore are best studied from a process perspective (Yukl 1981). Yet, much of the scholarship to date on authentic leadership has been theoretical, quantitative, and largely focused on the individual leader. This case study documents leadership as it occurs naturally within a social system contributing to a qualitative understanding of the concept of authenticity as it relates to design and emotion in the workplace. This study provides one example of how an authentic leader proactively managed her own emotions through the design of her workplace, illustrating how the physical environment supports sense-making across the organization.

Methodology

Research design

The research presented in this essay is part of a larger study entitled *Strategic Stories Shaping 21st Century Designing*: a collection of case studies which explored the role of workplace design in supporting leadership from a systems view of design impact. Utilizing narrative method in combination with a traditional case-study approach allows us to capture an integrative, holistic view of design as it relates to organizational life. Through narrative we are able to weave together a systems view of people and place, emotions, and aesthetics in an effort to better understand the interconnected nature of the physical and emotional elements of work. By constructing narratives of emotive workplace design, we are creating an accessible means of understanding critical incidents, and can begin to determine how leaders influence the attitudes and behaviors of followers (Yukl 1981). Narratives are particularly good at capturing emotions and revealing tacit forces of influence that cannot be captured through more traditional analytical methods (Boje 1991).

Narratives have three important attributes not found in other types of qualitative research. First, they are contextual, providing a framework of events and emotions from which to assess design intervention and impact. Second, they provide a systems view of the experience, often from multiple perspectives. Third, they allow the reader to experience the timing and sequence of critical events similar to the way the characters do – as they unfold. In this way, narratives guide the reader through their own process of discovery as they compare their own experiences with those in the story.

Data collection and analysis

All the cases were selected to meet the following three criteria. Cases had to be: (1) *authentic* – key players in real situations were interviewed and documented. This provided greater validity than would hypothetical composites created from multiple case sources; (2) *aspiring* – the organization approached design in a proactive way to promote positive change; and (3) *strategic* – the design impact had potential to impact the future course of the company. The case being presented is a 1,500-person investment services firm that recently redesigned its corporate headquarters (housing 400 employees) located in a major city in the northeast United States.

All interviews were audiotaped and transcribed verbatim to ensure accuracy. In addition to the recorded interviews, photographs were taken of the newly designed office space. Interview data were collected on site by the author at the headquarters site. Being on site while interviewing supported the internal validity in several ways. It provided the opportunity to see examples and actual outcomes referenced in stories as they were being told. It allowed the researcher to observe and corroborate portions of the story. Observations recorded through audio journals occurred throughout the interview process and proved invaluable for developing an intuitive feel for the organizational culture and for writing the narrative.

Inductive analysis with a focus on critical incidents was used to identify emergent issues and recurring themes throughout the case study. Final categories of analysis emerged from each interview rather than being determined a priori, an accepted procedure for narrative analysis (Atkinson 1998; Wolcott 1990). Several preliminary themes surfaced during this process: design and image, values clarification and communication, freedom to communicate personally held values, trust and leadership, decision-making as distinct from participation, and a sense of community. These themes formed the basic categories for further analysis and review after the narrative was created.

Creating the narrative

Creating the narrative was a separate and distinct phase in the research process. The raw interview data were reduced to the core narrative using those parts of the transcript that were central to the investigation. For example, extensive biographical material collected during the interview was not part of the core narrative used to generate the story. The core narrative was then segmented according to themes, then constructed using a six-part framework for organizing and interpreting narratives which included (1) abstract, (2) orientation, (3) conflicting action, (4) evaluation, (5) resolution, and (6) coda (Langellier 1989; Riessman 1993). This structure formed a mechanism for both the narrative analysis and construction. It proved invaluable for distilling the raw transcription data into several focused stories, each with a major theme, in this case authentic leadership. Unlike case-study reporting, which endeavors to provide a whole picture of the case with multiple issues and multiple voices, results presented using a story format intentionally focus on a particular issue in question and often a single voice (Wolcott 1990). The entire process of structuring raw interview transcripts into a meaningful story followed Lieblich's holistic-content approach (Lieblich, Tuval-Mashiach, and Zilber 1998).

Validity using narrative method is dependent on three primary characteristics: dependability, conformability, and transferability (Greene 1994). Dependability is achieved by the events being based on true-life experiences, where none of the events or encounters described are contrived. Conformability is established by building actual quotes into the storyline such that the conversation can be traced back to the original transcripts. Finally, transferability is achieved when the descriptive data embedded in the narrative enables readers to associate themselves with the narrative content. In other words, the narrative makes familiar linkages to the reader's world, allowing them to transfer the lessons to new contexts.

Results

The narrative, *A Sense of Purpose*, which follows represents the results of the inductive, critical incident analysis. It is based on a true story of an executive-level leader designing for emotional connection using artifacts, aesthetics, and symbolism in her office. This story is represented as largely told to the interviewer – not as a composite of unrelated events. Several key insights emerged from the narrative, highlighting the intersection of design and leadership and are presented in the discussion.

A Sense of Purpose narrative[1]

Some people have the courage to follow their heart instead of the crowd. Resisting pressures to conform, they choose instead to reveal a piece of their inner self, to share deeply held personal values and a commitment to their work in a way that touches our lives and our work too. They never do it to change us – but it does – in ways that defy explaining, or maybe needn't be explained. We leave our experiences with them, trusting something fundamentally deeper, almost spiritual in meaning. We feel more whole, our lives renewed in purpose.

Monica, a managing partner at a major financial planning firm, has that kind of courage. Her deeply held values about work are right there on public display in her office, full of emotion and passion. Though her office is largely identical to that of the other executives – same furnishings, same layout, same color scheme – Monica manages to redefine the bottom line for people each time they walk into her office. Not in words, but in symbols.

As the executive director of Valens Senior Living, a new start-up company within a large investment management firm, she is responsible for making this new senior housing venture a financial success. The pressure is real. Monica was brought in at the executive level and the clock is ticking for her to produce high returns for the clients of the firm. Toward that end, this woman is all business. She works in a conservative business environment and there is a no-nonsense approach to her. That's what makes her office all the more intriguing.

Monica's office is not grand or luxurious nor does it have any magnificent views. In fact, it is rather modest by industry standards. But step in and your attention is immediately drawn to a side wall where more than a dozen framed portraits hang. Simple, yet compelling, black and white photographs of elderly people – just their faces. Their expressions speak of happiness, contentment, longing, and reflection; their eyes seem to hide a veiled wisdom.

When asked, Monica talks about "the faces on the wall." "Some of these people are actual residents of our Valens senior communities," she says. "I like to have faces of seniors around because I know that one of the challenges of running a very service-oriented business in an investment management environment is that people forget who the main customer is." She's referring to the fact that in the day-to-day investment management environment where she works, the "main" customers are perceived to be the investors, clients who hire this investment firm to manage and grow their money. They are the people who visit and call on a daily basis. "So when I first came here a few years ago," she continues, "I put these pictures on my wall so I wouldn't lose sight of my real purpose. The comments I received, however, were really pretty interesting."

"It's been the evolution of the comments that has been so revealing to me. When I first came to the firm and folks saw these photos in my old office, I received lots of very cynical, snide comments about the pictures. Comments like, 'How many grandparents can one person have?' or 'Who is this motley crew?' or people just asking 'What's all this about?'" she recalls. Monica explained that while the photos clearly captivated attention, they were a source of jokes for many and seemed to even be a discomfort for some people. Her response would always calmly be, "I just think it's important for everybody here to remember who the other customer is."

Just past the last photo on the wall, on her side credenza, sits a rather whimsical tea set in the corner. "I brought the tea service in as a symbol to remind me that I'm in the business of hospitality," she says. "Again, it generated similar snide comments like, 'Oh, what are you going to do, have tea parties down here, or are you going to get some work done?' Very questioning, very challenging," she recalls. "But I really needed these symbols to remind myself that senior housing is as much a service business as it is a real estate business. When you're embarking on a new business, intellectually knowing it – and really understanding it, living it – are two very different things."

"So, I also brought in these books," she continues and points to three titles very prominently placed next to the guest chair. "*When I Am an Old Woman, I Shall Wear Purple* is a book about aging with grace and zest," explains Monica. "And *What Makes a Leader* was a gift given to me from my mentor and is now a guidebook for my team." The third title, *The Strong Living Program*, refers to an exercise and weight training program that we are

(Continued)

piloting in the Valens senior communities. "It's important to us that in our communities seniors view themselves as vibrant and are working and striving to stay active."

On the wall behind Monica's desk is a singular graphic statement that reads "So much more to experience." It turns out to be the tag line for Valens Senior Living. "That statement represents our competitiveness in the marketplace, that there's more to experience at our communities. It is also our philosophical underpinning. We believe that the senior years are a time when you are still working to reach human potential," she explained.

And what does "Valens" mean? "It's the Latin word for strong," says Monica.

Above her bookshelf a tender lithograph of two hands hangs, one old and one young, in loving embrace. It too has a story behind it. About a year and a half after Monica arrived, she went with several colleagues to an art auction when one of them spotted the lithograph of the hands and insisted that Monica buy it for her office. "That would go so great with the faces," she was told. Monica bought the piece. Shortly after, Monica was intrigued as people in the company heard about the "hands" artwork and came to visit in surprising numbers just to see it and where it was hung. It seemed no one was making fun of her wall anymore.

"All of these visual cues, all of these symbols in my office are reminders that there's a whole business that has to be successful in order for the investment management part of the business to be successful, and that we can't ever take that underlying part for granted. That's really been the message."

Monica has changed offices several times because of the phasing of office renovations for new space. Each time she has moved, everything would come down and then everything would go back up. The cynical comments subsided and were gradually replaced with genuine interest.

"But what really surprised me happened after we moved into the new space," Monica begins. "After we moved, we weren't allowed to put up any pictures ourselves. We were supposed to wait for the maintenance team to come around and put them up. So for a while the portraits were in piles against this wall. People kept stopping by and asking 'When are the faces going up? We miss the faces.' That was the first clue. As per our instructions, I put a number on the wall and a corresponding number on every photo indicating where each should go. One day, I left to go out of town on a business trip and when I came back, all the photos had all been put up exactly where they were supposed to be. I was delighted. But the maintenance staff were not. They came back later and said, 'It's up the way you want, but we really think they would look better if we hung them up this way.' And then they proceeded to describe a different arrangement of the faces on the wall."

"So I told them, reorganize it the way you want. And that's the way they are hung on the wall now. "The building maintenance people feel like they have a real sense of ownership of this wall," she says with pride.

Other people choosing artwork for her office? Concern over when her pictures will get hung? Suggestions of better ways to hang her pictures even though it meant redoing the work? It seems there was a lot more ownership of Monica's office symbols than she originally intended.

Later, Monica related one of the most surprising testimonials to the power of her symbols and their impact on the heart of the organization. It happened shortly after the company moved into the new space.

"One of our biggest business units was holding a special investor conference, so we decided to host a fancy reception downstairs on another floor. This was really the first time we invited a big group of investors to our new space since the move-in. We organized the staff to give tours through the new space and to talk about what it meant to us – about who we were as a company. Now, I was not involved in that reception, only that particular business group. So, as I was sitting in my office working, I realized, after the first few guided visits that I was on the tour. My office, was on the tour."

"It's been a really interesting lesson for me," she continued after a moment, "to watch the evolution of people's reactions and their levels of ownership of my office." Monica still seemed in awe of the experience. "Honestly, when I first brought all these things in they were symbols for me. I knew this new position was going to push me a little bit out of balance, a little bit off center of where I needed to be every day in my own thinking, in my own priorities. So the faces, the tea service, the books, the hands, the tag line – they were really visual cues for me. Ways to remember the real purpose behind my work and to balance that purpose against what it takes to be successful in the larger investment management business." Monica concludes, "What I learned is that just by being steadfast in having these cues around – the whole combination of them – is that people have over time really internalized some of the message and made it their own. They've made it part of the company's story, the company's purpose and are proud to tell it."

A sense of purpose isn't something we typically expect the physical environment to help us achieve in our professional lives. Perhaps we expect too little from our physical work environments, dismissing any truly high expectations of the role they might play in our growth as individuals. Instead, we settle for environments that merely support our work rather than nourish our souls or motivate us to greatness. We construct environments that facilitate process but neglect to build an environment of shared values. Perhaps we have been expecting too little. Perhaps with just a few heartfelt symbols, we can breathe new meaning into our lives and renew our sense of purpose.

Discussion

The narrative, *A Sense of Purpose*, traces the evolution of how meaning is communicated through artifacts and the aesthetics of space. It is a story about how individual values shape organizational values through the sharing of authentic emotions between leaders and followers. Through the narrative we see how leadership, followership, and design intersect to develop values alignment and emotional connection, both of which are fundamental to creative work.

Several important ideas emerge from the narrative relating the concepts of design, leadership, and the emotional organization. Framed as "design leadership constructs," they operationalize how to use design as a tool for leadership, either as a reflective, individual process or a process of engagement between leader and follower. The first construct (1) design as self-centering, represents an inward focus on design leadership, while the following three constructs, (2) design as provocateur, (3) design as a developmental process, and (4) designing for authenticity, shift to a distinctly outward, leader–follower focus. Together, they show how meaning and values embodied in the designed environment are transferred from the individual to the group and to the organization.

Authentic leadership by design: an inward focus

Design leadership construct #1: *Design as self-centering.*   The narrative reveals a leader's reflective, internal discourse focused on the need to align individual values and organizational values. In this case, the leader in the story, Monica, worried that financial performance issues would dominate her attention and undermine the more humanistic values that provided not only her intrinsic motivation for work, but ultimately the key to a successful business. Concerned about how she would maintain her commitment to financial performance *and* the well-being and vibrancy of the elderly people living in the communities that she finances, Monica designed a rich and varied array of artifacts – functional, aesthetic, and symbolic – into her office to help her balance these competing issues. Some of these artifacts were two-dimensional and pictorial, some were three-dimensional and abstract, but all were designed to connect her and others to the invisible stakeholders – the elderly and their caregivers who are directly affected by the business.

Monica's artifacts functioned as more than simple reminders or decorative objects; they functioned symbolically as interpretive tools to help Monica and her co-workers create new understandings of the meaningfulness of their work. Whether language-based, visual, or spatial, symbols help individuals generate new knowledge through a discursive, internal questioning process in which the viewer discovers new meaning by comparing their own experiences and memories with those embodied in the physical object. The tea service was just such a symbolic object. It was not used for the act of "serving tea," but rather to connect people with the concepts of service to others, help and kindness, civility, time, and a host of other emotional connections as varied as the people viewing them. The photographs of the elderly faces on the wall, though not abstract, functioned similarly, helping Monica and her co-workers relate their own personal experiences and understanding of the unique needs of the elderly to the stakeholders of the senior housing venture. "Physical objects." argue Leonard and Swap "can embody knowledge, often evoking emotion-laden personal memories or cultural connections. They come to symbolize who we are – our beliefs, our aspirations" (Leonard-Barton and Swap 1999).

Symbolic artifacts help us reframe problems (and sometime ourselves) in new and different ways. Schon refers to this process as problem-setting (Ortony 1979). Problem-setting is an important first step in any creative process. It is a frame of reference that guides (or limits) the problem-solving process. In this case, Monica's tea set symbolized an alternative frame of reference, a human service frame, from which to explore solutions to management or operational issues. Monica's tea service helped her reframe the problem from a financial frame to one that focused on customer service and growth. She understood that for the financial side of the business to succeed, she has to be successful in the human-centered side of the business, i.e., that of elder care and community-building. "When people become aware of conflicting frames of reference, perceptions are transformed and a new self-knowledge emerges" (Ortony 1979), which encourages us to think and act in new ways (Morgan [1997] 2006). The story reveals that this not only happened for Monica, but for many of her co-workers as well.

Design leadership: an outward focus

Design leadership construct #2: *Design as provocateur.*   As the narrative continues we see a shift in focus from inward reflection to outward engagement. What began as internal self-dialogue evolved into external discourse as co-workers pondered the nontraditional artifacts present in Monica's office and questioned her as to their meaning and purpose. Monica's need to be mindful of her core values blossomed into a leadership opportunity to help others to do the same. Surprised at the cynical responses elicited by the tea service and the faces of the elderly on the wall, Monica soon realized that her office could be used as a tool to provoke thinking and dialogue about corporate vision and values, shareholder needs versus stakeholder needs, and to challenge preconceptions about work. For Monica, design became a silent provocateur to facilitate emotional engagement.

Monica's symbols and artifacts provoked emotional engagement because they represented design dissonance – a nonconforming and disruptive relationship between object, function, and environmental context. No one expected to see a fanciful tea set on the work credenza of a VP in a financial investment firm. Nor did they expect to see multiple images of elderly faces prominently displayed on a wall, artwork that was highly emotive, or books about growing old gracefully. It was

Monica's contradictory design aesthetic – not the objects themselves, that was disruptive. This is an important distinction represented in the story. There was nothing inherently unusual or nonconforming in the selected objects. In fact, in another context these objects may have seemed quite ordinary. It was the intentional design contrast, the risk she took in representing herself and her values in a nontraditional way, which was key to engagement.

> Dramatic, symbolic actions emphasize key values in the vision…symbolic actions also demonstrate a manager's commitment to his or her vision, especially when the manager risks substantial personal loss, makes self-sacrifice or acts in ways that are unconventional. (Yukl 1981)

The story also highlights a unique aspect of designing with symbols – passive engagement. Monica did not have to say a word to engage people in a dialogue about values; the artifacts in her office began that process offering employees an important level of control over "if, when, and how" they might engage the reflective process. This allowed her to adopt an indirect leadership style with the tenor of an invitation; one that implied "these symbols are here for me now to help me reflect on my goals and purpose, but they are also here for you –when you are ready." The messages were not forced, nor were they hidden, but rather remained a latent opportunity to share her values until a co-worker chose to engage – or challenge – them.

Lastly, the many challenges to Monica's symbols and aesthetics illustrate the concept of creative abrasion. Creative abrasion results from a collision of opposing frames of reference among team members. The resulting tensions are a natural and critical part of a healthy process of innovation because they force divergent thinking (thinking from multiple perspectives) and critical evaluation of the contrasting solutions (Skilton and Dooley 2010). What is important from a design leadership perspective is the ability to manage these tensions constructively rather than destructively (Leonard-Barton and Swap 1999). A manager who understands the importance of creative abrasion finds ways to promote opposing solutions while diffusing the tension that results during evaluation, thereby avoiding the destabilizing forces that undermine new ideas and innovation.

Monica's calm and steadfast commitment to her symbols in the face of criticism and cynicism was critical to the values transfer that resulted. Monica managed *constructively* with patience, a lack of confrontation, and a willingness to continually re-explain. In so doing she gave people the time they needed to process the conceptual contrast with their old frame of reference. Her calm retorts provided a "safe space" for reflection, enabling others to grow into new levels of understanding.

Design leadership construct #3: *Design as a developmental process.* The narrative evidences design as a developmental process and illustrates the concept of organizations as living systems (Wheatley 2005). Though the symbols were inherently static, the process of self-discovery they nurtured was not. With each new query about their purpose and meaning, the symbols became part of a new storied reality of the organization, one that extended the meaningfulness and purpose of the work. For example, the person who suggested buying the lithograph of the "young and old hands in embrace" contributed to a new storied reality by adding a nuanced inter-generational quality to the mission; the maintenance staff who rearranged the faces on the wall contributed to a new storied reality through a shared pride of ownership; the people giving (and taking) the office tour contributed to a new storied reality by the telling and retelling of the story with outsiders "to talk about what it meant to us – about who we were as a company."

While the imagery and artifacts remained fixed in an individual office setting, the story behind them spread throughout the organization, becoming more widely understood and accepted. What the narrative helps us understand is that sensegiving and sensemaking is a slow and deliberative process that occurs over time. Once engaged, people need time to process the emotional discomfort as they let go of the old frames of reference and ways of thinking. Eventually they embrace the new as their own. "When people become aware of conflicting frames of reference, percep-tions are transformed (Ortony 1979). Monica's story evidences this transformational process as people's reactions shifted from cynical questioning to pride of place, ultimately including her office as part of the formal tour of the new headquarters.

Monica's office design became a form of organizational storytelling – not language-based, but design-based. Design is often perceived as a one-time static intervention because so much of the focus of design publicity is on the physicality of the product or space, the aesthetics of form, and the material sensuality. But the essence of design is not about forms or materiality, it is about the emotional con-nections design engenders, the relationships between people and objects that are created, and the subsequent behaviors that are choreographed. Good design is not just about physical space; it is about mind space. And it is in this psychological arena of mind space where the potential for transformation exists.

In the story, we see evidence of how an individual leader and her symbolic design elements laid the groundwork for transformation. Meaning emerged as people interacted not just with each other, but with the aesthetic qualities and elements of their surrounding environment. Morgan summarizes the symbiotic quality of emo-tional interactions and individual perceptions when he states:

> We are not passive observers interpreting and responding to the events and the situ-ations that we see. We play an important role in shaping those interpretations, and thus the ways the events unfold. (Morgan [1997] 2006)

Through the narrative, we begin to understand that organizational aesthetics – the physical space, the visual qualities, the artifacts, the symbols and metaphors – play a particularly important role because they can create a storied existence for the individual within the organization, i.e., the opportunity to see the part one plays in the grand scheme (Linstead and Höpfl 2000). Leaders frame events through the use of language choices and techniques such as metaphors, artifacts, stories, and myths (Deetz, Tracy and Simpson 2000). Monica's leadership tools were her tea service, her photos, her books, and her artwork – their transformational power came from her authentic self-expression and willingness to withstand criticism.

Design leadership construct #4: *Designing for authenticity.*   The story emphasizes that designing for emotional connection is about designing for authenticity. Authentic leadership is defined in the literature as more than inspired, charismatic leadership; authentic leadership is about being true to oneself, one's values and vision. This last construct underpins a key aspect of designing for emotional connection and organizational sensemaking, the importance of authentic expression through design.

Monica's story is not as much about symbolic artifacts as it is about her clarity of values and her authentic voice. Monica defied pressures to conform, to be concerned with the extent to which her perceived professional image fit organizational standards and culture. Assimilation was not her goal. Monica led from the inside out by giving herself permission to express her purpose in multiple unconventional ways and by having the courage to share her more vulnerable emotional self. Monica's leadership emanated from an internal moral compass, and this is what gave the design depth and resonance.

To design for authenticity means exhibiting a transparency in beliefs, values, and decision-making. It also means a willingness to share a deep sense of self with others in tangible ways that are perceived to be genuine. This concept can best be illustrated by considering a hypothetical comparison. What if Monica had purchased several motivational posters from a catalog, posters that perhaps admonished the viewer to "respect the elderly" or consider the "other stakeholders" in a business? How might the subsequent reactions by her co-workers have been different? In other words, what are the distinguishing design qualities that communicate "authenticity"?

Design authenticity comes from an individual, not from a store or service. Such intangible qualities are not easy to realize. In fact, they are the product of a self-reflective process that truthfully aligns a person's moral compass with his or her decision-making. Designers need to be reminded that they too are subject to pressures to conform – by clients, by standards, by resources, and a host of other limitations. Designing for authenticity is a product of an ongoing dialogue with oneself about how personal values are reflected in design decisions because authentic leadership by design goes beyond being true to yourself; it includes a commitment to developing others.

Conclusion: Beyond Aesthetics and Artifacts to Authenticity and Meaning-Making

The narrative, *A Sense of Purpose*, reveals an emotional journey beyond aesthetics and artifact to authenticity and meaning-making. What started with a single individual and a concern for being true to one's values ended with a shared passion of purpose at the organizational level. The narrative evidenced how artifacts, aesthetics, and symbolism support reflection and self-awareness, provoke dialogue and relational transparency, and develop the internal moral compass in others. It illustrated that design interventions can be more than superficial decoration; they can represent a depth of thinking about significant and conflicting issues important to the individual and to the organization and serve as a tool for emotional engagement and reflection. Through the narrative we come to understand that the designed environments in which we work are potentially powerful embodiments of ideas and values that undergird the individual and have the power to shape lives and the life of organizations. Most importantly, the narrative helps us see that at the core of the concept of design leadership is authenticity. But in order to achieve that authenticity it may be necessary to step outside of traditional expectations and professional identities to find one's own authentic voice.

Acknowledgments

The author wishes to gratefully acknowledge the thoughtful feedback and guidance of the following reviewers: Joy Dohr, Paul Eshelman, Richard Reich, Gary Evans, Alan Hedge, Jason Meneely, Deb Schneiderman, Rhonda Gilmore, Jan Jennings, Susan Chung, Robert Rich, and Jane Hexter.

Note

References

Albolafia, M. 2010. "Narrative construction as sensemaking: how a central bank thinks," *Organization Studies* 31(3): 349–367.

Atkinson, R. 1998. *The Life Story Interview*. Thousand Oaks, CA: Sage Publications.

Avolio, B. J. and Gardner, W. L. 2005. "Authentic leadership development: getting to the root of positive forms of leadership," *Leadership Quarterly* 16: 315–338.

Avolio, B. J. Gardner, W. L., Walumbwa, F., Luthans, F., and May, D. 2004. "Unlocking the mask: a look at the process by which authentic leaders impact follower attitudes and behaviors," *The Leadership Quarterly* 15: 801–823.

Boje, D. 1991. "Consulting and change in the storytelling organization," *Journal of Organizational Change Management* 4(3): 7–17.

Brief, A. P. and Weiss, H. M. 2002. "Organizational behavior: affect in the workplace," *Annual Review of Psychology* 53: 279–307.

Brotheridge, C. M. and Lee, R. T. 2008. "The emotions of managing: an introduction to the special issue," *Journal of Managerial Psychology* 23(2): 108–117. doi: 10.1108/02683940810850763

Cameron, K. S. and Caza, A. 2004. "Contributions to the discipline of positive organizational scholarship – introduction," *American Behavioral Scientist* 47(6): 731–739. doi: 10.1177/0002764203260207

Deetz, S., Tracy, S. J., and Simpson, J. L. 2000. *Leading Organizations through Transition : Communication and Cultural Change.* Thousand Oaks, CA: Sage Publications.

Elfenbein, H. A. 2007. "Emotion in organizations: a review and theoretical integration," *Academy of Management Annals* 1: 315–386. doi: 10.1080/078559812

Elsbach, K. D. and Pratt, M. G. 2007. "The physical environment in organizations," *Academy of Management Annals* 1: 181–224. doi: 10.1080/078559809

Fineman, S. 2003. *Understanding Emotion at Work.* Thousand Oaks, CA: Sage Publications.

Fineman, S. 2008. *The Emotional Organization: Passions and Power.* Malden, MA: Blackwell Publishing.

Fisher, C. D. 2010. "Happiness at work," *International Journal of Management Reviews* 12(4): 384–412. doi: 10.1111/j.1468-2370.2009.00270.x

Frijda, N. 1988. "The laws of emotion," *American Psychologist* 43: 349–358.

George, J. M. and Zhou, J. 2007. "Dual tuning in a supportive context: joint contributions of positive mood, negative mood, and supervisory behaviors to employee creativity," *Academy of Management Journal* 50(3): 605–622.

Gioia, D. A. and Chittipeddi, K. 1991. "Sensemaking and sensegiving in strategic change initiation," *Strategic Management Journal* 12(6): 433–448.

Gooty, J., Connelly, S., Griffith, J., and Gupta, A. 2010. "Leadership, affect and emotions: a state of the science review," *The Leadership Quarterly* 21(6): 979–1004. doi: 10.1016/j.leaqua.2010.10.005

Greene, J. C. 1994. "Qualitative program evaluation: practice and promise," in N. K. Denzin and Y. S. Lincoln (eds.), *Handbook of Qualitative Research.* Thousand Oaks, CA: Sage Publications, pp. 530–544.

Harter, J. K. 2003. "Well-being in the workplace and its relationship to business outcomes: a review of the Gallup studies," in J. K. Harter, F. L. Schmidt, C. L. M. Keyes, and J. Haidt (eds.), *Flourishing: Positive Psychology and the Life Well Lived.* Washington DC: American Psychological Association, pp. 205–224.

Hennessey, B. A. and Amabile, T. M. 2010. "Creativity," *Annual Review of Psychology* 61(1): 569–598.

Humphrey, R. H., Pollack, J. M., and Hawver, T. 2008. "Leading with emotional labor," *Journal of Managerial Psychology* 23(2): 151–168. doi: 10.1108/02693940810950790

Hussenot, A. and Missonier, S. 2010. "A deeper understanding of evolution of the role of the object in organizational process the concept of 'mediation object'," *Journal of Organizational Change Management* 23(3): 269–286. doi: 10.1108/09534811011049608

Langellier, K. M. 1989. "Personal narratives: perspectives on theory and research," *Text and Performance Quarterly* 9(4): 243.

Leonard-Barton, D. and Swap, W. C. 1999. *When Sparks Fly: Igniting Creativity in Groups.* Boston: Harvard Business School Press.

Lieblich, A., Tuval-Mashiach, R., and Zilber, T. 1998. *Narrative Research : Reading, Analysis and Interpretation.* Thousand Oaks, CA: Sage Publications.

Linstead, S. and Höpfl, H. 2000. *The Aesthetics of Organization.* Thousand Oaks, CA: Sage Publications.

Maitlis, S. 2005. *The Academy of Management Journal* 48(1): 21–49.

Maitlis, S. and Lawrence, T. B. 2007. "Triggers and enablers of sensegiving in organizations," *Academy of Management Journal* 50(1): 57–84.

Meyer J. P., Becker T. E., and Vandenberghe C. 2004. "Employee commitment and motivation: a conceptual analysis and integrative model," *The Journal of Applied Psychology* 89(6): 991–1007.

Meyer, J. P. and Maltin, E. R. 2010. "Employee commitment and well-being: a critical review, theoretical framework and research agenda," *Journal of Vocational Behavior* 77(2): 323–337. doi: 10.1016/j.jvb.2010.04.007

Morgan, G. [1997] 2006. *Images of Organization*. Thousand Oaks, CA: Sage Publications.

Ortony, A. 1979. *Metaphor and Thought*. Cambridge: Cambridge University Press.

Parker, S. K., Bindl, U. K., and Strauss, K. 2010. "Making things happen: a model of proactive motivation," *Journal of Management* 36(4), 827–856. doi: 10.1177/0149206310363732

Peterson, S. J., Walumbwa, F. O., Byron, K., and Myrowitz, J. 2009. "CEO positive psychological traits, transformational leadership, and firm performance in high-technology start-up and established firms," *Journal of Management* 35(2): 348.

Quick, J. C. and Quick, J. D. 2004. "Healthy, happy, productive work: a leadership challenge," *Organizational Dynamics* 33(4): 329–337. doi: 10.1016/j.orgdyn.2004.09.001

Rafaeli, A. and Pratt, M. G. 2006. *Artifacts and Organizations: Beyond Mere Symbolism*. Mahwah, NJ: Lawrence Erlbaum.

Rafaeli, A. and Vilnai-Yavetz, I. 2004. "Emotion as a connection of physical artifacts and organizations," *Organization Science* 15(6): 671–686. doi: 10.1287/orsc.1040.0083

Riessman, C. K. 1993. *Narrative Analysis*. Thousand Oaks, CA: Sage Publications.

Roberts, L. M. 2006. "Shifting the lens on organizational life: the added value of positive scholarship – response," *Academy of Management Review* 31(2): 292–305.

Rohan, M. J. 2000. "A rose by any name? The values construct," *Personality and Social Psychology Review* 4(3): 255–277.

Rubino, C., Luksyte, A., Perry, S. J. and Volpone, S. D. 2009. "How do stressors lead to burnout? The mediating role of motivation," *Journal of Occupational Health Psychology* 14(3): 289–304. doi: 10.1037/a0015284

Runco, M. A. 2007. *Creativity Theories and Themes: Research, Development, and Practice*. ScienceDirect (online service).

Skilton, P. and Dooley, K. 2010. "The effects of repeat collaboration on creative abrasion," *Academy of Management Review* 35(1): 118–134.

Smollan, R. K. and Sayers, J. G. 2009. "Organizational culture, change and emotions: a qualitative study," *Journal of Change Management* 9(4): 435–457. doi: 10.1080/14697010903360632

Walumbwa, F. O., Avolio, B. J., Gardner, W. L., Wernsing, T. S., and Peterson, S. J. 2008. "Authentic leadership: development and validation of a theory-based measure," *Journal of Management* 34(1): 89–126. doi: 10.1177/0149206307308913

Wheatley, M. J. 2005. *Finding Our Way: Leadership for an Uncertain Time*. San Francisco: Berrett-Koehler.

Wolcott, H. F. 1990. *Writing Up Qualitative Research*. Newbury Park, CA: Sage Publications.

Wright, T. A. and Quick, J. C. 2009. "The emerging positive agenda in organizations: greater than a trickle, but not yet a deluge," *Journal of Organizational Behavior* 30(2): 147–159. doi: 10.1002/job.582

Yukl, G. A. 1981. *Leadership in Organizations*. Englewood Cliffs, NJ: Prentice Hall.

9

Exploring the Schism: Toward an Empathetic Language

Shauna Corry Hernandez

Introduction

While shopping in the mall one afternoon I needed to use the ladies room. After hunting around for the obscure sign indicating its location, I hurried into the entryway of the women's restroom in J. C. Penny's. The room didn't have a door, with only a corner path providing separation from the sales floor and restroom. As I turned the corner and entered the sink area my eyes met those of another woman in the sink mirror. She was sitting on the toilet in the last stall with the door open. A wheelchair was lodged halfway between the stall opening and the restroom, causing the door to remain open. As our eyes met the woman immediately looked away and turned her head towards the wall. I hesitated, and then walked into the first stall.

I have often thought about that experience. It was obvious the woman felt her privacy had been invaded. Was she ashamed, angry, or just tired of the whole thing? As an interior designer and educator it raised questions in my mind about how the built environment is designed and why it still excludes a large segment of the population in the United States. Why is this true when it is federally mandated that all buildings must meet accessibility codes?

This experience, along with these unanswered questions, became the inspiration for the following research study that attempts to understand the apparent schism between users who are disabled and designers and managers of the built environment. It is suggested that by addressing these questions in a systematic way, a contribution can be made toward the development of an empathetic language for inclusive design that is understood by all members of the design community.

The Handbook of Interior Design, First Edition. Edited by Jo Ann Asher Thompson and Nancy H. Blossom.

Theoretical Overview

Social stratification in the built environment

David Grusky states that "the task of contemporary stratification research is to describe the contours and distribution of inequality and to explain its persistence despite modern egalitarian or anti-stratification values." Grusky continues to explain that "Inequality is produced by two types of matching processes: the jobs, occupations, and social roles in society are first matched to 'reward packages' of equal value, and individual members of society are then allocated the positions so defined and rewarded" (Grusky 1994). This, according to Grusky, results in unequal control over valued resources.

One's rank in a social hierarchy reflects cultural values, therefore status is determined by the possession of what society considers valuable. Amos Rapoport states that the "ideal" environment of a society is expressed in its buildings and settlements and that "The built environment is a direct and unselfconscious translation into physical form of a culture, its needs and values as well as the desires, dreams and passion of a people" (Rapoport 1994). An examination of Rapoport's theory provides valuable insights into why designers of the built environment are not adequately addressing the needs of people with disabilities. If a society or culture attaches value to its built environment, what messages about status are being sent to that segment of the population that cannot fully interact with the built environment, i.e., users who are disabled?

It is recognized that many in the design community are becoming more aware of, and responding to, the need to address the issues of social stratification and discrimination against users who are disabled in our built environment, and that they are becoming more cognizant of the fact that users who are disabled also need gracious and beautiful living, working, and commercial environments that not only satisfy functional needs, but feed the soul. These enlightened designers recognize that complex socio-cultural patterns define and control the use of space and ultimately contribute to conflict and inequality in the built environment. They believe that by designing inclusive environments, they can contribute to social change (Weisman 1992).

Meaning in the Built Environment

Discussions of space and meaning have inundated the social sciences and design disciplines in the last several years. Environmental designer Amos Rapoport, anthropologist Henrietta Moore, sociologists Durkheim, Bourdieu, and Giddens, and cultural theorist Foucault have all examined space in a social context. Their work confirms that spatial relations represent and reproduce social relationships.

The following quote by Moore from her book, *Space, Text, and Gender: An Anthropological Study of the Marakwet of Kenya*, eloquently describes the intersection of space and society, "It is now commonplace to say that the organization of space may be analyzed as a communication system or symbolic code analogous to language…Space is often analyzed as a reflection of social categories and systems of classification. The meanings assigned to elements of the spatial order in this kind of analysis are given and fixed by virtue of the relationship with the total cultural order." Moore continues her discussion by connecting the concepts of space and discourse: "if space can embody social meaning, then it can be treated as a kind of a language" (Moore [1986] 1996).

The idea that social and cultural phenomena can be interpreted as systems of signification was developed by the cultural critic and theorist, Roland Barthes, and is embraced by environmental designers today (Barthes 1977; Baird 1995). Through the use of semiotics to analyze interior spaces we can create spatial and linguistic metaphors that help us to understand not only how we use space, but what it means and how that meaning begins to classify and structure our lives.

Our built environment carries many meanings and messages. A well-designed space not only functions well, but it can satisfy a hunger in our souls with light, color, texture, and aroma. A space can embrace, comfort, and seduce. It can lead you from an inviting entrance through a sequence of passages into an anticipated destination.

On the other hand, interior spaces may not always elicit a strong response. They may be monotonous and ineffectual or may deny you pleasure and cause you pain by constricting your movements or annoying you. Depending on your physical and mental capabilities, you can be denied the right to enter a space. Such spaces may intimidate you. Although, at times, interior space can seem to be unobtrusive, it is never unseen.

Interior designers, architects, and facility managers all are actively involved in creating our public and private spaces. However, these spaces are generally designed to accommodate the physical needs of the majority of users; that is to say, users who do not have major problems negotiating the built environment. The resulting message, or meaning, these designs communicate to users with physical disabilities is the subject of this study.

Previous studies have addressed the need for increasing awareness, understanding, and application of universal design principles and the implicit meaning communicated to users with a disability (Hitch, Larkin, Watchorn, and Ang 2012; Saito 2006). In a comparative study of facility mangers in Japan and the United States researchers found that "although many facility managers recognized the advantages of applying universal design, most organizations currently provided accessible workplaces merely within the scope of legal requirements" (Saito 2006). Saito further found different perceptions of what the advantages are in applying universal design between cultures, and ultimately suggested that the key to promoting universal design practice in the workplace would be to enhance the understanding of the issues by top management.

A more recent study examined collaboration efforts between Australian occupational therapists and architects in relation to universal design and the built environment (Hitch et al. 2012). The results highlighted the need for increased collaboration in the workplace and professional education opportunities. Specifically the study called for an "earlier the better" approach.

The objectives of the study presented here were, first, to qualitatively identify commonalities and differences in the way design practitioners, facility managers, and users who are disabled experience the built environment and, secondly, to provide a collective profile, or cultural portrait, of current attitudes and beliefs. Specifically, the study attempted to determine the pattern language of each group and analyze differences and similarities in meaning and perception of the built environment.

In the seminal book *A Pattern Language*, C. Alexander suggests:

> A pattern language is, in short, a picture of a culture. And each personal version of the language is a work of art: a personal effort, by each person, to create a single picture of his culture, which fits together and makes sense of life. If all of us together, try to create such personal "languages," and share them, then the evolution of our shared language will be a continuous communal effort by all of us, to create an integrated picture of a future way of life, in which all of us can, communally, be whole. (Alexander, Ishikawa, Silverstein, et al. 1977)

The above quote reflects the primary goal of this study; that is, to explore the intersection of status and discrimination as it is seen and perceived in the built environment by users who are disabled compared to designers and managers. The qualitative nature of this study provided a richly textured description of how environments are perceived to be either inclusive or exclusive. In addition, the study helped clarify the nature of discrimination and status in designed environments and illuminated the complexity of meaning and symbolism that is attached to built environments by these two groups. It is suggested that by increasing our understanding of the symbolism and meanings that are routinely assigned to our built environments by both users who are disabled and designers and facility managers, we can begin to develop a cultural portrait that would help transform our built environment into more inclusive spaces.

Society's Edge

Traditionally, the built environment has been designed to facilitate the social purposes of a small segment of society. This powerful segment is composed of the people with the resources to design and build spaces (Weisman 1992). Unfortunately, these spaces often actively discriminate against various members of society. Whether the purpose of the design is to overtly discourage women from joining an all-male club by creating a feeling of psychological discomfort with over-scaled furniture and masculine design characteristics, or by providing the only accessible entrance to a restaurant through the back door of the kitchen, our built environment and those who design it can, and do, exclude certain segments of society.

A survey found that a disabled person is less satisfied with life, less educated, lives on a smaller income than average, and participates in fewer social activities. A major source of dissatisfaction is the difficulty that those with special needs have in finding accessible housing. Thus, individuals who are disabled find themselves on the edge of society, limited by the physical environment as well as the attitudes of the general public (LaPlante 1991).

Perception and Culture

Perception and culture play an important role in the way users who are disabled, and designers and managers, understand space. According to Carolyn Bloomer, author of *Principles of Visual Perception*, people project their own personal concerns onto established frameworks of meaning and selectively screen out other concerns. This screening process is a result of pre-existing mental models that program how a stimulus will be perceived (Bloomer [1976] 1990). People see things only in relation to categories already established in their minds. These categories are determined by the culture in which the person was raised, and that culture conditions the people living in it to share a fundamental concept of reality. As a consequence, humans do not experience everything in the world they perceive as having equal meaning.

Thus, non-disabled people do not perceive architectural barriers in their environments because they simply filter out things that are not meaningful to them. However, for users who are disabled, architectural barriers are a reality every day. These barriers are not screened out because they are a constant hindrance that negatively affects the quality of their lives. This lessened quality of life plays out in terms of the actual barriers, as well as the exhaustive sensory overload they are constantly bombarded with when dealing with these barriers.

In the essay "Spatial Organization and the Built Environment" Amos Rapoport, a noted environmental design educator, theorizes "Any consideration of built environments must take into account not only the "hardware" but also people, their activities, wants, needs, values, life-styles, and other aspects of culture" (Rapoport 1994). Rapoport further suggests in the book *House, Form, and Culture* that "The built environment is a direct and unselfconscious translation into physical form of a culture, its needs and values as well as the desires, dreams and passion of a people" (Rapoport 1969).

Thus, the "ideal" environment of a society is expressed in its buildings and settlements. Rapoport continues to say that an understanding of behavior patterns, including desires, motivations, and feelings, is essential to the understanding of built form. Built form is the physical embodiment of these patterns and, in turn, form affects behavior and the overall quality of life (Rapoport 1969). Rapoport defines the concept of built form to include space, time, meaning, and communication, and proposes the interaction of these elements is equal to spatial organization. This spatial organization, according to Rapoport, is composed of relationships among people and their physical surroundings (Rapoport 1994).

Rapoport's and Bloomer's theories may help explain why it seems that the design community is not adequately addressing the needs of users who are disabled – even though the law mandates attention to accessibility and design education programs go to great length to emphasize code requirements. Perhaps it is as Bloomer postulates. That is to say, since being unable to physically maneuver in a space is not part of designers' and managers' personal knowledge, it is not a part of their personal framework of meaning and they selectively screen it out. It is likely that when creating "ideal" environments, designers do not think about the fact that they may someday become disabled and have to deal with the very obstacles they have helped to create.

Methodology

Participants

A representative sample composed of 21 subjects participated in this study. The composition of the sample was eight users who were disabled, one disability advocate, four facility managers, four architects, and four interior designers. The ages of the five females and four males who represented the users who were disabled (Group 1) ranged from 30 to 57 with 53% having household incomes below $35,000. Seven out of nine were employed and all were high-school graduates, with four having earned Master's degrees. The ages of the six female and six male participants who represented the designers/facilities managers (Group 2) ranged from 28 to 53 with 83% having household incomes above $35,000. All were employed and 11 were college graduates, with three having earned Master's degrees.

Tools and Techniques of Data Collection

The following research tools and techniques were used in the study: (1) cognitive mapping, (2) autophotography, and (3) personal focused interviews.

Cognitive mapping

Researchers have long used cognitive mapping techniques to identify elements in our environments that have meaning and to highlight differences in perception (Altman and Chermers 1980; Lynch 1960). Altman and Chermers believe that cognitive maps are useful in determining cultural ecology. They note that culture refers to "beliefs and perceptions, values and norms, customs and behaviors of a group or society," and indicates "that cognitions, feelings, and behaviors are shared among a group of people in a consensual way," and that the term implies that values and the resulting behaviors are passed on to each new generation.

According to Zeisel and Baird, cognitive maps are the mental pictures we carry of our surroundings (Baird 1979; Zeisel 1981). These mental pictures structure the way we look at, react to, and act in the environment. Expressing these mental images graphically as sketches or diagrams can often assist those involved with the design and management of the built environment to better understand people's responses to, and use of, buildings.

Cognitive map analysis in this study illuminated the differences between both groups' perception of a public space. It should be noted, however, that this tool was difficult for Group 1 (participants who were disabled) to complete. Although Group 1 participants were able to effectively communicate their mental images, it was time-consuming for them and highlighted the differences between the graphic skills of Group 1 members and those in Group 2 (design professionals).

Autophotography

The use of autophotography as an investigative tool has been successful for researchers in sociology and anthropology for many years (Dollinger and Dollinger 1997; Thoutenhoofd 1998; Ziller 1990; Ziller and Lewis 1981; Ziller and Rorer 1985). Ziller believes that autophotography is "richly revealing" because it enables participants to construct a multi-dimensional view of their daily lives. Thoutenhoofd used autophotography to research the deaf community and culture and found that

> aspects of a particular, socially and culturally distinct visuality are manifest in visual data such as photographs…I have reached the conclusion that pictures contain a wealth of relevant visual information – often subject to structuring or patterning of sorts – only borne out by lengthy and repeated acts of looking, or after processes of visual analysis. (Thoutenhoofd 1998)

Dollinger and Dollinger used autophotographic essays to conduct research on identity status and identity style in relation to individuality in young adults (Dollinger and Dollinger 1997). The participants were asked to take photographs that answered the question "Who are you?" Dollinger and Dollinger's main objective "was to test whether the autophotographic measure of individuality reflected differences in identity exploration and crisis." They found that the autophotography technique worked well, with the results of their research showing that individuals who had had an identity crisis portrayed themselves in a more individualist manner.

Based on the literature, it was apparent that the use of autophotography as a tool of social and environmental investigation would enable participants in this research study to effectively communicate their perceptions of the built environment. However, it was soon discovered that image quality varied greatly from one participant to another and from one space to another. Oftentimes, low lighting levels negatively impacted some photographs and, although the photos were clear enough to be analyzed, they were not reproducible. In addition, some participants who were disabled were unable to take photographs and others had never used a one-time use camera and reported difficulty. Regardless of these technical problems, autophotography was found to provide valuable information in the final analysis.

Personal focused interviews

Personal interviews offer many advantages for the qualitative researcher, including understanding the meaning of the experience to the participants. They are also an excellent method to explore individual differences and commonalities among study participants (Sewell 2000). In particular, open-ended questions allow the respondent to expand on their thoughts and feelings in a narrative and provide a wealth of data.

When discussing the merits of personal interviews, Patton suggests that they "reveal the respondents' levels of emotion, the way in which they have organized the world...their experiences, and their basic perceptions" (Patton 1987). Kvale states that qualitative research interviews are "attempts to understand the world from the subjects' point of view, to unfold the meaning of people's experiences, to uncover their lived world prior to scientific explanations" (Kvale 1996).

In keeping with these researchers' views, personal interviews with participants in this study were found to offer many advantages for the qualitative researcher, including understanding the meaning of the experience to the participants. They were also an excellent method to explore individual differences and commonalities among the study participants

Data collection and analysis procedures

The study began by supplying each of the participants with a disposable camera (27 exposures) and asking them to photograph their daily environment for three weeks. This included their home, workplace, and other sites they visited (such as retail establishments). The participants were asked to include any areas that made them feel comfortable, along with areas that elicited discomfort. The participants were also asked to draw a cognitive map of the area's retail mall and then to visit the mall and take photographs.

At the conclusion of the autophotography exercise the photos and cognitive maps were analyzed for patterns and areas of interest that could be clarified or expanded on during the personal focused interview. Questions specific to the photographs and maps were generated, along with general questions concerning characteristics of the environments, and provided the framework for the personal interviews.

In the personal interviews the participants were asked to explain the environmental attributes they chose to highlight relative to the meaning or importance they held in their lives by discussing each photograph. They were then asked to describe an "ideal" and a "non-ideal" environment.

The information gathered from the cognitive mapping exercise, the autophotography exercise, and the personal focused interviews was examined and organized into common and discordant themes and patterns of spatial meaning among the participants, using Lynch's defining elements, Glaser and Strauss' research on developing emerging theory, and Windley and Scheidt's taxonomy of environmental attributes (Glaser and Strauss 1967; Lynch 1960; Windley and Scheidt 1980).

To organize the information obtained from the cognitive mapping exercises completed by the two groups of participants, Lynch's "defining elements" approach was used. Lynch suggests defining elements that repeatedly occur in cognitive maps in the following ways: (1) paths, (2) edges, (3) districts, (4) nodes, and (5) landmarks. Cognitive maps are spatial representations of the built environment and, as such, they are often incomplete, distorted, and at times augmented. People see what they have learned (through culture and experience) to be important (Bloomer [1976] 1990).

Glaser and Strauss' work in grounded theory focuses on analyzing data in an effort to develop an understanding of the meaning associated with a group's experience. Specifically, Glaser believes that grounded theory enables the researcher to discover the theory implicit in the data (Dick 2000). Glaser also suggests that "there are two main criteria for judging the adequacy of the emerging theory: that it fits the situation and that it works, e.g., that it helps the people in the situation to make sense of their experience and to manage the situation better."

Windley and Scheidt's taxonomy identifies eleven attributes that are perceived to contribute to environmental satisfaction (Windley and Scheidt 1980). They include sensory stimulation, comfort, activity, crowdedness, sociality, privacy, control, accessibility, adaptability, legibility, and meaning. These eleven attributes of environmental satisfaction provided a systematic, and previously validated, framework within which to organize the information provided by Groups 1 and 2 in their cognitive maps, autophotography and narrative exercises, and interviews (see Table 9.1).

To ensure the validity of the analysis and organization of the data, an independent reviewer was identified and asked to review and categorize the photographs and corresponding quotes that had been compiled by the researcher. Both the researcher and independent reviewer analyzed every tenth photograph and corresponding narrative. 100% validity was obtained between the researcher and the independent reviewer for the random analysis of data from Group 1 (users who are disabled)

Table 9.1 Windley and Scheidt's taxonomy of environmental attributes

Sensory stimulation	*Quality and intensity of stimulation as experienced by the various sensory modalities*
COMFORT	Extent to which an environment provides sensory and anthropometric "fit" and facilitates task performance
ACTIVITY	Perceived intensity of ongoing behavior within an environment
CROWDEDNESS	Perceived density level within an environment
SOCIALITY	Degree to which an environment facilitates or inhibits social contact among people
PRIVACY	Ability to monitor flow of visual and auditory information to and from others within an environment
CONTROL	Extent to which an environment facilitates personalization and conveys territorial claims to space
ACCESSIBILITY	Ease in locomotion through and use of an environment
ADAPTABILITY	Extent to which an environment facilitates personalization and conveys territorial claims to space
LEGIBILITY	Ease with which people can conceptualize key elements and spatial relationships within an environment and effectively find their way
MEANING	The extent to which an environment holds individual or cultural meaning(s) for people (e.g., attachment, challenge, beauty)

and 83% validity was obtained with the random analysis of data from Group 2 (design professionals).

Cognitive Map Analysis

A factor analysis of the cognitive maps was conducted to identify Lynch's defining elements of spatial perception (paths, edges, districts, nodes, and landmarks) and an attribute analysis of the personal interviews and corresponding photographs was used to identify symbolic elements within the built environment.

Regardless of the drawing ability of the participants, the cognitive maps served to provide important information about the spatial perceptions of the mall environment from members of both groups. As expected, the cognitive maps from Group 2 (designers and managers) were graphically more precise and enhanced with detail and color. In contrast, the cognitive maps from Group 1 (users who were disabled) were not embellished, either because the participants were unskilled in graphic communication or because it was a challenge for them to use a drawing instrument.

An examination of the cognitive maps of Group 1 and Group 2 revealed many similarities. In keeping with Lynch's defining elements, participants from both groups identified paths as the main public traffic corridors of the mall. The edge was noted as the building footprint or the boundary streets, and districts were denoted as the anchor department stores (Dayton's, Sears, J. C. Penny's, and Herbergers) and surrounding smaller retail corridors.

Nodes were identified as the gathering spaces in front of each anchor department store where public seating areas are provided. A major node and landmark denoted frequently was the fountain, a central gathering place in the mall. In fact, the majority of the participants from both groups identified the fountain as their starting place. Other areas identified by both groups were those of special note or meaning such as the museum, which is a source of pride for the community.

A cognitive map matrix was developed to determine how frequently the participants in each group denoted similar elements of the built environment (the mall). As can be seen in Table 9.2, both groups denoted Lynch's paths, edges, districts, nodes, and landmarks with approximately the same frequency, reinforcing the conclusion that all participants, regardless of whether they were disabled or not, perceived the major elements of the mall in much the same way.

Table 9.2   Cognitive map matrix

Categories	Elements	Frequency (%)	
		Group 1	*Group 2*
Paths	Main public corridors	15	13
Edges	13th Ave.; 1–29; 1–94; 42nd St.; 45th St.	4.5	11
Districts	Anchor wings; exterior; interiors	4.5	6
Nodes	Central fountain; J. C. Penny fountain	15	16
Landmarks	Central fountain; Roger Maris Museum, anchors; main entrance; secondary entrances; family bathrooms; accessible entrances; elevators	61	54

A comparison of the cognitive maps of Group 1 and Group 2 revealed that the most striking difference between the drawings was either the inclusion or exclusion of factors in the built environment that dealt with accessibility; (i.e., accessible/family bathrooms, elevators, and accessible entries). Group 1 always indicated the location of these elements on their cognitive maps, while Group 2 rarely indicated them, if at all.

Symbolic Element Analysis

A symbolic analysis of the content of the personal interviews and corresponding photographs was conducted to identify the underlying symbolic relationship structures. Differences and similarities in the symbolic elements were coded and placed into the following categories of meaning:

- *Concept* = underlying ideas that describe things and events, underlying ideas of similarity and difference by which events, people, and things are classified;
- *Icon* = symbolic element that is closely related to the concept (people, places, or things that concretely represent or portray an abstract concept or category); and
- *Theme* = a centerpiece of symbolic analysis; a theme is a person's assertion or comment about some aspect of reality.

As expected, and in accordance with the cognitive mapping results, this analysis also revealed that Group 1 focused on the theme of accessibility and function, while Group 2 focused on sensory and functional aspects of the spaces. Image and narrative analysis from Group 1 shows the icons of "door," "restroom," and "wheelchair" and the concept of "accessible" as the top symbolic elements in their environment. Group 2 participants identified the concepts of "lighting," "color," and "functional" as their top environmental symbolic elements. While both groups identified the icon of "door" in their top 10 symbolic elements, Group 1 ranked it as first and Group 2 ranked it as ninth.

Examples of the differences between the perception of the built environment by Group 1 and Group 2 can be seen clearly in narratives below. Each narrative corresponds to a photo taken by individuals in each group.

Group 1: Concept/icon examples of emerging themes

Theme: accessibility/function

Narrative: "[This] is a picture of my son standing on my wheelchair lift in my van and it illustrates how the lift opens up right down on that landing in the garage and I leave the van open like that so it's easy to get in and out. Our garage happens to be heated, which keeps everything warmer, heated to about 45/50 degrees and maybe colder next month because we just got our bill. That rather than fighting a parking place makes a difference."

Narrative: "This is a good bathroom. This is newly remodeled bathroom out at the mall. It works nice because this is a single stall bathroom and there is room to get in. If I need help, you know whoever is with me can come in. So if my husband is with me he can help, he wouldn't be in the women's restroom. I think they call it their family bathroom. It is really nice. I mean as far as going to the bathroom, the colors are nice."

Group 2: Concept/icon example of emerging themes

Theme: sensory/function

Narrative:"I took a picture of this front entry and I think it is just awful. Number one, it's dirty, and this is 9:00 in the morning before there's not even any traffic and it still is dirty. You can't see it very well but there's stains on the carpet. I think the way the sign is and stuff it's so busy and it blocks your view and you can't see a lot with some of the big stuff in the middle. And then I don't like the way they have this stuff set up around here, because it's like there's a lot of stuff in this area. But, it's hard to know where you are going. Confusing…the flow, the people flow."

Emergent Themes: Identification and Discussion

Five major themes were identified from analysis of the photographs and corresponding participant interview responses: (1) quality of life, (2) control and choice, (3) sensory stimulation, (4) meaning and values, and (5) similar preferences and "ideal" environments.

Quality of life theme

All participants took photographs of environments that either functioned well for them, thereby enhancing their quality of life, or that did not function for them, thereby lessening their quality of life. The primary difference between Group 1 and Group 2 was on the environmental characteristics that each group identified as facilitating the performance of a task. Group 1 commonly identified accessibility issues that focused on pathways of travel that severely limited their ability to interact with others or to complete a necessary bodily function such as going to the restroom. In contrast, participants from Group 2 identified general issues of function that were inconvenient, but did not hinder their performance.

The most common positive environmental characteristics identified by Group 1 were in their home environments. In particular, Group 1 identified most positively those areas in their home environments where they were able to make adjustments to meet their functional needs.

The autophotographic journals revealed numerous instances where Group 1 commonly encountered physical barriers that denied them access. When these physical barriers were brought to the attention of building owners they were oftentimes not dealt with in a timely manner, if at all. Thus, the data revealed that those individuals who designed or managed environments perceived accessibility as having less importance than did those who were disabled. This lack of affirmative responses from the able-bodied population and the design community at large negatively impacted the quality of life of the participants who were disabled.

The quality of life differences between Group 1 and Group 2 are exemplified by the following comparison of narratives from participants in each group when describing a photograph they took.

Quote from individual in Group 1:

"The front entrance to Phil Wongs…Well I can't get in, I mean there is a 6 inch rise to each entrance and there is no way I can enter that facility unless I get off my scooter and walk in with canes. I've lodged a complaint with the Mayor's Committee and if nothing happens soon I am going to lodge a complaint with the ADA coordinator. And what I understand [is] she usually sends a letter to the agencies to say, "What's the problem?" I don't know if anything happens, but…"

Quote from individual in Group 2:

"it's just the summer season porch and it is so pleasant to be out there because you feel like you're outside…it just feels like you're perched in a little tree house almost, when you are out there. And you can be outside and no bugs and you can see my husband's grill is out there. And the shape of the porch is like a Mondrian painting or something. It has as few support members as possible because we wanted as much visibility as possible, but it's a pleasant room to be in and a pleasant view. The only negative thing about it is sometimes the sun is so bright that we have to kind of hide in the shade of the corners, but other than that…"

Control and choice theme

The theme of "control and choice" emerged repeatedly from both groups. Participants in the study photographed spaces they could control and provided narrative about the positive aspects of those spaces. Comments regarding control and choice generally focused on qualities of ownership and their ability to change the environment, such as personalization of work environments, the design of a home work space, and the ability to choose where they would sit in a space.

Group 1 participants focused more on the issue of choice relative to accessibility, (e.g., whether or not they could sit at a particular table) than did Group 2. Preferred spaces for the participants who were disabled were ones that provided seating options and opportunities for choice. The difference in the perception of the built environment between disabled users and able-bodied designers and managers is best seen in a comparison of narratives describing a photo they had each taken.

Quote from Group 1:

"This is the eating area at M&H. It is booths and there are no chairs."

When asked if she would try and sit at one of tables the participant replied:

"no one could get by you. This is Taco Bell. They have a lot of booths…but they do have chairs too. So you can move a chair and get to a table."

Quote from designer in Group 2:

"This is my office. Put your feet up on the desk, I guess."

Sensory stimulation theme

Although Group 1 participants did not photograph environments that focused on sensory elements, they spoke about sensory elements in their narratives, especially when asked about their favorite and non-favorite spaces. Interestingly, however, during the personal interviews with participants who were disabled the focus again reverted to discussion of the functional issues that confront them on a daily basis. This indicates that the overarching concern for users who are disabled in the built environment is their ability to function. This implies that, by necessity, all other aspects of the built environment that might constitute a positive experience become secondary for users who are disabled.

Group 2 participants, on the other hand, spoke often about sensory elements in their workplaces, homes, and the public spaces they frequented. Sensory elements such as sound, smell, light quality, and the "look" of the space are all evident in the photographs and narratives.

Group 2 participants who had strong negative reactions to poorly maintained areas, clutter, dark spaces, and spaces that felt "dead" or lacked stimulation in terms of color, lighting, etc. demonstrate the sensory stimulation theme further. Participants in this group photographed positive spaces that often included natural plants, good friends and family, and attention to design detail. The emergence of this theme was not unexpected given the group's composition of individuals whose careers revolved around the design and creation of built environments.

Meaning and values theme

One of the prominent themes that emerged was an emphasis on "meaning" as it relates to personal values. For example, Group 1 participants expressed the theme of value and meaning in the photographs they took of the built environment and the narratives they supplied. However, the focus of the images and narratives identified a much different value than those seen in Group 2. Once again, the overarching issue for the users who were disabled was access and function – placing the most value and meaning on the concepts of exclusion, discrimination, and disregard for their needs.

In contrast, Group 2 participants photographed environments that had individual meaning and either reflected their personal values or countered their personal values but did not impact them on a daily basis. One participant identified the issues of sustainability and sense of place in his interview, and others in the group voiced concerns over changing morals and values as represented by security devices in public spaces.

Similar preferences for "ideal" environments theme

Many studies (Herzog 1998; Mauksch 1992; Nasar and Upton 1997; Newell 1997; Scott 1993) have been conducted on environmental influence and preference, building on theories developed in even earlier years (Mehrabian 1976; Nasar 1983). In 1997, Newell examined the impact cultural universals have on valued and favorite landscapes individuals interact with on a daily basis. In her study, Newell cautioned, "A point to bear in mind is that professionals, such as architects and landscape architects, appear to use different criteria from the general population. It is likely that the users place more emphasis on the affective meaning of the building, place, or landscape." Newell quotes Rapoport as stating designers "tend to react to environments in perceptual terms (which are meanings), whereas the lay public, the users, react to environments in associational terms."

This was indeed the case in this study with Group 1 and Group 2. When both groups were asked to identify their favorite spaces from the photographs they took and to describe their "ideal" environment, all participants, regardless of which group they were in, expressed a desire for similar elements. Those elements were identified as natural light, exterior views, large spaces, functional designs, plants, and a supportive environment in general. "Non-ideal" environments were identified as cold, institutional, impersonal, and – especially for Group 1 participants – nonfunctional.

For example, a participant in Group 1 described their "ideal" environment in this way:

> "Real light, real sunny, spacious, no carpet, an easy quick in and out. I could tell you what I really like, is a wheelchair accessible place in Arizona where I can get in and out easily. Lots of plants, lots of planters – my height. Low windows."

By comparison, a participant from Group 2 offered similar sentiments when asked to describe their "ideal environment":

> "Yeah, outside. Yeah I like that, the moon, full moon…try to be at the lake…I try to keep track of when the full moon is, so you can, when you are up at the lake, when you are sitting up in the loft, looking out the window, the big moon comes up and shimmers all the way across the lake, I would just sit down on the dock at night, look up at the stars…The exterior, my outer office does not have that. Actually I called my wife about 1:00 today and asked her if it was nice outside. I haven't seen it since I came this morning. So I kinda sense, I want to have a window, would like to have a view…I think personally, I'm somewhat energized by looking out at nature and seeing what's happening. I do enjoy urban scenes too where you have activity and people, cars, and see activity going, but my favorite would be when I'm at the lake, where you can see

nature, very relaxing. I would like to have space to have some of the things that I enjoy as far as art work. A comfortable couch, and access to a computer and probably a TV to watch, I don't watch too much TV though. I know it's not realistic, but I'd just as soon not have a telephone in that space. Actually, I think everything I'm telling you is a personal getaway. I like green colors, beige, true colors. There would be plants in my space. I'd like to probably even have a sky light in it so at night the when the moon is out you could see the moon and stars. Be able to adjust the lighting to whatever mood I happen to be in."

When asked to describe their "non-ideal" environments, again similarities emerged between the two groups. For example a participant in Group 1 described a "non-ideal" environment in this way:

"Spaces too small, ice and snow. The biggest frustration I have is bathrooms that I can't get into to use…I hate going downtown, because I don't know of a lot of buildings I can get in there…The Moorhead Theater, at Moorhead State, I mean that is appalling to me, for I have to sit in the walkways…another gentleman came in a wheelchair and had to crawl up the stairs. To me that is appalling. This is a state university, that I assume is getting federal dollars, I won't go there again, and I like going to plays with my wife. I don't want to be different, I'm different anyway, but I don't want to be more different than I have to be, from you or anybody else. I look obvious coming, I don't want to look more obvious by sitting in the alley or walkways where people have to rush by you, walking around you, that makes me uncomfortable."

Striking similarities exist between this quote from a participant who is disabled and an able-bodied design professional when speaking about their "non-ideal" environment:

"Yeah, worst space – all those cold institutional spaces. I guess the cold, a lot of metallic, marble, polished, you know I think would be beautiful, but seems sterile, and a general public location where, you know, like that bench, how many diapers have been changed on the bench, you don't know. A place that I don't have a relationship with, so I don't know its history. I don't know its use. I don't know anything about it and it's not even put there for me to get to know. It's like a place that occasionally, I have to use. Like a public restroom, who hangs out in there unless you are smoking cigarettes in tenth grade, you know."

Discussion

The results of this research study highlight the fact that although users who are disabled and designers and managers look for, and appreciate, many of the same attributes of the built environment, it is at the interface between what constitutes discrimination in the built environment and what does not where the two groups diverge. This study vividly points out that the issue of accessibility, and the potential of not being able to function in the built environment, carried a much more profound and personal meaning for those who were disabled than it did for the designers and managers in the study.

The social reality of this study is that a schism exists between users who are disabled and designers and managers of the built environment. The cultural portrait one can draw from this study suggests that this schism is evident to users who are disabled, but not so evident to the design community – which continues to reinforce the schism by creating built environments that discriminate.

Although designers consider function at all times, the majority view and define the term "function" from their personal perspective; in other words, whether it "meets code requirements" and, if it does, then it meets the accessibility goals of a project. Although users who are disabled uniquely view accessible space from their personal perspective, they are highly aware that "function for the majority" rules.

The emerging themes generated from this study offer a starting point for an improved dialogue between users who are disabled and management and design practitioners to help address discrimination in the built environment. Increased understanding of spatial perception and meaning can be effective in communicating user needs and wants in the built environment and help us move toward the creation of more inclusive environments.

The contrasting perceptions of the built environment between the two groups and the continued prevalence of the existence of exclusionary spaces in the built environment were documented throughout the study. Perhaps the most prominent, and disturbing result of this study was the evidence that there has not been as much change as is needed over the past several years – regardless of federal and state mandates such as the Americans with Disabilities Act (ADA, 1990). Discrimination of the disabled continues to exist in our built environments today and, although it may be unconscious, this discriminatory approach forces users who are disabled to either be seen as, or to feel as if they have been, stratified into a lower social class than able-bodied users. The resulting frustration, and at times rage, of these users is dramatically illustrated in their narratives and the photographs they took.

This study highlights the missed opportunity for the designers of the built environment to embrace "design as a instrument of social change." If, as Danko (2000), Presier et al. (1991), and Ganoe (1999) propose, design is an important part of enhancing life quality for users, then it must be inclusive design for all users, not just the able-bodied. According to Ganoe, "Designers…should…be aware that design…reveals meaning on three levels; behavior and function, power and status, philosophy and worldview."

The ramifications of failing to address the needs of users with a disability can be costly and affect all areas of the built environment, from the micro scale of product design to the macro scale of urban design. Bjork notes that the resistance of corporations in applying universal design principles to their development process is causing them to lose sales as they are not viewing people with disabilities, comprising 15% of the population of the Western world, as potential customers (Bjork 2009). Further, Skinner notes that East Asian countries have led the world in enhancing accessible public spaces and transportation infrastructure, and further believes universal design may become a necessity in managing travel populations in the future (Skinner 2008).

Bridging the Schism

How do we bridge the schism, the lack of collaboration, the lack of addressing the needs of all users? Knecht calls for incorporating universal design principles into the design process, so it is not just a solution to a problem, but a "framework for creating solutions" (Knecht 2004). This moves the concept from one of "have to" to a climate of access that encourages creativity and collaboration. Heylighen and Bianchin see the need for defining the relationship between inclusive design and good design not as just universal design, but "as a deliberative enterprise involving both designers and the people they design for" (Heylighen and Bianchin 2013). Specifically, they state, "we view design quality not simply as a matter of convergence of different perspectives, but as a matter of cooperative integration."

Monaghan notes that design for people with disabilities "has made only an intermittent, marginal impression on the world." However, he believes this will change because of the world's rapidly aging population. According to Monaghan, disciplines that are leading the way are product design (kitchen utensils and technology devices) and media designers (Monaghan 2010).

It is suggested that the results of this study can help bridge the schism between designers' and facility managers' perception of what is accessible design and what truly is inclusive design according to users with disabilities. Development of an empathetic language could be a step towards a common, shared language – a language that is inclusive and universal.

One of the things that this study most vividly illustrates is the fact that designers of the built environment and the users who are disabled each perceive spaces from their personal and individual perspectives and experiences. How the environment impacts their life in terms of function is the overriding issue for people with disabilities, while designers focus on a multitude of stimuli and address function at a much more abstract and less personal level. Although designers believe they are adequately addressing function and accessibility in the built environment when they adhere to "the rules" of ADA, it is apparent from this study that they are falling far short of creating inclusive spaces when seen from the perspective of users who are disabled.

It is suggested that if designers can develop and use a more empathetic language that becomes an integral part of the design process, change can and will occur. The foundation of this language is based in the concept of universal design. However, even that term is misunderstood. Welch reinforces this idea in the first Universal Design Education Project when she states,

Inaccurate use of language sometimes confused the basic goals of this project.

The ADA Standards for Accessible Design are the basis for universal design, but by themselves, constitute only one aspect of designing for all people…This problem is complicated by the popular trend in advertising and print media to use the terms barrier-free design, accessibility, and ADA interchangeably with universal design without understanding or explaining the requisite shift in perspective. (Welch 1995)

So what is an empathetic language? Is it a language based on perception and understanding of user needs or code definitions? The emerging themes of this study illustrate the need to develop a vocabulary of empathetic terminology. For example in "Theme I: Function and Accessibility," users who were disabled described spaces that they did not like in the following terms and phrases that exemplified what they can and cannot physically do in a space:

"I can't get in"; "no way I can enter"; "difficult to maneuver around in there"; "terribly narrow"; "I can barely fit through there"; "it is difficult and impossible to open"; "it's too high"; "This is labeled at our church as the accessible bathroom. And it is not"; "no one could get by you"; "had to crawl up the stairs."

In contrast, when designers and managers of the built environment talked about what they didn't like about spaces their focus was on inconveniences that make a space less enjoyable, rather than on whether or not they could physically do things in the space, such as move around comfortably:

"It just doesn't stay clean"; "The only negative thing about it is sometimes the sun is so bright that we have to kind of hide in the shade of the corners"; "at least it's shady for an outdoor seating space"; "I've had a couple of studios below ground and I've had to descend these stairs into that and, I don't know, somehow it's always been kind of cold."

An empathetic language for designers should incorporate a true understanding of what users who are disabled are experiencing as challenges in the built environment on a daily basis. It must go beyond the terms such as "accommodate," "accessible," "barrier-free," and "universal design." For example, instead of designing an "accessible bathroom" designers might say instead "inclusive bathrooms."

It is suggested further that changing the terminology from the perspective of the "other" (users who are disabled) versus "us" (able-bodied designers) to a perspective of "we" would help bridge the language gap. This approach would provide evidence to the disabled community that designers and managers are sensitive to the issues of discrimination in the built environment and willing to work towards design solutions that are inclusive of their needs and that strive for equality. The use of empathetic terminology that highlights the concepts of equity, sharing, and inclusion by designers and design educators would be a positive step toward transforming our built environment.

Future Research and Limitations of the Study

This research study is only a beginning step toward the development and adoption of an empathetic language for the design community. As such, it provides a starting point for many other research studies. For example, future research on the role of design as an instrument of social change could focus on the relationship between the designer/architect, building owner/manager, and the user who is disabled and the resulting negative social and economic impacts of continued discrimination by repeating this study with an expanded and more refined sample.

This study attempted to integrate a multitude of images and responses into a larger, collective mosaic of "the language of universal design." This mosaic is at times bold and definitive, and at other times blurred and undefined. Further study to develop and create an "empathetic language" that would communicate through symbols and an inclusive approach to creating our built environments would contribute to the body of knowledge necessary to underpin such an effort.

It is also suggested that further studies which expand the collective profile presented here would be of value. For example, a survey of top architectural and design firms and facility managers could be conducted to determine their level of understanding of universal design concepts. This, in combination with a study that focused on discovering more successful ways for people with disabilities to communicate their needs in an effective manner, would help bridge the schism between the design community and those with disabilities.

Additional studies of value to the design community at large could focus on the role of education in the design process. A methodology for how to increase three-way communication between designers, owners, and users would contribute to the transformation of our built environments into more inclusive environments. Further research documenting exactly what constitutes an inclusive environment would also contribute to the literature on universal design.

References

Alexander, C., Ishikawa, S., Silverstein, M., et al. 1977. *A Pattern Language*. New York: Oxford University Press.

Altman, I. and Chermers, M. 1980. *Culture and Environment*. New York: Cambridge University Press.

Baird, G. 1995. *The Space of Appearance*. Cambridge, MA: MIT Press.

Baird, J. C. 1979. "Studies of the cognitive representation of spatial relations," *Journal of Experimental Psychology* 108(1): 90–91.

Barthes, R. 1977. *Image, Music, Text*. New York: Hill & Wang.

Bjork. E. 2009. "Many become losers when the universal design perspective is neglected," *Exploring the True Cost of Ignoring Universal design* 21(4): 117–125.

Bloomer, C. M. [1976] 1990. *Principles of Visual Perception*. New York: Van Nostrand Reinhold.

Danko, S. 2000. "Beneath the surface: a story of leadership, recruitment, and the hidden dimensions of strategic workplace design," *Journal of Interior Design* 26(2): 1–24.

Dick, B. 2000. "Grounded theory: a thumbnail sketch." http://www.scu.edu.au/schools/gcm/ar/arp/grounded.html. Accessed May 2, 2014.

Dollinger, S. J. and Dollinger, S. M. C. 1997. "Individuality and identity exploration: an autophotographic study," *Journal of Research in Personality* 31: 337–354.

Ganoe, C. 1999. "Design as narrative: a theory of inhabiting interior space," *Journal of Interior Design* 25(2): 1–15.

Glaser, B. G. and Strauss, A. L. 1967. *The Discovery of Grounded Theory: Strategies for Qualitative Research*. New York: Aldive de Gruyter.

Grusky, D. B. 1994. "The contours of social stratification," in D. B. Grusky (ed.), *Social Stratification: Class, Race, And Gender in Sociological Perspective*. Boulder: Westview Press, pp. 3–35.

Herzog, T. R. 1998. "The role of mystery in perceived danger and environmental preference," *Environment and Behavior* 30(4): 429–450.

Heylighen, A. and Bianchin, M. 2013. "Designing as a deliberative enterprise," *Design Studies* 34(1): 93–110.

Hitch, D., Larkin, H., Watchorn, V., and Ang, S. 2012. "Community mobility in the context of universal design: inter-professional collaboration and education," *Australian Occupational Therapy Journal* 59(5): 375–383.

Jones, S. and Welch, P. 1996. "Power and place," *A&AA Review* 3 (Fall).

Knecht, B. 2004. "Accessibility regulations and a universal design philosophy inspire the design process," *Architectural Record* 192(1): 145–150.

Kvale, S. 1996. *Interviews: An Introduction to Qualitative Research Interviewing*. Thousand Oaks, CA: Sage Publications.

LaPlante, M. P. 1991. "The demographics of disability," *Medline* 69(suppl. 1–2): 55–77.

Lynch, K. 1960. *The Image of the City*. Cambridge, MA: MIT Press.

Mauksch, R. 1992. "Hospital visitors' perceptions of hospital waiting rooms," *IDEC International Conference Proceedings* 79–84.

Mehrabian, A. 1976. *Public Places and Private Spaces*. New York: Basic Books.

Monaghan, P. 2010. "Design for disability will become the norm," *Chronicle of Higher Education* 56(22): B6–B7.

Moore, H. L. [1986] 1996. *Space, Text, and Gender: An Anthropological Study of the Marakwet of Kenya*. Cambridge: Cambridge University Press.

Nasar, J. L. 1983. "Adult viewers' preferences in residential scenes: a study of the relationship of environmental attributes to preference," *Environment and Behavior* 15(5): 589–614.

Nasar, J. L. and Upton, K. 1997. "Landscapes of fear and stress," *Environment and Behavior* 29: 291–323.

Newell, P. 1997. "A cross-cultural examination of favorite places," *Environment and Behavior* 29(4): 495–510.

Patton, M. Q. 1987. *How To Use Qualitative Methods in Evaluation*. Newbury Park, CA: Sage Publications.

Presier, W. et al. 1991. *Design Intervention: Toward a More Humane Architecture*. New York: Van Nostrand Reinhold.

Rapoport, A. 1969. *House, Form and Culture*. New York: Prentice Hall.

Rapoport, A. 1982. *The Meaning of the Built Environment*. London: Sage Publications.

Rapoport, A. 1994. "Spatial organization and the built environment," in T. Ingold (ed.), *Companion Encyclopedia of Anthropology*. London: Routledge.

Saito, Y. 2006. "Awareness of universal design among facility managers in Japan and the United States," *Automation in Construction* 15(4): 462–478.

Scott, S. C. 1993. "Visual attributes related to preference in interior environments," *Journal of Interior Design Education and Research* 18(1–2): 7–16.

Sewell, M. 2000. "The use of qualitative interviews in evaluation," *CyberNet Evaluation*. http://ag.arizonia.edu/fcr/fs/cyfar/Intervu.5.htm.

Skinner, J. 2008. "Public places, universal spaces," *Planning* 74(7): 10–13.

Thoutenhoofd, E. 1998. "Method in photographic enquiry of being deaf," *Sociological Research Online* 3(2). http://www.socresonline.org.uk/socresonline/3/2/2.html.

Weisman, L. K. 1992. *Discrimination by Design: A Feminist Critique of the Man-Made Environment*. Urbana: University of Illinois Press.

Welch, P., ed. 1995. *Strategies for Teaching Universal Design*. Boston: Adaptive Environments Center.

Windley, P. G. and Scheidt, R. J. 1980. "Person–environment dialectics: implications for competent functioning in old age," in L. W. Poon (ed.), *Aging in the 1980s: Psychological Issues*. Washington DC: American Psychological Association.

Zeisel, J. 1981. *Inquiry by Design: Tools for Environment–Behavior Research*. New York: Cambridge University Press.

Ziller, R. C. 1990. *Photographing the Self: Methods for Observing Personal Orientations*. London. Sage Publications.

Ziller, R. C. and Lewis, D. 1981. "Self, social, environmental percepts through autophotography," *Personality and Social Psychology Bulletin* 7: 338–343.

Ziller, R. C. and Rorer, B. A. 1985. "Shyness–environment interaction: a view from the shy side through auto-photography," *Journal of Personality* 53: 626–639.

10

Ways of Knowing in Design: A Position on the Culture of Interior Design Practice

Janice Barnes

Introduction

It is often said that in the practice of law there are but three major achievements: (1) obtaining the law degree, (2) passing the bar exam, and (3) making partner and securing that corner office. In the practice of design, the list of accomplishments would also include winning a nationally recognized design award.

Over the last several years I have had the privilege of attending many of the top interior design industry-sponsored events where designers are recognized for their design talent and professional accomplishments. Each event draws hundreds, if not thousands, of participants, and a broad online following as the design industry comes together to celebrate its collective excellence. Winning such an award is considered a culminating and transformational achievement in terms of the value that the recognition brings to one's career.

I recently, however, began to question how the celebration of design talent at these events relates to the broader development of design knowledge within the practice of interior design. Do these events shape what we know about practice? As I considered the events, I also began to question the impact of our daily work more broadly. What makes up a day in the life of a designer? And, what in the daily life of a designer contributes to new knowledge, or how we know, in the profession? How do we know through our practice and its celebrations?

The Handbook of Interior Design, First Edition. Edited by Jo Ann Asher Thompson and Nancy H. Blossom.
© 2015 John Wiley & Sons, Ltd. Published 2015 by John Wiley & Sons, Ltd.

Ways of Knowing: Empiricism or Intuition?

Epistemology is the study of the scope and nature of knowledge, or "ways of knowing."[1] Much of the literature on epistemology focuses on the multivariate and often contradictory nature of knowledge. Nagel juxtaposes science and common sense. He describes science as a method of inquiry with a currently known truth (Nagel 1979). Common sense, comparatively, is a set of indeterminate, yet somehow known and accepted, values. Nagel's basic argument is to present the relative values of science against those of common sense. Science, he argues, allows for the growth of structured determinate knowledge. Common sense on the other hand provides a range of determinacy. Science provides value to those interested in advancing the state of knowledge about a particular subject. Common sense provides a lens for choosing how to proceed in a given moment, but is not contributory to the state of knowledge of a particular subject.

Nagel's best example of this is in his description of firearms expertise. He describes how numerous shooters might be ranked as firearms experts if they were able to hit the side of a barn at short range, assuming hitting the side of the barn was specific enough. Should the target be a 3-inch circle at twice the distance, the number of shooters who would hit the target – and thus be ranked as firearms experts – would decrease notably. His point is about specificity in the skill set. Science, or the specific contribution of precision sighting and aim, provides focus to the shooters, narrowing the target and raising the expectation of contribution. Common sense is hitting the side of the barn, an act that requires far less precision, but that is certainly an interesting leisurely exercise. Both norms have their place in our society, but in the first case we want the precision shooters to be in positions where their decisions about how and what to shoot are equally as precise as their ability to do so. In the second case, we simply want to make sure that we hit the barn.

"Ways of knowing" in practice are often defined by actions in practice. Bolan writes: "theorists are generally trying to abstract and generalize experience, while practitioners must confront the concrete uniqueness of actual situations" (Bolan 1980). Similarly, Argyris and Schon describe espoused theory as theory in use, which is simply another way of describing theory and practice (Argyris and Schon 1974). Ultimately, their point identifies the inherent contradictions that are often present in practice. For a designer this might be codified in contributing new knowledge to color theory versus using common sense in dealing with a client's expectations on a color palette. In the first case, the designer extends knowledge in the practice, and in the second case the designer uses knowledge and common sense in situ.

The work of Bolan and Nagel offers insight into the question of how designers come to know through their practice. While Bolan suggests learning through the active participation in work, Nagel disputes that work is contributing to the science of practice. Nagel's point isn't that common sense gained through participation is irrelevant, but simply that it doesn't contribute to the body of knowledge in practice.

In this Bolan's argument is similar. He describes "plagues of environmental turbulence that lead to the emergence of practices and conceptualizations that differ markedly from orthodox professional theory." Bolan's "plagues" are the random, but relatively frequent, experiences that designers engage in on a daily basis. Each of these experiences requires a designer to act in situ, drawing upon both espoused theory and the common sense realities of the client's situation.

Popper's World 2 and World 3 knowledge tackles the heart of this issue. His basic premise is that World 2 is subjective knowledge that will disappear with the passing of its creator. World 3 is objective knowledge that remains long after its creator has gone. From Popper's perspective, World 2 is the working knowledge of individual designers. World 3 is the shared body of knowledge that extends beyond any single designer to occupy independent intellectual space. It is a studied approach to advancing knowledge that will exist outside of any individual contribution (Popper 1972).

As designers, do we extend the body of knowledge of our discipline through a studied approach, or do we rely on our working knowledge, acting in the moment with its many variations? I believe that the latter is the case, which in my mind poses a challenge regarding how we contribute new knowledge in our practice.

Shifting Practices: Little Reflection

With global shifts in the nature of design practices, our professional futures rest on increasing agility and deepening knowledge of design in relation to broader societal issues. Shifting trends in professional services alter financing models, delivery models, and investments, and our clients expect us to bring both awareness and leadership on these issues (Barnes 2010). Examples include:

- Emergent norms in public–private partnerships that fundamentally change the nature of financing for design projects.
- Section 179D tax credits that alter the emphasis on investments in energy reductions.
- Cost segregation analyses that influence design decision-making at the level of technical attachment.
- Integrated project delivery that changes the nature of collaboration and the transparency of that collaboration with clients.
- Climatological changes and associated legislative oversight reframe the risk associated with design decision-making. Post-LEED, the Living Building Challenge is the new norm. A longer view focuses on regenerative design, or an emergence from green to blue design (Eagle and Barnes 2010).
- Evolutionary demographic shifts demand differentiated attention to generational expectations for design. Demographic shifts change the very nature of the workforce and vary by country, as Japan describes its Silver Leadership and America tackles both the Millennials and the retiring Baby Boomers.

- Global business practices increase awareness of global events and socio-cultural norms in design.

Many designers have faced project challenges on more than one of the issues above, but what do we actually do to advance disciplinary knowledge in these areas?

As designers, we often exceed American work-week norms by 20–50%. In busier times, that easily reaches 200%. With such work required for the delivery of services, there is little room in a work week for dialogue on the nature of design and the evolution of design practice, much less for a structured approach to advancing the body of knowledge. As a result, the research or scientific trajectory of design practice often falls to academic institutions wherein the majority of designers are not working on project delivery, but instead focus on teaching and research. While the academic contributions are enormously valuable, and in some cases conducted in concert with design firms focused specifically on advancing a particular aspect of practice, the broader question is how the profession beyond academe advances the body of knowledge.

Given the realities of maintaining design practice, with little free time and little free capital, designers increase their design knowledge when and where possible. Continuing education credits are the most common avenue, along with attendance at industry events and networking events. With the addition of the LEED Continuing Education Units (CEUs) on top of the National Council for Interior Design Qualification (NCIDQ) exam, many designers struggle to fit in the minimum requirements around the demands of work. In speaking recently with an owner of a small design practice, he noted that we fail to build a continuing education structure for ourselves, but instead simply grab what we can in order to maintain CEU minimums. Granted, for the most part these activities increase individual knowledge, but they do not necessarily contribute to the body of knowledge in the discipline.

With very busy professional calendars, it may be argued that one key means of investigating how designers grow their professional knowledge is through looking at how they spend their days, how they celebrate their successes, and how they reflect on career achievements. As a way of capturing knowledge through their practices, consider how designers spend the majority of their time. While practices certainly vary across scale of firm and market sector, it may be argued that designers spend most of their time on four other endeavors: (1) maintaining awareness of the peer activities in the design press; (2) marketing for and providing design services; (3) actively pursuing industry recognition for these services; and, to a lesser extent, (4) increasing their internal research capabilities. These endeavors comprise the majority of activities in design firms, and as such, offer a unique lens through which to understand practice and the means by which designers advance knowledge.

Research Framework

To understand how designers learn more about design, I conducted a content analysis of four relevant qualitative sources: (1) design press; (2) requests for proposals received by national design firms; (3) national design awards ceremonies; and (4) research arms within professional design firms. This analysis follows Guba and Lincoln's qualitative research methods approach (Guba and Lincoln 1981). Design press examines the structure and content of the major design publications (not including research journals). Requests for proposals emphasize client interest areas and professional service responses. National design award ceremonies identify incentives and evaluation criteria that meet the quality standards of the profession. Client requests and practitioners' responses, design awards, and publications are normative means for understanding the ways of knowing in design.

These sources offer insight into the reality of design practice, far from the academic experiences that define design research. Research within professional design firms focuses on the degree to which practitioners engage in structured dialogue to advance the body of knowledge of design and the applicability of research to practice. Research within professional design firms is emergent, but comparatively recent compared to the sources preceding.

Within each source, I identified: (1) messages about design practice evidenced in the source; (2) the source's contribution to the body of design knowledge; and (3) the ways in which designers use the source. While it may be argued that these are interpretive rather than causal references, the basis of the argument remains; that is, there is limited focus on structured scientific inquiry in design practice. As a result, the typical designer's "way of knowing" is through a common sense approach to design.

Nagel writes that science "arises out of daily living" (Nagel 1979). In the case of design practice, that is absolutely correct. For design practice to become scientific it must emerge from the known, the familiar, and become quite specific. With the exception of the research initiatives described later in this essay, design practice is currently much more about a growing body of common sense than a growing body of scientific research.

Nagel describes common sense as deeply connected to cultural and historical values, but not necessarily connected as a belief system. He describes common sense as vague and lacking in specificity, with limited experimental controls. He goes on to describe common sense as unaware of the framework that it works within and, therefore, of utmost value when there are many constants. He further notes that common sense remains incomplete.

Design practice in most cases is just as Nagel describes common sense – deeply tied to cultural and historical values, limited in terms of experimental controls, valuable in its ability to leverage many constants (typologies) and, arguably, incomplete.

Findings

Design press

Using *Contract Magazine* and *Interior Design Magazine* as the two primary sources of design press, I examined 12 months of recent issues. In each case, I compared the various message points, the contributions to new knowledge, and the ways in which designers use the source. As defined by Drab and Marian, the design publications have a significant influence both on practitioners and on public perception of design practice (Drab 1997; Marian 2009).

Contract Magazine is nominally recognized as the premier source of interior design news. Its website (www.contractdesign.com) describes its mission and audience in the following way:

> *Contract Magazine* and ContractDesign.com are at the hub of commercial interior design and architecture, connecting professionals and covering processes, products, projects and practice issues that set the standards in the industry. *Contract* elevates the relevance and value of commercial design by focusing on its power to transform business and institutional environments. *Contract* delivers the content and context in print, online, and face-to-face that design professionals need to create intelligent and inspired design solutions in the real world…*Contract* magazine addresses the key design, business, and technology issues currently shaping the practice of commercial and institutional interior design by the nation's architects, interior designers, and allied professionals…We also publish projects of the nation's most talented practicing interior designers and architects – both the emerging and the well-established.

Contract is typically organized as a series of cases that are placed in categories of project typologies. Each case offers excellent photography of the built spaces, oftentimes including floor plans and diagrams to help explain the design solutions. These cases form the basis for the publication, with source references and affiliated advertising comprising the remaining majority of the publication.

Interior Design Magazine provides this self-description: "*Interior Design Magazine* offers the latest interior design trends, ideas, contemporary architecture and design news." From its website (www.interiordesign.net), *Interior Design Magazine* describes its role:

> *Interior Design* is the magazine for the interior design professional marketplace…Each month, the magazine features a variety of outstanding projects, the latest new products across all disciplines, industry news and more. In fact, *Interior Design* offers the most editorial pages of any publication in the field. With a print circulation of more than 76,000 (paid), and over 170,000 monthly unique visitors online, *Interior Design* offers an unparalleled level of design-hungry readership…Every year, designers contact *Interior Design* with over 1 million product inquiries. As a result, designers trust *Interior Design* as a primary source, and interior furnishings manufacturers place more faith in the power of *Interior Design* than in all its competitors combined. Advertising in *Interior Design* is essential to reaching the enormous purchasing power of professional designers. And reading *Interior Design* is essential to staying inspired and informed.

Interior Design is organized in a similar manner to *Contract* with experiential cases and supporting information regarding product sourcing. New products also appear in *Interior Design*.

The basic message provided by the articles in each magazine focuses on the introduction of new projects with a brief overview of the solution. The secondary message is about new products or sourcing of shown products. With their respective website positions, *Contract* appears to be somewhat less product-focused than *Interior Design* and doesn't use product advertising as a key description of its role. *Interior Design* comparatively takes a strong position on product advertising in terms of exposure to designers who specify products.

As a result, it may be argued that the contribution that these sources make to the body of design knowledge is in increasing professionals' awareness of interesting new work and in introducing products to those same professionals, thereby providing real value to design practice. On the other hand, in terms of structured inquiry, there is a very limited approach to advancing knowledge.

A comparative example would be the use of cases in a research project in which precedent comparisons through structured inquiry advance our knowledge of a typology or of a client. These project overviews and product introductions are not presented in this way. We use these to build awareness and in so doing add to the common sense knowledge of the profession.

As Bolan would argue, the examples presented in these magazines offer insights into the normative structure of the discipline. Through the choices made for publication, they provide clues to the design community that a particular project is valued at an institutional level and gives status to its chosen designers (Bolan 1980). While such status doesn't contribute to the body of knowledge in the profession, it does establish a normative set from which to compare.

Requests for proposals

One basis for gaining work in most design practices is through the request for proposal (RFP) and earlier variations such as request for information (RFI) and request for qualifications (RFQ). Design firms receive RFPs because of their recognition within the industry in which the proposal originates or through a relationship with either the client or the program manager. Most typically these apply to larger design practices.

While relationships will always remain the strongest means by which to gain work, the way that designers learn about marketplace needs, beyond their existing relationships, is through reviewing the requests for services that clients currently require. Because these RFPs serve as strong indicators of client interests, it is appropriate to examine how the RFPs are written and what the performance indicators imply in terms of design practice.

Therefore, as part of this research I examined three RFPs that were simultaneously issued to several of the large design firms (as ranked by *Interior Design Magazine*) domestically. In each RFP, I identified the message about design, the source's contribution to the body of knowledge, and how designers use the source.

These three examples are indicative of the type of RFPs that leading design firms typically receive. Example 1 represents the large portfolio client that is looking for either a national or a global design firm or firms to use for all of its facility improvements. Example 2 represents the large firm with a one-off project that, through performance review, may lead to a larger portfolio of work. Example 3 represents a small regional practice that offers no further work beyond the initial request, but that may add to the coffer of typology experience.

In Example 1 (Nationwide Request for Information), the client sought information regarding company structure, experience in their specific industry, financial solvency, the firm's position on social responsibility and human resources, and project specifics such as staffing availability, software platforms, geographic coverage, and consultant relationships. The potential with this client is the design of millions of square feet in corporate offices throughout their domestic portfolio.

Responding to a request such as this allows a designer to reflect on the firm's ability to serve a national or global client and to collaborate with partners throughout the practice to identify how to present their argument to the client. Designers typically use this type of source to further refine their position in the client's industry and to better understand the degree of "bench-depth" in the practice.

In Example 2 (a Global Request for Proposal – South American site), the client sought information regarding life safety code application, occupancy, and associated utility limitations, building affordances, and base building detail integration. The design firms being considered had previously submitted a set of qualifications as described in Example 1, therefore this RFP offered more specifics in regard to the needs of a regional project. The potential with this RFP was just under 100,000 square feet of design work and access to perform services on their larger, multi-million-square-foot portfolio.

Responding to a request such as this allows a designer to enter into a broader dialogue with a target client and, through performance, open opportunities for additional services in other locations. For an international request specifically, exposure to the client's domestic operations and its comparative international operations offers additional insight into cultural nuances in both the client industry and the construction trade in various locales. Designers typically use this type of source to further refine their ability to deliver internationally and to reassess the practice exposure outside of their typical marketplaces. Designers also use this type of opportunity to further their network of collaborators from both an engineering and local design delivery perspective.

In Example 3 (a Regional Request for Qualifications and subsequent proposal) the client sought expertise to build a location strategy and overall approach to their portfolio. This was to be conducted in concert with a firm rebranding and potential repositioning to be more competitive with its peer group. The client initially sought information regarding the firm's qualifications with this project type. Subsequent follow-up included a specific request for approach to the project, and team members and overall strategy. The potential with this RFP was just over 150,000 square feet at one location.

Responding to a request such as this allows a designer to emphasize a particular area of expertise in the firm's portfolio, or to explore whether or not to move into that industry segment. Designers typically use this type of source to evaluate market position in a specific industry and/or the geographic reach of the firm.

What do these proposals offer in terms of opportunities to increase knowledge? Each of these examples offers the opportunity of a unique contribution. Example 1 encourages designers to further define their market share. Example 2 emphasizes evaluation of global reach and a type of courtship with a target client which requires global thinking. Example 3 urges introspection on new market interests.

In each of these ways, should designers choose to consider the requests for proposals through a meta-cognitive lens, each example may very well extend the body of knowledge. For the organizations wherein leadership recognizes the patterns established by RFPs such as these and responds accordingly with a structured approach to understanding and engaging the marketplace, there are significant opportunities to advance knowledge. While responding to these requests for proposals is not at all scientific, the potential of reflection on these as cases, or exemplars of shifting needs, offers the chance to learn a bit more about context and expectations in target client organizations, thereby extending the body of knowledge within the design practice (if not within the design community). However, there is often little reflection on the meta-structure behind these RFPs, the implications for practice, or the relation of these requests to how we reward ourselves for excellence.

National design awards

National design awards bestowed by *Interior Design* (Hall of Fame) and *Contract Magazine* (Contract Magazine Interior Awards) incentivize designers toward a particular kind of achievement – recognition for a design contribution. These awards define a community of like-minded participants who both value and pursue the recognition that the award signifies. But do these awards enable designers to know more about design, or is their contribution somewhat different? Research perspectives vary.

One recent research paper suggests that the Hall of Fame is particularly problematic for practice. In Marian's exploration of the value of Hall of Fame, she notes that "*Interior Design Magazine* explains that the purpose of the Hall of Fame Award is to recognize persons who have contributed to the development and prominence of the design field" (Marian 2009). However, through her research she reveals that the awards actually may negatively impact the profession. Marian's summary: "Data reveal that the award is a social rather than a professional event, that the interior design professional characteristics are minimally represented, and that the interior designers comprise 18 percent of the membership. Overall, the Award impacts negatively on the development of the interior design profession, even though the *Interior Design Magazine* considers the Hall of Fame to be the highest honor in interior design." Comparatively, the Contract Magazine Interior Awards, which are similarly recognized in the industry, exhibit like characteristics to the Hall of Fame. In both cases, design experiences are the focus of the awards, not the path of getting there or the performance thereafter. If Marian's assessment is correct in establishing the inherent contradictions in the awards and the need to advance the profession, what then do these awards offer?

Gemser and Wijnberg identify three distinct benefits of awards in design. These are: (1) the value of the award itself (money, exchange, etc.); (2) the value of the award as a signal to competitors; and (3) the value of the award as a signal to consumers (Gemser and Wijnberg 2002). Using these three lenses, do either Hall of Fame awards or Contract Design Interior awards offer distinct benefits?

Neither the Interior Design Hall of Fame, nor the Contract Design Interior award offers financial compensation. However, they clearly offer value in terms of sending a message to the competition within the industry. Peer recognition is quite valuable in this regard. The awards contribute to the prestige of the recipients, even though a historical review of the awards cycles suggests that the recipients, for the most part, are already recognized in the industry (Marian 2009). It is rare to see a practice win an award outside of the particular award category they have won in the past.

Other authors, such as English, argue that the production of cultural capital or the "geography of prestige" is an important trade value in the 21st century economy (English 2005). If this is the case, although most recipients are already recognized, perhaps the prestige bestowed by the awards provides additional value in the competitive landscape. As designers, we want it; we value it; we respect its recipients. But to what end?

Bolan describes a "conscious striving" for one or more of the following: (1) enhanced self-esteem, (2) mastery of professional domain, (3) cognitive and value consistency, (4) self-actualization, and (5) significant impact on the world of contemporaries (Bolan 1980). This summary of national design awards goes to the heart of what Bolan describes as "motivational relevance." It is easily argued that this is the case for designers seeking national design awards. Design awards equate to Bolan's "conscious striving" construct because they positively affect self-esteem and signal mastery in the discipline.

The trends evidenced annually in the awards do offer some degree of consistency and resonance to current trends in practice and thus raise awareness of these among contemporaries. But to the initial question: do these awards lead to new ways of knowing about the practice?

Perhaps the awards are more a means of establishing a stronger economic basis for a practice? Market research on the value of awards in driving new business is a significant area of exploration. It is unclear whether there has been any notable research tracking financial performance of awardees prior to the award and immediately following it, but perhaps there is unrecognized value there. English rallies around the "economics of cultural prestige," but he is quick to point out that there is no true economic exchange in the prestige award (English 2005). So, while the awards would act as a signal to the consumers of professional services, it is unclear the extent to which the awards would influence a client to choose a designer. Parallel research in other industries (Walsh, Roy, Bruce, and Potter 1992) suggests that there are economic performance benefits related to the receipt of design awards. However these are not focused on interior design per se.

With the awards offering the benefit of prestige within peer and aspirant groups, along with possible additional business, they most certainly provide value within the industry. Designers value the awards and continue to participate, actively seeking recognition for themselves and their firms. Designers use the recognition to leverage their marketplace position and to increase respect among their peers. A partner in a large design firm noted that awards are good for building exposure with other firms and as a result have a positive effect on recruiting. She also noted that awards are impressive to prospective clients and contribute to maintaining positive relations with the clients whose projects received the award.

Designers also use the awards to identify patterns of change. For example, when *Modern Healthcare* identified that in one year many of the awarded projects had a common characteristic of gardens, it was interpreted as a message regarding the potential for natural environments to promote healing (Pinto 1996). Such interpretations impact design practices as designers look to the projects that receive accolades for inspiration.

But awards rarely contribute substantially to the science of design practice. As such, they fall short in focusing the profession's intellectual growth. If publications, client responses, and awards fail to advance the body of knowledge, is there another avenue to do so?

Research in professional service firms

In 1967 Bourdieu focused his attention on the ways in which knowledge is gained through education and structured systems of thought. He described "intellectual clans" and their habits as critical to the development of knowledge in a particular area (Bourdieu 1967). In the design industry, Bourdieu's perspective is best captured in the emerging research groups within a small number of design practices. In these groups, intellectual clans provide focused, industry-specific research to advance the state of the practice. However, once again, this represents only a very small number of firms.

On the other hand, Mahdjoubi frankly juxtaposes science and design, giving numerous examples of the distinctive differences between scientific exploration and design exploration (Mahdjoubi 2003). His argument is that the theory of design falls short of theorizing – design is referenced as the transformation of a designer's tools and resources to create something new. Hillier, Musgrove, and O'Sullivan describe design as "the socially differentiated transformation of the reflexive cognition of the maker in terms of the latent possibility of his tools, materials and object types" (Hillier et al. 1984). Following Mahdjoubi's perspective would suggest that scientific inquiry is not appropriate for design epistemology. In fact, with this argument it runs counter to design intent. Certainly the accomplished design researchers would argue this point. But how about the clients?

As Rylander juxtaposes Knowledge-Intensive Firms (KIFs) and Design Firms, she makes an explicit comparison of the value of knowledge as an analytical, rational mindset armed with "data driven analysis" and the value of design as a creative mindset (Rylander 2008). She describes how consultants in KIFs align their language and their "way of knowing" with the general discourse in business, while designers produce "symbols of creativity [that] do not always speak the same language as clients. This is probably a contributing factor to the significantly lower profitability among design firms as compared to so-called KIFs in general and management consulting firms, in particular" (Johansson and Svengren 2008). What if Rylander is correct?

These opinions beg the question of the value of research in professional service firms in contributing to the body of knowledge in practice. Given that so few firms have true research capabilities, perhaps research in practice has failed to provide a value proposition. Or perhaps the investments are emergent because of the shifting landscape of practice as initially described.

In a recent overview of research in practice, Green, Kleusner, and Glenn (2011) identify three categories of "research." These are collecting information, collaborating on empirical work as a secondary support, and leading empirical work. Collecting information emphasizes non-empirical, yet somewhat structured, approaches to gaining insight into client industries as well as into our own industry.

Collection is often termed "research" in practice, but in fact it in no way resembles research. It is simply collecting information. Collaborating on true empirical work is less typical, but still evident. An example is the way in which firms support academic institutions in a research study wherein an accomplished researcher is the principal investigator and graduate students form the majority of the team.

Leadership of empirical work is actually quite rare in design firms. An example where this does exist is when a firm's researcher is the primary investigator on a grant or self-funded research. Using these categories, an examination was done of the practices of top design firms in North America to better understand to what degree these firms engaged in one form or another of research in practice.

The results were surprising. Almost all firms conduct some form of information collection (i.e., gathering materials and repackaging those to enable clients to see trends and their impacts). Collaborations with research institutions are far less frequent, but certainly evident across a number of firms. However only a handful of firms have embraced research leadership, and of these, two have started their research groups only recently. To be fair, perhaps some firms don't publicize their research in ways that make it accessible to such reviews. There could easily be more firms conducting research, but doing so with less public statement. However, if the work is happening and it isn't being shared, then is it really contributing to the body of knowledge of the discipline of interior design?

Rylander goes further by noting that "practically all design management research ends up in the functionalist paradigm. This implies relying on objectivist assumptions, a positivist epistemology, and a deterministic view of human nature. As such, it is in stark contrast to the basic principles of design thinking as described in the literature, as well as the design research literature in general." She concludes by stating that design firms could benefit from a more analytical approach to design thinking (Rylander 2008).

Rylander's work suggests that Mahdjoubi, more than Bourdieu, is aligned with current design practice, perhaps to his own detriment. This is not to suggest that empirical work is lacking; research conducted in academic institutions and provided to the design community is certainly welcomed. However, it could be argued that the work flows in only one direction, i.e., from researchers to practitioners. And, more often than not, the implications of that flow are just as Hillier, Musgrove, and O'Sullivan described some three decades ago when writing about the applicability gap between research and design (Hillier et al. 1984). Such difficulties certainly exist and, for now, research remains firmly grounded in the academic institutions with limited appearance in practice.

Implications

With limited research conducted in practice, an applicability gap between academic research and practice, industry press and awards focused on prestige, clients seeking more functional fit, and shifting landscapes for professional service delivery, designers face the dilemma of how to best contribute knowledge to the discipline and, in so doing, how to best grow as a discipline.

As we imagine Popper's World 2 contributions that the press, the awards, and client expectations afford, we realize that none of these really contribute to the type of objective knowledge that advances knowledge. Yet these activities fill our days, incentivize our behaviors, and establish industry recognition.

World 3 knowledge certainly exists in design. It resides in the empirical work conducted at academic research institutions and published in refereed journals. It exists in the handful of firms that engage in scientific inquiry. And it exists in those areas where science has been engaged to find a satisfactory explanation for whatever we, or our clients, have defined as important. But can anyone recall a recent design award that emphasized empirical work and its application to the solution?

With this juxtaposition of World 2/World 3 we find ourselves having to consider whether practice is doing enough to advance knowledge. How do we evaluate whether the prevailing common sense approach to design is good enough? Or do we instinctively know that it isn't?

Conclusion

As a partner in a large design practice that invests in research, I can definitively say that the common sense approach simply isn't enough. The complexity of the

environments in which we live/work/play grows daily. The enormous risks stem-
ming from plowing through that complexity with less than a full armature of
knowledge are not well understood. And so we invest in research and in researchers.
We do so to extend our knowledge, which in turn helps our clients, and we do so
to reduce our risks, our "Known Unknowns."

For an example, we have recently developed tools to extend knowledge about
health. These provide designers with easy access to the research on substances and
toxicity. Creating an easily accessible means with which to make decisions on environmental health is a true contribution to new knowledge in practice. It is a new
way of thinking about wellness and our responsibilities to it. And it is a belief that
we have as a firm about the value of research in design.

To advance the value of the discipline we must advance our knowledge. We must
drive practice into new ways of thinking that may not fit snugly into traditional
modes of practice. We have to prepare ourselves and our successors for a world that
is a bit different from business as usual. To do so, we simply must advance World 3
knowledge. And we must do so with a stronger affiliation to academe.

To reflect on the initial question, I believe that we do not spend enough time
thinking about thinking. We run ourselves ragged trying to keep up with client
demands, competition, public relations, and credential maintenance – and therein
lies the challenge. There's little left in a designer's day to give to broader questions
about World 3 knowledge. As a result, we do not purposefully and aggressively
consider ways to strengthen our theory and our practice. We leave the theorizing
to our colleagues in academe and in so doing reinforce the applicability gap that
Hillier, Musgrove, and O'Sullivan described. We offer little prestige (awards, publications, public relations) to those who seek to advance practice in this way. As
practitioners, we do not signal value for empirical work as our celebrations of successes tend to not include this work. As an unintended consequence, we fail to take
a leadership position in the shifting landscape around us and own it as a framework
for new ways of considering practice and extending knowledge. The complexity is
too great and our contribution remains too unclear. And we put our value to our
clients at risk as a result.

Note

1   Epistemology *n.*: the branch of philosophy that studies the nature of knowledge, its pre-
    suppositions and foundations, and its extent and validity. http://www.thefreedictionary
    .com/. Accessed May 2, 2014.

References

Argyris, C. and Schon, D. 1974. *Theory in Practice: Increasing Professional Effectiveness*. San
    Francisco: Jossey-Bass.

Barnes, J. 2010. "Pulling together value streams for building retrofits," *Green Biz*. http://www.greenbiz.com/blog/2010/08/05/pulling-together-value-streams-building-retrofits. Accessed May 2, 2014.

Bolan, R. S. 1980. "The practitioner as a theorist," *American Planning Association Journal* (July): 261–274.

Bourdieu, P. 1967. "Systems of education and systems of thought," *International Social Science Journal* 19: 338–358.

Drab, T. 1997. "The portrayal of interior design periodicals," in *Interior Design Educators Council Conference Abstracts*, pp. 72–73.

Eagle, P. and Barnes, J. 2010. "The future of design: blue is the new green," *Fast Company* http://www.fastcodesign.com/1662807/the-future-of-design-is-blue-the-new-green. Accessed May 2, 2014.

English, J. F. 2005. *The Economy of Prestige: Prizes, Awards, and the Circulation of Cultural Value*. Cambridge, MA: Harvard University Press.

Gemser, G. and Wijnberg, N. M. 2002. "The economic significance of industrial design awards," *Design Management Journal* 2(1): 61–71.

Green, D., Kleusner, G., and Glenn, P. 2011. Unpublished research. Perkins + Will.

Guba, E. G. and Lincoln, Y. S. 1981. "Epistemological and methodological bases of natural inquiry," *Educational Communication & Technology Journal* 30(4): 233–252.

Hillier, B., Musgrove, J., and O'Sullivan, P. 1984. *Knowledge and Design: Developments in Design Methodology*. New York: John Wiley & Sons, pp. 245–263.

Johansson, U. and Svengren, L. 2008. *Möten kring design: Om relationerna mellan designer, tekniker och ekonomer i fem svenska företag*. Lund: Studentlitteratur.

Mahdjoubi, D. 2003. "Epistemology of design: integrated design and process technology," *IDPT-Society for Design and Process Science*.

Marian, K. 2009, December. "Interior Design Magazine's Hall of Fame Award: What Does the Hall of Fame Tell Us about the Interior Design Profession?" Master's thesis, Washington State University, Department of Interior Design.

Miller, D. 1985. *Popper Selections*. Princeton: Princeton University Press.

Nagel, E. 1979. *The Structure of Science*. Indianapolis: Hackett.

Pinto, C. 1996. "Going natural by design," *Modern Healthcare* 26(45): 39–42, 44–45, 48–52.

Popper, K. 1972. *Objective Knowledge: An Evolutionary Approach*. Oxford: Oxford University Press.

Rylander, A. 2008. "Design thinking as knowledge work: epistemological foundations and practical implications," *International DMI Education Conference on Design Thinking: New Challenges for Designers, Managers, and Organizations*. Cergy-Pointoise, France: ESSEC Business School.

Walsh, V., Roy, R., Bruce, M., and Potter, S. 1992. *Winning by Design: Technology, Product Design and International Competitiveness*. Oxford: Blackwell Business Publishing.

11

Sustainable Life-Span Design: A New Model

Amber Joplin

Background

The US Census Bureau projects the number of people aged 65 and over will increase from 39 million in 2010 to 69 million in 2030, with the 85+ population, doubling by 2025 (Day 1996). Declining birth rates and increasing life-spans result in a shift in population age structure, with nearly one in five US residents expected to be 65 or older by 2030 (Vincent and Velkoff 2010). Individuals are aging in homes, neighborhoods, and communities designed for active, mobile, sighted adults. As their health and mobility begin to deteriorate, elders will no longer be able to operate successfully in the shared community environment. The magnitude of population aging challenges our current system of progressively relocating aging individuals from their homes and communities to senior-targeted environments, whether to amenity-rich retirement communities, near an amenable adult child's home, or an assisted living facility (Heumann 2001). The costs of our current system to individuals, families, society, and the natural environment are enormous (Landorf, Brewer, and Sheppard 2008).

Dramatic demographic changes require correspondingly dramatic changes in the built environment; however, implementing research into the design of environments for elders is challenging because aging, the effect of environments on individuals, and existing social and infrastructure systems are complex. Processes of aging differ in onset, duration, termination, direction, and order (Baltes 1987). Variables impacting elders range from place, space, and relocation (Litwak and Longino 1987); meaning and significant activities (Rubinstein and de Medeiros 2004), family

The Handbook of Interior Design, First Edition. Edited by Jo Ann Asher Thompson and Nancy H. Blossom.

and community connections, programs and policies, access to goods and services, stigma, poverty, safety hazards, crime and pollution (Dahlgren and Whitehead 1991; WHO 2001); access to nature (Ulrich 2002); and to spiritual connection (Sadler and Biggs 2006).

Introduction

This essay utilizes multidisciplinary theoretical models to integrate theories on "aging within the environment" as an initial step in developing a comprehensive model that can be flexibly applied to the design of living and community environments. Models are symbolic artifacts of knowledge used by all disciplines to create, hold, or transfer complex and/or developing information about relationships, processes, change, etc. (Ewenstein and Whyte 2007). In order to distill the primary concepts identified in behavioral and social sciences, education, health, sustainability, systems, and design literatures, I have focused my literature search on models of person and/or environment relationships and then deconstructed the model elements into tables. The resulting comparative tables identify relationships and significant issues that must be considered in person-centered, sustainable life-span design.

Three areas of literature are presented in this essay to identify indicators of sustainable environments for aging. The areas are models of: (1) contexts, (2) values, and (3) person–environment interaction. Organizing the review by models rather than by discipline highlights multidisciplinary factors of environments for elders. These selected models originate from the fields of design, sociology, gerontology, environmental psychology, geography, environmental science, and education. Most address multi-disciplinary relationships and several models are adopted across disciplines, particularly Lawton and Nahemow's (1973) Ecological Model of Aging.

Several key terms in the literatures were defined by combining the perspectives of various recognized scholars. Each model discussed relates to these terms.

Aging

Aging is a natural, developmental, life-course process (Baltes 1987) that involves bi-directional gains and losses over time in emotional, intellectual (Samanez-Larkin, Robertson, Mikels, et al. 2009), social, spiritual (Sadler and Biggs 2006) and physical arenas (Koncelik 2003).[1] US Census data show the continuation of good health "free of problems with personal and instrumental activities of daily living" ranges for women from the ages of 37 to 76, and for men from ages 45 to 80 with many individuals experiencing good health into their 80s and 90s (Kinsella and Velkoff 2001). However, there is a correlation of age with increasing levels of frailty and with chronic illnesses leading to functional limitations. Age-related physiological changes may include losses in mobility, intellectual functioning, and sensory acuity (affecting hearing, vision, touch, taste, and smell) as lung capacity, blood flow, muscle mass, and physiological efficiency decline (Ebersole, Hess, and Luggen 2004). Functional deficits occur at different rates for each individual and may be episodic, chronic, progressive, or cascading, as from a major illness or accident.

The literatures included in this review variously classify aging individuals using chronological age, health, work status, living situation, or other capacity. Most studies identify age ranges that are statistically, socially, or legally associated with their classification. For purposes of comparison between studies this review will demarcate "near old" (55–64), "young old" (65–74), "old old" (75–84), and "oldest old" (85 and above) (Brault 2008). Age classifications in built environment applications are lacking in the literature, essentially limited to the terms "active seniors" or "frail elderly," which latter is applied to people aged 65 and older with significant physical and/or mental problems (Kinsella and Velkoff 2001).

Disability

Contrasting with the typical usage synonymous with sensory, physical, and cognitive limitations (US Department of Justice 2005;[2] US Census Bureau 2005[3]); "disability" is defined as the consequence of the gap between individual capabilities and social or physical demands (WHO 2001). Significant disablement processes occur in and can be ameliorated by changes to the built environment (Verbrugge and Jette 1994).

Systems and sustainability

The literatures express the need for a systems approach to built environments for aging because of the dynamic, multi-directional interrelationships between elements of the environment and its inhabitants. Human systems are in the continuous process of being deliberately designed and redesigned through law or policy, as well as personal and cultural expression, need, and limits (Forrester 1991). A change in one system has an effect on others, and is in turn affected by subsequent changes in those individuals and systems. The concept of sustainability implies an enduring and balanced use of resources that values the needs of all persons (Chiras and Herman 1997).

Models of Contexts

Meaningful research on the interior environment as it relates to aging requires consideration of the multiple personal, social, and physical contexts in which aging occurs (Clarke and Nieuwenhuijsen 2009). These three context models emerge from seminal ecosystem thought in the 1970s categorizing domains and proposing dynamic relationships between them. Meadows' implementation of Daly's Hierarchy of Purpose Model uses economic language to illustrate linkages between environmental sustainability and human well-being (Meadows 1998). Bubolz, Eicher, and Sontag's (1979) Human Ecology Model integrates the subject matter of the evolving human ecology field.[4] Guerin (1992) focuses her Interior Ecosystem Model to frame integrative research in interior design. Together these models identify a framework capable of including a full range of factors relevant to aging.

The hierarchy of purpose model

The Hierarchy of Purpose Model (HOP), adapted by Meadows from the 1977 Daly Triangle, is used as a framework for organizing indicators of sustainability. The triangle is based on (1) the natural world as the "ultimate means" or source for the economy, (2) science and technology as the "intermediate means" for transforming the natural resources to "intermediate ends" (the goods and services which are distributed by the political economy), to achieve (3) the "ultimate ends" (well-being and transcendence, the *summum bonum* subject of theology and ethics (see Figure 11.1).

This model is used to organize the multiple contexts related to aging and the built environment because it provides easily visualized organization and multiple entry points to link additional content. Its major limitations are the hierarchical structure and flows between elements. A weakness of the model for designers is the lack of reference to the built environment. Economic terms such as "built capital" and "human capital" must be translated into the concepts of the design disciplines. The strength of this model is its explicit values orientation linking human well-being to sustainability.

The human ecology model

The Human Ecology Model (HEM) (see Figure 11.2) reframes the content of Meadows' hierarchy of purpose in non-linear, multi-directional constructs visualized in two separate images, a triangle showing major environmental categories with their inner workings, and a series of nested circles that illustrate how the environments are "embedded within each other" in the near environment (Bubolz 1979). Aspects of biological, physical, and social activity are included in each of the categories identified as the Natural Environment, the Human Behavioral Environment, and the Human Constructed Environment.

At the center of both versions is the Human Environed Unit (HEU), a placeholder element that represents any individual or body of humans that share an identity, needs, or goals, such as a family, work group, community, or state. Actual human corporeality and psychology – presence, actions, beliefs, and values – are classified within the behavioral and built environments.[5] Corresponding to Simon's artificial world, the Human Constructed Environment (HCE) category includes all of the "consequences of our collective artifice" (Simon 2001). By definition, this complex and rapidly expanding category is the domain of the designer. The second

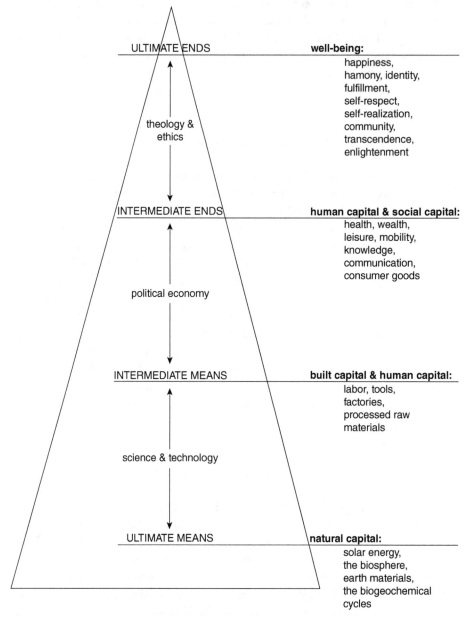

Figure 11.1 The Daly Triangle: Hierarchy of Purpose (Daly 1973 in Meadows 1998: 41). http://www.iisd.org/pdf/s_ind_2.pdf. Accessed October 17, 2008.

version of the Human Ecology Model (Figure 11.3) illustrates (in general agreement with the Hierarchy of Purpose Model) that behavioral and constructed environmental constructs occur within, and are dependent on, the natural environment (NE).

Comparing the two models (see Table 11.1) clarifies both sets of contexts. In addition to sharing the foundation of the natural environment, both models

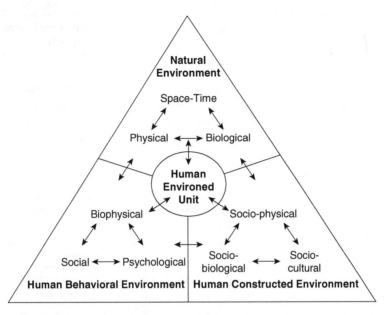

Figure 11.2 The Human Ecology Model (Bubloz, Eicher, and Sontag 1979: 28). Reproduced by permission of the American Association of Family and Consumer Sciences.

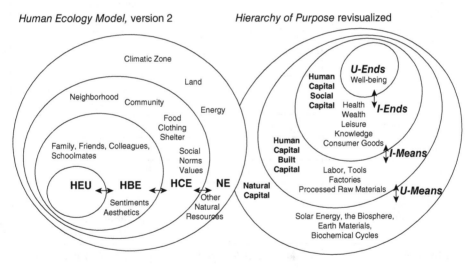

Figure 11.3 Comparison of Human Ecology Model with Hierarchy of Purpose (adapted from Bubloz, Eicher, and Sontag 1979: 29). Adapted with permission of the American Association of Family and Consumer Sciences.

are concerned with human well-being, although it is an implicit goal within the HEU. The major difference in organization is apparent between the HOP intermediate "ends" and "means" constructs organized by type of capital and which are reorganized in HEM into "behavioral" and "constructed" (human-created) environments, more familiar categories for environmental design.

Table 11.1 Hierarchy of Purpose/Human Ecology: comparison of ranges

Hierarchy of Purpose	Comments	Human Ecology
Ultimate Ends	Well-being is the goal of the designed environment	**Human Environed Unit (HEU)**
Well-being		(Implicit)
Happiness, Enlightenment	Internalized values are a significant component of personal well-being	**Human Behavioral Environment (HBE)**
Self-realization, Identity		Psychological: Sentiments, Aesthetics
Fulfillment, Self-respect		
Transcendence		
Intermediate Ends	Individuals and groups are valuable even if not productive	Social: Family, Friends, Colleagues, Schoolmates
Human capital, Leisure		
Health		Biophysical
Social capital	HBE and HCE include the non-desirable consequences of the HCE, on the individual, society, the built environment and the natural environment.	**Human Created Environment (HCE)**
Harmony, Communication		Socio-cultural: Social Norms, Values
Community		Community, Neighborhood
Mobility, Knowledge		Socio-biological
Wealth		
Consumer Goods		Socio-physical: Food, Clothing, Shelter
Intermediate Means		
Built capital:Tools,		
Production Facilities		
Processed Raw Materials		
Human capital: Labor		(socio-biological & socio-cultural)
Ultimate Means	NE does not include pollution, bioengineered crops, domesticated animals, etc. as these are in the HCE	**Natural Environment (NE)**
Natural Capital		Other Natural Resources
Earth Materials, Biosphere		Land, Energy
Biochemical Cycles		
Solar Energy		Climactic Zone
Unclear placement of space and time, although they are part of the natural environment, they are also cultural constructs		Space – Time

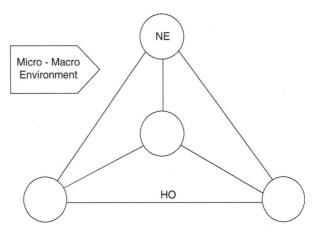

Figure 11.4   Interior Ecosystem Model (Guerin 1992: 257). Reproduced with permission of John Wiley & Sons, Inc.

The interior ecosystem model

Guerin streamlines the human ecology model as a guide for research, renaming and slightly modifying the constructs (see Figure 11.4). This model provides open categories, requiring the researcher to determine content; however, it has the capacity to adapt its structure and elements to accommodate the interacting issues under examination.

Discussion of context models

Meadows' Hierarchy of Purpose Model, Bubolz, Eicher, and Sontag's Human Ecology Model, and Guerin's Interior Ecosystem Model conceptualize relationships between humans and their multiple physical, social, and personal contexts. While all models provide a platform in which environmental issues of aging, such as frailty or disability, can be visualized, they are not specifically addressed. Values of human well-being and environmental sustainability are explicit in the HOP model, but implicit in the others. Values underlying intermediate constructs are not articulated, nor are values such as empowerment of individuals, or the impact of environments on disabled or fragile individuals, which are significant to aging.[6]

Values Model: Modal Patterns for the Treatment of the Aged

The literatures of aging and the built environment are concerned with values of access, empowerment, participation, well-being, aesthetics, efficiency, and sustainability; however, these values are rarely made explicit in models. Moody's Modal

Patterns for the Treatment of the Aged (MPTA) relates social values and perceptions to educational programming outcomes for seniors and has been applied to service design (Heumann 2001) and residential environments for seniors (Hofland 1990). Moody posits four distinct philosophical bases for treatment of older adults: (1) rejection, (2) social services, (3) participation, and (4) self-actualization. Each reflects "modal patterns," "ways society tends to regard old people" (Moody 1976), and exhibits specific characteristics (see Table 11.2).

Table 11.2 Modal patterns for the treatment of the aged (adapted)

Modal patterns for treatment of the aged			Types of values underlying attitudes
Modal pattern	*Characteristics*	*Basic attitude*	
Self-actualization (Stage 4)	Individuation, psychological growth, and self-transcendence	Wisdom, ego-integrity	Psychology, Spirituality (transcendence)
Participation (Stage 3)	Second careers (employment or volunteer activity); senior advocacy; autonomy	Social integration, "normalization"	Political (equality, freedom, happiness)
Social Services (Stage 2)	Transfer payments (welfare, social security); professional care, senior centers	Social conscience, liberalism	Liberalism, Welfare State (ameliorates)
Rejection (Stage 1)	Separation, mandatory retirement; poverty, neglect; family abandonment	Repression, avoidance	Economic (uncorrected abuses of capitalism)

Source: Moody, 1976. Reproduced by permission of Taylor & Francis Group, LLC.

Citing Spengler, Becker, and Mumford, Moody suggests "rejection" arises from a modern consciousness of functionality which prizes growth, development, and progress, but shuns decline and death (Moody 1976). Rejection excludes aging seniors from their places (both roles and locations) in society as their usefulness comes to an end. Moody posits rejection is based on economic values (Moody 1976). Limiting resource expenditures on over-priced and outdated workers, mandatory retirement requires that seniors withdraw from the workplace and accept the lower standard of living represented by a fixed income. In the built environment, successful retirees may enjoy the "gold coast" retirement communities, while the less successful are segregated in low-income apartments and facilities.

The second pattern, social services, is a welfare state response to the needs of aging individuals who have been marginalized (retired) and are identified to be in need of care. This pattern redistributes resources to ameliorate the worst excesses of rejection, but does not fundamentally challenge the prevailing institutions. Corresponding to the medical model, case managers and service providers assume that professionals are most qualified to assess needs and provide services (Putnam 2002). "Transfer payments such as social security, food stamps, or welfare, managed by providers are provided as a "safety net" and are monitored to maintain resource-limited individuals at the poverty level (Moody 1976). The structures of the stage 1 built environment (low-income housing, nursing homes) are supported by these transfer payments, as are senior centers and leisure activity programs.

"Characterized primarily by political values, the pattern of participation challenges age-graded distribution of power and status by demanding the rights of old people that have been denied them, sometimes through the policies alleged to be in their welfare" (Moody 1976). Similar to successful aging, this stage corresponds to the political civil rights and disability equality movements, requiring consciousness-raising within the aging community, retraining of providers, reducing ageism, and implementing built environment changes such as those enforced by the Americans with Disabilities Act 1990 (Putnam 2002). Built environments expressing the value of participation include cooperatives, mixed-age housing, participatory group homes, and programs facilitating aging in place.

The fourth pattern, self-actualization, differs from participation and the earlier patterns because it is not based on or reacting to the economic values of modern society, but is based on humanistic values. Old age constitutes a distinct phase of human development rooted in the particular experience of being aged and presents opportunities "uniquely possible in old age" (Moody 1976). The biological reality of aging is that over time many adults are no longer able to be involved in active and powerful ways, and thus are no longer capable of maintaining their middle-adult roles. Self-actualization "accepts aging on its own terms and discerns in the experience of growing old not a problem to struggle against but an opportunity to reach deeper levels of meaning."

"The prevailing values of Stage 4 are inner-directed and are psychological and spiritual in their orientation" (Moody 1976). Built environments expressing values of self-actualization evidence qualities of choice, meaning, and aesthetics, and provide for meaningful activities and roles. In a self-actualizing society the public built environment, as well as conventional housing, is designed to adapt and support human needs through the entire life cycle (Heumann 2001).

Comparing Moody's MPTA with the contextual models illustrates relationships between values and environmental categories (see Table 11.3). The most obvious link between Meadows' HOP and Moody's MPTA occurs at the self-actualization

Table 11.3 Modal Patterns for the treatment of the aged (adapted)

Hierarchy of Purpose	CONTEXTUAL MODELS		Comments	VALUES MODEL
	Human Ecology	*Interior Ecosystem / Construct of Interest*		*Modal patterns for treatment of the aged*
Ultimate Ends	**Human Environed Unit (HEU)**	**Human Organism (HO)**	*Strong Correlation: based on common terms:*	**Self-actualization**
Well-being, Transcendence	*(Implicit)*	*(Implicit) User-centered*	*Individuation transcendence*	*Spirituality, transcendence*
Enlightenment, Self-realization, Identity				*Wisdom, ego-integrity*
	Human Behavioral Environment (HBE)	**Behavioral Environment (BHE)**		
Fulfillment, Self-respect	*Psychological: Sentiments, Aesthetics*	*Psychological*	*Moody includes the value of "happiness" in the Participation stage*	*Psychology*
Happiness				**Participation**
Intermediate Ends	*Social: Family, Friends, Colleagues, Schoolmates*	*socio-behavioral*	*Strong Correlation: based on social and political constructs*	*Social integration, "normalization"*
Human capital, Leisure		*socio-political*	*[Each modal pattern has human created social and physical environments.]*	*Political (equality, freedom, happiness)*
Health	*Biophysical*	*bio-physical*		*Engaged*
Social capital	**Human Created Environment (HCE)**			
Harmony, Communication	*Socio-cultural: Social Norms, Values*			
Knowledge	*Socio-biological*			

	Community, Neighborhood	Built Environment (BTE)		Social Services
Community				
Wealth				
Mobility, Consumer Goods	Socio-physical: Food, Clothing, Shelter		Moody links leisure (in contrast to meaningful activity) with Social Services	
Intermediate Means				
Built capital: Tools,		site integration	Correlation: based on values such as efficiency oriented to meet the needs of service providers (Labor) and facilities.	Social conscience, liberalism
Production Facilities		energy system		Welfare State (ameliorates worst abuses of economic system)
Processed Raw Materials		building materials		
Human capital: Labor	(socio-biological & socio-cultural)	design		
Ultimate Means	Natural Environment	Natural Environment		**Rejection**
Natural Capital	Other Natural Resources	Resources (+availability)	Weak correlation: Desire to limit use of resources on marginalized populations.	Repression, avoidance
Earth Materials, Biosphere	Land,	Plants, Air, Water	Literal "dust to dust" image of burial, waste products	Economic values (uncorrected abuses of capitalism)
Biochemical Cycles				No services
Solar Energy	Energy Climactic Zone	Daylight, Energy, Climate		

level. Both models use virtually identical language to describe characteristics of this category. The relationship between MPTA participation and HOP's intermediate ends is also clear as the social and political constructs that promote engagement in society match positive social intermediate ends. MPTA social services and HOP intermediate means are linked by the production-related components (labor, facilities, and funding streams) of the bureaucratic systems created to provide services. Provision of services, whether in a nursing home or in the community, requires cost-benefit analysis similar to that used in manufacturing (Hofland 1990). Investment in facilities and costs for labor are managed to create maximum efficiencies for providers. In the built environment this translates into minimal spaces for consumers that are arranged for staff convenience. Phillipson and Powell (2004) describe this society as offering seniors two choices: living independently in a "no care zone" or receiving care in a "no identity zone."

Moody's rejection stage transpires when resource preservation is based on negative economic valuations of aging individuals. Since elders, particularly those representing failures of earning, savings, personal habits, and/or health, are no longer productive members of society, community resources are not invested to ensure full inclusion (Moody 1976). The resulting shared built environment, including housing and transportation, is inadequate, and necessary modifications become the responsibility of individuals, their families, or charities.

Discussion of values model

The MPTA links specific philosophical attitudes to patterns of treatment of aging adults. In the built environment these patterns are etched in wood, glass, and concrete. The pattern of rejection is expressed in a built environment that ignores the needs of elders. The pattern of social services creates facilities primarily designed to be efficient for providers (Heumann 2001). Participative built environment patterns include individualized, cooperatively planned, supportive living and activity spaces and aging-in-place modifications. The only examples I have found of self-actualizing built environments are in smaller closed communities such as religious orders (Snowdon 2001).

Moody's MPTA model is particularly relevant for frail and disabled seniors, as care and support options are identified under several modal patterns. In identifying social values underlying the built environment, this model integrates a significant element not articulated in other models. The MPTA also demonstrates how constructive values can be misapplied to create negative outcomes. All of the values identified in the four environmental constructs – resource preservation, efficiency, equality, and well-being – are in fact properly applied within the environments that they correspond to. Thus, for example, resource preservation is a sustainable approach to the natural environment, while efficiency operationalizes sustainability in the built environment.[7] Similarly, self-actualization is the sustainable value relating to human well-being; however, it is unsustainable when applied across all environments. Citizenship in society requires balancing individual desires (choice) with the common good, and preserving opportunities and benefits to all members, rather than only privileged individuals (Heumann 2001). Societies that prize all individuals invest resources to ensure social justice for all current and future members of society.

Person–Environment Interaction Models

Environmental gerontology is based on the concept that there is a relationship between persons and their environment and that this relationship can be described, explained, and modified in order to improve quality of life for aging individuals (Wahl 2004). Lawton and Nahemow's Ecological Model of Aging is the foundational person–environment (P–E) interaction, illustrating effects of congruence and incongruence between persons and their socio-physical environment. Wahl and Oswald's "person-environment processes with developmental outcomes" suggests means by which elements of the environment support the preservation of identity (self-actualization) and autonomy (social). Wahl and Lang's SPOT Analysis distinguishes changes in elders' value structures as their functionality diminishes. Values typically articulated in the person–environment literatures include the self-actualization values of well-being, autonomy, and identity, and political values of equality, often balanced with economic values of cost and efficiency.

The ecological model of aging (competence-press model)

Lawton and Nahemow's Ecological Model of Aging (see Figure 11.5), commonly referred to as the Competence-Press Model (CPM), represents individual competence within environmental demands. Competence (x-axis) is defined as "relatively stable capacities of biological health, sensory and motor skills, and cognitive function" that can change because of illness or injury (Lawton [1999] in Scheidt and Norris-Baker 2003). Environmental press (y-axis) includes both objective environmental conditions and subjective assessment of their impacts, consisting of external "forces appraised by the individual as possessing a demand or supporting quality" (Lawton [1999] in Scheidt and Norris-Baker 2003). Both competence and press are dynamic.

The mapping surface of the model shows alternative outcomes identified as behaviors and affect (mood) resulting from the level of match between the capacities of the person and the environment. An optimal match between personal competence and environmental press results in positive mood and behavior, while a poor match results in negative mood and behavior. Sub-zones such as the "zone of maximum performance potential" illustrate benefits of moderate challenge, and the "zone of maximum comfort" the relaxing experience of reduced press. To either side of the optimal area lie narrow marginal zones buffering the great negative expanse

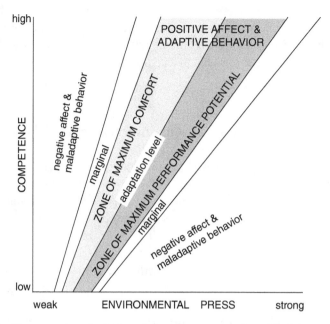

Figure 11.5 The general ecological model or Competence-Press Model as originally suggested by Lawton and Nahemow (1973); reproduced after Lawton 2000: 191. Reprinted with permission of the American Psychological Association.

where press is overwhelming (to the right), or conversely, demands are so low (on the left) that they result in helplessness. This model proposes that individuals with low competence require less demanding environments and have narrower optimal zones than individuals with high levels of competence; thus the former are more quickly overwhelmed or under-challenged.

Rubinstein and de Medeiros critique the CPM, contending it describes an organism's response to the environment rather than a person's response (Rubinstein and de Medeiros 2004). They posit that it is not the outside environment that directly presses on the individual, but that person's culturally influenced internal standard. An extension of the anthropological concept of cultural competence, the elder abstracts meanings from the originating culture and interprets it to establish standards for personal competence. Over the lifetime, these meanings become a sort of personal morality of the self; thus if the elder can no longer perform a personally distinguishing activity– which can be as simple as making tea – their identity is diminished.[8] Person–environment processes are linked to developmental outcomes.

Behavior, identified as an outcome in the CPM, has been repeatedly demonstrated to be affected by the ability to function, whether because of control, permission, or well-matched facilities (Clarke and Nieuwenhuijsen 2009). On the other

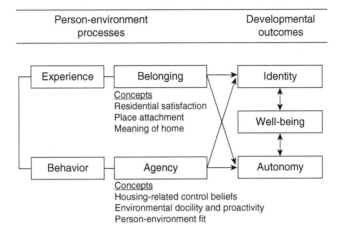

Figure 11.6 Overarching conceptual framework on person–environment relationships in later life. (Wahl and Oswald 2010: figure 8.1). Reproduced by permission of SAGE Publications Ltd.

hand, the equally significant personal experience of the environment at the level of meaning, satisfaction, and attachment over time is more difficult to access and measure, thus may be overlooked (Wahl, Fänge, Oswald, Gitlin, and Iwarsson 2009). Wahl and Oswald's person–environment processes with developmental outcomes (PEDO) addresses both personal identity (the self) as well as functionality (agency). Their flow diagram proposes that well-being emerging from autonomy is supported by P–E fit. However identity-based well-being is supported by experiencing meaning and belonging (see Figure 11.6). Poulet proposes that the self requires place and becomes one with place, just as the organism requires space for.[9]

The social-physical places over time model

The significance of agency and belonging changes over the life-span. Relocation research on the moves of older adults identifies that first moves are expected in the early years after retirement and are often selected to enhance agency (e.g., fewer stairs, close to places of activity, etc.). Second moves appear later in life and are motivated by desire for both support and continuity, for example relocation to be closer to one's children (Wahl and Lang 2004). Third moves, such as to a nursing home, are problematic as this move is required to provide care (agency) at a later time in life when the personal priority has shifted to belonging. Wahl and Lang's Social-Physical Places Over Time Model (SPOT) (see Figure 11.7 and Table 11.4) illustrates the trajectory of human motivation from prioritizing agency in middle adulthood, to valuing social-physical belonging for the oldest old.

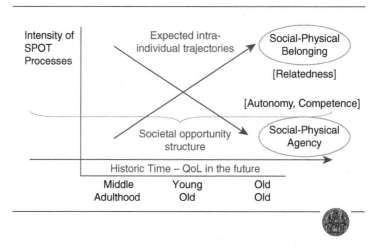

Figure 11.7 Social-Physical Places Over Time Model (SPOT): Implications for Future QoL in Old Age. Wahl and Lang (2006: 889). Reproduced by permission of Elsevier Academic Press.

The SPOT model is intended to integrate the developmental worldview with the environmental fit model. It is based on three concepts: place, its social construction, and its dynamic nature. Place is central, because "every aging person's day-to-day behavior is embedded within given physical and spatial surroundings" that have meaning rooted in characteristics and experiences (Wahl and Lang 2004).[10] These places are "socially constructed, socially filled out, and socially shaped physical environments" and consequently places are dynamic, showing stability and change over time as people age and environments are modified (Wahl and Lang 2004).

Table 11.4 Person–environment fit dynamics in SPOT

Stage of aging	Relevance of social-physical agency	Relevance of social-physical belonging	Person–environment fit dynamics in SPOT		
			Stimulation & activation	Safety & familiarity	Continuity & meaning
Middle adulthood	+++	+	+++	+	+
Early age/ "young old"	++	++	++	++	++
"Old-old"/ oldest old	+	+++	+	+++	+++

Source: Wahl and Lang 2004: table 1.2 (p. 24). Reproduced by permission of Springer Publishing Co. with kind permission from Springer Science+Business Media B.V.

A reference table of well-being precursors over time, such as person-environment fit dynamics (Table 11.4), an earlier presentation of SPOT, enriches the conversation for designers because it sheds light on the specific needs that should be accommodated in the environment for phases of adulthood. In middle age, when the relevance of agency is high, the need is for stimulation and action. For the young old, the relevance of agency and belonging is balanced, as are needs for stimulation, activity, safety, familiarity, continuity, and meaning. In old age, as the relevance of belonging increases and agency declines, the need increases for safety, familiarity, continuity, and meaning. A sustainable and humanistic approach to design would infuse essential elements required for safety, familiarity, continuity, and meaning into environments built for middle adulthood and early age to maintain well-being throughout the entire life-span. The reference table could expand to integrate the needs of disabled adults who lose agency earlier in the life course, and suggest strategies for populations with differing types of functional deficits.

Comparing terms from the person–environment models (Table 11.5) with those previously identified in the context and values models reveals their orientation to observable (external) behavior. The interface between the individual and the social and built environment neglects aspects of well-being related to self-actualization that are internal to the individual. The person–environment models essentially disregard the natural environment despite research showing the importance of access to nature in maintaining physical and mental health (Ulrich 2002). On the other hand, they clearly articulate multiple interacting levels of the social environment and demonstrate sensitivity to residential issues, including mention of neighborhoods and distances.[11]

Discussion of person–environment interaction models

Person–environment models from environmental gerontology provide a basis for understanding the centrality of the environment for individual agency and behavior. As such, they provide a theoretical underpinning for addressing social processes implicated in enabling and disabling behavioral environments, as well as providing justification for intervention in the built environment. Lawton and Nahemow's CPM is classic precisely because it continues to provide a clear presentation of foundational concepts, facilitating multi-disciplinary interaction regarding P–E fit.

Wahl and Oswald's PEDO integrates concepts from the psychology of aging and environmental psychology, proposing that interactive P–E processes can be pathways to well-being, thus extending the connection between person and environment into the self-actualization level. Person–environment fit dynamics in SPOT develop the connections identified in PEDO and add the dynamic elements of time and place significant to understanding P–E processes as part of a system. Without self-identity components, research centered on CPM, particularly for housing, actually supports existing materialistic systems (Moody 1993), modulating service

Table 11.5 Comparison of terms from person–environment models with the context and values models

CONTEXTUAL MODELS			VALUES	PERSON ENVIRONMENT
Hierarchy of Purpose	Human Ecology	Interior Ecosystem	Modal patterns	Terms from person–environment models
Ultimate Ends	**Human Environed Unit**	**Human Organism**	**Self-actualization**	
Well-being, Transcendence	(Implicit)	(Implicit) User- centered	Spirituality, transcendence	Well-being (PEDO)
Enlightenment, Self-realization, Identity			Wisdom, ego-integrity	Identity (PEDO)
	Human Behavioral Environment	**Behavioral Environment**		
Fulfillment, Self-respect	Psychological: Sentiments, Aesthetics	Psychological	Psychology	Affect (CPM) Continuity / Meaning (SPOT)
Happiness			**Participation**	(Positive affect)
Intermediate Ends	Social: Family, Friends, Colleagues, Schoolmates	socio-behavioral	Social integration, "normalization"	Behavior (CPM – P) Press (CBM – E) personal environment: the number of children and number of close friends (L) small-group environment: residents of an assisted living facility and employees of a small business (L) Relatedness (SPOT)
Human capital, Leisure		socio-political	Political (equality, freedom, happiness)	Autonomy (PEDO & SPOT) Simulation / Activation (SPOT)
Health	Biophysical	bio-physical	Engaged	Competence (CBM – P & SPOT) Comfort (CPM – P) Safety (SPOT)
Social capital	**Human Created Environment**			
Harmony, Communication	Socio-cultural: Social Norms, Values			Press (CPM – E, PxE)
Knowledge	Socio-biological			Familiarity (SPOT)

Table 11.5 (*Continued*)

CONTEXTUAL MODELS			VALUES	PERSON ENVIRONMENT
Hierarchy of Purpose	*Human Ecology*	*Interior Ecosystem*	*Modal patterns*	*Terms from person–environment models*
Community	*Community, Neighborhood*			*Press (CPM – E) supra-personal environment: age mix of one's neighborhood or range of health mix in a nursing home (L) physical environment: housing characteristics, the amount of seating space, and distances (L)Safety (SPOT)*
Wealth				
Mobility, Consumer Goods	*Socio-physical: Food, Clothing, Shelter*	*Built Environment*		
Intermediate Means			*Social Services*	
Built capital: Tools, Production Facilities Processed Raw Materials		*site integration energy system building materials*	*Social conscience, liberalism Welfare State (ameliorates worst abuses of economic system)*	mega-social environment: legislative regulations and liberal capitalism (L)
Human capital: Labor	*(socio-biological & socio-cultural)*	*design*		Performance (CPM – P)
Ultimate Means	**Natural Environment**	**Natural Environment**	**Rejection**	*Press (CPM – E)*
Natural Capital Earth Materials, Biosphere Biochemical Cycles Solar Energy	*Other Natural Resources Land Energy Climactic Zone*	*Resources (+availability) Plants, Air, Water Daylight, Energy, Climate*	*Repression, avoidance Economic values (uncorrected abuses of capitalism) No services*	

Key

CPM	Competence-Press Model
PEDO	Person-environment processes developmental outcomes
SPOT	Social-physical places over time
L	Environments identified by Lawton (quoted in Wahl and Lang, 2004: 7–8)

provision toward the participation level, by demonstrating positive behavioral and affective outcomes.[12] The models illustrate that over-support is equally disabling as lack of care, suggesting that facilities and services must be calibrated to the needs of individual persons.[13] The strength of the P–E fit models is illustrated in their application to residential structure and organization, particularly significant for identifying characteristics that create or reduce disability.[14]

Findings/Discussion

The findings of this literature review of models are multiple. Elders, aging, and contexts for aging are complex and are dynamically interrelated in interacting systems that affect individuals, society, institutions, the built environment, and the natural environment. The concept of the built environment as an expression of values is immediately usable for researchers and practitioners to consider in person-centered, sustainable design.

The comprehensive tabular model presented in this essay retains the intent and wording of the source models and can be used for interdisciplinary collaboration or to populate existing comprehensive design models such as those of Buboltz, Eicher, and Sontag, or Guerin. Additional work is needed to simplify the tabular model and create a visual structure that is effective in communicating essential concepts. Although the genesis of this study is the needs of aging populations and the elderly within the built environment, similar concerns, beyond the scope of this essay, are likely true for other populations, such as children or individuals with disabilities, not served by our current built environment.

This essay also illustrates how many forms of visualization can be labeled a "model." Models can be words, illustrations, tables, line drawings, three-dimensional objects, or computer simulations. While these models were discussed in terms of content and terminology, they could also have been reviewed for effectiveness in presentation. Some designs, such as the Lawton/Nahemow P–E fit model, were exceptionally comprehensible, while others, with equally significant content, such as the SPOT model, were very difficult to decipher, necessitating an explanatory table. It is likely that successful models that inspire years of debate are models that communicate well visually.

Conclusion

This essay presents aging as a natural aspect of human experience, integrating issues of aging populations and the elderly within the social and built community in order to improve individual well-being and environmental sustainability. The models of context suggest that the entire society and economic system is involved in our system for dealing with issues of aging populations and elders. Moody's model of values exposes the lack of capital investment that results in a built environment that effectively rejects aging and disabled individuals. The person–environment fit models illustrate the importance of matching environments to needs over time.

Aging seniors in Western society face a built environment that challenges well-being by progressively limiting their life activity space by excluding, and in some cases expelling, increasingly frail individuals from their environments of choice. Further, health effects, their economic consequences, and resource use are clearly interconnected; thus, the disabling impact of most existing built environments on aging individuals must be included in any meaningful discussion of urban sustainability.

While there is much research on aging and specific interior elements, there is a gap in the integration of knowledge from across the disciplines, and in its availability to designers. Planners and designers operationalize society's values as expressed in building codes, market preferences, and implicit expectations (Allen 2000); however, they are simultaneously positioned to be agents of systemic change (Buchanan 1992). In order to identify, design, and advocate for successful approaches to built environments for aging, researchers and practitioners need to integrate the complex range of elements making up current planning and design practice. Comprehensive environmental design research and planning, as well as design practice, must include life-span needs in order to serve individuals and the planet with holistic sustainability.

Acknowledgments

I gratefully acknowledge Nancy H. Blossom for practical and theoretical assistance in developing and articulating integrative approaches to complex systems.

Notes

1   "As a dynamic human factor, aging is a complex blending of physiological, psychophysical psychological and sociological change. Aging is a process of change personality through intensification of individual characteristics. People who have reached advanced years (75–95) will be a very diverse population with increased differences between individuals than younger populations" (Koncelik 2003: 121).
2   "An individual with a disability is defined by the ADA as a person who has a physical or mental impairment that substantially limits one or more major life activities, a person who has a history or record of such an impairment, or a person who is perceived by others as having such an impairment."
3   "The Census Bureau defines disability as a long-lasting sensory, physical, mental, or emotional condition. This condition can make it difficult for a person to do activities such as walking, climbing stairs, dressing, bathing, learning, or remembering. It can impede a person from being able to go outside the home alone or to work at a job or business, and it includes persons with severe vision or hearing impairments."
4   The authors suggest the Human Ecology Model as a comprehensive framework not only for the study of human behavior, but also as a basis for delineating and integrating the subject matter of their field. P. 28.
5   Any environment created by humans or adapted to human goals, including all modifications of physical, biological, social, and cultural constructs is included: the positive constructions of language, art, housing, and domesticated foods, as well as the less desirable outcomes of human action such as pollution or repressive cultural patterns.
6   Bubolz and Sontag write about the ethical underpinnings of the Human Ecology Theory in Boss et al. 1993: ch. 17.

7 Creating and managing the built environment efficiently typically requires greater initial resource inputs; however, the results are more sustainable (resource-preserving and waste-minimizing) over the long term, than designs based strictly on minimal resource use (Chiras and Herman 1997).

8 "Moreover, these activities and routines are at the core of the self and are symbolically significant to the person; they are what the person does and who she is. Routines and activities are embodied within the person through their unconscious nature and the habitus" (Bourdieu [1977, 1990] in Rubinstein and de Medeiros 2004: 72).

9 "Beings surround themselves with the places they find themselves, the way one wraps oneself up in a garment that is at one and the same time a disguise and a characterization. Without places, beings would be abstractions. It is places that make their image precise and that give them the necessary support thanks to which we can assign them a place in out mental place, dream of them and remember them" (Poulet [1977] in Chaudhury 2003).

10 "Having lived in a specific place implies an enormous amount of implicit knowledge related to everyday routines, geographical distances inside and outside the home, distinguishing neighbors from strangers, seasonal changes of the sunlight and community services" (Wahl and Lang 2004: 20).

11 Not discussed in this text, but included in the chart for robustness, are Lawton's five strata of an environment: physical, personal, small-group, supra-personal, and mega-social, four of which are social constructs (Wahl and Lang 2004: 7–8).

12 For examples applied to place experience see Calkins and Weisman 1999: 130–140.

13 For examples of expending resources on direct care rather than supporting self-care see Heumann 2001: 119–136.

14 For a comparison of therapeutic goals for environments for the elderly see Calkins and Weisman 1999: 134.

References

Allen, S. 2000. "Introduction: practice vs. project," in *Introduction to Practice, Architecture, Technique and Representation*. Australia: G+B Arts International.

Baltes, P. B. 1987. "Theoretical propositions of life-span developmental psychology: on the dynamics between growth and decline," *Developmental Psychology* 23(5): 611–626.

Boss, P. G. et al., eds. 1993. *Sourcebook of Family Theories and Methods: A Contextual Approach*. New York: Plenum Press.

Brault, M. 2008. *Review of the Changes to the Measurement of Disability in the 2008 American Community Survey*. Washington DC: US Census Bureau.

Bubolz, M. M., Eicher, J. B., and Sontag, M. S. 1979. "The human ecosystem: a model," *Journal of Home Economics* (Spring): 28–31.

Buchanan, R. 1995. "Wicked problems in design thinking," in V. Margolis and R. Buchanan (eds.), *The Idea of Design*. Cambridge, MA: MIT Press, pp. 3–20.

Calkins, M. P. and Weisman, G. D. 1999. "Models for environmental assessment," in B. Schwarz and R. Brent (eds.), *Aging, Autonomy, and Architecture: Advances in Assisted Living*. Baltimore: Johns Hopkins University Press, pp. 130–140.

Chaudhury, H. 2003. "Quality of life and place therapy," in R. J. Scheidt and P. G. Windley (eds.), *Physical Environments and Aging: Critical Contributions of M. Powell Lawton to Theory and Practice*. New York: Haworth Press, pp. 85–103.

Chiras, D. A. and Herman, J. 1997. "Sustainable community development: a systems approach," in I. Audirac (ed.), *Rural Sustainable Development in America*. New York: John Wiley & Sons, pp. 107–127.

Clarke, P. and Nieuwenhuijsen, E. R. 2009. "Environments for healthy aging: a critical review," *Maturitas* 64(1): 14–19.

Dahlgren, G. and Whitehead, M. 1991. *Policies and Strategies to Promote Social Equity in Health*. Stockholm: Institute for Future Studies.

Day, J. C. 1996. *Population projections of the United States by Age, Sex, Race, and Hispanic Origin: 1995 to 2050*. US Bureau of the Census, Current Population Reports, P25–1130. Washington DC: US Government Printing Office. http://www.census.gov/prod/1/pop/p25-1130.pdf. Accessed February 3, 2011.

Ebersole, P., Hess, P. A., and Luggen, A. S. 2004. *Toward Healthy Aging: Human Needs and Nursing Response*. St. Louis, MO: Mosby.

Ewenstein, B. and Whyte, J. K. 2007. "Visual representations as 'artefacts of knowing'," *Building Research & Information* 35(1): 81–89.

Forrester, J. W. 1991. "System dynamics and the lessons of 35 years," repr. 1993 in K. B. De Greene (ed.), *A Systems Based Approach to Policy Making* Boston: Kluwer Academic.

Guerin, D. A. 1992. "Interior design research: a human ecosystem model," *Home Economics Research Journal* 20: 4.

Heumann, L. F. 2001. "The role of the built environment in holistic delivery of home- and community-based care services to frail elderly persons," in L. F. Heumann, M. E. McCall, and D. P. Boldy (eds.), *Empowering Frail Elderly People: Opportunities and Impediments in Housing, Health, and Support Service Delivery*. Westport, CT: Praeger, pp. 119–136.

Hofland, B. F. 1990. "Value and ethical issues in residential environments for the elderly, " in D. Tilson (ed.), *Aging in Place: Supporting the Frail Elderly in Residential Environments*. Glenview, IL, pp. 287–309.

Kinsella, K. and Velkoff, V. A. 2001. *An Aging World: 2001*. US Census Bureau, p. 41. http://www.census.gov/prod/2001pubs/p95-01-1.pdf. Accessed September 29, 2009.

Koncelik, J. A. 2003. "Human factors of aging and the micro-environment: personal surroundings, technology and product development," *Journal of Housing for the Elderly* 46: 117–134.

Landorf, C., Brewer, G., and Sheppard, L. 2008. "The urban environment and sustainable aging: critical issues and assessment indicators," *Local Environment* 13(6): 497–514.

Lawton, M. P. 2000. "Quality of life, depression, and end-of-life attitudes and behaviors," in G. M. Williamson, P. A. Parmelee, and D. R. Shaffer (eds.), *Physical Illness and Depression in Older Adults*. New York: Plenum, pp. 147–171.

Lawton, M. P. and Nahemow, L. 1973. "Ecology and the aging process," in C. Eisdorfer and L. M. Powell (eds.), *The Psychology of Adult Development and Aging*. Washington DC: American Psychological Association, pp. 619–674.

Litwak, E. and Longino, C. F. 1987. "Migration patterns among the elderly: a developmental perspective," *The Gerontologist* 27: 266–272.

Meadows, D. H. 1998. *Indicators and Information Systems for Sustainable Development*. A report to the Balaton Group. Hartland, VT: The Sustainability Institute.

Moody, H. R. 1976. "Philosophical presuppositions of education for old age," *Educational Gerontology: An International Quarterly* 1: 1–16.

Moody, H. R. 1993. "Overview: what is critical gerontology and why is it important?", in T. Cole, W. Achenbaum, P. Jakobi, and R. Kastenbaum (eds.), *Voices and Visions of Aging: Toward a Critical Gerontology*. New York: Springer.

Phillipson, C. and Powell, J. L. 2004. "Risk, social welfare and old age," in E. Tulle (ed.), *Old Age and Agency*. New York: Nova Science, pp. 17–26.

Putnam, M. 2002. "Linking aging theory and disability models: increasing the potential to explore aging with physical impairment," *The Gerontologist* 42(6): 799–806.

Rubinstein, R. L. and de Medeiros, K. 2004. "Ecology and the aging self," *Annual Review of Gerontology and Geriatrics* 23: 59–84.

Sadler, E. and Biggs, S. 2006. "Exploring the links between spirituality and successful aging," *Journal of Social Work Practice* 20(3): 267–280.

Samanez-Larkin, G. R., Robertson, E. R., Mikels, J. A., et al. 2009. "Selective attention to emotion in the aging brain," *Psychology and Aging* 24(3): 519–529.

Scheidt, R. and Norris-Baker, C., eds. 2003. "The general ecological model revisited: evolution, current status, and continuing challenges," in *Annual Review of Gerontology and Geriatrics*, vol. 23. New York: Springer.

Simon, H. A. 2001. "'Seek and ye shall find': how curiosity engenders discovery," in K. D. Crowley, C. D. Schunn, and T. Okada (eds.), *Designing for Science: Implications from Everyday Classroom and Professional Settings*. Mahwah, NJ: Lawrence Erlbaum Associates, pp. 3–18.

Snowdon D. 2001. *Aging with Grace: What the Nun Study Teaches Us about Leading Longer, Healthier, and More Meaningful Lives*. New York: Bantam Books.

Ulrich, R. S. 2002. "Effects of gardens on health outcomes: theory and research," in C. Cooper Marcus and M. Barnes (eds.), *Healing Gardens: Therapeutic Benefits and Design Recommendations*, New York: John Wiley & Sons, pp. 27–86.

US Census Bureau. 2005. *American Community Survey: Subject Definitions*. Washington DC: United States Census Bureau, pp. 31–32.

US Census Bureau. 2009. *Disability Status and the Characteristics of People in Group Quarters: A Brief Analysis of Disability Prevalence among the Civilian Noninstitutionalized and Total Populations in the American Community Survey*. Washington DC: United States Census Bureau.

US Department of Justice. 2005. *A Guide to Disability Rights Laws*. US Department of Justice, Civil Rights Division, Disability Rights Section. http://www.ada.gov/cguide.htm. Accessed October 7, 2009.

Verbrugge L. M., and Jette, A. M. 1994. "The disablement process," *Social Science & Medicine* 38(1): 1–14.

Vincent, G. K., and Velkoff, V. A. 2010. *The Next Four Decades for the Older Population in the United States: 2010 to 2050*. Washington DC: US Department of Commerce, Economics and Statistics Administration, US Census Bureau. http://purl.access.gpo.gov/GPO/LPS126596. Accessed February 3, 2011.

Wahl, H.-W. 2008. *Environmental Gerontology and the Psychology of Aging*. Workshop at CASE in Lund, Sweden. April 10–11, Slide 26. Published in P. M. Conn (ed.), *Handbook of Models for Human Aging*. Amsterdam: Elsevier Academic Press (2006).

Wahl, H.-W., Fänge, A., Oswald, F., Gitlin, L. N., and Iwarsson, S. 2009. "The home environment and disability-related outcomes in aging individuals: what is the empirical evidence?" *The Gerontologist* 49(3): 355–367.

Wahl, H.-W. and Lang, F. R. 2004. "Aging in context across the adult life course: integrating physical and social environmental research perspectives," *Annual Review of Gerontology and Geriatrics* 23: 1–33.

Wahl, H.-W. and Lang, F. R. 2006. "Psychological aging: a contextual view," in P. M. Conn, (ed.), *Handbook of Models for Human Aging.* Amsterdam: Elsevier Academic Press, pp. 881–895.

Wahl, H.-W. and Oswald, L. N. 2010. "Environmental Perspectives on Ageing," in C. Phillipson and D. Dannefer (eds.), *The SAGE Handbook of Social Gerontology.* London: Sage Publications, pp. 111–124.

Weisman, G. D. and Diaz-Moore, K. 2003. *Vision and Values: M. Powell Lawton and the Philosophical Foundations of Environment-Aging Studies.* Binghampton, NY: Haworth Press.

WHO (World Health Organization). 2001. *International Classification of Functioning, Disability and Health.* ICF, Geneva: World Health Organization. http://www.who.int/classifications/icf/en/. Accessed October 24, 2008.

12

Frameworks for Decision-Making in Design for the Aging

Halime Demirkan

Introduction

Different aspects of design epistemology have been emphasized in the design literature for several years. Because of the nature of the design process, designers solve
problems that are not well defined and the methods that they use are not fully understood (Demirkan 1998, 2005). Although the final design goals may be unclear at the
beginning of the design process, the sub-goals must be well defined by the designer
throughout the entire design process (Akin 1986; Cross 2006; Lawson 1990).

As Cross explains, while designers deal with vague problems, their "mode of
thinking is constructive" and they use "codes that translate abstract requirements
into concrete objects" (Cross 1982). When Cross distinguishes design from other
ways of knowing, he emphasizes the importance of knowing, thinking, and acting
(Cross 2001). Further, Cross adds that designers develop an intellectual awareness
by making explicit analyses and comparisons of the paradigms by layering the
approaches of Simon's "rational problem-solving" and Schon's constructivism of
"reflective practice" (Cross 2001; Schon 1983, 1987; Simon [1969] 1996).

A "rational problem-solving" approach means that designers are "concerned with
how things 'ought' to be…in order to attain goals and to function." According to
Simon, "certain phenomena are 'artificial' in a very specific sense; they are as they
are only because of a system being molded, by goals or purposes, to the environment
in which it lives" (Simon [1969] 1996; Visser 2010).

Constructivism of "reflective practice" problem-solving, as explained by Schon,
is an approach that integrates or links thought and action with reflection. It involves

The Handbook of Interior Design, First Edition. Edited by Jo Ann Asher Thompson
and Nancy H. Blossom.
© 2015 John Wiley & Sons, Ltd. Published 2015 by John Wiley & Sons, Ltd.

thinking about and critically analyzing one's actions with the goal of improving one's professional practice. Engaging in reflective practice requires individuals to assume the perspective of an external observer in order to identify the assumptions and feelings underlying their practice and then to speculate about how these assumptions and feelings affect practice (Imel 1992).

In the following essay, the focus is on how designers solve problems in the conceptual design phase; a phase in which information-processing and decision-making are very intensive as a consequence of generating and evaluating alternative ideas. The aim is to demonstrate an epistemological and methodological approach that permits researchers to capture, describe, prioritize, act on, and evaluate alternative design solutions. Thus, the main emphasis of the essay is to provide a framework for understanding how methods and knowledge are linked within the cognitive strategies of design when creating interiors. For example, in design, the designer constructs a conceptual model of the artifact by abstracting knowledge from previous experiences and information stored in the memory. These conceptual representations are linked both with the external forms of knowledge as sketches or drawings and with the internal representations of the model as visual imagery.

The framework for understanding how this works is discussed through a focus on aging adults. This population was selected as the focus because of the complexity of issues that confront designers when creating interior spaces for maturing populations. Within the scope of this discussion, this complexity is addressed only to explain the framework; a complete study would involve many more layers of modeling.

A Framework for the Acquisition and Generation of Knowledge in the Conceptual Phase of Design Problem-Solving

Although design as a discipline has its specific characteristics, measures, and procedures, these have not been extensively analyzed, described, or formalized. Therefore, it can be stated that there is no theoretical knowledge base for design. Knowledge acquisition is a different process in design and yet there is no formal methodology that has proven effective. Knowledge is generated and accumulated through action. Designing for maturing populations and judging the results is the accepted general model. This is a cyclical process in which knowledge is used to create designs, and designs are evaluated to build knowledge.

As pointed out previously, designers construct a conceptual model of the built environment by abstracting knowledge from previous experiences and information stored in their memory (Demirkan, Pultar, and Ozguc 1992). Knowledge may be the truth or a rule of thumb that usually does not change over time, while the latter two can be modified according to the designer. Some of this knowledge is composed of facts and unlikely to change, while other knowledge is more nebulous and subject to change.

There are three major knowledge sources from which designers gather information when problem-solving: the relevant community of designers, experts, and clients; the relevant media, such as books, drawings, codes, journals, internet sources, and visual outlets; and the relevant domain accumulated by observing and modeling (Demirkan 1998).

In the acts of building and using design knowledge, questions are asked, answers are given, and decisions are made. The process through which these three factors are formed is the solution to success in building knowledge (Owen 2007). If the question in knowledge using or doing (building) is theoretical or methodological, in other words, if the designer is seeking to understand a phenomenon or process, the design is a conceptual model. The output of the design process is a design solution and not an artifact.

The design model describes how the conceptual model is realized with representational techniques that are the various drawings or computer representations of the artifacts. The conceptual models are more concerned with "finding" or discovering; design models are oriented toward "making" and inventing.

The process of knowledge using and building is fundamentally the same for the conceptual and design models. The differences are more in the purpose of the activity. The purpose of designing is to transform a concept into a design description in such a way that the artifact being described is capable of producing the determined function. Design requires a representational framework that has sufficient expressive power to capture the nature of the concepts that support the design process.

Certain aspects of maturing populations determine the decision-making processes used in the design of interior spaces. These aspects may involve age, sex, anthropometric dimensions, education level, ability level, use of assistive devices, and income level. Such important interacting and variable design elements must be considered in a design problem-solving process to satisfy the needs of maturing populations. Moreover, determining these requirements becomes a difficult process because of the imprecise and uncertain specifications and priorities of maturing populations (Afacan and Demirkan 2010). Thus, the requirements of the interior determine the decisions made in the design process. This being the case, knowledge is not a set of descriptions but an analytical abstraction (Demirkan 2005).

The conceptual design phase has four stages: concrete experience is followed by observations and reflections that lead to the formation of abstract concepts and generalizations, which are then tested through sketches. This is a circular process in which the actions are repeated until an optimum solution is found (Demirbas and Demirkan 2003).

Linking Methods and Knowledge within Cognitive Strategies

In order to provide an optimal design solution for maturing populations, designers need to operate within an effective cognitive strategy. Over the last four decades, design research has largely concentrated on designers' interactions with the design process and their engagement with design problems as a sequence of strategies (Akin 1986; Cross 1989; Lawson 1990; Schon 1983; Simon [1969] 1996). According to the literature, a cognitive strategy is the general plan of a sequence of particular actions employed by a designer throughout the design process (Afacan and Demirkan 2011). In other words, a designer's strategy refers to how a particular designer tackles a design problem.

The implementation of a design strategy varies from one designer to another because design problem-solving is based on the subjective interpretations of each designer (Demirkan 1998). This means that an effective cognitive strategy for one designer may be quite different from the cognitive strategy of another designer (Dorst and Cross 2001).

Even though design strategies may vary from designer to designer, according to Cross there are two primary types of cognitive strategies that designers rely upon: convergent and divergent (Cross 1989). The convergence-based design strategy is concerned with selecting the most appropriate solution from the alternatives regarding the objectives of the design problem; the divergence-based strategy deals with producing a wide range of alternatives (Afacan and Demirkan 2011). Cross suggests that convergent thinkers are successful in selecting the most feasible solution among the alternatives and in satisfying the requirements of the final design phase, while divergent thinkers are good at conceptual design and generate a wide range of alternative solutions (Cross 1989).

It is not possible to rely solely upon a convergence- or divergence-based strategy in the conceptual design phase. Hence, the ideal strategy in the conceptual design phase should be one which supports the dynamic nature of a design that will generate the most satisfactory solution. In this respect, Liu, Bligh, and Chakrabarti stated that it is important to carry out a thought process where as many different solutions as possible are explored for each task, and then, by moving to the convergent-thinking portion of the design process, the non-usable ones can be eliminated (Liu et al. 2003).

Liikkanen and Perttula maintain that during the conceptual phase of the design process idea generation involves repeated analysis and synthesis cycles to investigate problem decomposition. The completion of multiple divergent and convergent activities at each level of solution abstraction allows a designer to generate a reasonable number of concepts that are manageable at each level of the solution domain (Liikkanen and Perttula 2009).

According to Gero and McNeill, in a collaborative design process there are three micro-design strategies that designers use. These are: (1) analysis of a solution; (2) proposal of a solution; and (3) reference to explicit strategies (Gero and McNeill 1998). These strategies are related to application knowledge, knowledge and requirements of the design domain, and design strategies. The analysis of the solution refers to the application of knowledge, the proposal of a solution refers to the knowledge and requirements of the design domain, and the implementation of explicit strategies refers to overall design strategies and approaches.

Gero and McNeill's research showed that the designer was more involved in the micro-design strategy of "proposing a solution" in the conceptual phase, with the designer cycling between the "proposal of a solution" and the "analysis of a solution" when he or she spent almost equal time in both phases (Gero and McNeill 1998).

A research study conducted by Sagun and Demirkan examined Gero and McNeill's three micro-design strategies (Sagun and Demirkan 2009). The results showed that designers usually rejected immediately what were deemed to be unsatisfactory solutions, settling on a single solution instead of providing choices. Further, it was found that the greatest number of critiques focused on the first micro-design strategy proposed by Gero and McNeill (i.e., analysis of a solution).

In another study Demirkan found that the greatest number of critiques focused on the micro-design strategy of analysis (Demirkan 2005). In this same study Demirkan found that "reference to explicit strategies" occurred the second most frequently as opposed to Gero and McNeill's assertion that this micro-design strategy is least frequent. In a later study, Sagun and Demirkan found that the smallest number of critiques were related to explicit design strategies (Sagun and Demirkan 2009).

A Discussion of the Conceptual Phase of Designing for Maturing Populations

The following discussion is offered in an effort to increase understanding of how designers utilize knowledge and knowledge sources, and what strategies they use in design problem-solving during the conceptual phase. Understanding the human diversity of maturing populations is critical when creating interior environments for older adults. Because of the imprecise and uncertain specifications and priorities of a maturing population, the determination of requirements is a difficult process that challenges designers to seek information from knowledge sources both within and outside the parameters of most design problems (Afacan and Demirkan 2010).

This discussion, however, is not intended to address all the issues associated with the creation of interiors for maturing populations. Rather, it is intended, through the use of this example, to offer insights into how designers approach problem-solving and set priorities, while considering the significant differences that exist among maturing populations.

As a starting point in the design process, exploration of the knowledge domains associated with maturing populations is critical. These domains include information about such things as the personal and physical characteristics of aging adults and the social constructions of maturing populations. The data involve the age, sex, and anthropometric dimensions of the maturing population.

In humans, aging is a multi-dimensional process of physical and social change. The different age periods of the maturing population encompass different changes in physical and psychological characteristics, attitude, and behavior. The sex of the maturing population is important because of the different ways males and females use an interior based on cultural differences. Knowledge of human body size alone is not sufficient; information is needed about functional capabilities, mobility, and limitations in performing certain tasks.

By drawing from these knowledge sources, a designer develops a clearer picture of the type of environment best suited to a maturing population demographic. These knowledge domains fall under the general category of Design Knowledge and more specifically under the domains of Human and Interior Descriptions.

The knowledge domain of personal characteristics in maturing populations

The knowledge domain of Personal Characteristics provides insights for the designer during the conceptual phase of design regarding the idea of *functional status*. Functional status is a term that reflects a person's ability to handle the basic activities of daily living such as feeding, dressing, ambulating, bathing, transferring from bed to toilet, and grooming, and the ability to communicate. Such afflictions as arthritis, heart disease, diabetes, and restricted vision and hearing are common in maturing people and affect their functional status.

Further examination of the data in the knowledge domain of Personal Characteristics of maturing individuals reveals that people experience degenerative bodily changes at different time intervals. Also, as a maturing population continues to age, people may have problems moving around (mobility deficits), manipulating objects (dexterity deficits), and receiving sensory information (sensory deficits) (Demirbilek and Demirkan 1998).

Maturing populations often experience feelings of isolation because of the death of family members and peers. To help lessen isolation concerns, it is important that interior spaces for maturing populations include areas where people can meet and interact with each other. For example, in structures where the occupants are ambulatory the placement of benches on the staircase landing or in the corridors is a simple way to encourage interaction and interdependence among older adults (Demirkan 2000).

The knowledge domain of status in maturing populations

Income level and cultural background are two important aspects that determine the perceived status of maturing populations. Through an examination of the Status Domain of income and culture, designers gain an appreciation for the lifestyle, values, and subcultures of maturing populations that can be applied during the conceptual phase of design.

From an early age, shared meanings of the domains of income and culture are learned through social contact with others. As a result, cultural differences are learned factors, rather than genetic (Newell 1997). Thus, two people raised in

different cultures may have common needs or desires, but different ways of satisfying them. For example, sitting down is a worldwide activity, but whether one sits
on the floor or on a chair has major implications for the design of interiors for
maturing populations.

The Knowledge Domain of Abilities in Maturing Populations

The knowledge domain of Abilities in maturing populations falls under the umbrella
of universal design and within the context of "design for all." According to Story,
Mueller, and Mace, there are five important subcategories that must be taken into
consideration in the creation of a successful interior space for maturing adults.
These are: (1) cognition, (2) vision, hearing and speech, (3) body function, (4) arm
function and hand function, and (5) mobility (Story et al. 1998).

The subcategory of cognition in maturing individuals affects the usability of an
interior or a product. Therefore "the variety of abilities in receiving, comprehending,
interpreting, remembering, or acting on information" should be considered in the
conceptual phase when designing for maturing interior populations (Story et al.
1998b). Moreover, cognition level is dependent upon the age and ability level of the
population, as well as on the characteristics of the environment, or of the task conducted. Thus, it is important for designers to incorporate into their problem-solving
approach the understanding that maturing populations may include individuals
with diminished memory and reasoning skills, as well as individuals who may
become easily fatigued or distracted.

The subcategory knowledge domain that deals with vision offers useful insights
in the conceptual phase of design in regard to how older adults perceive visual
stimuli. For example, older adults may not be able to clearly perceive visual details,
focus on nearby and distant objects, discriminate objects from their background,
perceive contrasts in color and brightness, and adapt to high and low lighting
levels. Additionally, maturing populations may be distracted in a visual environment where stimuli are dense, and other individuals may feel fatigued by excessive
visual tasks or may have visual impairments such as presbyopia, glaucoma, or
cataracts.

Exploration of the knowledge domain subcategory of hearing and speech provides designers with information about the ability of maturing populations to local-
ize sound. For example, often older adults have difficulty in separating auditory
information from background noise, perceiving both high- and low-pitched sounds,
or carrying on a conversation (Story et al. 1998). In addition, the level of hearing
disability is often age-dependent and the attention of maturing populations may be
divided among several auditory sources.

Understanding the functioning level of the body/arm/hand category of older
adults informs the decision-making of a designer in the conceptual phase. In the
context of "design for all," "body function means consideration of the variety of
human abilities in performing common tasks...such as: physical exertion; achiev-

ing, maintaining and changing posture; maintaining equilibrium and breathing" (Story et al. 1998). Moreover, according to Story et al., the functional level of body/arm/hand is dependent on age, disability level of the population and the characteristics of the environment or task conducted.

Lastly, the subcategory of mobility is an important knowledge area that informs design decision-making. Central to design conceptualization for maturing populations is an understanding that there are a variety of possible mobility issues, and that even common tasks such as rising from a seated position, standing upright, walking, or kneeling often are challenging for older adults and maturing populations (Story et al. 1998).

The Knowledge Domain of the Built Environment: Physical and Social Environments

The physical and social environment subcategories of the knowledge domain of the Built Environment are important to consider when conceptualizing interior spaces for maturing populations. These two subcategories offer the designer insights into how to create environments for older adults that provide for the interaction of individuals with other people while still maintaining individual privacy.

It goes without saying that when dealing with the physical environment there are certain codes and regulations that must be considered in designing space for older adults. However, other design factors may be equally important to consider in providing a positive experience for older adults in their built environment. Such things as layout and configuration, functionality, maximum distances, ease of servicing, accessibility, and related technologies also have a bearing and must be part of the design conceptualization process.

As discussed earlier, as a designer moves from the conceptual phase into the design phase of a project, the focus necessarily shifts from theoretical to more pragmatic aspects associated with the physical environment. Primary among these is the selection of appropriate mechanical systems that will enhance and/or support the experience of maturing adults in their physical environment. For example, the specification of electrical systems that address illumination levels, glare control, increased stimulus contrast, and reduction in visual clutter should be a priority.

Other mechanical systems, which are the most supportive of an aging process, should also be selected. These include such things as heating/cooling, ventilation, communication, and security systems. For example, recognition of the fact that the body's ability to regulate its temperature declines with age supports the design decision to place thermostats where individuals with lessened mobility and visual acuity can easily see and control them.

The social environment subcategory of the Built Environment Domain informs the conceptualization process by introducing designers to knowledge sources that address the relationship between the patterns of an activity and the ability of a physical environment to support that activity. Issues like privacy, territoriality, personal space, and social interaction permeate these knowledge sources and are critical references when conceptualizing space for maturing populations.

The Prioritization of Requirements

As can be seen from the previous discussion, there are many variable and interacting design issues to be addressed when creating interior environments for maturing populations. The changing needs and diversity of maturing populations dictate that there will be some level of uncertainty about what is deemed to be a successfully designed interior environment for older adults.

The purpose of this essay is to provide a framework for understanding how methods and knowledge are linked within the cognitive strategies of design when creating interiors for maturing populations. Since all the requirements of such environments cannot be satisfied for each individual's situation, the designer must set priorities by tapping into the knowledge domain of "design for all" factors. Although "design for all" suggests a holistic approach that does not include individuals with disabilities as a specialized group (Demirkan 2007), it should be recognized that the accumulated knowledge of this domain can offer useful information during the conceptual design phase.

The "design for all" literature does not provide concrete answers to the kinds of systematic procedures and methods a designer should use to most effectively identify and set priorities and incorporate user needs into interior spaces for maturing populations (Canadian Human Rights Commission 2006; Center for Universal Design 1997, 2000). It has been suggested that, since all design requirements cannot be equally satisfied for this population, a designer should sift through the knowledge domains and sources available to them and make priority decisions based on the relative importance and order of each requirement (Ozkaya and Akin 2006).

An examination of the term *priority* shows that a priority is considered to be either the quantity and/or the importance of a requirement (Lehtola, Kauppinen, and Kujala 2004). The literature offers several examples of ways to set priorities that may be helpful to the design community when creating interiors for maturing populations (Karlsson, Wohlin, and Regnell 1998; Karlsson, Thelin, Regnell, Berander, and Wohlin 2007).

One such approach is called the Analytic Hierarch Process (AHP). In this approach to priority-setting, a designer compares two requirements to each other to determine which one is more important, and to what extent. The most obvious drawback to this approach is that it is time-consuming. Since all unique pairs of requirements have to be compared in this approach, the required effort can be substantial. In a design project, time is often of the essence, therefore this approach may make sense only for small-scale projects (Khari and Kumar 2013).

A less rigorous AHP approach is proposed by Wiegers and based on weighted assessments of perceived value, relative penalty, anticipated cost, and technical risks

(Wiegers 2003). The fundamental difficulty with Wiegers' approach is that the value assigned to a given requirement lacks the specificity necessary to determine whether or not the requirement meets core values.

In contrast to the AHP approach to setting priorities is the Value Oriented Prioritization (VOP) process. When using the VOP approach, a framework is established that identifies core values and the relative relationships among those values (Azar, Smith, and Cordes 2007).

The literature suggests that Quality Function Deployment (QFD) is another effective approach to set design requirement priorities. According to its developer, Dr. Yoji Akao, QFD is a "method to transform user demands into design quality, to deploy the functions forming quality, and to deploy methods for achieving the design quality into subsystems and component parts ... [QFD] is a way to assure design quality while the product is still in the design stage" (Akao 1994). By incorporating the voice of the users, QFD can help designers to transform the needs of users into characteristics that are appropriate – thereby establishing the design requirement priorities.

Lastly, the Planning Game (PG) technique can be used to help establish design priorities. According to the literature, PG is one of the most recognized prioritization techniques in use today (Lehtola and Kauppinen 2006). This approach involves end-users and proposes that priorities can be placed on an ordinal scale so that a ranked order among requirements can be established. In this approach requirements are written down by the end-users and divided into different piles.

Beck suggests that when using the PG technique for priority-setting there should be three piles: those requirements which are essential for functionality; those that are less essential but provide significant value; and those that would be nice to have. At the same time as the end-users sort the cards, the programmer (or in this case the designer) estimates how long each requirement will take to implement and sorts the requirements into three different piles of risk, i.e., the ones that can be estimated precisely, the ones that can be estimated reasonably well, and the ones that cannot be estimated at all. The end result of this sorting is a sorted list of requirements on an ordinal scale that is flexible and can be scaled up or down quickly to establish the order of priorities (Beck 2001).

The Application of Priority-Setting Techniques in Research

In the design of interior environments for maturing populations it may be necessary to apply variations of each of the priority-setting techniques previously discussed. For example, the PG technique may be chosen because it is user-friendly and quick and easy to implement. On the other hand, the AHP technique may be a more appropriate approach to priority-setting because of its precision, ability to be combined with other techniques, and capacity for creating a systematic formulation of complex requirements that is suitable for handling complex design requirements (Afacan and Demirkan 2010).

In a research study to explore how a QFD approach worked in the context of design problem-solving for maturing populations, Demirbilek and Demirkan classified all data, such as answers to pre-set questions, proposals, requirements, and ideas, according to the Quality Function Deployment system. The results of the study showed that the use of a QFD approach to priority-setting clearly established the relationships among the elderly users' requirements, their stated wishes, and the technical design specifications (Demirbilec and Demirkan 2004).

In another study, by Demirkan and Olgunturk, the aim was to determine and set priorities for the issues that are important for diverse user groups within the context of "design for all." A survey was conducted with four types of users: individuals with physical disabilities, individuals with visual impairments, the elderly, and fully functioning adults (Demirkan and Olgunturk 2013). The results of the survey were statistically tested to obtain a priority listing of essential items in interior environments designed for all. The following nine "design for all" factors resulted from the study and are listed below in priority order from highest to lowest:

1 Adequate illumination level in all spaces
2 Ease of use in the kitchen
3 Adequate space for approach and use
4 Adequate contrast between essential information and its surroundings
5 Ease of use in accessories
6 Functional vertical circulation
7 Provision of privacy and safety in bathroom
8 Safety of floors in all spaces
9 Accessibility to all spaces

Statistical analysis showed that there was a significant difference among user groups in all factors; however, all the groups did not differ significantly from each other in each factor.

Conclusion

The goal of this essay was to examine how methods and knowledge are linked within the cognitive strategies of the design process when creating interior environments for maturing populations. As discussed throughout, during the conceptual phase the designer constructs a mental image of the artifact to be produced by abstracting knowledge from previous experiences and information stored in the memory.

As stated by Liikkanen and Perttula, idea generation involves repeated analysis/synthesis cycles to investigate problem decomposition in the conceptual design phase. So, carrying out multiple divergent and convergent activities at each level of solution abstraction allows a designer to generate a reasonable number of concepts that are manageable at each level of the solution domain (Liikkanen and Perttula 2009).

The design process as a creative act should be explored within a model framework considering visual imagery and external representation. These conceptual representations are linked both with the external forms of knowledge (sketches) and with the internal representations (imagery) of the model. Sketches as external representations quicken the process, improve results, and aid the restructuring of the problem. This process is especially helpful for designers who have learned to use the sketch as a tool, and encourages the discovery of new information by combining new input and previous knowledge (Bilda and Demirkan 2003; Demirkan 2005; Suwa and Tversky 1997).

The design problem-solving process – consisting of the analysis, synthesis, and evaluation phases – utilizes acquired knowledge to support decision-making through cognitive design strategies. The systematic presentation and manipulation of design requirements is essential, requiring the selection of an appropriate priority-setting technique to best meet the needs of maturing populations.

References

Afacan, Y. and Demirkan, H. 2010. "A priority-based approach for satisfying the diverse users' needs, capabilities and expectations: a universal kitchen design case," *Journal of Engineering Design* 21(2–3): 315–343.

Afacan, Y. and Demirkan, H. 2011. "An ontology-based universal design knowledge support system for the conceptual design phase," *Knowledge-Based Systems* 24(4): 530–541.

Akao, Y 1994. "Development history of quality function deployment," in *QFD: The Customer Driven Approach to Quality Planning and Deployment*. Minato, Tokyo: Asian Productivity Organization, p. 339.

Akin, O. 1986. *Psychology of Architectural Design*. London: Pion.

Azar, J., Smith, R. K., and Cordes, D. 2007. "Value oriented requirements prioritization in a small development organization," *IEEE Software* 32–73.

Beck, K. 2001. *Extreme Programming: Explained* (7th ed.). Boston: Addison-Wesley.

Bilda, Z. and Demirkan, H. 2003. "An insight on designers' sketching activities in traditional versus digital media," *Design Studies* 24(1): 27–50.

Canadian Human Rights Commission. 2006. *International Best Practices in Universal Design: A Global Review*. CD-ROM. Canada: Betty Dion Enterprises.

Center for Universal Design. 1997. *The Principles of Universal Design*. Version 2.0. Raleigh: North Carolina State University.

Center for Universal Design. 2000. "Architecture and interior design," in *Universal Design Exemplars*. CD-ROM. College of Design, Raleigh: North Carolina State University.

Cross, N. 1982. "Designerly ways of knowing," *Design Studies* 3(4): 221–227.

Cross, N. 1989. *Engineering Design Methods*. Chichester: John Wiley & Sons.

Cross, N. 2001. "Designerly ways of knowing: design discipline versus design science," *Design Issues* 17(3): 49–55.

Cross, N. 2006. *Designerly Ways of Knowing*. London: Springer.

Demirbas, O. O. and Demirkan, H. 2003. "Focus on architectural design process through learning styles," *Design Studies* 24(5): 437–456.

Demirbilek, O. and Demirkan, H. 1998. "Involving the elderly in the design process," *Architectural Science Review* 41(4): 157–163.

Demirbilek, O. and Demirkan, H. 2004. "Universal product design involving elderly users: a participatory design model," *Applied Ergonomics* 35(4): 361–370.

Demirkan, H. 1998. "Integration of reasoning systems in architectural modeling activities," *Automation in Construction* 7(2–3): 229–236.

Demirkan, H. 2000. "A knowledge-based system for the design of elderly residences," in J. G. Mangin and M. Miramond (eds.), *Proceedings of 2nd International Conference on Decision Making in Urban and Civil Engineering*. Lyon: Université de Valenciennes, pp. 825–836.

Demirkan, H. 2005. "Generating design activities through sketches in multi-agent systems," *Automation in Construction* 14(6): 699–706.

Demirkan, H. 2007. "Housing for the aging population," *European Review of Aging and Physical Activities* 4(1): 33–38.

Demirkan, H. and Olgunturk, N. 2013. "A priority-based 'design for all' approach to guide home designers for independent living," *Architectural Science Review*. Under review.

Demirkan, H., Pultar M., and Ozguc, B. 1992. "A knowledge-based space planning system," *Architectural Science Review* 35(1): 3–7.

Dorst, K. and Cross, N. 2001. "Creativity in the design process: co-evolution of problem-solution," *Design Studies* 22(5): 425–437.

Gero, J. S. and Mc Neill, T. 1998. "An approach to the analysis of design protocols," *Design Studies* 19(2): 1–61.

Imel, S. 1992. *Reflective Practice in Adult Education*. ERIC Digest No. 122. Columbus, OH: ERIC Clearinghouse on Adult Career and Vocational Education.

Karlsson, L., Thelin, T., Regnell, B., Berander, P., and Wohlin, C. 2007. "Pair-wise comparisons versus planning game partitioning: experiments on requirements prioritization techniques," *Empirical Software Engineering* 12(1): 3–33.

Karlsson, J., Wohlin, C., and Regnell, B. 1998. "An evaluation of methods for prioritizing software requirements," *Information and Software Technology* 39(14–15): 939–947.

Khari, M. and Kumar, N. 2013. "Prioritization techniques for software requirements," *Journal of Global Research in Computer Science* 4(1): 38–43.

Lawson, B. 1990. *How Designers Think: The Design Process Demystified*. London: Butterworth Architecture.

Lehtola, L. and Kauppinen, M. 2006. "Suitability of requirements prioritization methods for market-driven software product development," *Software Process Improvement and Practice* 11(1): 7–19.

Lehtola, L., Kauppinen, M., and Kujala, S. 2004. "Requirements prioritization challenges in practice," in *Proceedings of 5th International Conference on Product Focused Software Process Improvement*. Kansai Science City, Japan, pp. 497–508.

Liikkanen, L. A. and Perttula, M. 2009. "Exploring problem decomposition in conceptual design among novice designers," *Design Studies* 30(1): 38–59.

Liu, Y. C., Bligh, T., and Chakrabarti, A. A. 2003. "Towards an 'ideal' approach for concept generation," *Design Studies* 24(4): 341–355.

Newell, P. B. 1997. "A cross-cultural aspects of environmental design," *Environment and Behavior* 29(4): 495–514.

Owen, C. 2007. "Design thinking: notes on its nature and use," *Design Research Quarterly* 2(1): 16–27.

Ozkaya, I. and Akin, O. 2006. "Requirement-driven design: assistance for information traceability in design computing," *Design Studies* 27(3): 381–398.

Sagun, A. and Demirkan, H. 2009. "On-line critiques in collaborative design studio," *International Journal of Technology and Design Education* 19(1): 79–99.

Schon, D. A. 1983. *The Reflective Practitioner: How Professionals Think in Action*. New York: Basic Books.

Schon, D. A. 1987. *Educating the Reflective Practitioner: Towards a New Design for Teaching in the Professions*. San Francisco: Jossey-Bass.

Simon, H. A. [1969] 1996. *The Sciences of the Artificial* (3rd ed.). Cambridge, MA: MIT Press.

Story, M. F., Mueller, J. L., and Mace, R. L. 1998. *The Universal Design File: Designing for People of All Ages and Abilities* (rev. ed.). Raleigh: North Carolina State University, Center for Universal Design.

Suwa, M. and Tversky, B. 1997. "What do architects and students perceive in their design sketches? A protocol analysis," *Design Studies* 18(4): 385–403.

Visser, Willemien. 2010. "Simon: design as a problem-solving activity," *Collection* 2 (Art + Design & Psychology) 11–16.

Wiegers, K. 2003. *Software Requirements* (2nd ed.). Redmond, WA: Microsoft Press.

13

Designing More Successful Social Spaces: Lessons Learned from a Continuing Care Retirement Community Study

Nichole M. Campbell

Introduction

Some places seem to draw people together – gathering them in for conversation and laughter. Sometimes places are designed and built specifically to serve this role. As exemplified by the following quote, when this is done, these social spaces can become lively, vibrant hubs of the community.

> Now that I look back, it seems to me that after the café closed, the heart of the town just stopped beating. Funny how a little knockabout place like that brought so many people together. (Flagg 1987)

Other times, these well-intentioned – and seemingly well-designed – spaces sit empty, not supporting community life.

Planned retirement communities are one place where this dynamic is played out again and again. Like small towns, Continuing Care Retirement Communities (CCRCs) often contain their own coffee shops, cafes, lounges, recreation rooms, and many other social spaces shared by CCRC residents. However, even with the current body of design research on social spaces (including post-occupancy evaluations) there is still inconsistency in how well these spaces are designed to meet the residents' needs.

In an attempt to address this phenomenon, this essay explores which factors drive how well retirement community social spaces are "liked" and "used." To uncover these factors, a correlational research strategy was conducted. The primary data source was resident ratings collected via surveys.

The Handbook of Interior Design, First Edition. Edited by Jo Ann Asher Thompson and Nancy H. Blossom.

Correlational studies on space utilization commonly use observational techniques to gather data. Whyte's study of urban public plazas provides a good example of an observational research strategy. In his studies, Whyte used direct observation to record and describe human behavior in urban plaza settings – observing everything from jaywalking patterns to "schmoozing patterns" (Whyte 1980).

While at first glance this approach seems an obvious strategy for the study of CCRC social spaces, it can be argued that the use of observation to study retirement communities may not be the only appropriate research tactic. As an alternative approach, a survey instrument was used in this study as the primary means of data collection.

A good precedent for the use of surveys in correlational design research can be found in Kim, Lee, and Bell's research on new urbanism (Kim et al. 2008). In their work, the principles of new urbanism are explored in relation to the design of new communities, as well as in relation to the regeneration of old communities in the State of Michigan. Through the use of a survey tool they examined community design and related programs, investigated the opinions of Michigan residents, business owners, and urban planners on the core new urbanism principles and, based on the survey results, were able to make recommendations for community design and planning.

In the study presented here, a survey was used to examine how well the social spaces in retirement communities were serving residents. Survey data were analyzed using multiple regression analysis to indicate which attributes were the best predictors of "like" and "use." In the process of identifying these attributes, several important questions were considered. These included:

- What components make up the social lives of retirement community residents?
- What is the relationship between independent living social space design elements and human needs, specifically social needs?
- What is the role of third places in the context of independent living in a CCRC?
- What is the relationship between how well spaces were "liked" versus how well they were "used"?

Important implication associated with the design of social spaces in CCRSs can be drawn from this study's findings for practicing designers and interior design educators.

Designing and Building to Suit People throughout Life

Designing to meet the needs of older adults does not mean designing only for older adults. By meeting the needs of the aged in the built environment, designed spaces then function better for users of all ages. For example, creating a no-step entrance into a building is a good strategy to help older adults negotiate an entry to a building safely. Yet this no-step entrance is also particularly useful for young mothers with strollers, wheelchair users of any age, and the visually impaired. The point here is that a no-step entrance creates easy access for users of most ages or ability levels, and design with the elderly in mind facilitates good "design for all."

It is important, nevertheless, to understand that disability commonly increases with age. These challenges may include reductions in mobility as well as decreases in vision and hearing acuity. We know that as people age – and their level of disability increases – the design of the built environment has a greater impact (Lawton 1974). Therefore, addressing the needs of the elderly in our built environment is of particular importance.

The body of literature on universal design that meets the needs of the aged/ elderly is expanding as that segment of the population in the US continues to grow. Given the increase in life expectancy, the need for designs that support the aged/ elderly is more pressing than ever. The US Census Bureau predicts the older adult population (aged 65+) will almost double to over 77 million persons by the year 2040 (Day, 2011).

With this exponential growth, the demand for spaces such as senior centers or planned retirement communities is expected to increase accordingly. Further, it is anticipated that there will be an increase in the need for supportive public spaces – from restaurants, to parks, to shops. In order to successfully address this demographic shift, the design professions must prioritize and utilize research that not only addresses the physical needs of an elderly population, but also more adequately addresses the social interaction needs of this population.

The Importance of Social Interaction at Any Age

Research suggests that while social participation decreases with advancing age, the influence of social interaction on older adults' health is greater than it is on the health of younger adults (Lee, Jang, Lee, Cho, and Park 2008). According to the literature, social interaction, particularly in later life, strongly impacts satisfaction and the quality of life (Aquino, Russell, Cutrona, and Altmaier 1996; Jang, Mortimer, Haley, and Graves 2004). MacNeil and Teague argue that "Life satisfaction among the elderly is strongly influenced by three variables – physical health, socioeconomic status, and the quality of social interactions" (MacNeil and Teague 1987).

Of these three variables, the built environment influences physical health and social interaction most directly. Its importance is further highlighted by the Active Aging Initiative of the World Health Organization (AAIWHO), the goal of which is to support the elderly population with "housing in communities that encourage daily social interaction" (WHO 2002).

The early retirement years typically are marked by many options for social interaction – as individuals choose where, with whom, and how to spend their time. As time passes, many older adults experience changes in physical abilities, such as declining vision and physical mobility, thus limiting their housing options. Often, this leads older adults to spend more time near or in their living quarters.

Recognizing this issue, directors of facilities for older adults strive to increase their residents' social connection within the facilities and the greater community (Cannuscio, Block, and Kawachi 2003). This trend presents a challenge for retirement community managers as they try to find a balance between their goal to increase the social connections of residents with the financial constraints associated with facilities that have too much unused or underutilized square footage. As a result, retirement communities offer fertile ground for the study of social spaces. These facilities provide a variety of spaces within which residents can have social interactions, such as lobbies, recreation rooms, lounges, and retail and coffee shops.

The Challenge of Affordable Social Space Square Footage

It is often noted that social spaces in CCRCs are not always well utilized. John Noreika, the chief executive officer of a non-profit retirement community, expressed frustration that while many of the social interaction spaces provided in his CCRC are in high demand, others sit empty the majority of the time (personal communication, January 2008). This issue of "wasted space" is challenging for both non-profit and for-profit CCRCs. The managers of CCRCs face having to balance their marketing efforts between advertising a healthy social scene with the actuality of underutilized social spaces in their facilities and communities.

Research on naturally occurring retirement communities (NORCs) helps illustrate the importance of offering a variety of spaces for social interaction. While the details regarding what constitutes a NORC vary, it is generally agreed by experts that NORCs are a distinct geographic area not planned specifically for that houses a significant proportion of older adults. In his study of a NORC, Hunt found that opportunities for social interaction were connected with resident satisfaction (Hunt 2001). This also led to word-of-mouth recommendations promoting the condominium or apartment complex to friends or relatives. This is in keeping with the work of Fiori, who found that, "Having a variety of people in one's network is better for psychological health" (Fiori, Antonucci, and Cortina 2006). In other words, both close friendships and acquaintances are important to a satisfactory social life.

It can be argued that careful research-based planning of CCRCs can promote and support social connections among residents because attention is paid to such things as programming aspects (e.g., planned activities offered), the place culture (e.g., the behaviors and beliefs of the residents and staff), and, finally, the attributes of the physical space itself.

Why Interaction with Friends Is Particularly Valuable

In addition to the importance of creating places suited for social interaction in a CCRC, there is great value in promoting relationships within individual facilities. Research suggests that over time relationships with friends within the retirement community come to hold greater value for residents than other interactions with friends and relatives outside the community. A study of social interaction in assisted living facilities showed that "contact with family and friends outside the facility did not significantly impact life satisfaction, but positive internal social relationships were associated with significantly higher life satisfaction" (Street, Burge, Quadagno, and Barrett 2007).

In addition to recognizing the importance of social spaces in CCRCs, designers must also be sensitive to the location of the social spaces within the retirement community. A 2001 study of a NORC provided evidence indicating that social spaces located in close proximity to individual residences were important. This study also suggested that proximity to services and shopping facilities, as well as to friends and family, were important factors in attracting older adults to this housing type (Hunt 2001). This idea can also be applied to CCRCs, and supports the conclusion that proximity to communal social spaces is an important factor in residents' satisfaction.

The Role of Place in Social Relationships

This essay presents the results of a study that focused on face-to-face communications and "in-person" social relationships. An essential concept to understand in this context is "sense of place." Rosenbaum argues that "places" can play one of three roles in the users' lives and categorizes these as: place-as-practical, place-as-gathering, and place-as-home (Rosenbaum 2006).

"Place-as-practical" is defined as a place that does not serve a social role, but instead meets a practical consumer need only. For example, this might be a fast food restaurant where the customer makes a quick stop to buy a soda before a long drive. While these are places that serve a predominantly consumption-oriented role, interaction between the consumer and the employee(s) still occurs. Since there is a small amount of social interaction, it is suggested that such places extend beyond simple consumerism to provide social tie interaction (albeit weak) for patrons. Weak social ties are described as "low levels of intimacy and relatively infrequent contact" (Krause 2006).

While weak social ties, such as those suggested in Rosenbaum's "place as practical" category, do not offer much in terms of supporting deep emotional connections, they can positively impact the elderly's health and well-being. According to Krause:

> The functions performed by weak social ties have important implications for the way older people cope with stress because the anonymity, low accountability, and diversity of views they provide typically cannot be found elsewhere. (Krause 2006)

Rosenbaum's second and third categories of "place-as-gathering" and "place-as-home" relate more strongly to social interaction and promote the idea of more emotionally invested interactions such as friendships and close attachments.

In related work, Oldenburg studied place-as-home establishments and coined the term "third places" (Oldenburg [1989] 1999). Oldenburg's work set the stage for Rosenbaum's examination of emotional attachment to place, where he argues that there is a clear delineation between third places (place-as-home) and place-as-gathering, based on the level of emotional support a patron receives in a venue.

In contrast to Rosenbaum's hypothesis that there are three categories of "place," it can be argued that "place" actually exists as a spectrum, rather than as distinct categories. For example, a "place-as-practical" (coffee shop) may provide almost no social interaction on a first visit, but when the patron becomes a repeat customer this interaction may well evolve from the category of "place-as-practical" into "place-as-gathering" space.

Making these delineations between place-types is useful in our overall understanding of "place" theory. However, there continue to be limited examples in the literature about how these theories about "place" can be applied specifically to the design of CCRCs – where richer levels of interaction would promote satisfaction.

Types of Engagement that Occur in Retirement Community Social Spaces

Social interaction within a retirement community can be classified into two varieties: formal and informal. Since these communities typically offer many organizationally planned social events and activities, formal social interaction usually occurs among residents around these activities and events. In contrast, informal social interaction does not revolve around organizationally planned activities. For example, informal social interaction can occur as a casual, impromptu conversation with a fellow resident or staff member.

Because most retirement communities have an array of planned activities and events, designated spaces and/or buildings are usually designed to serve these purposes. Oftentimes, however, these spaces are not suitable for informal social interaction. In a study of motivation and self-esteem in age-segregated venues, Percival remarks on the ill fit between planned social spaces and informal interaction:

> Communal lounges are popular locations for tenants' formal social activities, but appear to be of less interest as informal meeting places, because of their size, instrumental use, and tendency to emphasize loneliness and old age in this age-segregated setting. This suggests a need to critically examine whether the creation of smaller, partitioned areas within large lounges might enable both formal and informal social behaviors to be more self-contained, or whether greater emphasis should be put on establishing more informal meeting places away from the lounge. (Percival 2001)

As Percival explains, social spaces in age-segregated settings tend to support formal, programmed uses as opposed to informal, resident-initiated activities.

Consequently, there tends to be a lack of flexible space available for informal social interaction.

Defining Social Space Success

Even though there are retirement community examples where social spaces work well and the organization is thriving, several questions still remain. For example, how do we measure the success of social spaces? Is a space successful when residents prefer it? Is it successful when residents visit often? Is the length of time spent during visits relevant?

Generally there are two mechanisms that are used as a measure of the success of social spaces: (1) preference and (2) use. Preference deals with how much spaces are liked, and examines how well the space is used by the residents. In previous studies regarding preference, Scott (1993) and Kaplan and Kaplan (1989) presented guidelines for creating preferable environments. Later, Marsden investigated how the usability characteristics influenced preference (Marsden 2005).

While these studies help increase our understanding of preferences for certain types of spaces, they do not address the issue of why some social spaces for the elderly are underutilized. The conclusion that can be drawn is that the success of a social space cannot be solely based on whether or not a space is well liked. In other words, these studies do not address why certain preferred social spaces are not used to full capacity in senior communities.

In order to better understand how to create successful social spaces in CCRCs the following questions continue to be at issue: (1) Do people use the spaces they "like" and "like" the spaces they "use"? and (2) Do the same factors drive "like" and "use"?

The Social Lives of Retirement Community Residents

It is important to note that even when a CCRC includes social interaction spaces, the other components that make up the social lives of residents can either confound or further support interaction. If, for instance, the management prioritizes employee efficiency over employees interacting socially with residents, it is likely that will put a strain on the development of social ties among the residents.

A framework, called the Successful Social Space Attribute Model, is offered here to assist in our understanding of the most important components in the social lives of residents in retirement communities. The components of the model are: (1) factors unique to the individual; (2) communal environmental design factors; (3) place culture; and (4) programmatic factors (see Figure 13.1).

A fifth – and overarching – factor is time, which serves to influence all the other factors. For example, the time of day or time of year can impact space use dramatically.

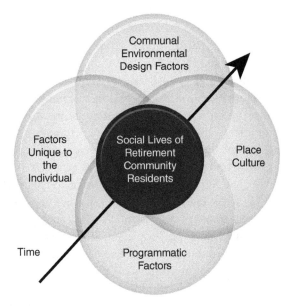

Figure 13.1 The Successful Social Space Attribute Model (SSSAM).

The factors unique to the individual (FUI) consist of built elements and other characteristics specific to each individual. These include components such as the convenience of a social space's location in relation to an individual's residence, whether the resident likes to be involved in informal activities in the space, and/or whether physical challenges (such as hearing or vision loss) impact the resident's use of a space. These aspects of the built environment are closely related to, though different from, the communal environmental design factors, which are defined as those characteristics of a social space that are shared by all the retirement community residents (e.g., nature views seen through the windows).

Place culture in this model is defined as the normative behaviors of retirement community staff and residents and programmatic factors cover such things as formally planned activities, rules, and volunteer opportunities. Each of these factors must be examined in light of the overarching factor of time.

How Well Spaces are "Liked" and "Used"

Even though the hierarchical nature of human needs has been well established (Maslow [1954] 1987), practitioners of the built environment rarely integrate this into their design thinking. More commonly, designers put their priority on physiological needs (e.g., accessibility, function, etc.) or informational needs (e.g., wayfinding, etc.)

Logic tells us that a person must first be able to safely enter and maneuver in a space before social interaction can take place. This being the case, it follows that designers first set as their priorities those things that meet basic human needs, rather than higher-level needs such as socialization. However, according to Marsden the importance of creating areas that feel more private and sheltered within a social space should not be overlooked (Marsden 2005).

Research studies suggest that people tend to approach scenes that have been judged favorably, therefore it follows that increasing our understanding of the preferences of older adults is an initial step toward creating more successful social spaces in retirement communities (Veitch and Arkkelin 1995). In addition, a clearer understanding of whether or not the factors driving preference for certain spaces have the same or similar impact on the utilization of those spaces is critical.

Carr, Francis, Rivlin, and Stone describe two types of activity that support space use in public spaces: (1) active engagement and (2) passive engagement (Carr et al. 1992). While passive engagement involves the satisfaction people take in a scene without being directly involved (e.g., people watching), active engagement is the user's direct involvement in an encounter. Active engagement involves interacting with others, as well as participating in physical activities. In the Carr study, these engagement types were examined in outdoor public spaces. In an interior scene, active engagement could, for example, be participating in a lively conversation or a card game.

Beyond the FUI, other components also serve as predictors of how well spaces are "liked" and "used." To understand how places can serve consumption needs, social interaction needs, and emotional support, Oldenburg's description of third places is particularly relevant (Oldenburg [1989] 1999). According to Oldenburg, third places are unpretentious and relaxed spaces where conversation is the main activity and which offer a playful, friendly, and welcoming atmosphere. Creating such a third place environment with these criteria is supported by Scott's preference research on interior space which identified the attributes of "relaxing," "warm," and "comfortable seating" as qualities of preferred social spaces (Scott 1993).

This research offers insights into how social spaces in retirement communities might be designed to better serve the residents and to help retirement community management meet their goals to build social spaces that are preferred by residents in CCRCs. Unfortunately, however, there is very little research in the literature that tells us whether or not social spaces in retirement communities have third place characteristics or if these characteristics are related to how well social spaces are liked and used.

Case Study: Oakwood Village Retirement Community

In this case study, the Successful Social Space Attribute Model (SSSAM) and the third place concept introduced in this essay were tested in a CCRC in Wisconsin. The study sought to advance understanding of FUIs, third places in CCRCs, and the relationship between "like" and "use." The following research questions were the focus of the study:

1   What factors unique to the individual and their experience of the spaces predict how well spaces will be "liked" and "used"?

2a   Do social spaces in retirement communities have the atmosphere (lively, playful, and welcoming) and décor characteristics (casual, well-worn, and home-like) of third places as defined by Oldenburg ([1989] 1999)?

2b   If third place characteristics exist in retirement community social spaces, how are these characteristics related to how well used and how well liked the social spaces are?

The predictor variables for each question were tested to see which factors could predict the two outcome variables of (1) informal social space usage and (2) how well spaces were "liked." Initially, informal social space usage was measured as two variables (number of resident-initiated visits and length of visits); however, it was decided that a better approach would be to combine them into one usage variable.

At the time of the data collection, the facility's 30 acre campus was located a few miles from the center of a mid-sized university town. The residents were chiefly Caucasian and upper-middle-class. Though the facility was a CCRC, which housed Alzheimer's care, nursing care, assisted living, and independent living, only the independent living residents were surveyed. Reflecting a 73% survey return rate, 303 of the 416 independent living residents that were sent surveys completed them. The respondents consisted of 213 women and 90 men who fell between the ages of 60 and 99. The majority of those (62%) were between 80 and 89 years old. In addition to the survey data, archival data were used to determine apartment sizes, which ranged from 488 to 2,285 square feet.

Given that this study focused on supporting informal social interaction, it is important to note how much residents liked to socially interact. To gauge this, a survey question was included that asked how much residents enjoyed social interaction. From the survey data, 267 respondents (88%) reported liking to interact socially moderately well to very much. Compared to the 29 residents (10%) who rated how much they like to socialize as "less than moderately well" to "not at all," it is apparent the majority of residents in this sample enjoyed interacting socially.

Methodology

To determine the spaces in the facility that would be the best to examine, a resident and staff focus group was conducted in which the group agreed by consensus on which social spaces were the three most and three least successful. These six spaces varied in size and amenities and were located on various floors throughout the independent living buildings. (See Table 13.1 for descriptions of the six spaces studied.)

Table 13.1   Description of the six social spaces in the study

Successful social spaces	*Underutilized social spaces*
1. *The Heritage Lobby.* This space is located on the interior "Main Street" in the campus' newest independent living building (built in 2006). Staffed by a receptionist throughout the daytime, Heritage Lobby is adjacent to one of the facility's main entrances and that building's resident mailbox area.	1. *The Oaks Community Room.* It is located in one of the campus' newer buildings, The Oaks, which was built in 2002. This space is adjacent to the building's entrance, mailbox area, elevators, and public restrooms but it is not located on Main Street.
2. *The Tower Lobby.* This space is located on the interior Main Street in the oldest independent living building, the Tower Apartments, which was built in the mid-1970s. Like Heritage Lobby, this space is adjacent to another of the facility's main entrances and hosts a receptionist during the day. The Tower Lobby is near many of the commercial facilities and is adjacent to a mailbox area; however none of these spaces is visually accessible from the Tower Lobby space.	2. *The Heritage 2nd Floor Lounge.* It is located on the 2nd floor of the Heritage Oaks building, the newest independent living building (built in 2006). The Heritage 2nd Floor Lounge is one floor directly above the Heritage Lobby and the facility's Main Street. Also this space is adjacent to staff offices, a staircase, and hallways.
3. *The Tower Bridge.* Located along the interior Main Street, this space bridges the Tower building to the Village Inn Dining Room and the campus Auditorium. Bulletin boards with activities schedules and sign-up sheets are hung here.	3. *The Tower 2nd Floor End Hall Sitting Nook.* This space is located in the Tower on the 2nd floor at the far end of the hall. On the floor below Main Street in the Tower, this space is near some resident apartments and adjacent to a couple staff offices and the fire stairs.

As mentioned previously, several examples exist in the literature of research studies of social spaces that use observation techniques rather than a survey approach. However, the most widely recognized studies focus on outdoor spaces and/or public plazas (Whyte 1980). It is suggested that such spaces have character-istics that make more observation more appropriate than survey. For instance, these spaces are open to everyone and no single person or group has more claim to a particular space than any other. Accordingly, a user does not expect to have privacy in those spaces. In addition, the sheer number of users in public spaces enables a researcher to blend into the crowd when collecting data so as not to impact the normal behaviors of users.

In contrast CCRC social spaces are more private than public plazas. While only the residents' apartments are totally private, the results of the focus groups indicated that residents exhibited a strong, nearly semi-private territorial claim to the CCRC communal social spaces. Consequently, while it may have been acceptable to videotape people for Whyte's studies, such an approach was not deemed appropriate for CCRC social spaces. Direct observation was also seen as an undesirable tactic given the strong feelings of privacy and territoriality expressed by the focus groups in regard to the social spaces. Lastly, it was determined that the presence of the researcher in the social spaces would disrupt the natural behavior patterns of the residents and skew the results of the study.

Thus, resident surveys were designed to uncover which variables from the SSSAM model had the most impact on how well the retirement community's social spaces were "liked" and "used." Variables drawn from the related research literature, as well as variables hypothesized to impact social space success, were operationalized in the resident survey. The questions regarding factors unique to the individual residents, as well as the third place characteristic questions, were combined into one survey instrument. After collection, the data from each of these sets of questions were analyzed separately.

The survey questions were formatted in one of two ways: multiple choice or Likert Scale rating format. To avoid unfairly impacting the results, six versions of the survey (with each version listing the space names in a different order) were randomly distributed to all independent living residents.

Prior to its use, the instrument's construct validity was addressed. Initially, the survey was created based on existing social space literature. After the instrument was reviewed by two experts in environment and behavior studies, the survey was adjusted to reflect the experts' consensus that the instrument measured what it was intended to measure. To further support construct validity, the clarity of the survey questions was examined in a pilot test.

Data analysis

In the first phase of the analysis, the predictor variables were grouped into three hierarchical need-based categories. Factors impacting basic needs were grouped as foundational factors, with second and third tiers ascending to a top tier of factors that focused on higher level needs (e.g., social needs). (See Table 13.2 for predictor variables that were tested.)

In the second phase of the analysis, the third place atmosphere and décor characteristics were tested. (See Table 13.3 for third place characteristics that were tested.)

In each analysis phase, the variables were examined within their subgroups as well as individually. In both phases, the same dependent variables were used. The dependent variables were Preference/Like and Informal Social Space Usage (visit length and how many resident-driven visits). Since there were two separate dependent variables a multiple regression analysis was done twice – once for each dependent variable.

Table 13.2 Predictor variables

Top tier needs variables

- Length of time in residence
- Resident living alone or with another person
- Professional interaction status (employed, regular volunteer, etc.)
- Sense of belonging/fitting in
- How well the space comfortably supports solo visits
- Reasons that make one want to use space that contribute to belonging/identity
  - Passive engagement activities
  - Active engagement activities

Second tier needs variables

- Gender
- Socializing space preference (within the CCRC or beyond it)
- How private a space felt

Foundational tier needs variables

- Apartment size
- Age
- Mobility
  - Transportation outside community
  - Physical mobility
- Sensory issues
  - Hearing
  - Vision/light needs
- Home range
  - Nearness to home
  - Nearness to daily routes

Table 13.3 Third place characteristics

Atmosphere variables

- Lively
- Playful
- Welcoming

Décor variables

- Casual
- Home-like
- New appearance (Note: the "New" variable was tested separately. The reasons for this will be discussed later)

Findings summary

Since this study was confirmatory in nature, some definitive conclusions may be drawn about design factors that contribute to the success of social spaces in CCRCs. In the first phase of the analysis, one variable was found significant in each subgroup of variables. These were:

- Active engagement opportunities (from the top tier of needs variables)
- How private a space felt (from second tier of needs variables)
- Home range (from the foundational tier of needs variables)

Interestingly, when the variables were tested while controlling for all the other variables, the privacy variable was no longer significant. This indicates that, while this variable matters, much of the variability explained by the privacy variable overlapped with the other two significant variables.

In the second phase of the analysis (i.e., third place characteristics), an assessment was made first of the extent to which the atmosphere and décor qualities were present in the six social spaces studied. As expected, the results showed that the presence of third place characteristics was related to how well spaces were "liked" and "used."

The atmosphere variables (lively, playful, welcoming) and the décor variables (casual and home-like) were positively correlated with the outcome variables. While both showed moderate correlations between "like" and "use," this relationship was stronger with the atmosphere variables than the décor variables.

A second layer of third place results came from a multiple regression analysis of the resident-reported data while controlling for age, gender, home range, and how much residents liked to interact socially. Even while controlling for other variables, the subdued vs. lively variable was a dependable predictor of "like" and "use."

Categorically, the atmosphere variables were better predictors of space "use" and "like" than the décor variables. Among the individual variables, the subdued vs. lively variable was the best predictor overall. The data showed this variable was a significant predictor of usage for five of the six spaces studied. Similarly the subdued vs. lively variable was a significant predictor of how "liked" a space was for four of the six social spaces.

Since this study separately measured both "like" and "use," the relationship between these two dependent variables was examined as well. In three of the spaces studied, there was a moderate positive correlation and a significant relationship between "like" and "use." In the remaining three spaces there was a low positive correlation between "like" and "use" and significant relationship. This means that while there was a relationship between "like" and "use," it was not a strong one. In other words, these two measures of success were different from one another.

Discussion and Lessons Learned

Factors unique to the individual

Using the Successful Social Space Attribute Model as the organizing framework, this study uncovered factors unique to the individual residents that predicted how well spaces were "liked" and "used." Earlier approaches to studying social spaces aimed at understanding features that supported either space use or preference (how well spaces are "liked"). Prior to this study, the connection between "use" and "like" had not been explored. In the six spaces studied, findings indicate there is only a low to moderate correlation between "like" and "use." While a relationship was found, the relationship between "like" and "use" was not robust enough to consider "use" synonymous with "like."

Based on the results of this study, it is suggested that a first step toward enticing residents into a social space is to locate the space within residents' home range; that is to say, within their daily path of travel. When residents pass by the space regularly, this provides the opportunity for the space to pique the curiosity of passersby, who may then stop in for a visit. The changes associated with aging, such as decreased mobility and balance, also support this suggestion because adjacencies are likely to be a priority.

The results of this study are in keeping with the research of Carr et al. (1992), who found two activity types (active and passive engagement) in outdoor social spaces. In this study the availability of active engagement opportunities in social spaces strongly predicted both "like" and "use" of the retirement community social spaces, Whether the action in a space is enjoying a cup of coffee or a conversation, this suggests that providing opportunities to get involved in the action of a space is crucial in social space design.

It is suggested that one way to support active engagement opportunities in the design of retirement community facilities is by centralizing social spaces and commercial services in an area with a lot of foot traffic. This reinforces Whyte's recommendation to cluster retailing and food establishments in interior public plazas (Whyte 1980), and reinforces Cooper Marcus and Francis' work (Cooper Marcus and Francis 1990) which argues for outdoor urban social spaces located near activity.

By creating activity hubs it is much easier for any individual passing by to find something or someone with whom to engage. If these activity hubs are located in the majority of residents' home range (e.g., in a main intersection in the building), residents pass naturally through these activity nodes on their way to other places in the retirement community. As they pass through these nodes, residents are more likely to make unexpected stops to interact socially.

The results of this study revealed that some social spaces felt more private and were better "liked" and "used" by the residents. This finding confirms Marsden's research that indicates that a sense of protective enclosure is key in fulfilling the human need to feel sheltered (Marsden 2005). The ideas of shelter and territoriality are linked closely with privacy. By addressing these needs in the built environment, emotional security issues are considered.

Privacy needs vary by individual and change depending on the situation (e.g., privacy needs increase when people are under stress) (Lang 1987). Supporting social interaction through the design of the space means offering options with various levels of privacy. In this way the resident can choose the level of privacy or social interaction desired. This supports Newman's earlier finding, which suggested the need for four levels of privacy in spaces (private, semi-private, semi-public, and public) to provide users the option to move between these to fulfill their individual need for interaction/privacy (Newman 1979).

It is suggested that one way to create different levels of privacy in social spaces is to provide seating in alcoves and other smaller, more sheltered areas. This should be done in addition to providing ample seating for areas where larger groups wish to gather. Research tells us that people most commonly gather in groups of two, therefore these smaller, cozier areas need to be readily available throughout the facility while maintaining at least partial views into nearby areas for security purposes (Whyte 1980).

Third place in independent living

This study found those social spaces that had third place atmosphere characteristics (lively, playful, and welcoming) were better "liked" and "used" than spaces not having those attributes. This further supports Oldenburg's findings regarding the atmosphere of third places (Oldenburg [1989] 1999). Additionally, social spaces that were characterized by residents as having third place décor (casual and home-like) were more highly used than spaces less characterized as such.

Although this study's results support Oldenburg's findings regarding the décor of third places, his idea that such spaces should be "comfortably worn" was not confirmed. Rather, the results of this study were that décor which was characterized as new had the most positive response to how well "liked" it was. (No association was found between new décor and how well a space was actually used, however.) This finding could be attributed to the high socio-economic status of this resident group in this study. Despite the preference for new décor, it is important to remember that a significant relationship was not found between new décor and space usage. In other words, new décor may attract residents, but has not been shown to impact how much residents use the space.

Of the third place characteristics related to "like" and "use," the atmosphere variables were better predictors than the décor variables. This implies that behavior research-based findings may help inform design solutions so as to better support social interaction among residents. In addition, the research implies it is important to create a design aesthetic that serves as a second layer of support to attain a successful social space design.

Lastly, the results of this study provide further incentive for retirement community organizations to take third place characteristics into consideration when incorporating social spaces into their facilities. Since third place characteristics were found to be related to how well "used" and "liked" spaces were, incorporating these features is an important strategy. Previous research on NORCs found that a lively social scene increases the retirement community's desirability as a housing option (Hunt and Ross 1990). Also, a lively social scene can help support resident satisfaction with the retirement community.

Unexpected findings – the relationship between "like" and "use"

Of the three unsuccessful spaces studied, one space was perceived quite differently from the other two spaces by the residents. While many residents used the Oaks Community room, other residents believed the space was unsuccessful. What caused this discrepancy?

The answer to this question proved to be quite straightforward. When the space was examined closely, residents living in the building that also housed their community room liked it more than residents who lived in other independent living buildings on campus. In addition, the residents used the community room much more than other building residents. While overall the residents liked the community room very much, residents who lived near it used it substantially more than residents who lived further away. Without such notably high usage by residents of the facility, this space would not have ranked nearly as high. The key implication of this finding is that locating social spaces in close proximity to residents' home range may be the most important factor in determining space usage.

This finding is crucial to note because it tells us that while the factors that drive "like" and "use" may be similar, there are distinct differences. These differences usually play out in how often a space is used. In other words, even though a space may be "liked" by the residents, it may not be "used" because it is too far away. Home range influenced how much a space was "used" much more than how much it was "liked." While "like" and "use" are often correlated, it cannot be presumed that a factor driving how much a space is used will equally push how much a space is "liked."

Practice Implications from This Study

While the findings from the study described in this essay can be translated into design recommendations, these findings are from a single case study thereby limiting the generalizability of the results. It can be said, however, that the results of this study can be used to inform design considerations for CCRCs that are similar to the one in this study. For such situations the following design recommendations for social spaces may apply.

Design recommendations

- Residents are more likely to "use" and "like" spaces where ample and socially comfortable informal activities take place (e.g., playing cards or conversing over a cup of coffee). This could be accomplished by clustering recreation, retail, or food service areas or other potential social spaces together so individuals are offered various options in which to engage.
- Locating social spaces in convenient and highly trafficked location(s) is critical for social spaces to be well liked and used. This could be by placing the commercial cluster (social hub) at a main circulation intersection within the facility that is in close proximity to residents' home or travel pathway.
- Spaces with areas that felt more private were liked more and used more than spaces not offering opportunities to choose more privacy. Within a social space, the incorporation of some smaller, more sheltered seating areas could serve residents better. The design of half walls or other means could be used to subdivide a large space and provide a sense of enclosure without sacrificing security.
- Spaces with third place atmosphere characteristics (lively, playful, and welcoming) were more well-used and liked than spaces not providing those characteristics. A lively, playful, and welcoming atmosphere could be created in a social hub with multiple ways to engage residents through such things as card games, puzzles, and interactive art. Locating these spaces close to areas that are conducive to conversation would enhance the opportunities for social exchange.
- Spaces with third place décor qualities (casual and home-like) were more well-used and liked than spaces not providing those attributes. Décor that appeared new was better liked than more worn décor. Third place décor should take into account what the resident group considers casual (e.g., stone fireplace) and home-like (e.g., varying furniture types, patterns, textures, lighting, and color to avoid an institutional appearance) and be designed with this aesthetic in mind.

Conclusion

This study's findings indicate the "factors unique to the individual" portion of the Successful Social Space Attribute Model was a suitable framework for examining retirement community social spaces. Also this study's findings suggest that it is crucial to take both physical and emotional needs into account when designing social spaces. Addressing people's needs in the built environment more holistically positions social space designs for greater success.

In order to inform and support the consistency of successful retirement community social space design, this study found factors that drive how well spaces are liked and used. These findings can be used as design tools to support social space success and provide a better understanding of the relationship between "like" and "use." The results of this study offer applicable insights for the design of vibrant and lively social spaces to address residents' higher-level need for social interaction.

References

Aquino, J., Russell, D., Cutrona, C., and Altmaier, E. 1996, October. "Employment status, social support, and life satisfaction among the elderly," *Journal of Counseling Psychology* 43(4): 480–489.

Cannuscio, C., Block, J., and Kawachi, I. 2003. "Social capital and successful aging: the role of senior housing," *Annals of Internal Medicine* 139: 395–400.

Carr, S., Francis, M., Rivlin, L., and Stone, A. 1992. *Public Space.* Cambridge: Cambridge University Press.

Cooper Marcus, C. and Francis, C. 1990. *People Places: Design Guidelines for Urban Open Space.* New York: Van Nostrand Reinhold.

Day, J. 2011. *Population Profile of the United States.* Washington DC: US Census Bureau Briefs.

Fiori, K., Antonucci, T., and Cortina, K. 2006, January. "Social network typologies and mental health among older adults," *The Journals of Gerontology* 61B(1): P25–P32.

Flagg, F. 1987. *Fried Green Tomatoes at the Whistle Stop Cafe.* London: Random House.

Howden, L. and Meyer, J. May 2011. *Age and Sex Composition: 2010.* Washington DC: US Census Bureau Briefs.

Hunt, M. 2001. "Settings conducive to the provision of long-term care," *Journal of Architectural and Planning Research* 18(3): 223–233.

Hunt, M. and Ross, L. 1990. "Naturally occurring retirement communities: a multi-attribute examination of desirability factors," *The Gerontologist* 30: 667–674.

Jang, Y., Mortimer, J., Haley, W., and Graves, A. 2004. "The role of social engagement in life satisfaction: its significance among older individuals with disease and disability," *Journal of Applied Gerontology* 23(3): 266–273.

Kaplan, R. and Kaplan, S. 1989. *The Experience of Nature: A Psychological Perspective.* Cambridge: Cambridge University Press.

Kim, S., Lee J., and Bell, R. 2008. *Informing the Debate: New Urbanism in Michigan.* Institute for Public Policy and Social Research, Michigan State University.

Krause, N. 2006. "Social relationships in late life," *Handbook of Aging and the Social Sciences* (6th ed.). San Diego: Academic Press.

Lang, J. 1987. *Creating Architectural Theory: The Role of the Behavioral Sciences in Environmental Design.* New York: Van Nostrand Reinhold.

Lawton, M. P. 1974. "Social ecology and the health of older people," *American Journal of Public Health* 64(3): 257–260.

Lee, H., Jang, S., Lee, S., Cho, S., and Park, E. 2008. "The relationship between social participation and self-rated health by sex and age: a cross-sectional survey," *International Journal of Nursing Studies* 45(7): 1042–1054.

MacNeil, R. and Teague, M. 1987. *Aging and Leisure: Vitality in Later Life.* Englewood Cliffs, NJ: Prentice Hall.

Marsden, J. 2005. *Humanistic Design of Assisted Living*. Baltimore: Johns Hopkins University Press.

Maslow, A. [1954] 1987. *Motivation and Personality*. (3rd ed.). New York: Addison-Wesley.

Newman, O. 1979. *Community of Interest*. New York: Anchor.

Oldenburg, R. [1989] 1999. *The Great Good Place*. New York: Marlowe.

Percival, J. 2001, November. "Self-esteem and social motivation in age-segregated settings," *Housing Studies* 16(6): 827–840.

Rosenbaum, M. 2006, August. "Exploring the social supportive role of third places in consumers' lives," *Journal of Service Research* 9(1): 59–72.

Scott, S. 1993. "Visual attributes related to preference in interior environments," *Journal of Interior Design* 18(1–2): 7–16.

Street, D., Burge, S., Quadagno, J., and Barrett, A. 2007, March. "The salience of social relationships for resident well-being in assisted living," *The Journals of Gerontology: Series B Psychological Sciences and Social Sciences* 62B(2): S129–134.

Veitch, R. and Arkkelin, D. 1995. *Environmental Psychology: An Interdisciplinary Perspective*. New York: Prentice Hall.

Whyte, W. 1980. *The Social Life of Small Urban Spaces*. Washington DC: Conservation Foundation.

WHO (World Health Organization). 2002. *Active Aging: A Policy Framework*. Geneva: WHO.

Ziegler. 2009. *Ziegler National CCRC Listing and Profile*. Ziegler Capital Markets Report.

14

Developing a Person-Centric Design Philosophy

Jill Pable

Introduction

The literature suggests that the creation of environments for vulnerable populations such as the poor, the homeless, the elderly, the displaced, and the disabled is a critical imperative that has not been fully embraced by the design community (Gamez and Rogers 2008; Hosey 2008). This movement, sometimes called "design for social justice," "socially conscious architecture," "public architecture," or "humanitarian design," promotes the idea that architecture and design can – and should – respond to the social concerns of disadvantaged users and, in so doing, substantiate the value of design by addressing the social compact it holds with the public (Anderson, Honey, and Dudek 2007; Sinclair 2008).

In this essay I argue that design professionals can benefit from intentionally adopting a philosophy that views human beings as cognitive, sensory-influenced, and emotional beings. Further, I will share my personal pursuit of such a philosophy.

Developing a Person-Centric Philosophy

When exploring various research questions, strategies, and tactics I have found it helpful to adopt a "person-centric" philosophical framework – one that lies outside of traditional design knowledge. My intent is not to suggest that this approach is appropriate for everyone, nor to direct others toward a specific worldview or system of inquiry. Instead, my intent is to suggest that a firm, intentional grounding in a

The Handbook of Interior Design, First Edition. Edited by Jo Ann Asher Thompson and Nancy H. Blossom.

relevant, person-oriented philosophy may be an invaluable orientation tool in the establishment of a research agenda. Further, I believe such an approach can provide balance to the full spectrum of human experience that designers must consider.

Framing the Question: The Needs of the Disadvantaged

How does one go about investigating the complex issues that face those who are disadvantaged? For example, the homeless, the mentally disabled, and victims of domestic violence face not only physical challenges, but significant psychological ones as well. Although all these groups fall under the social betterment umbrella, their needs vary greatly. In the case of the homeless, for example, they are typically under a state of heightened emotional crisis, are without substantial coping resources, and may fear interaction with others because they have been physically or mentally abused. They may exhibit defense mechanisms including anger, withdrawal, or denial. Stripped of the schedule of typical daily life, they may be out of touch with time.

All of these things may be aggravated by substance abuse issues or mental disabilities such as paranoia, depression, or schizophrenia. In some cases, the experience of "living rough" (essentially living outside) or life on the urban streets may have convinced a homeless person that she or he is not only invisible but less than human, and therefore deserving of the mistreatment she or he experiences (Burt, Aron, Douglas, Valente, et al. 1999; Rog and Buckner 2007).

In the case of creating built environments to accommodate the homeless, for example, it quickly becomes clear that a deep understanding of the lived experience of being homeless is critical to crafting an effective design response in either research or practice. Designers must understand the situational components that contribute to being homeless (e.g., domestic violence, mental disorder, lack of income, etc.). The lived experience of a person enduring a life crisis, such as homelessness, is characterized by their own perceptions of reality – something that an outsider's casual inspection of the situation can easily miss. Without this understanding, a gap is created between the designer's intuitive comprehension of the design challenges and the ability to effectively address the needs of disadvantaged populations.

Lack of an in-depth understanding of the human experience can be costly in design, a point long accepted by environmental behaviorists. Architects and designers who do not grasp the psychological scope of the experience and perceptions of their users run the risk of producing expensive built projects that fail. The need to understand the human experience is widely recognized in interior design programs of study, as evidenced by its inclusion in the accreditation standards established by the Council for Interior Design Accreditation (2011).

An often referenced example of a built environment that did not acknowledge the human experience and consequently failed is Pruitt Igoe, a low-income housing development in east St. Louis built in 1956. Its high-rise construction style ignored the residents' need for community and safety. While there were other issues and concerns also in play in the doomed Pruitt-Igoe project, its modernist architectural design is widely blamed for its failure (Montgomery 1985).

A smaller, but no less important, example comes from my own work with low-income housing. While working with a government agency that assists developers, I became aware of a project where all the low-income apartments had been sequestered together inside a larger residential development. In so doing, the developer failed to address the low-income residents' need for "normalcy" and "being just like everyone else." As a result, there was a perceived stigma and the low-income residents were less likely to be seen as part of the community.

Although in-depth reviews of the literature on disadvantaged populations, site visits, observations, and interviews are undoubtedly helpful in connecting designers to the lived experiences of disadvantaged populations, these things alone are not enough. They may get at the effect, but have less to offer in terms of understanding the cause.

For example, in my own research I have observed that homeless persons are sometimes critical of others as they wait to see if they will be admitted for the night. An understanding of the root of that behavior provides insights into ways to counteract this issue through the design of the space; that is, in this example, by creating thoughtful seating in small, non-confrontational arrangements.

Interior designers must regularly draw upon information from other fields in order to devise localized, specific solutions such as this example suggests. Because of this, I propose that a more foundational, broad level of understanding from other fields is necessary to achieve thoughtful and even-handed design outcomes.

A Case for the Intentional Person-Centric Philosophical Framework

I argue that data-gathering tactics such as observation, interview, and other research tools address small, isolated consequences or effects of the lived experience, while leaving out necessary, fundamental understandings about where the disadvantaged are "coming from." Further, I argue that these things alone overlook those choice-driving forces that are seldom easy to observe.

This being the case, I believe it is important to develop a philosophical design framework that speaks to people's holistic well-being. Questions such as the following underpin such a philosophical framework:

- What is a person's potential to be happy?
- How can people be emotionally complete and well-adjusted?
- How should aberrant or anti-social behavior be viewed, or to what should it be attributed?
- How should we view the built environment with regard to its potential to better the human experience?

I maintain that adopting a philosophical framework such as this will help ensure that design research includes an intentional "person-centric" approach to human mental and emotional well-being. The identification of one's philosophical world view is not a new idea, of course. A statement of philosophy that identifies one's values, priorities, and driving forces has for some time been considered an important component of a designer's portfolio (Bender 2008). Similarly, "mission statements" are commonly developed and promoted by interior design firms so that their clients can determine if there is a good match with their own priorities (such as expressing a commitment to sustainability or holding a global-scope perspective).

The philosophical framework I propose represents a step beyond these cursory conclusions, compelling the researcher/designer to craft their intent in an informed, thoughtful way, considering deeper questions such as those about human behavior, the nature of emotion, the source of aberrant action, and/or the nature of linear time.

A person-centric framework can spring from a number of fields and points of view including, but not limited to, psychology, sociology, and anthropology. For example, the school of ecological psychology places central priority on the influence of human beings' context or environment – that is to say, to fully understand behavior a full exploration of the environment where behavior takes place is necessary (Gibson 1979). Within this broad theory is the concept of "situated cognition," which claims that cognition, or knowing, cannot be separated from, and is heavily influenced by, environmental context, activity, people, culture, or language (Greeno 1989). These, along with other opportunities to form a person-centric design framework, open the door to a better understanding of perceived reality, and can broaden designers' understanding of ontology (the nature of reality) and epistemology (how we know).

A defined person-centric framework can ground a designer and/or design researcher, while at the same time providing an element of credibility to their work. Adopting a person-centric framework from a field outside of design can strengthen design decisions and conclusions because, as Cross explains, "[other fields] have much stronger histories of inquiry, scholarship and research than we have in design. We need to draw upon those histories and traditions where appropriate, while building our own intellectual culture, acceptable and defensible in the world on its own terms" (Cross 2001).

Of no less importance is the fact that the adoption of a person-centric framework provides a pathway for connecting design to other disciplines and moving design research toward its logical place as an "interdisciplinary discipline." According to Cross, this idea is the central challenge for design research, and mirrors the trend of design practitioners to collaborate with other disciplines (Council for Interior Design Accreditation 2010; Cross 1999).

I argue that a person-centric framework provides a lens through which human experience, behavior, and need might be holistically viewed. In addition, such a person-centric framework helps address the nature of research questions, strategies,

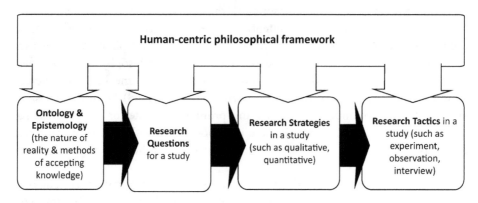

Figure 14.1

and tactics. Thus, a person-centric philosophical framework can operate alongside other choices in a research study, as shown in Figure 14.1.

The Personal Nature of a Person-Centric Framework

Although seldom discussed, it is usually the case that one's philosophical approach to a research problem is typically in agreement with one's personal worldview. How one believes the world works could and should encompass how one views truth, the nature of knowledge, and beliefs about how human beings interact with these concepts. Perceptions concerning these issues vary widely.

My own way of seeing such things is somewhat conventional, and predicated on my overt selection of a philosophical framework. Specifically, I am willing to accept that human perceptions vary, but ultimately the world possesses certain objective truths, some of which human beings have license to perceive and respond to in their own way. That is, certain properties do not rely on the cognizance of human minds to exist (e.g., the existence of gravity).

This being said, it is still true that subjective experience is compelling and at times cannot be captured by objective research approaches that discount these perceptual variations. As American philosopher Thomas Nagel artfully explains, "It is objectively impossible to describe what it is like to be a bat – one has to be a bat to really understand the point of view" (Nagel 1974). Put another way, one's consciousness has an inherently subjective nature to it. Thus, I accept that perceptions matter deeply to those that hold them, and as I am compelled to serve my clients (who hold these perceptions) in my design research, this fact must at times take precedence.

For me, this grounding in the nature of reality leads to a certain pragmatism when considering qualitative and quantitative methodologies for a study. While my primary research training was in quantitative methods, my personal evolution has led me to conclude that this approach sometimes lacks the richness of human experience that can lead to the discovery of important, often intimate human–environment points of view. Thus, my refusal to succumb to either wholesale qualitative or quantitative methods has led me to embrace a system of mixed methods as a means to determine and strengthen conclusions.

This decision, along with active searches of various theories, solidified my core belief in a person-centric framework and led me to my current research focus on homelessness. After much thought, I chose "humanistic psychology" as the person-centric framework to shape my research. This has proven to be a good choice for my worldview, as it is sufficiently universal to be applicable to a range of studies and, much like a design concept in an actual construction project, smooths the selection of future research studies.

What is Humanistic Psychology?

Sometimes called the "third wave" of psychology, humanistic psychology differs from the deconstructive psychoanalytic emphasis of Freud and his colleagues. It also offers a different view from the "black box" behaviorism of B. F. Skinner, which tied behavior to predictable responses prompted by stimuli (Bugental 1964). Humanistic psychology attempts to look beyond these strictly medical models of psychology and their reliance on controlled, clinical studies to a stance that concentrates not on the pathological aspects of the human condition, but instead the potential for good health.

This new point of view seeks to holistically explore the complexity of human beings and to serve as a science of the lived experience (Aanstoos, Serlin, and Greening 2000). Central to humanistic psychology is organismic theory, the idea that the total person is the natural unit of study (Hall and Lindzey 1978). The key components of humanistic psychology that are at the heart of my personal belief about human beings and their potential are listed below:

- Human beings are more than merely the sum of their parts. They cannot be reduced to component parts or functions.
- Human beings exist in a uniquely human context, as well as in a cosmic ecology.
- Human beings have some choice, and with that, responsibility.
- Human beings are intentional, aim at goals, are aware that they cause future events, and seek meaning, value and creativity (Bugental 1964).
- Art, poetry, literature, and philosophy are important to our understanding of the human experience and for healing and enriching one's inner life (Elkins 2009).

My initial exploration of humanistic psychology revealed that it had a significant impact on various disciplines including education, social work, and nursing (Elkins 2009) – fields that, like interior design, seek to offer positive progress relative to social betterment issues. In the words of prominent psychologist David Elkins, "Humanistic psychology is a psychology of liberation focused on change and growth, a passionate vision that all human beings have dignity and worth" (Elkins 2009).

After adopting humanistic psychology as my foundation, it was necessary to identify specific theories in humanistic psychology that could play a more visible and prominent role in my own research agenda. One such theory was self-actualization, a concept proposed by Abraham Maslow in his "hierarchy of needs" theory.

Self-actualization essentially holds that all human beings are capable of realizing their full potential, and that negative "psychopathologizing" experiences can hold people back from this full sense of being. As Søren Kierkegaard explained, self-actualization is the view that "a person [can] be that which one truly is" (Ewen 1984).

Maslow identified self-actualization as the central goal of therapy and suggested that "any means of any kind that helps to restore the person to the path of self-actualization and of development along the lines that his inner nature dictates" is a positive action (Maslow 1968). Implicit in this line of thinking is that elements of a human being's experience, including the built environment, can be agents of supportive therapy that assists one to self-actualization, or destructive to one's progress toward self-actualization.

Viewed in this light, physical environments for the homeless become much more than shelter, but rather a potential instrument of betterment. I suggest that in this realization lies the potential utility of humanistic psychology in design research (and more broadly, the usefulness of a human-centric framework to guide one's research agenda).

If we examine the example given earlier of the homeless person's anger toward others in the waiting room from a humanist psychology viewpoint, this anger can be seen as an expression of fear. Therefore, rather than being just managed, it is possible to eradicate it (Hall and Lindzey 1978). This fear can be treated as part of a process of healing; in this case, through the sensitive realignment of interior components in the waiting room. Thus, the full potential of the power of a person-centric framework can be seen. That is to say that not only can such a framework drive the nature of research questions, but it also becomes the means through which questions are answered.

Research strategies and tactics and their interface with the person-centric framework

With regard to specific research strategies (i.e., qualitative, quantitative, logical argumentation) and tactics (observation, interview, etc.), the humanistic psychology framework permits freedom in methodological choices, embracing both qualitative approaches that capture lived experience and quantitative a posteriori strategies that allow an idea to be considered without unduly generalizing the phenomena (Giorgi 2009). Essentially, the methodological pluralism of humanistic psychology provides a validated freedom to choose a research strategy that is based on the nature of the research questions. Such pluralism is in agreement with the authors of design discovery, who see design as different than either the objective/science paradigm or subjective/art paradigm and argue that a diversity of research methods has complementary strengths that have a better chance of serving the range of design activities (Cross 2001; Dorst 1997).

Another research strategy is to combine systems of inquiry within the same study; that is, to use a specific approach where it is most helpful, or as a means to triangulate findings. Johnston and Onwueguzie advocate this "mixed method" approach on the grounds that it can produce a more workable set of conclusions and gain a more balanced perspective on an issue (Johnston and Onwueguzie 2004). Equally important, having multiple strategies brings credence to intuitive processes which can then be subjected to verification by experience testing (Huitt 1998). This is a particularly useful strategy in cases with a small sample.

The Person-Centric Framework: Two Examples of Its Application in Design Research

The following examples of research studies were developed in response to the framework-methodology structures previously discussed. Both rely on humanistic psychology for their grounding, and demonstrate a range of methodologies. For clarity, these studies' methodologies are diagrammed using Wang's design diagramming method (Wang 2007).

Study #1. Design-decision research: design of a prototype
check-in patio for a homeless shelter

The first study springs not only from the general, subtle philosophy of humanistic psychology, but also uses the work of humanistic psychologist Abraham Maslow as its guiding principle for synthesis of tangible design guidelines (Maslow 1968). The study's focus was the design of a homeless shelter's intake patio. Its methods were akin to design-decision research that both assesses design decision-making and the actual implementation of those design decisions (Farbstein and Kantrowitz 1991). That is, the main goal of the study was to "develop a device that can inform reflective thinking about design action" (Groat and Wang 2002) by combining various theory systems into a "theory-to-action grid." Thus, the study occurred in two parts: first, the development of the theory-to-action grid as a design tool, then the application of the theory-to-action grid's recommendations in an applied design. Figure 14.2 graphically depicts the study's strategies and tactics.

The primary theory in the theory-to-action grid was Maslow's self-actualization theory (Maslow 1968). For example, Maslow asserts that a self-actualized person expresses interest in the social well-being of others. In the case of the homeless, one can assume that these individuals are in crisis and therefore not on a path toward

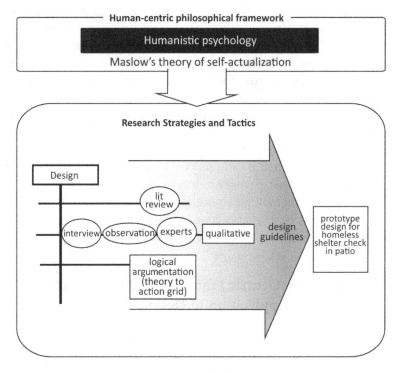

Figure 14.2

self-actualization. This characteristic is described in the theory-to-action grid (i.e., a person may feel animosity, frustration, or distrust of others).

This insight from Maslow's theory was coupled with ideas about ways that the built environment might counter these qualities from sources such as Alexander's *A Pattern Language* and Crowe's *Crime Prevention through Environmental Design* (Alexander, Ishikawa, and Silverstein 1977; Crowe 1991). Each of these theories supports the tenets of humanistic psychology of (1) self-determination and (2) the potential for betterment. The theory-to-action grid served to identify similarities in each theory system that then informed a set of specific and tangible design goals, as seen in Figure 14.3.

The second phase of this research study was to put the theory-to-action grid into practice by applying it to design guidelines for an actual homeless shelter's check-in area. Adherence to tenets of human wellness extracted from the various theory systems resulted in elements that catered to its users' psychological needs. For example, the intake area's enclosure had sufficient openness to permit a sense of psychological escape, a clock tower served as an anchor/organization device to provide the homeless with a reconnection to temporality, and seating placement acknowledged that users would prefer defensive protection. Figure 14.4 provides a perspective view of the proposed patio.

Self-Actualization characteristic	Explanation of the characteristic	Antithesis of this characteristic	Patterns response	CEPTD/Proxemics response	Patio design criteria
An accurate perception of reality	Self-actualizers are free of pessimism and defensive distortions. Can judge real from phony in people, events, and ideas.	Pessimistic, defensive. May be unable to make accurate judgments concerning truth and fiction in others' intent or events.	Patterns that relate to clarity in spatial experience and procedure: *#120: Paths and Goals.* Place goals at natural points of architectural interest. *#126 Something roughly in the middle.* Design space to draw people towards a center.	Provide clear definition of controlled space so that people recognize differences between public/private. An organization should stake claim to a space by creating well defined border and edges that imply ownership and control.	*Create a design that emphasizes clarity and legitimacy:* Patio should send cues of separation from the problems of the street and a sense of security, stability and refuge. Forms and textures that evoke an enduring presence will be used. Overhead forms will appear to be well supported. Overtly unsettling assemblies will be avoided. Be up front, easy to understand/clear, true and honest. Provide up to date accurate information on digital boards and bulletin boards. Provide a way to queue up for check-in that is fair and efficient.

Figure 14.3

Figure 14.4

The resulting design for the space is not strikingly novel; however, it possesses numerous small features that are attuned to the needs of a person in crisis through its proxemics, treatment of color, spatial circulation, and integration of staff. The nuanced nature of the design is not surprising because the lived experience of space is often local.

Study #2. Case study exploring family perceptions of a homeless shelter bedroom

The second study investigated further the "lived experience" of a homeless shelter. Like the first, the second study sprang from humanistic psychology; however, unlike the first study, the foundation of humanistic psychology more subtly underplays the research questions. That is to say, at its core the study explored the potential assistance that a built environment could offer to the homeless by, in effect, moving them toward self-actualization, but sought answers to questions that tested the specific means by which this might happen. The study's questions were crafted from informed a priori reasoning, gleaned from established psychological studies on crowding, sense of control, and helplessness. Focus groups of homeless residents at the shelter helped confirm the viability of questions before the study commenced.

Specifically, this study explored the "lived experience" of a bedroom for a homeless family and their perceptions of crowding, sense of control, and helplessness. The system of inquiry was both positivist, in that it included quantitative tactics, and naturalistic, in that it captured individual perceptions of the family using qualitative tactics. A pattern-matching case-study design was adopted, thus introducing qualitative measures in line with humanistic psychology. This design approach gathered data from a family occupying an altered bedroom and then measured effects against another "control" family, i.e., a family in an unaltered bedroom, over the course of six months. Differences in the two family's situations were acknowledged for the potential affect these might have on conclusions. Additionally, since the main objective of the study was theory-building, the limited generalizability of the small sample sizes was not considered significant.

Figure 14.5 provides a visual diagram of the study's overall method. The first of the two phases embraced literature review, focus group, and logical argumentation that resulted in guidelines that helped form the design priorities and features of the altered homeless shelter family bedroom. With the assistance of a $10,000 research grant, a bedroom at the shelter was renovated to include these new elements. Added features were intended to decrease sensations of crowding and increase sense of control.

The second phase of the homeless shelter bedroom study explored the families' reactions to the bedrooms and used interview, observation, and participant photographs, along with a quantitative questionnaire, to triangulate findings. The case-study method permitted the gathering of deep, rich information and enabled participants to descriptively report how the altered room's design reduced their

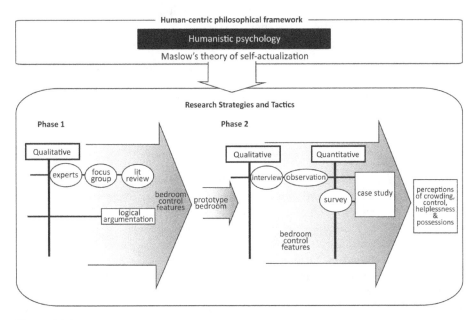

Figure 14.5

sense of crowding, and their perception of personal control. Further, the altered room's features reduced perceptions of crowding through the visual expansion of space.

Conclusions and Recommendations

In this essay I have argued that the adoption of a human-centric philosophical framework can assist design researchers who seek to embrace human welfare elements. This human-centric framework is particularly helpful when addressing disadvantaged populations whose life experiences are different from those of the researcher. I have further argued that the adoption of a philosophical framework supports the direction of design research and is in keeping with emerging trends in design practice.

In closing, I would like to leave the reader with three central points:

1   Elements such as safety, security, and privacy are critical parts of the human experience that must be acknowledged and planned for, and are critical to the lived human experience.
2   For staying power and full justification of the grounding for their work, design researchers must "leave the shallows" and recognize the foundations from which they design and reason, and on what basis they accept pre-existing knowledge and generate new knowledge. In effect, researchers must recognize that "knowing

a fact is not something that one does; it is a condition one has come to occupy in relation to information" (Rescher 2003).

3 Deep systemic connections of person-centric philosophical frameworks from other fields coupled with design field-specific knowledge can help guide choices and approaches to knowledge generation – and help design scholarship make its unique contribution to the betterment of society.

References

Aanstoos, C., Serlin, I., and Greening, T. 2000. "A history of division 32 (humanistic psychology) of the American Psychological Association," in D. Dewsbury (ed.), *Unification through Division: Histories of the Divisions of the American Psychological Association*, vol. 5. Washington DC: American Psychological Association. pp. 1–47.

Alexander, C., Ishikawa, S., and Silverstein, M. 1977. *A Pattern Language: Towns, Buildings, Construction*. New York: Oxford University Press.

Anderson, B. G., Honey, P. L., and Dudek, M. T. 2007. "Interior design's social compact: key to the quest for professional status," *Journal of Interior Design* 33(2): v–xiii.

Bender, D. 2008. *Design Portfolios Moving from Traditional to Digital*. New York: Fairchild.

Bugental, J. 1964. "The third force in psychology," *Journal of Humanistic Psychology* 4(1): 19–25.

Burt, M., Aron, L., Douglas, T., Valente, J., Lee, E. and Iwen, B. 1999. "Homelessness: programs and the people they serve," *Summary Report – Findings of the National Survey of Homeless Assistance Providers and Clients*. Washington DC: The Urban Institute.

Council for Interior Design Accreditation. 2010. *CIDA Collaborative Strategies Report*. Meeting conducted in Washington DC, November 12, 2010.

Council for Interior Design Accreditation. 2011. *Professional Standards 2011*. http://www.accredit-id.org/professional-standards. Accessed June 14, 2011.

Cross, N. 1999. "Design research: a disciplined conversation," *Design Issues* 15(2): 5–10.

Cross, N. 2001. "Designerly ways of knowing," *Design Issues* 17(3): 49–55.

Crowe, T. 1991. *Crime Prevention through Environmental Design*. Boston: Butterworth-Heinemann.

Dorst, K. 1997. "Describing Design: A Comparison of Paradigms." Doctoral dissertation, Technische Universiteit, Delft. Abstract retrieved from Proquest, AAT C627941.

Elkins, D. 2009. "Why humanistic psychology lost its power and influence in American psychology: implications for advancing humanistic psychology," *Journal of Humanistic Psychology* 49(3): 267–291.

Ewen, R. 1984. *An Introduction to Theories of Personality* (2nd ed.). New York: Academic Press.

Farbstein, J. and Kantrowitz, M. 1991. "Design research in the swamp," in E. Zube and G. Moore (eds.), *Advances in Environment and Behavior and Design*, vol. 3. New York: Plenum Press, pp. 297–318.

Gamez, J. and Rogers, S. 2009. "An architecture of change," in B. Bell and K. Wakeford (eds.), *Expanding Architecture: Design as Activism*. Singapore: Metropolis Books, pp. 18–25.

Gibson, J. 1979. *The Ecological Approach to Visual Perception*. Boston: Houghton Mifflin.

Giorgi, A. 2009. *The Descriptive Phenomenological Method in Psychology: A Modified Husserlian Approach*. Pittsburgh, PA: Duquesne University Press.

Greeno, J. G. 1989. "A perspective on thinking," *American Psychologist* 44: 134–141.

Groat, L. and Wang, D. 2002. *Architectural Research Methods*. New York: Wiley.

Hall, C. and Lindzey, G. 1978. *Theories of Personality* (3rd ed.). New York: Wiley.

Hosey, L. 2008. "Toward a humane environment: sustainable design and social justice," in B. Bell and K. Wakeford (eds.), *Expanding Architecture Design as Activism*. New York: Bellerophon Publications, pp. 34–41.

Huitt, W. 1998. "Measurement, evaluation, and research: ways of knowing," *Educational Psychology Interactive*. Valdosta, GA: Valdosta State University. http://www.edpsycinteractive.org/topics/intro/wayknow.html. Accessed December 23, 2010.

Johnston, R. and Onwueguzie, A. 2004. "Mixed methods research: a research paradigm whose time has come," *Educational Researcher* 33(7): 14–26.

Maslow, A. 1968. *Toward a Psychology of Being*. Princeton: Van Nostrand Reinhold.

Montgomery, R. 1985. "Pruitt-Igoe: policy failure or societal symptom," in B. Checkoway and C. V. Patton (eds.), *The Metropolitan Midwest: Policy Problems and Prospects for Change*. Chicago: Board of Trustees of the University of Illinois, pp. 229–243.

Nagel, T. 1974. "What is it like to be a bat?", *The Philosophical Review* 83(4): 435–450.

Rescher, N. 2003. *Epistemology: An Introduction to the Theory of Knowledge*. New York: Albany State University of New York Press.

Rog, D. and Buckner, J. 2007. "Homeless Families and Chidren," in D. L. Dennis (ed.), *Toward Understanding Homelessness: The 2007 National Symposium on Homelessness Research*. Washington DC: Department of Health and Human Services and US Department of Housing and Urban Development.

Sinclair, C. 2008. "I hope it's a long list," in K. Stohr and C. Sinclair, *Architecture for Humanity: Design Like You Give a Damn*. New York: Metropolis Books, pp. 10–31.

Wang, D. 2007. "Diagramming design research," *Journal of Interior Design* 33(1): 33–43.

15

In Support of Contemporary Identity: The Modern Palestinian Home

May Sayrafi

Introduction

Many Palestinians today live in places that barely satisfy their basic needs rather than dynamic places that convey cultural meanings and respond to the various forces that define the Palestinian context. In order to reconnect people with their home and identity, it is important to understand those aspects of the Palestinian home that enhance a sense of belonging and allow people to express their identity. To do this, an examination of the various forces that shape the Palestinian home is necessary and must include the exploration of cultural, historical, and identity contexts, as well as other extrinsic and intrinsic forces specific to the Palestinian experience such as political, economic, social, historical, and ecological conditions.

These extrinsic and intrinsic forces define a distinct character for the Palestinian home which can be developed into design strategies that respond to the current modes of living and the shared values of the Palestinians. A model for translation of these design strategies into the built environment is presented in this essay for a contemporary interior of a Palestinian house – one that reinterprets the past in a modern way while responding to the current needs of the community and restoring the occupants' identity and sense of place.

The Cultural Context

The home is shaped by the beliefs and practices of a certain group of people as they create an ordering system that reflects their modes of living, cultural expressions,

The Handbook of Interior Design, First Edition. Edited by Jo Ann Asher Thompson and Nancy H. Blossom.

and social standards (Rapoport 2001). The changes and variations in the form and spatial organization of the home reflect a continuous process that encompasses cultural and social forces. The cultural context is shaped by various aspects which include the family and their behavior patterns, the social norms and ordering systems, and the social interactions within a certain group. These aspects reflect their way of life, their symbols and meanings, and their strategies for survival (Altman, Rapoport, and Wohlwill 1980).

People also apply changes to the built environment in order to create physical spaces that meet their social needs and activities. The social activities of the occupants can give meaning to the home and transform it from a basic shelter into a place that communicates cultural messages (Lawrence and Low 1990).

In Palestine, the growth of the traditional home was determined by the social needs of the occupants. This organic nature created complex and rich residential units that included a variety of forms and informal organizations. The access to residential units was experienced through a sequence of spaces that protected the privacy of the homes. The interiors of the homes were also balanced between the private and public life of the occupants. Hence, the physical attributes of the space responded to the social organizations and systems, and also revealed embedded meanings that communicated the ideals and practices of the society (Bianca 2000; Rapport 2001).

Today, modern architecture is replacing the residential micro-communities and destroying the homogeneity and balance between the cultural patterns and the physical place. The modern residences are imported models that impose new social codes and behavioral patterns that are foreign and do not relate to the surviving traditions and cultural expressions. The new "street-facing" residential blocks are simply "detached objects" that do not consider the local materials, traditions, and needs of the society (Bianca 2000).

This lack of cultural meaning in the modern homes indicates the importance of attention to the non-verbal communications and cultural expressions of the Palestinian homes, and the need to include these symbolic meanings in the built environment of Palestinians. In so doing, a bridge between the principles of the traditional home and the current living patterns of the Palestinians is created.

The Historical Context

By exploring the historical styles and artifacts one better understands the various social and political forces influencing the development of a home. In Palestine, the changes in political forces throughout the history have had a direct influence on the form and interior organization of the home. These changes can be traced back through four historical periods: the Islamic period (the Mamluk influence, 1270–1516); the late Ottoman period (the European influence, 1841–1917); the British Mandate (1920–1948); and the Israeli occupation (1948–present).

During the early Islamic period (1270–1516), the traditional Palestinian house emerged from the traditional dwelling in the Arab region. The residential architecture during that time was based upon Islamic principles that regulated the social and cultural patterns within the house. An important aspect of the traditional house was the clear distinction between the private and public domains. Transitional spaces generated a hierarchical progression from public to private rooms and from the glare to dark spaces. The courtyard acted as a "nucleus" of the house, tying together the diverse units and activities (Ragette 2003).

During the mid-19th century under Ottoman rule, the Palestinian house was influenced by changes in political and economic conditions. The European presence and the advancement in transportation had a direct impact on the architecture and design elements of the Palestinian house. A new house style called the "central hall house" emerged (Scarce 1996). The new house had guest salons inspired by European drawing rooms, and each room had a distinct function and furniture that corresponded to it. The courtyard remained a central element that allowed social interaction between members of the extended family and maintained the balance between the public and private zones of the house (Safadi 2008).

Ottoman rule was followed by the British Mandate in the early 20th century. The British authorities preserved the architectural character of the Palestinian religious cities as they recognized the unique vernacular architecture that responded to the urban and social context (Fuchs 2000). British architects continued to use local materials and local methods of construction in order to respond to the traditional and climatic conditions of the region (Fuchs 2000).

The British Mandate ended with the declaration of the Israeli state in 1948. The 1948 war resulted in the expulsion of more than 750,000 Palestinians from their homes (Farsoun 2004). The new political and geographical boundaries directly influenced the architecture of Palestinian homes by creating a high urban density on a limited land resource. Housing projects responded to the high urban density by focusing on ways to make use of the limited land while housing thousands of people. Unfortunately, many of these projects did not take into consideration such things as the climate and social boundaries. This, along with the increasing use of the automobile, changed the orientation and functional organization of the Palestinian home.

The combination of social and political changes generated an architecture that is foreign to its context and that forced itself on the land. The buildings erected in Palestine after the Israeli occupation were mostly concrete blocks that provided the residents with affordable amenities and the comforts and conveniences of modern life; however, the spontaneous and scattered urban growth on a land under dispute has created fragmented communities that lack a cohesive political, religious, family, and communal structure. These dynamic changes that continue to occur in the Palestinian context influence the current character and identity of the home.

Home and Identity

People utilize the built environment in order to communicate their identity thereby strengthening their sense of belonging. The expressions of identity and the control of interior space contribute to place attachment and enhance the sense of belonging in the space. Many of the studies that focus on place attachment emphasize the dynamic nature of the identity process, and indicate how the physical space influences "the active construction and reconstruction of self-identity" (Manzo 2003).

In Palestine the continuous interruption of the identity-formation process has generated a fragmented community that is still of constructing its identity. The occupation of the West Bank and Gaza in 1967 has changed the identity of Palestine, and the Palestinian diaspora has created a new identity for the Palestinians who share the experiences of exile, dispersion, and loss of their land and home. The loss of a home disturbs the social bonds of the family, and hence the identity of the physical space is lost as well (Cox and Holmes 2000). The economic and political instability and the fragmentation in the occupied territories have created a stateless population that is denied a clear identity and boundary for existence.

There have been attempts to overcome this social fragmentation and disruption of the Palestinian identity. For example, a recent study reveals the work of several Palestinian artists who expressed their perception of the Palestinian identity by using natural materials from the land and references to memories of the lost land (Sherwell 2006). In order to ensure the continuity of the identity-formation process, it is important to examine current expressions of identity such as this, so that the home exceeds the physical boundary and becomes a living entity that supports the construction of a dynamic Palestinian identity and culture.

Revisiting the Palestinian Home

In order to examine the different dimensions that shape the Palestinian home, it is necessary to explore the relationship between people and their place of residence on a physical, social, and cultural level. These relationships were explored through a study conducted in the city of Nablus in Palestine. The study included the observation and documentation of the physical and aesthetic characteristics of 23 homes. In addition, semi-structured interviews were conducted with the residents of these homes. The themes that emerged from the interviews responded to historical, cultural, social, and identity aspects that were explored in the interviews. The study also revealed the Palestinian home's responses to changes in the political, economic, and ecological context.

The interviews and observations conducted in the Palestinian residences identified six core values that are shaped by the extrinsic and intrinsic forces of the Palestinian context. These six core values are: (1) family, (2) social networks, (3) privacy, (4) patterns of daily life, (5) cultural symbols, and (6) the land. Through the incorporation of these core values into design strategies a distinct home that is sensitive to the Palestinian context can emerge.

Design value #1. Family

The extrinsic changes that occurred because of the Israeli occupation of Palestine disrupted the economic, cultural, and political institutions in the region, leaving the family as the only remaining structure that provides a sense of security and supports the Palestinian identity (Schulz 2003). However, the Israeli occupation changed the structure of the family, and today many extended families are broken down into nuclear families. Despite the changes that occurred in the structure of the family, the social norms continue to support the unity of the family as they emphasize its hierarchical order and strengthen ties between members of the extended family.

The observations carried out in both the historical and modern residences revealed a recurrent theme for family gatherings. In modern residences, the kitchen is a central space that encourages all members of the family to work and gather in that space. In the historical residences, the courtyard is a central space that provides a comfortable microclimate and facilitates most of the domestic and family activities.

The home needs to support the family by providing similar opportunities for interaction, and incorporating central spaces in the home can facilitate family gatherings. Furthermore, generating a sequence of clustered units around these central spaces can strengthen family bonds as they continue to expand in order to adapt to the needs of the family.

Design value #2. Social networks

Palestinian social practices and customs are intrinsic values that aim to encourage social networks, which achieve group solidarity and reinforce Palestinian identity. These social customs include culture-specific occasions and celebrations, which entail seasonal gatherings, and receptions that strengthen the ties between members of the community. These networks became even more prevalent after the Israeli occupation as a great majority of Palestinians were displaced from their homes. During that time, the displaced Palestinians who shared similar experiences of dispersion and exile started forming their own residential communities, and each community became an extension for the family.

Providing public social spaces within the home can facilitate both formal and informal social gatherings. The responses in the interviews revealed the importance of the guest room as a social space. A spacious reception/guest room is necessary in each house, and its generous dimensions allow more furniture to be placed against the wall, enabling more people to be engaged in the same conversation.

Design value #3. Privacy

The desire for privacy and protection has remained an important theme for every home during the different historical periods. During the Islamic and Ottoman periods, the spatial organization of the home was informed by the desire to seclude women: hence public zones were associated with males, and private zones were associated with females (Safadi 2008; Scarce 1996).

It was not until the British Mandate and the Israeli occupation that women joined the labor force and took part in the "public" life of the home. This influenced the spatial organization of the home, and the public zones became associated with guests and strangers, and the private zone became associated with the entire family instead of just the women.

Social values have always prescribed the protection of the home from any undesired intrusion and aimed to achieve a balance between the private and public lives of the occupants. The design of a home needs to respond to these values, as it should include spaces that proceed gradually from public to increasingly private areas. Semi-public zones connect the private and the public, and form a buffer between the different domains. Provision of a double circulation system can help maintain the balance between private and public spaces and separate the private family circulation paths from the public areas. Interior elements such as movable partitions and screens can also control the level of privacy and provide various degrees of enclosure within the home.

Design value #4. Patterns of daily life

The patterns of daily life are shaped by the social and domestic activities, which take many forms and vary in duration. The spaces of the home usually adapt to the different behavioral patterns and social norms associated with each type of activity. Throughout the interviews, the occupants demonstrated the diurnal and seasonal activities that take place in the home. The diurnal activities include domestic activities that are carried out during the daytime, and social and family gatherings that usually occur after sunset. The seasonal activities include a range of formal and informal seasonal gatherings.

Ecological changes such as those in wind direction and solar radiation influence the patterns of daily life, as the distribution of the activities shifts during different times of the day and over the different seasons. In both the modern and historical residences, the occupants define certain rooms as summer and winter rooms, and they perform seasonal migrations to these rooms to achieve thermal comfort. In addition to seasonal shifts in climate, there are also diurnal changes in solar radiation and wind direction which influence the type of activities carried out in each space.

As the patterns of daily life of the family shift in time and space, the spatial organization of the home can also adapt itself to the rhythm of activities of the family and accommodate the changes that occur in the surrounding environment. The home needs to include flexible spaces that have the ability to adapt to the different seasons and events. Movable partitions and furniture enable temporary transformations of the space, and allow it to contract or expand in response to the climate, social events, and family cycles. Partly enclosed spaces enable the home to accommodate climatic changes as they facilitate the movement between the outdoor and indoor environments and enable users to adjust to the different light levels of these environments.

Design value #5. Cultural symbols

Symbolic gestures are guided by intrinsic values shared by the Palestinians, and they communicate meanings in the space and establish environments that reinforce their shared beliefs. The occupants use these symbols to guide behavior, regulate interactions, and reinforce identity. The study conducted in Palestinian homes indicates that modern apartments in Palestine lack these symbolic gestures, which forces many of the occupants to use movable objects and other semi-fixed elements in order to convey cultural meanings and establish a character for their homes.

Cultural symbols became more significant as the Palestinians who lost their homes employed them to maintain their identity. The homes of the past became mental images that are out of reach, and people started reconstructing the details of the past to give form and structure to their shared experiences and hopes. The detailed descriptions included interior elements such as archways, courtyards, green-painted door panels, and built-in cupboards of the lost homes. The use of such elements in the home can communicate meanings and establish environments that facilitate activities in the home. The use of traditional structures and historical interior elements can facilitate the transformation to new physical environments and create a link to the past, reinforcing the sense of continuity and belonging in the home.

Design value #6. Identity and the land

The land is a symbol of permanence and is often referred to as the ancient land. The historical buildings acquired the same sense of permanence as the domes of the traditional houses imitated the ancient surrounding hills (Amiry 1989). The building materials used in the historical residences were also extracted from the land, and their natural color blends with the ancient land. Occupants who live in modern apartments often refer to their residences as temporary structures because of the contrast they create with the land. The new apartment buildings are built from smoothly cut white limestone which contrasts with the earthy colors of the surrounding hills, and the form of these buildings does not relate to the context as it imposes itself on the ancient land (Amiry 1989).

The Israeli occupation is the main extrinsic factor that influenced the Palestinian perception of the land. The Israeli occupation separated the Palestinians from their land, and tightened the boundary around each city. The loss of the land, the confiscation of more lands, and the displacement from the land generated a shared experience that shaped the national identity for Palestinians and set them apart from the rest of the Middle East region. It is the "lack of the homeland rather than the homeland itself that shaped the Palestinian identity" (Schulz 2003). Palestinians define themselves by the land, even though the land evokes painful memories of dispersion and loss; but maintaining the connection with the land brings hope for a better future.

The home plays a significant role in reconnecting Palestinians with the land. Interplay between outdoors and indoors connects outdoor spaces with the interior of the home and provides more visual and physical access to the land. The building material itself can suggest rootedness in the land, and the use of limestone and other local materials that are extracted from the surrounding mountains creates a harmonious relationship with the land.

Towards the Future: A Model for a Contemporary Palestinian Home

The main objective of this model is to establish an interior environment that responds to the needs and life patterns of Palestinians. The model emphasizes the powerful role of the home, and reveals how the home becomes a place that maintains traditions and provides continuity for the dynamic Palestinian identity.

The model for the contemporary Palestinian home is based upon incorporating the six main design values in a historical palace located in the old city of Nablus in Palestine. The historical palace is a traditional Palestinian courtyard house that used to house three or four generations of an extended family. Choosing a historical site for this model provides an opportunity to reuse the traditional structures in a manner that is more sensitive to the modern needs of society, and it also reveals how traditional structures can support a contemporary lifestyle while still maintaining references to the historical context.

The model preserves the historical character of the palace and, at the same time, introduces new functions and spaces that meet the modern needs of the occupants. The model consists of light structures and movable partitions that subdivide the house and define new spaces. The new additions do not disturb the integrity of the palace, and provide modern solutions that respond to the family life-cycle. The six core design values that are reflected in this model – (1) family, (2) social networks, (3) privacy, (4) patterns of daily life, (5) cultural symbols, and (6) the land – are key elements, and each one of these values informs the interior environment and spatial organization of the proposed model.

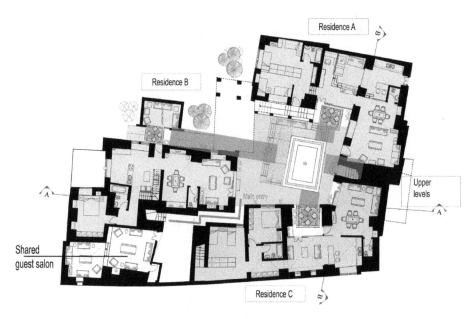

Figure 15.1

Family

The design of the model focuses on the organic nature of the Palestinian home that continues to grow in order to support the growth of the family. The changes that have occurred in family structure are reflected in the spatial programming of the design, as it proposes five residences for nuclear families. These residences are represented as major nodes (see Figure 15.1) around the courtyard, and each node has the ability to evolve into a sequence of clusters that adapt to the needs of a nuclear family. Three nodes lead to three residences located on the first level, and the fourth node connects to a staircase that leads to two more residences located on the upper levels (see Figure 15.1).

The delicate balance between the private and public realms reveals itself as each nuclear family has its own individual access and independent living unit; meanwhile all the families continue to share a main courtyard and a reception hall. The courtyard remains the nucleus which ties all the families together and maintains social networks along the family line. The sharing of spaces and the compactness of the clusters strengthen the bonds between the families and provide opportunities for more family interactions.

Social networks

The model provides special spaces that respond to the different forms of gathering that occur within the Palestinian community. Each residence includes a guest room

Figure 15.2

that is intended for different social events for the members of the nuclear family. The furniture in the guest room supports the contemporary lifestyle of the family and also references elements from the past. The arrangement of the furniture and the generous size of the room encourage more human interaction and facilitate these social meetings. The more formal gatherings take place in the shared reception hall, which is intended for seasonal gatherings and celebrations shared by members of all the families (see Figure 15.2).

Privacy

The floor plan in Figure 15.1 demonstrates how the spaces of the residences proceed gradually from public to increasingly private. The semi-public spaces and the double circulation system allow the family to link or separate different activities and regulate between the different domains. Movable screens control the level of enclosure in the space and act as "veils" protecting the privacy of the family spaces when needed (see Figure 15.2). The movable screens offer flexibility, and allow the family to control the degree of privacy in these spaces.

Patterns of daily life

The model proposes a series of central family spaces that respond to the daily domestic cycle of the family. Each room becomes a central space that can expand

Figure 15.3

or contract depending on the activity it fosters and the different times of the day. The living room, for example, is a multi-functional family space that provides intimate gathering spaces, seasonal seating areas, and study areas. The kitchen, another family space, connects to the living area and supports the rhythm of family activities.

The movable partitions establish settings that foster a variety of activities and allow different forms of enclosure in response to the patterns of daily life. The movable wood screens used in the living room enable temporary transformations of the space in response to the physical and social environments (see Figure 15.3). During the summer, the screen can open up and create a summer seating area that is connected to the main courtyard; at other times the screen can be closed, providing more enclosure for the living room, and create a more intimate family area. Wood screens are used in outdoor spaces to create semi-public zones that are partially enclosed and enable the occupants to adjust to the different light levels as they move between the outdoor and indoor environments.

Cultural symbols

The interior elements and finishes of the proposed model represent shared values and ideals that support values and traditions of the past and are essential for the identity-creation process. The selection of materials and objects in the design was guided by the cultural meanings associated with them; the use of specific patterns, colors, and pieces of furniture can convey powerful non-verbal messages and provide a sense of continuity in the cultural process. The intricate patterns of Palestinian floor tiles and Palestinian embroidery reflect a tradition that is still alive and continues to support the Palestinian identity. The historical objects and pieces of furniture also convey strong cultural messages as these objects are not only a historical record for the family but also an extension of the family, and they maintain the family's identity and the heritage.

The land

The proposed model emphasizes the strong relationship between the home and the land. The home model consists of wood screens, vegetation, and indigenous materials that connect the home with the land. The plants and vegetation features in the courtyard generate symbolic images associated with the land, and the mature grapevines rooted in the land suggest history and signify the strong connection with the land. The link to the land is further emphasized by the use of materials and structures that are extracted from the land; the limestone, extracted from the surrounding mountains, creates a harmonious relationship with the land and suggests rootedness.

The proposed model also focuses on integrating outdoor spaces and gardens in the interior environment by the use of movable wood screens that connect the occupants with elements of the land and transport them between domestic environments and the microclimates of the courtyard.

Overall, the model addresses the dynamic changes that have occurred in the cultural practices and identity-formation process of Palestinians. The proposed model draws from the principles of the past, and at the same time introduces new elements that did not exist before but are important for the continuity in the cultural and identity-formation process. It achieves a harmonious balance between old and new, private and public, indoor and outdoor, temporary and permanent, and the parts and the whole.

Conclusion

This essay has explored the forces that shape the home, and communicated the powerful role of the home as a living object that conveys meanings, regulates interactions, adapts to life patterns, and supports group identity. It also has revealed how cultural and historical forces can inform the design process, and create thriving and living entities that frame the home environment. The design values and proposed model emphasize the organic nature of the Palestinian home and provide a unique perspective on the dynamic life of the Palestinian family. In addition to that, study of the current Palestinian context raises awareness of significant values that have accumulated over the centuries and continue to be core values that are important for the survival of the Palestinian culture.

This issue is of great importance to Palestine, especially at a time when people are still in the process of constructing their identity and continue to live in modern residences that are imposed on them. The younger generation of Palestinians is disconnected from Palestine, and only knows Palestine through stories about the lost homeland and lost homes. In order to face modernity and make use of its advantages, it is essential to define the strong base that makes Palestine a culture, a community, and a country. When this identity becomes clear, the core elements that define the culture and reinforce the identity of Palestinians become clear as well. Technology and modern amenities are tools that can be used to satisfy current needs, yet these tools should be informed by the historical, political, and cultural forces that shape the Palestinian community.

References

Amiry, S. 1989. *The Palestinian Village Home*. London: British Museum Publications.

Altman, I., Rapoport, A., and Wohlwill, J. F., eds. 1980. *Human Behavior and Built Environment: Advances in Theory and Research*, vol. 1. New York: Plenum Press.

Bianca, S. 2000. *Urban Form in the Arab World: Past and Present*. New York: Thames & Hudson.

Cox, H. and Holmes, C. A. 2000. "Loss, healing, and the power of place," *Human Studies* 23(1): 63–78.

Farsoun, S. 2004. *Culture and Customs of the Palestinians*. London: Greenwood Press.

Fuchs, R. 2000. "Representing Mandatory Palestine," *Architectural History* 43: 281–233.

Lawrence, D. and Low, S. M. 1990. "The built environment and spatial form," *Annual Review of Anthropology* 19: 453–505.

Manzo, L. 2003. "For better or worse: exploring multiple dimensions of place meaning," *Journal of Environmental Psychology* 25: 67–86.

Ragette, F. 2003. *Traditional Domestic Architecture of the Arab Region*. Sharjah: American University of Sharjah.

Rapoport, A. 2001. "Theory, culture and housing," *Housing, Theory and Society* 7: 145–165.

Safadi, S. 2008. *Wall and Ceiling Painting in Notable Palestinian Mansions: Late Ottoman Period*. Ramallah: Riwaq.

Scarce, J. 1996. *Domestic Culture in the Middle East: An Exploration of the Household Interior*. Great Britain: National Museum of Scotland.

Schulz, H. 2003. *The Palestinian Diaspora: Formation of Identities and Politics of Homeland*. London: Routledge.

Sherwell, T. 2006. "Topographies of identities: soliloquies of place," *Third Text* 20(3/4): 429–443.

16

Creativity in Interior Design: Cross-Cultural Practitioners' Reviews of Entry-Level Portfolios

Siriporn Kobnithikulwong

Global Attention to Creativity

We live in "a world of change" and increasingly find that what we normally do may not work anymore. In this situation, creativity becomes essential for us to achieve our goals as individuals, as organizations, and as countries (Glăveanu 2010). Creativity has become one of the key qualities for people and products to be successful, especially these days when many countries have encountered difficulties such as natural disasters and economic recessions.

Organizations and governments across the world fully promote creative ideas and processes to enhance the productivity of their services, businesses, and national economies (Baldoni 2010; Oliver and Jung 2010). Since 2005, the United Kingdom has developed a strategy called "creative economy" to address the global competitive challenge by encouraging creativity in businesses. To compete in the current worldwide marketplace, others, such as the United States, Australia, Ireland, South Korea, and Thailand, have tried hard to develop initiatives to harness creativity (Development of Creative Economy in Different Countries, 2009; Lee 2012; Percival 2012).

Creativity in Design

Design commonly represents a creative profession, involving designers who are capable of creating innovative design works (Lawson 2006). In design disciplines,

The Handbook of Interior Design, First Edition. Edited by Jo Ann Asher Thompson and Nancy H. Blossom.

creativity appears fundamental not only in business but also in education. In looking at design education, we often find creativity as one of the most important aspects in curricula. In the practice sector, the role of design has become recognized as a creative industry that plays a significant part in many countries' economic capability (Hokanson 2010). As a result, research on design creativity has been increasingly called for to provide a better understanding of creativeness in design. According to Mooney, creativity is a multi-faceted phenomenon found in products, processes, persons, and environments (Mooney 1963). Researchers across disciplines have examined the phenomenon in relation to these four aspects; however, researchers in design fields have paid the most attention to creative design processes or products (e.g., Christiaans 2002; Demirkan and Hasirci 2009; Goldschmidt and Smolkov 2006).

Problem Statement

There is no doubt that design disciplines worldwide recognize creativity; however, characteristics of design creativity are still vague. People often consider design as a combination of the arts and sciences (Buchanan 1992). Design shares similarities with the other disciplines; nonetheless, Cross argues, "design practice does indeed have its own strong and appropriate intellectual culture" (Cross 2001). To indicate specific attributes of creativity in the design domain, we need to address crucial questions regarding design creativity that have not been fully answered. The most imperative of these are: How is creativity defined in design disciplines? How do experts in design disciplines assess creativity? and What do these stakeholders perceive as the most important attributes of creativity?

Another gap in knowledge on creativity is the cultural context. Since the majority of creativity research has been conducted in the West and represent Western points of view, this knowledge may not apply to other areas of the world (Baer and Kaufman 2006; Kim 2007). Although the number of cross-cultural studies has been increasing in the current literature (e.g., Chen, Kasof, Himsel, et al. 2005; Kim 2005; Leung, Au, and Leung 2004; Paletz and Peng 2008), the scope of research contexts clearly needs further expansion. Focusing on the design domain, a review of articles published in top-tier design journals including *Journal of Interior Design*, *Design Issues*, and *Design Studies* showed few cross-cultural studies conducted so far. As Westwood and Low state, "[c]ultures are creative and innovative within the context of their own systems and to the extent that circumstances require creative and innovative solutions" (Westwood and Low 2003). Thus, to fully gain insight into creativity, we need to examine cultural impacts on the phenomenon.

Based on the issues outlined above, this essay presents research that attempts to explore creativity in interior design across two cultures, Thailand and the US, with an emphasis on the assessment, attributes, and definitions of creativity. As argued by Mooney, creativity involves a product, process, person, and/or environment

(Mooney 1963) and creative individuals utilize creative processes to produce creative products, all of which are enhanced by creative environments. Moreover, other researchers, such as Simonton (1990) and Mumford, Scott, Gaddis, and Strange (2002), have proposed an additional aspect, persuasion, to emphasize the ability to convince others about one's creative talent. In regard to the notion that the design product is the evidence of a designer's creativity and the outcome of a creative design process (Demirkan and Hasirci 2009), the research presented in this essay emphasizes only the creative product.

Relevant Studies on Creative Design Products

A review of precedent reveals that little systematic research on creative products has been conducted in allied design fields (Cho 2007; Christiaans 2002). However, a few existing studies on the evaluation of design products are worth thoroughly reviewing. Levins examined interior designers' assessments of entry-level interior design portfolios by assessing creativity in terms of novelty, resolution, and style (Levins 2006). She also added overall creativity and hiring potential to link the portfolio evaluation to its actual role in the hiring process. Levins employed survey and interview methods and the results revealed that overall creativity had the strongest relationship to novelty. Interestingly, a creative portfolio had a significant influence on an applicant's potential to be hired.

Barnard also explored qualities relating to creativity by adapting Amabile's criteria to assess creativity, technical skills, and aesthetic aspects of interior design projects (Amabile 1983; Barnard 1992). She asked design educators and practitioners to rate the projects. The findings showed that while educators and designers gauged overall creativity similarly, they viewed creative attributes differently. Educators associated creativity with artistic and aesthetic merits while designers, conversely, valued the technical and functional qualities of creativity.

Examining creativity in artworks across cultures, Niu and Sternberg recruited a sample of US and Chinese judges to evaluate artworks created by US and Chinese college students based on creativity, likeability, appropriateness, and technical quality (Niu and Sternberg 2001). Creativity had the strongest correlation to likeability, which is one of the aesthetic qualities in the artworks. There was no indication that the judges made more favorable ratings for one culture over another. However, Chinese judges showed higher consensus on their judgments than their counterparts and US judges seemed to have a higher standard than Chinese judges when evaluating creativity, likeability, and technical quality. Similarly, Chen, Kasof, Himsel, et al. asked US and Chinese judges to assess drawings created by US and Chinese undergraduate students on creativity, uniqueness, technical quality, and liking (Chen et al. 2002). They found that all aspects were highly correlated, and the relationships were similar across groups.

Introduction to the Study

To assess the creative design product, the current research employs Amabile's Consensual Assessment Technique (CAT), which has been applied widely in diverse disciplines, such as psychology, business, art, and design (Amabile 1982, 1996; Dollinger and Shafran 2005; Kaufman, Plucker, and Baer 2008). The CAT requires experts to judge levels of creativity from their own concepts of creativeness; this basically reflects real-world judgments of creative works based on the notion that the consensus of experts in a given domain results in the best creativity measure (Kaufman, Lee, Baer, and Lee 2007). The role of experts also appears to be significant in Csikszentmihalyi's systems theory of creativity, which comprises three factors: the individual, the domain, and the field (Csikszentmihalyi 1988). Experts take part in the field, influencing and assessing the individual's creative outcomes in the domain. Consequently, in this study experienced Thai and US designers were recruited as the experts to evaluate creative design products.

To suitably employ the CAT as an assessment method, an assessed product must meet the following criteria: it must be appropriate to be evaluated; it must allow for flexibility and novelty in responses; and it should not represent participants' different skill levels in baseline performances (Amabile 1996). This study utilizes a sample of entry-level design portfolios as the assessed product, since it meets all of the three requirements. The portfolio also represents a passport, enabling students who are graduating from design schools to cross from the educational to the professional world. Therefore, employing a set of portfolios as the assessed product in this research should help to reveal evaluation criteria in the actual hiring process. For the purposes of this study, the domain consists of the interior design discipline and culture, which offers knowledge and skill sets that shape perceptions of the individual and field, which are represented by Thai interior design graduates and Thai and US senior-level designers, respectively. The students created a sample of entry-level design portfolios as creative outcomes to be assessed by the practitioners.

The primary purpose of this study was to conduct a cross-cultural investigation into creativity in the context of interior design. Another objective was to explore Thai and US designers' assessments of design portfolios. Last but not least, this research aims to help define creativity and its attributes in interior design. To scrutinize the assessment, dimensions, and definitions of creativity across cultures, this study employed a sample of Thai and US experienced designers to assess creativity levels in a sample of Thai entry-level interior design portfolios.

In order to thoroughly examine similarities and differences between Thai and US practitioners' assessments and perceptions of creativity, the research questions aimed to: (1) examine designers' assessments of overall creativity, hiring potential, and the creative attributes: novelty, appropriateness, technical merit, and aesthetic appeal; (2) compare Thai and US practitioners' judgments of the portfolios to indicate cultural similarities and/or variations; and (3) qualitatively explore portfolio assessments, hiring considerations, and definitions of creativity supplied by Thai and US designers.

Methodology

This study employed field-based research and utilized a systematic methodology to thoroughly examine creativity in the context of interior design. Survey and semi-structured interview methods were combined into a portfolio assessment procedure. The methodology for evaluating entry-level design portfolios drew on the CAT involving the agreement of senior-level designers as expert judges who independently assessed the sample of design portfolios. After the portfolio assessment, a semi-structured interview was conducted with each designer to gain the qualitative insight into the evaluation process. Additionally, a field-based research approach required the researcher to collect data from participants in an actual setting. Such an approach provided a better understanding of the issues under observation and enhances the generalizability of findings to real-world situations (Bogdan and Biklen 1998).

Portfolios as the assessed product

Figure 16.1 illustrates the overall methodology employed in this study. The first step was to develop a set of portfolios to evaluate. Six pilot judges with experience in practicing and reviewing portfolios in interior design reviewed 23 digital portfolios received from Thammasat University, Thailand, and selected 12 portfolios as a sample to assess. The chosen portfolios were sorted into groups exhibiting high (n = 4), medium (n = 4), and low creativity (n = 4). Each of the portfolios

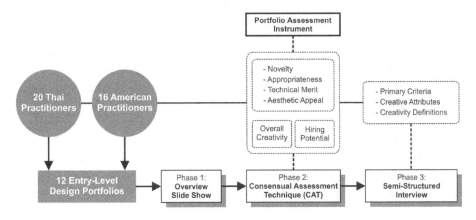

Figure 16.1

contained similar projects, including a corporate and hospitality project, a product design work, as well as an individualized thesis project. Twelve student portfolios were presented to judges in a timed Microsoft PowerPoint format show. The researcher developed three randomized sets of the slide shows to reduce sequential order effects and potential viewing fatigue.

Experienced designers as the expert judges

The next step was to recruit appropriate expert judges. The panel consisted of a total of 36 designer participants from 17 design firms selected based on specific criteria: location, services, and professional stature. The researcher chose Bangkok and Atlanta as the research settings because of their compatible characteristics. Bangkok is Thailand's capital and most populous city, locating the economic center and housing national major businesses including a comprehensive design district ("The Largest Cities" 2007). Atlanta is the capital city in the state of Georgia and one of the fastest-growing urban areas in the US, and offers a competitive design market in the southern region (Apple 2000).

Both cities have similar design cultures that focus on international design styles in medium-sized urban areas. Twenty Thai participants were recruited from nine Bangkok-based firms, while the 16 US participants were recruited from eight Atlanta-based firms. The scope of services in the selected firms was similar and included corporate, hospitality, residential, retail, education, healthcare, government, mixed-use design, cultural, and transit design. Importantly, all of the firms had received national and/or international design awards and had projects featured in national and/or international trade publications.

The data-collecting process

The researcher scheduled a one-hour block with each practitioner for assessing the sample of portfolios. The data collection involved three stages. First, designer judges watched a four-minute slide show to get an overview of the portfolios. The overview offered the judges a glimpse into the overall quality of the portfolios before they evaluated each one independently. The judges viewed the slide show on a lap top computer with a 14″ screen. The slide presentation illustrated eight images from each portfolio, and slides advanced automatically after two seconds.

In the second stage, the judges viewed the timed slide show and independently evaluated each portfolio using a locally developed assessment instrument designed to assess novelty, appropriateness, technical merit, aesthetic appeal, overall creativity, and hiring potential. These six criteria were developed based on a review of relevant studies on the judgment of creative products in the art and design fields.

As shown in Figure 16.2, concepts of novelty, appropriateness, technical merit, and aesthetic appeal often appear as relevant aspects of creative products. In

	# of Products	# of Judges	Creativity	Novelty	Appropriate	Technical Merit	Aesthetic Appeal	Others
Levins (2006)	12 portfolios	21 Design Practitioners	•	•	•		•	Hiring Potential
Barnard (1992)	18 Design Projects	13 Design Educators 31 Design Practitioners	•			•	•	
Dorst & Cross (2001)	9 Product Designs	5 Design Educators	•		•	•	•	Business Aspects
Christiaans (2002)	44 Product Designs	10 Design Educators 12 Design Students 12 Mathematics Students	•		•	•	•	Interest Expressiveness Integrating Capacity
Niu & Sternberg (2001)	139 Collages and Drawings (76 American and 63 Chinese Students)	9 American Psychology Graduate Students 9 Chinese Psychology Graduate Students	•		•	•	•	
Chen, Kasof, Himsel, Greenberger, Dong, & Xue (2002)	294 Drawings (50 American and 48 Chinese Students)	6 American Students 8 Chinese Students	•	•		•	•	
Averill, Chon, & Hahn (2001)	N/A (Literature Review and Proposed Framework)	N/A (Literature Review and Proposed Framework)		•	•			

Figure 16.2

addition to the four creative dimensions, this study also considered overall creativity and hiring potential, representing the possibility that a student would have an interview for employment, in the assessment criteria to connect the accomplishment of a portfolio to its primary purpose.

A seven-point Likert scale, from 1 (poor) to 7 (excellent), was used to assess each portfolio based on the assessment criteria. The portfolios were formatted into a single presentation containing 184 portfolio slides. Each slide was set up to advance automatically to the next slide after 10 seconds. Following each portfolio, a slide instructing the judges to evaluate the previously viewed portfolio was added; this slide was timed to last 15 seconds. The practitioner judges spent approximately 35 minutes in total to complete the assessment.

Upon completion of the second stage, judges participated in semi-structured interviews, providing them with the opportunity to elaborate on the process of reviewing portfolios. To assist the practitioners in recalling their assessment, 12 boards of 14″ x 17″ heavy stock paper featuring eight images from each portfolio were created. This procedure was implemented because the designers could only view each portfolio once during the assessment and this meant that they might not recall which portfolio to reference in the interviews.

Research Findings

Table 16.1 shows the Cronbach's coefficient alphas indicating the inter-judge reliability. According to Amabile, prior to analyzing any data collected by using the CAT, it is necessary to verify whether the judges' subjective evaluations are reliable (Amabile 1996). A high alpha value signifies a high level of agreement among judges. Across all judges, 16 out of 18 coefficients were higher than .70, which is an acceptable value. Only the reliabilities of appropriateness and aesthetic appeal rated by US judges were slightly less than the acceptable level. However, these two aspects also showed greater variation than other criteria in previous studies on assessments of creative products (e.g., Casakin and Kreitler 2008; Runco and Charles 1993). Moreover, studies in social sciences that usually seek experimental findings rather than rigidly precise results tend to accept slightly lower inter-rater reliabilities. Given the exploratory nature of the present study, data points from all six criteria were used in subsequent analyses.

Table 16.1 Inter-judge reliabilities of assessment criteria

Dimensions	Thai practitioners (n = 20)	US practitioners (n = 16)	Total sample (n = 36)
Novelty	.871	.772	.846
Appropriateness	.894	.658	.845
Technical merit	.796	.729	.816
Aesthetic appeal	.843	.667	.770
Overall creativity	.878	.755	.839
Hiring potential	.916	.796	.884

Combined samples' evaluations of the assessed criteria

To examine the combined samples' assessments of overall creativity, hiring potential, and the creative attributes, the researcher first employed a correlation analysis. The analysis revealed positive and significant associations among the six criteria. Overall creativity had a positive and strong correlation to hiring potential ($r = .84$, $p = .000$). Concerning the creative dimensions, overall creativity had the strongest association with novelty ($r = .85$), while having the weakest, but still significant, correlation to technical merit ($r = .71$). Hiring potential also had the strongest relationship with novelty ($r = .84$) and the weakest, but still strong, association with technical merit ($r = .72$).

According to Field, significant correlations between variables do not permit strong inferences about causality in the data (Field 2005). However, we can analyze correlation coefficients further by squaring them to understand the variance between two variables. As Figure 16.3 illustrates, the r^2 values between overall creativity and hiring potential suggest creativity accounted for 71% of the variance in hiring potential. This result implies that judges considered overall creativity in design portfolios as a strong predictor of hiring potential.

Focusing on the creative dimensions, novelty accounted for 72% of the variability in overall creativity, followed by appropriateness at 67%. Aesthetic appeal and tech-

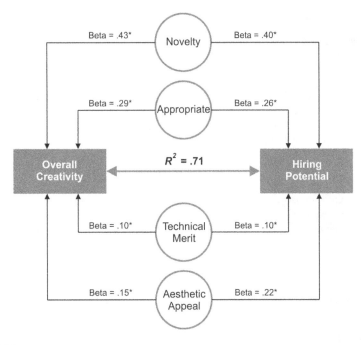

Figure 16.3

nical merit accounted for 58% and 50% of the variance in overall creativity, respectively. In line with this, novelty accounted for 71% of the variability in hiring potential. Finally, appropriateness, aesthetic appeal, and technical merit accounted for 66%, 61%, and 52% of the variance in hiring potential, respectively.

Since all the correlations were significant, a regression analysis was performed to further examine the attributes that would explain the relative importance of the creative aspects to overall creativity and hiring potential. Table 16.2 shows the influence of novelty, appropriateness, technical merit, and aesthetic appeal on overall creativity. The regression analysis also specified the R^2 value, which is the coefficient squared for multiple regression, of .79. The results of the regression analysis suggest that the set of variables could explain 79% of the variance in overall creativity.

Moreover, the standardized coefficient or beta value for each significant variable was examined to further assess its individual impact. As seen in Figure 16.3, novelty had the highest beta value (.43), followed by appropriateness (.29), aesthetic appeal (.15), and technical merit (.10). These values suggest that novelty had four times more impact on overall creativity than technical merit. Table 16.3 illustrates the impact of novelty, appropriateness, technical merit, and aesthetic appeal on hiring potential. The R^2 value of .79 suggests that this set of variables could explain 79% of the variability in hiring potential. As shown in Figure 16.3, the beta values suggest that novelty (.40) had 1.5 times more influence on hiring potential than appropriateness (.26), with aesthetic appeal (.22) closely following. Technical merit (.10) had the least influence on hiring potential.

Table 16.2   Multiple regression analysis of overall creativity

Predictor variables	Slope (b)	Std. error	Beta	t	Sig.
Novelty	.434	.042	.429	10.235	.000*
Appropriateness	.331	.047	.293	7.074	.000*
Technical merit	.109	.040	.097	2.745	.006*
Aesthetic appeal	.153	.039	.150	3.970	.000*

* Significance at the 0.05 level ($p < .05$).
$R = .886$, $R^2 = .785$.

Table 16.3   Multiple regression analysis of hiring potential

Predictor variables	Slope (b)	Std. error	Beta	t	Sig.
Novelty	.453	.047	.401	9.722	.000*
Appropriateness	.333	.051	.264	6.469	.000*
Technical merit	.119	.044	.095	2.732	.007*
Aesthetic appeal	.247	.042	.217	5.825	.000*

* Significance at the 0.05 level ($p < .05$).
$R = .889$, $R^2 = .791$.

Thai and US designers' assessments of the creative portfolios

To explore how Thai and US designers perceived overall creativity and the creative dimensions in design portfolios, as well as potential to hire graduates who created the portfolios, the researcher scrutinized inter-rater reliabilities of the assessed criteria. Then, correlation analyses and Independent-Samples *t* tests were employed to determine whether there were associations between the groups' judgments and variations in the assessments, respectively.

An examination of the inter-judge reliability score (.84) confirmed that there was strong agreement between Thai and US designers in terms of their assessments of overall creativity in portfolios (see Table 16.1). The coefficient of .88 indicates that Thai and US designers had high consensus in their perception of hiring potential. Similarly, the reliabilities of novelty, appropriateness, technical merit, and aesthetic appeal confirmed that practitioners from the two cultures agreed on their assessments of the portfolios.

Focusing on overall creativity and hiring potential, the researcher analyzed the correlations between the two groups' ratings using simple scatterplots and correlation analyses. The scatterplots, showing each portfolio's average score rated by Thai designers against its average score rated by US designers, revealed positive relationships between evaluations of the groups on overall creativity and hiring potential.

Moreover, a correlation analysis confirmed a significant relationship between the groups' assessments on the two variables (overall creativity: r = .80, p = .000; hiring potential: r = .74, p = .006). By squaring the *r* values, the results indicated that Thai practitioners' evaluations on overall creativity accounted for 64% of the variability in US practitioners' evaluations; correspondingly, Thai designers' ratings on hiring potential explained 55% of the variance in US designers' ratings.

Table 16.4 presents the means and standard deviations of each criterion by culture. Although the two groups of designers seemed to agree on their judgments of the portfolios, the *t* tests indicated that Thai professionals gave significantly lower average scores to the portfolios on all criteria than the US designers did: overall creativity, hiring potential , novelty, appropriateness, technical merit, and aesthetic appeal.

Table 16.4 Means and standard deviations of assessment criteria by culture

	Thai practitioners (n = 20)	US practitioners (n = 16)
	M SD	M SD
Overall creativity	4.40 1.30	4.89 1.43
Hiring potential	4.17 1.52	4.79 1.49
Novelty	4.22 1.29	4.84 1.38
Appropriateness	4.23 1.15	4.84 1.23
Technical merit	4.43 1.25	5.09 1.11
Aesthetic appeal	4.36 1.28	4.67 1.43

The researcher further explored whether Thai and US designers perceived creativity expressed in design portfolios as an indicator of potential to hire their creators by separately analyzing Thai and US practitioners' evaluations using correlation analyses. After that, results from the correlation analyses were compared to investigate the similarities and/or variations between the two groups.

Starting with Thai practitioners' assessments, correlation analyses revealed positive and significant relationships among overall creativity, the four creative dimensions, and hiring potential. Overall creativity had a significantly high interaction with hiring potential. Among the four creative attributes, novelty correlated most strongly with hiring potential. Appropriateness appeared almost identical as novelty, with aesthetic appeal closely following, and technical merit at the least.

The researcher further examined the relationships between the variables using multiple regression. Novelty, appropriateness, and aesthetic appeal significantly influenced hiring potential, whereas only technical merit did not. For US designers' assessments, correlation analyses showed that overall creativity and all the four creative attributes had positive and significant relationships with hiring potential.

Overall creativity had a significantly high association with hiring potential. In looking at the creative dimensions, the strongest relationship appeared between novelty and hiring potential, followed by appropriateness, aesthetic appeal, and technical merit, respectively. Further, multiple regression revealed that all of the four dimensions significantly influenced hiring potential.

The results from the two groups showed both similarities and differences across the cultures. In both Thai and US designers' evaluations, overall creativity and the four creative dimensions appeared significantly correlated to hiring potential. Nevertheless, the regression analyses disclosed some differences between the groups. Thai practitioners' assessments showed that novelty, appropriateness, and aesthetic appeal – not technical merit – significantly influenced hiring potential. On the other hand, US practitioners' evaluations revealed that all of the creative attributes significantly influenced hiring potential, with novelty having a noticeably larger impact than the other dimensions.

Thai and US designers' interview responses on the portfolio assessment, hiring considerations, and creativity perceptions

Supplementing the statistical results, three open-ended questions were posed after the portfolio assessment to seek a better understanding of designers' views on creativity, especially in relation to portfolio reviews. Thirty-five of the thirty-six judges attended the interview session. One Thai practitioner could not participate in the interview. The qualitative data collected from the interview were transcribed, interpreted, coded, and classified into main themes.

The first question asked judges to identify the criteria they considered important while assessing the portfolios. The responses were coded and organized into groups in relation to: overall creativity; the creative dimensions novelty, appropriateness, technical merit, aesthetic appeal; and other factors.

Based on a total of 55 responses from the Thai sample, 75% of them related to creativity and its attributes, while the other 25% included other aspects, such as clarity, articulation, and the composition of a portfolio. Excluding these factors, when rating portfolios, Thai practitioners favored creativity (23.64%) as much as aesthetic appeal (21.82%), followed by appropriateness (16.36%), technical merit (9.09%), and novelty (3.64%).

Based on a total of 46 answers from the US sample, 72% referred to creativity and the creative dimensions, and the other 28% mentioned other criteria. Focusing on creativity and its attributes, the US designers recognized creativity first (28.26%), technical merit second (15.22%), followed by appropriateness (13.04%), aesthetic appeal (10.87%), and novelty (4.35%). When reviewing portfolios, Thai designers looked for both creativity and aesthetic appeal almost equally, while US practitioners considered creativity as the foremost aspect. Interestingly, both groups regarded novelty as less important than the other creative criteria.

The second question asked judges to describe criteria they considered in the actual hiring process. With reference to the criteria involved in making a hiring decision, 68.42% of the Thai practitioners (n = 13) agreed that they often suggested an applicant with a creative portfolio for an interview and sometimes even recommended hiring him or her. All of the 16 US designers unanimously agreed on the importance of a creative portfolio in the hiring process. However, practitioners from both cultures noted that, in addition to reviewing the portfolio, they needed to assess the person as well.

In line with this, based on the total of 62 answers from Thai designers, 24.19% cited the portfolio aspects (creativity, technical skills, and aesthetic sense), while 43.55% emphasized the personal characteristics. Thai designers also referred to work capability and communication skills 17.74% and 14.52% of the time, respectively. Similarly, based on the total of 79 responses from US practitioners, 31.65% highlighted the portfolio aspects, while 40.51% referred to the personal characteristics. US practitioners discussed the work capability 18.99% of the time, though only 8.86% of the responses included communication skills.

In summary, Thai and US designers generally viewed creativity in a portfolio as important as an applicant's work capability and his or her personal characteristics when making a hiring decision. Additionally, Thai designers emphasized communication skills more than their US counterparts.

The final question asked judges to discuss their own personal definition of creativity. Their responses were organized in relation to novelty, appropriateness, technical merit, aesthetic appeal, and other considerations. Eighty four percent of the Thai designers' responses cited novelty, appropriateness, technical merit, and aesthetic appeal, while the other 16% referenced other criteria. The majority of the responses (40.54%) described creativity in terms of novelty; "A creative design has to challenge the norm and the ordinary standards" (TH-13). Slightly less than novelty, 37.84% of the supplied definitions cited appropriateness; "a creative solution should be flexible and serve the function" (TH-03). Only 5.40% of the definitions related to aesthetic aspects. Interestingly, no definitions involved technical merit.

Seventy-four percent of the US practitioners' definitions were associated with novelty, appropriateness, technical merit, and aesthetic appeal, while the other 26% included other considerations. The majority of the definitions (34.21%) viewed creativity as novelty: "I think creativity in design is really, really based on solving your client's problem in a unique way" (US-05). Further, 26.32% of the answers related to appropriateness. Judge US-09 underlined that "in the world of design and architecture, [a creative idea] has to create, elicit, an emotion, negative or positive, while still being fully functional." In addition, 7.90% and 5.26% of the definitions involved technical merit and aesthetic appeal, respectively.

Interpretation of Results

The results of this study appear to reinforce three premises: creativity as a discipline-specific phenomenon, the universal perception of creativity in interior design, and the importance of persuasion in design creativity.

Creativity as a discipline-specific phenomenon

Simon posits that creativity generally appears in "usual processes of human think-ing... to produce something that is new and valuable" (Simon 2001). Baer argues that creativeness possibly occurs in a general situation; however, to create a creative performance in any discipline, expertise, knowledge, and skill sets in that discipline certainly appear necessary (Baer 2010). The findings of this study support Baer's argument, in that expertise in a specific domain affects how creativity is assessed and perceived. In looking at the realm of interior design, the current research rein-forces essential roles of the domain and the field as the social aspects of creativity regarding Csikszentmihalyi's systems theory (Csikszentmihalyi 1988).

In this study, Thai and US experienced practitioners – the gatekeepers to and also the experts in interior design – showed consensus on their judgments of crea-tive portfolios and defined creativity in design by sharing similar criteria, including but not limited to novelty, appropriateness, technical merit, and aesthetic appeal. Numerous aspects have been proposed to define creative outcomes across disci-plines; nonetheless, the majority of scholars agree upon novelty and appropriateness (Averill 2005; Gruber and Wallace 1999; Hokanson 2010; Jackson and Messick 1965). In allied design fields, Barnard (interior design), Casakin and Kreitler (archi-tecture), and Christiaans and Dorst and Cross (industrial design) recommended technical and aesthetic merits as discipline-relevant considerations to identify creative works (Barnard 1992; Casakin and Kreitler 2008; Christiaans 2002; Dorst and Cross 2001). This study reinforces these previous studies, in that design creativ-ity involves novelty, appropriateness, and other domain-relevant aspects, including technical and aesthetic merits.

In discussing the results further, this research supports the importance of domain-relevant knowledge. As Csikszentmihalyi posits, to define creativity, one needs to have information that has been stored in "the symbol system of the culture, in the customary practices, the language, [or] the specific notation of the domain." The following examples of creativity definitions supplied by designers in this research clearly support the previous notion.

> Creativity, in my view, is initially derived from the understanding of the fundamentals. It is a collection of experiences in design, whether it is the great design that you have seen, the understanding of spaces or color schemes, or even the understanding of the overall composition. (TH-13)

> Creativity is taking a space and making it work for the client, but also doing something unusual, something that you would not expect. That still works technically and will hold up over time in that it is unique to that space. (US-12)

Universal perception of creativity in interior design

We clearly see in this study that Thai and US practitioners showed a high level of agreement on their assessments of creative portfolios and their definitions of creativity. When reviewing creative portfolios, both groups of designers were mostly concerned with novelty, appropriateness, technical merit, aesthetic appeal, and other domain-relevant criteria, such as articulation and composition. Thus, the findings basically reinforce the universal perception of creativity in interior design, and imply that experienced designers from different cultures do share similar considerations in identifying creative design works.

Moreover, when discussing creative design works, Thai and US designers often mentioned visual design elements and associated the creative dimensions of novelty, appropriateness, technical merit, and aesthetic appeal with the design elements. For example, one practitioner described it as: "not just planes of color. It has textures…that had been considered as well as the shape of the space, and creativity and thoughts going further" (US-13).

Practitioners viewed a portfolio as novel because "the [concept] was unique and stood out from the others." They considered a portfolio as appropriate when its content "responded to the reality limitation." When evaluating technical merit, designers looked for "techniques that added [dimensions] to the work." They considered "a good sense of [scale and proportion] and also a very good sense of [materials and color]" to assess aesthetic appeal.

Figure 16.4 condenses designers' perceptions of creativity in relation to the discipline and culture. Both Thai and US designers referred to novelty, appropriateness, aesthetic appeal, exploration, design recognition, and organization in their conceptions of creativity. The results support Portillo's study indicating originality and exploration as related to creativity in allied design areas (Portillo 2002).

Most importantly, although this study considers interior design and culture as the domain influencing individuals' perceptions and abilities to identify creative outcomes, the findings disclose the stronger role of the discipline of interior design in shaping practitioners' perceptions of creativity by universal canons, values, and foci. This implies that designers seem unlikely to be completely insular. They do share similar fundamentals and standards even though they work in different areas of the world.

Although culture plays a weaker role in this study, it still influences practitioners' perceptions, including their own personal concepts of creativity. Thai and US designers generally agreed on their definitions of creativity; nonetheless, minor cultural distinctions emerged in their concepts. As Figure 16.4 illustrates, Thai designers considered flexibility and design solutions in their conceptions of design creativity; on the other hand, US designers recognized technical merit, emotional impact, imagination, and simplicity in theirs.

Additionally, cultural differentiation in practitioners' discernment of the portfolios was found. Although designers were unaware of where the portfolios were collected from, US participants could discern that they did not belong to US students. In assessing the Thai portfolios, Thai practitioners showed higher consensus in their judgments than did US designers. This implies that culture is a market-differentiating factor in the context of interior design. Designers from different countries seem to share similar standards in creating and judging design works

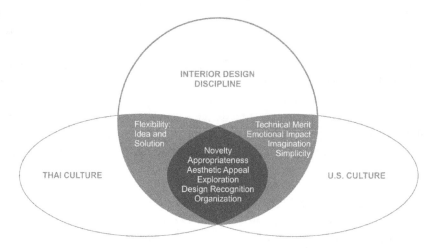

Figure 16.4

(Ledoux and Ledoux 2010); however, culture still has an impact on design styles in each country.

Persuasion as an important factor in discipline-specific creativity

In finalizing their hiring decisions, both Thai and US designers did not only assess creativity in portfolios; they also evaluated applicants' work capability, communication skills, and personality characteristics. Candidates should "present themselves in a way that clearly conveys their own identities" (TH-17) and must have "a sense of the person and their ability to work" (US-08). Interestingly, these findings reinforce the vital role of persuasion, the ability to communicate with others and persuade them of one's creative work, in design creativity (Simonton 1990).

MacKinnon (1962) supported this premise in a study exploring the personal characteristics of creative architects. He found that architects were "possessed of those qualities and attributes which underlie and lead to the achievement of social status." In further examination of living architects in MacKinnon's research, Dudek and Hall revealed that the architects' success in the late stage of their careers necessarily involved commitment, drive, and persuasive skills (Dudek and Hall 1991). In line with this, Guest proposed a list of basic knowledge and skills that design practitioners consider essential for entry-level designers (Guest 2010). The top of the list consisted of "communication abilities" which distinguish "the successful designer from others," "understanding and willingness to contribute to a team," and "willingness to continue to learn." Thus, to be creative in the design realm, designers should be able to solve design problems creatively as well as be capable of presenting and selling the solutions to co-workers and clients.

Conclusions

The findings of this research support the domain specificity and universal perception of creativity in interior design. They also suggest that persuasion is important in design creativity. Thai and US designers both considered novelty, appropriateness, technical merit, and aesthetic appeal as important aspects in determining overall creativity in portfolios. However, these dimensions did not stand alone, but were interrelated with other discipline-specific criteria. More importantly, the results confirm that a creative portfolio could enhance an applicant's potential to be called for an interview or even be hired. Nonetheless, designers also considered the applicant's work capability, communication skills, and personal characteristics when making a final decision.

Although judging creative design works and selecting creative designers involves several considerations, experienced professionals seem to share similar criteria, including but not limited to novelty, appropriateness, technical merit, and aesthetic appeal. Other discipline-specific factors influence designers' perceptions of creativity as well; however, these four creative attributes can be guidelines for educators to develop creativity that meets practitioner expectations.

References

Amabile, T. 1982. "Social psychology of creativity: a consensual assessment technique," *Journal of Personality & Social Psychology* 43: 997–1013.

Amabile, T. 1983. *The Social Psychology of Creativity*. New York: Springer.

Amabile, T. 1996. *Creativity in Context*. Boulder, CO: Westview.

Apple, R. W., Jr. 2000, February. "On the road; a city in full: venerable, impatient Atlanta," *New York Times*. http://www.nytimes.com/2000/02/25/arts/on-the-road-a-city-in-full-venerable-impatient-atlanta.html?sec=travel. Accessed May 5, 2014.

Averill, J. R. 2005. "Emotions as mediators and as products of creative activity," in J. C. Kaufman and J. Baer (eds.), *Creativity Across Domains: Faces of the Muse*. Mahwah, NJ: Lawrence Erlbaum Associates.

Averill, C. and Hahn, D. 2001. "Emotions and creativity, East and West," *Asian Journal of Social Psychology* 4(3): 165–183.

Baer, J. 2010. "Is creativity domain specific?", in J. C. Kaufman and R. J. Sternberg (eds.), *The Cambridge Handbook of Creativity*. New York: Cambridge University Press.

Baer, J. and Kaufman, J. C. 2006. "Creativity research in English-speaking countries," in J. C. Kaufman and R. J. Sternberg (eds.), *The International Handbook of Creativity*. New York: Cambridge University Press.

Baldoni, J. 2010, January 29. "How to encourage small innovations," *Business Week*. http://www.businessweek.com/managing/content/jan2010/ca20100129_077398.htm. Accessed May 5, 2014.

Barnard, S. S. 1992. "Interior Design Creativity: The Development and Testing of a Methodology for the Consensual Agreement of Projects." Dissertation, Virginia Polytechnic Institute and State University.

Bogdan, R. C. and Biklen, S. K. 1998. *Qualitative Research for Education: An Introduction to Theory and Methods* (3rd ed.). Needham Heights, MA: Allyn & Bacon.

Buchanan, R. 1992. "Wicked problems in design thinking," *Design Issues* 8(2): 5–21.

Casakin, H. and Kreitler, S. 2008. "Correspondences and divergences between teachers and students in the evaluation of design creativity in the design studio," *Environment and Planning B: Planning and Design* 35(4): 666–678.

Chen, C., Kasof, J., Himsel, A. J., et al. 2002. "Creativity in drawings of geometric shapes: a cross-cultural examination with the consensual assessment technique," *Journal of Cross-Cultural Psychology* 33: 171–187.

Chen, C., Kasof, J., Himsel, A. J., et al. 2005. "Effects of explicit instruction to 'be creative' across domains and cultures," *Journal of Creative Behavior* 39: 89–110.

Cho, M. 2007. "Portfolio development in a secondary teaching credential art program," in T. Rayment (ed.), *The Problem of Assessment in Art and Design*. Chicago: Intellect Books, University of Chicago Press.

Christiaans, H. 2002. "Creativity as a design criterion," *Creativity Research Journal* 14(1): 41–54.

Cross, N. 2001. "Designerly ways of knowing: design discipline versus design science," *Design Issues* 17(3): 49–55.

Csikszentmihalyi, M. 1988. "Society, culture, and person: a systems view of creativity," in R. J. Sternberg (ed.), *The Nature of Creativity: Contemporary Psychological Perspectives*. Cambridge: Cambridge University Press.

Demirkan, H. and Hasirci, D. 2009. "Hidden dimensions of creativity elements in design process". *Creativity Research Journal* 21(2): 294–301.

"Development of creative economy in different countries." 2009, January. *Creative Thailand*. http://www.creativethailand.org/th/articles/article_detail.php?id=3. Accessed May 5, 2014.

Dollinger, S. J. and Shafran, M. 2005. "Note on the Consensual Assessment Technique in creativity research," *Perceptual and Motor Skills* 100: 592–598.

Dorst, K. and Cross, N. 2001. "Creativity in the design process: co-evolution of problem-solution," *Design Studies* 22: 425–437.

Dudek, S. Z. and Hall, W. B. 1991. "Personality consistency: eminent architects 25 years later," *Creativity Research Journal* 4(3): 213–231.

Field, A. 2005. *Discovering Statistics Using SPSS* (2nd ed.). Thousand Oaks, CA: Sage Publications.

Glăveanu, V. P. 2010. "Paradigms in the study of creativity: introducing the perspective of cultural psychology," *New Ideas in Psychology* 28(1): 79–93.

Goldschmidt, G. and Smolkov, M. 2006. "Variances in the impact of visual stimuli on design problem solving performance." *Design Studies* 27: 549–569.

Gruber, H. E. and Wallace, D. B. 1999. "The case study method and evolving systems approach for understanding unique creative people at work," in R. J. Sternberg (ed.), *Handbook of Creativity*. Cambridge: Cambridge University Press.

Guest, R. C. 2010. "Expectations of new graduates: a view from practice," in C. S. Martin and D. A. Guerin (eds.), *The State of the Interior Design Profession*. New York: Fairchild Books.

Hokanson, B. 2010. "Beyond function: creativity in interior design," in C. S. Martin and D. A. Guerin (eds.), *The State of the Interior Design Profession*. New York: Fairchild Books.

Jackson, P. W. and Messick, S. 1965. "The person, the product, and the response: conceptual problems in the assessment of creativity," *Journal of Personality* 33(3): 309–329.

Kaufman, J. C., Lee, J., Baer, J., and Lee, S. 2007. "Captions, consistency, creativity, and the consensual assessment technique: new evidence of reliability." *Thinking Skills and Creativity* 2(2): 96–106.

Kaufman, J. C., Plucker, J. A., and Baer, J. 2008. *Essentials of Creativity Assessment*. Hoboken, NJ: John Wiley & Sons.

Kim, K. H. 2005. "Learning from each other: creativity in East Asian and American education," *Creativity Research Journal* 17(4): 337–347.

Kim, K. H. 2007. "Exploring the interactions between Asian culture (Confucianism) and creativity," *The Journal of Creative Behavior* 41(1): 28–53.

Lawson, B. 2006. *How Designers Think: The Design Process Demystified*. Burlington, MA: Elsevier/Architectural.

Ledoux, K. A. and Ledoux, F. 2010. "Entering the global design market," in C. S. Martin and D. A. Guerin (eds.), *The State of the Interior Design Profession*. New York: Fairchild Books, pp. 341–345.

Lee, S. S. 2012, October 18/20. "Park suggests paradigm shift toward 'creative economy'," *The Korea Herald*. http://nwww.koreaherald.com/view.php?ud=20121018000858. Accessed May 5, 2014.

Leung, K., Au, A., and Leung, B. W. C. 2004. "Creativity and innovation: East-West comparisons with an emphasis on Chinese societies." in S. Lau, A. N. N. Hui, and G. Y. C. Ng (eds.), *Creativity: When East meets West*. Singapore: World Scientific Publishing.

Levins, K. E. 2006. "The Impact of Creativity on the Evaluation of Entry-Level Interior Design Portfolios: Examining the Relationships among Creative Novelty, Resolution, and Style." Thesis, University of Florida.

MacKinnon, D. W. 1962. "The nature and nurture of creative talent," *American Psychologist* 17: 484–495.

Mooney, R. L. 1963. "A conceptual model for integrating four approaches to the identification of creative talent," in C. W. Taylor and F. Barron (eds.), *Scientific Creativity: Its Recognition and Development*. New York: Wiley.

Mumford, M. D., Scott, G. M., Gaddis, B., and Strange, J. M. 2002. "Leading creative people: orchestrating expertise and relationships," *The Leadership Quarterly* 13(6): 705–750.

Niu, W. and Sternberg, R. J. 2001. "Cultural influences on artistic creativity and its evaluation," *International Journal of Psychology* 36(4): 225–241.

Oliver, C. and Jung, S. 2010, January 28. "Lack of innovation clouds Samsung's future," *Financial Times*. http://www.ft.com/cms/s/0/2988943c-0c31-11df-8b81-00144feabdc0.html.

Paletz, S. B. F. and Peng, K. 2008. "Implicit theories of creativity across cultures: novelty and appropriateness in two product domains," *Journal of Cross-Cultural Psychology* 39(3): 286–302.

Percival, G. 2012, October 16. "Creativity vital to Irish recovery, says economist," *Irish Examiner*. http://www.irishexaminer.com/business/creativity-vital-to-irish-recovery-says-economist-210962.html. Accessed May 5, 2014.

Portillo, M. 2002. "Creativity defined: implicit theories in the professions of interior design, architecture, landscape architecture, and engineering," *Journal of Interior Design* 28(1): 10–26.

Runco, M. A. and Charles, R. E. 1993. "Judgments of originality and appropriateness as predictors of creativity," *Personality and Individual Differences* 15(5): 537–546.

Simon, H. A. 2001. "Creativity in the arts and the sciences," *The Kenyon Review* 23(2): 203–220.

Simonton, D. K. 1990. "History, chemistry, psychology, and genius: an intellectual autobiography of historiometry," in M. A. Runco and R. S. Albert (eds.), *Theories of Creativity*. Newbury Park, CA: Sage Publications.

"The largest cities in the world by land area, population and density." 2007. *City Mayors*. http://www.citymayors.com/statistics/largest-cities-area-125.html. Accessed May 5, 2014.

Westwood, R. and Low, D. R. 2003. "The multicultural muse," *International Journal of Cross Cultural Management* 3(2): 235.

17

Human Responses to Water Elements in Interior Environments: A Culture and Gender Comparison

Gwo Fang Lin

Background and Contextual Information

Water is the most common substance on Earth, covering more than 70% of the planet's surface. The location of water has helped to determine where humans settle and grow crops for food. The human body is about two-thirds water, and without water the longest any human can expect to live is 10 days.

This life-giving substance has played an important role in the religion, literature, and art of every culture. For example, the ancient Greeks had springs where only the immortal gods were privileged to imbibe (Moore 1994b), and in Christianity the Bible makes frequent mention of the mystical and religious powers associated with water: "A river flowed out of Eden to water the garden, and there it divided and became four rivers" (Genesis 2:10).

The simple yet interesting physical characteristics of water stimulate our senses, and the mental connections these help us make. According to the literature, these connections are important and can also be used to create experientially rich and meaningful places. Almost unanimously, studies have shown that water is one of the most powerful elements in enhancing human preferences (Brush and Shafer 1975; Civco 1979; Hammitt, Patterson, and Noe 1994; Kaplan and Kaplan 1982; Palmer 1978; Palmer, Schloss, and Sammartino 2013; Penning-Roswell 1979; Shafer, Hamilton, and Schmidt 1969; Strang 2006; Syme and Nancarrow 1992; Ulrich 1981; Yang and Brown 1992; Zube, Pitt, and Anderson 1975).

For example, in Yang and Brown's study in Korea the characteristics of preferences for three landscape elements – water, vegetation, and rock – were analyzed.

The Handbook of Interior Design, First Edition. Edited by Jo Ann Asher Thompson and Nancy H. Blossom.
© 2015 John Wiley & Sons, Ltd. Published 2015 by John Wiley & Sons, Ltd.

The main purpose of the study was to compare the characteristics of preferences of a group of Korean citizens and Western tourists, with special emphasis on the general patterns of preference and the relationships of landscape preference to landscape styles and elements. The research results showed that water was the most preferred landscape element, regardless of the cultural differences of the people (Yang and Brown 1992).

More evidence of the strong connections between people and water is provided by a study by Syme and Nancarrow. This longitudinal study was done to assess the level of demand and the motivations for participating in urban water planning in three Australian cities. The research concluded that there is a strong demand for involvement in water-related planning (Syme and Nancarrow 1992).

In her book *The Meaning of Water* (2006), Strang suggests that there is a highly complex relationship between people and water in which "physical, sensory and cognitive experiences articulate with cultural meanings and values." In a systematic research model, Strang used ethnographic data (collected via classical anthropological research methods of long-term fieldwork, in-depth interviews, observation and mapping of social, spatial, and environmental relations) to examine this complex relationship. The results of her study showed that the meanings people associate with water are highly consistent over time and that these meanings exert influence over every decision involved in how water is used. In addition, she found that the associations people have with water are difficult to alter.

Throughout time, special meanings such as life, purity, fertility, security, hospitality, and communion with God have been associated with water (Douglas 1970). It is suggested that water has a physical hold on the lives of every one of us, carrying mental images that have meaning for us – from birth in the amniotic fluid to death in the mythical waters of the river Styx (Moore 1994b).

In addition to water's association with special meanings and symbols, the literature cites the basic human need to be close to – and feel part of – nature. For instance, according to Fitzsimmons and Salama, a water-related recreation facility can help improve the physical and mental health of the users (Fitzsimmons and Salama 1977). Several studies have shown that water has a positive therapeutic effect. Alexander argued that going into the water might bring a person closer to the unconscious process in their life and closer to their dreams (Alexander 1977). In psychoanalysis, it is common to consider the appearance of water in people's dreams as associated with special meanings. Jung and the Jungian analysts consider the great bodies of water as representing the dreamer's unconscious.

For many of us, water has a great attraction. People often visit places with water such as rivers, lakes, waterfalls, or swimming pools. Water touching our skin is the most personally intimate experience we can have. Degrees of contact range from being misted by warm steam, to being splashed by a waterfall, to being completely immersed in a bath. Immersion is a kind of escape or disconnection from the world outside the water.

People often say that water makes them feel relaxed or that water can enhance a living environment. In recent years a variety of small to large-scale water fountains for living environments have become available in the marketplace, with retailers extolling the virtues of a fountain to create an ambience of relaxation that sets the mind at ease and refreshes the senses. According to these marketing tactics, fountains can also take you away to a distant place, improve your concentration, rest your body, and restore the balance between your mind, body, and soul.

Today, from shopping malls, to hotel lobbies, to fish tanks in our living rooms, water continues to be used throughout our interior environments. Recognizing this, some fundamental questions arise. Does the use of water in interior spaces elicit positive human responses, as the literature seems to indicate? Does the use of water in interior spaces have different meanings depending on gender and cultural orientation?

These questions are not easily answered and depend upon many variables. In an attempt to gain a better understanding of the relationships between people and water Lin conducted an initial exploratory study (Lin 1999). The purpose of the study was to examine human responses to water features in public interior spaces and to determine the extent to which people modified their behavior as they moved through public spaces where water features were included.

This non-participant, observational study was conducted in 10 public interiors with a major water feature. Observational data were collected on the behavior of people as they passed through each public space with a water feature. Notes and mapping techniques were used to document behaviors such as whether people looked at the water feature, and, if so, for how long; if people tried to interact with the water feature by touching or playing in the water; whether people appeared to modify their pathway to better interact with the water feature; and if there were differences between the genders in their behavior toward the water feature.

The results showed surprising differences in the way people of different genders and ages responded to the water features. In general, and contrary to expectations, the study showed that people's physical response to water features in public interiors was very low, with most people paying little to no attention to the water feature as they passed through a space. Additionally, and contrary to expectations and the literature, male subjects tended to consistently respond to water more frequently than female subjects.

To more fully explore the responses people had to water features in interior spaces, a new study was designed to examine how people from two different countries, the US and Taiwan, reacted to water features. Since water has played an important role in Taiwanese culture, one aspect of the study was to examine the cultural differences between Taiwanese and American preferences for the use of water features in interior environments. Also, because the results from the previous study on gender differences and preference were inconclusive, this study set out to examine in more depth the differences between men's and women's preferences. Lastly, a goal of the study was to investigate, and possibly challenge, preconceived notions about the use of water in interior spaces (i.e., both the use of the image of water versus the use of real water).

Overview of the Relationship between Water and Humans

As noted earlier, water has played an important role in the religion, literature, and art of every culture, and throughout time special meanings have been associated with water. Ancient philosophers regarded water as the symbol of life and as one of the four basic elements of the universe along with earth, air, and fire (Moore 1994b), and through the ages water has been used as a design element in a multitude of ways, presenting a complexity and interweaving of function and symbolism (Campbell 1978).

Modern artists and designers have used water as a source of inspiration or as a major design element. For instance, Claude Monet spent his final years painting impressions of the transcendent pond that resulted in the water lily series with the intention of bequeathing his last peaceful opus to the people of France (Moore 1994b) and Frank Lloyd Wright, in the Hollyhock House in Los Angeles, used water throughout the house to create specific moods.

Our associations with water today have been shaped by our ancestors, so that the lapse of centuries adds to the symbolism (Moore 1994b). Campbell wrote, "I seriously doubt that any of the sounds created by water could be considered distressing or annoying" (Campbell 1978). The effectiveness of the audio element of water is demonstrated in the design of the Hospital Santa Engracia in Monterrey, Mexico, where a sunken fountain is used to mask street sounds (Tetlow 1997).

A design enhancement such as a decorative fountain with splashing water has also served as a way-finding device in certain spaces, with the sound of the fountain providing orientation cues (Patterson 1997). In addition to these qualities, designers have used water for its reflective properties to provide depth and taken advantage of the infinite surface of water for relief of claustrophobia and expansion of personal space (Moore 1994b).

The human relationship with water involves understanding not only environmental behavior but also our biological roots. It is a central contention of anthropology that humans are different by culture, but fundamentally the same by nature. Our DNA takes the form of innate propensities, things we do unthinkingly and without having to learn from our parents. For example, regardless of culture differences, humans seem to be biologically prepared to look for very specific cues about the natural world. Biologists believe that the way our ancestors lived has shaped our DNA, and the strings that tie us to our past may stretch back more than 2 million years.

It is believed that over thousands of years of evolution humans recognized certain features of the landscape as offering greater chances for survival (Conniff 1999). In addition to providing a physical necessity for survival, bodies of water also provided a defense from most natural enemies and attracted other animals and plant life on which humans depended.

Through time, there is no doubt that the meaning of water has grown and developed along with many different human cultures. Research across many disciplines supports the hypothesis that there is a fundamental basic human need to connect closely with nature. This condition is known as biophilia. If this biophilia hypothesis has merit, it provides a framework across different disciplines for the investigation of the meaning of water and the relationships humans have with it (Kahn 1999).

Another idea appropriate for consideration when examining the relationship between humans and water is the "involvement theory" proposed by Goffman in the early 1960s. The involvement theory suggests that humans and animals have the capacity to divide their attention between main and side involvements. A main involvement is the major focus of one's attention and interest, visibly forming the principal current determinant of one's actions. A side involvement is an activity that an individual can carry on in an abstracted fashion without interrupting or confusing the main involvement: for example, singing while working, and knitting while listening (Goffman 1963).

When applying the involvement theory to questions about the relationship between humans and water in interior environments, the use of a water feature would be considered a side involvement. This is in keeping with Goffman's idea that people in a public space sustain minimal main involvement to avoid the appearance of being totally disengaged – whether a main involvement is present or not.

Other examples of side involvements include the use of such things as magazines and newspapers in waiting rooms and the incorporation of water features in parks, waiting areas, and lobbies. According to the involvement theory, the use of water features in these environments plays an important role, providing a source of minimal involvement to fulfill a basic human need.

The use of water features in our built and natural environments has been of longstanding interest to researchers. There are several studies that have examined the use of water on the exterior of buildings, and in landscapes, that have shown it to be an important element that enhances the human response to a building or environment (e.g., Brush and Shafer 1975; Civco 1979; Kaplan and Kaplan 1982; Palmer 1978; Penning-Roswell 1979; Shafer, Hamilton, and Schmidt 1969; Ulrich 1981; Zube, Pitt and Anderson 1975). However, water as a component of interior environments, and its interrelationship with human behaviors, has received only limited attention – with the majority of such studies being done in relation to healthcare facilities. For example, a study in a Swedish university hospital investigated whether exposing heart surgery patients in intensive care units to nature pictures improved outcomes (Ulrich, Lundèn, and Eltinge 1993). Those patients assigned a landscape with trees and water experienced less anxiety, and required fewer strong pain doses, than control groups assigned no pictures.

Gender Considerations

Like any social institution, gender exhibits both universal features and chronological and cross-cultural variations that affect individuals' lives and their social interactions in major ways. Lorber claims that gender is an institution that establishes patterns of expectations for individuals, orders the social processes of everyday life, is built into the major social organizations of society, such as the economy, ideology, family, and politics, and is also an entity in and of itself (Lorber 1994).

Most people find it hard to believe that gender is constantly created and re-created out of human interactions and social life. Yet gender, like culture, is a human production that depends on everyone constantly "doing gender" (West and Zimmerman 1987).

In almost every encounter, human beings produce gender, behaving in the manner they learned as appropriate for their gender status, or resisting or rebelling against these norms. Coser claims that women and men spend much of their time with people of their own gender because of the way they work and how their families are organized. This spatial separation of women and men reinforces gendered differentness, identity. and ways of thinking and behaving (Coser 1986).

In a study conducted by Weisman and Birkby women were asked to draw their environmental fantasies in workshops conducted across the United States. The participants were chosen to be diverse in age, lifestyle, experience, and education. After Weisman and Birkby collected hundreds of drawings from the workshops, they began to notice patterns of shared experiences and common characteristics among the participants. One of the four themes resulting from the study was the importance of contact with nature and natural materials to soothe and stimulate the senses (Weisman 1992).

Many studies support the idea that women are: (1) more sensitive than men and (2) looking for relief from environmental stress, especially in public environments (Gardner 1989; Goffman 1963; Mozingo 1989). Ortner suggests that a woman's psyche is closer to nature and that the female personality tends to be involved with concrete feelings, things, and people rather than with abstract entities, thereby tending toward personalism and particularism (Ortner 1996).

Culture Considerations

According to Amos Rapoport, a noted authority on the interface between people and built environments, valid generalizations about this relationship must be based on a broad sample, covering a wide variety of situations both in space and time and thus requiring both cross-cultural and historical studies (Rapoport 1976). Rapoport claims that built environments are much more than physical objects or economic devices, and that in order to understand human–environment relationships one must get beyond material aspects of the environment by using a cross-cultural and historical approach, with the nature of cultural environments and their relationships playing a central role (Rapoport 1980).

Methodology

The purpose of this study was to examine human responses to water features used in interior environments and to determine the extent to which the incorporation of water features may influence people's preference for those environments. To test this concept, the following hypotheses were developed:

- *Hypothesis 1.* Overall, the preference score for photographic images emphasizing water will be higher than a preference score for photographic images that do not emphasize water.
- *Hypothesis 2.* The preference score for photographic images emphasizing water will increase when a water fountain is present in the interior environment.
- *Hypothesis 3.* Female subjects will have a higher preference score for images emphasizing water than male subjects.
- *Hypothesis 4.* Taiwanese subjects will have a higher preference score for photographic images emphasizing water than subjects from the United States.

Sample

To test these hypotheses, data were collected from a sample of 400 college students. A convenience sample of 200 subjects from the Pacific Northwest of the United States of America (100 male and 100 female) was selected from students at an institution of higher education. Another convenience sample of 200 Taiwanese subjects (100 male and 100 female) was selected from universities in Taiwan. The identity of the subjects was kept confidential and anonymous.

Photographic images of public interiors

Six pairs of photographic images of public interiors were developed, with each pair showing a different interior environment. Four of the six pairs consisted of an image of a public interior where a water feature was emphasized and an image of the same interior without the water feature emphasized. Each pair of photographic images was duplicated as closely as possible, with the only exception being the emphasis or de-emphasis on the water feature.

In addition to these four pairs of images, a fifth set of images where a water feature was not included and a sixth pair of images where a water feature was included were developed and included in the packet that subjects reviewed. The purpose of the fifth and sixth pair of images was to prevent subjects from determining the purpose of the experiment and behaving differently than they would if they were unaware of the purpose of the experiment (demand characteristic).

Because the photographic images were a key part of the study, the content and quality were important. Interior design experts was asked to review the images and recommend six pairs that, based on their design expertise, they felt were most appropriate for this study. The criteria for these recommendations were: (1) the consistency of contemporary design characteristics; (2) the consistency in scale of the water features; and (3) the consistency in function of the interior environment.

The final six pairs of images recommended for the use in the study by the design experts were developed into $8'' \times 10''$ color photographs.

Room setting and viewing order

A small room (approximately $10' \times 15'$) was set up for the subjects to view the six pairs of images of interior environments with and without water features. In room setting W (water), a small portable water fountain ($W8'' \times D8'' \times H10''$) with water flowing was placed in the room. In room setting NW (no water), the fountain was removed from the room. In other words, the only difference between the two room settings was the presence or absence of the water fountain. In each culture and gender group, an equal number of subjects was exposed to each room setting.

In addition, to counteract an order effect, the images were presented to the subjects in two different random orders (coded as A and B). One-half of each subject group viewed the images in random order A and the other half viewed the images in random order B. For example, within the 50 American male sample group (S_1) 25 subjects viewed the images in random order A and the other 25 viewed the images in random order B. The overall design is summarized in Table 17.1.

Table 17.1 The overall experiment design

Room setting with flowing water fountain present (W)				Room setting without flowing water fountain present (NW)			
US (A)		Taiwan (T)		US (A)		Taiwan (T)	
Male (M)	Female (F)	Male (M)	Female (F)	Male (M)	Female (F)	Male (M)	Female (F)
$S_1 = 50$	$S_2 = 50$	$S_3 = 50$	$S_4 = 50$	$S_5 = 50$	$S_6 = 50$	$S_7 = 50$	$S_8 = 50$

Photo questionnaire and test administration

The photo questionnaire included the following items:

- Brief instructions for completion of the questionnaire
- A place for the investigator to mark code information
- A short demographic profile for the subject to complete; i.e., age, gender, and education
- Preference indicators that each subject could mark when viewing the images

To ensure that the Taiwanese subjects had a clear understanding, a Chinese version of the photo questionnaire was also developed.

The room setting had two chairs and a table. Each subject was invited into the room and asked to sit down across the table from the investigator. In room setting

W, the room also included a fountain with flowing water that was within a 3-foot radius of the table. The room setting NW was the same but did not include the water fountain.

The investigator reviewed the instructions with each subject, assured them of confidentiality and anonymity, and then asked them to complete the demographic information. Once that was done, the investigator showed them each a set of the six pairs of photographic images with and without water. Each subject was asked to indicate their preference for one of the two images in each pair they were shown. After responding to all six pairs of photographic images the subject was thanked and the next participant invited into the room.

Findings and Analysis

The average age of the 400 subjects was 21years with a range between 18 to 31 years, and 342 (85.5%) were under the age of 23. The dependent variable was the number of preference marks (preference score) made by each subject for images of an interior environment with a water feature emphasized. Since two out of the total of six pairs of photos were used to prevent subjects from determining the true purpose of the experiment, only the data from the four applicable pairs were counted. This meant that the range of the preference scores was from 0 to 4. The closer a subject's score was to 4, the higher their preference for the interior environment with a water feature shown. Table 17.2 shows the mean preference score and standard deviation for the eight sample groups.

Table 17.2 Mean preference score and standard deviation

	US		Taiwan	
	Male	*Female*	*Male*	*Female*
With water fountain				
Sample size	50	50	50	50
Standard deviation	0.87	0.76	1.31	1.25
Mean	3.32	3.44	1.62	1.94
Without water fountain				
Sample size	50	50	50	50
Standard deviation	1.06	0.92	1.35	1.20
Mean	3.18	3.36	1.76	2.02

The null hypotheses tested were:

1   The preference score for the photographic images emphasizing water will be the same as the preference score for the photographic images that do not emphasize water features.

2   The preference score for the photographic images emphasizing water will not change when the water fountain is present.
3   Male and female subjects will have the same preference score for the photographic images emphasizing water.
4   Taiwanese subjects will have the same preference score for the photographic images emphasizing water as American subjects.

A *t*-test was administered to test the first null hypothesis of indifference (in this study, mean = 2) to determine if there was a significant difference between the subjects' responses to images of interiors with water and images of interiors without water. The result of this test was a *t* of 8.69. Since a *t* over 1.65 is required for rejection of the null hypothesis at the .05 level of significance the hypothesis was rejected. Rejection of the null hypothesis supports the idea that there was a significant difference in the subjects' responses to interiors with and without water features. In addition to the results of the *t*-test, an examination of the mean scores supports the conclusion that there was a higher preference for the interiors where water was included (see Table 17.3).

Table 17.3   *t*-test of overall mean = 2 (null hypothesis of indifference)

H0: $\bar{X} = 2$	
H1: $\bar{X} > 2$ or $\bar{X} < 2$	
Mean	2.58
Observation	400
t	8.69
t Critical one-tail	1.65

A three-way analysis of variance (ANOVA) was used to analyze the results of both the main effect and the interaction effect of the following three factors: *water* (with or without real water flowing in the test room), *culture* (US versus Taiwan), and *gender* (male versus female). The three-way ANOVA results are shown in Table 17.4.

In Table 17.4, if the F score is above 1, it is significant at .05 level. The "Sig." column gives the probability (p) value of the F test. The results of this three-way analysis of variance yielded no significant three-way interactions between culture, water, and gender (F = .073, p = .787), and there was no significant two-way interaction between culture and water (F = .982, p = .322); culture and gender (F = .398, p = .529); or water and gender (F = .000, p = 1.000).

The main effect for culture was found to be significant (F = 180.257, p = .000) indicating that the preference score of US subjects and the preference score of Taiwanese subjects tended to be different. The main effect for gender was also

Table 17.4   Tests of between-subjects effects

Source	*Type III Sum of Squares*	*df*	*Mean Square*	*F*	*Sig.*
Dependent Variable: SCORE					
Corrected Model	228.640[a]	7	32.663	26.520	.000
Intercept	2662.560	1	2662.560	2161.813	.000
CULTURE	222.010	1	222.010	180.257	.000
WATER	.000	1	.000	.000	1.000
GENDER	4.840	1	4.840	3.930	.048
CULTURE * WATER	1.210	1	1.210	.982	.322
CULTURE * GENDER	.490	1	.490	.398	.529
WATER * GENDER	.000	1	.000	.000	1.000
CULTURE * WATER * GENDER	9.000E-02	1	9.000E-02	.073	.787
Error	482.800	392	1.232		
Total	3374.000	400			
Corrected Total	711.440	399			

a. R Squared = .321 (Adjusted R Squared = .309).

significant (F = 3.930, p < .05) indicating the preference score of female subjects and the preference score of male subjects also tended to be different.

The difference between the overall mean score of males and the overall mean score of females was only −.22. This indicates that if groups of 100 males and 100 females were compared, the females would prefer a photo emphasizing water a total of 22 more times than the males. This relatively small difference suggests that the substantive importance of this finding may need further examination.

Lastly, the main effect when a water fountain was present in the test room had an F value below the .05 level and therefore was not significant (see Table 17.4). The means are shown in Figures 17.1 and 17.2 (with Figure 17.1 representing the room setting with real water flowing and Figure 17.2 representing the room setting without real water flowing).

From Figures 17.1 and 17.2 an examination of the main effects of real water flowing in the test room on culture and gender can be done. Contrary to expectations, the presence of real water flowing in the test room did not significantly affect the mean preference scores. Figures 17.1 and 17.2 show that the mean preference scores were similar in both room settings (with and without real water flowing.) Also, unexpectedly and contrary to what was hypothesized, subjects from the United States had higher preference levels than Taiwanese subjects regardless of whether real flowing water was present or not. Lastly, as anticipated, female subjects had higher preference levels than male subjects in all settings regardless of cultural background.

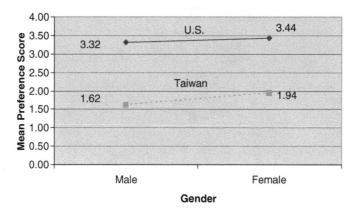

Figure 17.1 Effect of gender on the preference score by culture (with real water flowing in the test room).

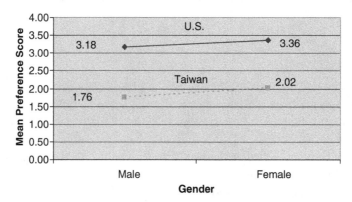

Figure 17.2 Effect of gender on the preference score by culture (without real water flowing in the test room).

Figures 17.1 and 17.2 also show the interaction effect between and among the following variables: (1) real water flowing in the test room and culture; (2) real water flowing in the test room and gender; (3) culture and gender; (4) real water flowing in the test room, culture, and gender. An examination of these interaction effects shows that the cultural difference between Taiwanese subjects and US subjects was greater in the test room with real water flowing than it was in the test room without real water flowing. Unexpectedly, the effect of real water flowing in the test room was positive for American subjects, but negative for Taiwanese subjects.

Figures 17.1 and 17.2 also indicate that there was very little interaction between the presence of real water flowing in the test room and gender and there was very little interaction effect between culture and gender. When the interaction effect was examined among the three variables of real water, culture, and gender, there was also very little interaction.

Conclusions

The literature indicates that water is one of the most powerful elements that can be used to enhance the human experience (e.g., Brush and Shafer 1975; Civco 1979; Hammitt et al. 1994; Kaplan and Kaplan 1982; Palmer 1978; Penning-Roswell 1979; Shafer, Hamilton, and Schmidt 1969; Syme and Nancarrow 1992; Ulrich,1981; Yang and Brown 1992; and Zube, Pitt and Anderson 1975). For example, Moore claims that water touching our skin is the most personally intimate experience we can have (Moore 1994b). Also, Campbell claims that we must feel the water in order to complete our experience (Campbell 1978).

The literature also supports the notion that water carries special meanings and associations for people of different ethnic, cultural, and social backgrounds. By the same token, the literature shows that gender, and the way that it is interpreted by different social and cultural groups, is an extremely powerful component of our everyday lives (Gardner 1989; Goffman 1963; Mozingo 1989; Ortner 1996; Whyte 1980). As such, it is a powerful design element when used in our built environment.

Overall, the fact that the subjects, regardless of gender or culture, preferred interior images where water features were emphasized supports the literature that suggests people's experiences are enhanced by the presence of water. Additionally, in keeping with the literature on gender which points out that women are more sensitive to their surrounding environment, the study found that female subjects, again regardless of culture, had a significantly higher preference level for images of interiors with water emphasized than male subjects.

Contrary to expectations, overall the presence of real running water had little to no effect on the subjects' preferences for an interior image. There are several possible explanations for this result. For instance, perhaps the size of the fountain (water element) in the test room was not sufficiently large that people noticed it. Or, perhaps, the sound of the water was actually annoying rather than pleasant for most of the subjects. It could also be because the overall design of the water fountain was not integrated well into the whole setting or the design of the fountain itself was not attractive to the subjects.

In a previous exploratory study that examined the use of existing water features in public spaces (Lin 1999), contrary to the literature and what was expected, it was found that the frequency of people's responses to water features in public interiors was very low. In addition, there were surprising differences in the way the genders responded to the water features, with male subjects tending to respond more frequently than female subjects.

In an attempt to further examine these results, the experimental setting for this study used a small, private, and enclosed interior space where the variables could be more controlled. The results of the study were contrary to those of the earlier exploratory study, showing that, indeed, female subjects had a higher preference for interior environments with water features than male subjects.

One explanation for these contradictory results is not only that the experimental setting was more controlled but also that, as the literature points out, females may be more conscious of their safety when in open public environments and therefore less apt to stop or display their response to water features. In addition, as part of a social order or norm, there is evidence that suggests that women in general more tightly define how they behave in public spaces than men (Gardner 1989; Goffman 1963; Mozingo 1989; Ortner 1996; Whyte 1980). These studies have concluded that sometimes women display certain attitudes and behavior, yet may shun others.

On the other hand, the literature also suggests that women are more sensitive to their surrounding environment. As stated earlier, the result of the study conducted by Weisman and Birkby shows that women felt it was important to have contact with nature and natural materials that soothe and stimulate the senses (Weisman 1992). Based on the results of the controlled experiment and the literature on gender and social norms, it can be concluded that although women are actually more sensitive to their surrounding environment, they are less prone to openly respond to water features in public spaces.

One unforeseen and interesting result of this controlled study was that American subjects had a significantly higher level of preference for the images with water features than the Taiwanese subjects. In addition, a closer examination reveals that the effect of real water flowing in the test room was positive for American subjects, but negative for Taiwanese subjects. It is suggested that this may be the result of unanticipated variables between the test room in the United States and the test room in Taiwan such as overall design of the room, lighting, layout, background noise, and other such variables – even though the size, scale, level of sound, and distance of the flowing water from each subject was tightly controlled in both settings.

Another possible explanation for the greater preference of subjects from the United States for water than Taiwanese subjects may be related to media focus in the United States on the benefits of "feng shui," making the incorporation of water features into interior environments very trendy. In contrast, feng shui is an integral part of the Taiwanese culture. Therefore, it may be that since water is an important element of feng shui, it is not unusual for water features to be incorporated into Taiwan's built environment. For Taiwanese people, the use of water elements is just something that is always there. In other words, having water elements in the built environment is normal and not unusual, whereas for the subjects from the United States it is less common.

The geographical location of the two cultures could be another explanation for subjects from the United States' preference for water features. The North American continent is so large that it does not allow everyone to be exposed to a big body of water on a daily basis, while Taiwan is a tropical island with the total area of $32,260\,km^2$, and water is a constant part of daily life.

Lastly, since all of the images used in this study were of contemporary interiors, the low preference level of Taiwanese subjects might indicate a preference for more traditional interiors reflecting the Taiwanese culture. In other words, perhaps the images of interiors with water features shown in the study were not attractive to most of the Taiwanese subjects

Implications for Future Study

The results of this study emphasize the complex nature of design issues that surround the use of water in public interiors. It is suggested that a study focusing on the design of interior water features would add to our understanding of these issues. The purpose of such a study could be: (1) to identify the most favorable design for interior water features for specific settings including design aspects such as scale, color and material used; and (2) to examine the sound of water, including the level and kind of sound appropriate for specific settings.

In addition, it is suggested that a study similar to this one including only Taiwanese subjects could be conducted to further explore the reason for the lower preference level of Taiwanese subjects for water features in interior environments. The focus of such a study would be on the incorporation of traditional Taiwanese design elements versus non-traditional, contemporary design elements and water features.

According to an old saying, "Water can either float or sink a boat." This and many other studies reinforce the idea that water is a powerful element in human experience. This study represents only a small contribution to our understanding of the complex relationship between humans and water and, in many ways, has raised more questions than it answered. Such is the nature of research. Regardless, the results suggest that the use of water in interior environments should be carefully considered by designers and it should not be assumed that all people will respond positively and at the same level to its inclusion.

References

Alexander, C. 1977. *A Pattern Language: Towns, Buildings, Construction.* New York: Oxford University Press.

Brush, R. O. and Shafer, E .L. 1975. "Application of a landscape-preference model to land management," in E. H. Zube, R. O. Brush, and J. G. Fabos (eds.), *Landscape Assessment: Values, Perceptions and Resources.* Sydney: Halstead Press, pp. 168–181.

Campbell, C. S. 1978. *Water in Landscape Architecture.* New York: Litton Educational Publishing.

Civco, D. S. 1979. *Numerical Modeling of Eastern Connecticut's Visual Resources.* Proceedings of Our Natural Landscape: A Conference on Applied Techniques for Analysis and Management of the Visual Resource (General Technical Report PSW-35, pp. 263–270).

Berkeley: USDA Forest Service, Pacific Southwest Forest and Range Experiment Station.

Conniff, R. 1999, November. "The natural history of art," *Discover* 94–101.

Coser, R. L. 1986. "Cognitive structure and the use of social space," *Sociological Forum* 1(1): 26.

Douglas, M. [1970] 2002. *Natural Symbols*, London: Barrie & Rockliff.

Fitzsimmons, S. J. and Salama, O. 1977. *Man and Water: A Social Report*. Boulder, CO: Westview.

Gardner, C. B. 1989. "Analyzing gender in public places: rethinking Goffman's vision of everyday life," *The American Sociologist* 20: 42–56.

Goffman, E. 1963. *Behavior in Public Places: Notes on the Social Organization of Gathering*. New York: Free Press.

Hammitt, W., Patterson, M., and Noe, F. 1994. "Identifying and predicting visual preference of southern Appalachian forest recreation vistas," *Landscape and Urban Planning* 29 (2–3): 171–183.

Kahn, P. H., Jr. 1999. *The Human Relationship with Nature: Development and Culture*. Cambridge, MA: MIT Press.

Kaplan, S. and Kaplan, R. 1982. *Cognition and Environment*. New York: Praeger.

Lin, G. F. 1999. "Behavioral Responses to Existing Uses of Water Elements in Public Interior Environments." Master's thesis, Washington State University.

Lorber, J. 1994. *Paradoxes of Gender*. New Haven: Yale University Press.

Moore, C. 1994a. "The potential for wonder," *Architecture and Water*. London: VCH Publishers.

Moore, C. W. 1994b. *Water and Architecture*. New York: Harry N. Abrams.

Mozingo, L. 1989. "Women and downtown open spaces," *Places* 6(1): 38–47.

Ortner, S. B. 1996. *The Politics and Erotics of Culture*. Boston: Beacon Press.

Palmer, J. F. 1978. *An Investigation of the Conceptual Classification of Landscapes and its Application to Landscape Planning Issue*. Priorities for Environmental Design Part 1. Washington DC: Environmental Design Research Association.

Palmer, Stephen E., Schloss, K., and Sammartino, J. 2013."Visual aesthetics and human preference," *Annual Review of Psychology* 64: 77–107.

Patterson, M. 1997, November. "Accessible to accessible through," *Buildings* 91(11): 60–63.

Penning-Roswell, E. C. 1979. *The Social Value of English Landscapes*. Proceedings of Our National Landscape. (General Technical Report PSW-35, pp. 249–255). Berkeley: USDA Forest Service, Pacific Southwest Forest and Range Experiment Station.

Rapoport, A., ed. 1976. *The Mutual Interaction of People and Their Built Environment: A Cross-Cultural Perspective*. Chicago: Mouton.

Rapoport, A. 1980. "Cross-cultural aspects of environment design," *Human Behavior and Environment: Advances in Theory and Research* 4: 7–46.

Shafer, E. L., Hamilton, J. F., and Schmidt, E. A. 1969. "Natural landscape preference: a predictive mode," *Journal of Leisure Research* 1: 1–19.

Strang, Veronica. 2006. *The Meaning of Water*. Oxford: Berg.

Syme, G. J. and Nancarrow, B. E. 1992. "Predicting public involvement in urban water management and planning," *Environment and Behaviour* 24: 738–758.

Tetlow, K. 1997, June. "Hospital Santa Engracia," *Interiors* 156(6): 100–105.

Ulrich, R. S. 1981. "Natural versus urban scenes: some psychophysiological effects," *Environment and Behavior* 13: 523–556.

Ulrich, R. S. 2000. "Environmental research and critical care," in D. K. Hamilton (ed.), *ICU 2010: Design for the Future*. Houston: Center for Innovation in Health Facilities, pp. 195–207

Ulrich, R. S., Lundén, O., and Eltinge, J. L. 1993. *Effects of Exposure to Nature and Abstract Pictures on Patients Recovering from Heart Surgery*. Paper presented at the thirty-third meeting of the Society for Psychophysiological Research, Rottach-Egern,Germany. Abstract published in *Psychophysiology* 30 (suppl. 1): 7.

Weisman, L. K. 1992. *Discrimination by Design: A Feminist Critique of the Man-Made Environment*. Chicago: University of Illinois Press.

West, C. and Zimmerman, D. 1987. "Doing gender," *Gender and Society* 125(1): 51.

Whyte, W. H. 1980. *The Social Life of Small Urban Spaces*. Washington DC: Conservation Foundation.

Yang, B.-E. and Brown, T.J. 1992. "A cross-cultural comparison of preference for landscape styles and landscape elements," *Environment and Behavior* 24: 471–507.

Zube, E. H., Pitt, D. G., and Anderson, T. W. 1975. "Perception and prediction of scenic resource values of the Northeast," in *Landscape Assessment*. Stroudsburg: Dowden, Hutchinson and Ross.

18

Concerns with Daylight and Health Outcomes

Michael D. Kroelinger

Introduction

Daylight, through properly designed strategies, creates a superb, dynamic quality of light that enhances the human experience of buildings and spaces while at the same time supporting a sustainable environment. Historical examples demonstrating the potential value of daylight for healthful spaces are reflected in the accounts of hospitals designed with large glass areas "to take maximum advantage of available sunlight" (Sternberg 2009). Sternberg reflects on the 19th-century actions of Florence Nightingale and the early 20th-century hospital designs of Alvar Aalto and Richard Neutra and their emphasis on natural views and daylight, thus implying the importance of daylight in the healing process.

Heerwagen and others discuss the impact of daylight on mood, alertness, stress, reduced pain levels, and other attributes relating to health and wellness (Alimoglu and Donmex 2005; Figueiro, Rea, Stevens, and Rea 2002; J. Heerwagen 2009; J. H. Heerwagen 1990; Walch, Rabin, Williams, Choy, and Kang 2005). Application of light and health knowledge has been identified as evolutionary, with relationship to the need for interdisciplinary work that leads to a strong knowledge foundation which can be applied to design and the provision of quality healthcare (Veitch 2005).

Environmental attributes, including daylight, have a documented impact on human health and performance. For example, extensive literature reviewed by Boyce, Hunter, and Howlett outlines the following key points concerning daylight and health: "daylight is an effective stimulant to the human visual system and the human circadian system; daylight and a view are much desired; people will take

The Handbook of Interior Design, First Edition. Edited by Jo Ann Asher Thompson and Nancy H. Blossom.
© 2015 John Wiley & Sons, Ltd. Published 2015 by John Wiley & Sons, Ltd.

action to reduce or eliminate daylight if it causes discomfort or increases task difficulty; and exposure to daylight can have both positive and negative effects on health" (Boyce et al. 2003).

The purpose of this essay is to identify, briefly, how daylight should be utilized in interiors and to define key issues which impact healthful interiors in relation to daylighting. The essay attempts to provide factual findings from research across many disciplines and demonstrate why daylight is instrumental in supporting human health. An additional goal is to document the importance of future research in the continued evolution of what constitutes a healthful space through the use of daylight.

Why Daylight?

The use of good daylight strategies was essential to well-designed buildings before and as electric lighting emerged late in the nineteenth century. The Rookery Building in Chicago, by Burnham and Root, with its light court and expanses of glass in the exterior masonry wall construction, is an example. As electric light evolved during the 20th century as a result of more efficient and long-lasting sources combined with low electricity rates, daylight was supplanted in many, but not all, situations. With greater concern for energy costs, beginning in the 1980s and increasing to the present day with concerns for sustainability and green design, daylight strategies have become more essential for good design in many building types. In short, humans want visual contact with the outdoors and welcome the attributes of daylight inside buildings (Heerwagen and Heerwagen 1986).

A general goal is to get as much daylight as possible deep into a building while controlling contrast, brightness, glare, and heat gain. Climate, geographic location, sky conditions, building type, space use, occupants, and other issues must be considered along with techniques for introducing daylight through top-lighting, side-lighting, or other strategies (Kroelinger 2002). Design of daylight openings should vary based on building orientation and compass direction of each facade. As an example, north-facing openings in cool-cold climates should be minimized. Other rules of thumb apply for each compass direction and climate type (hot-humid, hot-arid, temperate, cool-cold). (See Figure 18.1, lighting in a bookshop in Finland.)

While acceptable design practices often vary for different building types, design criteria for using daylight commonly include:

- avoiding direct skylight and sunlight
- bouncing daylight into spaces
- filtering daylight
- bringing daylight from above for deeper penetration
- optimizing ceiling height for better daylight distribution
- separating view from daylight glass
- creating low contrast between windows and adjacent walls for reduction of glare

Figure 18.1 Top lighting in the Academic Bookshop, Helsinki. Designer: Alvar Aalto. Photo: M. Kroelinger.

- locating as many spaces as possible near daylight openings
- promoting distribution of daylight through space configuration and building geometry
- integrating building systems with daylight control systems (Kroelinger 2002)

Use of bi-lateral or multi-lateral design strategies potentially reduces glare and creates better distribution of daylight compared with single side-lighting. Top-lighting approaches can achieve more uniform light distribution and benefit from high wall surfaces but are limited to the upper floors of multi-story buildings. Artificial lighting and control systems also must be designed to integrate with day-light. Finally, daylight may be the primary or a secondary source of light within an interior space. (See Figure 18.2, lighting in a Chicago store.)

Daylight and Visual Performance

The literature generally indicates that daylight creates a better visual environment than, for example, fluorescent sources because it more closely matches the way humans, throughout evolution, have identified with all sources of light (Franta and Anstead 1994). Good visual performance can be diminished through poor contrast and brightness variations between surfaces which lead to glare and veiling reflec-tions. The physical condition of the eye and the occupants' age also impact visual

Figure 18.2   Skylighting in the Apple Retail Store, Chicago. Designer: Bohlin Cywinski Jackson. Photo: M. Kroelinger.

performance. Speed and accuracy are important when critical task performance is involved and vary depending on task detail size, contrast, and illuminance levels. Boyce, Hunter, and Howlett indicate that "performance deteriorates dramatically...when any of these factors get low enough" (Boyce et al. 2003). Poor lighting design often limits worker satisfaction. For example, Hedge (discussed in Guzowski) found that "the quality of the lighting environment correlates directly to the frequency of vision-related symptoms such as headache, eyestrain, and visual discomfort" (Guzowski 2000).

Daylight, in comparison with artificial light, varies widely in continuous spectrum characteristics in the visible spectrum. Daylight differs throughout the day, season, latitude, and with other conditions, a fact that does not apply to electric light. Because the rods and cones of the eyes have wide spectral responses of differing wavelengths of light, daylight is not "superior to other light sources" as "a stimulus to the visual system" (Boyce et al. 2003). Thus, positive benefits of daylight generally result from glare control based on how daylight is distributed and from better color discrimination due to the spectral qualities of daylight. Well-designed daylight strategies also illuminate vertical surfaces more effectively and, therefore, help achieve better light distribution within small to medium-sized spaces.

Daylight and View

Occupants of spaces without windows tend to indicate that lack of view and natural light affect them as well as their work (Ruys 1971). A study by Hartkopf, Loftness, and Duckworth demonstrated the benefits of windows for persons close to exterior walls (Hartkopf et al. 1994). Health complaints were 20% to 25% lower for those individuals with view and daylight. Studies by others about daylight and view in vastly different building types show that view and windows resulted in fewer sick calls, fewer days in hospital, less confusion, and higher preference for windows with a view (Keep and Inman 1980; Moore 1981; Ulrich 1984; Verderber 1986).

Much research has documented that people prefer to sit by windows (Brill et al. 1985; Cuttle 2002, 2003; Heerwagen and Heerwagen 1986). Good daylight strategies must be used or people will find the resulting conditions of glare, excessive brightness, or heat gain inappropriate and take action to reduce the objectionable conditions (Maniccia, Rutledge, Ray, and Morrow 1999). While individuals desire daylight and view, it can often compromise effective task performance if good lighting design strategies are not followed (Boyce, Beckstead, Eklund, Strobel, and Rea 2003).

The Human Circadian System, Seasonal Affective Disorder (SAD), and Mood

The occurrence of the sleep and wake cycle is directly impacted throughout the 24-hour day by light as a signal through photoreceptor cells and a nerve system to the biological clock (van Bommel 2006). This circadian system is impacted by human hormonal rhythms which add to the complexity of understanding human performance and physiological functions (CIE 2004; Edwards and Torcellini 2002). Cawthorne studied occupants and light exposure in two settings: (1) a deep plan office and (2) a daylit laboratory (Cawthorne 1994). The study results emphasized the significant difference in illuminance levels in the two settings – higher in the daylit laboratory. Czeisler et al. pointed out the importance of the intensity of light and time of day of exposure on the synchronizing value of light for circadian rhythm (Czeisler et al. 1989). Daylight outdoors is usually the primary key in determining the phase of the circadian rhythm (Boyce et al. 2003). Utilization of properly distributed daylight indoors, as noted in the above study by Cawthorne, demonstrates that higher levels of daylight in an interior space likely contribute to maintaining circadian rhythm. A study of visual and biological responses to daylight and artificial light indicated that illuminance ratios and vertical planes are important for "visual performance as well as biological stimulation and circadian rhythm" (Begemann, van den Beld, and Tenner 1996).

The hypothalamus regulates our activity and sleep cycles. This "twenty-four hour body clock" resetting for the day-night cycle is impacted by bright light, meaning that daylight triggers secretion of serotonin and melatonin. Melatonin increases and drowsiness occurs with low light levels or at dark each day, while increased daylight "suppresses the production of melatonin and fosters an alert state of mind by increasing secretion of serotonin" (Boubekri 2008). Boubekri continues by indicating that windowless environments or places without adequate light may cause a continual disruption of the body clock. As described by Cvengros and Wyatt (2009), bright morning light has been used as a treatment for circadian rhythm disorders including irregular sleep-wake syndrome (Czeisler et al. 1989).

Rea, Figueiro, Bierman, and Bullough have proposed a mathematical model for quantifying circadian light that allows researchers and designers to effectively address daylight and circadian rhythm. Rea et al. emphasize the need to further develop this definition "for quantifying the photic stimulus for the human circadian system" (Rea et al. 2010). Veitch indicates that "a more broad definition of lighting quality" also must include "maintenance of good health." Veitch further indicates that first prescriptions should contain a higher "daily light dose," "healthy darkness," be "rich in the regions of the spectrum to which the nonvisual system is most sensitive," recognize the importance of the light dose received by the eye, and the "time of light exposure" and its impact on dose (Veitch 2003). The researcher also emphasized the need for "dynamic daylight performance metrics" which replace the "static metrics" that are currently used in daylighting design (Veitch 2005).

Extensive research has focused on Seasonal Affective Disorder (SAD) and has established a direct correlation between exposure to daylight and vulnerability to SAD (Nayyar and Cochrane 1996). Depression from SAD for people living in northern latitudes has been well documented (Liberman 1991). Figueiro and Rea suggest that greater access to evening daylight may actually disrupt the sleep patterns of adolescent children and that sleep patterns were shorter in spring than in winter for the study sample and geographic location (Figueiro and Rea 2010). These findings question what school start-stop schedules should be, given the relationship between evening daylight exposure and phase levels of the circadian system.

SAD symptoms fall into two distinct categories: (1) melancholic and (2) atypical/ vegetative, and typically appear late in the fall or early in the winter in northern climates (Terman and Terman 1985). Liberman for example, reports that children with SAD suffer declines in concentration and performance in school, fatigue, sadness, and irritability (Liberman 1991). Another Canadian study determined that children in daylit elementary school classrooms had fewer absences per year along with positive health effects when compared to children in conventionally illuminated classrooms (Hathaway 1995).

Lighting impacts on mood are often discussed within the research literature on Seasonal Affective Disorder and circadian rhythm. A review by Stone, while exploring effects of light on circadian rhythms and mood states, asserts that prolonged exposure to abnormal lighting conditions does affect rhythms and possibly impacts mood (Stone 1999). Stone points to work by Lewy, Kern, Rosenthal, and Wehr which showed that bright light could alter the mood cycle of manic depressive patients (Lewy et al. 1982). Stone also indicates that everyday lighting conditions "including excursion into daylight" may not impact circadian rhythms and related mood states. The author also indicates that "low levels of daylight will induce depressive feelings, but these are usually transitory and may be rapidly dispelled by a more cheering environment" (Stone 1999). Wirz-Justice explores circadian rhythm disturbances and mood disorders and notes that a relationship between the two is not clear (Wirz-Justice, Graw, Krauchi, Gisin, and Jochum 1993).

Tonello looked specifically at environmental psychology and lighting with a focus on attributes of Seasonal Affective Disorder (Tonello 2008). A key conclusion reinforced the need for more definitive work investigating unique conditions like SAD and of mood and behavior in general. Tonello notes that there are many lighting aspects that depend on psychology instead of physiology, including "mood, motivation and behaviour." The comments reinforce the work of others which imply that these aspects are impacted by many factors, thus there is a need for more holistic viewpoints if the desire is "to achieve efficient and healthy built environments" (Tonello 2008).

Veitch and Gifford investigated the beliefs about lighting on respondents' mood, work performance, health, and social behavior. A component of the multi-dimensional method used to investigate lighting beliefs assessed daylight and "determined that 65% of the respondents reported that the quality of light is important to their well-being" (Gifford and Gifford 1996). A larger percentage (80.5%) agreed that "natural light indoors improves their mood" (Gifford and Gifford 1996).

Research findings suggest that mood is influenced by daylight but, as noted by Veitch, there are "not yet enough absolute statements about the light and dark needs for good human health." This includes mood. Boyce et al. indicate that the link between mood, productivity, and daylight is weak due to the large number of influencing factors. For example, research by Gutkowski did not show changes in mood in experimental settings with and without windows (Gutkowski 1992). Boubekri indicates that mood may be more impacted in spaces where dramatic changes in light result from manipulation, including religious and social settings (Boubekri 2008). In settings with less subtle lighting, like offices and workplaces, mood change may not be as dramatic.

Perhaps the most consequential research regarding the relationship between light and psychological issues, including evaluative impressions, was the 1970s work of John E. Flynn and his fellow researchers. While this body of work was related to artificial light and not daylight, the general objective was to measure subjective impressions from lighting modes in interior spaces (Flynn 1979; Flynn, Spencer, Martyniuk, et al. 1973). The research defines patterns of light that might be responded to by occupants of spaces in consistent ways. The initial work, (Flynn et al. 1973) reinforced the concept that lighting can alter "the content of the visual field, and that this intervention has some effect on behavior and on sensations of well-being." The greatest strength of the series of Flynn-led studies lies in their research methods and "the theory that the experience of lighted space is, to some extent, a measurable

Figure 18.3 End wall daylight detail in the Kimbell Museum, Fort Worth, Texas. Designer: Louis I. Kahn. Photo: M. Kroelinger.

experience" (Flynn 1979). Extensions of this work to include daylighting and psychological attributes, including mood, are worthy of more in-depth and rigorous exploration. (See Figure 18.3, daylight in a museum.)

Daylight and Biological Functions

Daylight may positively or negatively impact human biological functions. The majority of the literature is focused on exposure to sunlight outdoors vs. transmission of light into the interiors of buildings through daylight openings. Glass and other transmission materials vary in how they transmit solar radiation into interior spaces. While details of these materials are beyond the scope of this essay, architects and designers must consider the attributes and the potential beneficial and harmful effects that may result. This is also an area of potential research regarding healthful interiors.

Most are aware of the potential harmful impact of sunlight on the skin as a result of excessive exposure. The skin must also receive radiation from sunlight or vitamin

D deficiency will result (Dowdy, Sayre, and Holick 2010). Hathaway, Novitsky, Thompson, et al. reinforce the importance of daylight for human biological functions and emphasize the importance of the visible wavelength range from 290 to 770 nanometers and the impact on vitamin D synthesis, tanning, and pigmentation of the skin, reduction of dental cavities, bilirubin degradation, and sensitivity of human vision to light (Hathaway et al. 1992). According to Wurtman, the physiological benefits of light are in two categories: (1) light on the skin, and (2) impact of light on endocrine, hormone, and metabolic states (Wurtman 1975).

Researchers have acknowledged the potential health benefits regarding ailments. Sunlight has often been a key to curing rickets in children and osteomalacia in adults because of vitamin D development (Holick 1985; Liberman 1991). The benefits of ultraviolet light, called UV-B, in the 290 nm to 400 nm range were determined to produce vitamin D through photosynthesis (Goldblatt and Soames 1923). Vitamin D also contributes to bone development and growth (Glerup, Mikkelsen, Poutsen, et al. 2000) and is often called the sunshine vitamin (Boubekri 2008). Romagnoli, Caravella, Scarnechia, et al. determined that variation in vitamin D occurred across seasons because of the variation in sunlight by season or by location in more northern latitudes – vitamin D amounts were higher in summer than in winter (Romagnoli et al. 1999). Similar findings have been confirmed by others (Brustad, Edvardsen, Wilsgaard, Engelsen, et al. 2007; Gillie 2006; Saadi, Kazzam, Ghurban, and Nicholls 2006).

Researchers have confirmed the relationship between vitamin D and aging, bone density, pregnancy, regulation of calcium absorption, and heart disease among differing groups (Chen, Ni, and Humphreys 2005; Holick 2004; Holick, Matsuoka, and Wortsman 1989; MacLaughlin and Holick 1985). Other research has confirmed the benefit of vitamin D in treating kidney diseases, normalizing blood pressure, and regulating calcium and phosphorus levels in the blood (Prasad, Nash, and Zaltman 2001).

Additional health conditions that are impacted by sunlight through vitamin D development include diabetes, multiple sclerosis, and cancer. Studies have shown the effect of sunlight on insulin secretion, which is used in treating type 1 diabetes (Brown, Dusso, and Slatopolsky 1999; Colas, Garabedian, and Fontbonne 1988; Sorenson 2006). Multiple sclerosis (MS) is also believed to be impacted by lack of sunlight in northern latitudes. The US geographical distribution, for example, reflects higher levels of MS in northern states than in other states (Boubekri 2008). Hutter and Laing investigated latitude, MS, and sunlight, and impacts on melatonin secretion and on fatty acids in the retina. As a result of their findings, the researchers suggest a re-examination of the consequences of sunlight on the retina (Hutter and Laing 1996). Hayes and Acheson indicate that insufficient sunlight exposure and MS are linked and that a unified approach to develop new methods to treat or prevent the disease is needed (Hayes and Acheson 2008). Finally, Mehta investigated sunlight, geographic variability, and MS and the central nervous system. Mehta stressed the need to continue research to confirm vitamin D, vitamin A, and melatonin roles in MS (Mehta 2010).

Robsahm, Tretli, Dahlback, and Moan investigated the possible improvements in the prognosis of breast, colon, and prostate cancer through vitamin D_3 from sunlight. The researchers determined that there was a significant variation in fatalities based on the season in which the cancer was diagnosed, which "coincides with the seasonal variation of in UV-induced vitamin D_3" (Robsahm et al. 2004). Holick also noted the association between vitamin D and breast, colon, and prostate cancer (Holick 2000). Finally, Kampman, Slattery, Caan, and Potter confirmed an inverse relationship between high colon cancer risk and calcium intake but did not determine that sunshine exposure was importantly associated with colon cancer (Kampman et al. 2000).

Daylight and Performance

Extensive research related to light, productivity, and stress has appeared in the literature, including the controversial Hawthorne studies begun in the 1920s by Elton Mayo and later by Mayo and Roethlisberger (Brannigan and Zwerman 2001; Hart 1943; Mayo 1933; McQuarrie 2005). The early experiments, focusing on electric lighting levels on a factory floor and increases in productivity, have resulted in much additional evaluation of Mayo's methods and original intentions with the research. There is also much apprehension regarding the actual impact of lighting on productivity, especially in situations where workers are being observed in a newly revised luminous environment.

More recently, work by others has addressed performance, productivity, users' response, and user behavior in work settings (Boubekri 2008; Boubekri, Hull, and Boyer 1991; Schuster 2008; Wang and Boubekri 2009). Boubekri et al., for example, determined that window size and sunlight penetration do have an effect on workers' feelings and environmental satisfaction and therefore affect their productivity because the quality of the workplace is affected. Schuster concluded that differences in lighting quality and openness of space can be impacted by levels of perception of brightness. He indicates that "as productivity is directly linked to comfort and well-being, the matter of subjective impression should not be neglected when designing and planning new working spaces" (Schuster 2008).

A comprehensive study of light and health investigated daylight and room depth looking specifically at stress among other factors (Cakir 1994; Cakir and Cakir 1998). The study concluded that "the distance of the workplace from the nearest window constitutes the main influencing factor in determining stress caused to humans by spatial conditions" (Cakir and Cakir 1998). The study determined that "too little daylight" increases stress through visual impairments and visual fatigue and that the lowest strain in workplaces was found closest to windows.

The Lockheed facility in Sunnyvale, California was designed in an open office layout which integrated daylighting strategies by Leo O. Daley in 1979 and was occupied in 1983. Studies demonstrated that the workers in the facility had an increase in productivity, due to a reduction in absenteeism by 15%, and this was believed to be a result of the integrated daylighting strategy (Bouchey 2001; Fountain and Benton 1990; Hein 1996; Pierson 1995). The project also saved 75% on electric lighting operation costs (Pierson 1995).

A study of second- through fifth-grade elementary school students by Heschong, Wright, and Okura was designed to "establish a statistically significant association between daylighting and student performance" (Heschong et al. 2002). The researchers studied three different schools in California, Washington, and Colorado and considered variables including age of school, classroom type and size, population, and size and presence of skylights and windows. In the researchers' words, "we were able to identify statistically significant effects of daylighting on human behavior, as evidenced in the standardized test scores for elementary school students" (Heschong et al. 2002: 110). Heschong concluded that "students in classrooms with the most window area or daylighting were found to have 7% to 18% higher scores on the standardized tests than those with the least window or daylighting." The study was based on a study by the authors for the California Public Utilities Commission and the Pacific Gas and Electric Company (1999a). Plympton, Conway, and Epstein documented several school case studies where a result was improving student performance and health (Plympton et al. 2000). In this latter case, all four case-study schools were able to cost-effectively create settings for improved student performance through daylight.

A related study on retail spaces, funded by the California Public Utilities Commission and the Pacific Gas and Electric Company (1999b), was designed around the same general goals as the schools study, discussed above. The retail skylight study focused on the sales index, as a measure of productivity, for over 100 chain stores owned by the same retailer. Two-thirds of the stores had skylights and one-third did not have skylights. Skylighting was one of the five significant variables in predicting gross sales per store. While these results apply to the chain of retail stores that was studied, the authors concluded that there was a strong positive and significant effect of skylighting on sales.

Other work suggests that daylight and view might alter short-term mood and happiness among workers but may do little to change individual workers' dispositions (Boyce et al. 2003). Boyce, Hunter, and Howlett review the work of researchers in organizational productivity and offer the following conclusion: "Unfortunately, there is no obvious mechanism by which working in a daylit environment could be expected to change a worker's disposition, although a daylight environment might be less likely to produce a negative mood state." Clearly, additional in-depth research across disciplinary boundaries is needed to more thoroughly address these complex phenomena.

Conclusions

The Illuminating Engineering Society (IES) has published a position paper on the known relationships between optical radiation and human health (IES 2008 [TM-

18-08]) and has established a position statement on the effects of exterior lighting on human health (IES n.d. [PS-03-10]). The latter document states the following:

> As with any research concerning human health, the information is complex and difficult to place in context. This is due in part to the complexity of investigations, the lack of experimental control, the ability of results to be generalized, and finite resources that make it impractical to explore relevant hypotheses.

This statement captures the current inconsistent status of research that precisely documents the complex relationship between daylight and issues associated with health and, therefore, healthful interiors. Certainly, relationships between daylight and healthful spaces exist but much future research is required to clearly ascertain relationships and causal effects, and to establish resulting design criteria based on reliable and valid findings. Work will also be required to bridge the gap between the research findings and the requisite design criteria which will be needed for good design decision-making in creating healthful spaces.

A statement by Sternberg captures the challenge presented by this complex concept of the relation between light and health: "How can we avoid too much short-wavelength exposure (and possibly skin cancer), while getting enough sunlight to activate the Vitamin D we need for growth and healing?" (Sternberg 2009). Good health through lighting represents a powerful new research area in need of extensive and innovative research methods, cross-disciplinary collaboration, and new findings that ultimately shape how we design healthful spaces.

This essay has established some, but not all, of the current health and daylight issues which have been addressed by a wide range of researchers from across a variety of disciplines. As noted, more in-depth review and analysis is required to clearly establish a meaningful research agenda for the future. Further exploration of these phenomena is encouraged!

References

Alimoglu, M. K. and Donmez, L. 2005. "Daylight exposure and the other predictors of burnout among nurses in a university hospital," *International Journal of Nursing Studies* 42: 549–555.

Begemann, S. H. A., van den Beld, G. J., and Tenner, A. D. 1996, July 17. "Daylight, artificial light and people in the office environment, overview of visual and biological responses," *Industrial Ergonomics* 20: 231–239.

Boubekri, M. 2008. *Daylighting, Architecture and Health Building Design Strategies* (1st ed.). Jordan Hill, Oxon.: Architectural Press.

Boubekri, M., Hull, R. B., and Boyer, L. L. 1991. "Impact of window size and sunlight penetration on office workers' mood and satisfaction," *Environment and Behavior* 23(4): 474–493. doi: 10.1177/0013916591234004

Bouchey, L. M. 2001, December. "Daylighting: big energy savings," *Plants, Sites and Parks* 28(7): 6.

Boyce, P. R., Beckstead, J. W., Eklund, N. H., Strobel, R. W., and Rea, M. S. 1997. "Lighting the graveyard shift: the influence of a daylight-simulating skylight on the task performance and mood of night-shift workers," *Lighting Research and Technology* 29(3): 105–134.

Boyce, P., Hunter, C. and Howlett, O. 2003, September 12. *The Benefits of Daylight through Windows*. Troy, NY: US Department of Energy.

Brannigan, A. and Zwerman, W. 2001. "The real 'Hawthorne effect'," *Society* 38(2): 55–60.

Brill, M. et al. 1985. *Using Office Design to Increase Productivity*. New York: Workplace Design and Productivity.

Brown, A., Dusso, A., and Slatopolsky, E. 1999. "Vitamin D," *American Journal of Physiology* 277(2): 1757–1775.

Brustad, M., Edvardsen, K., Wilsgaard, T., Engelsen, O., Aksnes, L., and Lund, E. 2007. "Seasonality of UV-radiation and vitamin D status at 69 degrees north," *Photochemical & Photobiological Sciences* 6(8): 93–98.

Cakir, A. C. 1994. *Does Lighting Influence Health and Well-Being?* Paper presented at the IES Triannual Conference. Toronto.

Cakir, A. and Cakir, A. 1998. "Light and health," *The Project*. http://www.healthylight.de/Light_and_Health/Start.html. Accessed December 21, 2010.

California Board for Energy Efficiency. 1999a. *Skylighting and Retail Sales: An Investigation into the Relationship between Daylighting and Human Performance*. Pacific Gas and Electric Company For the California Board for Energy Efficiency Third Party Program.

California Board for Energy Efficiency. 1999b. *Daylighting in Schools: An Investigation into the Relationship between Daylighting and Human Performance*. Pacific Gas and Electric Company For the California Board for Energy Efficiency Third Party Program.

Cawthorne, D. 1994. *Daylight and Occupant Health in Buildings*. Cambridge: University of Cambridge.

Chen, S., Ni, X. P., and Humphreys, M. H. 2005. "1,25 dihydroxyvitamin D amplifies type A natriuretic peptide receptor expression and activity in target cells," *Journal of the American Society of Nephrology* 16: 329–339.

Colas, C., Garabedian, M., and Fontbonne, A. 1988. "Insulin secretion and plasma 1,25(OH)2D after UV-B irradiation in healthy adults," *Hormone and Metabolic Research* 21: 154–155.

CIE (Commission Internationale de l'Éclairage). 2004. *Ocular Lighting Effects on Human Physiology and Behavior*. Vienna: CIE.

Cuttle, C. 2002. "Identifying the human values associated with windows," *International Daylighting* 5: 3–6.

Cuttle, C. 2003. *Lighting by Design*. Burlington, MA: Architectural Press.

Cvengros, J. A. 2009. "Circadian rhythm disorders," *Sleep Medicine Clinics* 4(4): 495.

Cvengros, J. A. and Wyatt, J. K. 2009. "Circadian rhythm disorders," *Sleep Medicine Clinics* 4(4): 495–505.

Czeisler, C. A. et al., eds. 1989. "Bright light induction of strong (type 0) resetting of the human circadian pacemaker," *Science* 244.

Dowdy, J. C., Sayre, R. M., and Holick, M. F. 2010. "Holick's rule and vitamin D from sunlight," *The Journal of Steroid Biochemistry and Molecular Biology* 121(1–2): 328–330.

Edwards, L. and Torcellini, P. 2002, July. *A Literature Review of the Effects of Natural Light on Building Occupants* (NREL/TP-550-30769). Golden, CO: US Department of Energy. http://www.osti.gov/bridge. Accessed October 10, 2010.

Figueiro, M. G. and Rea, M. S. 2010. "Evening daylight may cause adolescents to sleep less," *Chronobiology International* 27(6): 1241–1258.

Figueiro, M. G., Rea, M. S., Stevens, R. G., and Rea, A. C. 2002. *Daylight and Productivity – A Possible Link to Circadian Regulation*. Paper presented at the EPRI/LRO 5th International Lighting Research Symposium, Palo Alto, CA.

Flynn, J. E. 1979. "A guide to methodology procedures for measuring subjective impressions in lighting," *Journal of the Illuminating Engineering Society* 8(2): 95.

Flynn, J. E., Spencer, T. J., Martyniuk, O., et al. 1973. "Interim study of procedures for investigating the effect of light on impression and behavior," *Journal of the Illuminating Engineering Society* 87–94.

Fountain, M. and Benton, C. C. 1990. "Successfully daylighting a large commercial building: a case study of Lockheed Building-57," *Progressive Architecture* 71(11).

Franta, G. and Anstead, K. 1994. "Daylighting offers great opportunities," *Window & Door Specifier-Design Lab* (Spring): 40–43.

Gifford, J. A. and Gifford, R. 1996. "Choice, perceived control, and performance decrements in the physical environment," *Journal of Environmental Psychology* 16: 269–276.

Gillie, O. 2006. "A new government policy is needed for sunlight and vitamin D," *British Journal of Dermatology* 154(6): 1052–1062.

Glerup, H., Mikkelsen, K., Poutsen, R., et al. 2000. "Common recommended daily intake of vitamin D is not sufficient if sunlight exposure is limited," *Journal of Internal Medicine* 247: 260–268.

Goldblatt, H. and Soames, K. N. 1923. "A study of rats on a normal diet irradiated daily by the mercury vapor quartz lamp or kept in darkness," *Biochemical Journal* 17: 294–297.

Gutkowski, J. M. 1992. "The Impact of Windows on Positive Affect and Cognitive Performance in Work Settings." Manuscript, Rensselaer Polytechnic Institute, Troy, NY.

Guzowski, M. 2000. *Daylighting for Sustainable Design*. New York: McGraw-Hill.

Hart, C. W. M. 1943. "The Hawthorne experiments," *The Canadian Journal of Economics and Political Science / Revue Canadienne d'Économique et de Science Politique* 9(2): 150–163.

Hartkopf, V., Loftness, V., and Duckworth, S. 1994, December. *The Intelligent Workplace Retrofit Initiative: DOE Building Studies*. Washington DC.

Hathaway, W. 1995. "Effects of school lighting on physical development and school performance," *The Journal of Educational Research* 88(4): 228–242.

Hathaway, W. E., Novitsky, D., Thompson, G. W., et al. 1992. *A Study into the Effect of Light on Children of Elementary School Age – A Case of Daylight Robbery*. Edmonton: Alberta Education.

Hayes, C. E. and Acheson, D. E. 2008. "A unifying multiple sclerosis etiology linking virus infection, sunlight, and vitamin D, through viral interleukin-10," *Medical Hypotheses* 71(1): 85–90. doi: 10.1016/j.mehy.2008.01.031

Hedge, A. n.d. *Indoor Air Quality and "Sick" Building Syndrome in Offices*. www.meadhatcher.com. Accessed July 28, 2010.

Heerwagen, J. 2009. *Biophilia, Health, and Well-Being*. http://www.nrs.fs.fed.us/pubs/gtr/gtr-nrs-p-39papers/04-heerwagen-p-39.pdf. Accessed October 15, 2010.

Heerwagen, J. H. 1990. "Affective functioning, light, hunger and room brightness preferences," *Environment and Behavior* 22(5): 608–635.

Heerwagen, J. H. and Heerwagen, D. R. 1986. "Lighting and psychological comfort," *Lighting Design & Application* 16: 47–51.

Hein, K. 1996. "Let the sunshine in," *Incentive* 170(7): 6.

Heschong, L., Wright, R. L. and Okura, S. 2002. "Daylighting impacts on human performance in schools," *Journal of the Illuminating Engineering Society* 31(2): 101–114.

Holick, M. F. 1985. "The photobiology of vitamin D and its consequences for humans," *Annals of the New York Academy of Sciences* 453: 1–13.

Holick, M. F. 2000. "Sunlight and vitamin D: the bone and cancer connections," *Radiation Protection Dosimetry* 91(1–3): 65–71.

Holick, M. F. 2004. "Sunlight and vitamin D in the prevention of cancers, type 1 diabetes, heart disease, and osteoporosis," *American Journal of Clinical Nutrition* 79: 362–371.

Holick, M. F., Matsuoka, L. Y., and Wortsman, J. 1989. "Age, vitamin D, and solar ultraviolet," *The Lancet* 2(8671): 1104–1105.

Hutter, C. D. and Laing, P. 1996. "Multiple sclerosis: sunlight, diet, immunology and aetiology," *Medical Hypotheses* 46(2): 67–74.

Illuminating Engineering Society. 2008, November. *Light and Human Health: An Overview of the Impact of Light on Visual, Circadian, Neuroscience, and Neurobehavioral Responses.* IES.

Illuminating Engineering Society. n.d. *Effects of Exterior Lighting on Human Health.* New York: IES.

Kampman, E., Slattery, M. L., Caan, B., and Potter, J. D. 2000. "Calcium, vitamin D, sunshine exposure, dairy products and colon cancer risk (United States)," *Cancer Causes & Control* 11(5): 459–466.

Keep, J. P. and Inman, M. 1980. "Windows in intensive therapy units," *Anaesthesia* 35: 257–262.

Kroelinger, M. 2002. "Daylight in buildings," *Implications* 03(3). http://www.informedesign.org/_news/mar_v03-p.pdf. Accessed July 12, 2010.

Lewy, A., Kern, H., Rosenthal, N., and Wehr, T. 1982. "Bright artificial light treatment of manic-depressive patients with seasonal mood cycle," *American Journal of Psychiatry* 139: 1496–1498.

Liberman, J. 1991. *Light: Medicine of the Future: How We Can Use It to Heal Ourselves.* Santa Fe, NM: Bear & Co.

MacLaughlin, J. and Holick, M. F. 1985. "Aging decreases the capacity of the human skin to produce vitamin D_3," *Journal of Clinical Investigation* 76: 1535–1538.

Maniccia, D., Rutledge, B., Rea, M. S., and Morrow, W. 1999. "Occupant use of manual lighting controls in private offices," *Journal of the Illuminating Engineering Society* 28: 42–56.

Mayo, E. 1933. *The Human Problems of an Industrial Civilization.* New York: Macmillan.

McQuarrie, F. 2005. "How the past is present(ed): a comparison of information on the Hawthorne studies in Canadian management and organizational textbooks," *Canadian Journal of Administrative Sciences* 22(3): 230.

Mehta, B. K. 2010. "New hypotheses on sunlight and the geographic variability of multiple sclerosis prevalence," *Journal of the Neurological Sciences* 292(1–2): 5–10.

Moore, E. O. 1981. "A prison environment's effect on health care service demands," *Journal of Environmental Systems* 11: 17–34.

Nayyar, K. and Cochrane, R. 1996. "Seasonal changes in affective state measured prospectively and retrospectively," *British Journal of Psychiatry* 185(5): 627–632.

Pierson, J. 1995, November 20. "If sun shines in, workers work better, buyers buy more," *The Wall Street Journal* B1, B7.

Plympton, P., Conway, S., and Epstein, K. 2000, June 16. "Daylight in schools: improving student performance and health at a price schools can afford," *NREL/CP-550-28049*. Golden, CO: US Department of Energy.

Prasad, G. V., Nash, M. M., and Zaltman, J. S. 2001. "Seasonal variation in outpatient blood pressure in stable renal transplant recipients," *Transplantation* 72(11): 1792–1794.

Rea, M., Figueiro, M., Bierman, A., and Bullough, J. 2010. "Circadian light," *Journal of Circadian Rhythms* 8(1): 2.

Robsahm, R. E., Tretli, S., Dahlback, A., and Moan, J. 2004. "Vitamin D_3 from sunlight may improve the prognosis of breast-, colon- and prostate cancer (Norway)," *Cancer Causes and Control* 15(2): 149–158.

Romagnoli, E., Caravella, P., Scarnechia, L., et al. 1999. "Hypovitaminosis D in an Italian population of healthy subjects and hospitalized patients," *British Journal of Nutrition* 81(2): 133–137.

Ruys, T. 1971. "Windowless offices," *Man-Environment Systems* 1: 49–50.

Saadi, H. F., Kazzam, E., Ghurban, B. A., and Nicholls, M. G. 2006. "Hypothesis: correction of low vitamin D status among Arab women will prevent heart failure and improve cardiac function in established heart failure," *European Journal of Heart Failure* 8(7): 694–696.

Schuster, H. G. 2008. "Dim office buildings – the user's response," *Journal of Green Building* 3(1): 102–111.

Sternberg, E. M. 2009. *Healing Spaces: The Science of Place and Well-Being*. Cambridge, MA: Belknap Press of Harvard University Press.

Stone, P. T. 1999. "The effects of environmental illumination on melatonin, bodily rhythms and mood states: a review," *Lighting Research and Technology* 31(3): 71–79.

Terman, M. and Terman, J. 1985. "A circadian pacemaker for visual sensitivity," *Annals of the New York Academy of Sciences* 453(1): 147–161.

"The Rookery History," *The Rookery Building*. http://therookerybuilding.com/building-timeline.html. Accessed May 20, 2014.

Tonello, G. 2008. "Seasonal affective disorder: lighting research and environmental psychology," *Lighting Research and Technology* 40(2): 103–110.

Ulrich, R. S. 1984. "View through a window may influence recovery from surgery," *Science* 224.

van Bommel, W. J. M. 2006. "Non-visual biological effect of lighting and the practical meaning for lighting for work," *Applied Ergonomics* 37: 461–466.

Veitch, J. A. 2001. "Psychological processes influencing lighting quality," *Journal of the Illuminating Engineering Society* 30(1): 124.

Veitch, J. A. 2003. "Principles of healthy lighting: a role for daylight," *International Daylighting RD&A* 5: 5–6.

Veitch, J. A. 2005, October. *Light, Lighting, and Health: Issues for Consideration*. Ottawa: National Research Council Canada.

Veitch, J. J. A. 1996. "Assessing beliefs about lighting effects on health, performance, mood, and social behavior," *Environment and Behavior* 28(4): 446–470.

Verderber, R. 1986. "Dimensions of person-window transactions in the hospital therapeutic environment," *Environment and Behavior* 8: 450–466.

Walch, J. M., Rabin, B. S., Williams, J. N., Choi, K., and Kang, J. D. 2005. "The effect of sunlight on postoperative analgesic medication use: a prospective study of patients undergoing spinal surgery," *Psychosomatic Medicine* 67: 156–163.

Wang, N. and Boubekri, M. 2009. "Behavioral responses to daylit space: a pilot study," *Journal of the Human-Environment System* 12(1).

Wirz-Justice, A., Graw, P., Krauchi, K., Gisin, B., and Jochum, A. 1993. "Light therapy in seasonal effective disorder is independent of time of day or circadian phase," *Archives of General Psychiatry* 50: 929–937.

Wurtman, R. J. 1975. "The effects of light on man and other mammals," *Annual Review of Physiology* 35.

19

Healthy Interiors for the Visually Impaired

Dak Kopec

Introduction

The United States is home to an aging population, many of whom develop chronic health conditions that impede their ability to live on their own. The 2008 United States (US) Census Bureau projections stated that approximately 22% of the nation's population would be over 65 years of age by the year 2050. The last of the baby boomers, born from 1946 to 1964, will reach the age of 85 by the year 2050 (US Census Bureau 2008), thereby increasing the percentage of older Americans by 125% from the year 1900. Rather than place an older family member into an assisted living facility, many have opted to care for the older person. Termed "informal caregivers," family members of the aged population currently provide 75–80% of all long-term care in the US (Wright 2005).

William Glasser states that behavior is a result of a person's fears and desires at a given point in time. Control, for the older person, is the fear of freedoms lost and the desire to retain past freedoms (Glasser 1985). These fears and desires become omnipresent as the individual encounters activities of daily living (ADL) that have become more difficult or impossible. For the older person, the loss of control can then lead to a condition called "learned helplessness." The fundamental idea behind learned helplessness is that motivation becomes diminished as attempts to control one's surroundings are met with futility. The goal for design then is to facilitate autonomy-supportive environments that maximize the older person's freedom to negotiate his or her environment with a high degree of success and safety.

The Handbook of Interior Design, First Edition. Edited by Jo Ann Asher Thompson and Nancy H. Blossom.

To keep older family members safe and to provide regular assistance as needed, many families have opted to construct a "granny flat." The term granny flat is not new to the English vernacular; it is at the core of a long tradition where housing multiple generations and extended families in a single home or on a parcel of land was the norm (El Nasser 2004). Unfortunately, once the American suburb gained in popularity, the granny flat lost its appeal and many cities banned them (El Nasser 2004; Jarmusch 2005). Today in the US, we know granny flats by the name "guest suites or houses" in more affluent communities, "in-law suites" in middle-class communities, and by the term "accessory unit" in the newer master-planned communities (El Nasser 2004; Wedner 2008). The granny flat can take the form of a free-standing dwelling that shares a parcel of land with a primary existing structure, or the re-segmenting of an existing home. For many, this is an important housing option for the growing number of aging adults who would rather forgo senior- or assisted-living facilities (El Nasser 2004; Miller 1994; Wedner 2008).

Granny flats, however, are unique environments because they must be designed and constructed to accommodate age-related disabilities and promote independent living. Independent living includes the ability for the occupant to control his or her environment as well as actively ensure his or her safety and well-being. While there are universal guidelines related to universal design and aging-in-place that benefit an older population, the granny flat is often pursued (constructed or renovated) for a specific person with a specific condition. Designers of these environments must become knowledgeable about that person and his or her physical and psychological strengths and limitations when occupying an environment; recall, the goal is to maximize individual control. For example, let's consider the following situation:

> Bula is an 83-year-old Caucasian woman who was diagnosed with macular degeneration. She had surgery to correct the problem but ended up with a condition called *unilateral mydriasis*. Because Bula's health was steadily declining, her family opted to pursue "parasitic architecture" and construct a granny flat onto their existing home. Bula was in her new home for less than a month when she fell and fractured numerous bones in her face. When recovering in the hospital she indicated that she experienced eyestrain and frequent headaches.

Given this situation, it would be logical to conduct a post-occupancy evaluation (POE) to determine what, if anything, could be done to prevent future falls – and how the environment could be modified to reduce eyestrain and headaches.

A POE is a form of research intended to assess an environment's efficacy in meeting its occupant's needs and allow him or her to freely perform ADLs within an autonomy-supportive environment. In order to adequately perform a POE on an environment for a person or group of individuals with a health condition, the evaluator must know about the occupants and their respective health conditions and symptom manifestations. This is a systemic process that necessitates an:

- Understanding of the problem
- Understanding of the condition along with symptom manifestation
- Understanding of the client
- Understanding of the existing environment and
- Understanding of how design can affect the environment

Understanding the Problem

We experience the world through an aggregation of information obtained through our combined five senses. It is through these sensory abilities that we have been able to thwart danger and thrive as a species. Among the most important sensory abilities for all primates is vision. Nearly one-third of our brain is dedicated to this sense, and the physical structure of the human eye is among the most complicated in the animal kingdom. However, optimal performance of human vision is dependent upon the provision of light. The iris, which is one of three sphincter muscles in the body, contracts and dilates to control the amount of light entering the eye. When light passes through the pupil it proceeds to the retina, which contains rods and cones. Rods allow us to see in low lighting levels, and cones allow us to see in color and to detect detail. The central area of the retina is called the macula and it contains a high concentration of cones. It's this area that allows us to perceive sharp and detailed images.

Recent estimates from the National Eye Institute indicate that almost 14 million Americans suffer from visual impairments (National Eye Institute 2010). These impairments can be congenital, result from damage or injury to the eye or brain, or occur as part of the natural aging process. In many respects the gradual loss of vision is discounted and simply regarded as normal. However, current population forecasts suggest that by 2050 the United States will be home to 88 million people aged 65 and older. Fifty percent of this population will be living alone, 26% will be living with a spouse, 22% will be living with family members and 2% are expected to be living with non-family members (US Census Bureau 2008). Given that the Americans with Disabilities Act (ADA) protects age-related disabilities, including the decline of vision, the burden of knowledge pertaining to these disabilities and proficient implementation of accommodation strategies for equal accessibility is the responsibility of those who design the built environment (Kopec 2006).

Common visual impairments, other than blindness, include difficulties with depth perception, reduced visual field, sensitivity to glare, and difficulties adjusting from dark to light (Kopec 2007). With age, the lenses of our eyes become less flexible, thereby causing us to experience difficulties focusing when shifting our attention from a distant vista to one that is near. Similarly, as the lenses thicken they take on a yellowish hue from the build up of carotene. This means that older people will experience difficulties distinguishing between blues, purples, and greens (Tilly and Henry Dreyfuss Associates 2002). To accommodate the older person's decline in vision, experts have recommended an increase in lighting levels by 20% while simultaneously bringing about color contrast. (Tilly and Henry Dreyfuss Associates 2002).

When developing designs for people with visual impairments the goal is to compose designs that will maximize a person's ability to perform all of the tasks that he or she desires. The level of one's perceived mastery, or control, over the environment will directly affect belief in one's abilities. Recall that repeated failed attempts at a task will lead a person to develop learned helplessness – and to omit that task within their daily routines. For example, during the interview with Bula she said:

> "I used to curl my hair every morning with a curling iron. After the eye surgery, I would sometimes get dizzy when I looked in the bathroom mirror to curl it. See this mark? [she points to a burn scar on her wrist] This is where I burnt myself with the curling iron because I thought I was falling and went to grab the counter top. The hot curling iron fell and burnt my arm. I'm lucky there wasn't any water in the sink because that is where the iron fell. After that I said to myself, enough of this and threw the curling iron away."

As a result of this incident, Bula doesn't curl her hair anymore because she is afraid she may experience dizziness and fall, and she's afraid that she might burn herself again.

Because morning or evening ablutions are ritualistic, we tend to perform them without thought. Hence, accommodating ideas such as the addition of a vanity table and chair where one can sit while applying make-up or curling their hair may be overlooked. For Bula, who now hates her straight hair, the loss of her ability to control it through curling is another example of something age has taken away from her. Yes, Bula could have someone else curl her hair, she could get a perm, etc., but the point is that Bula wanted to curl it herself and believes she no longer can. This is the premise of learned helplessness. If the environment had been designed to include the vanity table from the time Bula had moved into the space, sitting at the table to curl her hair might have been incorporated into her ritual. Then, when she experienced the dizziness, she would have been sitting and a different outcome may have occurred.

As designers of the built environment, it is important that we don't over-generalize visual impairments as a singular condition with only one perceptual manifestation. Likewise, we need to concede that we have two eyes and as part of the normal aging process each eye may not age in the same way (i.e., a condition may affect vision in only one eye). Because of the multitude of conditions that result in visual impairments, and the variety of perceptual manifestations, the designer must first understand the condition and how it affects the individual's visual understanding of a space. The first step is for the designer to review what is known about vision and its processes through an exploration of the literature. From these baseline data, interviews with individuals who suffer from the condition can be performed to gain greater insights into and understanding of unique variations. This information will help the designer to identify unique conditions and situations pertaining to the environment in question and thereby begin to develop the most appropriate design.

Understanding the Condition

Visual processing

Vision is a process that requires a series of mechanical movements within the eyeball followed by a series of cognitive interpretations that take place in the visual processing centers of the brain (Kopec 2008). This means that a visual impairment may manifest from a physical deficit or from a cognitive misinterpretation. Understanding the difference will determine the most appropriate design initiatives. A physical deficit might result in changes to lighting or contrast. A cognitive deficit may require the omission of patterns and specific color combinations within certain instances.

The physical eye is much like a balloon filled with water. The fluid within the eye is called vitreous fluid, which has a thicker consistency than water. The center black portion of the eye is called the pupil. This is where images first enter the eye. The colored ring around the pupil is called the iris and it controls how much light enters the eye. The iris is a sphincter muscle that dilates to allow additional light into the eye and contracts to reduce the level of light. With age the sphincter muscle weakens. This means that we can expect a decrease in the effectiveness of the iris to constrict – allowing too much light to enter the eye in some situations.

Once light has entered the eye it is converted into electrical impulses by rods, cones, and ganglion cells. Cones are responsible for depth perception, color, and intensity of light. The rods are extremely sensitive to light and enable us to see at night by signaling the iris to either constrict or dilate. In conditions where the rods are damaged or lost, such as with macular degeneration, the message to constrict the pupil may be lost. This results in mydriasis – when one or both irises fail to constrict. The result is over-exposure to light, subsequently causing periodic episodes of momentary blindness (Kanski 2007; Schwartz 2004). One study showed that patients with photoreceptor rod dysfunction had lower pupil responses, thereby further supporting the connection between light, rod function and pupil diameter (Kawasaki, Anderson, and Kardon 2008). The ganglion cells are used with mesopic vision (low contrast conditions such as at dawn and dusk) and unconscious sight (Kanski 2007), a phenomenon in which the brain registers an object, but the person does not cognitively focus on that object. In low contrast environments, an elderly person with a visual impairment may register an object at an unconscious level, but not respond to it (Shepherd 1994).

In Bula's situation damage to the cones resulted in a permanently dilated pupil which affects the level of light detected by her eyes' cones. This, in turn, affects her depth perception and visual detection of color contrast. High levels of light on the cones also decrease perception of contrast, thus increasing the possibility of unconscious sight, which increases the probability of an accident.

When the physical eye is damaged or impaired, the way in which the person sees the built environment differs from when they have a fully functional eye, and from condition to condition. For example, wet macular degeneration will result in a varying number and size of black spots, while dry macular degeneration will result in a blurring of the center portion of the visual field. Glaucoma, on the other hand, will result in a clouding of vision, with some areas more opaque than others.

Another way in which vision can be impaired is through the malfunctioning of the neural connections within the various visual-processing centers in the brain. These impairments can range from temporal delays in which the world appears as if one were perpetually in a dark room with a strobe light, to dilutions or hallucinations in which the individual merges visual input with ideas or concepts formed within the brain. A third condition is when there has been damage to the brain resulting in a person not being able to see despite a fully functioning eye.

Clearly, these visual impairments require more forethought and understanding of the related conditions that influence visual perception. When a designer understands the condition and how that condition affects sight, he or she can design better living spaces that facilitate a high degree of control for individuals who may suffer from these impairments.

Lighting

We are able to see and interpret the world around us because of natural and artificial light. Natural light has long been seen as advantageous and has been a fundamental tenet of the sustainable design movement since the 1970s (Cohen 2005). There are some environments such as nightclubs, restaurants, and theaters where the value of natural lighting has been overstated (Baker and Steemers 2002). This means that designers must remain judicious in the application of natural and artificial lighting, and ensure such applications are appropriate to the population constituency and corresponding environment.

While it is difficult to mimic the full spectrum of natural lighting – albeit full-spectrum fluorescent lighting does come close (Hathaway, Hargreaves, Thompson, and Novitsky 1992) – the benefits of natural lighting to humans are well established. Natural light helps with vitamin D synthesis, reduces dental caries, enhances visual detection and discernment, and keeps levels of billirubin low – a brownish yellow substance produced when the liver breaks down old red blood cells (Hathaway et al. 1992). Other benefits associated with natural lighting include elevated mood, better balance of circadian rhythms, and increased energy (Boyce 1981). Notwithstanding these benefits, we must concede that some visual deficits may be exacerbated with too much light or lighting orientation and creative mitigation may be necessary.

Understanding the effects of lighting on visual perception of an illuminated environment requires special attention from the designer, particularly when designing for an aging population. For example, washing an interior environment with excessive daylight can actually decrease visual sharpness and increase visual fatigue through the introduction of glare. Contemporary studies show that excessive light causes great discomfort and cognitive impairment to people with age-related macular degeneration or other similar forms of ocular motor deficits (Cheong, Legge, Lawrence, et al. 2007). This discomfort and cognitive impairment may lead individuals to conclude that they cannot control certain factors that contribute to their safety, thus causing them to alter their behaviors. In such cases steps must be taken to guard against high levels of direct light and to avoid applying general rules to unique situations, thus overstating a theory or concept (Baker and Steemers 2002).

Similarly, material selection and uses must be understood in relation to the use of natural lighting (Van Kesteren, Stappers, and de Bruijn 2007). Floor and wall coverings, other surface finishings, along with personal artwork and other items of display, all have a direct relationship with lighting and light performance within the built environment. With regard to individual occupants, the use of, or means by which, natural lighting is facilitated must be tempered with the occupant's unique conditions. For example, high windows are likely to encourage an occupant to stand on a chair or climb a ladder to clean the windows, and people with certain visual problems may have difficulty filtering out excess light.

Understanding the Client

Interview preparation

Interviewing is a research method used in social science to gain information from an individual's unique perspective. When this interview is conducted prior to an examination and intervention, it is commonly called a needs assessment. Designers can use a needs assessment as part of the pre-design research or POE. To prepare for an interview, designers should craft questions intended to gain greater insights into:

- The occupant's goals and aspirations within the environment.
- How the environment has influenced the way the occupant behaves (i.e., has excessive heat in the evening or bright light in the morning changed the person's sleeping patterns?)
- How the occupant ranks various elements within the environment (important – not important; good – bad; convenient – not convenient; etc.).
- How a person achieves his or her goals (i.e., do they run a long extension cord to a favorite reading area?)
- Personal, social, and cultural rituals an occupant brings to the environment (i.e., prayer patterns, reading in the evening with a cup of tea, etc.).
- How the user's previous knowledge and experience influences what he or she does and how it is done (i.e., prior experience with too many lights tripping the

breaker switch, so the person limits the number of lights turned on during evening hours) (Hackos and Redish 1998)

By crafting three to four questions per topic area the most in-depth and accurate information can be obtained. However, care should be taken in the interview process because the person who is being interviewed may interpret a question differently than what was intended. For example, the occupant often performs rituals without much thought. Hence, many rituals may not be revealed without proper questions aimed at extracting that information.

Observation is another important component of the interview process. A designer must be observant of the nuances of the occupant. For example, the occupant may slouch in a chair, may put on and take off eyeglasses, or may continually place items in specific areas (on the coffee table, end table, on adjacent furnishings, or on their lap). If there is a pet in the environment, notice should be taken of where the pet is (in the same room, by the person's feet, on the person's lap, etc.). Observations such as these provide the basis for additional impromptu questions, which can be asked during the interview to gain a more thorough understanding of the occupant's needs.

In many situations a pre-design and POE interview will involve more than one person. If the purpose of the interview is for a child or elderly parent, another family member may be present. Likewise, adults tend to ask for their significant other to be present during an interview. These additional perspectives can be of great value in the creation of a final living environment; however, caution should be exercised not to allow the additional person to dominate the responses. Oftentimes the subject occupant with a health-related concern will be more timid during an interview. In such cases it may be necessary to conduct two interviews, one with the family member as an active participant and one where he or she only observes.

Ideally the interview will be videorecorded for later viewing and in-depth analysis, but if this is not possible an audio recording will suffice. Occupant verbal authorization and acceptance of being recorded is essential. Recording the interview allows a designer to listen to the dialogue as a third party at a later time. It is important to understand that while the interview is taking place the designer is an active participant. This means that critical physical or verbal clues may be overlooked during the interview process itself. By watching or listening at a later time, the designer then becomes an observer and is able to more keenly understand and interpret the information provided during the interview.

The subject client

Depending upon the building typology, a designer may have to consider the unique needs of a single person or the aggregate needs of a group with one or more common denominators. Bula's family sought out design assistance in response to a recent accident that they blamed on macular degeneration. By studying Bula during the interview it was clear that she suffered from a visual impairment called unilateral mydriasis.

Mydriasis is a condition characterized by prolonged abnormal dilatation of the iris causing the pupil to appear large. Unilateral means that only one eye is affected. Noticing the differences between Bula's pupils prompted the question of how she acquired this condition. Bula developed unilateral mydriasis as a result of corrective surgery for macular degeneration. A review of the literature revealed that mydriasis often leads to headaches and blurred vision (Hallett and Cogan 1970). Many people with this condition experience light sensitivity and are significantly affected by glare, which often leads to various halo effects (Ritschel, Ihrke, Frisvad, et al. 2009). The manifestation of a halo effect results in a false image appearing around a brightly illuminated object (Schwartz 2004).

Because Bula experienced mydriasis in only one eye, her visual impairment was compounded by the conflicting signals derived from each eye responding differently to lighting levels. During bright conditions one set of visual information came from the fully functional eye that constricted, limiting the amount of light into the pupil, while another set of visual information came from the eye that was permanently dilated, allowing excessive levels of light into the eye (Toy, Simpson, Pleitez, Rosenfield, and Tintner 2008). The brain therefore receives two similar but different sets of visual signals. This is analogous to the phenomenon known as "flicker vertigo" whereby the visual processing centers within the brain receive an imbalance in activity (Brandt 1999; Moore and Harris 2006; Rash 2004).

The high levels of light entering the one eye would thus affect the degree of contrast detected between various elements and colors contained within the environment. It also influences the detection and processing of specular reflections (mirror-like reflection of light from a surface object) and retro-reflections (a reflection of light that creates a glow). Depending on the elements within the environment, the effect can be similar to a fun house that uses an assortment of reflective devices. This is because reflections often influence peripheral vision, which has a slower processing speed (Cheong et al. 2007), prompting a Thorndike halo effect. This halo effect results from a cognitive bias that causes the visual perception of a current object to be influenced by the perception of a former object in a sequence of interpretations (Schwartz 2004). The inconsistent visual processing caused by incongruent visual detection along with specular and retro-reflections and halo effects would likely lead to multiple cognitive misinterpretations causing dizziness and bumping into, or tripping over, various environmental elements.

Not surprisingly, the interview revealed that Bula had routine occurrences of headaches, eye fatigue, difficulties detecting edges, and periodic vertigo. On the end table next to where Bula sat was a pair of prescription sunglasses. She said that she often wore them inside because they helped her with the headaches. Interestingly, Bula seemed embarrassed to reveal that she wore sunglasses inside of her home. This nuance was important because it goes to the development of learned helplessness. Bula believed she had no control over the conditions in her environment except to wear sunglasses inside. However, she was embarrassed by this action. As a result, she altered her daily routine of reading and started to listen to television (she could close her eyes), and she limited her movements within the home because she was afraid of injury. In the US over one-third of adults aged 65 and older fall each year (Hornbrook, Stevens, Wingfield, et al. 1994; Hausdorff, Rios, and Edelber 2001), and in 2005, 15,800 people aged 65 and older died from injuries related to accidental falls, with approximately 1.8 million treated in emergency departments (CDC 2008). Given these numbers and Bula's recent fall, her fear of falling again in the future is understandable.

When a person feels as though he or she has lost control over one or more of his or her freedoms, they will attempt to reassert control, which can lead to dangerous conditions or situations. Bula started to wear sunglasses inside of her home, and whenever possible she spent more time in her daughter and son-in-law's living room, which has a northern orientation making that room darker than her space. Bula wasn't able to articulate why she had adopted these two new behavioral patterns, she just knew that they brought her greater comfort.

Summary

Understanding the client, and having a solid foundation of vision, visual conditions, and aging, revealed five issues of concern that pertained to Bula's environment. These issues are as follows:

- *Issue 1.* As part of the normal aging process the lenses of the eyes take on a yellowish hue thus leading to inaccurate perception of color. Bula routinely wore sunglasses inside of the home. The tinted lenses of the sunglasses would exacerbate color distortion and significantly reduce the detection of contrast. Caution must be exercised to use colors that continue to contrast even when a yellowish hue is cast over the colors.
- *Issue 2.* One of Bula's irises is permanently dilated. Since the iris controls the amount of light going into the eye and one iris is not working, environmental luminosity must be controlled manually. Bula's attempt to control light manually can be seen in her desire to wear sunglasses inside of the home during the daytime. Caution must be exercised not to make an environment so bright as to inspire an occupant to engage in compensation measures.
- *Issue 3.* Excess light causes color to lose vibrancy. A dilated iris equates to excess light which means vibrancy will need to be increased throughout the space. Similarly, because Bula does wear sunglasses inside, color is further distorted by the tint of the sunglasses. Attention will need to be directed at reducing interior brightness as a means to mitigate the desire to wear sunglasses inside of the home.
- *Issue 4.* Because it is only one eye that is compromised and a visual image is composed of information obtained from two eyes, inconsistent information can lead to perceptual errors. Special attention will need to be given to sources that

can facilitate perceptual errors such as reflections. Also potential trip hazards and items used for stabilization should be assessed for the potential of injury.

- *Issue 5.* The occupant had macular degeneration and now unilateral mydriasis, which means that her peripheral vision was likely compromised. Following from issue 4, special attention will need to be given in the assessment of potential trip hazards as well as reflections.

Understanding the Environment

Site analysis preparation

After reviewing the literature pertaining to the condition or circumstance of the occupant it is important to develop a list of variables that will need to be included in a site analysis. These variables come from the review of literature and are augmented by information obtained from the interview.

Significant variables to be considered for those with a visual impairment are the type, level, and source of lighting (artificial or natural) as well as the color and color combinations of lighting. Traditional artificial lighting requires bulbs, which often produce a yellow tinge that can distort contrast and color perception as well as contribute to glare. Recall from the review of literature that as people age the eye's lens thickens and takes on a yellowish hue. The yellowish tinge common to many types of artificial lighting thereby becomes enhanced with the older person because of the yellowing of the eye's lens.

The best artificial lighting sources for those with visual impairments are those that simulate the effects of natural lighting by producing the full spectrum of colors. Natural lighting is much easier on the eyes (Edwards and Torcellini 2002) because the iris is not required to continually constrict and dilate, and natural lighting increases contrast and clarity while reducing glare (Gordon 2003). However, caution should be exercised to evaluate sources and levels of natural lighting within individual environments because the interior environment's use of colors and materials will affect perceptual manifestations within the space. Thus, a designer should place special attention on all reflective surfaces (tile or porcelain, granite and marble, surfaces painted with glossy paint or that contain a smooth plastic veneer, flooring with a polyurethane finish, polished metals, and glass table tops, picture frames, and vases) to avoid specular or retro-reflections. When performing the site analysis a designer should note and document current light sources (artificial or natural) along the originating point and pathway of that light. This information can then be analyzed in relation to the identified and perspective reflective surfaces.

As part of the site analysis attention should be directed to low-contrast or monochromatic colors between two or more elevations. For example, a green pedestal sink placed on a green floor can lead to conflicts in depth perception and boundary delineation. One common issue with depth perception derived from a monochromatic design is a white porcelain commode placed on a white tile floor.

The white-on-white can lead to location detection errors (i.e., missing the top of a counter and dropping a cup to floor). Similarly, special attention should be given to elevation changes regardless of height. For example, there may be less than a quarter-inch difference between the abutment of two flooring materials. This minuscule change in elevation is enough to bring about a moment of cognitive confusion, especially when one has just awakened, that could then lead to a fall.

Another variable of concern is the assortment of edges found within the built environment. Right-angled or knife-edges from doors and doorframes, counter and tabletops, and bookcases and other furnishings can pose a significant threat. Because of the distorted spatial awareness that often accompanies visual impairments, people tend to bump into or fall against these edges, often leading to bruising or more severe injuries. Ideally, bull-nosed edging should be used throughout the environment. An example of a tool that one might use when performing a site analysis for the purpose of redesigning a space for a person with a health-related issue can be seen in Figure 19.1. Although this example applied to a specific client (Bula) the categories exemplified are generic (i.e., room location, date, time, weather, and outside temperature).

ROOM ASSESSMENT TOOL		
Room:	**Location:**	
Date:	**Time:**	
Weather conditions:	**Outside temperature:**	
Window placement, size, and orientation		
Location	Item	Type
Notes:		
Lighting		
Location	Item	Type
Notes:		
Flooring materials		
Location	Item	Type
Notes:		
Wall coverings including art		
Location	Item	Type
Furnishings		
Location	Item	Type
Edging		
Location	Item	Type
Color/Contrast		
Location	Item	Type
Obstacles		
Location	Item	Type
Notes:		

Figure 19.1   Example of a room assessment tool.

Summary

A site analysis for a client's specific issues will demand special attention. In Bula's situation specific issues that needed to be addressed included:

- *Issue 1.* Types of artificial lighting will need to be identified. Bulbs that produce light with a yellowish hue will exacerbate the yellowish hue that is produced from the lens of the eye, thus distorting color.
- *Issue 2.* Numerous lighting sources will be needed to maintain a balance of light throughout the environment in order to reduce the need for the iris to continually contract and dilate.
- *Issue 3.* Reflections will need to be minimized to limit the number of visual messages required for processing within the brain.
- *Issue 4.* Assessment of color uses will need to be analyzed in relation to depth perception and spatial awareness.
- *Issue 5.* Safety measures will need to be identified in relation to periodic bouts of vertigo and the mechanisms used for stabilization and support.
- *Issue 6.* Distance between "safe areas" (places to safely hold on to something should a person experience dizziness or disorientation) will need to be identified and analyzed.

The Environment

Bula's environment was analyzed from the two aforementioned section summaries with special attention given to the maintenance of personal freedom and control. Her environment consisted of a newly constructed, three-room, 500 square foot, rectangular space attached to a primary structure on the eastern side. The three rooms consisted of a bathroom on the north end, a bedroom in the middle, and a combined living/dining/kitchen area on the south end. The environmental assessment was focused on three primary areas of concern. The first was Bula's sensitivity to light, the second was an abundance of glare in relation to direct and ambient lighting levels, and the third was degree of color contrast.

Using the tool illustrated in Figure 19.1, each of the three interior spaces was assessed individually and then as an aggregate whole. The tool provided basic information related to window and door placements, natural lighting levels, as well as light permeation from one room to another. For example:

- *Space One*
  - Bathroom. One small W3′ x H2′ etched window built into the eastern wall. Average levels of light come through the doorway from the middle room.
- *Space Two*
  - Bedroom. Two W3′ x H4′ windows were located on the eastern wall. Full-length mirrored sliding closet doors (3′ x 6′) abutted the northern wall and

were positioned perpendicularly to the eastern wall – directly across from the entryway to the living/dinning/kitchen area. Above-average lighting levels came into the middle room from the doorway to the southern side, and direct lighting from the windows was way above average during the morning hours.

- *Space Three*
  - Living/dining/kitchen. Two windows on the eastern wall. One was a 2′ x 2′ hexagon-shaped window and the other was a W3′ x H4′ standard rectangle. Next to this window was the door leading to the exterior of the building. There were no screens or security devices that would allow for this door to remain open. On the southern wall were two windows – both W3′ x H4′. This room received well above average lighting levels throughout the course of the day.

The tool also allowed for identification of environmental attributes that would contribute to illumination levels. These included the use of color, surface materials, and artifacts contained within the environment. For example:

- *Space One*
  - Bathroom. White ceiling, walls, and fixtures (commode, sink, and counter top) and shower stall. The floor consisted of a low-contrast beige tile, and the shower pan was white with a three-inch ledge requiring a step over when entering or exiting the shower stall. The combined porcelain fixtures and polished tiled walls led to many reflections.
- *Space Two*
  - Bedroom. White ceiling and walls, beige carpet, a double bed covered with a white comforter and three pillows contained within white pillowcases. Straddling the bed were white wicker end tables with clear glass tops, and at the end of the bed – against the eastern wall and under the two windows – was a white wicker dresser with a clear glass top.
- *Space Three*
  - Living/dining/kitchen. Oak hardwood flooring with a large white and blue Asian-style circular area carpet. Bula's chair and her coffee, end, and dining tables were composed of white wicker. The chair had a back and seat cushion composed of light blue patterns on a white background. The coffee, end, and dining tables had clear glass tops with white doilies. Throughout the 500 square foot environment were numerous glass-framed photographs (Bula was a photographer in her prime), porcelain vases, and figurines.

The environment's high luminance in conjunction with the overuse of the color white, and numerous reflective objects generated numerous hazards for Bula. Stellman notes that reflections can lead to periodic episodes of vertigo and moments of disorientation (Stellman 1998). In Bula's case, the environment likely compromised her lateral inhibitions. In essence, the eye and brain have special mechanisms for seeing edges clearly. These mechanisms allow the eye to see sharp boundaries between objects (e.g., a person standing against a building) and the background (Nabet and Pinter 1991).

Generally, concerns associated with lateral inhibition are the accidental creation of optical illusions. For Bula, who had a visual deficit, there were insufficient visual clues needed to stimulate these cells and thus Bula experienced difficulty identifying boundaries between objects and the background, or walls that protruded. In essence, the environment's high levels of lighting negatively combined with low levels of contrast interfered with Bula's body awareness in relation to objects and features contained within her environment (Wazen and Mitchell 2004). It is this combination of environmental factors that likely led to her initial fall and subsequent learned helplessness behaviors.

Understanding Environmental Design

The combined knowledge gained from the review of literature, interview, and site analysis allows the designer to better understand and address environmental attributes that are contrary to a healthy and empowering environment for people with specific visual impairments. The objective is to gain a comprehensive understanding of the joint nature of the occupant's condition and his or her environment. From the analysis comes the identification and prioritization of actions related to design modification and retrofits. Different people prioritize differently, and some might generate a list based on the prevention of future falls. Another professional might prioritize according to cost and overall budget concerns. Some might even prioritize according to initiatives that can be implemented without hiring a third party. When designing healthy environments, prioritization must be done according to optimal physical and psychological health.

Bula's physical health was compromised by excess light. She complained of headaches, eye strain, and periodic episodes of dizziness. These are all physical health issues that likely contributed to a recent fall requiring hospitalization. On some level, Bula concluded that she could not control her environment, which meant that she could not control nor be proactive with regard to personal safety. The result was an alteration in behaviors and she began to engage in learned helplessness.

A superficial analysis might conclude that the first priority for Bula's environment should be a reduction in lighting levels. However, through a deeper understanding of design principles we know that levels of interior illumination may not be a result of lighting per se. More likely, they are a result of the high reflectivity commonly associated with white and other light colors. Also, natural lighting has many beneficial qualities that we do not want sacrificed too quickly. Before reducing the lighting levels, the priorities should be remediation of elements that enhance luminosity such as color and reflections.

Given Bula's visual deficit and her interior environment the first priority for environmental modification should be the introduction of highly saturated and contrasting colors, particularly between the wall and floor abutment. One area in Bula's environment where color and color contrast should be addressed as soon as possible is the shower stall. High-gloss reflective white ceramic tile walls coupled with a matching built-in bench, also composed of white ceramic tile, and a 4″ ledge that must be traversed while entering and exiting the shower increase the potential of perceptual errors thus risking an accident. Ideally the shower stall should be reconstructed with rough-cut stone and designed with a slight slope to the floor, thereby eliminating the need for a ledge. The bench seat should be redesigned so that the seating area uses a rough-finish material that contrasts with the walls and flooring for easy visibility. Finally, the stall should be fitted with appropriately placed and anchored grab bars.

The second priority should be the reduction of reflective surfaces. This would include using matt-finish paint on the living/dining/kitchen area walls, or using non-reflective wallpaper. This priority should also entail etching all of the clear glass tabletops so that they appear frosted as well as changing the glass in all of the framed artwork to non-glare glass. The mirrored closet doors in the bedroom should be replaced with opaque doors, preferably made from wood. Kitchen and bathroom hardware should be changed from polished to brushed stainless steel, and the bathroom floors and counter tops that have polished ceramic tile should be replaced with rough-cut stone.

The third prioritization should be the reduction of illumination and the balancing of light. One method could be the use of interior window treatments to block out excess light during the brightest times of the day. Other methods might be the use of exterior awnings or a similar shading device to limit levels of direct lighting, the use of window tinting to reflect direct sunlight, or, as a last option, interior window films that diminish the quantity of natural light entering the environment.

Levels of color contrast, reflections, and lighting are all elements that can exacerbate vertigo, but vertigo itself can present irrespective of these elements – albeit, with less frequency and severity. This means that non-reflective grab bars should be strategically placed and incorporated into the overall design scheme for enhanced safety. Also, recessed lighting with compact fluorescent light bulbs that emit a white light should be installed throughout the environment to help even out lighting levels, as well as incorporating task lighting for areas requiring greater visual acuity. Other accommodations should be made, such as the provision of a grooming table located in either the bathroom or bedroom, the use of lighting and electrical face plates that contrast with the wall, and comforter, pillows, and seat cushion covers that are composed of more saturated colors.

Discussion

This environmental analysis was performed on an environment for an elderly woman whom we called Bula. Bula suffers from unilateral mydriasis and experienced a fall within her environment that required hospitalization. Bula's condition, combined with her fall, facilitated the belief that she has limited personal control within her environment. This caused her to alter her behaviors because she feared for her safety. Bula's family recognized the importance of providing care outside of an institutional environment. What they did not know was that older people respond better to autonomy-supportive environments because they are able to retain a high degree of control over their environment and their person. Lost freedoms and abilities symbolize the loss of an active role in our destinies, and behaviors begin to be modified as the person engages in learned helplessness.

What this analysis demonstrates is that whether it is an accessory dwelling for an older family member or an institution, the environment itself can enhance or impede one's sense of control and subsequent behaviors. If the environment is poorly designed the individual may not be able to function effectively within it – thus diminishing his or her sense of control. Once a person no longer believes that he or she has control, learned helplessness will set in and lead to an alteration of behaviors. In Bula's case, she stopped reading because she was experiencing eyestrain, she sat more often because she was afraid of falling, and she wore sunglasses inside of the home. These behavioral changes arose from environmental factors related to high levels of illumination, low levels of contrast, and high levels of reflectivity within the environment.

The family was given a priority list of design initiatives. This list was based on the joint nature of Bula's condition combined with the environmental design. The first priority was to introduce saturated colors as a means of diffusing light intensity. Priority two was the elimination of reflections to reduce the rebounding of light and false images that can induce confusion. Lighting levels, which may seem like the obvious first priority, was listed third because lighting, natural in particular, has many beneficial qualities. However, given the choice between lack of real or perceived control and subsequent learned behaviors in response to lighting levels, perceived control and subsequent behavioral responses must be placed first.

Key Terms

In order to promote a clear understanding of the terms used in this essay, definitions of several key terms are provided below:

Congenital   A condition that has been present since birth.

Activities of daily living (ADL)   All of the activities that person would like to do throughout the course of a day.

Americans with Disabilities Act (ADA)   A law that was enacted by the US Congress in 1990 to guarantee those with disabilities equal access to the built environment.

Autonomy-supportive environment   The ability to perform activities of daily living within an environment.

Cognitive misinterpretation   Conflict between what is present in the world and what the brain perceives as real.

Cones   Responsible for depth perception, color, and intensity of light.

Flicker vertigo   When the visual processing centers within the brain receive an imbalance in activity from two similar but different sets of visual signals.

Ganglion cells   Transmit signals of light and color to the brain for interpretation.

Halo effect   A false image appearing around a brightly illuminated object.

Lateral inhibitions   Mechanisms within the eye and brain that allow us see edges clearly.

Learned helplessness   A condition that occurs as a result of a person experiencing a negative outcome after repeated attempts.

Needs assessment   An assessment of user needs prior to a design concept.

Ocular motor deficit   Faulty component or multiple components found within the eye.

Parasitic architecture   The attachment of a new structure to an older pre-existing structure.

Physical deficit   A disability that results from a faulty organ or organ system.

Post-occupancy evaluation (POE)   An evaluation performed on an environment after the intended occupant has assumed occupancy.

Retro-reflections   A reflection of light that creates a glow.

Rods   Sensitive to light and enable us to see at night by signaling the iris to either constrict or dilate.

Specular reflections   A mirror-like reflection of light from a surface object.

Sphincter muscle   A circular muscle that constricts and dilates to control the passage of light, or solid/liquid substances.

Temporal delay   When the brain processes.

Thorndike halo effect   A cognitive bias that causes the visual perception of a current object to be influenced by the perception of a former object in a sequence of interpretations.

Unilateral mydriasis   When one iris is permanently dilated.

References

Baker, N. and Steemers, K. 2002. *Daylight Design of Buildings: A Handbook for Architects and Engineers.* London: Earthscan.

Boyce, P. R. 1981. *Human Factors in Lighting.* London: Applied Science Publishers.

Brandt, T. 1999. *Vertigo: Its Multisensory Syndromes* (2nd ed.). Basel, Switzerland: Birkhäuser Publishing.

CDC (Centers for Disease Control and Prevention), National Center for Injury Prevention and Control. 2006. *Web-Based Injury Statistics Query and Reporting System (WISQARS).* www.cdc.gov/ncipc/wisqars. Accessed June 7, 2009.

Cheong, A. M. Y., Legge, G., Lawrence, M., et al. 2007. "Relationship between slow visual processing and reading speed in people with macular degeneration," *Vision Research* 47(23): 2943–2955.

Cohen, M. 2005. "Ecological modernization and its discontents: the American environmental movement's resistance to an innovation-driven future," *Future* 38(5): 528–547.

Edwards, L., and Torcellini, P. 2002. *A Literature Review of the Effects of Natural Light on Building Occupants*. (Task No. BEC2.4002). Springfield, VA: US Department of Commerce: National Technical Information Service.

El Nasser, H. 2004, January 5. "'Granny flats' making a home in a tight market," *USA Today*. www.usatoday.com/news/nation/2004-01-05-granny-flats_x.htm. Accessed November 19, 2008.

Glasser, W. 1985. *Control Theory: A New Explanation of How We Control Our Lives*. New York: Harper & Row.

Gordon, G. 2003. *Interior Lighting for Designers, Fourth Edition*. Hoboken, NJ: John Wiley & Sons.

Hackos, J. T. and Redish, J. C. 1998. *User and Task Analysis for Interface Design*. Hoboken, NJ: John Wiley & Sons.

Hallett, M., and Cogan, D. G. 1970. "Episodic Unilateral Mydriasis in otherwise normal patients," *Achieve of Ophthalmology* 84(2): 130–136.

Hathaway, W. E., Hargreaves, J. A., Thompson, G. W., and Novitsky, D. 1992. *A Study into the Effects of Light on Children of Elementary School Age: A Case of Daylight Robbery*. Edmonton: Alberta Education, Policy and Planning Branch, Planning and Information Services Division.

Hausdorff, J. M., Rios, D. A., and Edelber, H. K. 2001. "Gait variability and fall risk in community-living older adults: a 1-year prospective study," *Archives of Physical Medicine and Rehabilitation* 82(8): 1050–1056.

Hornbrook, M. C., Stevens, V. J., Wingfield, D. J., et al. 1994. "Preventing falls among community-dwelling older persons: results from a randomized trial," *The Gerontologist* 34(1): 16–23.

Jarmusch, A. 2005, January 30. "'Granny flat' winners make additions flat-out appealing," *San Diego Union Tribune*. www.signonsandiego.com/uniontrib/20050130/news_1h30granny.html. Accessed June 7, 2009.

Kanski, J. J. 2007. *Clinical Ophthalmology: A Systematic Approach* (6th ed.). Woburn, MA: Butterworth-Heinemann.

Kawasaki, A., Anderson, S. C., and Kardon, R. H. 2008. "Pupil light reflexes mediated by outer retinal versus inner retinal photoreceptors in normal subjects and patients with neuroretinal visual loss," *Acta Ophthalmologica* 86(s243): 0. http://dx.doi.org/10.1111/j.1755-3768.2008.432.x. Accessed May 6, 2014.

Kopec, D. 2006. *Americans with Disabilities Act and the Elderly Population*. Washington DC: ASID Monograph Series.

Kopec, D. 2007. *Designs that Protect: Incorporating Culturally Diverse Perspectives in Long-Term Care Facilities*. Washington DC: NCIDQ Monograph Series.

Kopec, D. 2008. *Health, Sustainability, and the Built Environment*. New York: Fairchild Books.

Miller, M. March 24, 1994 "Granny flats keep families close," *Boston Globe*, p. A-1.

Moore, R. and Harris, B. 2006, October 26. *Esperanza Fire: Factual Report: Accident Investigation*. Riverside County, CA: Esperanza Investigation Team.

Nabet, B. and Pinter, R. B. 1991. *Sensory Neural Networks Lateral Inhibition*. Danvers, MA: CRC Press.

National Eye Institute. 2010. *Report of the Visual Impairment and Its Rehabilitation Panel.* www.nei.nih.gov/resources/strategicplans/neiplan/frm_impairment.asp. Accessed July 27, 2010.

Rash, C. 2004. "Awareness of causes and symptoms of flicker vertigo can limit ill effects," *Human Factors and Aviation Medicine* 51(2): 1–6.

Ritschel, T., Ihrke, M., Frisvad, J. R., et al. 2009. "Temporal glare: realtime dynamic simulation of the scattering in the human eye," *Eurographics* 28(2): 1–10.

Schwartz, S. 2004. *Visual Perception: A Clinical Orientation* (3rd ed.). New York: McGraw-Hill Medical.

Shepherd, G. M. 1994. *Neurobiology* (3rd ed.). Carey, NC: Oxford University Press.

Stellman, J. M., ed. 1998. *Encyclopaedia of Occupational Health and Safety.* Geneva: International Labour Organization.

Tilley, A. and Henry Dreyfuss Associates. 2002. *The Measure of Man and Woman: Human Factors in Design.* Hoboken, NJ: Wiley.

Toy, E. C., Simpson, E., Pleitez, M., Rosenfield, D., and Tintner, R. 2008. *Case Files: Neurology.* New York: McGraw-Hill Medical.

US Census Bureau. Population Division. 2008, August 8. *Projections of the Population by Selected Age Groups and Sex for the United States: 2010 to 2050* (NP2008-T2). http://www.google.com/url?sa=t&rct=j&q=&esrc=s&source=web&cd=3&ved=0CDcQFjAC&url=http%3A%2F%2Fwww.census.gov%2Fpopulation%2Fprojections%2Ffiles%2Fsummary%2Fnp2008-t2.xls&ei=ztp7U-7VBJSKqAbgo4GIBw&usg=AFQjCNEupVpb-T4PQQvvqER4S8ZmiXTRww&bvm=bv.67229260,d.b2k. Accessed May 20, 2014.

Van Kesteren, I. E. H., Stappers, P. J., and de Bruijn, J. C. M. 2007. "Materials in products selection: tools for including user-interaction in materials selection." *International Journal of Design* 1: 3, www.ijdesign.org/ojs/index.php/IJDesign/article/view/129/78. Accessed December 13, 2008.

Wazen, J. J. and Mitchell, D. R. 2004. *Dizzy.* New York: Simon & Schuster.

Wedner, D. 2008, November 15. "'Granny flats' let aging relatives live close – but not too close," *Los Angeles Times.* www.latimes.com/news/local/valley/la-hm-granny15-2008nov15,0,6802085.story. Accessed June 7, 2009.

Wright, L. June 2, 2005. "Report of findings: the growing shortage of in-home caregivers," *2005 White House Conference of Aging; Schmieding/ ILC Solutions Forum on Elder Caregiving & Schmieding Conference on Elder Homecare.* http://webarchive.library.unt.edu/eot2008/20090106200842/http:/www.whcoa.gov/. Accessed May 20, 2014.

20

Interior People Places: The Impact of the Built Environment on the Third Place Experience

Dana Vaux

Introduction

This study provides through example an application of research methods to interior design topics. The purpose of this study is to establish a better understanding of how students and faculty on college campuses utilize public interior plazas for social gathering, and to identify the design attributes and properties of those spaces most widely used. The author viewed these third places in the context of sense of community and place attachment theories to determine the impact of the built environment on present-day socializing trends and preferences. As a non-participant observer, the author conducted two series of observations on two sites of a state university campus, one urban and one rural, over a five-month period. The study was qualitative in nature and included non-participant observation and behavioral mapping techniques. The objective of this study was to further the understanding of design attributes that were most common, deriving design guidelines for other such spaces.

Overview

Among public interior plazas on college campuses with high levels of public use, the physical environment affects behavior (Jarrett 2006). More than the physical structures that fill locations, the built environment is also a setting where emotional ties bind and build community relationships. The theoretical framework established

The Handbook of Interior Design, First Edition. Edited by Jo Ann Asher Thompson and Nancy H. Blossom.

by McMillan and Chavis defines sense of community as a process that provides opportunity for membership, power to influence, an environment of reciprocity, and "shared emotional ties and support" (McMillan and Chavis 1986).

As designers, we have the capacity to create built environments that support community. However, all too often the built environment instead becomes a barrier to community. In their 1986 study, Chavis and Newbrough ask if community psychologists – psychologists whose focus of study and practice is the dynamics of interactions between people within the context of community – can afford to overlook the potential of "intentional development of community" as a primary contributor to human health and well-being (Chavis and Newbrough 1986). As designers, we may need to be asking ourselves a similar question: Can designers afford to overlook intentional design of environments that support community?

Along with a sense of community, stronger relationships result in places where people establish attachment. Place attachment is the emotional connection of a person to a specific physical environment as the result of personal experience (Low and Altman 1992). Research suggests that people–place bonding is interconnected (Riley 1992) and that place attachment enhances the cultural identity of people and groups (Low 1992).

While the importance of place attachment and sense of community appear clearly significant to human well-being, the loss of the ability for people to connect on a community level continues to be a concern of social scientists. Many social researchers contend that the "disappearance" of public life and resulting loss of community is a consequence of the privatization of American society (Chidster 1988; Jacobs 1961; Putnam 2000). Sociologists Oldenburg and Brissett claim that loss of community is in actuality a loss of opportunity for "social relationships and experiences with a diversity of human beings." They maintain that third places provide the opportunities for community experiences that have been lost in present-day society (Oldenburg and Brissett 1982).

Third places, defined as "the utilization and personalization of places outside the workplace and home" (Oldenburg and Brissett 1982), provide opportunities for social relationships and experiences in settings other than those two primary environments. Oldenburg describes them as contemporary counterparts to the informal social gathering places of the past. They are environments accessible to home and work, yet separate from them.

Third places as described by Oldenburg are models based on typologies that industrialized cultures have relied upon for centuries: English pubs, Viennese coffee houses, French cafés, and Main Street, USA. Oldenburg looks to successful social spaces in past generations, arguing that creating similar contemporary environments provides a viable present-day solution to loss of social connection. More likely, with American society moving beyond a post-industrial era to global economies, a new paradigm needs to be addressed. As modern life has become more privatized and socialization takes place more within the private and micro-environments of society, a need arises to look more closely at design factors that contribute to or detract from the existing social environment. For designers, these factors raise questions and opportunities for design research and practice.

Research studies relate design factors to human health (Evans and McCoy 1998), work environments (Kupritz 1998), educational environments (Abu-Ghazzah 1999), and housing for the elderly (Zaff and Devlin 1998). The fields of urban planning and landscape architecture offer extensive research on connections between the physical environment and community (Handy, Sallis, Weber, Maibach, and Hollander 2008; Jacobs 1961; Katz 1994; Lund 2002; Marcus and Francis 1998), yet a literature search reveals little available information that focuses on interior spaces. This gap in the literature offers tremendous research opportunities. For example, designers need information about where people are socializing, where they find settings to form informal relationships, and what attributes and properties make these environments social settings.

The study presented in this essay was conducted to further the understanding of design attributes that are common among public interior plazas on college campuses with high levels of public use. Nearly every college campus building has interior public spaces with casual seating, in essence public interior plazas. A "public interior plaza" is defined as those spaces within the interior of public buildings intended to provide opportunities for gathering, socializing, and respite – an interior counterpart to exterior plazas. While not "away from work and home" as Oldenburg would describe third places, they are away from the classroom, library, and home.

Some of these spaces are always full of people with lively activity. Others remain vacant. Why? What design attributes and properties are common among the well-used interior plazas? Are those same attributes and properties missing in the less used interior plazas? Can a design language be developed that will aid designers in creating third-place spaces where people want to be? The design intent of the study was to determine design criteria for a social gathering space on a college campus that might serve as a third place and to provide design guidelines for other such spaces. The objective of the study was to determine if there are common design attributes among public interior plazas on college campuses. The results of the study revealed that several design attributes do exist in common among social gathering places on college campuses.

Literature Review

This study viewed third places in the context of sense of community and place-attachment theories in order to consider the impact of the built environment on present-day socializing trends and preferences. Researchers exploring sense of community study the relationship between people in the context of community, while those studying place attachment consider the relationship between people and place in community settings. Both are important components of third places because these social gathering places are environments that rely on people-to-people interaction as well as people-to-place association. Availability of research on sense of community and place attachment is extensive, while literature on interior social gathering places and third places is limited.

Sense of community

As social scientists became concerned about loss of community in America, community psychologists began to examine ways to measure the degree to which a person feels a sense of connection to their community, or a "sense of community". McMillan and Chavis developed a theory and definition, providing four descriptors to measure sense of community: membership (sense of belonging), influence (empowerment within the community), reciprocity (fulfillment of needs), and collective experiences (McMillan and Chavis 1986).

These four categories of definition were later reinterpreted by McMillan as spirit, trust, trade, and art (McMillan 1996). Each of these attributes, as measured by the Sense of Community Index (SCI) developed by Chavis, Hogge, McMillan, and Wandersman, combines to create a shared sense of community in a setting (Chavis et al. 1986). Together they enable individuals to form a "system of friendship, kinship & associational networks," defined by Kasard and Janowitz as community (Kasard and Janowitz 1974).

Three themes emerge in reviewing the literature on sense of community: psychological environments, social environments, and physical environments. Some overlap occurs, but a gap exists in connections between all three (Waxman 2006). If, as Oldenburg contends, third places are a means to promote community, then sense of community is an important aspect to consider (see Figure 20.1).

In addition to dozens of seminal research projects that explore, establish, and define "sense of community theory," other studies speak to psychological aspects and include research, indicating that sense of community is a pathway to wellness

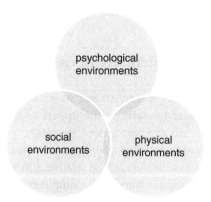

Figure 20.1

(Herrero and Gracia 2007), creates a sense of mutual aid (Unger and Wandersman 1985), emotional safety (McMillan and Chavis 1986), and an increase in confidence levels among parents of small children (Martinez, Black, and Starr 2002). Those addressing the social environment suggest that sense of community contributes to social and political participation (Chavis and Wandersman 1990), neighborhood satisfaction (Martinez et al. 2002), and residents' commitment to sustainable practices (Valeria and Guardia 2002). Additionally, findings are positively associated between sense of community and community interventions to generate opportunities for social life, which consequently promote social integration (Gracia and Herrero 2004). Clearly, the research supports the conclusion that a strong sense of community enhances personal and social well-being.

Research also supports the hypothesis that the design of the built environment can assist individuals within communities in developing a sense of community. While most studies identify variables that contribute to the psychological or social aspects of sense of community without consideration of the contextual setting, researchers suggest that sense of community is largely "setting-specific" (Hill 1996). In fact, Hill proposes that because sense of community includes variables beyond individual relationships and behavior, the most effective studies will combine research of sense of community with research of a particular setting. Puddifoot's findings that sense of community relates not only to the individual but to the shared aspects of community as well, supports Hill's suggested approach (Puddifoot 2003). Additional studies on public spaces in rural environments (Salamon 2003) and garden-style apartments in housing for the elderly (Zaff and Devlin 1998) confirm this combined research approach. Research suggests a strong sense of community enhances social and personal well-being, as well as a relationship between physical design of the built environment and sense of community. Addressing the two issues in the context of one another is important when considering design of social spaces.

Place attachment

Place attachment is the emotional connection of a person to a specific physical environment as the result of personal experience (Low and Altman 1992). Place is different from space in that it refers to a specific context rather than a general environment. Research reveals that it contributes to well-being and life satisfaction (Gustafson 2001) and differs according to individual experience (Ryan 2005).

Studies of place attachment in the context of the built environment suggest place attachment affects behavior and that the built environment affects place attachment. Recent research positively correlated place attachment to concern and care of the local environment (Vorkinn and Hanne 2001), demonstrated connections between physical factors of the built environment and place attachment (Sugihara and Evans 2000), and revealed a relationship between transit-oriented developments and higher levels of neighborhood satisfaction and place attachment among

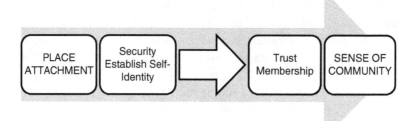

Figure 20.2

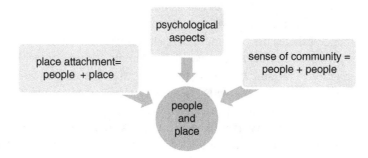

Figure 20.3

riders (Brown and Werner 2009). With these connections, it is important to understand the role place attachment plays in integrating the individual into community life. Place attachment is integral to community and self-identity, providing individuals with stability and security (Brown and Perkins 1992). A review of McMillan and Chavis' descriptors for sense of community reveals a connection between place attachment and sense of community. (McMillan and Chavis 1986). The security provided by place attachment contributes to an individual's ability to trust or mutually influence, and to trade or experience a reciprocal integration and fulfillment of needs. The ability to establish self-identity within community aids in membership and sharing of experiences, a key component of sense of community (see Figure 20.2).

Place attachment is similar to sense of community. Both theories deal with psychological aspects relating to people and place, yet place attachment refers to the relationship "between" people and place while sense of community deals with the relationship between people in the context of place (see Figure 20.3).

Because third places rely on people-to-people interaction as well as people-to-place association, both sense of community and place attachment are important components of third places (see Figure 20.4).

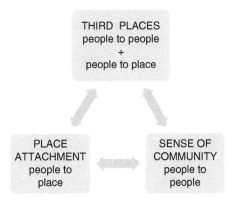

Figure 20.4

Third places

Oldenburg and Brissett argue that it is not the loss of community in American society as much as the conditions of social life resulting in a lack of availability of social experiences that adversely affect socialization (Oldenburg and Brissett 1982). They offer the "third place" as a solution. Third places, by definition, possess the following qualities: diversity and novelty, spontaneous "free-wheeling" social experiences, an encouragement of emotional expressiveness, and "color," defined as "the familiar and personal backdrop against which new experience is made meaningful."

Central to the definition is the idea that the major activity of a third place is conversation, and that the main reason for frequenting it is socializing, particularly within the context of a localized setting. Additionally, third places are described as a public gathering place, an informal venue, away from home and work, that accommodates the infrastructure capable of facilitating social attachments. To Oldenburg, a lack of purpose, other than establishing and supporting friendships, is also a requirement, and no formal membership requirements exist (Oldenburg 1989). The third place is "the antithesis of a group therapy session," yet offers the same opportunities for "sharing of problems or elations." Individuals meet spontaneously, without requirements of membership or performance. The benefits attributed to third places include a social support network developed through friendships, essentially a place of sociability.

In a study on third-place coffee shops, Waxman found positive correlation between the length of coffee-shop patronage and sense of community (Waxman 2006). Results also suggested that physical factors influence place attachment in coffee shops. Patrons attributed trust, support, sense of ownership, and personal growth to a positive social environment, while properties such as cleanliness, adequate lighting, views, aroma, and comfortable furniture contributed to attachment.

However, contrary to Oldenburg's definition of a third place, Waxman found that many patrons were content to sit alone, not needing to participate in conversation to feel connection to the social atmosphere.

Recent studies look at new types of venues for third places, including those relating virtual space to third places (Ducheneaut and Moore 2007; Hampton and Gupta 2008; Soukup 2006). Researchers also studied grower-only markets (Tiemann 2008) restorative environments chosen by urban elementary teachers (Gulwadi 2006) and libraries as third places (Harris 2007; Lawson 2004), discussing ways they contribute to social capital and sense of community. Glover and Parry studied a non-institutional setting designed for people with cancer, Gilda's Club of Toronto, in relationship to its function as a third place (Glover and Parry 2009).

While aspects of these environments contradict Oldenburg's definition, the researchers regard them as legitimate third places because of the ways the social environment reflects third-place characteristics. For example, Gilda's Club is not a place away from home and work, but rather a place away from home and hospital and is somewhat exclusive, not a public gathering place. The obvious hindrance of considering cyberspace in the realm of third places is that it is not a "place" with physical properties. Nevertheless, these venues serve as informal gathering places, encourage friendship, focus on sociability, and allow people to "check their troubles at the door" or "confront common problems" with a community of support (Oldenburg 2003).

While each of these environments is beyond the boundaries of Oldenburg's paradigm for third places, the literature supports the conclusion that these settings may act as present-day third places. As a new generation creates "virtual communities and home [pages] in cyberspace" (Lawson 2004) the concept of expanding the definition of third places is one that deserves significant attention.

Several seminal works on the relationship of the design of the built environment to human behavior are informative to our understanding of social gathering spaces. Alexander et al. published a collection of design patterns based on their observations of human interaction with the designed environment (Alexander et al. 1977). Designers across disciplines consider these patterns as recommendations for creating optimal spaces for human use. Sociologist William H. Whyte studied urban plazas in New York City in order to understand user preferences (Whyte 1980). Through observations, he discovered that the plazas most widely used had similar design characteristics. The results are largely transferable to interior public plazas. Marcus and Francis (1998) furthered Whyte's research on plazas by outlining design guidelines for urban outdoor spaces (Marcus and Francis 1998). However, an extensive literature search revealed only two studies that related physical factors of the built environment to third places, with only one of these suggesting connections to place and community theory in interior environments.

Although the literature suggests third places are positive for reinforcing a sense of community, clearly several gaps exist in the literature. While we know that sense of community is multidimensional, with numerous personal, interpersonal, and situational variables (Herrero and Gracia 2007; Tartaglia 2006) we do not know how those factors integrate in public gathering spaces. In addition, research has not shown that third places enhance sense of community or that place attachment is necessary to connect the two; findings only suggest it. Considering the potential of the interaction between place and community theory and the design of the built environment, the need for further studies relating the three is apparent.

Research Overview

Several exploratory research studies were conducted on two different campuses at the same university, one rural campus and one urban campus. The objective was to determine if common design attributes existed among public interior plazas on two college campuses. In the first study, non-participant observation, behavior mapping, and visual documentation techniques were used to document the total number of people entering two locations over a one-hour period, the activities they engaged in, how long they stayed, and how they interacted with the designed environment. A floor-plan diagram of each setting that included permanent and semi-permanent design features was created to document the observations.

A second observational study of three interior gathering places was completed in one-hour segments over a three-month period at the urban campus. The one-hour segments of activity were recorded on behavioral maps. In addition, the number of people using the space and their locations within the space were recorded in 10-minute increments. Diagrams noted the furniture layout, window placement in relationship to seating, seating arrangement, lighting, entrances, and amenities of the space. The results of the studies revealed that several design attributes did exist in common among social gathering places on the two college campuses.

Non-participant observation was selected as the primary research tool for all the studies. This allowed for observations to occur of the behavior of individuals in the natural setting (public gathering spaces) without risk of the subjects altering their behaviors. Further, non-participant observation allowed for the identification and recording of individuals' routine paths, actions, interactions, and responses to the built environment without interference.

The Studies

Study 1

The first study was conducted in four different venues on a rural university campus. Two of the venues were centrally located on campus and two were within a short walking distance of the campus. The two on-campus locations were interior plazas of buildings frequented by students. One was an open area designated by a coffee bar, tables, and chairs. The other was in a central location easily accessed from several entrances with food nearby. The two off-campus locations were coffee shops –

one an international chain and one locally owned. All four sites had internet access, although only one – the locally owned coffee shop – offered access free to all patrons. The role of technology as a place of sociability was also examined in this study through connections with Facebook.

Results of Study 1

Table 20.1 provides an overview of the results of Study 1. The results of the study suggest that some of Oldenburg's criteria may not fit present-day socializing trends, in particular those of campus social spaces. Oldenburg believed that true third places did not have technology of any kind available because it detracted from the social environment. However, the results of this study suggest that technology plays an important role in 21st-century socializing, and therefore access to technology may be an important criterion of contemporary third places. (See Table 20.1 for comparison results.)

Table 20.1   Results of Study 1

Criteria	Campus 1	Campus 2	Coffee Shop 1	Coffee Shop 2	Facebook
Neutral (not class-dependent)	X	X		X	X
Leveler (inclusive, public)			X	X	X
Conversation main activity					X
Accessibility/ accommodation (no responsibilities- can go alone)	X	X	X	X	X
Regulars (patrons who visit often)	X		X	X	X
Low-profile (not "designed")				X	X
Playful mood (conversation not heavy)	X	X	X	X	X
Home away from home (people notice if you don't show)			X	X	X

Study 2

The second study was completed on the urban campus and focused on three interior plazas. Over a three-month period, behavioral maps were used to record the number of people and the activities taking place in each of the interior gathering places during one-hour increments. Diagrams noted the furniture style and layout, window placement in relationship to seating, seating arrangement, electric lighting design, availability of natural light, entrances, and amenities the space provided. Two of the spaces are located in a building dedicated to the study of design and night courses. The third space is in a separate building used primarily by health sciences students and faculty. The campus is wireless throughout, so computer use is available to students in all three.

Interior Plaza 1. In this plaza the seating arrangement, style, and lack of variety make it difficult to be "alone in a crowd" or to gather as a group. Additionally, the poor lighting, both electric and natural, minimizes the ability to accomplish student-related tasks such as reading and computer use – an important part of campus life. While food is available nearby, it is not visible from the seating area and the facility is only open for a few hours in the early evening. Food was therefore not considered to attract users, and was determined as one of the unsuccessful characteristics (see Figure 20.5).

Interior Plaza 2. While Plaza 2 is centrally located and the furniture is moveable, the lighting is poor and the furniture uninviting causing the space to be rarely used as a social gathering space. Also, with no food available other than from vending machines, there is nothing to encourage students to gather and stay in the space (see Figure 20.5). This examination implies that students will use spaces that are less than optimal when there are no others available, but choose differently when they can.

Figure 20.5 Plazas 1 and 2.

Figure 20.6   Plaza 3.

Interior Plaza 3. Despite the fact that food was not available in close proximity to this space, it appeared to be widely used by students. The comfortable, moveable seating that can be rearranged by students to optimize their socializing needs, as well as the ample natural and artificial lighting, contribute to the attraction of this interior plaza as a social space (see Figure 20.6).

Results of Study 2

Seven design criteria for successful social gathering spaces were developed from the literature review and compared to the results of this study. The data derived from the observations were first analyzed within the context of each setting to determine which physical attributes were present or not. The successful features are noted in Table 20.2 with a "yes" and the unsuccessful features are noted with a "no".

Table 20.2   Results of Study 2

SITE	Location	Path	Entrance	Food	Seating	Lighting	Technology
Plaza 1	Yes	No	No	No	No	No	Yes
Plaza 2	Yes	No	No	No	No	No	Yes
Plaza 3	Yes	Yes	Yes	No	Yes	Yes	Yes

These seven design features were then compared to the criteria established in four seminal publications dealing with the design of public social spaces: William Whyte's *The Social Life of Small Urban Spaces* (1980), Marcus and Francis' *People Places: Design Guidelines for Urban Open Spaces* (1990), Christopher Alexander's *A*

Pattern Language (1977), and Oldenburg's (1989) third place theory as described in *The Great Good Place*. The results of this comparison can be seen in Table 20.3.

Table 20.3 Results of Study 2 comparison

Criteria	Observation outcomes	Whyte (1977)	Marcus (1990)	Alexander (1977)	Oldenburg (1989)
Location	**Yes** Central to activity of building or campus	**Yes** Places w/ People	**Yes** Attracts variety of people	**Yes** Center-heart of building(s)	**Yes** Away from home and work
Path	**Yes** Space is on people's path	**Yes** People need to see it to use it	**Yes** Circulation meshes w/ current patterns	**Yes** "On the way"	**Yes** Between home and work
Entrance	**Yes** Able to "see in" before entering	**Yes** Smooth transition between path and entrance	**Yes** A distinct yet separate space	**Yes** More than one and tangent to path	
Seating	**Yes** Varied (tables and chairs; comfy chairs)	**Yes** Moveable chairs	**Yes** Many kinds	**Yes** Varied and comfortable	**Yes**
Food	**Yes**	**Yes**	**Yes**	**Yes**	**Yes** Beverages
Lighting	**Yes** Adequate for multiple purposes, appropriate for scale of the room, and natural	**Yes** Sun/ southern exposure	**Yes** Maximize sun year-round	**Yes** Light on two sides of room; south-facing	

Interestingly, the criteria that emerged from the observations as important to the success of a public space for social gathering coincide with the design guidelines outlined in the four publications. For example, although the language is slightly different – Whyte says southern sun exposure is important and Marcus and Francis recommend maximizing sun year-round – the observational studies confirmed that these general design principles are transferable to widely used public interior plazas. A final analysis was made comparing the design features established in the literature and the results of this study to Oldenburg's social criteria for third places. The results of this analysis are seen in Table 20.4.

Table 20.4 Results of final analysis

Oldenburg's criteria	Observations	Whyte	C.M & Francis	Alexander
Neutral not class-dependent	**Yes**	**Yes**	**Yes**	
Leveler Inclusive, public	**No** patrons are university students and faculty	**Yes** although "the unwanted" are often not welcome	**Yes**	
Conversation main activity	**No** varied activities in groups and alone	**No** Many reasons for a person to be there	**No** space is divided to support varied activities	**No** multiple activities, patrons often go alone to people-watch
Accessibility/ accommodation No responsibilities, could go alone	**Yes**	**Yes**	**Yes**	**Yes**
Regulars Patrons who visit often	**Yes**	**Yes**	**Yes**	
Low profile Not "designed"	**No**	**No**	**No**	**No**
Playful mood Conversation not heavy	**Yes**	**Yes**	**Yes**	**Yes**
Home away from home People notice not there	**Yes**	**Yes**	**Yes**	

Although some of Oldenburg's criteria are still relevant, this analysis reinforces the suggestion that present-day socializing trends represent a different paradigm for third places. In keeping with Oldenburg's criteria, an environment with a playful mood that is a "home away from home" and accessible with regulars remains is an important aspect of a third place. However, 21st-century third places appear to be multi-purpose with many activities, including technology. Evidence also reveals that current third places are often purpose-driven, intentionally designed spaces, which are not necessarily public. Additionally, today's third places appear to be seen as appropriate for both socializing as well as being alone in a crowd.

Emergence of design criteria

Seven design criteria emerged from the studies conducted for evaluating social gathering spaces: location, entrance, path, seating, food, and lighting. The following list provides relevant questions and considerations for application of these criteria:

- *Location*. Is the space centrally located and casually encountered daily by many potential users? The location of an interior plaza is of primary importance. It must be central to activities and accessible to all (Alexander et al. 1977; Oldenburg 1989).
- *Path*. Is the space "on the path" without being too open or too closed? In order for a space to attract occupants, they must first be aware it is there, and then encounter it often on their daily path. The more accessible it is without effort, the more likely people are to occupy it (Alexander et al. 1977). "Sightlines are important. If people do not see a space, they will not use it" (Whyte 1980).
- *Entrance*. Can a person assess the room and the people in it without first making a commitment to enter? The entrance of a space is a key to success or failure (Whyte 1980). Ideally, the transition from the path to the space should be indistinguishable. Marcus and Francis state, "A plaza must be perceived as a distinct place, and yet it must be visible and functionally accessible to passers-by" (Marcus and Francis 1998). This leads to the ability for a person to first assess the environment without committing to enter and then do so "without" having made a conscious decision" (Whyte 1980).
- *Seating*. Is it sociopetal or sociofugal? Comfortable and moveable? Are there varied types available? Research shows that successful plazas have seating that is comfortable, moveable, and varied in type. Marcus and Francis found that large open spaces without clear subdivisions are intimidating to most people, causing them to pass through quickly or not enter. They found that subtle subdividing of the space encouraged use (Marcus and Francis 1998).
- *Food*. Is there food available within the space or nearby? Whyte states, "If you want to seed a place with activity, put out food" (Whyte 1980). Marcus and Francis also suggest that to increase the liveliness of a plaza is to provide food (Marcus and Francis 1998).
- *Lighting*. Is there adequate and appropriate artificial light and natural daylight? Just as use increases in outdoor plazas south-facing with sun (Marcus and Francis 1998; Whyte 1977), people gravitate to rooms with natural light (Alexander et al. 1977). In addition, adequate and appropriate electric light attracts users.

- *Technology.* Is its use acknowledged and encouraged through the design? As noted in the research, technology is an important part of American social life in the 21st century. Successful third places incorporate technology, and this is especially important on a college campus.

These seven criteria, along with the results of the research studies conducted, provide guidelines for the design of a third place as a social gathering space.

As demonstrated by these studies, third places can and should be part of college campuses. Interior public plazas can provide venues for social connection, providing college students and faculty with a sense of community and place attachment. Additionally, students as well as professional designers can easily transfer the guidelines to other venues.

When designers create barriers instead of bonds in social environments, it is often because they do not design with information. If Putnam and Oldenburg are right that American communities are experiencing a loss of social capital and need new ways to provide connections among individuals, then understanding how design decisions impact those spaces can only aid the process. Understanding connections between sense of community and place attachment in the context of third places could assist designers in creating social environments that promote human well-being by providing venues for social connection.

Social scientists and community psychologists have increased awareness of the need for social capital and community in American public life. Americans need public environments where they can make informal social connections and build social networks (Putnam 2000). Studies connecting sense of community to social spaces suggest a relationship between the physical design of the built environment and sense of community, yet researchers have noted the disparity of research relating these two factors (Hill 1996; Lund 2002; Sugihara and Evans 2000; Waxman 2006).

Research on sense of community suggests a strong connection between the environment and sociability. The connection needs verification by more research within the context of specific environments (Hill 1996). Understanding how the built environment enhances people-to-people connection and consequent application in the built form begins with understanding human use and preferences, allowing those understandings to inform design, resulting in more venues for social connection. Designing environments, in particular social gathering spaces, to augment social connections is a valuable pursuit. Waxman states that "designers should consider the value the built environment holds for creating community-gathering places that enhance the ability of people to connect with their community" (Waxman 2006).

Third places, as a current and future social trend, provide a viable venue for exploring the design of social spaces. As designers, we have the capability to design spaces that promote human well-being as well as places where people want to live, work, and play – or not. The potential for designers to contribute to the enhancement of settings that support community through intentional design – interior people places – and consequently enhance people-to-people connections deserves attention.

References

Abu-Ghazzah, T. M. 1999. "Communicating behavioral research to campus design: factors affecting the perception and use of outdoor spaces at the University of Jordan," *Environment and Behavior* 31(6): 764–804.

Alexander, C. et al. 1977. *A Pattern Language: Towns, Buildings, Construction.* New York: Oxford University Press.

Brown, B. and Werner, C. M. 2009. "Before and after a new light rail stop: resident attitudes, travel behavior, and obesity," *Journal of the American Planning Association* 75(1): 5–12.

Brown, B. B. and Perkins, D. 1992. "Disruptions in place attachment," in I. Altman and S. Low (eds.), *Place Attachment.* New York: Plenum Press, pp. 279–304.

Chavis, D. M., Hogge, J. H., McMillan, D. W., and Wandersman, A. 1986. "Sense of community through Brunswick's lens," *Journal of Community Psychology* 14: 24–40.

Chavis, D. M. and Newbrough, J. R. 1986. "The meaning of 'community' in community psychology," *Journal of Community Psychology* 14(4): 335–340.

Chavis, D. M. and Wandersman, A. 1990. "Sense of community in the urban environment: a catalyst for participation and community development," *American Journal of Community Psychology* 18: 55–79.

Chidster, M. 1988. "Reconsidering the piazza: dramatic changes in city form and living require new design models and inspirations for public experience," *Landscape Architecture* 78(1): 40–43.

Ducheneaut, N. and Moore, R. J. 2007. "Virtual third places: a case study of sociability in massively multiplayer games," *Journal of Collaborative Computing* 16(1–2): 129–166.

Evans, G. W. and McCoy, J. M. 1998. "When buildings don't work: the role of architecture in human health," *Journal of Environmental Psychology* 18: 85–94.

Glover, T. D. and Parry, D. C. 2009. "A third place in the everyday lives of people living with cancer: functions of Gilda's Club of Greater Toronto," *Health & Place* 15: 97–106.

Gracia, E. and Herrero, J. 2004. "Determinants of social integration in the community: an exploratory analysis of personal, interpersonal and situational variables," *Journal of Community & Applied Social Psychology* 14(1): 1–15.

Gulwadi, G. B. 2006. "Seeking restorative experiences: elementary school teachers' choices for places that enable coping with stress," *Environment and Behavior* 38: 503–520.

Gustafson, P. 2001. "Roots and routes: exploring the relationship between place attachment and mobility," *Environment and Behavior* 33(5): 667–686.

Hampton, K. N. and Gupta, N. 2009. "Community and social interaction in the wireless city: wi-fi use in public and semi-public spaces," *New Media & Society* 10(6): 831–850.

Handy, S., Sallis, J., Weber, D., Maibach, E., and Hollander, M. 2008. "Is support for traditionally designed communities growing? Evidence from two national surveys," *Journal of the American Planning Association* 74(2): 209–221.

Harris, C. 2007. "Libraries with lattes: the new third place," *Australian Public Library Information Services* 20(4): 145–152.

Herrero, J. and Gracia, E. 2007. "Measuring perceived community support: factorial structure, longitudinal invariance and predictive validity of the PCSQ (Perceived Community Support Questionnaire)," *Journal of Community Psychology* 35(2): 197–217.

Hill, J. L. 1996. "Psychological sense of community: suggestions for future research," *Journal of Community Psychology* 24(4): 431–438.

Jacobs, J. 1961. *The Death and Life of Great American Cities*. New York: Random House.

Jarrett, C. 2006. "Is there a psychologist in the building?," *The Psychologist* 19(10): 592–594.

Kasard, J. and Janowitz, M. 1974. "Community attachment in mass society," *American Sociological Review* 39: 328–329.

Katz, P., ed. 1994. *The New Urbanism: Towards Architecture of Community*. New York: McGraw-Hill.

Kupritz, V. W. 1998. "Privacy in the workplace: the impact of building design," *Journal of Environmental Psychology* 18: 341–356.

Lawson, K. 2004. "Libraries as virtual third places," *New Library World* 105(3/4), 125–130.

Low, S. 1992. "Symbolic ties that bind: place attachment in the plaza," in I. Altman and S. Low (eds.), *Place Attachment*. New York: Plenum Press, pp. 165–184.

Low, S. and Altman, I. 1992. "Place attachment: a conceptual inquiry," in I. Altman and S. Low (eds.), *Place Attachment*. New York: Plenum Press, pp. 1–12.

Lund, H. 2002. "Pedestrian environments and sense of community," *Journal of Planning Education and Research* 21(3): 301–312.

Marcus, C. C. and Francis, C. 1998. *People Places: Design Guidelines for Urban Open Spaces*. New York: John Wiley & Sons.

Martinez, M. L., Black, M., and Starr, R. H. 2002. "Factorial structure of the Perceived Neighborhood Scale (PNS): a test of longitudinal invariance," *Journal of Community Psychology* 30(1): 23–43.

McMillan, D. 1996. "Sense of community," *Journal of Community Psychology* 24(4): 315–325.

McMillan, D. and Chavis, D. M. 1986. "Sense of community: a definition and theory," *Journal of Community Psychology* 14: 6–23.

Oldenburg, R. 1989. *The Great Good Place: Cafes, Coffee Shops, Bookstores, Bars, Hair Salons and Other Hangouts at the Heart of the Community*. New York: Marlowe.

Oldenburg, R. 2003. "Third places," in K. Christenson and D. Levinson (eds.), *Encyclopedia of Community*. Thousand Oaks, CA: Sage Publications, pp. 1373–1376.

Oldenburg, R. and Brissett, D. 1982. "The Third Place," *Qualitative Psychology* 5(4): 265–284.

Puddifoot, J. E. 2003. "Exploring 'personal' and 'shared' sense of community identity in Durham City, England," *Journal of Community Psychology* 31(1): 87–106.

Putnam, R. D. 2000. *Bowling Alone: The Collapse and Revival of American Community*. New York: Simon & Schuster.

Riley, R. B. 1992. "Attachment to the ordinary landscape," in I. Altman and S. Low (eds.), *Place Attachment*. New York: Plenum Press, pp. 13–32.

Ryan, R. L. 2005. "Exploring the effects of environmental experience on attachment to urban natural areas," *Environment and Behavior* 37(1): 3–42.

Salamon, S. 2003. "From hometown to nontown: rural community effects of suburbanization," *Rural Sociology* 68(1): 1–24.

Soukup, C. 2006. "Computer-mediated communication as a virtual third place: building Oldenburg's great good places on the world wide web," *New Media & Society* 8(3): 421–440.

Sugihara, S. and Evans, G. 2000. Place attachment and social support at continuing care retirement communities. *Environment and Behavior* 32(3): 400–409.

Tartaglia, S. 2006. "A preliminary study for a new model of sense of community," *Journal of Community Psychology* 34(1): 25–36.

Tiemann, T. K. 2008. "Grower's only farmer's markets: public spaces and third places," *The Journal of Popular Culture* 41(3): 467–487.

Unger, D. G. and Wandersman, A. 1985. "The importance of neighbors: the social, cognitive, and affective components of neighboring," *American Journal of Community Psychology* 13: 139–169.

Valera, S. and Guardia, J. 2002. "Urban social identity and sustainability: Barcelona's Olympic Village," *Environment and Behavior* 34(1): 54–66.

Vorkinn, M. and Hanne, R. 2001. "Environmental concern in a local context: the significance of place attachment," *Environment and Behavior* 33: 249–263.

Waxman, L. 2006. "The coffee shop: social and physical factors influencing place attachment," *Journal of Interior Design* 31(3): 35–53.

Whyte, W. H. 1980. *The Social Life of Small Urban Spaces*. Washington DC: Conservation Foundation.

Zaff, J. and Devlin, A. S. 1998. "Sense of community in housing for the elderly," *Journal of Community Psychology* 26(4): 381–398.

21

Places in the Virtual and Physical Continuum: Examining the Impact of Virtual Behaviors on Place Attributes of Wireless Coffee Shops

Newton D'Souza and Yu Fong Lin

Introduction

Places are characterized by physical features (i.e., furniture, window placement, etc.) and by the corresponding behaviors of people who occupy them (i.e., eating, sitting, walking). In the digital world, places are also characterized by the virtual behaviors and activities of people (i.e., internet browsing, checking emails, etc.). Although virtual behaviors usually occur in computer-mediated formats, these behaviors are no different than conventional forms of behavior where people interact with each other, exchange ideas, share information, conduct business, or engage in discussion.

This means that in today's world of telecommunication and technological advances virtual behaviors can – and do – occur any place where wireless connections are available. It can be assumed, then, that the classical "place attributes" of sociality, control, community, and privacy apply to both physical and virtual places (Axtell, Hislop, and Whittaker 2008; Oblinger and Oblinger 2005; Wilson and Peterson 2002).

Virtuality and Physicality

Any discussion regarding virtual behaviors must first address the ongoing debate in the literature regarding the concepts of "virtuality"[1] and "physicality." Although the literature contains many research studies that explore the physical attributes of places,[2] research studies that examine the virtual attributes of places are far less frequent (Canter 1997; Cresswell 2004; Weisman 2001).

The Handbook of Interior Design, First Edition. Edited by Jo Ann Asher Thompson and Nancy H. Blossom.
© 2015 John Wiley & Sons, Ltd. Published 2015 by John Wiley & Sons, Ltd.

Virtuality is an umbrella term that refers to the nature of human interaction with virtual tools and is defined as "the cultural perception that material objects are interpenetrated by information patterns" (Hayles 1999). According to Hayles, virtuality is normally associated with computer simulations that put the body into a feedback loop with a computer-generated image. This definition suggests the duality of virtuality as being materiality on the one hand, and information on the other. In contrast, the term physicality usually is used to refer to the tangible physical world and the physical space that is occupied while conducting activities such as conversation, eating, and sitting.

The difference between virtuality and physicality is the focus of debate among scholars. Those who fall into the virtuality school of thought suggest that virtual reality technologies make visually immediate the perception that a world of information exists parallel to the "real" world, the former intersecting the latter at many points and in many ways (Hayles 1999).

Advocates of physicality, in contrast, usually proclaim phenomenology as the dominant school of thought. Phenomenology enthusiasts argue that the character of "place" is embodied in its physical rootedness. This way of thinking proposes that because an individual is bound by their body to a place, the physicality of the human body immediately regularizes the world in terms of here-there, near-far, up-down, above-below, and right-left. Further, they argue that physicality equates to authenticity, suggesting that any simulation of the physical world is inauthentic – often referring to such places as pseudo-places (e.g., Disneyland) or as non-places (e.g., an airport) (Relph 1976). According to this way of thinking, when people are sitting at their computer and looking at the screen they are merely "pretending" to be in a "real" place, much like people pretend to be at a "real" French café when dining in Disneyland (Turkle 1996). In extreme cases phenomenology advocates suggest that any relationship between virtuality and "sense of place" is insignificant in relation to the properties of physicality.

This debate among scholars about the dichotomy between virtuality and physicality reflects a long-standing tension in the environment and behavior literature where phenomena are often cast in outright opposition to each other; for example, form versus function, environment versus behavior, and people versus place. Various scholars have challenged such dichotomous views, suggesting that such stances are detrimental to a holistic understanding of phenomena (Altman and Rogoff 1987).

Critique of Physical Rootedness

Physicality, as a place determinant, stems from a nostalgic view of place as suggested by phenomenologist Heidegger (1962) and his followers. Moores observes that physical determinism as a criterion of place suffers from an excess of idealism, and, as such, negates the possibility of different, perhaps competing, place-making practices occurring among people who occupy the same physical location (Moores 2006; see also Massey 1995; May 1996).

In keeping with Moores' assertion, Kendall proposes that much like physical locations, virtual behaviors allow for near-instantaneous responses from physically distant others, and can provide a particularly vivid sense of place. At the same time, however, Kendall maintains that virtual determinism should not be considered the sole criterion of place. She notes that while engaged in a virtual behavior, there is still a physical environment in which the body resides and, hence, there is the potential for two experiential worlds to coexist simultaneously (Kendall 2002).

Extending the idea of virtual behaviors to urban environments, Linda Baker observes a new sense of place, terming it the "new new urbanism," a fusion of telecommunications technology and urban design (Baker 2004). Baker postulates that with the new generation of wireless devices, GPS locators, and ubiquitous networking, digital space will facilitate the communal public places where people interact with friends or strangers. She observes that the wireless services emphasize proximity over connectivity, the local over the global, and the adage of "here and now" rather than "anytime, anywhere" of the internet's former purpose.

The Virtual–Physical Continuum

This essay extends the prior arguments of virtual–physical coexistence by going beyond the simplistic dichotomy of virtuality and physicality, and framing it as a virtual–physical continuum. Consider, for instance, that person A visits a coffee shop with person B. This means that persons A and B are operating in the same physicality. If person A connects with person C through a social networking site such as Facebook, person A is operating in virtuality. Thus, person A is operating both in physicality (as he engages with person B) and virtuality (as he engages with person C). This interaction could be further intensified if person B connects virtually with another person, D. Now both A and B are floating between physicality and virtuality.

These different scenarios create different space-time geographies which can only be described through environments which are on a virtual–physical continuum. Spaces which are on the virtual–physical continuum have been referred in educational and information sciences as blended spaces which, by definition "blend" physical environments (face-to-face) with virtual environments (wireless computer technology) (Oblinger and Oblinger 2005).

Classroom environments and wireless coffee shops can be considered as existing in the central portion of this virtual–physical continuum because they consist of a nearly equivalent blending of virtual and physical places. Other environments can be at the extremes: that is, either overtly virtual such as social networking sites or overtly physical such as a neighborhood park, an assisted living facility, or any environment where online activities are kept to a minimum. While a strict demarcation between these three modes is difficult to make, suffice it to say that with the rapid advancements of digital technologies, distinctions between them are continually blurred.

Emerging Place-Types in the Virtual–Physical Continuum

While not many studies have explored place-type attributes of the virtual–physical continuum, in recent studies of the virtual behaviors of computer users, Ito, Okabe, and Anderson identified two types of behaviors – "camping" and "cocooning" (Ito et al. 2009). "Camping" consists of moving from place to place and "cocooning" consists of being stable in a place for a specific duration. A certain degree of cocooning behavior may be part of camping behavior on a temporary basis (i.e., when needing to stop in order to complete a task before moving on).

In an examination of the behaviors of wireless café users, Gupta observed them to be either mobilizers or socializers (Gupta 2004). For mobilizers, the wireless café is the background for a principal activity. Socializers, on the other hand, camp out with their laptops in the hope of connecting physically with co-present others. In addition to Gupta's study, other researchers also identify socializer behaviors as prevalent in wireless establishments (Brown and O'Hara 2003; Hislop and Axtell, 2009; Kakihara 2003).

These altered behaviors, to some extent, can be described by the differences of perception between older and younger generations regarding computer technology. For example, studies conducted in coffee shops during the 1970s by Oldenburg and Seamon suggested that "whatever interrupts conversations" lively flow is ruinous to a sense of place, citing the example of electronic gadgets as such an interruption (Oldenburg 1989). Similarly, in 1979 Seamon contended that "technology and mass culture destroy the uniqueness of places" (Seamon 1979).

In contrast, more recent studies of users who visit coffee shops have found that one of the main reasons for going to a café is to work on, or with, their electronic gadgets. According to Nimon, perhaps the most predictable development in today's generation has been in regard to their attitudes towards technology itself (Nimon 2007). To the baby-boomer generation (those born between 1946 and 1964) and Generation X (those born between 1965 and 1979), phenomena such as mobile phones and the internet represent tools that, while useful, are not essential. For the current generation, referred to as Generation Y (those born after 1980), these tools are as inseparable from their daily existence as the clothes they wear or the food they eat. Dobbins also notes that the world of Generation Y is a "24/7" world – meaning that their expectation is for immediate responses within a rapid time frame (Dobbins 2005).

Place Attributes and Their Measurement

According to Weisman, place attributes are qualities that are attributed to places in the context of our interactions with them. Although few studies have been done that examine the attributes of places that exhibit a virtual–physical continuum, related studies reveal that the ambience of the space and the services offered within, or adjacent to, the hotspot (such as print and copy services) are critically important (Forlano 2008). In another, related, study, Doyle identified behavioral and physical attributes of places in terms of patterns. These patterns include "wings of light," positive outdoor spaces, private terraces, windows overlooking life, low sills, main entrances, pedestrian density, activity pockets, and "common areas of the heart" (Doyle 2011).

A good example of a place-type that illustrates emerging place attributes is the MIT steam café. The goal of the café is to augment technology with physical space in order to bring people together to discuss and improve the continuing creation of food and space as an inspirational reflection of a community (Wilson and Peterson 2002). This wireless café includes an active website and a plasma monitor. The website allows visitors to review the daily menu, check ingredients, and submit feedback or new recipe ideas. Through the use of the plasma monitor, visitors are encouraged to participate in public discussions about the content of the Web, thereby building a sense of ownership and empowerment.

Methodology

The purpose of this research study was to identify the place attributes that are impacted by virtual behaviors. The following research questions were the foci of this inquiry:

1   In the context of wireless coffee shops, are there differences in the importance of place attributes between computer users (engaged in virtual behaviors) and non-computer users (not engaged in virtual behaviors)?
2   What are the prevalent virtual behaviors of computer users and what is the impact of their behavior on place attributes?

Research setting and subject population

The research setting for this study was a Midwestern town in the USA with a population of approximately 100,000 people. The boundaries between the downtown and campus areas have blurred over time, with several wireless coffee shops appearing over a short stretch of street close to the downtown and campus. Over the space of three years, a total of seven wireless coffee shops were designated as the "place" settings for this study. The subjects of the study were users of coffee shops along this stretch of street, most of whom spent two to three hours per day in one of the shops. Among all the users, most were university students between 20 and 29 years of age (n = 143).

The close proximity of the coffee shops, the resemblance in size of each shop, and the similarity of users provided a measure of control over the demographic and physical variables. At the same time, these factors helped to maintain a certain level of control over variations in the "place" experience of customers/users.

The sample included a total of 233 coffee shop customers/users, consisting of both computer users (n = 163) and non-computer users (n = 70), with the latter used as a control group. The unequal sample sizes are a result of a shift in the focus of the study from one of simply examining the behavior of computer users in coffee shops to a more comprehensive examination of the relationship between virtual behaviors and place attributes. In order to do this, a control group of computer users was necessary, resulting in the hypothesis that there would be significant differences in the way these two groups perceived the relative importance of place attributes.

Definition of concepts and terms

Since the intention was to examine the impact of virtual behaviors on place attributes, the dependent variables consisted of place attributes that were operationalized into behavioral and physical attributes. Thus, behavioral attributes were defined as those properties of the place that included psychological and socio-physical aspects that might impact how users experienced the "place." Physical attributes were defined as those properties of a place that included physical and tangible objects as well as interior/architectural features that might impact the users' experience of the place.

The virtual behaviors independent variables were operationalized as those activities that computer users engaged in while at the coffee shops, as compared to non-computer users. Computer users were defined as customers who came into the coffee shop with a computer device such as a lap-top and engaged in virtual behaviors. Hand-held or mobile devices were not included in the study. Virtual behaviors included such things as interaction with other people online, the exchange of ideas, information-sharing, social support, conducting business, directing actions, creating art, playing games, and engaging in political discussion, among others. These activities were accomplished through computer-mediated formats such as instant messaging, emails, and Web browsing, among others. In addition, the independent variable of "time spent in the coffee shop," measured in terms of hours per week, was included in the study to provide further insights into the place experience of people in the coffee shop.

Measures and instruments

The physical and behavior attributes of the place were measured through the use of a questionnaire. Data from the questionnaire were supplemented by information resulting from a photo-voicing technique that captured the visual characteristics of the place attributes through the eyes of each subject. In addition, data were gathered that identified the nature, order, and length of time of spent on virtual behaviors using a cognitive mapping exercise of each subject's personal learning environment (PLE).

The User Analysis questionnaire used in the study was developed by ASTM to measure workplace performance (Becker and Sims 1990).[3] This instrument identifies the behavioral attributes as degree of privacy, accessibility of location, opportunity to meet friends, density of people, noise level, and crowd character. The physical attributes are identified in the questionnaire as space size, arrangement of furniture, quality of lighting, color of room, and overall image. Because the intent of the study was to discern whether or not the nature of place attributes changed when applied in the context of a virtual–physical continuum, no attempt was made to distinguish place attributes as solely physical or solely virtual.

Photo-voicing interviews were conducted with five customers per coffee shop (a total of 40 customers), targeting subjects of diverse age, profession, and gender. To complete the photo-voicing portion of the study, subjects were provided with a camera and asked to photograph elements that they liked in a specific coffee-shop setting. The investigators accompanied each subject on the photo journey. After the photo-journey, the participants were shown pictures of the photographs they had taken and asked why they selected them in relation to their experience in the coffee shop.

In addition, further insights were provided from the cognitive mapping exercise, completed by each subject, of their personal learning environment (PLE). A PLE, as used in this study, follows the definition proposed by Graham Attwell in his paper, "The Personal Learning Environments – the future of eLearning?" (2007). According to Attwell, a PLE is:

> any social software that lets people rendezvous, connect or collaborate by use of a computer network. It supports networks of people, content and services that are more adaptable and responsive to changing needs and goals. Social Software adapts to its environment, instead of requiring its environment to adapt to software…allowing the internet to be used for creating and sharing information and knowledge, rather than merely accessing external artifacts.

Such internet or software tools are used by learners to take control of and manage their own learning and includes systems such as wiki, blogs, and Facebook (Milne 2006).

To complete the cognitive mapping exercise of their virtual behaviors, subjects were asked to draw a flow chart of the internet sites they visited, their activities while on the site, and the order and frequency of each visit.

Analysis and Findings

The objective of the study was to examine the differences between non-computer users and computer users in terms of the importance of physical and behavioral place attributes. To test the effects of virtual behaviors in the form of computer usage on place attributes a sample t test was computed. Because the place attribute scores were negatively skewed, a log transformation of the scores was conducted to transform the data of place attributes into a normal distribution. Further, because the sample size of the two groups was unequal (n = 70 for non-computer users and n = 149 for computer users), it was necessary to check for homogeneity of variances. This test revealed that the standard deviations were within the range of 0.2 and 0.3 of each other and therefore were not significant.

The results of the t test showed that the place attribute variable of "opportunity to meet friends" was significant. The t test (t (231), p = .017) revealed a significant difference in this variable between computer users (M = 0.28, SD = 0.23) and non-computer users (M = 0.20, SD = 0.23). Contrary to what might be expected as suggested by the literature, computer users placed higher importance on the opportunity to meet friends than non-computer users did. The photo-voicing exercise clarified that the opportunity to meet friends was referring to having a space available in the coffee shop that would facilitate interaction among small and large groups. The results were inconclusive as to whether the opportunity to meet friends was meant to be with those individuals who were physically present, those who were virtually present, or both. It is suggested that future study is needed to pinpoint this further.

While the opportunity to meet friends was found to be the most important place attribute, it should be noted that another place attribute found to be of high importance was the arrangement of furniture. Although not statistically significant, the results showed that computer users valued the importance of furniture arrangement (M = 0.38, SD = 0.18) more than non-computer users (M = 0.33, SD = 0.19). This view was also reflected in the photo-voicing exercises where subjects pointed out the placement, functionality, and role of furniture in accomplishing specific virtual and physical tasks. In addition, the results of the t test revealed that for the variable of "time spent" in the coffee shop, computer users spent more time in the coffee shop (M = 2.2, SD = 1.3) than non-computer users (M = 1.7, SD = 0.9).

The cognitive maps derived from the personal learning environments of computer users provided data relative to the order and frequency of virtual behaviors being conducted by computer users in the coffee shops. When all the PLEs from all computer users (n = 163) were tabulated, it revealed that the computer users engaged in a variety of virtual behaviors, resulting in nine different prevalent activities: (1) using email, (2) using social networks, (3) studying, (4) browsing, (5) online chatting, (6) listening to music, (7) watching movies, (8) shopping online, and (9) viewing pictures/photographs. The frequency of use of virtual behaviors shows that most users were engaged in emailing, followed by social networking, studying, and browsing.

Although emailing was the most dominant virtual behavior, computer users seldom did this activity in isolation from other activities. Most users undertook a cluster of virtual behaviors/activities. These clusters were identified and then categorized based on the level of formality in the nature of the behavior:

- Predominantly formal virtual behaviors (16%)
  (study, browsing, emailing)
- Predominantly a mix of formal and informal virtual behaviors (23%)
  (study, social networking, chat, browsing, emailing)
- Predominantly informal virtual behaviors (30%)
  (social networking, chatting, browsing, emailing)

The remaining activities were dispersed and could not be clustered in any meaningful way. Overall, users engaged in predominantly informal virtual behaviors as compared to a mix of formal virtual behaviors.

An examination of virtual behavior clusters and the importance of the cluster to specific place attributes was completed using a standard multiple regression analysis. (No violations of multi-colinearity were found in that the correlations of independent variables were smaller than 0.7 and tolerance >1.) When all three virtual behavior clusters were simultaneously used to predict the relative importance of the 11 place attributes, the independent importance of each one emerged in the resultant standardized beta weights.

In the regression model, formal virtual behaviors and informal virtual behaviors accounted for a significant variance in the importance of the place attribute of privacy. In other words, privacy was valued by coffee shop computer users who were predominantly engaged in the formal cluster of virtual behaviors and informal cluster of virtual behaviors, while no significance was found for mixed virtual behaviors.

It is interesting to note that the place attribute variable of "noise level" was not significant for computer users who were engaged in formal virtual behaviors such as "study." It is suggested that this may be because computer users have found ways to neutralize this place attribute through the use of earphones and other gadgets.

Informal virtual behaviors accounted for a significant variance in the importance of the place attribute of "meeting friends," and mixed virtual behaviors accounted for a significant variance in the importance of the place attributes of "size of the space" and noise levels. In these cases the beta value was negative, indicating that lower space size and higher noise levels were undesirable for informal virtual behaviors. This could be explained by the need for more flexibility and the diversity of these activities.

Interestingly, none of the virtual behaviors significantly predicted the importance of physical place attributes such as color or furniture arrangements (compared to behavioral place attributes), indicating that these features were not as important for computer users as convention would assume.

Using a standard multiple regression analysis, the variable of "time spent" by computer users in the coffee shop was examined to see if it could serve as a predictor of the frequency of specific virtual behaviors. It was found that spending more time in the coffee shop was a significant predictor of the frequency of virtual behaviors such as watching movies, viewing pictures, and listening to recordings.

Interestingly, the "time spent" in coffee shop was not a significant predictor of the frequency of virtual behaviors such as studying, browsing, social networking, and shopping.

The variable "time spent" by computer users was examined further to see if it could serve as a predictor of the importance given to the place attributes of the coffee shops. Statistical analysis of the results revealed that the time spent in the coffee shop was a significant predictor of the importance given to the place attributes of density and size of the space. This finding suggests that among computer users, more time spent in the coffee shop was associated with less density (fewer people) and smaller space size. Contrary to expectations, "time spent" in the coffee shop was not associated with other physical place attributes such as lighting, color, and image – elements which are traditionally considered important by designers.

In this study an attempt was made to reconceptualize places in a physical–virtual continuum in order to measure virtual behaviors and their impact on place attributes. Data collected from eight wireless coffee shops over a three-year period using various research tools revealed that the opportunity to meet friends and the arrangement of furniture were the most important place attributes for customers who engaged in virtual behaviors. The study also reinforced the assumption that computer users would spend more time in the coffee shop compared to non-computer uses.

Although the PLE maps completed by the computer users in the coffee shops showed a wide variety of virtual behaviors, emailing was found to be the most prominent virtual behavior, with social networking coming in second. An important finding related to these behaviors was that computer users tended to conduct these behaviors as clusters of activities, rather than in isolation from other behaviors/ activities. Three clusters of behaviors were identified: (1) predominantly formal, (2) predominantly informal, and (3) predominantly a mix of formal and informal.

It should be noted that computer users whose activities fell into the formal cluster valued their privacy more in comparison to those who fell into the informal cluster, who valued meeting their friends more. Those users who fell into the mixed cluster rated the size of the space and the noise level as most important to their experience in the coffee shop.

Lastly, among computer users the findings revealed that the time spent in the coffee shop was a significant predictor of the place attributes of density (number of people in the space) and the size of the space.

While it is not possible to predict the impact of virtual behaviors on place attributes based solely on the results of this study, an examination of the findings provides interesting insights into the importance of place attributes in the experience of computer users. When examining the virtual–physical continuum of place attributes, this study found that computer users assigned more importance to the virtual attributes of the coffee shop than the physical attributes. (It is important to note that place experience in the virtual–physical continuum includes a range of awareness from minimal attentive contact to more intense encounters. This being the case, these variations of space-time geographies of environments in the virtual–physical continuum are difficult to comprehend, let alone measure.)

Conclusion

Traditionally, place as a construct has been addressed in several different domains.[4] The question is whether the role of virtual behaviors should be situated within these existing place models or, instead, be reconceptualized. According to the literature, when virtual behaviors are introduced into the existing models of place, they can be viewed as an additional layer that maps onto physical place (Graham and Marvin 1996). This approach argues for augmentation or evolution, rather than substitution – suggesting that no matter how "real" virtuality may appear, physicality continues to impact and shape the individual experience. Therefore, physicality remains relevant in any new conception of place and supports the growing belief that virtuality and physicality are complements to each other rather than substitutes for each other (Mokhtarian 2002).

A new framework for place attributes can be illustrated through a modification of one of the place models suggested by Weisman (2001). Weisman's model defines place as the interaction between people (individuals, groups, or organizations), program (purpose and patterns of use), and building (sensory and spatial properties, as well as physicality of the setting). By augmenting virtuality to this model, it is reconceptualized to fit the virtual–physical continuum. This reconceptualization of Weisman's place model adds virtual people to the people component (for e.g. friends in Facebook), virtual functions to the program component (for e.g. emailing) , and virtual interfaces (computers and mobile devices) to the building component. Place then becomes the fusion of all the components of virtuality and physicality.

The reconceptualization of place in terms of a physical–virtual continuum avoids the simplistic notions associated with extreme physicality and extreme virtuality of place models. As anthropologists Wilson and Peterson suggest in their work with online communities, the conventional analytical emphasis on a community's boundedness and isolation usually masks significant interactions between individuals as well as the heterogeneity of the community itself. They contend that there exists a wide range of virtual communities – from small groups engaged in tightly focused discussions of specific topics, to complex created worlds with hundreds of simultaneous participants, to millions of users linked by exchange networks. In other words, a more fluid concept of community, one that explores multi-sided situations, is spatially diverse and consists of trans-local sites (Wilson and Peterson 2002).

According to Forlano, the "Anytime, Anywhere" adage promoted by mobile companies is untrue when one looks at the actual habits of the users (Forlano 2008). Doyle contends that the conventionally touted distinction in the place literature between "here" and "there" is also a myth. That is to say, just because an activity can be performed as easily in space A as in space B it does not mean that the experience of doing that activity will be the same in each space. Kakihara argues that the locational aspect of a place (where) should take on greater importance only when one considers other variables such as interaction (with whom) and organization (with what) (Kakihara 2003). For example, an individual who works at home may decide to go to a neighborhood café to do their work because the café provides a positive ambience that enables them to concentrate on their work.

The purpose of this chapter was to introduce the reader to a new way of thinking about place attributes and to introduce the concept of the virtual–physical continuum as a mechanism for the reconceptualization of existing place models. The research study discussed here was limited by the specific type of place (coffee shops) used as the setting for the research. Thus, further research is necessary in other place settings to gain a better understanding of how the virtual–physical continuum affects one's sense of place and to address the following questions raised by the research study:

- How can environments that demand a continuum of space-time geographies be best supported and designed?
- How can place attributes be measured, especially when consideration is given to a rapidly changing technological context?
- How much do traditional physical "design" elements (color, texture, focal points) affect the meaning and value of a place?
- How does the physical design of a place impact the facilitation or disruption of virtual behaviors?

Notes

1   The term "virtuality" can be associated with different terms such as "cyberspace," "computer-mediated communication," "information technology" (IT), and "communication technologies" (CT), to name a few. Cyberspace has come to describe anything associated with diverse internet culture, often referring to a global network of interdependent IT infrastructures, telecommunications networks, and computer-processing systems. As a social experience, individuals interact, exchange ideas, share information, provide social support, conduct business, direct actions, create artistic media, play games, and engage in political discussion. Computer-mediated communication (CMC) is a much more narrow terminology referring to communicative transaction through the use of two or more networked computers. While CMC traditionally refers to those communications that occur via computer-mediated formats (e.g., instant messages, emails, chat rooms), it has also been applied to other forms of text-based interaction such as text messaging. Information and communications technology (ICT), is often used as an extended synonym for information technology, but is a more general term that stresses the role of integration of telecommunications, intelligent building management systems, and audio-visual systems.

2   Weisman refers to these as attributes of place experience, which include stimulation, accessibility, crowdedness, privacy, control, legibility, comfort, adaptability, sociality, and

meaning. Tofle (2009) identifies impairing attributes of place (safety, function, comfort), enabling attributes (identity, meaning), and opportunities (control preference, choice, adaptation, autonomy, and sensory perception). Evans and McCoy (1998) suggest attributes such as stimulation, coherence, affordances, control, and restorative qualities important to healthcare settings. Bennett (1977) has suggested other attributes such as safety, health, performance, comfort, and aesthetic pleasantness. Oldenburg and Brissett (1982) refer to these attributes in terms of sociability, spontaneity, community-building and emotional expressiveness, and the power of place to be regenerative/restorative. Besides these references, one can find the description of place attributes, sometimes referred as human factors, in concepts such as privacy (Altman 1975), personal space (Sommer 1969), territoriality (Brown 1987), environmental stress (Evans and Cohen 1987), environmental press (Lawton 1986), aesthetics (Weber 1995), preference (Kaplan 1988), meaning (Csikszentmihalyi and Rochberg-Halton 1981), spatial behavior (Holahan 1982), legibility/imageability (Lynch 1960), spatial nostalgia (Hester 1979), and way-finding (Passini 1984) among others.

3   This survey instrument, although geared toward assessing building performance, provided a macro-level framework to understand place attributes. The ASTM scales are Likert-type scales for physical and behavioral attributes, in which participants are asked to indicate the relative importance of specific place attributes in the range from 1 to 5. Not all questions from ASTM were used. Only those items which had content validity to place attributes and coffee shops were used. Alpha reliability ranged for all items ranged from 0.72 to 0.73.

4   Domains such as environment-behavior (Mazumdar and Mazumdar, 1993; Seamon 1979; Tofle, 2009), anthropology (Oldenburg 1989), sociology (Gustafson 2001), human geography (Creswell 2004) , psychology (Canter 1997), and architecture (Norberg-Schulz 1986; Weisman 2001). One could view these place models deriving from their respective epistemological positions, for example: positive science (in which place is a tangible objective construct), interpretivism (in which place is reified in meaning and values), and constructivism (place as an active construction rather than a passive state of mind).

Acknowledgments

Many thanks to the students from Human Factors Class at the University of Missouri, Department of Architectural Studies, 2007–2012, who were instrumental in collecting these data.

References

Agnew, J. 1987. *Place and Politics: The Geographical Mediation of State and Society.* Allen and Unwin, London.

Altman, I. 1975. *The Environment and Social Behavior.* Monterey, CA: Brooks/Cole Publishing.

Altman, I. and Rogoff, B. 1987. "World views in psychology: trait, interactional, organismic, and transactional perspectives," in D. Stokols and I. Altman (eds.), *Handbook of Environmental Psychology.* New York: John Wiley & Sons, vol.1, pp. 7–40.

Attwell, Graham 2007. "The personal learning environments – the future of eLearning?", *eLearning Papers* 2(1).

Axtell, C., Hislop, D., and Whittaker, S. 2008. "Mobile technologies in mobile spaces: findings from the context of train travel," *International Journal of Human-Computer Studies* 66(2): 902–915.

Baker, L. 2004. "Urban renewal, the wireless way." www.salon.com/2004/11/29/digital _metropolis. Accessed July 20, 2014.

Becker, F. and Sims, W. 1990. "Assessing building performance," in F. Becker (ed.), *The Total Workspace: Facilities Management and the Elastic Organization*. New York: Van Nostrand Reinhold, pp. 269–300.

Bennett, C. 1977. *Spaces for People: Human Factors in Design*. New York: Prentice Hall.

Brown, B. 1987. "Territoriality," in D. Stokols and I. Altman (eds.), *Handbook of Environmental Psychology*. New York: Wiley, pp. 510–531

Brown, B. and O'Hara, K. 2003. "Place as a practical concern of mobile workers," *Environment & Planning A* 35(9): 1565–1587.

Canter, D. 1997. "The facets of place," in G. T. Moore and R. W. Marans (eds.), *Advances in Environment, Behavior, and Design 4*. New York: Plenum.

Cresswell, T. 2004. *Place: A Short Introduction*. Oxford: Blackwell.

Csikszentmihalyi, M. and Rochberg-Halton, E. 1981. *The Meaning of Things: Domestic Symbols and the Self*. Cambridge: Cambridge University Press.

Dobbins, K. W. 2005. "Getting ready for the Net Generation Learner," *Educause Review* (September/October): 8–9.

Doyle, M. R. 2011. "Designing for mobile activities: wifi hotspots and users in Quebec City." Master's thesis, University of Laval, Quebec.

Evans, G. and McCoy, M. 1998. "When buildings don't work: the role of architecture in human health," *Journal of Environmental Psychology* 18: 85–94.

Evans W. G., and Cohen, S. 1987. "Environmental stress," in D. Stokols and I. Altman (eds.), *Handbook of Environmental Psychology*. New York: Wiley, p. 15.

Forlano, L. 2008. *When Code Meets Place: Collaboration and Innovation at WiFi Hotspots*. New York: Columbia University.

Graham, S. and Marvin, S. 1996. "Telecommunication and the city," *Electronic Spaces, Urban Places*. London: Routledge.

Gupta, N. 2004. "Grande Wi-Fi: Understanding What Wi-Fi Users Are Doing in Coffee-Shops." Master's thesis, Massachusetts Institute of Technology, Cambridge, MA.

Gustafson, P. 2001. "Meanings of place: everyday experience and theoretical conceptualizations," *Journal of Environmental Psychology* 21: 5–16.

Hayles, Katherine N. 1999. *How We Became Post-Human: Virtual Bodies in Cybernetics, Literature, and Informatics*. Chicago: University of Chicago Press.

Heidegger, M. 1962. *Being and Time*. Oxford: Blackwell.

Hester, R. 1979. "A womb with a view: how spatial nostalgia affects the designer," *Landscape Architecture* 69: 475–481.

Hislop, D. and Axtell, C. 2009. "To infinity and beyond: workspace and the multi-location," *New Technology and Work Employment* 24(1): 60–75.

Holahan, C. J. 1982. *Environmental Psychology*. New York: McGraw-Hill.

Horan, Thomas A., 2000. *Digital Places: Building Our City of Bits*. Washington DC: Urban Land Institute.

Ito, M., Okabe, D., and Anderson, K. 2009. "Portable objects in three global cities: the personalization of urban places," *Journal of Industrial Ecology* 6(2): 43–57.

Kakihara, M. 2003. *Emerging Work Practices of ICT-Enabled Mobile Professionals*. London: London School of Economics.

Kaplan, S. 1988. "Where cognition and affect meet: a theoretical analysis of preference," in J. Nasar (ed.), *Environmental Aesthetics*. Cambridge: Cambridge University Press.

Kendall, L. 2002. *Hanging Out in the Virtual Pub: Masculinities and Relationships Online*. Berkeley and Los Angeles: University of California Press.

Lawton, M. P. 1986. *Environment and Aging*. Albany, NY: Center for the Study of Aging.

Low, S. M. and Altman, I. 1992. "Place attachment: a conceptual inquiry," in I. Altman and S. M. Low (eds.), *Place Attachment*. New York: Plenum.

Lynch, K. 1960. *Image of the City*. Cambridge, MA: MIT Press.

Massey, D. 1995. "The conceptualization of place," in D. Massey and P. Jess (eds.), *A Place in the World? Places, Cultures and Globalization*. Oxford: Oxford University Press.

May, J. 1996. "Globalization and the politics of place: place and identity in an inner London neighbourhood," *Transactions of the Institute of British Geographers* 21: 194–215.

Mazumdar, S. and Mazumdar, S. 1993. "Sacred space and place attachment," *Journal of Environmental Psychology* 13: 231–242.

Milne, A. J. 2006. "Designing blended learning spaces to the student experience," in D. Oblinger (ed.), *Learning Spaces*. Boulder, CO: Educause.

Mokhtarian, P. L. 2002. "Telecommunications and travel: the case for complementarity," *New Technology, Work and Employment* 24(1): 60–75.

Moores, S. 2006. "Media uses and everyday environmental experiences: a positive critique of phenomenological geography," *Particip@tions* 3(2). Online journal http://www.participations.org/index.htm. Accessed May 7, 2014.

Nimon, S. 2007. "Generation Y and higher education: the other y2k?," *Journal of Institutional Research in Australia* 13(1): 24–41.

Norberg-Schulz, C. 1986. *Architecture: Meaning and Place*. New York: Rizzoli.

Oblinger, D. and Oblinger, J. 2005. "Is it age or IT? First steps towards understanding the Net generation," in *Educating the Net Generation*. Boulder, CO: Educause.

Oldenburg, R. 1989. *The Great Good Place: Cafés, Coffee Shops, Community Centers, Beauty Parlors, General Stores, Bars, Hangouts, and How They Get You through the Day*. New York: Paragon House.

Oldenburg, R. and Brissett, D. 1982. "The third place," *Journal of Qualitative Sociology* 5: 265–284.

Passini, R. 1984. *Wayfinding in Architecture*. New York: Van Nostrand Reinhold.

Relph, E. 1976. *Place and Placelessness*. London: Pion.

Schönhammer, R. 1989. "The Walkman and the primary world of the senses," *Phenomenology + Pedagogy* 7: 127–144.

Seamon, D. 1979. *A Geography of the Lifeworld: Movement, Rest and Encounter*. New York: St. Martin's Press.

Seamon, D. 2006. "A geography of Lifeworld in retrospect: a response to Shaun Moores," *Particip@tions* 3:2. Online journal. www.participations.org/. Accessed May 7, 2014.

Sommer, R. 1969. *Personal Space*. Englewood Cliffs, NJ: Prentice Hall.

Tofle, R. 2009. "Creating a place for dying: gerontopia," in B. Schwarz, and D. P. Oliver (eds.), *Journal of Housing for the Elderly* 23(1–2): 66–91.

Turkle, S. 1996. "Virtuality and its discontents," *The American Prospect* 4(24).

Urry, J. 2002. "Mobility and Proximity," *Sociology* 36: 255–274.

Weber, R. 1995. *On the Aesthetics of Architecture: A Psychological Approach to the Structure and the Order of Perceived Architectural Space*. Aldershot: Avebury.

Weisman, G. 2001. "The place of people in architectural design," in A. Pressman, (ed.), *The Architect's Portable Design Handbook: A Guide to Best Practice*. New York: McGraw-Hill, pp. 149–170.

Wilson, S. M. and Peterson, L. C. 2002. "The anthropology of online communities," *Annual Review of Anthropology* 31(1): 449–467.

22

The Relationship between Historic Preservation and Sustainability in Interior Design

Lisa Tucker

Introduction

The historic interior is a place where principles of preservation and principles of sustainable design inevitably overlap. As such, the interior of a historic building is a perfect vehicle in which to explore the synergies between historic preservation and sustainable design. As Peter Zumthor suggests,

> Every new work of architecture intervenes in a specific historical situation. It is essential to the quality of the intervention that the new building should embrace qualities that can enter into a meaningful dialogue with the existing situation. For if the intervention is to find its place, it must make us see what already exists in a new light. (Zumthor 2010)

The underlying purposes of historic preservation (to retain historic fabric) and sustainability (to reduce the human footprint) are inherently similar. Both require a focus on reducing the use of newer materials in buildings and a greater appreciation for the use of older materials in structures. Therefore a case can be made that retaining, rather than replacing, historic materials with new ones directly reduces the ecological footprint of a building.

In today's construction environment it is most likely that materials selected for use in buildings will be rapidly renewable, locally harvested, extracted, or manufactured, and non-toxic. However, for builders of historic structures concern about whether or not their sources were renewable or toxic was not at the forefront of their thinking. As a result, most historic structures are composed of local materials which are predominantly natural – thereby providing ample opportunities for the successful overlap of preservation and sustainable design principles.

In the case of historic buildings the interior of a structure will likely change significantly over time. Layers of surfaces and resurfacing continuously change the historic interior space to reflect its social history. How all of this is preserved, restored, adapted, or otherwise interpreted is at the core of what an interior designer does. As such, it is important that the designer's work not only reflect the new uses and occupants of a historic interior but, at the same time, honors the changes in taste and social mores that have occurred over time.

The Palimpsest Approach

I suggest that the essence of a historic interior is like a palimpsest – or multi-layered record. While the original meaning of the word refers to a manuscript that has been erased or scraped and re-layered with writing over time, the concept can be applied easily to the interior of a historic building. Diverse layering over time contributes to the current essence of a space and can provide the basis for an environment that helps us remember what has come before and enjoy what takes place in the present as a new layer for future reflection.

A thorough review of the literature reveals that little research has been undertaken to explore the idea of historic interiors as a palimpsest. In most part, the literature reflects an emphasis on the materials, structural components, and facade details of a building's shell. Further, most of the literature is found in preservation briefs that describe how to technically do the work, not why we make the choices we make. This being the case, it follows that while much has been written about the synergies between historic preservation and sustainable design, little emphasis has been placed on these synergies as they might occur in the interior.

In his article for the *Forum Journal*, practitioner Carl Elephante suggests a framework adopted from Stewart Brand of *How Buildings Learn* fame, that proposes that we look at existing buildings in terms of four areas: structure, envelope, interior, and systems. Of the four areas outlined by Elephante, it is safe to say the interior changes the most frequently. Like the fashion industry in some regard, interiors change with the times and new color palettes, materials, furnishings, and even spatial considerations change continuously.

Few guidelines exist on how to deal with this record of change in the interior within a historic building. Although *Preservation Brief 18* addresses the interior by providing 10 general guidelines, and other briefs discuss interior paint, ceramic tile floors, plaster work, and ornamentation of the interior, there is no attention paid to the importance of preserving the essence of a historic space through what I have called a palimpsest approach; that is, as a multi-layered record of the past.

Similarly, although the *Interiors Handbook for Historic Buildings* investigates several facets of a historic interior including planning, architectural features and materials, finishes and accessories, systems and fixtures, fire protection and codes, adaptive reuse and manufacturers, and sources and literature, no information is provided about how to preserve the changing roles of a historic building as they are reflected through the interiors (Fisher, Auer, and Grimmer 1988).

At the time the *Interiors Handbook for Historic Buildings* was developed, Associate Professor Jim Morgan (Pratt Institute) lamented the lack of information on historic interiors: "No academic framework exists for teaching interior preservation design nor to my knowledge, does a book exist on the subject." This complaint is as true today as it was then. Like the remainder of the information contained in the *Handbook*, the information that does exist focuses on specific materials, historic windows, and plaster ornamentation. In other words, little theoretical or philosophical guidance about how to approach a historic interior is suggested.

Having established that there is little available information in the literature to help guide a palimpsest approach to historic interiors from a preservationist point of view, it is also true that there is even less written about how to complete a historic interior from a sustainability point of view. As suggested earlier, nearly all the current literature addresses more general issues associated with the building itself.

The Intersection of Sustainability and Historic Preservation Work for the Interior: A New Framework

I propose a new framework for dealing with the specific issues associated with the history of interiors in a building. This framework for sustainable historic interiors proposes a more expansive conversation – one that includes the European sensibility of conservation, that is, conservation as defined by English Heritage as "the careful management of change" (Holden and Meek 2011).

In keeping with this European sensibility and recognizing the need for economic and socially viable projects, the Cadw (Welsh Government Historic Environment Service) established the following series of six principles to guide conservation work:

- Historic assets will be managed to sustain their values.
- Understanding the significance of historic assets is vital.
- The historic environment is a shared resource.
- Everyone will be able to participate in sustaining the historic environment.
- Decisions about change must be reasonable, transparent, and consistent.
- Documenting and learning from decisions is essential. (Cadw 2011)

These principles are in concert with the palimpsest approach to a historic interior which recognizes that a historic interior represents a series of changes throughout the life of a building.

The palimpsest approach offers a new way of looking at interior sustainable preservation. Although a palimpsest approach has been used to describe the exteriors of historic buildings designed by architects such as Carlo Scarpa, Peter Zumthor, and others at the Harvard School of Design (2011) and at Ryerson (2011), until now – unfortunately – the discussion has not been expanded to include historic interior spaces. By viewing the historic interior as a palimpsest, the space can be recognized as a series of layers where parts are removed to allow for new interventions. Such interventions, therefore, have some level of importance in telling the complete story.

Action Outline for a New Palimpsest Framework

Evaluation of a historic interior for significance and rehabilitation guidelines

To understand how a palimpsest framework can be applied to a historic interior it is important to first have a clear understanding of how a historic interior is evaluated for significance. Several documents exist that discuss the question of significance within a historic building. These include, *Bulletin 16A*, *Preservation Brief 17*, and *Preservation Brief 18* (Jandl 1988).

According to these and other sources, historic character is defined as the tangible elements that convey a sense of time and place. The Secretary of the Interior suggests that the following things must be assessed to determine historical significance: (1) association with historic events or activities; (2) association with important persons; (3) distinctive design or physical characteristics; and (4) the potential to provide important information about prehistory or history.

According to *Preservation Brief 17*, there are several things that determine the architectural character of a building which inform a historic interior. These include individual spaces, related spaces and sequence, interior features, surface finishes and materials, and exposed structure. In a similar vein, *Preservation Brief 18* suggests that establishing which interior spaces play a primary role versus those of a secondary nature is important. By identifying these roles it can be determined which spaces contribute to the significance of the building and which might not.

Generally, primary spaces include foyers, elevator lobbies, assembly spaces, stair halls, and parlors. These are often the most costly spaces with the most highly designed interiors. Secondary spaces, such as bathrooms and kitchens, are more utilitarian. According to Jandl, the sequence of spaces and the interrelation between them can also be of significance (Jandl 1988).

Once the various roles of the spaces have been reviewed and established, the next step in evaluating the significance of a historic interior is the assessment of finishes. For example, do the interior spaces feature wood graining and marbleizing, or fine plasterwork? In addition, note should be taken of any alterations that may have been done over time and attention should be paid to the state of deterioration of the materials and finishes.

Whenever possible, *Preservation Brief 18* further suggests that interiors that have been deemed historically significant should be rehabilitated by carefully retaining and preserving floor plans and interior spaces that are important in defining the overall historic character of the building. According to *Brief 18*, the subdivision of spaces that are characteristic of a building type that is directly associated with specific persons or patterns of events should be avoided.

Further, when rehabilitating significant historic interiors *Preservation Brief 18* cautions against making new cuts in floors and ceilings where such cuts would change character-defining spaces and the historic configuration of such spaces. And it is recommended that the installation of dropped ceilings be avoided below ornamental ceilings or in rooms where high ceilings are a part of the building's character.

In addition to these considerations, when rehabilitating significant historic interiors it is important to retain the interior features that help define the overall historic character of the building and to maintain, whenever possible, the visible features of early mechanical systems that are important to the overall historic character of the building such as radiators, vents, fans, grilles, plumbing fixtures, switch plates, and lights.

It is recommended further that interior elements such as stairs should be kept in their historic configuration and location and that care should be taken when insulating perimeter walls. Lastly, caution should exercised with the removal of paint and plaster from traditionally finished surfaces to expose masonry and wood and the use of destructive methods such as propane and butane torches or sandblasting to remove paint or other coatings from historic features should be avoided.

Nomination of property to the National Register

In order to fully understand the history of a property to be nominated to the National Register, several types of research must be conducted. This often starts with archival research into land tax records, deeds, and local histories for dating purposes. Local libraries often contain genealogical information, personal diaries and accounts, historic photographs, and often sketchbooks or other documentation of historic properties.

A second level of archival research can be done in conjunction with the State Historic Preservation Office (SHPO). In many parts of the US, surveys that were conducted as a part of the Historic American Building Survey (HABS) in the 1930s and 1940s, and again later under the auspices of the state to record state historic properties for planning purposes, offer invaluable insights into the history of a building. Because any federal monies that were used for new roads and highways required an architectural and archeological survey of the area prior to construction, the SHPO records offer the most thorough and accurate picture of the historic significance of buildings that have been surveyed.

Once the research has been completed, several key elements must be included in order to nominate a property to the National Register. The nomination must include a thorough review of the building's historic significance, historic integrity, and historic context. Historic integrity extends to include the location, the design, the setting, the materials, the workmanship, the feeling, and the association, while historic context covers such issues as theme, place, and time. The combination of all these factors creates a holistic picture of the building and its significance as a historic property.

The palimpsest approach to a historic interior: rehabilitation, restoration, preservation, or reconstruction?

Approaching the historic interior as a palimpsest, the interior designer recognizes that any intervention must realize that the interior changes on a regular basis. It reflects new uses, new occupants, new materials and workmanship, and changes in style and taste. How all of this is preserved, restored, adapted, or otherwise interpreted is in the purview of the interior designer.

One of the biggest challenges of a historic interior for an interior designer is how to reflect the constant record of change encapsulated in the space. Every occupant and owner makes changes to the interior – big or small. Unlike the architecture of a building, which tends towards permanence, the interior changes regularly and for many reasons. The question, from a preservation point of view, is: What is the period of significance? And if there is more than one significant time, how should this be retained and interpreted to show all periods as well as that which is new? How can multiple layers be expressed simultaneously and with clarity? When was the interior significant? What were the significant events that took place? Are there any significant personages tied to the place?

It is important to understand that the embodied energy of existing materials in a historic building has been estimated to equate to 65 years in the life of a newly designed high-performance sustainable building (Armitage 2010). This being the case, a complete evaluation of the extant materials is warranted. Such an evaluation will reveal those materials which need remediation, those that are beyond repair, those that are significant, and a host of other issues. Once a complete examination has been conducted, decisions about restoration, consolidation, or replacement can be made.

According to Brosseau (2006) there is a lack of information on how to document a historic interior in the HABS and the National Park Service information. To address this concern, an outline for gathering and documenting information on a historic interior is provided in Figure 22.1.

• **Room #**	• **Door elements and materials**	• **Window elements and materials**	• **Wall elements and materials**
Name of room:	Notes:	Notes:	Notes:
Source:	Frames and trim	Frames and trim sets:	Base shoe:
Location:	sets:	Window (A, B, or C)	Base:
Description:	Door (A, B, or C)	Inside trim height:	Base molding:
Height:	Inside trim height:	Outside trim height:	Measured
Width:	Outside trim	Inside width:	drawing:
Length:	height:	Outside width:	Field:
	Inside width:	Hardware	Chair rail:
• **General notes:**	Outside width:	Window (A, B, or C)	Field:
	Measured	Condition:	Picture
• **Flooring**	drawing	Operation:	molding:
Elements	Operation:	Window (A, B, or C)	Frieze:
Material:	Door (A, B, or C)	(Example: A (w) is a fixed	Cornice:
Notes:	Hardware	window)	Condition:
Condition:	Door (A, B, or C)	Window (A, B, or C)	
	Condition:	Projection:	• **Ceiling**
		Fenestration patterns:	**elements and**
		Hardware:	**materials**
		Window (A, B, or C)	Notes:
		Condition:	Field:
			Molding:
			Filler:

Figure 22.1   Interiors checklist

While most historic building analysis tools focus on the more permanent components of the building, this tool can be used to capture the physical state of the interior. While this instrument is helpful in recording the physical detail and conditions of each room, it fails to collect the more intangible properties and characteristics of the space. How does it feel? And why? How many layers are discernible? What are the dates/periods of these layers?

Interpretive and disappearing historic interiors

Significant historic properties have long been preserved, restored, and reconstructed to interpret a particular event or moment in time. Examples of this are Colonial Williamsburg, Monticello, Mount Vernon, and many others. However, while these buildings and monuments have their place, most buildings do not meet this level of significance. A more common situation is when the historic interior has disappeared. In such cases the interior preservationist must consider several questions. Should it be reconstructed? Or are there other ways to interpret a lost environment through a photographic record, 3D drawings, and/or video flythrough?

In the case of all historic interiors – be they interpreted, preserved, or disappeared – it can be assumed that changes and additions will be necessary to make a building meet today's needs. Therefore consideration must be given to how new systems and needs can be sensitively and sensibly integrated. For example, since materials experience wear and tear, should these be replaced in kind or with the next generation of material?

According to the standards set by the Secretary of the Interior, new interventions in material and workmanship should be made in a way that is obvious, while not disturbing the historic integrity. In keeping with the palimpsest framework, as well as European conservation ideology, reasonable, consistent, and transparent decisions should be made and documented in this process.

The final component of the palimpsest framework involves a post-occupancy evaluation to test the propositions and to add to the body of knowledge through published findings and lessons learned. Research throughout all steps of the process is an important feature of this framework. Historic research, case-study research, and environment and behavioral research all play an important role.

To create a body of knowledge in the specific area of interior sustainable preservation, designers must record their thinking in regard to the overall historic record, the multiple layers, and the justification for design decisions. Time and evaluation will be the final judges of which decisions were correct and which ones could have been improved.

As demonstrated here, much of the existing knowledge about historic interiors and how to approach them falls into the domain of "how to." This new framework proposes that the questions of "Why?" and "Within what context?" are much more important first considerations. A historic interior challenges our very relationship with our past and what we can learn from it. Allowing the interior to tell us its history through layering over time, i.e., a palimpsest approach, offers a more sensitive methodology to guide our efforts.

Sustainability: What Historic Buildings Can Teach Us

According to Shirazi, "In architecture, I would rather palimpsestic design, where we encounter an old historical building. In this case, we have a remarkable, text-in-between, but [one that] appreciates it and accompanies...it. The logic of palimpsestic design is interaction and conversation, not imposition and conquering" (Shirazi 2004).

Instead of looking at how to make historic buildings more sustainable, as most of the existing literature does (imposing and conquering), lessons can be learned from historic buildings – and these lessons can teach us how to be more sustainable (interaction and conversation). In much the same way that the interior responds to changes in use, owner, style, workmanship, materials, and other factors, vernacular building traditions evolve from local variations in weather, site, available materials and skilled workers. Letting the interior guide the sustainable preservation process provides invaluable direction to the designer.

Tucker's research has identified several examples from historic houses that replicate current guidelines for sustainable houses (Tucker 2008). For instance, the single-pile plan type allows for natural cross-ventilation and the interior transoms and stair halls draw hot air up and out of the house during hot summer months. The single-pile (one room deep) form also allows for maximum daylight and views and, by planting deciduous shade trees, the front-facing southern facade is protected from direct sunlight in the summer thereby reducing solar gain.

Several other practices can be identified in historic structures that echo today's sustainable guidelines. Things such as the use of local lumber, stone, and brick and the inclusion of a cistern for on-site water catchment mirror the sustainability guidelines for houses. End chimneys, as found in the I-House throughout Virginia and North Carolina – were used in historical houses to provide thermal mass – absorbing heat from the sun during the day and retaining heat created by fires during the winter. This concept is again seen in current sustainability guidelines, where thermal mass walls are recommended to retain heat that can be given back to the space at night when the temperature drops.

A look at historic houses and their adaptations to the specific locale can provide much-needed guidance in this area. Knowledge formed over many decades in response to a specific region, as seen in historic buildings, has been lost in most locales. As traditions have changed, specific skills and normative processes have been replaced with technology and standardization. Allowing historic buildings to teach us provides a new approach to intervention with new designs.

These historic applications are in concert with the considerations that today inform the Green Building Rating Systems. This is to say that such things as daylight and views, site orientation, natural ventilation, and locally available materials are all important factors in gaining LEED certification for buildings.

Learning from History: Net Zero Housing

It can be argued that single family houses in today's market should be more affordable, sustainable, and well designed. This being the case, a serious examination of the work of a group of early 20th-century architects, known as the Architects Small House Service Bureau (ASHSB), is warranted, The express purpose of this group was to create small, affordable, and well-designed houses.

Located all over the US and focusing on house design for the middle and lower classes, the ASHSB produced hundreds of designs based on basic design principles. These principles included the proper positioning of a house on a site and maximization of the house's efficiency through a small building footprint and the use of technological innovations. Between 1919 and 1943, the organization sold hundreds of plans all over the US and in other countries. As part of their guidelines, it was suggested that each homeowner contract with a local architect to customize the design to a specific site, thus taking advantage of local conditions for passive solar.

Additionally, each of the divisions produced designs that were suited to the part of the country within which they were operating.

In today's vernacular, a net-zero house is one that minimizes the use of energy from outside sources and is designed for sustainable living. According to Tucker, the Architects' Small House Service Bureau offers guidelines for net-zero housing, thereby providing a model for sustainable housing for the 21st century (Tucker 2012). In keeping with this, the following ASHSB guidelines are presented as examples that could inform the design of net-zero houses today:

- Small and efficient housing is better than large and inefficient housing
- Built-ins maximize space usage
- Materials should be chosen to last
- Good Design upfront eliminates waste during the construction process
- A trained design professional providing a complete plan and building services saves time and money
- Builders are not designers
- Choosing a house is one of the biggest decisions a prospective homeowner will ever make
- Design adds value and quality
- The ASHSB and its advice are practical
- Good design shows

Conclusion

The thesis of this essay – that sustainable preservation is the realm of the interior designer – challenges the current view of historic preservation in the US that is predominantly in the domain of architecture. As specialists in interior environments, it is logical that this be a specialization within interiors. The interior is a multi-layered canvas expressing the changes in occupation, use, and period. An understanding of the many people who shaped the interior and the many ways in which it has functioned is within the domain of interior design. Additionally, as the case studies mentioned demonstrate, history is important and can inform what we do today both in terms of the preservation and sustainability of buildings. The interior is the vehicle where preservation and sustainable design inevitably overlap. Through a thorough understanding of both approaches, interior designers are the professionals to create a truly sustainable preservation intervention.

References

APT (Association for Preservation Technology). 2005. *APT Bulletin: The Journal of Preservation Technology* 36: 4.

Armitage, S. 2010. "Historic preservation meets sustainable development," *Yale Globalist.* http://yaleglobalist.wordpress.com/2010/07/14/historic-preservation-meets-sustainable-development/. Accessed May 8, 2014.

Brosseau, T. L. 2006. "Historic Interior Documentation: A Case Study." Master's thesis, Cornell University.

Cadw (Welsh Government Historic Environment Service). 2011. *Conservation Principles.* http://cadw.wales.gov.uk/historicenvironment/conservation/conservationprinciples/?lang=en. Accessed May 8, 2014.

Chicago School of Media Theory. 2003. *Palimpsest.* University of Chicago. http://lucian.uchicago.edu/blogs/mediatheory/keywords/palimpsest/. Accessed May 7, 2014.

Elephante, C. 2007. "The greenest building is...one that is already built," *Forum Journal* 21(4): 26–38.

Fisher, C., Auer, M., and Grimmer, A. 1988. *The Interiors Handbook for Historic Interiors.* Prepared for the Historic Preservation Education Foundation.

Holden, P. and Meek, J. 2011. *Roch Castle, Pembrokeshire: A Study in Significance.* www.buildingconservation.com. Accessed May 7, 2014.

Jandl, W. H. 1988. *Preservation Brief 18: Rehabilitating Interiors in Historic Buildings: Identifying and Preserving Character-Defining Elements.* Washington DC: National Park Service.

Shirazi, M. R. 2004. "Notes on palimpsest," *Architecture and Construction Quarterly,* Tehran, Iran. http://www.tu-cottbus.de/theoriederarchitektur/wolke/eng/Subjects/Shirazi/NOTES-ON-PALIMPSEST_text.pdf. Accessed May 8, 2014.

Stevenson, M. D. 2004. "Post-Industrial Palimpsest: Maintaining Place and Layers in History." M.Arch. thesis. University of Cincinnati.

Tucker, L. M. 2008. "18th and 19th century building technologies in Virginia and single-family house sustainable design rating systems," *Environmental Design Research Association* 39: 23–29.

Tucker, L. M. 2012. "Net zero housing: the architects' small house service bureau and contemporary sustainable single-family house design methods for the United States," *Journal of Interior Design* 37: 1–16.

US Department of the Interior. 1983. *The Secretary of the Interior's Standards for Rehabilitation and Guidelines for Rehabilitating Historic Buildings.* Washington DC: Preservation Assistance Division, National Park Service, US Department of the Interior.

US Department of the Interior National Park Service Cultural Resources. 1997. *Bulletin 16A.* The National Park Service: Washington DC. http://yaleglobalist.wordpress.com/2010/07/14/historic-preservation-meets-sustainable-development/. Accessed May 7, 2014.

Zumthor, P. 2010. *Thinking Architecture.* Basel: Birkhauser.

23

Forging Empathetic Connections to Create Compatible Designs in Historic Buildings

Jessica Goldsmith

Introduction

Interior design is a specialty field of professional practice and inquiry that addresses the design and condition of the interior environment of buildings. Interior designers create environments that balance the needs of the people who will occupy those environments with the pre-existing conditions of a building and its site. Interior designers are professionals who must be educated and licensed in order to ensure their ability to protect the health, safety, and welfare of the public (NCIDQ 2009).

Interior design usually takes place within the walls of a pre-existing building, either in new construction or an older building that has perhaps gone through various owners and renovations. Designing new interiors for older, historic buildings is challenging; designers must address the historic architectural and aesthetic style(s), construction, and finish materials, and signs of layers of use. Then they must design for new uses and users. Although interior designers rarely have control over the pre-existing conditions of an older building, they must recognize what character-defining features to save, continue, or eliminate in their interventions and rehabilitation.

This essay analyzes recent research, asking: What shapes the interior designer's experience? What internal factors drive the interior designer and how is their outward manifestation (the design of an interior) affected by the designer's experience? Like materials, artifacts, and technology, interior designers are another resource to be applied in the creation of interior environments. How do these human utensils (designers) work and create? This essay presents a psychology-based

The Handbook of Interior Design, First Edition. Edited by Jo Ann Asher Thompson and Nancy H. Blossom.

theoretical model to support contemporary designers working with existing and, in particular, historic buildings.

New Designers in Old Buildings

Historic preservation is the preservation and maintenance of historic structures and sites, particularly those that are over 50 years old (NPS n.d. (b)). Historic preservation can occur in ways that range from the meticulous safeguarding and restoration of a historic home as a house museum to the regular rehabilitation of a downtown storefront for new renters. Maintaining buildings as museums ensures the future of significant historic buildings, such as Mount Vernon and Monticello. However, most historic buildings will remain in use and be repeatedly reused as a vital part of rural and urban communities.

Functioning historic buildings need to be maintained as a result of both human and environmental events that can degrade them over the years. When a historic building is renovated or rehabilitated, its function may change (e.g., when a historic warehouse is converted into loft apartments). These changes from the original function can keep a historic building in use by rehabilitating it, even though such functional changes can present challenges to designers, who must plan how to integrate the new building functions with existing conditions.

Many buildings undergo repeated major rehabilitations, forcing designers to deal with multiple layers of restoration, redesign, and removal of building elements. In the best designs with compatible elements, new functions integrate smoothly with the existing older building. These new designs are not historical replicas, but a recognizable part of the reused building. Significant features are preserved, and new designs are informed by the past, while also retaining the character of their own time and place.

Designers and design educators recognize the need to prepare future designers to work on projects in historic structures. In their review of the state of architectural education, Boyer and Mitgang cited being able to work with existing structures as an important educational goal (Boyer and Mitgang 1996). Historic and older existing buildings are a significant percentage of US building stock. The American Institute of Architects (AIA) estimates that 80% of future design work will take place within the context of a historic building (Futurevisions 2004).

Currently, any significant building constructed before 1960 is considered a historic building (NPS n.d. (b)); less significant buildings are often referred to as older or existing buildings. For the purposes of this discussion, a historic building is one that is over 50 years of age, regardless of its currently recognized level of significance and whether or not it has been placed on the National Register of Historic Places or is located within a historic district.

Historic and older existing buildings do not usually receive special protections unless they are on the register or in a protected district. Despite the buildings' lack of legal protection, a large percentage of professional design work is expected to come from historic/older buildings. Preparing interior designers to work compatibility with these structures will be important to their success in professional practice.

Despite the challenges, the continual preservation of historic buildings is important for many reasons. Historic buildings provide a physical record of a community's history, development, and dynamic change over time. They show an area's evolution and allow residents to connect in the larger community by maintaining a diverse physical environment that illustrates the past visions of many residents (NTHP 2009). Living and working in historic structures allows people to enjoy places that matter to them and that may have mattered to the community for generations (NTHP 2009).

Preservation success stories across the country often begin when a community comes together to protect the continued existence of a shared built environment (NTHP 2009). For example, community support led to the preservation of Cincinnati's historic public schools (Flischel 2001). Community members held fundraisers and public events in support of the city's 19th- and early 20th-century schools. Public action encouraged the school system to stop closing and demolishing its historic schools and led to the reopening of some school buildings.

From a sustainability standpoint, reusing historic structures is better for both the natural and built environments. The maintenance and reuse of historic buildings encourages urban areas to remain within their existing footprint and not to continue sprawling into undeveloped land. This allows communities to slowly develop an integrated residential and commercial infrastructure. New building materials, such as wood, metal, cement, and gypsum, are energy- and resource-intensive to develop. New building construction is wasteful; for example, about 4 pounds of building material enters a landfill for every square foot of new construction (NTHP 2009). By continuing to use existing buildings and only updating the interiors when needed, millions of pounds of construction materials will not be created or enter landfills.

New buildings can be more energy-efficient to maintain, but because so much energy is needed to build them it may be many years before genuine energy savings begins. Keeping existing buildings in use through preservation, maintenance, and rehabilitation provides space for human activities, maintains the vitality of urban neighborhoods, and curbs unchecked growth in undeveloped areas.

Designing new interiors for historic buildings requires interior designers to work with an existing building, just as they do with almost all projects. But with historic buildings there are additional considerations; historic buildings can present unique challenges since they are already part of a community with some longstanding residents who remember past owners and uses. Historic buildings have shared in the social and physical life of a community. These buildings were built with aesthetic principles that may be unfamiliar to contemporary designers and design students. For example, designers of Colonial Revival buildings were deliberately working to create buildings that evoked feelings and images of America's past. In contrast, modern designers created buildings for a new future, opposed to historical associations. Undercurrents of architectural theory and ideology inform past and present design decisions. Inexperienced designers may unknowingly be working with the interiors of buildings with one or more design foundations that are different from their own contemporary experience.

Decades of use, aging, changing owners, and renovations may leave many historic building interiors in need of a new compatible rehabilitation. The challenges of preserving historic buildings and the pressure of popular contemporary architectural design often encourage designers to simply gut interiors. Designers need help, not just with the technical aspects of historic materials, but also with how to design within a historic structure and – through continuity or transformation – use significant design elements of the historic structure in their new designs.

Compatibility

Interior designers create architectural spaces within existing buildings, including new buildings and those that may be undergoing their first or fiftieth renovation or rehabilitation. Interior design professionals are distinguished by their ability to work with existing structures and as part of a larger design team that may include architects, engineers, and tradespersons. Working with historic structures can be a daunting and sometimes confusing task because of the different building systems, the aesthetic preferences of multiple owners and users, and the layers of outdated interior materials and finishes. What should be kept for the next iteration of the building? Should everything be removed, allowing a fresh start? Should spaces be meticulously preserved as they are, with equal treatment given to every design feature and material? How should the building be changed and rehabilitated to serve its new purpose? If the building should be changed, then how does one proceed?

Preservationists, including interior designers who work primarily in historic preservation, struggle with these and other questions (Murtagh 2006; Stipe 2008). In the early decades of preservation efforts, emphasis was placed on meticulous preservation, even re-creation, of historic materials and features (Murtagh 2006; Stipe 2008). While prominent public buildings and sites, such as Mount Vernon and Colonial Williamsburg, benefited from being fixed in time and place, there are thousands of buildings that need to remain in use to serve their owners and communities. These buildings need regular maintenance and appropriate alterations to remain functional and relevant for contemporary uses and standards. For buildings that are both historic and actively used structures, preservationists depend on a guiding design goal of "compatibility" (NPS n.d. (a)).

Compatibility seeks to combine and recognize the importance of the old and new physical architectural features of a building. Compatibility allows alterations and additions to be made to a building while guiding designers and owners to preserve the most significant, noteworthy, elements of the historic features. For example, after the restoration of historic Anderson Hall on the University of Florida campus, classrooms were stocked with new furniture and lighting, against a backdrop of original wood paneling. New lighting was comparable with historic lighting in size, scale, and material finishes, but it was distinctly new in appearance and functionality. New furniture was typical of other campus classrooms, allowing the uniqueness of the historic paneling to stand out. Significant spaces, such as the entrance, were preserved and fully integrated into the new design and function.

This combination of old and new into a contemporary, functional design is the focus of this essay. The essay examines the challenges designers encounter when designing rehabilitations for existing historic structures and explores how developing an emotional connection with their project site may help them understand the structures' unique elements. Understanding may then lead to the creation of new interiors that reflect the best of the past and the present.

Defining compatibility through preservation literature

Communities across the country have developed preservation literature, primarily in the form of historic district design guidelines, to aid owners and designers who are modifying existing structures or building new ones in or near historic buildings. When a designer is working in a recognized historic area, historic district design guidelines are the primary tool available to develop new designs. Most guidelines are based on a set of federal standards and enhanced to address the area's context (NPS n.d. (a)).

Within both the federal standards and local district guidelines, compatibility is the overarching design goal. Compatibility is primarily presented as a designed, architectural response to the physical parameters of a building's character-defining features. Character-defining features are the physical and/or architectural features that distinguish a building, or give it character (NPS n.d. (a); Jandl 1988; Nelson n.d.). For example, the roofline, interior paneling, and fireplace or a particular sequence of interior spatial layouts with traditional proportions could all be character-defining features on one building, but less significant in another building.

Distinguishing a building's character-defining features is part of the task of designing in an older building. The *Secretary of the Interior's Standards for Rehabilitation* and the National Park Service's preservation briefs series provide general guidelines to owners and designers in the identification of character-defining from less significant features (Jandl 1988; Nelson n.d.; NPS n.d. (b)) These sources provide general knowledge, but since each historic building and project site is unique, applying general information may be daunting.

Once owners and designers have a specific project site, identifying the specific context and design elements can help them develop locally compatible designs. Local guidelines may be important tools for designers working in historic districts. If a project building or new construction infill site is located in a historic district, there should be a local set of guidelines for the historic district. A historic district is an area of land protected at either the local, state, or federal level (NPS n.d. (b)). Historic districts can range in size and composition from a fairly unified college campus to a sprawling rural community. Some historic districts have buildings constructed over several decades or centuries; others contain only buildings constructed within a shorter time span.

In most historic districts, the exterior of existing and new construction is protected and changes must be approved, usually by a local Historic District Commission or Board. The lack of current legal protection for historic interiors does not negate their significance; it is a reflection of the extent of US private ownership rights. Historic districts on university campuses are currently leading the way toward protection of interiors and including interiors in their historic district guidelines (see John Muir College 2008; Darbee, Rechie, Rickey, Williams, and Loveridge 2009 [Miami University]; Tate, Dixon, et al. 2007 [University of Florida]).

In this research the contents of over 30 historic district guidelines were examined to inform the discussion. Previously, the author of this essay helped write guidelines through a Getty Campus Heritage Grant for the historic University of Florida campus (Tate, Dixon, et al. 2007) as part of a fieldwork experience in the City of Gary, led by Professor Roy Graham in 2005. As part of those projects and this study, an examination of the content of historic district guidelines was done to assess how that content might relate to and guide the creation of compatible interiors and be used to assess the compatibility of design solutions. Figure 23.1 illustrates ways in which knowing the content of historic district guidelines may help interior designers and students create more compatible interiors.

Like interiors in most historic buildings, historic structures that are not recognized individually or as part of a historic district currently receive no formal protection. However, both information and methods developed to design compatibility for protected buildings could be used to design for unprotected ones as well. This essay expands the boundaries of current preservation practice by emphasizing compatible new designs inside historic buildings, regardless of their protected status. Interiors are a vital part of buildings' architecture and users' experiences in the built environment (Malnar and Vodvarka 1992). By expanding the standards of compat-

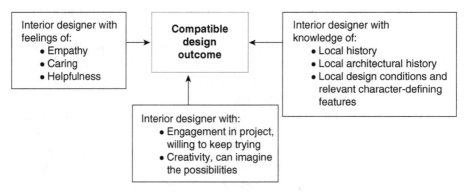

Figure 23.1 Conceptual framework illustrating how designers may create relatively more compatible design outcomes.

ible design to include interiors, people can gain a holistic and pleasurable experience as they move through a refurbished building.

Local historic district guidelines can be particularly helpful because such guidelines provide specific detail about recognized features and techniques for working compatibility in a district. Many historic district guidelines for rehabilitation, alterations, and new construction share a similar content structure that requires the designer to investigate the district's social history, identify its major architectural styles, and also analyze its most significant architectural elements. The history section should include information about noteworthy individuals, the community's growth, and shared social history, that is, the human story (for examples, see City of Bolivar n.d.; Tampa Architectural Review Commission 2002 [Hyde Park]).

For example, the Ybor City historic district guidelines include both pictures and the history of the community's historic clubs (City of Tampa 2010). In the early 20th century, major immigrant groups, including Italians, Sicilians, and Greeks, each ran a social club; membership included invitations to social events, free access to a staff doctor, life insurance, and mortuary services. Clubs vied with each other to create grand, ornate buildings. These historic district guidelines help readers appreciate the grandiose architecture of club buildings as a combination of influences from popular American and home-country styles, and a significant statement of social cohesion and group success in the New World.

The stories and histories told in historic district guidelines do more than provide information; these stories also help owners and designers connect with the district and their project site. Historical narratives help explain the significance of the district; that is to say, why the place matters (Allison and Allison 2008; Dohr and Portillo 2011; NTHP 2011).

Caring about historic buildings and working to preserve places that matter have been significant elements in many successful preservation stories. For example, the ongoing Place Matters program in New York City allowed locals to nominate the historic places that they care about (Place Matters 2007). This process has led to a broader understanding of the significance of New York City's history and added new historic literature and protection for some nominated structures (Allison and Allison 2008).

By learning local history, interior designers and students may better connect with their project site and see it as a real place with significance before and after they complete their project. These insights lead designers to greater engagement with their work and feelings of empathy, caring, and helpfulness for the historic project building (Frantz, Mayer, Norton, and Rock 2005). (See Figure 23.1 for a list of ways in which engagement with a project helps create compatible interiors.)

Section 2 of many historic district guidelines discusses prevalent architectural styles and may include labeled drawings of a typical building in each major style. Labeled drawings or photographs call out significant features of each style, as expressed in the historic district, and demonstrate how to discuss the style (for an example, see City of Portland Bureau of Planning 2008 [Skidmore and Old Town Historic Districts]).

The concept of architectural styles has come under criticism within the preservation community in recent years because identifying buildings by style may over-simplify the complex and varied history of architectural aesthetics (Longstreth 1999). However, style sections and their terminology can be helpful to teach design students and practitioners the importance of a major architectural style and its evolution in the context of the historic district (Blakemore 2005; Blumenson 1990).

In their text on those qualities and experiences that most impact the design process and interior environment, Dohr and Portillo noted that place identity, including the qualities that give a building a sense of place, was significant for imparting meaning and engaging users and designers (Dohr and Portillo 2011). Significant local architectural features contribute to sense of place and provide cues to identify the local place. For example, decorative iron balcony railings immediately conjure up images of New Orleans' French Quarter, while wooden shot-gun houses with carpenter Gothic detailing suggest New Orleans' Ninth Ward. In these examples, altering the significant architectural features changes place identity, history, and a host of connected meanings. Interior designers working in a historic context need to know and understand the character-defining features of the local district. Then designers can create new interiors that respond to significant existing features to maintain and develop an ongoing place identity.

Section 3 of most historic district design guidelines includes sketch drawings demonstrating specific design elements and showing both compatible and incom-patible new design features. The exact features illustrated vary by historic district, but typical examples include: scale, massing, fenestration, roofs, entrances, and materials (see the National Alliance of Preservation Commissions' [n.d.] *Online Design Guidelines* for access to multiple examples). Although the design elements and principles in Section 3 are primarily applied to a building's exterior, they have the potential to expand into building interiors (Ching 2007).

Compatibility and creativity

As an interior design educator, I frequently hear students express their concern that historic preservation projects limit their original input and creative expression. Students say they don't want to copy something old, but feel that they must to respect the historic building. Copying historic features and retaining the original principles seem like the safest solutions. Feeling that creativity and compatibility are at odds with one another may also be evident among experienced designers and design instructors.

This apparent dichotomy between compatibility and creativity shows a lack of understanding of compatibility and creativity. A creative design solution is one that is novel and appropriate (Hennessey and Amabile 1988). Preserving elements of a historic building is appropriate, but how historic elements are transformed into a new design allows opportunity for novelty, in addition to the creativity needed to create a contemporary interior. Successful compatible designs require a designer's full creativity and skills to see and develop the potential of what is already in place and imagine new ways to use that potential. See Figure 23.1 for a framework that illustrates some of the elements necessary for being engaged and working creatively on a historic building project.

Compatible designing has the potential to push interior designers to their creative boundaries. In a monograph on creativity for teachers, Hennessey and Amabile explain that in addition to interest and motivation, creativity needs domain knowledge and the recognition of constraints and opportunities to develop and grow (Hennessey and Amabile 1987). The challenges of acquiring the technical knowledge needed to design compatibility for historic buildings can provide designers with the extra momentum they need to strengthen their creative design skills.

Too few criteria or constraints for a project can result in limited challenges, challenges which could push creativity further. By designing compatibility, design options are constrained, but not eliminated. Indeed, significant spaces and features should be enhanced as designers explore molding and harmonizing their design in partnership with the historic building. These types of explorations could push designers to fresh, creative constructions (Carmel-Gilfinen and Portillo 2010; Hennessey and Amabile 1987; Nakamura and Csikszentmihalyi 2009).

In their research on flow, defined as "an enjoyable psychological state of harmonious creative working," Nakamura and Csikszentmihalyi state that to enter flow a person must be challenged to stretch their existing skills. Compatibility and creative design solutions go together. The struggle to design compatibility forms the challenge that stretches a designer's skills and pushes him or her forward to find creative solutions (Nakamura and Csikszentmihalyi 2009).

Creativity is significant because working creatively and experiencing flow are enjoyable processes that engage the creator. Engaged designers may be less likely to settle for their first solution. They will return to their project and continue developing their solution; ultimately, this may lead to a more compatible design outcome. Creative, compatible designs can preserve the best of the past, provide a harmonious experience for users, and showcase the best in contemporary design.

Sense of Connectedness

Working with the historic built environment requires engagement in the design project and knowledge of the history and architectural features of the site. Knowledge alone, however, might not be enough to engage designers in the process of creating compatible designs. Designers' ability and desire to create compatible designs may be improved by a feeling of connection to the historic built environment. An emotional sense of connection may inspire local stakeholders to want to preserve their historic structures (Dohr and Portillo 2011; Place Matters 2007). If designers share in a sense of connection, the designer may be able to combine design skills and site knowledge with an empathic sensitivity to create a compatible design.

Through research into a historic project site, designers may learn that they can work with a historic building to create a compatible design that reflects the best of today and the past. By learning about and analyzing their project building before developing a design, designers may be able to recognize the building's significant qualities and visualize opportunities to integrate both new and existing features into a compatible whole.

If designers can imagine ways they can work with the existing building, connect their new designs to it through appropriate transitions, and emphasize the best features of the old and new, they will have succeeded in creating a compatible design. While much of the design will be informed by their knowledge and ability, the potential importance of creating an emotional connection between the historic building and designer is underscored in recent research in environmental psychology.

Frantz, Mayer, Norton, and Rock researched feelings of connectedness to nature and pro-environmental impulses. For example, participants with a higher sense of connection recycled, donated to environmental charities, and voted for pro-environmental measures (Frantz et al. 2005). Frantz's work begins with an extensive review of psychological literature findings in which one person's feeling of connectedness to another person was shown to increase empathy, caring, and helpfulness. Simply stated, we help those we feel a connection to. Frantz asked if this impulse to help where we feel connected could be extended from a person-to-person connection to one of person-to-environment (Frantz et al. 2005). Through multiple studies it was revealed that people who feel connected to nature, a "we-ness", also show more pro-environmental impulses. Those who do not feel a connection to nature exhibited significantly lower pro-environmental impulses; those with the lowest feeling of connection were anti-environment.

The logical conclusion from this research is that if designers can make historic buildings part of their "we-ness", then buildings will benefit. Through their work, designers have the potential to help or damage historic buildings. However, Frantz's research raises the nagging question: "What happens when designers are not connected?" Figure 23.2 illustrates how sense of connection may contribute to compatible design outcomes.

Measuring a sense of connectedness

Mayer and Frantz (2004, 2009) introduced their "Connectedness-to-Nature" scale (CNS) as a measure of individuals' feelings of connectedness and community with nature (Frantz et al. 2005). In their study, they tested their 14-question instrument on large classes of students and members of the community. The CNS was administered as part of a larger study to examine the positive relationship between finding time in nature beneficial and a high CNS score. The test has since been used in several other studies.

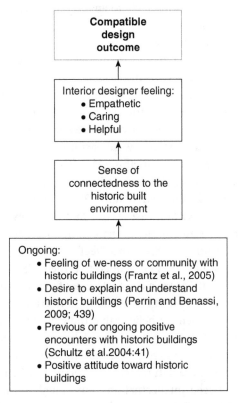

Figure 23.2 Conceptual framework illustrating how the study's compatibility and sense of connectedness theory combine to support relatively strong compatible design outcomes.

Frantz used the scale to examine the connection between nature and a feeling of community or "we-ness." They found that individuals who can feel a larger connection to nature can also feel a greater connection to the larger community and are less individualistic. This is significant because individuals who feel a connection are more capable of making decisions during difficult environmental dilemmas. Further, these individuals profit from own-group biases toward positive evaluations and greater moral consideration and rights (Devine-Wright and Clayton 2010; Tajfel and Turner 1986).

The results suggest that designers who feel a greater connection to the historic built environment should be better able to make design decisions and consider the historic building more in their decision-making process. This kind of connection could help designers make more sensitive and compatible design decisions in the historic built environment. Nisbet, Zelenski, and Murphy provide further support for the idea that individuals' sense of connection may explain their personal behavior (Nisbet et al. 2009). In their research they found that individuals with a greater sense of connectedness were more likely to engage in pro-environmental behaviors such as recycling, donating, and voting for environmental measures.

Milfont and Duckitt have reviewed several measures of environmental attitudes, beliefs, and/or feelings. Almost every instrument they have reviewed is not applicable to other studies because each instrument tests for multiple factors, usually both general and topical concerns, knowledge, and beliefs (Milfont and Duckitt 2010). Unlike other environmental attitude scales, Mayer and Frantz's CNS is particularly appropriate for future interior design research applications because of its single factor (connectedness) analysis, wide past use, and ability to be transformed to test sense of connectedness to something else (Gosling and Williams 2010).

In 2009, Perrin and Benassi published a critical review of the CNS measure based on their five-part study (Perrin and Benassi 2009). They agree with Mayer and Frantz's assessment that the CNS measures one factor; however, Perrin and Benassi argue that the factor is less an emotional than an intellectual connection to nature. Their analysis is based on how the word "feel" is used in the scale and cross-examined with similar scales. They concluded that the CNS "is not a measure of an emotional connection," but "it taps a connectedness to nature dimension" and "provides a measure of people's beliefs about their connection to nature" (Perrin and Benassi 2009). Perrin and Benassi believe that the CNS may tap a more cognitive, rather than emotional, interest in nature, and elaborate on their analysis by saying it is a useful tool because "an interest in nature motivates a desire to explain and understand phenomena in the natural world" (Perrin and Benassi 2009).

The relationship between intellectual and emotional connections is still being understood in this context. Returning to the historic built environment, it is suggested here that "a desire to explain and understand" the historic built environment could be an excellent first step for a designer trying to develop a compatible design for a historic building. It is suggested that a type of Connectedness-to-Nature scale could be adapted for historic buildings using Frantz's CNS as a guide. Such an adaptation of Frantz's CNS can be seen in Gosling and Williams' test of connectedness among farmers to their farms, and demonstrates how to modify the context of the CNS instrument while maintaining it as a reliable measure of connectedness (Gosling and Williams 2010).

In their adaptation of the CNS instrument, Gosling and Williams found that farmers who felt a greater sense of connectedness with their farms managed native vegetation differently than those who did not. This finding and Gosling and Williams' literature review further suggest that connectedness and CNS instruments may be correlated to behavior as well as feelings – all of which are important elements of an interior designer's mental engagement with a historic project.

Significance of a sense of connectedness

The literature indicates that current history-teaching practices may not foster a feeling of connection to the historic built environment. Beecher found that history textbooks and class lectures feature a collection of the "unique and elaborate" (Beecher 1998), and Lichtman similarly found that the masterpiece canon focused on exceptional pieces, and textbooks presented each masterpiece as something unique, unrelated to most people's lives either then or now (Lichtman 2009). The masterpiece canon is criticized because it focuses on the products of Caucasian, Euro-American culture; however, unfortunately most attempts to remedy this situation only add examples of the unique and elaborate from other cultures or female designers (Brandt 1998).

Lichtman's research offers a review of several textbooks that discuss furniture and/or objects created by female designers and non-Western cultures in their introduction. Her findings revealed that these books contained only a few new examples and continued to emphasize the exceptional nature of all pieces. In Brandt's case study of an interior design history class it is postulated that the masterpiece canon of Caucasian, male, Euro-American designers and artifacts is increasingly irrelevant to diverse classes of minority and female students (Brandt 1998). To counter this, Brandt introduces designs from diverse sources that highlight different cultures and designers, and presents each site within a set of themes, rather than in chronological order.

In a review of Lichtman's work, Dilnot explains why developing a more diverse collection of masterpieces will not solve the essential problems with this teaching methodology. Underlying the masterpiece collection is the implicit idea of the "other," and it is this separateness that keeps students from finding relevancy in masterpieces, regardless of the culture or creator (Dilnot 2009). Beginning with two essays, Dilnot has called for faculty to explore teaching methods and content that encourage students to see themselves in history and see historical designs as a source of inspiration, rather than memorization (Dilnot 1984a, 1984b). This philosophy is particularly relevant for historic preservation practice: a designer who feels a connection to historic buildings and history will be more inclined to design for historic structures with empathy.

According to the literature, a feeling of empathy may be significant to the design process. While reviewing designers' experiences working with clients, Dohr and Portillo state that "design thinking and the experience of interiors are remembered well where empathy is in force" (Dohr and Portillo 2011). Designers feeling empathetic can holistically work with and respond to their clients' needs; they also remember the project well, and can learn from it (Dohr and Portillo 2011). An emotional connection, including the feeling of empathy, is the extra puzzle piece that helps a project come alive for a designer and affects their design processes over time.

One way to increase connectedness to historic buildings for interior designers and interior design students is by involving them in an historic building project. In a review of environmental research on increasing connectedness to nature, Schultz found that "a considerable amount of environmental research has demonstrated the transforming ability of encounters with nature" and calls for educational activities that will promote a sense of connectedness (Schultz, Schriver, Tabanico, and Khazian

2004). By having a design encounter with historic buildings in a university design studio or through continuing education courses, designers may be positively transformed, thereby increasing their sense of connectedness to the historic built environment and more apt to create compatible design outcomes.

It is suggested that future research could be done that would enhance teaching and learning strategies by building upon Frantz's research and the importance of a feeling of connectedness and "we-ness" – particularly if modified to address a historic built environment model. Further, just as with Frantz's call for researchers to develop strategies to help people increase their feeling of connectedness to the environment, such a call could be made in regard to historic buildings. Current research suggests that as people learn more about the environment and become more comfortable with it, they may increase their feeling of connectedness; however, further research is needed to confirm these suggestions and develop strategies to increase that feeling (Frantz et al. 2005).

The literature shows that the development of a positive attitude is important for pro-environmental behavior. Hinds and Sparks found the strength of an individual's emotional connection with nature to be a strong predictor of environmental engagement, such as spending time outside and supporting environmentalist causes (Hinds and Sparks 2008). Costarelli and Colloca found attitudinal ambivalence to be one of the strongest predictors of behavioral intentions (Costarelli and Colloca 2004). In other words, unless individuals care, they will not assert themselves in a positive manner. In a related study Whitmarsh found that people who were genuinely concerned with the environment made seemingly pro-environmental life changes (Whitmarsh 2009). However, ignorance of how their actions contribute to global warming led study participants to make life changes with no real beneficial impact on the environment. This finding underscores the need to increase caring and knowledge.

If individuals and designers lack the technical knowledge to truly help, it is not likely that their "best guesses" will have a positive impact. Similarly, Brent, Eubank, Danley, and Graham found that the empathy and desire to help persons with disabilities greatly increased among the interior design students and professionals who participated in their ADA workshop; however, participants' technical knowledge only increased by 25% after completing the program (Brent et al. 1993). (Follow-up examinations were not conducted to see how time, and practice, affected participants' knowledge.)

Without more technical knowledge, designers may care about universal design; however, their design decisions will lack the best-practice information that would have allowed them to use their professional capacity to make a positive difference for others. For this reason, one of the main points of this essay is to underscore the significance of caring and learning in relation to the design of historic buildings. It is suggested that through university and continuing education courses designers could become more informed about the relevancy of historic buildings to their design practice and help them develop a connection to the historic built environment.

Frantz's psychological literature review of studies that increased empathy and connectedness between people suggests several sources for inspiration: changing perspectives, stories of personal distress, group identification, finding similarities, and a sense of interdependence. Multiple studies support the effectiveness of each factor to increase connections between people. For example, Story and Forsyth also used person-to-person psychology in an environmental application where they framed environmental engagement with a local watershed as helping behavior (Story and Forsyth 2008).

Psychological factors that increase helping, caring, and empathy could inspire assignments in interior design courses. Many could be integrated within a master-pieces and/or chronological history survey or continuing education course. For example, within a history course, students could change their perspective and write the story of a building's history from its point of view, what it has seen and experienced, or the point of view of its original designers, who saw it when it was new. Through this exercise, students could discover that what they first may have viewed as a dilapidated old dump is instead a building that has a rich history and was loved and created by real people.

Many masterpieces as well as vernacular structures have stories of distress. Some survived bombing in the world wars (European cathedrals), some were used to store explosives and then bombed (the Parthenon), and others experienced vandalism after regime or religious changes (English cathedrals, Afghan Buddhist shrines, Versailles, Incan cities). If history instructors share vivid stories, or designers learn through their own investigation about a building's personal stories, they may become sympathetic and gain personal knowledge of history. In studio projects, design students could learn these stories about their project building, giving them a chance to learn local history while they practice creating a compatible new interior design.

Human and environmental psychological research has identified factors that may increase feelings of empathy, connectedness, and helpfulness. Using this research, interior design faculty could design assignments and present course material to help students develop a sense of connectedness. With a sense of connectedness, students may find relevancy in their learning and practice, connecting their content learning to their studio practice. In turn, students who feel a connection to the historic built environment should be more inclined to work compatibly with it in studio and professional practice.

Compatibility through Connectedness Framework: Unifying the Literature

Historic preservation practice relies on individuals who care about the historic places in their community (Allison and Allison 2008; Dohr and Portillo 2011; NTHP 2011; Place Matters 2007). For decades, preservation, including adaptive reuse of historic structures, has occurred because individuals cared. They wanted to save their historic buildings and help them to remain as active parts of the built community. If an interior designer possesses the same feelings that motivate locals to preserve, their design solutions may show caring and empathy toward the historic building and therefore be more compatible with it.

In this essay, literature was discussed that helps to build a framework for how compatible interior design solutions may be created. As shown in Figure 23.3, the design goal (a compatible design solution) is created by an interior designer with (1) feelings of empathy, caring, and helpfulness and (2) knowledge of the local history and architectural conditions.

In addition to these two components, the designer also needs to be engaged in the design process, with a willingness to keep trying new ideas and to work creatively. An examination of the preservation literature, including texts on how to preserve through architecture and community engagement, revealed the presence of these three qualities – feelings, knowledge, and design process engagement.

If compatibility is a design goal for historic structures, along with the three qualities of feelings, knowledge, and design process engagement, how are these qualities encouraged? Can they be developed? To address these questions, an examination of the relationship between feelings and engagement was undertaken.

According to the literature, feelings of empathy, caring, and helpfulness strengthen people's connections between each other. Feeling empathetic can also improve a designer's ability to work with a client and learn from their design process (Dohr and Portillo 2011). The literature also supports the conclusion that when empathy, caring, and helpfulness exist together a sense of connection is established. This phenomenon is shown as applied to historic structures in Figure 23.3.

These qualities – a feeling of community, desire to understand and explain, positive encounters, and a positive attitude toward historic buildings – may take longer than one project or course to develop; however, practice and learning can form the foundation for interior designers' burgeoning sense of connectedness.

If these ideas are applied to the historic built environment, designers with a positive emotional connection with historic buildings may spend more time discovering the positive aspects of their historic project building and developing designs to showcase its potential. Both the natural and built environments need active, positive individuals to manage their preservation and future. Having practitioners who care and are passionate about working on historic buildings will result in more compatible designs and more satisfied users and clients. Ongoing education and design practice experiences will also increase the opportunities interior designers need to reconnect with the historic built environment.

Key Terms

The following terms have been provided in an effort to help clarify the discussion and arguments presented in this essay:

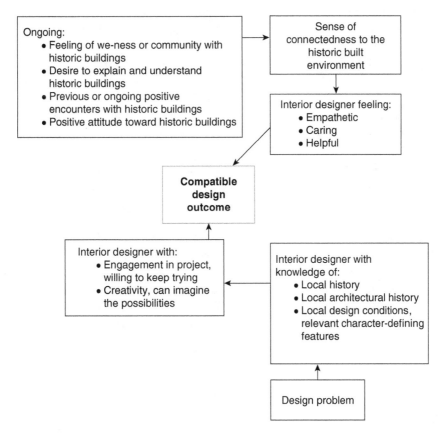

Figure 23.3   Conceptual framework illustrating how the study's compatibility, learning theory, and sense of connectedness combine to support more compatible design outcomes.

Character-defining spatial features   The physical features of a building or site that are important to its architectural significance. Example features include roof type, fenestration, ornamentation, materials, or spatial layout. Features can be physical, such as roofing material, or spatial, such as the size and proportions of an auditorium. "Rehabilitation standards focus attention on the preservation of those materials, features, finishes, spaces, and spatial relationships that, together, give a property its historic character" (NPS n.d. (a)).

Compatibility   A significant criterion for new construction and rehabilitation in historic buildings and districts. The Secretary of the Interior's *Standards* do not define compatibility; most local guidelines do not either. The researcher uncovered only two guidelines that directly address the word compatibility. The City of Bolivar historic district guidelines explain compatibility as when a feature is "similar in character to existing or known historic examples" (City of Bolivar n.d.: 2). The University of Florida guidelines explain that compatibility is "based not on individual preferences but on accepted principles of design. These include scale, proportion, massing, materials, color and value, texture, geometric form, and context. Further, understanding of the extant language of detail and form is key to compatibility" (Tate, Dixon, et al. 2007).

Compatibility is *not* recreating or mimicking a historic or faux-historic interior. Compatibility is the combination of a contemporary interior with the best elements of the historic building. Both historic and contemporary elements are distinct halves of one design. Contemporary interior elements exist in their own right while showcasing the best, most significant, elements of the historic building.

Connectedness   An emotional construct explaining a person's feeling of inclusion, we-ness, or connection with other. This term is most often used to explain interpersonal feelings; however, recent research discussed above is exploring how it can be expanded to environments.

Historic building   The US Secretary of the Interior's *Standards* (NPS n.d. (b)) uses the 50-year mark as a guideline to help define significant historic buildings. For the purposes of this study, a historic building refers to any existing building 50 years old or older, regardless of its currently recognized significance. Today, buildings built in the 1960s will qualify as historic structures. Soon, buildings from the 1970s, 1980s, and so on will become historic structures.

References

Allison, E. W. and Allison, M. A. 2008. "Preserving tangible cultural assets: a framework for a new dialog in preservation," *Preservation Education and Research* 1: 29–40.

Beecher, M. A. 1998. "Toward a critical approach to the history of interiors," *Journal of Interior Design* 24(2): 4–11.

Blakemore, R. 2005. *History of Interior Design and Furniture: From Ancient Egypt to Nineteenth-Century Europe* (2nd ed.). Hoboken, NJ: Wiley.

Blumenson, J. 1990. *Identifying American Architecture: A Pictorial Guide to Styles and Terms, 1600–1945* (rev. ed.). New York: W. W. Norton.

Boyer, E. and Mitgang, L. 1996. *Building Community: A New Future for Architecture Education and Practice*. Princeton: Carnegie Foundation for the Advancement of Teaching.

Brandt, B. K. 1998. "A thematic approach to teaching design history in a multicultural setting," *Journal of Interior Design* 24(2): 17–24.

Brent, R., Eubank, W., Danley, M., and Graham, C. 1993. "Hands-on approach to the Americans with Disabilities Act," *Journal of Interior Design* 19(1): 47–50.

Carmel-Gilfinen, C. and Portillo, M. 2010. "Creating mature thinkers in interior design: pathways of intellectual development," *Journal of Interior Design* 35(3): 1–20.

Ching, F. 2007. *Architecture: Form, Space, Order*. Hoboken, NJ: Wiley.

City of Bolivar. n.d. *Historic District Standards and Guidelines*. http://www.cityofbolivar.com/HistoricDistrictStandards&Guidelines[1].pdf. *Accessed May 8, 2014.*

City of Portland Bureau of Planning. 2008. *Skidmore/Old Town Historic District Design Guidelines*. http://www.portlandonline.com/bps/index.cfm?a=213931&c=48640. Accessed May 8, 2014.

City of Tampa. 2010. *Ybor City Historic District Design Guidelines and District Map.* http://www.tampagov.net/dept_Historic_Preservation/information_resources/Design _Guidelines/Ybor_Design_Guidelines.asp. Accessed May 20, 2014.

Costarelli, S. and Colloca, P. 2004. "The effects of attitudinal ambivalence on pro-environmental behavioral intentions," *Journal of Environmental Psychology* 24: 279–288.

Darbee, J., Rechie, N., Rickey, B., Williams, J., and Loversidge, Jr, R. 2009. *Miami University Campus Heritage Plan.* https://oneness.scup.org/asset/53664/Miami_U_Campus _Heritage_Plan.pdf.Accessed July 11, 2011.

Devine-Wright, P. and Clayton, S. 2010. "Introduction to the special issue: place, identity and environmental behavior," *Journal of Environmental Psychology* 30: 267–270.

Dilnot, C. 1984a. "The state of design history. Part I: mapping the field," *Design Issues* 1(1): 4–23.

Dilnot, C. 1984b. "The state of design history. Part II: problems and possibilities," *Design Issues* 1(2): 3–20.

Dilnot, C. 2009. "Some futures for design history?", *Journal of Design History* 22(4): 377–394.

Dohr, J. and Portillo, M. 2011. *Design Thinking for Interiors: Inquiry, Experience, Impact.* Hoboken, NJ: Wiley.

Flischel, R., ed. 2001. *An Expression of the Community: Cincinnati Public Schools Legacy of Art and Architecture.* Cincinnati, OH: Art League Press.

Frantz, C., Mayer, F. S., Norton, C., and Rock, M. 2005. "There is no 'I' in nature: the influence of self-awareness on connectedness to nature," *Journal of Environmental Psychology* 25: 427–436.

Futurevisions. 2004. *2000 Symposium: Historic Preservation and Architecture Education: A Dialogue.* American Institute of Architects: Washington DC. http://www.aia.org/ practicing/groups/kc/AIAS076343. Accessed May 20, 2014.

Gosling, E. and Williams, J. H. 2010. "Connectedness to nature, place attachment and conservation behavior: testing connectedness theory among farmers," *Journal of Environmental Psychology* 30: 298–304.

Hennessey, B. and Amabile, T. 1987. *Creativity and Learning: What Research Says to the Teacher.* Washington DC: NEA Professional Library.

Hennessey, B. A. and Amabile, T. M. 1988. "Story-telling: a method for assessing children's creativity," *Journal of Creative Behavior* 22: 235–246.

Hinds, J. and Sparks, P. 2008. "Engaging with the natural environment: the role of affective connection and identity," *Journal of Environmental Psychology* 28: 109–120.

Jandl, H. W. 1988 *Preservation Brief 18: Rehabilitating Interiors in Historic Buildings, Identifying and Preserving Character-Defining Elements.* Washington DC: US Government Printing Office.

John Muir College. 2008. *Historic Resources Inventory and Preservation Plan.* http:// muir.ucsd.edu/_files/about/MCPP_Preservation.pdf. Accessed May 20, 2014.

Lichtman, S. 2009. "Reconsidering the history of design survey," *Journal of Design History* 22(4): 341–350.

Longstreth, R. 1999. "Architectural history and the practice of preservation in the United States," *Journal of the Society of Architectural Historians* 58(3): 326–333.

Malnar, J. M. and Vodvarka, F. 1992. *The Interior Dimension: A Theoretical Approach to Enclosed Space.* New York: Van Nostrand Reinhold.

Mayer, F. S. and Frantz, C. M. P. 2004. "The connectedness to nature scale: a measure of individuals' feelings in community with nature," *Journal of Environmental Psychology* 24(4): 503–515.

Mayer, F. S. and Frantz, C. M. P. 2009. "Why is nature beneficial? The role of connectedness to nature." *Environment and Behavior* 41(5): 607–643.

Milfont, T. L. and Duckitt, J. 2010. "The environmental attitudes inventory: a valid and reliable measure to assess the structure of environmental attitudes," *Journal of Environmental Psychology* 30: 80–94.

Murtagh, W. 2006. *Keeping Time: The History and Theory of Preservation in America* (3rd ed.). Hoboken, NJ: Wiley.

Nakamura, J. and Csikszentmihalyi, M. 2009. "Flow theory and research," in C. R. Snyder and S. J. Lopez (eds.), *Oxford Handbook of Positive Psychology*. New York: Oxford University Press, pp. 195–206.

NAPC (National Alliance of Preservation Commissions). n.d. *Online Design Guidelines.* http://www.uga.edu/napc/programs/napc/guidelines.htm. Accessed July 11, 2011.

NCIDQ (National Council for Interior Design Qualification). 2009. *NCIDQ Exam Eligibility Requirements.* http://www.ncidq.org/Exam/EligibilityRequirements.aspx. Accessed May 20, 2014.

Nelson, L. H. n.d. *Preservation Brief 17. Architectural Character: Identifying the Visual Aspects of Historic Buildings as an Aid to Preserving their Character.* Washington DC: US Government Printing Office.

Nisbet, E. K., Zelenski, J. M., and Murphy, S. A. 2009. "The Nature Relatedness Scale: linking individuals' connection with nature to environmental concern and behavior," *Environment and Behavior* 41: 715–740.

NPS (National Park Service). n.d. (a). *Introduction: Choosing an Appropriate Treatment for a Historic Building.* http://www.nps.gov/history/hps/tps/standguide/overview/choose_treat.htm. Accessed May 7, 2014.

NPS (National Park Service). n.d. (b). *The Secretary of the Interior's Standards for the Treatment of Historic Properties.* http://www.nps.gov/history/hps/tps/standguide/. Accessed October 4, 2010.

NTHP (National Trust for Historic Preservation). 2009. *Issues.* http://www.preservationnation.org/. Accessed October 20, 2009.

NTHP (National Trust for Historic Preservation). 2011. *This Place Matters.* http://www.preservationnation.org/take-action/this-place-matters/. Accessed May 7, 2014.

Perrin, J. L. and Benassi, V. A. 2009. "The connectedness to nature scale: a measure of emotional connection to nature?", *Journal of Environmental Psychology* 29: 434–440.

Place Matters. 2007. *Place Matters.* http://www.placematters.net/. Accessed May 7, 2014.

Schultz, P. W., Schriver, C., Tabanico, J. J., and Khazian, A. M. 2004. "Implicit connections with nature," *Journal of Environmental Psychology* 24: 31–42.

Stipe, R. 2008. *A Richer Heritage: Historic Preservation in the Twenty-First Century.* Chapel Hill, NC: University of North Carolina Press.

Story, P. A. and Forsyth, D. R. 2008. "Watershed conservation and preservation: environmental engagement as helping behavior," *Journal of Environmental Psychology* 28: 305–317.

Tajfel, H. and Turner, J. C. 1986. "The social identity theory of intergroup behavior," *Psychology of Inter-Group Relations* 7–24.

Tampa Architectural Review Commission. 2002. *Hyde Park Design Guidelines: A Guide to Rehabilitation and New Construction in the Hyde Park Historic District*. Tampa Architectural Review Commission: Tampa. http://www.tampagov.net/dept_Historic _Preservation/information_resources/architectural_review_commission/hyde_park _design_guidelines.asp. Accessed March 11, 2010.

Tate, S., Dixon, L., et al. 2007. *The University of Florida Campus Preservation Plan with Guidelines for Rehabilitation and New Construction in the Historic Impact Area*. Gainesville: University of Florida. http://www.ppd.ufl.edu/HistoricCampusWebsite/pdf/ UFPreservationPlan.pdf. Accessed March 11, 2010.

Whitmarsh, L. 2009. "Behavioral responses to climate change: a symmetry of intentions and impacts," *Journal of Environmental Psychology* 29: 13–23.

Section III

Considerations of Education in Interior Design

The Phenomenological Contribution to Interior Design Education and Research: Place, Environmental Embodiment, and Architectural Sustenance

David Seamon

In simplest terms, phenomenology is the description and interpretation of human experience (Finlay 2009; Seamon 2000; van Manen 1990). Its central aim is "always to question the way we experience the world, to want to know the world in which we live as human beings" (van Manen 1990). Phenomenology has potential value for interior design research because it provides one conceptual and methodological means for examining the spatial, environmental, and architectural dimensions of human life. For example, why are places important to people and how does interior design contribute to architectural place-making? What is the experience of at-homeness and dwelling and how do designable qualities play a role in making home life satisfying or awkward? How do aspects of interior space – for instance, corridor layout, spatial dimensions, color, sound, or lived aspects of furnishings – support or stymie particular architectural and place experiences? How do personal, social, and cultural qualities contribute to the lived meanings of interior spaces and places?

In this essay, I review the origins and nature of phenomenology and delineate some of its key philosophical assumptions. I then indicate the relevance of phenomenological research for interior design by focusing on the three themes of "place," "environmental embodiment," and "architectural sustenance." I emphasize that a major value of phenomenological research for interior design is revealing aspects of environmental and place experience that are typically unnoticed so that they might be pondered and made better use of in the design process.

The Handbook of Interior Design, First Edition. Edited by Jo Ann Asher Thompson and Nancy H. Blossom.

Origins of Phenomenology

The principal founder of phenomenology was Edmund Husserl (1859–1938), a German philosopher and mathematician who focused his professional life largely on questions of epistemology. In other words, what is the nature of knowledge and how can one be certain that what he or she knows is trustworthy and real? Husserl worked to establish a discipline and method that would describe how the world is constituted and encountered through conscious acts. Husserl argued that, behind the ever-shifting dynamic of everyday human experience and awareness, there are certain unchanging structures of intellectual consciousness that he claimed a phenomenological method could clarify by setting aside all taken-for-granted notions and preconceptions, whether arising from conventional philosophy, science, or common sense. Husserl viewed consciousness as a pure "region" coming before and grounding the lived realm of human experience; his approach, therefore, came to be known as "transcendental" or "constitutive" phenomenology.

Other phenomenological philosophers argued, however, that Husserl's transcendental structures of consciousness were incomplete conceptually and provided no interpretive place for the wide range of ways in which human beings actually live in, experience, and understand the world in which they find themselves. In his 1927 *Being and Time*, German philosopher Martin Heidegger (1889–1976) suggested that consciousness is not separate from but is interwoven experientially with the world in which human beings find themselves – an existential situation that he termed "being-in-the-world" (Heidegger [1927] 1962).In his 1945 *Phenomenology of Perception*, French phenomenologist Maurice Merleau-Ponty (1908–1961) argued that an integral part of this intimate entwining between people and their worlds is what he called "body-subject"; i.e., the pre-reflective but learned intentionality of the body expressed through action and typically enmeshed in and in sync with the world in which the action unfolds (Merleau-Ponty [1945] 1962; see also Finlay 2006).

This so-called "existential turn" by Heidegger and Merleau-Ponty marked a significant conceptual shift from Husserl's realm of pure intellectual consciousness to the realm of lived situations, experiences, and meanings (Moran 2000). Because Heidegger and Merleau-Ponty emphasized the nature and qualities of human existence in its everyday typicality, their approach came to be known as "existential phenomenology." Generally, this style of phenomenology is more useful for interior design researchers, since a central interest is the human experience of real-world environments, buildings, and interior spaces and their contents (Graumann 2002; Seamon 2000).

From the vantage point of this existential perspective, phenomenology can be defined as the exploration, description, and interpretation of phenomena, which refers to any experiences, situations, or things that human experiencers can experience. Any event, process, living thing, or object that a person can see, hear, touch, taste, smell, sense, know, feel, intuit, think about, undergo, or encounter is a potential focus for phenomenological study. There can be a phenomenology of light, of color, of fabrics, of architecture, of sitting and sitting devices, of home, of journey, of learning, of privacy, of community, of sexuality, of less-abledness, and so forth (Seamon 2000; van Manen 2002). The aim is to describe the phenomenon in its own terms as it is encountered and known through real-world experiences. The aim, however, is not idiosyncratic explication of unique experiences, but the identification and interpretation of underlying, lived patterns and relationships shared by many lived instances of the phenomenon (Finlay 2009).

Phenomenological Assumptions

A first important assumption of phenomenological research is that, to better know ourselves as human beings, we must anchor that knowledge in a conception and terminology that arise from and return to human experience and meaning (van Manen 1990). There is no world "behind" or "beneath" the world of lived experience, and the phenomenologist must be skeptical of any conceptual, ideological, or methodological system that transcribes human life and meaning into some second-hand, reason-based account – for example, scientific studies that reduce the lived complexity of human experience to tangible, measurable units and relationships that are then quantitatively correlated and explained (Moran 2000). Rather, the phenomenological aim is to generate a thorough interpretive description of some aspect of human experience, while never forgetting that lived experience is always more complex and robust than any second-hand description can ever reveal. In short, phenomenological explication is always under way in the sense that human experience is inexhaustible in its lived richness, and any vicarious portrait, phenomenological or otherwise, can never exactly or completely grasp or reproduce the actual experience.

A second important phenomenological assumption is that human experience, action, and awareness are always intentional – in other words, they are always and necessarily directed toward and finding their significance in a world of continually shifting experience, encounter, and meaning (Moran 2000). Human beings are not only aware, but always aware of something, whether a thing, an idea, a feeling, an imagination, a person, an event, or something else. All thinking is thinking about something, just as grasping is grasping something, hearing is hearing something, or imagining is imagining something. All human actions and encounters are directed toward something, which in turn contributes to the particular manner of the directedness.

Intentionality is central to a phenomenological conception of human experience because it means that people are inescapably bonded to and enmeshed in their world, which always appears as ready-made and already there – Heidegger's being-in-the-world. The everyday lived structure through which being-in-the-world expresses itself is termed the "lifeworld" – the day-to-day world of taken-for-grantedness to which, typically, people give no attention because they are caught up in their ordinary, daily pursuits (Moran 2000). In turn, the unquestioned acceptance of the lifeworld is called the "natural attitude" (Moran 2000), and one phenomenological aim for interior design research is to identify and depict the lived dimensions and dynamics of the lifeworld and the natural attitude, which always include environmental, architectural, and spatial aspects.

A Phenomenology of Place

To illustrate more specifically how phenomenology can have value for interior design research, I highlight three relevant topics that have received phenomenological attention: "place," "environmental embodiment," and "architectural sustenance." Research on place, including phenomenological work, has proliferated in the last two decades (Janz 2004; Patterson and Williams 2005), partly because of its gathering, synthesizing quality to hold people and their worlds intimately together (Casey [1993] 2009; Malpas 1999). One of the most revealing starting points for understanding a phenomenological approach to place is to identify a favorite place in one's own experience and to describe it as fully as possible.

For example, Sidebar 24.1 reproduces a place description written by a second-year undergraduate design student in a course I teach at Kansas State University entitled "The Designed Environment and Society." From a phenomenological perspective, this account of a popular St. Louis music club named "Off Broadway" can be understood as one experiential description to be probed for generalizable themes and qualities that mark the underlying, lived structure of the "phenomenon of place." Notice, for example, that the account indicates an intimate relationship between physical and experienced qualities: the spatial density of the club contributes to a sense of camaraderie and vibrancy, just as the lighting, difference in floor levels, closeness of functions, and unique sensuous and performative qualities evoke a singular ambience that "lets you know this place is special." A next step would be to study other favorite-place accounts and locate common themes and patterns that point toward the lived crux of place experience (Manzo 2005).

Sidebar 24.1 Student description of a favorite place: "Off Broadway," St. Louis, Missouri

"Off Broadway"
One of my favorite places is a music venue in St. Louis, Missouri, called "Off Broadway." It's a small bar with a stage and lofted area. You enter a small room that serves for ticketing during concerts. You then make an immediate left and right to arrive in the music room, which consists of a bar area, stage, and

loft in back. You enter this space with the bar to your left and stage to the right. The bar follows the left wall all the way back to a narrow stair leading to the loft, where there are more tables and chairs. "Off Broadway" is a relatively old venue, so there is lots of wood and bricks, with all sorts of photographs, posters, and other memorabilia acquired by management over the years.

The entire space is warm and accepting. Everyone there, even the bands waiting to perform, shares the same space and nothing is more than a few steps away. Participating in the concert crowd or standing idly in back is only a difference of a few feet. If you want a place for conversation or greater privacy, you climb up to the loft, which allows you to get away while still watching the show. If a performer needs another drink, all he or she needs do is look left and say, "bartender, give me another pale ale…"

The most important aspect of this place is its relationship with patrons. As a person who has lived all over the country and known many different types of people, I can say there are few places more interesting than the local music scene on a Saturday night. People come from all over town and from all walks of life to share a mutual appreciation for music. Skinheads, punk rockers, mods, rudeboys, kids, urbanites, and suburbanites all share the floor. The smell of hardwood, sweat, alcohol, and cigarettes; the low light; the people, the tension, and the gigantic framed poster of Johnny Cash giving you the middle finger – all these elements let you know this place is special.

– Eric Wencel

To provide readers with one picture of what a more comprehensive phenomenology of place might be, I highlight phenomenological geographer Edward Relph's *Place and Placelessness*, still perhaps the most accessible phenomenology of place so far written (Relph [1976] 2009). Relph defined place phenomenologically as a fusion of natural and human-made order and a significant center of a person or group's life. He argued that the lived crux of place is the experience of "insideness" – in other words, the more deeply a person or group feels themselves inside an environment, the more so does that environment become, existentially, a place. The deepest experience of place attachment and identity is what Relph termed "existential insideness" – a situation where the person or group feels so much at home and at ease in place that they have no self-conscious recognition of its importance in their lives, unless it changes in some way, for example one's home and neighborhood is destroyed by natural disaster. Relph identified several other modes of place insideness and its lived opposite, "outsideness" – a situation where the person or group feels separate or alienated from place in some way (see Sidebar 24.2).

Sidebar 24.2   Relph's modes of insideness and outsideness

1   Existential Insideness

An experience of place involving deep identification and attachment; one feels thoroughly "at home" in this place but, because of the natural attitude, is typically unaware of the strong sense of belonging. Only when the place changes dramatically in some way (e.g., one's home is destroyed by flood) does one realize a deep sense involvement.

2   Existential Outsideness

An experience of place in which the person feels in some way separate from that place or "out of place." The place may seem oppressive, unreal, or alienating. Examples include homesickness and homelessness.

3   Objective Outsideness

An experience involving an intentional dispassionate attitude of separation from place. The place is objectified in some way – for example, it becomes a thing to be studied and manipulated for practical ends. The typical scientific or planning approach to places and environments.

4   Incidental Outsideness

An experience in which place is little more than a background or mere setting for activities – for example, the landscapes and places that a driver passes through as she commutes from home to work each day.

5   Behavioral Insideness

An experience involving the intentional attending to the appearance of place for some lifeworld end – for example, moving to a new city and learning to get around by giving direct attention to streets, landmarks, and other elements of orientation.

6   Empathetic Insideness

An experience in which a person unfamiliar with place works to be open to that place and encounter and understand it more deeply.

7   Vicarious Insideness

An experience in which the person comes to know place through second-hand encounter. One learns of place through imaginative presentations – for example, through poetry, novels, paintings, or films.

Based on Relph [1976] 2009: 51–55.

Phenomenologically, Relph's conceptual structure of place is useful because the various modes of insideness and outsideness provide a flexible, conceptual means for distinguishing the lived experience of place from its material, environmental qualities (Seamon 2008). These modes provide a way to keep sight of the existential facts that: (1) the same physical place can involve a wide range of differing experiences for different individuals and groups involved with that place; and (2) the same physical place can, over time, involve vastly different place experiences for the same individual or group – for example, a well-loved home that suddenly feels alienating because one's significant other has just died.

Today, phenomenological research on place is wide-ranging (Janz 2004).[1] On one hand, phenomenological philosophers (Casey [1993] 2009; Janz 2009; Malpas 1999; Mugerauer 1994; Stefanovic 2000) have written book-length works demonstrating the foundational significance of place and emplacement for understanding human being-in-the-world. On the other hand, a related body of research focuses on phenomenologies of particular places and their associated place experiences (Janz 2009; Seamon 2000). In regard to phenomenological work on place directly relevant to interior design, one can mention studies of workplaces (Horan 2000), hospitals and healing facilities (Hammer 1999; Moore 2009; Sternberg 2009), learning environments (Foran and Olson 2008; Rothbauer 2009), commercial establishments (Oldenburg 2001; Rosenbaum 2007), performance spaces (Blesser and Salter 2007; Filmer 2006), sacred spaces (Barrie 2010), and homes, domestic interiors, and domestic furnishings (Cloutier-Fisher and Harvey 2009; Cooper Marcus 1995; Percival 2002; Rechavi 2009; Shenk, Kuwahara, and Zablotsky 2004).

For example, Moore examined how hospice day-care patients experienced the hospice as a place in the context of their illness, while Oldenburg explored the community-making value of "third places" – i.e., public establishments like taverns and cafés where people informally gather and socialize (Moore 2009; Oldenburg 2001). Foran and Olson drew on teacher descriptions to understand the places and situations in school environments where students experience more engaging and stimulating learning experiences, while Horan and Moores, in examining the impacts of cyberspace on contemporary society, considered whether physical places and environments still hold significance in human life or might be largely superseded by virtual environments and realities (Foran and Olson 2008; Horan 2000; Moores 2006).

A Phenomenology of Environmental Embodiment

A phenomenology of "environmental embodiment" examines the various lived ways, sensuously and motility-wise, that the body as a pre-reflective intentionality encounters, understands, and synchronizes with the world at hand (Finlay 2006). One important aspect of environmental embodiment is what can be called the "body-as-given" – i.e., the ways that bodily size, structure, and modes of sensuous encounter sustain environmental and place experiences. Casey, for example, examined how bodily qualities contribute to our taken-for-granted sense of direction and orientation, while Pallasmaa, McCann, and Malnar and Vodvarka considered the need to reintroduce a deeply sensuous dimension into environmental design (Casey [1993] 2009; Malnar and Vodvarka 2004; McCann 2005; Pallasmaa 1996, 2009).

A second important aspect of environmental embodiment relates to the "body-as-learned," a lived situation referring to the pre-cognitive intelligence of the body manifested through action and intertwining with the world at hand – what Merleau-Ponty ([1945] 1962) termed "body-subject." Body-subject has significance for interior design because one can point toward its wider-scaled movements, behaviors, and actions extending over time and space (Seamon 1979, 2007). Two such bodily patterns are, first, "body-routines" – sets of integrated gestures, behaviors, and actions that sustain a particular task or aim, for example preparing a meal, driving a car, doing home repairs, and so forth; and, second, "time-space routines" – sets of more or less habitual bodily actions that extend through a considerable portion of time, for example a getting-up routine or a weekday going-to-lunch routine (Seamon 1979).

Because interior designers regularly fashion the spatial and architectural environments in which body- and time-space routines transpire, an understanding of body-subject is important so that there is a smooth, comfortable "fit" between lived body and surroundings. One way, phenomenologically, that one can become better attuned to body-subject is to observe what happens experientially when one attempts simple lifeworld experiments that change everyday taken-for-grantedness in some way – for example, moving a thing that has a place to a new place; or walking to a destination by a route different from what they typically use (Seamon 1979). Another way, phenomenologically to better understand body-subject is using passages from imaginative literature as an interpretive context for recognizing dimensions of body-subject.

For example, a passage from Columbian novelist Gabriel García Márquez's *One Hundred Years of Solitude* describes how a woman named Ursula copes with progressive blindness. Sidebar 24.3 presents interpretations of this passage written by students in my "Designed Environment and Society" class mentioned earlier. Drawing on the phenomenological notions of body-subject and lifeworld, these two interpretations highlight the habitual dimension of Ursula's home life and recognize qualities of body-subject as its lived foundation. In emphasizing the household's quotidian regularity, the two interpretations recognize the lived intimacy of relationship between family members' environmental embodiment and their dwelling. Both students point out how, in Ursula's unusual situation, a seeming disadvantage – being blind – can make one more aware and thus better able to "see."

Sidebar 24.3   Two student interpretations of the passage from Gabriel García Márquez's *One Hundred Years of Solitude*

Student Interpretation 1
This account is about Ursula, who, because of increasing blindness, necessarily becomes conscious of her lifeworld, especially the bodily routines of her home. By making herself aware of the habits and daily patterns of herself and

other family members, she is able to conceal her blindness. Obviously, she is a complete insider in her home; she knows every part of it and is comfortable there. Her bodily awareness is so well developed that she can continue to do what she has always done: her hands already have the knowledge of sewing and locations; her feet know where to go, and her senses of smell and sound have grown sharp (boiling milk, voices), thus everything can be done without eyes directing it.

Her entire family is bound up in their habits and routines – so much so that they rarely deviate from them. It might be said that Ursula makes an unselfconscious phenomenological discovery when she realizes this regularity. In some ways, her discovery gives her an advantage over the others as, for example, when Fernanda loses her ring.

Fernanda's routines are so structured that when she deviates from them – by airing the mattress and losing her ring in the process – she never considers going to look for the ring where she normally never goes. In contrast, Ursula is aware of Fernanda's routines and is able to look in a place where no one else would think of looking.

The passage provides another example of how Ursula becomes aware of her lifeworld through her blindness. Amaranta is in the habit of sitting in a certain spot on the porch at a certain time of day, unaware of the slight changes she makes to compensate for the shifting sun. Ursula is unaware of this slow change until she makes another unintentional phenomenological disclosure after bumping Amaranta on the porch. At first she thinks Amaranta has deviated from her normal routine, but then she links the shift with the changing sun. This insight allows her to make conscious changes in her own bodily routine.

I have tried to interpret this passage phenomenologically, and I think it is basically about the regularity of Ursula's lifeworld and how the dramatic change of her going blind allows her to "see" it in a way she couldn't before. The passage also points out some of the advantages of being observant.

– Miriam Marsh

Student Interpretation 2

We are creatures of habit. For a long time, this statement seemed to me to be just another adage like those in *Poor Richard*. But when looking at habit from the viewpoint of Ursula or from what each of us would like to think of as a unique lifestyle, the unveiling of our day-to-day experiences reveals the considerable magnitude of habitual behavior.

It seems impossible that the characters in the selection could let themselves succumb to what appeared to me as a sort of methodical oppression brought on by their particular way of life and accepted without question. This is quite

(Continued)

a hypocritical viewpoint coming from someone who becomes upset when the least little thing breaks up the pattern of his routine. "Routine" is the key word here because it is the very fact that a routine exists that constitutes the center of my interpretation or, rather, the awareness that the behavior exhibited by Ursula and myself has a common thread, though we are quite remote from each other in most other ways. I maintain that when it comes to getting through the day, all of us have a lifeworld that is very much sustained by habit.

I love this selection about Ursula because it is the blind woman in the household who can really see. In one sense, it is sad that such a tragedy was the prerequisite for the insights she acquired, but still her story is enlightening. I love the selection for its irony – the very thing that made Ursula aware of the patterns of the household was also the handicap that she guarded from detection. Her blindness gave her the ability to let the material world speak. She did not search for indicators and household landmarks; rather, they came to her. I'm sure in the beginning we all accept our lifeworld at face value with little contemplation about the true identity of our patterned existence. It is when Ursula became aware of the unfolding of daily activities and began to question them that she really began to see.

I could make some sociological assumptions about Ursula's condition – for example, her socio-economic status and how that probably led to her decision to keep her failing eyesight a secret. But the heart of the passage is marked in the last paragraph, where her awareness reaches almost uncanny proportions. It is here that the reader sees that the world – and not just a blind woman's living room – is all a matter of perception. If we applied the diligence of Ursula, we might attain her degree of perception. As it is, however, we are the ones who are blind.

– Steve Murphy

In regard to environmental embodiment and interior design research, one significant body of work has focused on the environmental experiences of less able and differently abled individuals, including the blind (Allen 2004), the deaf (Finlay and Molano-Fisher 2007), paraplegics (Cole 2004), persons with multiple sclerosis (Toombs 1995), the elderly (Stafford 2009), and infants and children (Simms 2008). For example, neurophysiologist Jonathan Cole and philosopher Kay Toombs explored how less-abled individuals' loss of mobility leads to a changed interaction with the surrounding physical and human world, while phenomenological psychologist Eva Simms delineated "some of the key experiences of early childhood" (Cole 2004; Toombs 1995; Simms 2008). For interior design research, one of the most instructive introductions to the design importance of environmental embodiment is sociologist Galen Cranz's *The Chair*, which argues that many chairs are uncomfortable because designers are not typically attuned to the lived dimensions of sitting (Cranz 1998). The key to bodily-attuned design, Cranz demonstrated, is changing posture often and keeping the body moving: "We need to consider not just different ways to sit, but also ways to incorporate a variety of postures – including lying and standing – into our lives" (Cranz 1998).

Architectural Sustenance

"Architectural sustenance" refers to the ways that elements of the designable environment contribute to human well-being. A phenomenological perspective recognizes that, existentially, people and environment are not separate and two but indivisible and one. This lived fact has immense significance for interior design, since it suggests that the specific material, designable constitution of the world contributes to sustaining or undermining human life. A central question is whether, through thoughtful design and policy, we can re-create, self-consciously, places and environmental experiences that, in the pre-modern past, typically arose unselfconsciously and spontaneously, for example robust town centers, lively city neighborhoods, and life-enhancing buildings and interiors.

In regard to architectural sustenance, this means asking if qualities of the built environment, just by being what they are, contribute in various ways to a more pleasurable, sustaining way of life. One eye-opening study is Thomas Thiis-Evensen's *Archetypes in Architecture*, which can be described as a phenomenology of architectural experience (Thiis-Evensen 1987). This architect's aim was to understand "the universality of architectural expression" and his interpretive means was what he called architectural archetypes – "the most basic elements of architecture," which he identified as floor, wall, and roof. Echoing Relph's interpretation of place, Thiis-Evensen argued that the lived commonality of floor, wall, and roof is their making of an inside in the midst of an outside, though in different ways: the floor, through above and beneath; the wall, through within and around; and the roof, through over and under.

Thiis-Evensen proposed that a building's relative degree of insideness and outsideness in regard to floor, wall, and roof can be clarified through what he calls the three existential expressions of architecture (Thiis-Evensen 1987): motion, weight, and substance. By motion, he meant the architectural element's expression of dynamism or inertia – i.e., whether the element seems to expand, to contract, or to rest in balance. In turn, weight refers to the element's expression of heaviness or lightness, while substance involves the element's material expression – whether it seems soft or hard, coarse or fine, warm or cold, and so forth. Using examples from architectural history as descriptive evidence, Thiis-Evensen generated an intricate language of architectural-elements-as-experienced. For example, he discussed stairs as one kind of directed floor and explored how a stair's material and spatial qualities of slope, breadth, groundedness, and form contribute to contrasting lived experiences and meanings (Thiis-Evensen 1987). His interpretation offers a powerful demonstration of the tacit ways in which architectural elements sustain or undermine specific modes of environmental and architectural experiences.

Though not explicitly phenomenological, the work of architect Christopher Alexander is a second important example of research relating to architectural sustenance. Throughout his career, Alexander has sought to understand the designable qualities of environments and places that evoke a sense of wholeness, healing, and life. His influential *Pattern Language* can be described as an implicit phenomenology of design elements that contribute to making place (Alexander, Ishikawa, and Silverstein 1977).

This book presents a method for envisioning and programming a design problem whereby, moving from larger to smaller scale, one identifies designable qualities – what Alexander calls "patterns" – that contribute to an environmental and architectural robustness. In his more recent four-volume *The Nature of Order*, Alexander integrates his pattern language with the much larger aim of understanding and making wholeness, particularly as environments and buildings can be imagined and designed as dense centers of human meaning and life (Alexander 2002–2005). Alexander's work is a masterly demonstration of the powerful ways that architectural sustenance plays a major role in making the world a better place.

Shaping Worlds

I highlight the work of Thiis-Evensen and Alexander because both architects, though working at somewhat different environmental scales, strongly believe that the material and designed environments play a central role in the quality of human life. Both assume that, by exploring and understanding architectural elements and qualities that we normally take for granted, we will more suitably and effectively envision and design future environments, whether they be neighborhoods, buildings, interiors, or furnishings. One aim is re-creating self-consciously the kind of exuberant, serendipitous place ambience illustrated earlier in the colorful student account of the music venue "Off Broadway."

In this sense, the most important value of a phenomenological approach to interior design is its power to make us more aware of our lived relationship with physical and spatial environments. Qualities of the material world make a difference in human lives, often in ways we don't see because we are caught up in the lifeworld and natural attitude. All phenomenological work calls the obvious and taken-for-granted into question so they can be seen in the light of empathetic description and interpretation. For interior design, a major phenomenological aim is to understand the lived nature of inside places and their parts and to use that understanding as one springboard for better interior design.

Notes

The author thanks Kansas State University students Miriam March, Steve Murphy, and Eric Wencel for permission to publish essays written as assignments for courses taught by the author.

1 Though most of the real-world studies I highlight in this essay are explicitly phenomenological in their conception, method, and results, some (e.g., Galen Cranz's or Christopher Alexander's) are more broadly qualitative and interpretive. I include these studies because their style of working closely parallels a phenomenological approach and their conclusions can readily be accepted as phenomenological.

References

Alexander, C. 2002–2005. *The Nature of Order*, 4 vols. Berkeley, CA: Center for Environmental Structure.

Alexander, C., Ishikawa, S., and Silverstein, M. 1977. *A Pattern Language*. New York: Oxford University Press.

Allen, C. 2004. "Merleau-Ponty's phenomenology and the body-in-space: encounters of visually impaired children," *Environment and Planning D: Society and Space* 22: 719–735.

Barrie, T. 2010. *The Sacred In-Between: The Mediating Roles of Architecture*. London: Routledge.

Blesser, B. and Salter, L. 2007. *Spaces Speak, Are You Listening? Experiencing Aural Architecture*. Cambridge, MA: MIT Press.

Casey, E. [1993] 2009. *Getting Back into Place* (rev. ed.) Bloomington: Indiana University Press.

Cloutier-Fisher, D. and Harvey, J. 2009. "Home beyond the home: experience of place in an evolving retirement community," *Journal of Environmental Psychology* 29: 246–255.

Cole, J. 2004. *Still Lives: Narratives of Spinal Cord Injury*. Cambridge, MA: MIT Press.

Cooper Marcus, C. 1995. *House as a Mirror of Self*. Berkeley, CA: Conari Press.

Cranz, G. (1998) *The Chair: Rethinking Culture, Body, and Design*. New York: Norton.

Filmer, A. R. 2006. "Backstage Space: The Place of the Performer," Doctoral thesis, Department of Performance Studies, University of Sydney.

Finlay, L. 2006. "The body's disclosure in phenomenological research," *Qualitative Research in Psychology* 3: 19–30.

Finlay, L. 2009. "Debating phenomenological research methods," *Phenomenology & Practice* 3: 6–25.

Finlay, L. and Molano-Fisher, P. 2007. "Transforming self and world: a phenomenological study of a changing lifeworld following cochlear implant," *Medicine, Health Care and Philosophy* 11: 255–267.

Foran, A. and Olson, M. 2008. "Seeking pedagogical places," *Phenomenology & Practice* 2: 24–48.

Graumann, C. F. 2002. "The phenomenological approach to people-environment studies," in R. Bechtel and A. Churchman (eds.), *Handbook of Environmental Psychology*, New York: Wiley, pp. 95–113.

Hammer, R. M. 1999. "The lived experience of being at home: a phenomenological investiga-tion," *Journal of Gerontological Nursing* 10(Nov.): 10–18.

Heidegger, M. [1927] 1962. *Being and Time*, trans. J. Macquarrie and E. Robinson. New York: Harper & Row.

Horan, T. 2000. *Digital Places: Building Our City of Bits*. Washington DC: ULI – the Urban Land Institute.

Janz, B. 2004. "Walls and borders: the range of place," *City & Community* 4: 87–94.

Janz, B. 2009. *Philosophy in an African Place*. New York: Lexington Books.

Malnar, J. M. and Vodvarka, F. 2004. *Sensory Design*. Minneapolis: University of Minnesota Press.

Malpas, J. E. 1999. *Place and Experience*. Cambridge: Cambridge University Press.

Manzo, L. 2005. "For better or worse: exploring multiple dimensions of place meaning," *Journal of Environmental Psychology* 25: 67–86.

Márquez, G. G. [1967] 2006. *One Hundred Years of Solitude*. London: Folio Society.

McCann, R. 2005. "On the hither side of depth: an architectural pedagogy of engagement," *Environmental and Architectural Phenomenology* 16(3): 8–19.

Merleau-Ponty, M. [1945] 1962. *Phenomenology of Perception*, trans. C. Smith. New York: Humanities Press.

Moore, A. J. 2009. "Space, Place and Complementary Therapy in Hospice Day Care," Doctoral dissertation, University of Central Lancashire.

Moores, S. 2006. "Media uses and everyday environmental experiences," *Particip@tions* 3; www.participations.org/. Accessed June 20, 2010.

Moran, D. 2000. *Introduction to Phenomenology*. New York: Routledge.

Mugerauer, R. 1994. *Interpretations on Behalf of Place*. Albany: State University of New York Press.

Oldenburg, R. 2001. *Celebrating the Third Place*. New York: Marlow.

Pallasmaa, J. 1996. *The Eyes of the Skin: Architecture and the Senses*. London: Academy Editions.

Pallasmaa, J. 2009. *The Thinking Hand*. London: Wiley.

Patterson, M. E. and Williams, D. R. 2005. "Maintaining research traditions on place," *Journal of Environmental Psychology* 25: 361–380.

Percival, J. 2002. "Domestic spaces: uses and meanings in the daily lives of older people," *Ageing and Society* 22: 729–749.

Rechavi, T. B. 2009. "A room for living: private and public aspects in the experience of the living room," *Journal of Environmental Psychology* 29: 133–143.

Relph, E. [1976] 2009. *Place and Placelessness* (2nd ed.). London: Pion.

Rosenbaum, M. 2007. "A cup of coffee with a dash of love," *Journal of Service Research* 10: 43–59.

Rothbauer, P. 2009. "Exploring the placelessness of reading among older teens in a Canadian rural municipality," *Library Quarterly* 79: 465–483.

Seamon, D. 1979. *A Geography of the Lifeworld*. New York: St. Martin's.

Seamon, D. 2000. "Phenomenology in environment-behavior research," in S. Wapner (ed.), *Theoretical Perspectives in Environment-Behavior Research*. New York: Plenum, pp. 157–178.

Seamon, D. 2007. "A lived hermetic of people and place: phenomenology and space syntax," in A. Sema Kubat et al. (eds.), *Proceedings, 6th International Space Syntax Symposium 1*. Istanbul: ITU, Faculty of Architecture, pp. iii, 1–16. www.spacesyntaxistanbul.itu.edu.tr/papers.htm. Accessed June 20, 2010.

Seamon, D. 2008. "Place, placelessness, insideness, and outsideness, in John Sayles' *Sunshine State*," *Aether* 3: 1–19. http://130.166.124.2/~aether/. Accessed June 20, 2010.

Shenk, D., Kuwahara, K., and Zablotsky, D. 2004. "Older women's attachments to their home and possessions," *Journal of Aging Studies* 18: 157–169.

Simms, E. M. 2008. *The Child in the World*. Detroit: Wayne State University Press.

Stafford, P. B. 2009. *Elderburbia: Aging with a Sense of Place in America*. Denver: Praeger.

Stefanovic, I. L. 2000. *Safeguarding Our Common Future*. Albany: State University of New York Press.

Sternberg, E. M. 2009. *Healing Spaces*. Cambridge, MA: Belnap Press.

Thiis-Evensen, T. 1987. *Archetypes in Architecture*. New York: Oxford University Press.

Toombs, S. K. 1995. "The lived experience of disability," *Human Studies* 18: 9–23.

van Manen, M. 1990. *Researching Lived Experience: Human Science for an Action-Sensitive Pedagogy*. London, Canada: Althouse.

van Manen, M., ed. 2002. *Writing in the Dark: Phenomenological Studies in Interpretive Inquiry*. London, Canada: Althouse.

25

Testing a Culture-Based Design Pedagogy: A Case Study

Abimbola O. Asojo

Introduction

Previous authors have discussed the significance of integrating non-Western design forms into design curricula as a means of addressing diversity and global issues (Boyer and Mitgang 1996; Elleh 1997; Fairbrass and Harris 1986; Grant 1991; Guerin and Mason 1993; Guerin and Thompson 2004; Leigh and Tremblay 2002). However, few studies exist that examine instructional approaches that use non-Western design forms. Research findings from a study by Jani and Asojo of interior design educators indicated the need for design discourse and instructional approaches on non-Western cultures that promote diverse multicultural perspectives in education (Jani and Asojo 2007).

To help address this issue, a cultural framework of five constructs was developed and applied in third- and fourth-year interior design studios. Students were assigned the task of design problem-solving for spaces in Nigerian, South African, and Native American settings (Asojo 2011). This essay provides insights into this cultural framework and instructional approach.

A Cultural Framework of Five Constructs

The results of a study conducted by Asojo on design problem-solving in different cultural settings revealed five constructs. These constructs were used to develop a cultural framework for the design of interiors in cultural settings (Asojo 2011). The constructs are: social dynamics; juxtaposition of traditional and contemporary

The Handbook of Interior Design, First Edition. Edited by Jo Ann Asher Thompson and Nancy H. Blossom.

culture; visual and performance arts; elements and principles of design; and sustainability.

In this study, the constructs of social dynamics and juxtaposition of traditional and contemporary culture were deemed to be abstract, while visual and performance arts, elements and principles of design, and sustainability were seen as concrete constructs. In other words, the abstract constructs were considered more theoretical, while the concrete constructs were considered more grounded in the physical world. The data revealed strong connections – even overlap – among the five constructs.

Abstract Construct 1: Social Dynamics

Specific components were identified that characterize the social dynamics construct. These are: ethnicity and cultural diversity; philosophy and religion; government and iconic people in the cultures; and community, social interaction, and family (Asojo 2011). In this study it was found that ethnicity and cultural diversity were important considerations in the design of interior spaces for non-Western settings. This is not surprising when one considers the large number of diverse ethnic groups found in non-Western settings. In Africa, for example there are multiple ethnic groups within the various countries, with Nigeria alone representing over 250 different ethnic groups. It stands to reason that the philosophical and religious beliefs, which are closely aligned with the concepts of ethnicity and cultural diversity, also were seen as important considerations that impact the art and architecture of a country.

In order to create meaningful interior spaces in non-Western settings, an understanding of the entire context of the region is needed. Such things as ideas about community, social interaction and family, and the balance among spiritual, cultural, and artistic elements – in conjunction with the government structure and the existence of iconic cultures – are often reflected in the built environment and must be taken into consideration. For example, in Nigeria, Ghana, and some other West African countries, the impluvium-style houses with their multiple courtyards and functions arranged around them were designed to support the coexistence of the extended family.

Abstract Construct 2: Juxtaposition of Traditional and Contemporary Culture

"Juxtaposition of traditional and contemporary culture" is the second abstract construct that was identified. The notion of juxtaposing traditional with contemporary culture implies a consciousness of the indigenous influences and the importance of their interpretation in a non-literal and non-stereotypical way, as opposed to what is often perceived in the media's depiction of non-Western cultures as impoverished and underdeveloped.

Particularly in Africa, this construct demonstrates aspects of Mazrui and Elleh's "triple heritage" theory regarding the history and architecture of African countries (Elleh 1997; Mazrui 1986). Mazrui suggests that African culture is deeply rooted in a "triple heritage" reflecting indigenous, Western, and Islamic influences. Later, Elleh observed the "triple heritage" phenomenon in the architecture of most Nigerian and South African cities. It can be argued that these factors make African cities different from those in most parts of the world because their built environments have been influenced by three different heritages.

In addition, the availability of real-time global communication has increased cross-cultural exchanges, thereby further impacting the architecture of many non-Western cultures. This makes the "juxtaposition of traditional and contemporary culture" a very significant construct to be considered in the design of interior spaces in non-Western cultures.

Concrete Construct 1: Visual and Performance Arts

"Visual and performance arts" is the first of three concrete constructs (Asojo 2011). Visual art is a term used to collectively characterize artifacts, arts, and crafts – all of which are important aspects of a culture and influence its built environment. In most non-Western cultures the visual arts have a strong connection with the performance arts (dancing and music), and therefore must also be considered as important influences on the built environment of non-Western cultures.

Individual elements of the visual and performance arts such as specific motifs and attributes of dress, fabrics, hairstyles, body decoration, metalwork, carving, pottery, basketry, beadwork, and wall decoration can be observed in the built environment of most non-Western cultures. This relationship between visual and performance arts is consistent with the notion that art is an extension of architecture in the African built environment and that the arts cannot be separated from architecture in an African cultural context. Balogun explained this phenomenon in the following way:

> African artistic genius was strongly asserted in the decorative embellishment of the built environment. Varying decorative patterns could be found sculpted or painted on walls and wooden doors, which ranged from figurative designs to complex abstract patterns which revealed an exquisite balance of form, color and shading. Painting was carried out as an extension of architecture rather than an independent medium. (Balogun 1979)

Concrete Construct 2: Elements and Principles of Design

"Elements and principles" of design is the second concrete construct. Most design students begin their programs of study with introductory courses in the basic elements of design (i.e., point, line, form, shape, space, texture, and color) and design principles (i.e., balance – symmetrical or non-symmetrical – rhythm, emphasis, proportion, scale, unity/harmony, and movement) (Ching 2007). However, the notion that African and other non-Western cultures demonstrate principles of rational planning has not been widely endorsed in literature. For example in the case of pre-colonial African cultures, Hull observed the following:

> Another misconception about pre-colonial Africans is that their settlement patterns were a disorganized, cacophonous, sprawling scramble of random structures, exhibiting little or no regard for the elements of rational planning. Oral and written evidence reveals the importance of human relationships as a major determinant in the placement of buildings. They also suggest that utilization of space was hardly haphazard. Nevertheless, it was not space that mattered so much as the relationship of its occupants. Space was seen as a medium in which to express relationships of a social, religious, ethnic, political, or occupational nature. (Hull 1976)

More recent studies, however, have shown that indigenous African motifs are based on geometric designs that incorporate basic principles of design through the use of lines, shapes, textures, and rhythms (Asojo 2011). For example, among the Hausa in sub-Saharan Africa motifs can be found that are predominantly geometric patterns which emphasize the intricate volumetric vaulting of the Hausa mosque ceilings, and the Yoruba and Igbo in West Africa routinely incorporate rectangular, circular, and organic shapes in their spatial organization.

In other examples, certain Nigerian cultures create hierarchy among spaces that are dependent upon the religious and social structure of the group (i.e., the king's palace is more elaborate in form, shape and height than others). In South Africa one can see the incorporation of vibrant, warm textures and colors in the built environment. The Zulu culture, a prominent South African culture, is strongly dependent on music and includes the design principle of rhythm to organize the spatial elements of Zulu buildings and interiors.

Given this background, a noteworthy conclusion can be drawn. Contrary to what Western literature seems to imply, design precedents from non-Western cultural settings can be used to inform design discourse and, as such, they can be used pedagogically to discuss elements and principles of design. In so doing, a more inclusive design education can be promoted.

Concrete Construct 3: Sustainability

"Sustainability" is the third concrete construct identified by Asojo in her study. Sustainability manifests itself in the importance of the natural environment; local materials; climatic considerations; and natural lighting among indigenous non-Western cultures. Many of the early practices of non-Western indigenous cultures were synonymous with today's sustainable practices because these cultures were very earth-centered and in tune with the natural environment. Unfortunately, many of these sustainable practices have been abandoned as indigenous societies have become more urbanized. The application of this construct in interior design classes can help bridge the gap between the old and new, thereby reinforcing notions from the past in contemporary practices with strong emphasis on the earth-centered nature of non-Western cultures.

Case Study 1: Nigerian and South African Design Project

The Nigerian and South African project was incorporated into a third-year interior design studio course. The task assigned to the students was to design the interior and lighting for a restaurant in either Nigeria or South Africa within a six-week period. The students were given the option of setting the restaurant in Lagos, Nigeria or Johannesburg, South Africa. (These locations were chosen because each offered an urban setting with a strong influx of tourists and multiple opportunities for the exploration of cultural attributes.) The project was completed in teams of five students each, identified as Groups A, B, C, D, and E.

Student design solutions: Groups A, B, C, D, and E

Group A set out to integrate the three predominant ethnic groups in Nigeria (the Yoruba, Igbo, and Hausa) through the creation of a "melting-pot atmosphere." Ceiling elements from Hausa vaults and arches and the indigenous materials, fabric, textiles, art, and sculpture derived from Yoruba and Igbo served as inspiration for the design of their restaurant. The architecture, design, furniture, and décor from Yoruba, Igbo, and Hausa informed their conceptual sketches that were subsequently translated into their design solution.

Group B derived their solution from the vibrant colors, arts, and traditions of Swazi, South African, and Swaziland culture. This group's solution was mainly influenced by geometric patterns from Swazi baskets. The geometric patterns from Swazi baskets were integrated into the stained patterns on the flooring, columns, room dividers, patio fence, and ceiling. This group emphasized the importance of this abstraction so as to avoid any stereotypes.

The beadwork and use of color of the Yoruba were the primary inspirations for Group C's solution. Patterns in the space, including the layout of the floor plan, were inspired by a beaded painting by prominent Yoruba artist Jimoh Buraimoh, and resulted in an open-plan solution. A water wall feature was used to reflect light into their space.

Group D started their design process by studying the Yoruba philosophy which emphasizes the significance of the earth and sky's concave shapes. These shapes were used as space defining elements in the design of their restaurant. As a focal point, they created an undulating ceiling with prominent tree branches. The tree was located in a central place inside the restaurant to represent Oduduwa, the founder of the Yoruba, and to symbolize growth and energy through the many branches. Sustainability was another key concept this group integrated in the use of materials (e.g., recycled bottles with LED lights as fixtures). They named their restaurant

Omnomnom Restaurant, Bar and Lounge, a name that was an amalgamation of Nigerian words.

Lastly, Group E focused on the Zulu ethnic group of South Africa. Since community is an important aspect of the Zulu culture, it became a major component of the design thinking of this group. The use of large tables with lots of seating reinforced the notion of community, with some of the tables being shaped in the form of a leaf to emphasize the Zulu culture's connection with nature. Other inspiration for the design of the restaurant was drawn from images of Zulu children, warriors, baskets, and dome huts, resulting in a beaded column as a prominent feature in the space. The importance of performance arts and dance to the Zulu culture was reinforced by the inclusion of a stage, and the vibrant color palette of the Zulu culture was exhibited in a variety of circular forms, curved lines, and organic shapes.

An analysis of the student projects revealed that each group relied on elements that fell under the umbrellas of abstract and concrete constructs (see Tables 25.1, 25.2, and 25.3 for a synopsis of how the students used these constructs in their design solutions).

Case Study 2: Native American Community College Library Project

The Native American community college library project was included in a fourth-year interior design studio course. The students were asked to create a design for a library for a Native American community college. A primary goal of the space was that it would reflect the heritage, artistic expression, culture, and colors of a specific Native American culture. The students worked individually and were allowed to choose the Native American culture they were designing for as well as the location of the library.

Student design solutions

One student decided to create a library for the Ojibwe tribe in White Earth Community College in Mahnomen, Minnesota. After studying the culture of the Ojibwe tribe, the student's solution incorporated several diverse areas into the plan which included individual, communal, educational, and informal spaces. In keeping with the Ojibwe philosophy and connection to nature, the majority of the public spaces were organized around a window to emphasize the natural landscape and maximize daylight exposure. In terms of artistic expression, a combination of soft curves and rigid geometric characteristics of traditional Ojibwe patterns were integrated into perforated screens to depict the beadwork patterns of the tribe. Photographs emphasizing the tribe's history and the artifacts of the Ojibwe were prominently displayed in a gallery format.

Another student proposed a library for the Pequot tribe in Connecticut. The boldness and confidence of the Pequot tribe were reflected in the bold and angular

Table 25.1 A synopsis illustrating the abstract constructs

Group	Culture(s)/ country	Abstract construct 1: Social dynamics	Abstract construct 2: Juxtaposition of traditional and contemporary culture
A	Yoruba, Igbo, and Hausa, Nigeria	The idea of Lagos as a melting pot and a multicultural metropolis led to this group using three cultures, from southwest, southeast, and north. Creating spaces to foster social interaction, reinforcing the importance of community, and focus on extended family were prominent notions to this group	The notion of Western and Islamic influences impacting Nigeria architecture along with the indigenous influences. Emphasis placed on influences from mosque architecture
B	Swazi, South Africa and Swaziland	Idea of emphasis on family and community. Balance between spiritual, cultural, artistic, and family life. Nelson Mandela as an iconic person to South African culture	The idea that contemporary buildings still reflect culture
C	Yoruba, Nigeria	Design inspiration derived from the artwork of Jimoh Buraimoh, an iconic Yoruba artist	An emphasis on developing contemporary solutions based on Yoruba culture
D	Yoruba, Nigeria	Design inspiration derived from the mythology and philosophy of the Yoruba. Oduduwa, the spiritual leader of the Yoruba, as an iconic person	The idea that government whether democratic or imperial was reflected in city, urban planning, and architecture
E	Zulu, South Africa	Derived inspiration from Shaka Zulu, a prominent Zulu king and Zulu philosophical beliefs. Community and social interaction were major design determinants	The idea of creating a contemporary expression of Zulu design in their design solution

Table 25.2 A synopsis illustrating the concrete constructs (Groups A and B)

Group	Culture/country	Concrete construct 1: Visual and performance arts	Concrete construct 2: Elements and principles of design	Concrete construct 3: Sustainability
A	Yoruba, Igbo, and Hausa, Nigeria	Design solution highlighted artwork and fabric of three cultures. Inspiration for space planning and furniture design were derived from geometric patterns of Hausa, Igbo, Yoruba doors, drums, and fabrics. Performance stage was integrated to enliven the environment. Restaurant was named "Durojaiye," meaning "wait and enjoy life," evoking a feeling of entertainment and reviving traditional music	Open planning, vaulted ceilings creating emphasis, hierarchy in radial spaces, courtyard, and circular vestibule are elements from indigenous spaces that inspired this solution. Color and artwork were important solutions using a neutral background in the restaurant to highlight the colors of the artwork and fabric. Geometric patterns from Hausa and Igbo doors inspired details for the carved tabletops, furniture, and other spatial forms. Organic forms came from the Yoruba as well as the artwork and design of the bar Motifs in the space were large patterns made up of smaller patterns similar to fractals	Emphasis on natural forms and materials Extensive research on indigenous materials. Adobe was used in the design of the entry vestibule and booth in the restaurant Natural lighting integrated in design solution. Emphasis on sustainability being part of indigenous cultures and have abandoned sustainable practices as they urbanized
B	Swazi, South Africa and Swaziland	Swazi baskets, and artwork impacted space planning and volumetric design for this restaurant	Bright colors, vibrant textures, warm tones, geometric shapes, circular forms and patterns derived from Swazi baskets were major design concepts Spaciousness a key concept. Strong interior and exterior relationship Volumetric abstraction of hut forms in interior	

Table 25.3 A synopsis illustrating the concrete constructs (Groups C, D and E)

Group	Culture/ country	Concrete construct 1: Visual and performance arts	Concrete construct 2: Elements and principles of design	Concrete construct 3: Sustainability
C	Yoruba, Nigeria	Forms from Jimoh Buraimoh's beadwork served as an inspiration for the design solution	Colors in Nigeria had meaning; opening planning; non-symmetrical form; geometric patterns and forms from beaded painting inspired space planning; color psychology of the Yoruba, warm colors, patterns and natural colors from Buraimoh's beaded painting	A water wall was a prominent natural feature in the space
D	Yoruba, Nigeria		Concave shapes of earth and sky in Yoruba philosophy used as space-defining element in ceiling plane. Prominent undulating ceiling and tree branches in the space	Sustainability a key concept of this group in use of materials. Recycled bottles with LED lights integrated into it at the bar wall a major sustainable feature of the space
E	Zulu, South Africa	Dancing, music and performance arts considered important aspects of Zulu culture were highlighted. Small stage incorporated Zulu traditional dancing, a form of entertainment prominent in Zulu culture.	Curved forms, earth tones, and vibrant colors from ethnic arts and crafts; red color from arts and crafts prominent; rhythm is evident in patterns; asymmetry; round forms; and dome shapes were major design determinants. Large tables with shapes derived from nature to promote community	

layout of the design. The community-based philosophy of the Pequot tribe was reinforced by a central communal area, and the ceiling design was inspired by the wigwam shape of the traditional Pequot home. The Pequot love of self-expression through body paint, bold colored clothing, and mohawks was incorporated in the vibrant colors integrated throughout the design. Lastly, the angular shapes and strong lines of Pequot pottery, necklaces, and clothing were prominently displayed and integrated into the final solution.

The Cheyenne tribe was the focus of study for another student. This student found the Cheyenne arrow ceremony to be of particular fascination and used this as inspiration for the design solution. The Cheyenne arrow ceremony, with its half-moon arrangement, served as the catalyst for the curvilinear spatial organization of the space. Group seating areas were provided to accommodate the activity of storytelling, an important component of Cheyenne culture where members of older generations pass down history to younger generations. The colors, materials, and shapes used in this student's design of the library were based on Cheyenne artwork and clothing, utilizing warm yellows, reds, and natural tones derived from Cheyenne traditional wear.

In her research on the Arapahoe tribe, another student found that the tribe was nomadic and roamed throughout the Midwest region of the United States. A reflection of this characteristic of the Araphahoe tribe became the primary focus of her design concept. Synonymous with the characteristics of the Arapahoe as travelers and traders, she used angular walls in the library space to indicate movement. These unusual angles of the walls also served to enhance the flow from one space to another. Other strong focal points were used to evoke a sense of movement using references to legends and other traditional elements of the Arapahoe culture. For example, because the Arapahoe tribe was known as gemstone jewelry traders who told great stories and legends that mystified those they came across, the space was designed to illustrate three elements: the movement of the traveling traders and the river in the creation story, the spider trickster found in children's legends, and the beautiful gemstones and turquoise they traded.

Lastly, the focus of another student's design of the library was the Algonquin tribe located in Ottawa in Ontario, Canada. Research into the Algonquin people revealed that their culture tended to incorporate large gathering spaces into their living environments. To reflect this, as well as illustrate the equality philosophy of the Algonquin people, a large central gathering space was used as a focal point in the library. Birchwood, the type primarily used by the Algonquin people, was selected for finishes throughout the library, and the children's area of the library was designed to reflect the rivers that the Algonquin people traveled. An analysis of the student projects revealed that each group relied on elements that fell under the umbrellas of abstract and concrete constructs.

As with the previous case study and analysis of student designs set in African countries, the student designs for a Native American library revealed that each student relied on different elements that fell under the umbrellas of abstract and concrete constructs (see Tables 25.4 and 25.5 for a synopsis of how the students used in these constructs in their design solutions).

Table 25.4 A synopsis illustrating the abstract constructs

Tribe	Abstract construct 1: Social dynamics	Abstract construct 2: Juxtaposition of traditional and contemporary culture
Ojibwe	The Ojibwe lived in groups and were community oriented. Most Ojibwe lived a sedentary lifestyle. They mainly lived in wigwams. Their spiritual beliefs were passed down by oral tradition	The notion of spaces organized corresponding to traditional patterns The combination of soft curves and rigid geometry characteristic of traditional Ojibwe patterns Photography used to emphasizes connection to historic culture
Pequot	Pequot were bold and confident people. The tribe was very community-based. The Pequot people loved to express themselves through body paint, bold colored clothing, and Mohawks The "red fox" was an animal that they honored and they often called themselves fox people. The tribe lived on the shoreline and spent time fishing	Drawing inspiration from tradition, the ceiling design is inspired by the wigwam shape of the traditional Pequot home
Cheyenne	The Cheyenne tribe originally lived in the Great Plains in South Dakota, Wyoming, Nebraska, Colorado, and Kansas. Today there are two Cheyenne tribes, one in Oklahoma and the other in Montana. The Cheyenne arrow ceremony was a big part of the culture and belief. The ceremony was set up in a half-moon arrangement, with a main tepee in the middle and two more off to the side. Another part of the culture is the traditional Cheyenne legends and fairy tales. Storytelling is very important to the Cheyenne Indian culture	Inspiration is derived from traditional ceremonies and storytelling of the Cheyenne tribe
Arapahoe	The Arapahoe were nomads in the Midwest region of the United States As travelers the Arapahoe were known to be gemstone jewelry traders that told great stories and legends that mystified those they came across	The space evokes movement through strong focal points derived from legends and the traditional culture of the Arapahoe. For example, the children's legend of the spider trickster inspired web-like patterning
Algonquin	Algonquin people were located in the northern woodlands spanning Canada and the northern US. The area had abundant wildlife, forests, rivers, and lakes	Drawing inspiration from the lifestyle of the Algonquin people and the notion of equality of people, a concept the Algonquin believed in

Table 25.5 A synopsis illustrating the concrete constructs

Tribe	Concrete construct 1: *Visual and performance arts*	Concrete construct 2: *Elements and principles of design*	Concrete construct 3: *Sustainability*
Ojibwe	Actual art and artifacts of the Ojibwe tribe are displayed in a gallery like format	The combination of soft curves and rigid geometry characteristic of traditional Ojibwe patterns presents itself most clearly in the form of perforated screens reminiscent of beadwork patterns	The majority of public space is organized along a curtain wall to emphasize the natural landscape, and make use of daylighting. The interior space supports engagement with the nature
Pequot	The Pequot tribe created pottery, necklaces, and clothing with bold designs, angular shapes, and strong lines which informed the design parti	The tribe lived on the shoreline and fished. The importance of the shoreline is implemented through the use of curvilinear lines. Orange and teal, which were prominent colors in the tribe, were incorporated in the space. These colors reflected the idea of fire and water, which were important symbols in the tribe	Natural materials of wood and stone derived from Pequot homes which were made of wood beams
Cheyenne	Cheyenne artists are famous for their fine quill embroidery, beadwork, pipestone carving, and pottery. Design parti was derived from the Cheyenne ceremony	The arrow ceremony, which is a big part of the culture and belief, with a half-moon arrangement inspired the curvilinear spatial organization. Warm colors such as yellows, reds and natural tones were derived from the traditional wear and art	Natural materials and proximity to nature
Arapahoe	The Arapahoe tribe were gemstone jewelry traders that told great stories and legends that mystified those they came across.	The space is abstracted to combine three main guiding concepts; movement of the traveling traders and the river in the creation story, the spider trickster found in their children's legends and gemstones and turquoise they traded. Juxtaposition of geometric forms and the curved waves informed the design parti	Proximity to nature and the environment
Algonquin	Red- and birchwood from clothing integrated in the furniture and artwork	A central focal area based on the idea of equality of all people sharing one circular gathering space	Natural elements utilized to reflect lifestyle of Algonquin

Conclusion

This essay provides educators with a pedagogical model to help students view the world from multiple perspectives. In so doing, they will be better equipped to be actively engaged in solving design problems in a diverse, global society. The cultural framework discussed in this essay can serve as a starting point for design educators who are interested in integrating global concerns, diversity issues, and cultural settings into their design studios. Exercises such as those presented in each case study can be easily integrated into an existing curriculum. However, in order for global and diversity issues to become routinized in design education, such approaches need to be included in a separate required course in a design studio curriculum. An important resource for this type of course is the book *Diversity in Design Perspectives from the Non-Western World*. This book focuses on the culture, architecture, and philosophies of India, China, Turkey, Egypt, Nigeria, Algeria, Saudi Arabia, and United Arab Emirates and is written to appeal to design students and educators interested in learning about indigenous and contemporary aspects of non-Western cultures.

Another approach that is suggested to increase understanding and appreciation of non-Western cultures is to create a global design history course that recognizes the contributions of many world cultures. This type of lecture course could be taught as a companion course to a design studio course that emphasizes non-Western settings.

The abstract and concrete constructs of social dynamics, juxtaposition of traditional and contemporary culture, visual and performance arts, elements and principles of design, and sustainability discussed in this essay offer one lens through which educators can study and incorporate multicultural and non-Western concepts into their design studios. However, this alone is not enough. Design educators must go beyond one approach, or one course, to make a difference that will better prepare design students for work in global and non-Western settings.

References

Asojo, A. O. 2011. "A Culture-Based Design Pedagogy for Nigerian and South African Spatial Forms." Retrieved from UMI Proquest Dissertations and Theses (3488023).

Balogun, O. 1979. "Form and expression in African arts," in A. I. Sow, O. Balogun, H. Aguessy and P. Diagne (eds.), *Introduction to African Culture: General Aspects*. Paris: UNESCO, pp. 33–80.

Boyer, E. and Mitgang, L. 1996. *Building Community, A New Future for Architecture Education and Practice*. Princeton, NJ: Carnegie Foundation for the Advancement of Teaching.

Ching, F. D. K. 2007. *Architecture Form Space and Order*. Hoboken, NJ: John Wiley & Sons.

Elleh, N. 1997. *African Architecture Evolution and Transformation*. New York: McGraw-Hill.

Fairbrass, A. and Harris, R. 1986. "Designing internationally," *Journal of Interior Design Education and Research* 12: 9–16.

Grant, B. 1991. "Cultural invisibility: the African American experience in architectural education," in T. A. Dutton (ed.), *Voices in Architectural Education Cultural Politics and Pedagogy*. New York: Bergin & Garvey, pp. 149–164.

Guerin, D. and Mason, B. 1993. "An experiential framework for international interior design education," *Journal of Interior Design Education and Research* 18: 51–58.

Guerin, D. and Thompson, J. 2004. "Interior design education in the 21st century: an educational transformation," *Journal of Interior Design* 30(1): 1–12.

Hull, R. 1976. *African Cities and Towns before the European Conquest*. New York: Prentice-Hall.

Jani, V. 2011. *Diversity in Design*. New York: Fairchild.

Jani, V. and Asojo, A. 2007. "Design and social justice: an investigation of non-Western perspectives in interior design curriculum," *Proceedings of Interior Design Educators Council Conference*, 38–47.

Leigh, K. and Tremblay, K. 2002. "A global agenda," *Journal of Interior Design* 28(1): IV–V.

Mazrui, A. 1986. *The African: A Triple Heritage*. New York: Little, Brown.

26

Connecting the Scholarship of Teaching and Learning to the Discipline of Interior Design

Isil Oygur and Bryan D. Orthel

Introduction

For many new educators, the teaching approach they use when first entering a classroom is a reflection of how and what they learned as a design student or as a design practitioner. Although new educators often question how well this approach is working, there have been relatively few attempts to rigorously examine teaching methods and student learning. In the case of interior design education, neither the discipline nor teaching methodologies are straightforward. In addition, interior design pedagogy is complicated by the following factors:

- the ambiguity of the cognitive process of design (Lawson 1990; Rowe 1987)
- the debate about the discipline's body of knowledge (Guerin and Martin 2004)
- the continuing reappraisal of the interior design profession (Guerin and Martin 2004; Kucho, Turpin, and Pable 2009; White 2009)
- the misconceptions about the interior design profession (Marshall-Baker 2005)
- the pedagogical questions about skills training versus knowledge-based education (Poldma 2008) and
- the institutional challenges to the value of interior design education (Boyer and Mitgang 1996; White 2009)

In this environment, achieving teaching excellence is a difficult and complex endeavor – an endeavor which is further complicated by the lack of progressive and cumulative studies about teaching and learning in interior design. This, in combina-

The Handbook of Interior Design, First Edition. Edited by Jo Ann Asher Thompson and Nancy H. Blossom.
© 2015 John Wiley & Sons, Ltd. Published 2015 by John Wiley & Sons, Ltd.

tion with fast-paced changes in the educational environment – as well as changes in the practice of interior design – creates a situation where interior design educators must struggle to keep up.

We suggest that the "scholarship of teaching and learning" (SoTL) offers a new perspective on interior design pedagogy. Further, we propose that SoTL's collective and rigorous approach to pedagogy can be used as a tool to advance teaching and learning in interior design. We believe that when used as a tool, SoTL supports the development of interior design pedagogy, practice and, ultimately, the advancement of the discipline and profession. In defense of this position, the following basic questions will be addressed in this essay:

- What does SoTL offer to interior design?
- What are the characteristics of a high-quality SoTL-based study in interior design?
- How can future generations of interior design educators benefit from understanding SoTL?

Through a review of the literature and the examination of two cases studies, answers to these questions are postulated – and the value of a SoTL approach demonstrated.

A Perspective on Interior Design Pedagogy

As the interior design field has grown from a craft and vocational tradition into an autonomous discipline, the pedagogy of interior design has followed a similar course. In the last few decades, the field has developed a "disciplinary" pedagogy in interior design (Vischer and Poldma 2003) and educators have begun to question the content of interior design education (e.g., Asojo 2001; Beecher 2006; Zuo, Leonard, and MaloneBeach 2010) and to focus on effective ways of communicating this content to students (e.g., Carmel-Gilfilen and Portillo 2010; Nussbaumer 2001; Zollinger, Guerin, Hadjiyanni, and Martin 2009). Pedagogical studies addressing these issues reflect the development of broader discussions within the discipline on its body of knowledge and professionalism. As a result, disciplinary design knowledge has become a concern for interior design educators in terms of how to govern the studio and the classroom, how to transfer knowledge to students, and how to address the design process and outcomes (Guerin and Thompson 2004; Klassen 2003; Poldma 2008).

While these efforts have opened opportunities for dialogue, they are far from sufficient in creating a common movement for the advancement of interior design pedagogy (Blossom, Oygur, and Orthel 2011; Vischer and Poldma 2003). This limited emphasis on the advancement of interior design pedagogy suggests that teaching is undervalued as a scholarly activity in our disciplinary context. Consequently, interior design education and academia are often criticized by practitioners and others as being far behind the contemporary practice of interior design, as being unable to educate competent interior designers, and as inadequately addressing student needs (Danko 2010; Guerin and Thompson 2004; Poldma 2008).

We argue that teaching is undervalued as scholarship because of a common misconception that this type of scholarship does not create new knowledge (Blossom, Oygur, and Payne-Tofte n.d.). This misconception is reinforced by the fact that, until recently, the majority of pedagogical investigations have ignored the topic of teaching and learning as an area appropriate for investigation. For instance, in a survey which questioned interior design faculty about their attitude towards research, none of the questions or responses related to research that focused on teaching and/or learning. Instead, the survey's focus was on programming and the development of professional practice and theory (Dickinson, Anthony, and Marsden 2009). This lack of attention to teaching and learning as scholarship is unfortunate since, as with other applied disciplines, the development and growth of the interior design profession depends on the academy and its educational approach to teaching and learning (Anderson 2008; Guerin and Thompson 2004; Zhu 2008).

As suggested by various scholars, a systematic investigation of teaching and learning provides critical improvement to instruction and strengthens disciplinary pedagogy through the continuous generation and flow of knowledge (Boyer [1990] 1997). This type of collective knowledge development, rather than individualistic effort, is a recognized area of study in many disciplines and exists under the umbrella of the "scholarship of teaching and learning" (SoTL). By contextualizing pedagogical studies under the wider SoTL literature and tradition, disciplinary and interdisciplinary pedagogical progression increases, enriches, and supports collective new knowledge (Healey 2000; Huber and Hutchings 2005; McKinney 2007; Weimer 2006). We advocate that interior design would benefit from using SoTL as a tool to collectively study the pedagogical, institutional, and professional elements of interior design as a discipline.

A Common Ground: Scholarship of Teaching and Learning

As a new and maturing field, SoTL has no single or widely accepted definition (Huber and Hutchings 2005; Huber and Morreale 2000; Shulman 1999; Weimer 2006). The adoption of SoTL across disciplines can be traced to Ernest Boyer's critique of the traditional American post-secondary education system in which success, productivity, and tenure and promotion mechanisms are measured by research and publication – with little to no recognition of achievement in teaching (Boyer [1990] 1997). Boyer argued for a redefinition of scholarship to include the "scholarship of teaching" as a practice requiring shared, career-long, critical learning. Huber and Hutchings stated that "such work has the potential to transform higher education by making the private work of the classroom visible, talked about, studied, built upon, and valued" (Huber and Hutchings 2005: ix).

It is important to distinguish SoTL from the wisdom-of-best-practices and educational research (Hutchings 2000; McKinney 2007; Weimer 2006). Best practices (good teaching or scholarly teaching) develop from experience and informal recognition of teaching methods and content that seem to work in the classroom. Although SoTL recognizes the importance of these things, in addition it requires a systematic and self-reflective analysis that publicly demonstrates the benefit of instructional practices (Agouridas and Race 2007).

Educational research is also distinct from SoTL (Kreber 2002; Tsang 2010). Whereas educational research defines broad educational theories, SoTL builds from specific cases to strengthen disciplinary pedagogy, improve teaching practice, and ultimately to define the profession. More specifically, educational research builds a third-party examination of theory and practice, while SoTL develops from first-person-based research of a researcher's own practice (Hutchings 2000).

This being the case, we propose that SoTL is particularly beneficial for educating new teachers in interior design. The structure of SoTL methodologies requires the researcher to rigorously self-evaluate teaching and learning, rather than repeat "best practices." Furthermore, the focus on analysis and investigation promotes an increasingly equal mentorship relationship between new educators and seasoned educators.

SoTL-based studies that meet these criteria tackle different kinds of questions because it "is deeply embedded in [each] discipline; its questions arise from the character of the field and what it means to know it deeply" (Hutchings 2000). Typically, SoTL research questions include: "what works" in teaching and learning, "what is the advantage and disadvantage" of a teaching and/or learning method, "what is the vision for the future" of teaching and learning, or "what might be new frameworks" for the practice of teaching and learning (Hutchings 2000). For interior design, these questions can be coupled with the disciplinary context to build new knowledge about "what we teach" and "how we teach."

Two Courses, Two Pedagogical Pathways

The value of SoTL can be seen through an examination of two case studies that were conducted in a program accredited by Council for Interior Design Association (CIDA), at a public research university. These case studies serve as examples that illustrate the potential impact of SoTL on interior design pedagogy and the profession. Each case study approached different research questions and educational contexts (see Table 26.1). Case Study 1 concentrated on ways of fostering better communication in the design process of interior design studios. Case Study 2 focused on the implementation of disciplinary interior design knowledge into the graphic design context of a portfolio course.

Table 26.1   Overview of cases

	Case 1	*Case 2*
Research question	How can studio instruction improve student learning and awareness of design thinking processes?	How can interior design students' disciplinary knowledge be used within a portfolio class to make the transition from interiors to graphics easier?
Context	Fourth-year studio class	Upper-division portfolio design class
Data-collection tools	Observation, work product analysis, peer observation, student survey	Observation, focus groups, peer-review survey, student survey

Case Study 1: Interior Design Studio

After teaching a fourth-year interior design studio (Studio A), questions were raised in regard to the impact of grading criteria on student work and about how well students were able to explain the projects they had created. Reinforcement for the need to explore these questions more thoroughly came from feedback from design critiques done by practicing designers. These critiques indicated that although the students presented well-designed portfolios with good content, they did not show process and could not explain how they thought about the presented projects.

According to the literature, student awareness of design thinking and process skills promotes their ability to actively engage in a professional practice that values such leadership (Danko 2010; Marshall-Baker 2005; Pable 2009). To explore how to improve the teaching and learning that takes place during the design process in an upper-division design studio, a SoTL research project was developed and implemented as a subsequent, fourth-year studio (Studio B).

Purpose and research question

Teaching interior design requires more than technical skill development (e.g., building codes, drafting) and aesthetic training (e.g., design history, material selection). Similar to a humanities education, interior design develops an integrative mixture of thinking skills, informational knowledge, and intellectual context (Marshall-Baker 2005). If studios fail to challenge students to cohesively understand the learned skills, knowledge, and context within the process of resolving example design problems, the studio becomes merely rote practice.

Through the exploration of concerns about assessment criteria and student self-awareness, Studio A became a baseline for understanding such teaching and learning. Studio A focused on a large, multi-story, mixed-use design program that required integration of technical design issues within an aesthetic whole.

The students produced interesting, visually compelling, and critical designs, but could not individually explain how they did what they did. Similarly, when their design processes stalled, the students were frequently unable to see alternative approaches to the problem and adapt their processes. Studio A students had learned how to design, but were not necessarily aware of what they knew. They had learned, but were not truly educated. This observation framed the question: "How can studio instruction improve student learning and awareness of design thinking processes?"

Context

Only a handful of SoTL articles have been published about interior design studios specifically. These studies can be contextualized with SoTL research on design studios from similar fields (e.g., architecture, landscape architecture). While several SoTL articles were found which discussed different approaches to preparing design problems (Fernando 2006; Klassen 2003; Ozturk and Turkkan 2006), student information-gathering and -processing (Akalin and Sezal 2009; Bilda and Demirkan 2003; Kvan and Yunyan 2005; Sachs 1999), and methods of instructor–student feedback (Al-Qawasmi 2006; Bender and Vredevoogd 2006) the focus was on the goal of improving the studio rather than specifically aimed at improving the students' design process.

One example, from landscape architecture (Bose, Pennypacker, and Yahner 2006), was found that documented curricular and instructional changes to build students' ability to independently make design decisions. These studies, in combination with the work of de la Harpe, Peterson, Frankham, et al., provided the framework for developing the Case Study 1 SoTL project that was used in Studio B (de la Harpe et al. 2009).

According to de la Harpe et al., studio assessment preferences (e.g., design thinking, technical skills, communication) vary by the type of design education (de la Harpe et al. 2009). For example, art education places the highest priority on process over product while architecture and interior design emphasize the product. The Studio A assessment criteria weighted grading to emphasize product-oriented results: technical thinking (e.g., building codes, system integration) (45%), final design product (21%), design process (14%), and communication (6%). As a consequence, these criteria affected where students focused their attention. Students' time and thought focused on crafting representations and resolving detailed issues (e.g., code requirements). Although the instruction integrated the issues, the students understood that the assessment criteria and school culture emphasized something else. Therefore, unless instruction and/or assessment criteria changed, the students were unlikely to redirect their studio efforts.

Research design

The SoTL research plan consisted of revisions in instructional approach and assessment criteria and research data-gathering methods. Although Studio B instruction remained similar to that of to Studio A, it included dedicated time for dialogue about design processes. This was augmented with focused student-by-student discussion of individual design processes. Studio assessment criteria were reapportioned in the following way: design process (35%), technical/criteria thinking skills (25%), communication/graphics (25%), and design product (15%). These revised assignment submission standards were supported by the assessment criteria. For example, the new assignments added self-reflective activities that focused on process, demonstrated in examples of student work found in Figure 26.1.

The rationale for this assessment scheme was explicitly explained to Studio B participants. Studio B completed a similarly complex project in terms of scope, issues, and duration as the project done in Studio A. SoTL data for research validation were gathered using instructor self-reflective notes, outside faculty feedback on student performance, and student surveys. The Web-based surveys included a baseline survey during the first week of the course and a post-studio survey after the final assignment was completed. The survey documented students' perceptions and recognition of their design abilities.

Emergent findings

Analysis of teaching and learning in Studio B demonstrated that: (1) students recognized the value of developing their individual design processes; (2) the focused and individual instruction on design process improved student confidence when working with "mildly challenging" and "difficult" design problems; and (3) instruction about the design process provided a link between student practices and design process language and structures.

Students in Studio B were initially reticent and uncertain about the unfamiliar assessment criteria. The criteria were different than those used in previous studios and concurrent sections at the same studio level. As the term progressed, five students specifically communicated their appreciation in being challenged to express ideas rather than simply produce work. Most of these students' comments referenced specific improvements the student had made to his or her design process.

The baseline and post-studio surveys (n = 9, 60% response, and n = 8, 53% response, respectively) revealed that Studio B students recognized development in their abilities to improve potential design solutions, to resolve conflicts within solutions, and, specifically, increased confidence in their ability to solve more difficult problems. The survey also revealed continuing student discomfort with linking design process to professional practice.

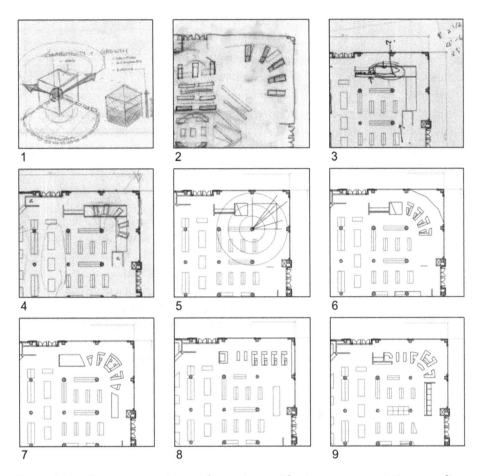

Figure 26.1 Design process images demonstrating ideation, re-representation, recycling, and development commonly observed within the design process of Studio A and Studio B. Images adapted from Studio A design process images, 2009. Original images by C. Brewe, A. Congdon, and H. Usui.

Review of the finalized work, including design graphics and student-documented process images, suggested that most students were actively engaged in the typical components of the design process and design thinking (e.g., re-representation of ideas, abstracted communication). However, the students were typically unaware of their actions or approach until the components were pointed out. Individual, situation-based instruction regarding a student's design process showed improvement in the student's ability to describe and alter his or her process. It was found that, while demonstrably valuable, this process-focused instruction approach was time-consuming and limited the time available to work with students on technical design issues.

Case Study 2: Portfolio Design Class

This case study was conducted during a portfolio design course for interior design students. SoTL research in Class A focused on defining the obstacles affecting students' portfolio design process and learning experience. Lack of systematic design processes, including a deeper understanding of design principles, and use of a different terminology were two issues affecting students' comprehension in the portfolio design class. In order to ease the students' knowledge transfer from interiors to graphics, the course was restructured the subsequent year (Class B).

Purpose and research question

Every design field practices similar "designerly ways" of developing solutions (Archer 1984; Cross 1982). Disciplinary design principles, processes, history, and theory refer to similar backgrounds. Hence, interior design students are expected to realize the commonalities between interior design and graphic design and to use their design knowledge from interiors to solve graphic design problems. However, the teaching experience in Class A showed that the students who were successful in applying design principles in interior design struggled to apply the same principles to the graphic design of portfolios. Rather than developing their portfolio through a systematic process, students tried to develop a graphic design solution immediately. Furthermore, students were not utilizing their knowledge about design principles while solving graphic design problems. For example, while students were utilizing negative space within an interior design solution, they lost their appreciation of negative space in the design of their portfolios.

Through observations in interior design studio, two main differences were noted between the studio and the portfolio class: (a) the implementation of design process and (b) the use of terminology. While interior design students were familiar with terms such as "program" and "parti," in the portfolio class these terms were replaced with "self-analysis" and "visual identity."

The effect of disciplinary language as a communication and knowledge-exchange barrier has previously been addressed within interdisciplinary contexts (Brotman, Kelliher, and Spicer 2008; Kolodner 1995; Lawson, Franz, and Adkins 2005). However, the impact of terminology on teaching across disciplinary content has not been studied in depth. None of the existing portfolio design books (e.g., Bender 2008; Mitton 2010) was found to define the portfolio design process as an interior design project. So, the question became, "How could interior design students' disciplinary knowledge be used within a portfolio design class to make the transition from interiors to graphics easier?"

Context

In order to address the problems observed in Class A, Class B was restructured. Students were introduced to portfolio design process using terms from interior design. Design process was also introduced as a criterion for grading (10%). All the submission dates were defined by the end products using standard interior design phases. For example, at the end of programming, students submitted a programming document reporting their professional and personal goals together with portfolio objectives. At the end of conceptual design, students submitted two visual identity concepts for their portfolio solutions.

Of the 40 students who were enrolled in Class B, 36 (90%) volunteered for this study. All of the students were fourth-year interior design students with no previous background in graphic design.

Research design

The main research methodology was design ethnography; a research "process that sits at the intersection of participatory action research, critical ethnography, and socially responsive instructional design" (Barab et al. 2004). Design ethnography is different from ethnography in the sense that design ethnographers are not only passive observers, but also are actively involved in trying to transform the education of others (Barab, Thomas, Dodge, et al. 2004).

Data were collected from three sources. First, observations in the class were recorded in a journal. Second, student focus groups, which were conducted at week 13, were followed by a student survey at the end of the semester. Third, eight interior design faculty members participated in a peer-review survey at which they were asked to evaluate representative students' work (five cases from Class A and five case from Class B) based on design principles. Examples of this survey are found in Figure 26.2.

Emergent findings

Analysis of the data from Class B showed that the introduction of the portfolio design with interior design terminology and process helped students to: (1) focus on the process of building a portfolio rather than only the end product; (2) better handle the portfolio design process; (3) develop knowledge about how to solve other graphic design problems; and (4) appreciate the significance of graphics for visual communication.

Still, the intervention in Class B brought new challenges. Students were observed having difficulties applying the steps of an interior design project in portfolio design and they struggled to make the transition from 3D to 2D. For example, the majority of students had difficulty defining a concept or reasoning for their portfolio design solution.

The qualitative analysis of the student survey, focus groups, and peer-review survey helped evaluate the class from other perspectives. From the perspective of peer reviewers, students from Class B were slightly more successful in transferring knowledge from interiors to graphics (here the knowledge transfer was evaluated

Figure 26.2   An example from the data-collection instrument created to collect insights from peer reviewers. Source: Isil Oygur.

based on the use of universal design principles such as harmony, hierarchy, and proportion). The application of design principles in the initial layout concepts and final layout solutions were found to be more successful than in Class A. On the other hand, according to peer reviewers, Class B students' application of design principles improved less from initial layout solution to final solution than Class A's.

In the student surveys, students listed the scale difference, 2D versus 3D, not having a client (designing for oneself), detailing, and not having a definitive space to work with as five major differences between interior design and portfolio design. Seventy-eight percent of students reported having difficulty developing a concept and defining a portfolio based on personal and professional goals.

As a general rule the students in both classes spent the most time on the design development phase, followed by preparation of the final deliverables, while less time was spent on the conceptual design and pre-design phases. Compared to Class A, Class B students experimented more with layout solutions and improved their design gradually throughout the semester, thereby demonstrating that students gained a better understanding of the portfolio design process. At the end of the semester, 62% of the students stated their perception of graphic design problems that they tackled outside of the class had changed (e.g., presentations).

While the intervention in Class B had some positive results, knowledge transfer was only improved to a limited extent. It was concluded that because graphic design and interior design are so different, to obtain a more complete transfer of knowledge between disciplines would require more than simply adjusting terminology and process.

Relationship to Interior Design Pedagogy and Profession

The results of both case studies have had immediate application in how we, and hopefully others, teach interior design. More importantly, both cases produced new knowledge about ways of teaching and learning interior design, created a platform to exchange knowledge about pedagogy, and revealed information about the practice of interior design. With these things in mind, let us return to the SoTL questions posed earlier.

What does the field of SoTL have to offer interior design?

Our SoTL-based research experience and research findings are in line with the literature that describes SoTL as a venue for collective pedagogical development (Huber and Hutchings 2005; Hutchings 2000; Weimer 2006). Our research agenda has given us the chance to discuss and exchange knowledge and ideas on different – and otherwise unrelated – courses that we normally approached in an isolated manner. In so doing, we realized that, in spite of the contextual differences, our challenges and research questions were similar. In asking how to improve teaching and learning in interior design, the questions became about how we know, what we know, what we need to know, and how we receive knowledge. In our case studies, these questions were transformed into questions about design process and design knowledge.

Case Study 1 provided insight into how we know what we do by identifying what students already knew and how that knowledge was demonstrated to others. With a similar approach, Case Study 2 more specifically examined how what we know was transferred between contexts. Our studies made it possible for us to discuss these issues together, learn from each other's experiences, apply existing literature to these issues, and work towards answers to our problems. This collective value of SoTL serves to continuously improve interior design pedagogy. As explained by scholars from other disciplines (Healey 2000; Huber and Hutchings 2005; McKinney 2004; Weimer 2006), both of the case studies discussed are longitudinal and illustrate that SoTL is not a straightforward process.

Our first teaching experience in these courses helped us to refine some ideas – which we then sought to address in our second year of teaching the courses. While the second-year experiences resolved some of the issues, we also realized several misconceptions and soon developed new ideas for further research. Consequently, the case studies yielded more questions, while at the same time not fully answering all of our initial questions.

For example, although Case Study 1 showed that instruction could improve students' understanding of studio design processes, we noted that students were still confused when it came to transferring design process skills to other problems. Similarly, while Case Study 2 suggested the positive impact of disciplinary terminology and process on knowledge transfer, it also raised questions about what things were the most important to emphasize in an interdisciplinary work environment.

Both SoTL case studies suggested ways to develop and improve our "disciplinary" knowledge. Case Study1 applied general design knowledge to an interior design-specific situation to reveal unique issues within the discipline. Case Study 2 demonstrated that the translation of design principles between disciplinary projects complicates learning. Both situations directed us to reconsider how interior design was taught and furthered our understanding of how interior design relates to other design disciplines.

These conclusions demonstrated the need for repetition to verify results and deepen knowledge. In other words, we were able to clearly see that SoTL research cannot – and should not – be a series of single studies. We believe that our case studies should be reported, analyzed, and linked with other interior design SoTL research done by other educators and practitioners engaged in SoTL research. We believe our case studies reinforce the collective value of SoTL and that the application of SoTL research methodologies goes beyond the simple improvement of an individual educator. Our experience with SoTL research has led us to conclude that its application will strengthen interior design knowledge and understanding within the academy and ultimately contribute to the professional identity and practice of interior design.

What would be the characteristics of a high-quality SoTL-based study in interior design?

Distinct from other well-established disciplines, the discussion in interior design regarding "vocation versus discipline" affects the characteristics of SoTL-based research studies. While existing SoTL-based studies include experiential and systematic approaches to teaching and learning (Weimer 2006), the case studies discussed here demonstrate the need to conduct systematic, rigorous, and critical pedagogical studies in order for interior design to grow as a discipline. The types of research methods will vary based on the questions, researchers, and context, but must always be carefully selected and implemented to ensure the validation of the research outcomes as legitimate knowledge. Subjective "best practices" research based on a single experience, or biased by viewpoint, provides only limited advancement of interior design knowledge.

As suggested by Huber and Hutchings, disciplinary issues in interior design can be reflected in SoTL-based studies (Huber and Hutchings 2005). Our case studies demonstrate that research questions in interior design extend pedagogical issues specific to teaching while at the same time providing questions relevant to the interior design profession and the nature of designing.

We argue that SoTL uniquely addresses practice as part of the fundamental questions regarding how students and teachers think about the discipline. Researching how we know, or what methods affect learning, provides opportunities to examine closely held doctrines about the design process – all of which are learned design processes and serve as the foundation of professional practice.

The SoTL perspective promotes asking questions that follow ideas from practice into pedagogy. For example, the implementation of new technology (e.g., three-dimensional digital modeling) in practice transforms how we work. SoTL research related to how we learn to use such new technology can reveal how it also changes how we think. Furthermore, although interior design is similar to other design disciplines, both cases studies questioned how we are similar and unique as a design discipline (e.g., "Is an interior design studio the same as a graphic design studio?"; "Are learning characteristics distinct for interior design students in comparison to architecture students?"). Consequently, high-quality SoTL-based studies can serve to address pedagogy along with important professional and disciplinary issues.

Lastly, although SoTL offers a structure for pedagogical studies, it cannot impact broader professional and disciplinary issues unless it is shared and valued (Huber and Hutchings 2005; Shulman 1999; Weimer 2006). The lack of rigorous forums for discussing interior design-specific SoTL research limits knowledge exchange and integration. Although some discussion of SoTL research occurs at professional conferences, the availability of proceedings and records of these discussions is limited – thereby limiting the effectiveness of conference presentations to build a referential set of knowledge.

In both of our case studies, our search for previous SoTL studies required looking to other disciplines' SoTL publications because there was no existing SoTL platform in interior design to be found. We believe a solid interior design SoTL platform would allow the discipline to learn more effectively from others' experiences and to increase the pace of pedagogical development. Such common ground would also open new opportunities for cross-disciplinary communication. Sharing and exchanging knowledge with other disciplines would ease interior design's institutional issues within the academy by broadening the dissemination and public discussion of interior design research.

How can future generations of interior design educators benefit from training that includes SoTL?

The SoTL case studies presented here address developing knowledge unique to interior design. In this sense, we have illustrated how future generations of interior design educators can use pedagogy as a tool to advance interior design teaching and learning, maintain disciplinary boundaries, and identify cross-disciplinary knowledge exchange.

Even though we taught the same courses for two consecutive years, our teaching experiences were quite different. Approaching the studio and class as research cases to be rigorously studied and analyzed prevented the teaching from becoming tacit repetition. Instead, we felt like strangers in the classroom. This heightened awareness, gave us the chance to observe more clearly and to learn from each day. We believe this aspect of SoTL-based studies can be particularly helpful to both new instructors and more experienced educators.

Knowledge unique to interior design is shared between pedagogy and practice. The critical questioning of what we know in both arenas should be a central activity for educators and practitioners. SoTL can foster such questioning by forcing us to state how we know and how we think about problem-solving. For example, evidence-based design knowledge develops through both practice and academic-based research. Teaching design courses that integrate evidence-based design knowledge is not as simple as assembling puzzle pieces. A student cannot simply do everything that the evidence suggests and produce a design that is appropriate to the given problem. SoTL provides a way to investigate how students and designers navigate the integration of evidence with design process into a comprehensive project. This flow of knowledge between pedagogy and practice moves both forward.

Our argument here should not be interpreted as a statement about the relative roles of education and the profession. Although we advocate for the "scholarship of teaching" and learning within the academy, a parallel track of process-knowledge research can occur in other forums (e.g., the Interior Design Experience Program [IDEP], continuing education, inter-office communication) that would complete a cycle of knowing, doing, and transferring knowledge.

Final Words

Through mentorship relationships early in our teaching careers, SoTL became the context for us to critically self-evaluate our teaching experiences. We did not expect our research to lead us to suggest a way forward for the interior design pedagogy and profession; however, we are eager to share our learning experience in the hope of extending the discussion and cross-fertilization. Through SoTL research, we found that we were able to develop a platform to discuss issues on different courses, to establish a common ground to communicate with instructors from other disciplines, and to learn from others' teaching experiences.

We used two case studies to demonstrate how SoTL was used to improve teaching through continuous research within the classroom. The field's unknowns and the wicked nature of the professional act of design make it hard to solely focus on one's teaching and students' learning. This dilemma is apparent in our cases as well. Extrapolating case-specific results from the grounded processes and knowledge of the classroom to disciplinary ideas requires continuous effort. However, we firmly believe that linking pedagogy and the profession through process and knowledge is essential to advancing interior design education. How we teach affects knowledge and questioning that influences practice; practice changes what and how we teach. The pursuit of SoTL research in interior design demonstrates how fundamental questions about how we know, what we know, and how we transfer what we know define the profession.

In both case studies, our research results must be generalized with great caution because of unanticipated external factors that may have affected students' learning. For example, a change in department policy meant that Class A was a requirement for its students while Class B was an elective course. This change did not affect the course content, but did affect the dynamics within the classroom. Similarly, students in Studio B, compared to Studio A, had a wider range of prior design education experience, but a narrower set of cultural references. In-depth conversation with students helped delineate these differences, but the precise impact on the class cannot be fully known. Regardless of such limitations, the emergent results from the case studies demonstrate the benefits and promise of SoTL to impact interior design.

Regardless of these limitations, we advocate that a SoTL research agenda would strengthen interior design and help bridge disciplinary boundaries. Setting new SoTL research agendas begins by defining "what we know, what we do not know, and what we need to know" (McKinney 2004). We assert that asking these questions can – and will – address issues of pedagogical scholarship, as well as the professional future of interior design as a discipline.

Acknowledgements

We thank Nancy Blossom for her mentorship and for introducing us to SoTL.

Note

The two authors contributed equally to the conceptualization and writing of this essay.

References

Agouridas, V., and Race, P. 2007. "Enhancing knowledge management in design education through systematic reflection practice," *Concurrent Engineering* 15(1): 63–76.

Akalin, A. and Sezal, I. 2009. "The importance of conceptual and concrete modeling in architectural design education," *Journal of Art & Design Education* 28(1): 14–24.

Al-Qawasmi, J. 2006. "Transformations in design education: the paperless studio and the virtual design studio," *Open House International* 31(3): 95–102.

Anderson, B. G. 2008. "Letter: theoretical and practical expertise," *Journal of Interior Design* 33(3): iii–iv.

Archer, B. 1984. "Systematic methods for designers," in N. Cross (ed.), *Developments in Design Methodology*. Chichester: John Wiley & Sons, pp. 57–82.

Asojo, A. O. 2001. "A model for integrating culture-based issues in creative thinking and problem solving," *Journal of Interior Design* 27(2): 46–58.

Barab, S., Thomas, M., Dodge, T., et al. 2004. "Critical design ethnography: designing for change." *Anthropology & Education Quarterly* 35(2): 254–268.

Beecher, M. A. 2006. "Designing criticism: integrating written criticism in interior design education," *Journal of Interior Design* 31(3): 54–61.

Bender, D. M. 2008. *Design Portfolios: Moving from Traditional to Digital*. New York: Fairchild Books.

Bender, D. M., and Vredevoogd, J. D. 2006. "Using online education technologies to support studio instruction," *Educational Technology & Society* 9(4): 114–122.

Bilda, Z., and Demirkan, H. 2003. "An insight on designers' sketching activities in traditional versus digital media," *Design Studies* 24(1): 27–50.

Blossom, N., Oygur, I., and Orthel, B. D. 2011. "A new perspective for interior design pedagogy: the scholarship of teaching and learning" in *Proceedings of the Interior Design Educators Council's 2011 Annual Conference*, Denver, CO, March 16–19, pp. 362–366.

Blossom, N., Oygur, I., and Payne-Tofte, E. n.d. "A critique of design pedagogy: scholarship of teaching and learning in design." Unpublished paper.

Bose, M., Pennypacker, E., and Yahner, T. 2006. "Enhancing critical thinking through 'independent design decision making' in the studio," *Open House International* 31(3): 33–42.

Boyer, E. L. [1990] 1997. *Scholarship Reconsidered: Priorities of the Professoriate* (1st ed.). Princeton, NJ: Carnegie Foundation for the Advancement of Teaching.

Boyer, E. L., and Mitgang, L. D. 1996. *Building Community: A New Future for Architecture Education and Practice. A Special Report*. Princeton, NJ: Carnegie Foundation for the Advancement of Teaching.

Brotman, R., Kelliher, A., and Spicer, R. 2008. "Well, how would you do it? Facilitating the transfer of knowledge in collaborative design environments," in *Proceedings of the IDSA International Education Symposium*, pp. 29–36.

Carmel-Gilfilen, C., and Portillo, M. 2010. "Creating mature thinkers in interior design: pathways of intellectual development," *Journal of Interior Design* 35(3): 1–20.

Cross, N. 1982. "Designerly ways of knowing," *Design Studies* 3(4): 221–227.

Danko, S. 2010. "On designing change," *Journal of Interior Design* 36(1): v–x.

de la Harpe, B., Peterson, J. F., Frankham, N., et al. 2009. "Assessment focus in studio: what is most prominent in architecture, art and design?" *Journal of Art & Design Education* 28(1): 37–51.

Dickinson, J. I., Anthony, L., and Marsden J. P. 2009. "Faculty perceptions regarding research: are we on the right track?", *Journal of Interior Design* 35(1): 1–14.

Fernando, N. A. 2006. "Design as exploration: an integrative model," *Open House International* 31(3): 10–16.

Guerin, D. A., and Martin, C. S. 2004. "The career cycle approach to defining the interior design profession's body of knowledge," *Journal of Interior Design* 30(2): 1–22.

Guerin, D. A., and Thompson, J. A. 2004. "Interior design education in the 21st century: an educational transformation," *Journal of Interior Design* 30(1): 1–12.

Healey, M. 2000. "Developing the scholarship of teaching in higher education: a discipline-based approach." *Higher Education Research & Development* 19(2): 169–189.

Huber, M. T. and Hutchings, P. 2005. *The Advancement of Learning: Building the Teaching Commons* (1st ed.). San Francisco, CA: Jossey-Bass.

Huber, M. T. and Morreale, S. P. 2002. *Disciplinary Styles in the Scholarship of Teaching and Learning: Exploring Common Ground*. Sterling, VA: Stylus Publishing.

Hutchings, P., ed. 2000. *Opening Lines: Approaches to the Scholarship of Teaching and Learning*. Stanford, CA: Carnegie Foundation for the Advancement of Teaching.

Klassen, F. 2003. "Tangible to intangible," *Journal of Art & Design Education* 22(1): 92–99.

Kolodner, J. 1995. "Design education across the disciplines," in *Proceedings of the ASCE Specialty Conference, 2nd Congress on Computing in Civil Engineering*, pp. 318–333.

Kreber, C. 2002. "Teaching excellence, teaching expertise and the scholarship of teaching," *Innovative Higher Education* 27(1): 5–23.

Kucho, J., Turpin, J. C., and Pable, J. 2009 "A single interior design professional association: the time is now," *Journal of Interior Design* 34(3): vii–xx.

Kvan, T. and Yunyan, J. 2005. "Students' learning styles and their correlation with performance in architectural design studio," *Design Studies* 26(1): 19–34.

Lawson, B. 1990. *How Designers Think: The Design Process Demystified*. London: Butterworth Architecture.

Lawson, G. M., Franz, J. M., and Adkins, B. A. 2005. "Rhetoric of landscape architecture and interior design discourses: preparation for cross-disciplinary practice," *IDEA Journal* 41–49.

Marshall-Baker, A. 2005. "Knowledge in interior design," *Journal of Interior Design* 31(1): xiii–xxi.

McKinney, K. 2007. *Enhancing Learning through the Scholarship of Teaching and Learning: The Challenges and Joys of Juggling*. San Francisco: Jossey-Bass.

Mitton, M. 2010. *Portfolios for Interior Designers*. Hoboken, NJ: John Wiley & Sons.

Nussbaumer, L. L. 2001. "Theoretical framework for instruction that accommodates all learning styles," *Journal of Interior Design* 27(2): 3–15.

Ozturk, M. N., and Turkkan, E. E. 2006. "The design studio as teaching/learning medium – a process-based approach," *Journal of Art & Design Education* 25(1): 96–104.

Pable, J. 2009. "Interior design identity in the crossfire: a call for renewed balance in subjective and objective ways of knowing," *Journal of Interior Design* 34(2): v–xx.

Poldma, T. 2008. "Interior design at a crossroads: embracing specificity through process, research, and knowledge," *Journal of Interior Design* 33(3): vi–xvi.

Rowe, P. 1987. *Design Thinking*. Cambridge, MA: MIT Press.

Sachs, A. 1999. "'Stuckness' in the design studio," *Design Studies* 20(2): 195–209.

Shulman, L. S. 1999. "Taking learning seriously," *Change* 31(4): 11–17.

Tsang, A. 2010 "Pitfalls to avoid in establishing a SoTL academic pathway: an early career perspective," *International Journal for the Scholarship of Teaching and Learning* 4(2): 1–9.

Vischer, J. and Poldma, T. 2003. "Growing a discipline: evolving learning practices in interior design," *IDEA Journal* 173–184.

Weimer, M. 2006. *Enhancing Scholarly Work on Teaching and Learning: Professional Literature that Makes a Difference*. San Francisco: Jossey-Bass.

White, A. C. 2009. "What's in a name? Interior design and/or interior architecture: the discussion continues," *Journal of Interior Design* 35(1): x–xviii.

Zhu, Y. 2008. "Letter: scholarship of application and discovery," *Journal of Interior Design* 33(3): iv–v.

Zollinger, S. W., Guerin, D. A., Hadjiyanni, T., and Martin, C. S. 2009. "Deconstructing service-learning: a framework for interior design," *Journal of Interior Design* 34(3): 31–45.

Zuo, Q., Leonard, W., and MaloneBeach, E. E. 2010. "Integrating performance-based design in beginning interior design education: an interactive dialog between the built environment and its context," *Design Studies* 31(3): 268–287.

27

Engaging Voices within a Dynamic Problem-Based Learning Context

Tiiu Poldma

Introduction

Designing interiors for people's activities and situations is a complex process. Alongside the usual client requirements and protocols are circumstances in designing interior spaces that vary from context to need, and from situation to situation. Increasingly, complex issues and situations are changing how today's dynamic interior environments are designed.

In a universal sense, interior environments play a large role in the relative success of people of all ages and stages of life. The reality is that people are not uniform; they are large and small, culturally and physically different, and of all ages and at all stages of life. In other words, there is no such thing as an "average" person; however, our interior spaces continue to be designed with criteria and references to the "average" person's physical body type (Panero and Zelnik 1979; Pheasant 1996). Furthermore, access issues are determined by codes, rather than how people experience the space or how an interior might facilitate social interactions.

Rehabilitation Living Lab: Creating Inclusive Environments for Persons with Disabilities

This essay presents a design studio that is informed by context and research. The studio is part of a major research project called the Rehabilitation Living Lab:

The Handbook of Interior Design, First Edition. Edited by Jo Ann Asher Thompson and Nancy H. Blossom.

Creating Enabling Physical and Social Environments to Optimize Social Inclusion and Social Participation for Persons with Physical Disabilities.[1] The project, referred to as a Living Lab and supported by local government and institution funding, is an interdisciplinary and multi-sectorial research study that explores the principal obstacles, either physical or psychosocial, to social participation and inclusion for persons with disabilities in a commercial mall environment.

According to Ballon et al., a Living Lab is "an experimentation environment in which technology is given shape in real life contexts and in which [end] users are considered 'co-producers.'" In a Living Lab, technology and concepts are tested in a real-life context and end-users are important informants in the testing process. The Living Lab concept refers to methodologies where innovations, such as services, products, or application enhancements, are created and evaluated with a human-centric approach in real-world environments involving a mix of user representatives (Ballon et al. 2005).

The goal of the Rehabilitation Living Lab project is to initiate and develop technological and participatory/collaborative research that facilitates social inclusion and social participation for persons with disabilities. More specifically, the purpose of the Living Lab is "to contribute comprehensively to the autonomy and social integration of persons with physical disabilities, through basic research as well as through clinical, epidemiological, evaluative and applied research in both the biomedical and psychosocial domains, on all aspects of the handicap production process" (Living Lab n.d.) In an effort to include as many voices as possible in the research construction, the methodological approaches used in the Rehabilitation Living Lab project include constructivist forms of inquiry such as participatory action and pragmatist approaches (Guba and Lincoln 1994).

An urban shopping mall was chosen for the Rehabilitation Living Lab project because it provides an ecologically valid example of a societal microcosm where complex transactions and activities involving persons with and without disabilities routinely take place. It is within this context that the design studio case study presented here was conducted, challenging the students to create interior space in the mall that was inclusive of the lived experiences of people from all walks of life, and to incorporate into their thinking the voices of those who are not always heard in an aesthetic-driven design studio.

Understanding Voice

When designing interior spaces visual languages often dominate the process. However, such languages alone cannot always sufficiently address how people experience the interior spaces that designers create. These experiences are best understood by listening to the voices of the people who live, play, and work in an interior environment. In other words, only by incorporating into the design process an understanding of how people's experiences frame their worldview can the design of an interior space be truly meaningful.

In the Rehabilitation Living Lab mall project the stakeholders' "voices" underpin all research activities. Thus it was that the students, as participants in the project, quickly became attuned to the importance of paying attention to these "voices" during the design process. For the purposes of the design studio learning experience, the concept of "voice" was framed as Elliot Eisner suggests – as an exploration of how people experience everyday situations. According to Eisner, "[people] use language to reveal what paradoxically words can never say. … the reason for emphasizing "voice" … is to serve epistemological purposes. What we look for, as well as what we do or say, is influenced by the tools we know how to use" (Eisner 1991). Eisner also refers to how languages, both visual and verbal, frame how we understand ways of knowing. Because the concept of "voice" takes into account how people of all ages and at various stages of life experience diverse situations, Eisner maintains it is through listening to their "voices" that ways of knowing can be better understood. Belenky, Clinchy, Goldberger, and Tarule agree, and propose that new and different knowledge types are constructed when situational and actual experiences are considered. (Belenky et al. 1997; Poldma 2013).

Therefore it can be said that the voices of people form the crux of understanding human-situated problems in physical and social environments. These voices may be those of the designer, the user, or the researcher, each contributing to the design context (Eisner 1991; Ely, Vinz, Downing, and Anzul 1997).

It is with this understanding of "voice" that the students in the Rehabilitation Living Lab design studio were asked to produce designs for the mall that acknowledged the voices of the multiple users and stakeholders (i.e., users who were disabled, users who were not disabled, management representatives, employees, etc.) During the design studio these voices were shared as a form of cooperative inquiry (Heron and Reason 2001).

The Research Approach

As part of the Rehabilitation Living Lab project, the design studio incorporated a constructivist/pragmatic inquiry approach, with the data collection predicated on participatory action research. Participatory research, a form of action research, "aims to contribute both to the practical concerns of people in an immediate problematic situation and to further the goals of social science simultaneously… [Action research] requires the active collaboration of researcher and client, and stresses the importance of co-learning as a primary aspect of the research process" (Gilmore, Krantz, and Ramirez 1986).

O'Brien asserts that what separates action research from general professional practices is the emphasis on scientific study; that is to say that a problem is systematically studied and solutions are informed by theoretical considerations. In action research much of the researcher's time is spent refining the methodological tools to suit the situation, and on collecting, analyzing, and presenting data on an ongoing and cyclical basis (O'Brien 1998).

Such an approach was in keeping with the goals of the Rehabilitation Living Lab, whereby research is conducted while actively participating in a change situation, emphasizing principles of collective inquiry and experimentation grounded in experience and social history. In this type of research Creswell suggests that

> knowledge claims arise out of actions, situations and consequences rather than antecedent conditions (as in postpositivism). There is a concern with applications – "what works" – and solutions to problems…Instead of methods being important, the problem is most important and researchers use all methods to understand the problem. (Creswell 2003)

Several research tools were used to document information and record the physical issues of the mall. Action research approaches and grounded theory techniques and interviews were used to glean user needs. Analytic methods included visual content analysis for the physical visual documentation (Rose 2001), phenomenological reading and interpretive methods of reflection using reflective and analytic memos for analyzing the data (Ely et al. 1997), and grounded theory development of categories that emerged in the analyses conducted (Charmaz 1990; Poldma 2013; Price 1999).

The Phenomenological Walkabouts in the Living Lab

To be able to capture the voices of various people in ways that are authentic and trustworthy, conversations are vital. One way to record this more tacit form of knowledge empirically is through the documentation of lived experience, as supported by a phenomenological perspective (Creswell 2003; Price 1999). People's experiences are best understood as they use the space in real time.

In order to do this, researchers in the Rehabilitation Living Lab accompany users and stakeholders in "walkabouts" of the mall environment. The students in the design studio completed similar exercises, accompanying designers, researchers, stakeholders, and persons with disabilities as they moved through the mall. In this way, they learned the issues, both personal and social, at first hand by experiencing the spaces in the mall in real time with real users. Discussions and conversations during the walkabouts were conducted and recorded using an open-ended interview process (Ely et al. 1997; Rubin and Rubin 2005).

The Social Construction of Space and
Subsequent Experiences

Voices, as a reflection of personal experience, cannot occur in isolation. Everyone engages, in one way or another, with everyday life – whether it is through the way we move in and within various types of interior spaces or through the way we experience social situations. This engagement is varied and subjectively situated within each person's experience. How people use and experience space is vital to the relative success of a designed interior. Confrontations with the social construction of reality are necessary to situate how things actually work in real-world settings and how people actually feel about their experience within interior spaces.

An individual's social construction of reality is, in essence, the construction of the reality that happens within the context of the real environment. As Berger and Luckmann suggest in *The Social Construction of Reality*, "The world of everyday life is structured both spatially and temporally" (Berger and Luckmann 1966). According to these authors, social constructions are manifested in the inter-subjective experiences that everyone has as they go about living their lives. These experiences and activities are framed by how each person's own personal and social constructions are situated, how spaces and places are located within those experiences, and how this reality is shared with others (Berger and Luckmann 1966).

From the moment of birth, spaces contribute to how people see their own reality. The social constructions of space and place, at least in part, create the social roles and relationships that govern how people live, work, and play (Spain 1992; Vaikla-Poldma 2003). Spaces influence social relationships and contribute to the constructions that govern social and political interactions. These value constructions influence how space is designed, and contribute to the reproduction of values. (Spain 1992; Vaikla-Poldma 2003). Starting at home within the family, these social constructions and relationships continue and expand as people engage in the realms of work, leisure, and community.

Problem-Based and Project-Based Learning in Design

Incorporating the concepts of voice and social construction of space into design studio learning helps students to reflect on situations and to develop empathetic – yet aesthetic – design solutions. The use of problem-based and project-based modules set in reality as a learning tool helps students understand theories of design juxtaposed against the realities that drive professional problem-solving in real-world contexts. The important nuances to understand about project-based learning are context and subject (De Graaff and Kolmos 2007; Kolmos, Fink, and Krogh 2004; Savin-Baden and Major 2004).

In this type of learning exercise, the teacher acts in the role of facilitator rather than in the more traditional role of teacher-as-expert or teacher-as-deliverer-of-information. In such an instructional approach the teacher's role is to provoke students to teach themselves. This type of learning experience is "voice-situated" and occurs when students are allowed to unfold the activities of the studio while the teacher, acting as a facilitator, assists them in the process. (Kolmos et al. 2004; Savin-Baden and Major 2004). Such an approach is student-centered and puts the students in an active role in their learning experience, acknowledging the students' voices as central to the learning experience and requiring students to be responsible participants (Essential Schools n.d.).

An important aspect of this learning approach is the interaction between and among the students, the users and/or clients, and the real-world setting. As Savin-Baden and Major suggest, this can be accomplished by "an integration of theory and practice…a focus on processes…and…concepts" such as "case-based lectures…where students meet with a client in some form of simulated format where free inquiry is allowed to take place" (Savin-Baden and Major 2004).

In the Rehabilitation Living Lab design studio, students analyzed the information that they collected, met with the various stakeholders and users as simulated "clients," and discussed issues during the walkabouts that occurred in the mall. This required the students to confront how their theory-informed concepts could be applied in practical situations. (Botti-Salitsky 2009; Nussbaumer 2009). In addition, through their interactions with the Rehabilitation Living Lab researchers, students began to clearly understand the difference between research and information-gathering – situating research in a different context entirely from programmatic information-gathering.

The Design Project

At the beginning of the studio, the students were introduced to the project (i.e., a branded commercial interior public space for a shopping mall) and exposed to where the mall was situated (i.e., an urban environment bordered by both an upscale residential neighborhood and a subsidized-housing, lower-income neighborhood). Next, the students were exposed to the research of over 45 researchers, collaborators, and stakeholders from design, anthropology, architecture, rehabilitation, occupational therapy, medicine, sociology, and psychology involved in the Rehabilitation Living Lab project.

As an initial exercise, students were asked to examine how the current design of the mall responded (or did not respond) to people's experiences, to issues of way-finding, and to universal issues of access for people with disabilities. This was accomplished in several ways, through interviews and discussions with the users on site, and by poring over the research data of the physical characteristics provided by the researchers and their students. As part of the Rehabilitation Living Lab project the students interacted repeatedly in the mall space with different project collaborators, including the mall manager, Master's and doctoral students and designers, and users with disabilities. All the conditions and experiences gleaned during these exchanges were discussed and documented.

Once the exercise was completed and the students returned to the studio they were asked to reflect on what they had seen and experienced. Technological and visual considerations such as way-finding tools and signage from a universal design perspective were discussed and considered as possible tools for transforming the space (Lidwell, Holden, and Butler 2003).

A major contextual issue that students had to consider was the commercial aspect of the mall complex and determining the relative importance of the diverse points of view from users and other stakeholders. Confronting diverse views and reflecting on decision-making is a vital aspect of interior design practice – the simulation of which in an academic design studio is difficult to do. The difficulty in simulation comes from the impossibility of providing students with all the inherent complexities that are found in a situated context and the contradictions that these generate.

In the Rehabilitation Living Lab design studio these different voices were situated in the realities of practice, rather than created by the instructor to represent client-based needs and user types. The reality of these contradictions was evident and the students soon became aware of how such contradictions are often intertwined with individual wants and needs. For example, while the shopping complex was a place understood by some to be a destination place of necessity (service), it was also seen as a destination for shopping, social get-togethers, meetings, and even exercising. This was in contrast to the mall owners and manager, who still saw the mall as a place where commerce was primary and, in fact, vital.

In these contexts, design intention and marketing realities may seemingly be in contradiction with the needs of people with disabilities. By exposing the students directly to this issue, the learning that occurred was focused on the complexity of user dynamics. In this type of learning, the dynamics that form the backdrop for design intentions and the aesthetic ideas that ensue.

Discussion of the Pedagogy

It is important to remember that the pedagogical goal of the Rehabilitation Living Lab design studio was to help students understand complex problem-based learning in a context-based studio project. From the teacher's perspective, the implementation of a project that took into account multiple contextual variables and worked *in situ* with existing physical conditions and real constraints added value to the learning experience.

Encouraging students to design by means of actual problem-solving requires that the students' design concepts are responsive to a specific mandate. The teacher in the Rehabilitation Living Lab design studio explains his approach in the following way:

> The ultimate aim is to help the student realize that design, and/or the designer's intervention, does not start and end with the concept…[students need to develop an] understanding that the design process begins with the client, responds to a mandate and concludes with the end-user.

With this in mind, the teacher – acting in the role of facilitator – provided a learning framework to help integrate the voices of users and other stakeholders into the design thinking of the students. In this case, the learning framework included:

- The establishment of procedures, protocols, and priorities
- The identification and organization of a preliminary schedule of activities
- The production of programs that explicated the different requirements and identified the various phases of work
- The articulation of concerns, needs, and/or specific criteria expressed by the client
- The gathering of all relevant technical and regulatory data

Throughout the studio experience, students were encouraged to collaborate with the Rehabilitation Living Lab researchers and to have conversations with different stakeholders in the mall to acquire an in-depth understanding of how to frame their design concepts. Collaboration between the students in the design studio and the Rehabilitation Living Lab participants provided them with cutting-edge information about the development of various physical and virtual platforms and infrastructures that could be used to create enabling environments for social inclusion and social participation of people with disabilities of all kinds. This collaboration included exposing the students to innovative technological tools and practices (Kehayia, Swaine, Poldma, and Desjardins 2012).

Through conversations and interviews with stakeholders involved in the Rehabilitation Living Lab project, the students (as designers) were able to put into context the issues underpinning their design choices and were able to co-construct with users through their experiences, spaces in the mall that were both aesthetic and functional.

According to the literature, contextual design such as this studio learning experience is a situated method that emphasizes interviews conducted in the user's context, co-designing with the user, building an understanding of the user's context, and summarizing conclusions (Wixon, Holtzblatt, and Knox 1990).

Voice-situated studio learning

As discussed earlier, the design studio learning experience was situated within the context of a real project (the mall) with real users (people with disabilities and other stakeholders). In keeping with this approach, the voices of various users and participants became an important component of the "voice-situated" studio learning experience. It was through listening and interpreting these voices that the students were confronted with conflicting perspectives and faced with the challenge of reconciling what they were hearing from these constituent groups with the commercial, consumer, and cultural needs of the mall, as well as with their own aesthetic design intentions.

Because the design studio's focus was on "voice-situated" learning, a "voice-centered" understanding of peoples' intersubjective experience in the mall was necessary to determine their actual, specific, and intimate needs. This was accomplished primarily through the walkabouts.

The walkabouts were predicated on a phenomenological approach where together researchers, designers, and participants shared their actual lived experiences as they occurred in the space in real time (Poldma 2013; Price 1999). The inquiry modes of this approach are situated in action research wherein informal conversational interviews guide the inquiry (Ely et al. 1997; Rubin and Rubin 2005). According to the literature, such walkabouts are participatory forms of inquiry that seek to uncover and transform practices (Creswell 2003).

This inquiry approach allowed the students to reflect on their own experiences and to integrate the empirical results they uncovered into their design conceptualization. Such reflections stimulated the students to examine for themselves the way they approached design problem-solving. The facilitator role of the studio instructor in this learning exercise supported a process whereby students' design solutions unfolded in accordance with the voices of the people with whom they spoke in the walkabouts.

During the studio experience examples of student projects and the results of ongoing research were shared. These discussions provided the students with insights into cooperative inquiry and participatory action research using problem-based learning in a practice-based scenario. In this way, knowledge was constructed when theory and practice came together, voices were heard, and design concepts of interest to all stakeholders and users were generated.

Discussion

The goal of Rehabilitation Living Lab design studio was to help students understand the complex dynamics of universal design issues, corporate needs in public spaces, and how design processes and solutions contribute to these contexts. In this learning exercise, students were confronted with several issues and were challenged to construct their understanding of the design problem through collaboration with researchers, listening to the voices of users, and gathering information.

In this situated design exercise, the studio served as the place where knowledge was built from the perspectives of inquiry (theory) and a pragmatic approach of thinking-as-doing – in this case, using the commercial shopping mall as the scenario (practice). It was necessary, in this circumstance, for students to reflect on theory and then engage in solutions driven by practice – while being able to return to theory to reflect on the design solution's impact on the people that their design was to serve (Poldma 2013).

There were several learning outcomes that resulted from this situated design studio approach, serving to increase the students' understanding and appreciation for

- participatory action research as a useful tool in the co-construction of knowledge;
- the importance of understanding the social constructions of interior environments;

- how to deal with the complexity of multiple and dynamic voices in a real setting;
- how problem-based and project-based learning can help to clarify disparate issues (e.g., universal design and commercial branding).

In addition to these learning outcomes, the students in the Rehabilitation Living Lab design studio enhanced their skills in critical self-awareness and judgment by reflecting on their practices as they occurred. Small, informal group critiques and regular discussions with peers and teachers allowed for the problems and practices to be discussed, interpreted, and better understood.

Conclusion

In a process such as this, questions inevitably occur. For example: Who decides the best or most aesthetic design solution? Which voices are the most important? Who determines what is a successful design? These are the type of value judgments that designers make on a routine basis. Margolin and Buchanan suggest that who decides is influenced by the competitive environment within which decision-making is made, and that this is imbued with values and value judgments (Margolin and Buchanan 1995). According to Margolin and Buchanan, this is the "fourth discovery of design," and they explain it in this way:

> The fourth discovery of design is a domain of contested principles and values, where competing ideas about individual and social life are played out in vivid debate through material and immaterial products…It is not a question of which principles and values should guide design…Rather, the key issue is, who shall judge? Should it be the designer, the manufacturer, or critics of taste, or scientific and technical experts, or segments of the population, or the individual customer, or society and culture at large? Increasingly, this translates in design literature into a struggle to determine who is the designer and how the activity of designing can best represent the interests and values of the human user. (Margolin and Buchanan 1995)

In reality, the designer, the user, and the recipient all have a stake in the process of design. It is through a situated design problem that students confront these issues in a real context (Poldma 2013). Direct contact with clients, users, and various stakeholders makes the design problem real and facilitates their questioning of how designs are conceived.

The instructor of the Rehabilitation Living Studio design studio reflected on his own experience in this way:

> Working with and from a specific mandate, along with existing conditions, helped to focus the students a lot better than other studios that I've initiated in the past, whereby projects where primarily hypothetical and or mainly conceptual.

Positive feedback received from the Rehabilitation Living Lab participants in regard to the activities of the students in the design studio reinforced the benefits of a problem-based situated design teaching approach. One participant expressed it this way, "The students are the future and they are very interested in our problems – which we appreciate."

The response of students to the learning exercise was equally positive, pointing specifically at the importance of access to the users and stakeholders of the mall in their design thinking. Students further expressed appreciation for the opportunity to work with the researchers in the Rehabilitation Living Lab, citing how this exposure had improved their understanding of the problem and helped them to sort through the contradictions they faced, thereby enriching their learning experience. With the help of their teacher-facilitator, students were able to reflect on (and make sense of) the information they had collected, to interpret their findings, and to organize the information and propose protocols that suited the project issues in a final design solution.

Student learning is engaged and innovative when they are confronted with real people with real experiences, contexts, and learning situations that put the problem first. The situated contexts of both the real-life settings and the Rehabilitation Living Lab research project added richness to the design studio. Final design presentations and critiques which included the perspectives of the users and other stakeholders of the mall constructively added to students' understanding of the relative success of their proposed design solutions.

Solving complex problems situated in real-life settings means considering issues that are divergent, and yet necessary to reconcile. In this case study, students were able to grasp how to integrate design intent and aesthetics with issues of diverse user needs as a means of problem-solving. Problem-based learning and project-based situations integrate both theory and practice, generate innovative and new ideas as possibilities for both improving the space and its use, and help students to rethink the value of diverse users and how they can add value to designed environments.

Notes

Some of the concepts of this essay were presented at the DRS Cumulus Design and Education Conference with co-author Michael Joannidis, in Oslo, Norway, in May 2013.

1 The Rehabilitation Living Lab is a four-year (2011–2015) research project funded by the FRQ-S, Government of Quebec, Canada. This project is a multi-sectorial research project headed by Dr. Eva Kehayia (McGill University) and Dr. Bonnie Swaine (Université de Montréal) and includes the following co-researchers: Sara Ahmed (McGill University), Philippe Archambault (McGill University), Joyce Fung (McGill University), Guylaine LeDorze (Université de Montréal), Dahlia Kairy (Université de Montréal), Anouk Lamontagne (McGill University), Hélène Lefebvre (Université de Montréal), Olga Overbury (Université de Montréal), and Tiiu Poldma (Université de Montréal). This project is made possible by a grant from FRQ-S (Government of Quebec) and is also supported by the management team of the Place Alexis Nihon shopping complex in Montreal. All research is still ongoing and several articles on other aspects of the project have been previously published in peer review journals and books.

References

Ballon, P., Pierson, J., and Delaere, S. 2005. *Open Innovation Platforms for Broadband Services: Benchmarking European Practices.* Proceedings of 16th European Regional Conference, Porto, Portugal, September 4–6, 2005.

Belenky, M. F., Clinchy, B. M., Goldberger, N. R., and Tarule, J. M. 1997. *Women's Ways of Knowing: The Development of Self, Voice, and Mind.* New York: Basic Books.

Berger, P. L. and Luckmann, T. 1966. *The Social Construction of Reality.* New York: Anchor Books.

Charmaz, K. 1990. "Discovering chronic illness: using grounded theory," *Social Science & Medicine* 30(11): 1161–1172.

Creswell, J. 2003. *Research Design: Qualitative, Quantitative and Mixed Methods Approaches.* (2nd ed.). Thousand Oaks, CA: Sage Publications.

De Graaff, E. and Kolmos, A., eds. 2007. *Management of Change: Implementation of Problem-Based and Project-Based Learning in Engineering.* Delft University of Technology, The Netherlands and Aalborg University, Denmark: Sense Publishers.

Eisner, E. W. 1991. *The Enlightened Eye: Qualitative Inquiry and the Advancement of Educational Practice.* New York: Macmillan.

Ely, M., Vinz, R., Downing, M., and Anzul, M. 1997. *On Writing Qualitative Research: Living By Words.* London: Falmer Press.

Essential Schools. n.d. *The Coalition of Essential Schools.* http://www.essentialschools.org/benchmarks/10). Accessed July 31, 2013.

Gilmore, T., Krantz, J., and Ramirez, R. 1986. "Action-based modes of inquiry and the host-researcher relationship," *Consultation: An International Journal* 5(3): 160–176.

Guba, E. G. and Lincoln, Y. S. 1994. "Competing paradigms in qualitative research," in N. K. Denzin, and Y. S. Lincoln (eds.), *The Handbook of Qualitative Research.* Thousand Oaks, CA: Sage Publications.

Heron, J. and Reason, P. 2001. "The practice of co-operative inquiry: research 'with' rather than 'on' people," in P. Reason and H. Bradbury (eds.), *Handbook of Action Research: Participatory Inquiry and Practice.* Thousand Oaks, CA: Sage Publications.

Kehayia, E., Swaine, B., Poldma, T., and Desjardins, M. 2012. "Mall as Living Lab: Creating Enabling Environments for Persons with Disabilities." Workshop at the Science and Society Conference, Berkeley, CA.

Kolmos, A., Fink, F., and Krogh, L. 2004. "The Aalborg model-problem-based and project-organized learning," in *The Aalborg PBL Model: Progress, Diversity and Challenges.* Aalborg, Denmark: Aalborg University Press, pp. 9–18.

Lidwell, W., Holden, K., and Butler, J. 2003. *Universal Principles of Design.* Gloucester, MA: Rockwell Publishers.

Living Lab. n.d. *A Rehabilitation Living Lab: Creating Inclusive Environments for Persons with Disabilities.* http://crir-livinglabvivant.com/synopsis_projects-en.html. Accessed July 31, 2013.

Margolin, V. and Buchanan, R. 1995. *The Idea of Design.* Cambridge, MA: MIT Press.

Nussbaumer, L. 2009. *Evidence-Based Design for Interior Designers.* New York: Fairchild Books.

O'Brien, R. 1998. *An Overview of the Methodological Approach of Action Research.* University of Toronto. http://www.web.ca/robrien/papers/arfinal.html. Accessed July 31, 2013.

Panero, J. and Zelnik, M. 1979. *Human Dimension and Interior Space*. New York: Whitney Library of Design.

Pheasant, S. 1986. *Bodyspace: Anthropometry, Ergonomics, and the Design of Work*. Abingdon, Oxon.: Taylor & Francis.

Poldma, T. 2009. *Taking Up Space: Exploring the Design Process*. New York: Fairchild Publications.

Poldma, T. 2013. *Meanings of Designed Spaces*. New York: Fairchild Books.

Price, J. 1999 "In acknowledgement: a review and critique or qualitative research texts," in R. Josselson and A. Lieblich (eds.), *Making Meaning of Narratives*. Thousand Oaks, CA: Sage Publications, pp. 62–87.

Rose, G. 2001. *Visual Methodologies: An Introduction to the Interpretation of Visual Materials*. London: Sage Publications.

Rubin, H. J. and Rubin, I. R. 2005. *Qualitative Interviewing: The Art of Hearing Data*. Thousand Oaks, CA: Sage Publications.

Savin-Baden, M. and Major, C. H. 2004. *The Foundations of Problem-Based Learning*. Maidenhead, UK: Open University Press/McGraw-Hill Education.

Spain, D. 1992. *Gendered Spaces*. Chapel Hill: University of North Carolina Press.

Vaikla-Poldma, T. 2003. "An Investigation of Learning and Teaching Processes in an Interior Design Class: An Interpretive and Contextual Inquiry." Doctoral thesis. McGill University, Montreal.

Wixon D., Holtzblatt K., and Knox, S. 1990. "Contextual design: an emergent view of system design," in *Proceedings of CHI'97*. New York: ACM Press, pp. 329–336.

28

Aesthetic Theory and Interior Design Pedagogy

Ji Young Cho and Benyamin Schwarz

Introduction

Interior design pedagogy and aesthetics have multifaceted relationships. Among designers and educators one can find diversity of responses to the significance of aesthetics in the practice and teaching of interior design. The curricula in interior design and architecture programs rarely, if ever, address the subject of aesthetics. In fact, the discourse among interior design educators has been dominated by commentary on almost every aspect of design except aesthetics. While the collective message that can be found in interior design discourse is that a beautiful appearance of an interior setting is a desired quality, the linkage of interior design with the pursuit of beauty and attractiveness is sometimes misinterpreted by critics as lacking intellectual depth.

Most noteworthy interior spaces are judged by their capacity to produce an aesthetic experience; however, the pedagogy of most design programs is not guided or generated through a process that is engaged with aesthetic features or visual thinking. It seems that the artistic features of interior design are often undermined in the current discourse in favor of the more rational, pragmatic, economic obligations of the profession, and consequently professionals in the field rarely address the multifaceted relationships between interior design pedagogy and aesthetics. Consequently, interior design is predominantly discussed in terms of ethics (protecting client health, safety, and welfare) and functional considerations of content or activity, and much less in terms of its image, composition, or visual effect.

The Handbook of Interior Design, First Edition. Edited by Jo Ann Asher Thompson and Nancy H. Blossom.

The current discourse on interior design education is "far from harmonious" but "the diversity of voices is a registration of interior design's struggle to emerge as a nonhomogeneous discipline and practice" (Preston 2012).

According to some researchers and professional practitioners interior design education is in a state of identity crisis or at a crossroads. Mitchell and Rudner, for example, claim that interior design is disadvantaged by the general perception that it is an inferior design profession to architectural practice (Mitchell and Rudner 2007). This perception is propagated by "the proliferation of numerous, popular television programs which are labeled as 'interior design,' but are in fact glorified exercises in decorating." Other critics argue that in the process of professionalizing interior design and the efforts to gain recognition as a positivistic, pragmatic, and knowledge-based occupation, interior design education lost its clarity (Weigand and Harwood 2007).

The authors of this essay are aware of the claims of autonomy that govern the disciplines of architecture and interior design dialogue. However, we wish to address design aesthetic theory by bridging the interior and the exterior and diminishing the place where the interior and the exterior begin or end. In the discussion about aesthetics, interior design and architecture should be treated as a continuous design discipline that takes a unique place among the arts because it has a distinctive place by virtue of being useful. We believe that anyone involved in the act of design can benefit from the discourse about the physical form and its impact on the individual and society at large. Thus this essay adds another perspective to the disordered discussion about interior design pedagogy in an attempt to offer its audience a broader point of view. It is our opinion that aesthetic theory is essential to interior design education. This is true not because aesthetics needs to prescribe rules and norms for guiding budding designers, but rather because interior design and architecture need aesthetic education to provide capacity for reflection, which the professions are hardly able to attain on their own (Adorno 1977).

Background

Formal education in interior design began in the late 19th/early 20th century. Before that time, interior designers had little or no formal training, if any; they acquired the principles of interior decoration through apprenticeship or a training in the fine arts (Beecher 2012). However, the field transformed itself within few generations from a vocation focused on the arrangement of home furnishings and decoration into a practical profession that takes on numerous branches of contemporary culture. Correspondingly, interior design education shifted over a short time from a residential emphasis to new territories with the intention of expanding student expertise for designing environments such as commercial spaces, healthcare facilities, workplaces, and hospitality venues. Throughout the evolutionary process, the pedagogy in interior design programs embraced more technical content and higher professional standards to meet consumers' and employers' expectations and satisfy the accreditation requirements of the Council for Interior Design Accreditation (CIDA).

Interior design educational programs have been traditionally situated in one of the following: (1) an art department in connection with art practice; (2) home economics schools which evolved into human ecology programs; or (3) within established architectural programs (Beecher 2012). Interior design programs in art schools emphasize artistic expression and interior decoration. Grounded in human behavior, home economics-based programs focus on domestic science and consumers of design (Hildebrandt 2010). Architecture-allied interior design programs center on common denominators between the discipline and provide foundation studios and basic courses attempting to view the professions as a continuum rather than distinct occupations (Beecher 2012). Most CIDA-accredited interior design programs are taught in one of these three settings. Their focus may vary according to each setting, but overall the pedagogical content exhibits similarities because of CIDA's strict accreditation guidelines.

Historically interior design was rooted in domesticity and homemaking, decoration, upholstery, and home economics. The profession's relation to interior decoration is well known. So are its efforts to transform itself into a science-based profession in order to undo the historical associations with a perceived feminine, superficial, and mimetic discipline. Thus "in a body of public and anecdotal discussions that range from scorn and cautiously couched historical respect to positions for and against 'curtains and cushions', the discipline of interior design expresses overall desire to confront and/or transcend the cultural burden and image generated by this heritage" (Preston 2012). Beecher notes that the pedagogy of interior design has lately been preoccupied with "space planning" – the organization of areas based on functional factors rather than formal considerations – and concern with the impact of the built environment on human behavior from an evidence-based perspective (Beecher 2012). Current education of interior designers promotes "the emphasis on determining users' functional needs," which "has led to the development of a specific design methodology in which elements like light and color are employed as theoretical and technical tools to enhance the comfort, functionality, and aesthetics of lived spaces" (Beecher 2012).

According to the National Council for Interior Design Qualification (NCIDQ), interior design is:

> A multi-faceted profession in which creative and technical solutions are applied within a structure to achieve a built interior environment. These solutions are functional, enhance the quality of life and culture of the occupants and are *aesthetically attractive*. (NCIDQ n.d.; emphasis added)

This definition was endorsed by CIDA, the accrediting body for interior design education (Weaver 2010). Thus, nurturing students' ability to produce functional and aesthetically attractive interior environments is a central goal of interior design education. However, little discussion has taken place on the pedagogy of aesthetics in interior design education. For instance according to CIDA's professional standards, which outline the expectations for interior design programs and learning outcomes, *aesthetics* is explicitly mentioned in only one standard, standard 10, labeled "Color":

Student Learning Expectations

Student work demonstrates *understanding* of:

a) color principles, theories, and systems.
b) the interaction of color with materials, texture, light, form and the impact on interior environments.

Students:

c) appropriately select and *apply* color with regard to its *multiple purposes*. (CIDA 2011: II-9; emphasis added)

As an example of multiple purposes, aesthetics is listed in the footnote once. This should not come as a surprise because the accreditation process is predisposed to the measurable aspects of a program. Aesthetics may appear in the column of the immeasurable, to use one of the famous distinctions of Louis Kahn in reference to the measurable act of design in contrast to the feelings and the thoughts that a great building elicits (Twombly 2003). Ironically, during the accreditation team visit, the immeasurable aesthetics of student work plays a significant role in the overall impression of the quality of a reviewed program and may determine whether it is accredited.

In her analysis of interior design education, Preston points to four conditions that influence the current teaching of interior design. First, the "mixture of unequal and varying portions of embarrassment over and embracement of its origins in the decorative arts." Second is "design's conception as an applied practice and commercial enterprise." Third is the unsettled relation to architecture, and fourth, "interior design's engagement with interiority, spatial experience, performance, and temporal inhabitation" (Preston 2012). Detailed discussion of these conditions is beyond the scope of this essay; however, it is apparent that interior design education interior design education needs to address the relationships between the act of design, its subsequent outcomes, and their aesthetic influence on the individual and the collective political impact on society.

Aesthetic Theory and the Design Disciplines

In architecture and interior design, aesthetics occupies a unique position compared to painting, sculpture, and other visual arts. Because of the characteristics of architecture, which blends artistic and practical purposes, the discussion of aesthetics in architecture cannot be debated completely separately from its purpose, function, performance, or usage (Hillier 1996; Lagueux 2004). This is especially true in the discourse about interior spaces where the spatial experience links the space's purpose with its aesthetic character. Any definition of aesthetics as it pertains to interior design needs to encompass (1) the design process and product (i.e., outcome), (2) formal and symbolic aesthetics, and (3) the objective nature of the interior space itself and the subjective nature of people's emotions and perceptions (Cho 2011).

The dictionary definition of aesthetics includes two meanings: "(a) a set of principles concerned with the nature and appreciation of beauty, especially in art; and (b) the branch of philosophy that deals with the principles of beauty and artistic taste" (*OED* 2003). The two parts of the definition link the arts and philosophy as the arenas in which discussions of aesthetics occur. In the arts, the discussion revolves around appreciation of art as it relates to the psychological aspects of aesthetics, specifically the nature of art that arouses aesthetically pleasing responses and the principles of aesthetics.

In philosophy, the discussion of aesthetics involves how to define art. To illustrate, the nature of art comprises three broad subjects: (1) the intention of art (how to define a work as art), (2) standards of taste (whether universality exists in aesthetic judgment), and (3) the nature of aesthetic judgment (whether aesthetic judgment is a matter of taste or a cognitive function) (Wartenberg 2007). Aesthetic theory is a relatively recent branch of philosophy which lacks a clear definition, and its contemporary reach is difficult to delineate. Harrington notes:

> Deriving from the Greek word for "perception" – *aesthesis* – aesthetics refers to the study of *pleasure in perception*. Although some of its meanings have changed since its first appearance in eighteenth century Enlightenment thought, aesthetics remains the key term today for that branch of philosophical inquiry that is concerned with the grounds for experience of pleasure in sensory objects. In particular, aesthetics refers to the grounds for intersubjectively valid "judgements of taste" about sensory objects. (Harrington 2004)

The discussion of the nature and appreciation of beauty treats the psychological aspect of aesthetics, that is, whether a particular form arouses a certain aesthetic response and experience. The psychological aspect of aesthetics has been treated in environmental psychology using empirical research methods. Researchers in environmental psychology have explored the relationship between the environment and human response (Carlson 2006). Jon Lang discusses three types of aesthetics – sensory, formal, and symbolic aesthetics – based on Santayana's three values in aesthetics – sensory values, formal values, and expressions or associational values. Formal aesthetics is concerned with "the appreciation of shapes and structures of the environment" (Lang 1987), and symbolic aesthetics deals with "the associational meaning of the patterns of the environment that give people pleasure" (Lang 1987).

The desire for beauty in architecture is fundamentally rooted in human experience from the dawn of history (Pallasmaa 2010). In *De Architectura* (On Architecture), the only noteworthy survivor of architectural theory and practice from the ancient world, Marcus Vitruvius Pollio stresses the significance of aesthetics as one of the essential qualities of architecture. Although the precise date of the publication is unknown, it was probably written during the second decade of the first century BC, and has influenced two millennia of architectural theory and practice. Vitruvius defined "beauty" (*venustas*) along with firmness (*firmitas*) and utility (*utilitas*) as the three requirements for architecture:

> And all these buildings must be executed in such a way as to take account of durability, utility and beauty. Durability will be catered for when the foundations have been sunk down to solid ground and the building materials carefully selected from the available sources without cutting corners; the requirements of utility will be satisfied when the organization of the spaces is correct, with no obstacles to their use, and they are suitably and conveniently oriented as each type requires. Beauty will be achieved when the appearance of the building is pleasing and elegant and the commensurability of its components is correctly related to the system of modules. (Vitruvius [20 BC] 2009)

Alberti noted that "every aspect of building, if you think of it rightly, is born of necessity, nourished by convenience, dignified by use; and only in the end is pleasure provided for, while pleasure itself never fails to shun every excess" (Alberti [1486] 1988). It is one of the earliest testaments to the uneasy balance of the forces that act in architecture and by extension in interior design. In his classic text *The Architecture of Humanism*, Geoffrey Scott writes about the difficulty of studying the art of architecture in comparison to the science and history of architecture, claiming that the difficulty stems from a lack of agreement about the concept of the beautiful:

> Too many definitions of architectural beauty have proved their case, enjoyed their vogue, provoked their opposition, and left upon the vocabulary of art their legacy of prejudice, ridicule, and confusion...Not only do we inherit the wreckage of past controversies, but those controversies themselves are clouded with the dust of more heroic combats, and loud with the battle-cries of poetry and morals, philosophy, politics, and science. (Scott 1924)

To the Greek philosophers the product of architecture was perceived as a work of art, which permitted them to think that, outside in the macrocosmos, an objective criterion of the "beautiful" exists. But even then the "beautiful" was never defined purely and simply by the subjective pleasure it produces. The idea of the "beautiful" was generally associated with the need to measure and apply the rules of proportion as a device or as the reflection of an order external to the human being. Socrates talked about the harmony that characterizes the work of artists and architects, and several centuries later Alberti wrote in response "We should follow Socrates' advice, that something that can only be altered for the worse can be held to be perfect," a theme he repeats: "Beauty is that reasoned harmony of all the parts within the body, so that nothing may be added, taken away, or altered, but for the worse" (Alberti [1486] 1988: bk. 6, ch. 2).

The proposition according to which the architect should search for harmony did not disappear in modern aesthetics. But this harmony was no longer thought of as based on objective criteria. The "beautiful" was no longer central because the work of architecture was intrinsically beautiful but rather because it provided a certain type of pleasure that could be coined as beautiful (Ferry 1993). The break with antiquity with regard to the "beautiful" may be traced to the treatise published in 1750 by the Prussian rationalist philosopher Alexander Gottlieb Baumgarten, who is credited with the creation of the term "aesthetics." Baumgarten defined beauty as the sensation of pleasure that accrues from arrangements of forms in harmony with reason and logic. He used the term "aesthetica" as an analogue to "logica," maintaining that while logic seeks to establish the principles that should govern the implementation of reason, aesthetics search for the principles that should govern judgments of taste (Harries 1997). The analogy implies that the pleasure we take from viewing a painting is similar to the enjoyment we experience when smelling a rose. In other words, Baumgarten maintained that taste resembles reason.

The concept of aesthetics is central to *The Critique of Judgment* by Immanuel Kant, arguably the most influential philosopher of the modern era. Published in 1790, it is the last of his three philosophical treatises. Although architecture was not essential to Kant's exposition in his aesthetic theory, his seminal book influenced the philosophical discipline of aesthetics and consequently affected the theoretical architectural debate in the next two centuries. In the first part of the text, Kant probes into the subjective act of perceiving something as beautiful. He contends that beauty is independent of any concept one may associate with the things one judges to be beautiful (Mitrovic 2011). "Kant argues that aesthetic judgments neither communicate any information about the physical properties or causes of their object, nor express any judgment about the moral worth or practical utility of their object. They express purely the pleasure of the spectator on apprehending the object" (Harrington 2004). Kant excludes any concept of function from the judgment of beauty and introduces his famous hypothesis that our pleasure in beauty is due to the "free play" of the cognitive powers of imagination and understanding. In other words, beauty is not an "objective" property of a beautiful thing. Rather, the judgment of beauty is subjective; it is inherent in the person's cognitive mental processes, or is in the mind of the beholder, as David Hume claimed in 1777. Andrew Ballantyne offers the following explanation:

> Despite the passing of generations since that realization, it has not passed into common sense, so we still have not developed a habit of saying "that object produces in me a feeling of beauty." What we still say is: "that object is beautiful," even though we know it's only a manner of speaking. This isn't to say that architecture is altogether personal without objectivity, because within any given culture we can expect a degree of consensus in the responses, and one can design with expectation that some gesture will be recognized – there is an element of unpredictability involved, but we can set in place conditions that favor an appropriate response. (Ballantyne 2002)

Kant's definition of architecture and its aesthetic potential appears in the following passage:

> [Architecture] is the art of presenting concepts of things which are possible only through art, and the determining ground of whose form is not nature but an arbitrary end – and of presenting them both with view to this purpose and yet, at the same time, with aesthetic finality. In architecture the chief point is a certain use of the artistic object to which, as the condition, the aesthetic ideas are limited. (Kant [1790] 1911)

Readers of this statement often think that Kant claims that architecture cannot be art due to its usefulness. However, Kant maintains that architecture has a place in his systems of the arts despite its utility. Accordingly, we may evaluate how well a building performs its function, which in the judgment of fine arts will be irrelevant because it will be a judgment of reason and not an aesthetic judgment. Richard Hill explained why Kant wished to separate his theory of aesthetic experience from our ordinary pleasure of objects. He writes:

> The explanation lies in his desire to explain how aesthetic judgements can arise from subjective experience and yet have objective validity. He wished to account for the fact that the pleasures of art can involve something more than an assertion of a personal taste. This led him to the thought that if aesthetic judgements are to have objective validity they must be universally held by humans. Therefore they cannot be dependent on the immediate feelings of pleasure we have when confronted with objects. These by definition are individual, of "private validity" only. Then he makes the suggestion that aesthetic satisfaction is based on a universal feature of the mind, one that we all possess by virtue of the fact that we are able to understand the world at all. (Hill 1999)

In spite of Kant's short and scattered discussion of architecture, his contribution to the philosophy of architecture played a significant role, transforming it from a discipline focused on the Vitruvian values of beauty and utility to a post-Vitruvian discipline concerned with understanding architecture's expressive dimension. Kant's theory opened the door to the conception of architecture as expressing ideas. While he assumed that architecture must express moral ideas, Kant opened the door to scholars who argued that architecture should express ideas of its own function (Schelling), ideas of the nature of physical forces and its own construction (Schopenhauer), or metaphysical ideas (Hegel) (Guyer 2011).

Shifting Norms of Aesthetic Judgment

Aesthetic judgment in general and of interior design in particular is never fixed forever. Change is the norm. With the evolution of modernism in the late 19th century and the manifestation of the modern in architecture, the theory of aesthetics shifted radically. Modern architectural thinkers repudiated traditional restrictions and decoration and reconceptualized space-time following the logic of function. "Modernist architecture embodied modern modes of living, thinking, and production based on rationality, efficiency, calculation, and the obsession with novelty and abstraction" (Lu 2012).

The modern aesthetics of architecture claimed a basis in psychology that led to the stipulation for an empirical proof, prescriptions for practice, and normative concepts of form. Colin Rowe maintained that the emphasis on "objectivity" led architects to argue that their architecture was founded on facts, data, analysis, programs, function, and other scientific, measurable precepts (Rowe 1994). In his book *The Architecture of Good Intentions*, Rowe notes:

> From Mies van der Rohe there follows possibly the most succinct statement of what – until not very long ago – was to be considered modern architecture's avowed aim: Essentially our task is to free the practice of building from the control of aesthetic speculators and restore it to what it should exclusively be: building. (Rowe 1994)

Modern architects' refusal to recognize the role of individuality and subjective will in the design process became the dominant attitude in architectural discourse. The popular mantra pursued by architects in Europe and America was "form follows function," which devalued the image of buildings unless they carried a strong social and political mission or a "utilitarian task" (Reisner 2010).

Architecture and design schools were not unaffected by the new attitudes toward aesthetics. By the late 1920s, modernism began to shape architectural education in the US through the influential pedagogical model of the Bauhaus. Due to turbulent political times in Germany the school existed for only few years (1919–1933), yet its influence on design education is still felt in design schools around the world. It was predicated on a radical approach to design pedagogy which embraced "learning by doing," collaboration, formal and technical experimentation, and social responsibility (Simon 2012). When the Nazis disbanded the Bauhaus, many of the school's teachers emigrated to the US and relocated to American design schools. The influence of the Bauhaus masters – Josef Albers, Walter Gropius, Ludwig Mies van der Rohe, and László Moholy-Nagy, and their collaborators – on design education in North America cannot be overstated. In a few years their ideas revolutionized the design pedagogy in design schools. In particular, there was the course on "Basic Design," which consisted of two hours of lectures six days a week, plus 20 hours a week in the workshop, where students using their hands and power tools undertook a series of two- and three-dimensional exercises investigating form, space, and perception with variety of materials and media, endorsing the concept of a unified beginning for students in all fields of design (Simon 2012).

In due course, the ideological attitudes of the founders of the canonical modern history of the mid-20th century such as Sigfried Giedion and Nikolaus Pevsner lost credibility, and by the 1980s new approaches to architectural aesthetics such as postmodernism surfaced. With the publication of *Complexity and Contradiction in*

Architecture (1966) and *Learning from Las Vegas* (1972), Robert Venturi and Denise Scott Brown "became the most prominent debunkers of the formalist aesthetics of modernism by explaining what architects could learn from the popular built environment" (Macarthur and Stead 2012). The thirst for philosophy or some form of cerebral authority changed aesthetic discourse toward content and meaning rather than pure aesthetics in the 1980s. The tendency for architectural theory at the end of the 1980s to open itself to other disciplines such as philosophy, literature, and gender studies was not unique to architecture. Other disciplines in the humanities were looking to cultural studies and literary criticism for their theoretical models. "But in order for architecture to take its place among other humanities disciplines, it had to be reconceived as a kind of discursive, text-based practice itself" (Allen 2012). Two strains of architectural theory were predominantly influential on academic practice in this period: first, the critical project, which consisted of a fusion of "Marxian critical theory and post-structuralism with architectural modernism" (Gage 2011). Second, the introduction of the computer as a design tool, which "allowed designers to organize large bodies of data in the forms of various new diagrams and mapping; its graphic capabilities gave designers access to new illustrative and collage tools, and provided a means of producing entirely new families of form" (Gage 2011).

Interior design education was influenced by these developments to a lesser degree. However, it is obvious that the rapid technological and social changes since the 1990s – the speed of information exchange, and the use of creative technologies – presents new, complex challenges to the design disciplines' practice and education.

A Research Study on the Pedagogy of Aesthetics in the Design Studio

In order to explore the pedagogy of aesthetics in the design studio, a research study was conducted in three design studios in architectural and interior design programs at a major university in the US (Cho 2011). The primary objective of the study was to examine how aesthetics (the discussion of beauty) is taught in design studios and how instructors and students understand the current status of aesthetic education. Three design studios were selected as research sites based on two criteria: those taught by professors "(a) who received at least one teaching award from their respective university," and "(b) who were recommended by each school's associate dean/ department chair for their ability to help students produce design outcomes with high aesthetic qualities" (Cho 2011). Each of the three studios was observed once a week throughout one academic semester. Data garnered from these observations were supplemented with insights gained from interviews with each of the three studio professors and 40 of the students. The three studios included one undergraduate interior design, senior-level, CIDA-accredited studio, one elective graduate architecture studio, and one graduate architecture core studio, all in NAAB-accredited programs. Students voluntarily participated in the research.

Photographs of student work were taken regularly and used to document the design evolution and outcomes. Discussions that took place during desk critiques between each student and the instructor were audio-recorded. In addition, all lectures, class discussions, and reviews done during the semester-long study were audio-recorded. Students were interviewed once in the middle of the semester to explore their perceptions of aesthetics, and at the end of the semester they completed an open-ended questionnaire where they were asked to reflect on their studio experience. Interviews with the instructors focused on each person's teaching philosophy, strategies, and understanding of aesthetics. Interviews were conducted primarily in a semi-structured format with all the data from the recordings transcribed. The verbal transcriptions and visual materials were analyzed qualitatively using a grounded theory method.

According to Glaser and Strauss, a grounded theory method is "the discovery of theory from data – systematically obtained and analyzed in social research" (Glaser and Strauss 1967) and is "a qualitative research method that uses a systematic set of procedures to develop an inductively derived grounded theory about a phenomenon" (Strauss and Corbin 1990). Further, a grounded theory method is seen as appropriate when no theory exists to be tested or when a theory exists, but is too abstract to be tested (Suddaby 2006).

As shown by the discussion at the beginning of this essay, there is very little information, dialogue, or debate to be found about aesthetic education in design studios in the literature. Therefore, the grounded theory method was determined to be an appropriate approach for this study since no theory exists regarding the pedagogy of aesthetics (Cho 2011). It was also determined that the use of multiple data-collection tools (i.e., observations, student interviews, instructor interviews, and visual material reviews) would provide important insights that would help in understanding if, when, and how aesthetic education was integrated into each studio.

The design studio is central to interior design and architecture programs. One-third to one-half of the required professional coursework for interior design and architecture students takes place in the studio. The essence of the studio experience is the development of design solutions under criticism. It follows the dictum of Aristotle, who maintained that "What we have to learn to do we learn by doing." In the studio setting and during the learning process, the instructor typically poses a problem and then works individually by coaching the students as they develop their design solutions. The inherent problem in the coaching process is that the instructor cannot make the solution clear because there is no single-track agenda and because there are no right answers. The student must put different things together and bring new ideas into being while dealing in the process with many variables and constraints.

Aesthetics is part of the dialogue that takes place between the instructor and the student as the design process ensues. The process makes use of words and actions.

While the instructor is explaining and demonstrating, the student is listening and imitating (Schon 1987). The studio setting enables students to experiment in a safe place and it is where students are expected to synthesize the information they learned in previous architectural history, basic design, technology, or studio courses (Anthony 1991; Demirbas and Demirkan 2003). The design studio is a world with its own culture, language, norms, and rituals.

Among other findings, in this study Cho found that the design studio does provide students with an environment where they can apply aspects of aesthetics that complement their studies in other courses, such as history of interior design or architecture, visual design, photography, drawing, or design communication. However, both students and instructors noted that there was very little actual discussion of aesthetics in the design studio. The informants listed possible reasons for this conundrum, pointing to the negative connotations associated with the term "aesthetics," insufficient time, and the difficulties of discussing aesthetics in the context of the studio. Students and instructors stated that placing too much emphasis on aesthetics would take too much time at the expense of other important considerations such as use, social aspects, and/or human behavioral aspects. In addition, the instructors stated that the course content required by the accrediting bodies did not provide enough room for dedicated discussion of aesthetics in the curriculum, and concern was expressed that the term "aesthetics" was unclear – noting that "beauty is in the eye of beholder." Perhaps this lack of attention to the topic of aesthetics can be explained by the point of view that aesthetically pleasing design solutions are the result of an innate ability rather than something that can be taught.

These findings support Scott's argument that the difficulty in studying the art of architecture derives from the lack of an agreement on what constitutes beauty (Scott 1924). These findings also reconfirm the tendency in architecture to avoid discussions about subjective aspects of architecture such as aesthetics and focus, rather, on more objective aspects such as utility and function (Rowe 1994).

It seems that the assumption inherent in most design programs is that aesthetics is a contentious subject which should be avoided in design discourse and that students can absorb the ideas of form and beauty by osmosis or through the creative process of the studio environment. Consequently student work in the studio is predominantly discussed in terms of ethics, content, activity, and use, and much less in terms of imagery, look, visual values, composition, or other design language aspects. Unfortunately, this lack of attention to aesthetics devalues one of the key aspects of a design education, as pointed out by Johnson, who argues that aesthetics are one of the important issues in the fields of architectural and interior design:

> The worry is that informed discussion of esthetics as an interpretive issue is now almost absent from professional architectural journals and from open public debate, even though it is warranted as a public concern of the highest order among architects, planners, fine arts commissions, and design review boards. (Johnson 1994)

The Nature of Aesthetics: Subjective vs. Objective and Visual vs. Experiential

In this study Cho found that the language used during design studio discussions about the nature of aesthetics was twofold, comprising: (1) formal attributes, such as appearance, looks, form, shape, and proportion, and (2) emotional attributes, such as impressive, interesting, intriguing, powerful, or preferable. This is in keeping, on the one hand, with Bell's ([1914] 2007) argument of "significant form," whereby aesthetics resides in the objective attributes of the form of the architecture or interior space. On the other hand, it also supports the arguments of Kant ([1790] 1911) and Hume ([1777] 1985), whereby aesthetics has subjective attributes that relate to the emotional responses of the viewer (audience or user). For example, Kant argued that aesthetic judgment involves feelings that are subjective in nature.

In addition to the twofold nature of aesthetic discussions, the language used by the instructor and students occupied two primary realms: (1) the visual and (2) the spatial. In other words, discussion of the aesthetics of architecture and interior design occurred primarily when people talked about the visual aspect of a space, that is, color, finishes, materials, exterior, facade, and form or shape of the space or building; or when they described spatial experience, such as spatial quality, spatial organization, and sequence of spaces.

Figure 28.1 shows two representative natures of aesthetics and two realms where aesthetic discussions took place in the studios.

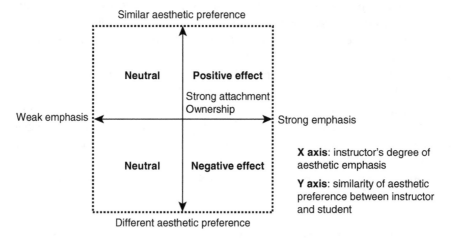

Figure 28.1   Two natures of aesthetics and the realms of aesthetics of architecture (modified from Cho 2011).

Aesthetic Education in the Design Studio:
A Place Open to New Aesthetics

Clearly, the way aesthetics was introduced in the studio varied with each instructor's teaching philosophy, methods, and strategies; however, several themes emerged in the study. First, instructors tended to use precedents and examples to illustrate their aesthetic preferences. Three types of sources for precedents were normally used in design studios: (1) visual materials from architecture and interior design books, drawings of buildings, and artwork; (2) written materials that the instructors distributed to the students, such as book chapters and articles about aesthetic theories and principles; and (3) verbal communication in the form of storytelling, discussions regarding concepts, and descriptions of design work of particular designers or architects. In the use of precedents, instructors tended to reiterate their "hero architects or designers" works in an attempt to encourage students to study their special qualities. The precedents and examples were introduced at different stages throughout the design process, such as in the early conceptual stages, during design development, or in final presentations. Precedents were used as a way "to expose students to good examples and further develop students' ideas" (Cho 2011).

A second emergent theme for teaching aesthetics in the studio was found in deliberations made about the proper use of materials and finishes and prototypes of space. Oftentimes the instructors used verbal and visual articulations to enhance the students' design vocabulary – encouraging students to engage and articulate their ideas and design intentions in a clear verbal or graphic way using the aesthetic principles of design.

Interestingly, although aesthetics were seldom discussed overtly in desk critiques or discussion in the studios, conflicts were observed to arise between the instructors and students about aesthetic preference. Such conflicts were most prevalent when the instructor maintained a strong preference for particular aesthetic characteristics and tried to impose his aesthetics on the students by virtue of his authority. Figure 28.2 shows a diagram of students' reactions to conflict over aesthetic preference. The x-axis indicates the instructor's degree of aesthetic emphasis, and the y-axis depicts the degree to which the aesthetic preferences of the instructor and student were similar or dissimilar. When an instructor imposed his or her own aesthetic, students reacted, feeling that the project was no longer theirs.

As a result of this study, it can be concluded that the design studio is a place where students are exposed to aesthetics in new ways and that it is also a place where students must learn to negotiate aesthetic dilemmas with instructors, clients, and/or reviewers. The educational challenge is to invent a workable symbiosis between applied science and artistry and to provide a venue whereby students can be acculturated into the design community (Cho 2011).

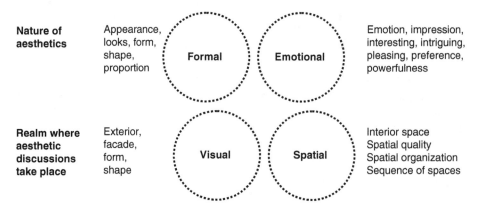

| **Nature of aesthetics** | Appearance, looks, form, shape, proportion | Formal | Emotional | Emotion, impression, interesting, intriguing, pleasing, preference, powerfulness |

| **Realm where aesthetic discussions take place** | Exterior, facade, form, shape | Visual | Spatial | Interior space Spatial quality Spatial organization Sequence of spaces |

Figure 28.2   The conflict between students' emotional attachment to their projects and the instructor's aesthetic preferences (Cho 2011: 206).

Lessons: Implications for Design Educators

Studio instructors do not have the luxury of being able to always rely on empirically measurable "facts." The challenge in dealing with aesthetic values in design education is the need to clarify the reasons for supporting certain solutions without the comfortable certainty of reliable truth. In architecture and interior design there are numerous contradictory measures of values that must be reconciled in the educational process – with aesthetic discourse being a fundamental component of these values. Clearly the absence or marginalization of aesthetic theory in interior design and architecture education exacerbates problems of critical thinking in the disciplines. In addition, the exclusion of discussion about aesthetics in interior design and architecture curricula intensifies tendencies of students to embrace fashionable trends too hastily, and dismiss more subtle theoretical propositions.

Issues covered in this essay offer several suggestions to design educators regarding the pedagogy of aesthetics. First, instructors need to understand that students' aesthetic preferences may differ from their own. In particular, students in advanced school years tend to have a clearer preference for certain aesthetics than beginning students; thus, instructors need to approach studio instruction while considering students' varying levels of knowledge and design experience.

Second, educators need to deal with both the objective and subjective aspects of aesthetics. Even though aesthetics involve subjective preference, certain objective commonalities and principles exist in aesthetics, and students want to know why some designs are more aesthetically attractive than others. As Ballantyne pointed out, there is a certain degree of consensus in the aesthetic response (Ballantyne 2002). Thus, instructors must deliver the objective principles of aesthetics and formal aspects relating to aesthetic judgment, such as proportion, balance, principles of color, and the nature and proper use of material.

Third, educators need to know the unique nature of the aesthetics of interior design and architecture. As opposed to other domains in which aesthetics is discussed, such as philosophy, art, or sculpture, in interior design and architecture, function, performance, and utility are important elements that explain the rationale of their existence. Basically, the aesthetics of interior design occurs both in visual and spatial realms. Compared to the aesthetics of architecture, in interior design the spatial experience of interior space is even more important and should not be neglected in any discussion of aesthetics.

Hence, the pedagogy of the aesthetics of interior design needs be based on: (1) an acknowledgment of possible differences in the aesthetic preference of the instructor and the students; (2) an understanding of subjective preference in aesthetics and its objective principles and nature; and (3) an understanding of aesthetics in terms of both the visual and the spatial. It is our hope that this essay will stimulate a beneficial discussion, draw attention to the pedagogy of aesthetics, and provide insights for design educators interested in advancing interior design and architectural education.

Last Words

The last words belong to Mark Foster Gage:

> Architecture today faces multiple master-narratives that seek to further transform it into a sustainable-cum-scientific endeavor. Undoubtedly our buildings must be sustainable. They must be efficient, power saving, resource responsible, and easily maintained. To propose anything less is to abdicate our responsibility to our limited resources. This responsibility to our resources, however, should not be confused as the only way in which we can judge our architecture. There must be an equally significant way to judge architectural values in nonscientific terms as well – that is to say in terms of its physical, formal, and aesthetic impact. Aesthetic theory is the obvious starting point through which to understand this distinction. (Gage 2011)

In this passage, interior design could easily be substituted for architecture. Good design is essentially valued for its formal properties. Other conceptual properties can be significant and worthy endeavors, but they are not the primary reasons for which design is culturally valued. Design "must be more than what it does, how little it costs, how quickly it was built, or how much energy it can save" (Gage 2011). Aesthetic theory has long been absent from the curricula of design schools. "Nonetheless, aesthetic theory is not a frivolous pursuit: as it is the branch of philosophy that deals with not only artistic categories of the beautiful but also the forms and products of architecture and design as they directly relate to individual and collective users" (Gage 2011). Clearly, aesthetic theory should be an integral part of design pedagogy.

References

Adorno, T. 1977. "Aesthetic theory," in T. Adorno and R. Tiedemann, *Aesthetic Theory*. Minneapolis: University of Minnesota Press, pp. 131–153.

Alberti, L. B. [1486] 1988. *On the Art of Building in Ten Books*, trans. J. Rykwert, N. Leach, and R. Tavernor. Cambridge, MA: MIT Press.

Allen, S. 2012. "The future that is now," in J. Ockman (ed.), *Architecture School: Three Centuries of Educating Architects in North America*. Cambridge, MA: MIT Press, pp. 203–229.

Anthony, K. H. 1991. *Design Juries on Trial: The Renaissance of the Design Studio*. New York: Van Nostrand Reinhold.

Ballantyne, A. 2002. "Commentary: the nest and the pillar of fire," in A. Ballantyne (ed.), *What Is Architecture?* New York: Routledge, pp. 7–52.

Beecher, M. A. 2012. "Interiors. between art and practicality," in J. Ockman (ed.), *Architecture School: Three Centuries of Educating Architects in North America*. Cambridge, MA: MIT Press, pp. 347–350

Bell, C. [1914] 2007. "Art," in T. E. Wartenberg (ed.), *The Nature of Art: An Anthology*, New York: Thomson and Wadsworth, pp. 118–124.

Carlson, A. 2006. "The aesthetic appreciation of environmental architecture under different conceptions of environment," *Journal of Aesthetic Education* 40(4): 77–88.

Cho, J. Y. 2011. "Pedagogy of Aesthetics: A Study of Three Architectural Design Studios." Doctoral dissertation. University of Missouri, Columbia.

CIDA (Council for Interior Design Accreditation). 2011. *Professional Standards II-1*. Professional Standards, II-9 http://accredit-id.org/wp-content/uploads/Policy/Professional%20Standards%202011.pdf. Accessed May 11, 2014.

Demirbas, O. and Demirkan, H. 2003. "Focus on architectural design process through learning styles," *Design Studies* 24(5): 437–456.

Ferry, L. 1993. *Homo Aestheticus: The Invention of Taste in the Democratic Age*. Chicago: The University of Chicago Press.

Gage, F. M. 2011. *Aesthetic Theory: Essential Texts for Architecture and Design*. New York: W. W. Norton.

Glaser, B. and Strauss, A. 1967. *The Discovery of Grounded Theory: Strategies for Qualitative Research*. London: Weidenfeld & Nicolson.

Guyer, P. 2011. "Kant and the philosophy of architecture," in D. Goldblatt and R. Paden (eds.), *The Aesthetics of Architecture: Philosophical Investigations into the Art of Building*. Chichester: John Wiley & Sons, pp. 7–17.

Harries, K. 1997. *The Ethical Function of Architecture*. Cambridge, MA: MIT Press.

Harrington, A. 2004. *Art and Social Theory: Sociological Arguments in Aesthetics*. Cambridge: Polity.

Hegel, G. W. F. [1886] 1993. *Introductory Lectures on Aesthetics*, trans. Bernard Bosanquet. London: Penguin.

Hildebrandt, H. P. 2010. "Sustaining interior design pedagogy: structure and content of interior design programs and an emerging academic context," in C. S. Martin and D. A. Guerin (eds.), *The State of the Interior Design Profession*. New York: Fairchild Books, pp. 424–429.

Hill, R. 1999. *Designs and Their Consequences*. New Haven: Yale University Press.

Hillier, B. 1996. *Space Is the Machine*. Cambridge: Cambridge University Press.

Hume, D. [1777] 1985. "Of the standard of taste," in E. Miller (ed.), *Essays, Moral, Political and Literary*. Indianapolis: Library Fund, pp. 226–249.

Johnson, P.-A. 1994. *The Theory of Architecture: Concepts, Themes & Practices*. New York: Van Nostrand Reinhold.

Kant, I. [1790] 1911. *The Critique of Judgement*, trans. James Creed Meredith. Oxford: Clarendon Press.

Lagueux, M. 2004. "Ethics versus aesthetics in architecture," *The Philosophical Forum* 35(2): 117–133.

Lang, J. 1987. *Creating Architectural Theory*. New York: Van Nostrand Reinhold.

Lu, D. 2012. "Entangled modernities in architecture," in C. Greig Crysler, S. Cairns, S. and H. Heynen (eds.), *The SAGE Handbook of Architectural Theory*. Los Angeles: Sage Publications, pp. 231–246.

Macarthur, J. and Stead, N. 2012. "Introduction: architecture and aesthetics," in C. Greig Crysler, S. Cairns, S. and H. Heynen (eds.), *The SAGE Handbook of Architectural Theory*. Los Angeles: Sage Publications, pp. 123–135.

Mitchell, T. C. and Rudner, S. M. 2007. "Interior design's identity crisis: rebranding the profession," in J. Gigli et al. (eds.), *Thinking Inside the Box: A Reader In Interiors for the 21st Century*. London: Middlesex University Press, pp. 67–76.

Mitrovic, B. 2011. *Philosophy for Architects*. New York: Princeton Architectural Press.

NCIDQ (National Council for Interior Design Qualification). n.d. http://www.ncidq .org/AboutUs/AboutInteriorDesign/DefinitionofInteriorDesign.aspx. Accessed May 12, 2014.

OED. 2003. *Oxford English Dictionary* (2nd ed.). Oxford: Oxford University Press.

Pallasmaa, J. 2010. "Beauty is anchored in human life," in Y. Reisner and F. Watson (eds.), *Architecture and Beauty: Conversations with Architects about a Troubled Relationship*. Chichester: John Wiley & Sons, pp. 77–87

Preston, J. 2012. "A fossick for interior design pedagogies," in K. Kleinman, J. Merwood-Salisbury, and L. Weinthal (eds.), *After Taste: Expanding Practice in Interior Design*. New York: Princeton Architectural Press, pp. 92–109.

Reisner, Y. 2010. *Architecture and Beauty: Conversations with Architects about a Troubled Relationship*. Hoboken, NJ: Wiley.

Rowe, C. 1994. *The Architecture of Good Intentions: Towards a Possible Retrospect*. London: Academy Edition.

Schon, D. A. 1987. *Educating the Reflective Practitioner*. San Francisco: Jossey-Bass.

Scott, G. 1924. *The Architecture of Humanism: A Study in the History of Taste*. New York: Charles Scribner's Sons.

Simon, M. 2012. "Design pedagogy: changing approaches to teaching design," in J. Ockman and R. Williamson (eds.), *Architecture School: Three Centuries of Educating Architects in North America*. Cambridge, MA: MIT Press, pp. 276–285.

Strauss, A. and Corbin, J. 1990. *Basics of Qualitative Research*. Newbury Park, CA: Sage Publications.

Suddaby, R. 2006. "From the editors: what grounded theory is not," *Academy of Management Journal ARCHIVE* 49(4): 633–642.

Twombly, R., ed. 2003. *Louis Kahn: Essential Texts*. New York: W. W. Norton.

Venturi, R. 1966. *Complexity and Contradiction in Architecture*. New York: Museum of Modern Art.

Venturi, R., Scott Brown, D., and Izenour, S. 1972. *Learning from Las Vegas*. Cambridge, MA: MIT Press.

Vitruvius [20 BC] 2009. *On Architecture (De Architectura)*, trans R. Schofield. London: Penguin Books.

Wartenberg, T. E. 2007. *The Nature of Art: An Anthology* (2nd ed.). New York: Thomson & Wadsworth.

Weaver, C. D. 2010. "Allied profession or subset of architecture: the dilemma," in C. S. Martin and D. A. Guerin (eds.), *The State of the Interior Design Professions*. New York: Fairchild Books, pp. 444–448.

Weigand, J. and Harwood, B. 2007. "Position paper: defining graduate education in interior design," *Journal of Interior Design* 33(2): 3–10.

29

Interior Design Teaching and Learning in Elementary and Secondary Education (K-12)

Stephanie A. Clemons

Introduction

Children learn and create everywhere. They learn on the streets, in classrooms, at the park, from the television and Internet, through their teachers, and with friends. They create in the same places through play, experimentation, structured tutoring, and innovative exercises. While research from E. O. Wilson indicates that the best learning often occurs when children spend unplanned hours exploring and playing outside – labeled by David Orr of Oberlin College as the "spontaneous design of their own curriculum" – the classroom remains the place supported by federal funding as the classic learning environment (OWP/P 2010).

Youth – their thinking, learning, creativity, and work ethic – ensure the future success of any country. The United States competes daily in a global economy. The quality and effectiveness of teaching and learning, measured through student assessment and qualifications, are publicized and compared against other nations' student achievements as indicators of the country's ability to compete successfully in a world market. Yet, according to the literature, "Every 29 seconds another student gives up in school, resulting in more than one million American high school students dropping out every year" (OWP/P 2010).

Many people with associated resources are strategically placed throughout the world to develop and deliver a structured, formal education to children and youth. In the United States alone there are 97,382 public schools where more than 76.3 million people are enrolled, and the "U.S. national average for annual

The Handbook of Interior Design, First Edition. Edited by Jo Ann Asher Thompson and Nancy H. Blossom.

expenditures per student [is] $10,418. By 2013, spending on construction, renovation, and maintenance of U.S. schools reached nearly $30 billion annually." Further, about 4.7 million people are employed as elementary and secondary school teachers or as college faculty. In addition, $5.6 million is dedicated to support staffing for schools and colleges (NCES 2011).

The US Constitution mandates that the responsibility for public elementary and secondary education (K-12) resides with the states. However, through the legislative process, the federal government provides financial assistance and resources to the states and schools in an effort to supplement, but not supplant, state support (US Department of Education 2005). Thus, federal funding and national education reform acts shape school programs and curriculum in K-12 at the state level.

In order to provide a context for understanding the place of interior design research and content in the K-12 environment, the three most recent national acts are outlined in this essay. These ever-changing education acts explain the moving target both teachers and school districts must respond to in an effort to remain viable, visible, and successful in securing federal funding to support their curricula and programs.

National Education Acts

Historically, the primary source of federal funding for K-12 education emerged in 1965 with the enactment of the Elementary and Secondary Education Act (ESEA). Today, this act continues to guide what the US Department of Education can and cannot do in regard to K-12 education (US Department of Education 2005). Since 1965, each education reform act, signed by the current US president, serves as a reauthorization of the ESEA and is enacted through the US Department of Education.

In 1994 the School-to-Work (STW) Opportunities Act was signed into law by President Bill Clinton. The purpose of STW was to raise achievement for all students and to align the nation's educational system with the modern workplace in order to better prepare students for a full range of post-secondary education and employment opportunities. Concerned that many young people were not interested in school and were ill prepared for the workforce, a system was created to make academic learning more exciting and relevant to all students, while at the same time equipping them with workplace skills. While the school-to-work systems varied from state to state, each allowed students to explore different careers of their choice (see Table 29.1) (http://www.dol.gov/elaws/esa/flsa/scope/ee15astw.asp).

Table 29.1 Three United States national education acts

Act	Year	President	Purpose	Sampling of programs
School-to-Work Opportunities Act (STW)	1994	Clinton	Provide seed money to states and local partnerships of business, labor, government, education, and community organizations to develop school-to-work systems.	*School-based learning*: classroom instruction based on high academic and business-defined occupational skill standards *Work-based learning*: career exploration, work experience, structured training, and monitoring at job sites. *Connecting Activities*: courses integrating classroom and on-the-job instruction, matching students with participating employers, training of mentors and building bridges between school and work.
No Child Left Behind Act (NCLB)	2001	Bush	Raise achievement for all students and to close the achievement gap. This was done through accountability, research-based instruction, flexibility, and options for parents, so that no child was left behind.	*Title I*: improvement of academic achievement of children in high-poverty schools *Reading first*: promote the use of scientifically based research to provide high-quality reading instruction for grades K-3. *English language acquisition*: to assist schools in improving the education of limited English-proficient children by teaching them English and helping them meet state academic standards.
A Blueprint for Reform Act (Blueprint)	2010	Obama	By 2020, the US will once again lead the world in college completion. To ensure that every student graduates from high school well prepared for college and a career.	*Race to the top*: incentives for excellence by encouraging state and local leaders to work together. Incentives for systemic reforms at the state level and expand the program to school districts that take on bold, comprehensive reforms. *Investing in innovation*: support local and non-profit leaders as they develop and scale up programs that have demonstrated success, and discover the next generation of innovative solutions. *College-and-career-ready students program*: Improved assessments used to accurately measure student growth; to better measure how states, districts, schools, principals, and teachers are educating students.

The No Child Left Behind (NCLB) Act of 2001 was signed into law by President George Bush in 2002. This law was the most comprehensive revision of federal education programs since the ESEA. NCLB programs included Title I – the largest federal K-12 program to that date – which provided $13 billion to local districts with high-poverty schools (US Department of Education 2005). Academic achievement standards for all students were raised through accountability, research-based instruction, flexibility, and options for parents to ensure that no child was left behind. Unfortunately the NCLB was only partially successful. Evidence of this can be seen in the fact that 4 out of every 10 new college students, including half of those enrolled in two-year institutions, continue to need remedial courses to successfully compete with other students at the college level. Additionally, many employers continue to comment on the inadequate preparation of high-school graduates to enter the careers they choose (US Department of Education OPEPD 2010).

In 2010, A Blueprint for Reform Act (commonly referred to as "Blueprint") was signed into law by President Barack Obama. The goal of this act was to ensure that, by 2020, the United States will once again lead the world in college completion and that every student will graduate from high school well prepared for college and the career they choose (US Department of Education OPEPD 2010).

Interior Design Presence in K-12: National to Local

In order to better understand the research that has been completed on interior design's place in elementary and secondary education – and to fully comprehend the research gap that exists – it is important to examine the connections between curriculum development and the US Department of Education. Of particular importance is the fact that the Department of Education serves as the umbrella organization that provides the financial support for interior design-related courses offered in high schools and establishes standards that guide the content of such courses.

Interior design-related content and its place in the US Department of Education

While there is little content taught in elementary schools that is specific to interior design or its career path, research indicates that many art- and design-related topics are incorporated into kindergarten through sixth-grade curricula. These topics (e.g., color theory) serve as a foundation for many design-related careers, including interior design. Standard topics such as math, natural sciences, and social sciences also assist in preparing students for the interior design profession (Clemons 2001). The curricula for such classes are guided by national academic standards, some of which fall under the rubric of the visual or fine arts.

Research indicates that visibility for the career of interior design dramatically increases at the secondary education level. Its first appearance is in junior high or middle school as a topic taught in life skills courses. Beginning in the ninth grade, a stand-alone, elective course in interior design at the high-school level is available at some schools (Clemons 2001). Depending on the popularity of such courses, certain high schools may offer between one and four interior design courses.

Within the US Department of Education the Office of Vocational and Adult Education (OVAE) exists, where the Career and Technical Education (CTE) programs reside. The CTE programs direct states to create courses of study that lead to industry-recognized credentials or associate/baccalaureate degrees. Historical connections within the Family and Consumer Sciences (FCS) programs (formerly referred to as Home Economics) have made it possible for the profession of interior design to fall under the auspices of CTE.

Funding for secondary education interior design-related courses: Perkins Act

The Carl D. Perkins Career and Technical Education Act of 2006 (Perkins Act) focuses on career readiness and is administered through the CTE offices. The Perkins Act has a congressionally supported budget-line item for career and technical education that provides resources for career-related high-school classes such as interior design. Perkins funding receives approximately $1.14 billion in annual subsidy through the OVAE (US Department of Education OVAE 2012). Although these dollars are allocated to state education agencies, national programs, and related associations, only state boards for vocational education are eligible to apply (www2.ed.gov/offices/OVAE/CTE/perkins.html).

On the national level, a number of organizations are funded by the Perkins Act. The Association of Career and Technical Education (ACTE) is one organization that is partially funded by the Perkins Act. It is the largest national association dedicated to the advancement of education that prepares youth and adults for careers and is the professional organization that represents CTE (https://www.acteonline.org/vision.aspx#.U30G7IdOWM8). ACTE is composed of 27,000 career and technical educators, administrators, researchers, and guidance counselors whose core purpose "is to provide leadership in the development of an educated and competitive workforce" (www.acteonline.org).

ACTE offers resources for teacher education, represents career-related legislative issues, funds lobbyists to create public awareness, and offers business internships. Its state-driven associations, such as the Colorado Association of Career and Technical Education (CACTE), offer professional development and annual conferences to high-school teachers, which are also Perkins-funded. The presence of interior design at the middle and high-school levels, therefore, is directly related to and reliant upon Perkins funding.

Interior Design-Related Content and Courses in Secondary Education

At the state level, interior design is taught as a semester-long, elective course in high schools throughout the nation, typically under the title of "Housing and Interiors." The number of interior design-related courses differs from community to community and state to state. Research indicates that a central database does not exist that tabulates the enrollment numbers of students in high-school interior design courses in the United States. The fact that each state employs a different location and method of compiling such numbers makes it difficult to assess the presence of interior design in courses offered at the high-school level. National statistics are being gathered through a national survey and personal phone calls from the Interior Design Educators Council (IDEC) K-12 Task Force. Securing accurate data has proven to be a challenge for the Task Force, with the biggest obstacle being to locate the appropriate state representative with access to enrollment numbers (IDEC 2012).

In this discussion it is important to remember that states administer elementary and secondary education. Therefore, the teaching of interior design at the high-school level is decentralized across the nation and facilitated at the state level by Family and Consumer Science curriculum specialists. This being the case, some states (e.g., New Mexico) have indicated that no interior design-related courses are offered in their high schools. This is not surprising, since New Mexico is one of the few states that does not offer a post-secondary interior design program. In contrast, other states, such as Indiana and Florida, have reported the presence of as many as four interior design courses at one high school.

Research shows that when only one course is offered at the high-school level, it is usually an introductory course that outlines career paths in the fields of housing and interiors. In a few rare instances an introductory "Housing and Interiors" course is followed by separate residential and commercial interior design courses.

Some states (e.g., Colorado) have 40+ high-school, state-approved interior design programs. This means that the state, after review, has given 40 high schools permission to teach a semester-long interior design-related course. However, this should not be interpreted to mean that all 40 of the schools have enough enrollments to offer the course each semester or year.

Other states (e.g., New York) require every youth to complete at least one FCS course before graduation, with FCS serving as the umbrella subject-matter area for interior design. As a result, in New York State alone approximately 12,000 students annually decide whether or not to take an interior design course as their FCS course of choice.

Larger states (e.g., California) have decentralized state-administered interior design-related curricula and report that 1,350 students took housing and interior design courses in 2011 and 700 students in 2012. In Texas, also a state that has centralized, state-administered, interior design-related curricula, 9,500 students took housing and interior design courses in 2012 and 9,000 in 2011.

As can be seen from these two examples, both California and Texas have seen a decline in the number of students enrolling in interior design-related courses in the last several years. This decline in enrollment correlates to enrollment numbers at the collegiate level in this same time frame. In contrast to this, however, is the state of Pennsylvania, which reports that enrollment numbers in interior design-related courses have increased and appear to be continuing to increase. Although there are no data available to ascertain why some states have increasing enrollment and others do not, funding from the Perkins Act continues to be a key component in the promotion and continuation of interior design-related courses in high schools.

In order to receive Perkins funding a course must meet the CTE requirements. Therefore, teachers must make sure the interior design-related courses meet these standards. In addition, they must continually market the courses to their students and negotiate with administrators to receive funding. In an environment where state and school district budgets are being cut, interior design-related courses are continually at risk.

Secondary Education Teachers of Interior Design

High-school interior design-related courses are taught predominantly by those professionals who have earned a four-year baccalaureate degree in Family and Consumer Science. FCS teachers educate students for life management and a variety of careers such as child development, food production, hospitality management, apparel, and interior design. Therefore, graduates of collegiate FCS programs vary in the amount of exposure they have had to interior design in their college programs. For example, in some FCS collegiate programs future teachers are required to take only one introductory interior design course, while in other FCS collegiate programs they are required to complete several interior design-related courses such as textiles, introduction to interior design, lighting, and color. This poses a consistency and relevancy challenge for college-level interior design programs and the professional field of interior design.

National Interior Design Competition in High Schools

As mentioned earlier in this essay, the Perkins Act funds career and technical education programs on a national, regional, and local level for both students and teachers. The goal is to provide better service to students, to better prepare teachers and counselors, and to address the priorities of business and industry. In regard to student needs, career and technical student organizations (CTSOs) receive financial support for activities at the state and local levels that are targeted to help improve student learning and assist students in achieving their career goals. One such CTSO program related to interior design is the Family, Career and Community Leaders of America (FCCLA). This nonprofit association of over 205,000 youth in nearly 6,500 chapters is for young men and women who are enrolled in FCS classes in public and private schools through grade 12.

The FCCLA is endorsed by the US Department of Education (Office of Vocational and Adult Education) and the American Association of Family and Consumer Sciences (AAFCS). It offers programs such as competitive events, national outreach projects, career connections, community service, leadership training, and financial workshops. The purpose of AAFCS is to promote personal growth and leadership development in high-school students through Family and Consumer Sciences education.

The STAR event is an important AAFCS-sponsored annual student competition that assesses student learning in such careers as entrepreneurship, fashion design, culinary arts, interior design, hospitality, tourism, and recreation (FCCLA 2012). Sponsored in part by the National Kitchen and Bath Association, the interior design STAR event is an individual or team event that recognizes participants who apply interior design skills learned in FCS courses. Students who are taking an interior design-related course or courses that are federally funded by a Perkins grant are required to participate in the FCCLA STAR event at the local level. Local winners are then required to compete at the national level.

Students participating in the STAR event competition are given a client profile and program for the design of a residence prepared by members of the Interior Design Educators Council, and the American Society of Interior Designers (ASID; www.asid.org). IDEC is an organization of interior design educators which focuses on the advancement of interior design education and research, and ASID is the oldest and largest organization of practicing interior designers working in the areas of commercial and residential design.

Each student competing in the STAR event is given the challenge to design a space plan, draw elevations, select interior finishes, and make a graphic and oral presentation to judges. Since its inception the focus of the competition has been on residential design; however, the inclusion of a commercial design scenario is planned for the near future. It is anticipated that this change, adopted by the FCCLA, will encourage high-school interior design instructors to teach commercial design in their courses.

National Examination: High-School Interior Design

In order to satisfy the growing emphasis on assessment and accountability in secondary education, AAFCS determined that a national interior design assessment at the high-school level was needed. Also in support of the idea was the National Standards for Family and Consumer Sciences Education and the National Career Clusters Initiative (NASDCTEc n.d.).

With funding support from 29 states, AAFCS solicited a partnership with ASID and IDEC to develop a Pre-Professional Assessment and Certifications (Pre-PAC) for interior design fundamentals (AAFCS 2012a, 2012b). Leaders of ASID and IDEC initially had reservations about developing a partnership with ASFCS because of the stigma of AAFCS' historical link to Home Economics; however, the decision was made that it was better to help guide the AAFCS process rather than ignore the effort or to have the Pre-PAC developed by other practitioner resources (Clemons 2010). As a result, by working together AAFCS, ASID, and IDEC had developed an agreement with over 30 states to write the Pre-PAC for interior design by 2009.

The agreed-upon purpose of the Pre-PAC national-standards-based competency assessment was to measure the knowledge and skill levels students had attained in interior design at the pre-professional and/or para-professional level. It was determined that when a student had successfully completed the assessment, a certificate of completion would be awarded. The assessment program was targeted at students who had expressed an interest in entry-level to mid-level positions in interior design-related fields, including furnishings or equipment sales associates, computer-aided drafting, interior design assistants, modelers, showroom assistants, photo stylists, furnishings buyers, commercial/residential furnishings coordinators, and renderers (AAFCS 2012b).

The composition of the Pre-PAC development board for interior design was made up of 15 interior design practitioners (e.g., commercial/residential design), representatives from potential employment paths (e.g., IKEA), and educators (e.g., secondary and post-secondary) (Clemons 2010). The six domain areas identified to guide assessment questions were: career paths, design fundamentals, factors influencing design, design communications and skills development, interior design application and analysis, and professional practice (AAFCS 2012b).

Bloom's *Taxonomy of Educational Objectives* was used to guide the composition of the assessment. Created in 1956 under the leadership of educational psychologist Dr. Benjamin Bloom, a taxonomy of learning was developed to promote higher forms of thinking in education, such as analyzing and evaluating, rather than rote learning. The taxonomy identified three domains of learning: cognitive: mental skills (*knowledge*); affective: growth in feelings or emotional areas (*attitude or self*); and psychomotor: manual or physical skills (*skills*) (Bloom 1956). Working within these three domains, the Pre-Pac assessment was targeted to serve those students who expressed a desire to: (1) earn college credit toward an associate or bachelor degree in interior design or (2) earn a design credential to enhance employment potential upon graduation from a high-school or post-secondary program.

The first Pre-PAC Interior Design Fundamentals assessment exam was given in the fall of 2010. It consisted of 80 multiple-choice questions (with three cognitive difficulty levels) and was administered via a computer-based testing program that provided valid and reliable competency measurement. As predicted, the student scores from the first two years in which the Pre-Pac assessment was offered were low. The low scores confirmed the expectation that there would be a significant difference between the FCS-related standards and the interior design industry-driven standards of the National Council of Interior Design Qualification (NCIDQ) exam (taken by those who are entering the profession after completing a baccalaureate degree in interior design and who have completed a specified number of years working in the field).

Education Standards Impacting K-12 Interior Design: National, State, and Local

As explained earlier in this chapter, standards that are related to national education acts, as well as the standards that are set by professional organizations such as AAFCS, drive the development of new K-12 education programs, curriculum development, and the content that is taught in specific courses. K-12 curriculum specialists and teachers are required to respond to these standards.

Over the years, each of the national education acts has set curricular standards that guide the development of state standards. Likewise, these curricular standards have guided the development of standards for specific K-12 school districts within each state. The three major national education standards that are currently used to guide interior design-related high-school course content are: the Common Core State Standards, the National Career Clusters Framework, and the Framework for 21st Century Learning. These standards are augmented by the National Association of State Administrators of Family and Consumer Sciences (NASASFACS) Housing and Interior Design Standards.

Because of the variety and constantly changing nature of these standards at the national, state, and local levels, it is a continuing challenge for K-12 teachers and curriculum specialists to respond to the standards. The curricula of post-secondary education programs, in contrast to K-12, are set by the faculty and are usually guided by the standards set by only one professional organization.

All public schools in the US have been encouraged to comply by 2014 with the Common Core State Standards (www.corestandards.org) that were introduced in June 2010. These standards represent a set of expectations for student knowledge and skills that high-school graduates should master in order to be college- and career-ready (National Governors Association Center for Best Practices 2010). Compiled by the Council of Chief State School Officers (CCSSO) and the National Governors Association (NGA), these standards emphasize English language arts (ELA) and mathematics standards. They represent the culmination of an extended effort to fulfill the charge issued by states to create the next generation of K-12 standards to ensure that all students are college- and/or career-ready by the end of high school. In addition to English language arts, the Common Core State Standards also set expectations for literacy in history/social studies, science, and technical subjects. These have been integrated by some states (e.g., Texas) into the development of an interior design curriculum, and by publishers such as Goodheart-Willcox, Inc. into high-school textbooks per mandate of the state.

While the Common Core State Standards guide schools in the overarching educational goals in reading, writing, and listening, the US Department of Education uses a Career Cluster framework to help students connect with courses of study and careers via career assessments. The Career Cluster initiative of 1996 was initially known as the Building Linkages Initiative. It was a collaborative effort between the US Department of Education, the Office of Vocational and Adult Education, the National School-to-Work office, and the National Skill Standards Board. The goal was to develop connections among federal and state educational agencies, employers, industry groups, and secondary and post-secondary educational institutions to create curricular frameworks in broad career clusters.

Now known as the National Career Clusters Framework with 16 Career Clusters, and administered through CTE, these standards improve student achievement by providing them with relevant contexts, linking school-based learning with the knowledge and skills required for success in the workplace. One of the 16 clusters relates to interior design: architecture and construction (NASDCTEc n.d.).

In 2010, industry and textbook corporations (e.g., Apple Inc., Crayola, Intel Corporation, and McGraw-Hill) supported the development of the Framework for 21st Century Learning, commonly referred to as P21 (Partnership for 21st Century Skills 2011). This framework offers descriptions of the skills, knowledge, and expertise that students should master in order to succeed in today's workplace and in life. P21 highlights such things as critical thinking, problem-solving, communication, and collaboration as essential skills. Specifically, it emphasizes:

- Learning and innovation skills (e.g., creativity and innovation)
- Information, media, and technology skills (e.g., media literacy)
- Life and career skills (e.g., social and cross-cultural skills)

In addition to the three educational standards just outlined, NASAFACS has developed and published curricular standards specific to housing and interior design (NASAFACS 2010: Area of Study 11.0: Housing and Interior Design). Revised in 2009/2010 and projected for revision in 2019, the NASAFACS Housing and Interior Design Standards are used in every state to guide the development of housing and interior design courses.

Analysis and research of these standards indicates they are skewed heavily toward the residential sector (Clemons 2001). Almost exclusively, the spaces designed, evaluated, and studied are housing-related. However, in the few instances where an interior design-related course is not linked to housing content, the national interior design industry standards set by the Council for Interior Design Accreditation (CIDA) may be used (CIDA 2011). These standards offer guidance to educators who want to prepare high-school students to successfully make the transition into a collegiate-level interior design program.

As mentioned earlier, in addition to responding to the overarching standards just reviewed, each state can develop its own set of standards for interior design-related courses in order to best meet the needs of its constituency and communities.

Some states administer their standards (and subsequent assessments) in a centralized manner (e.g., Texas) while others use a decentralized method (e.g., Colorado). If the administration is decentralized, the decision-makers reside at the local level.

Educational Learning Theories

Of equal importance to the context and content of interior design-related high-school courses is an understanding of *how* the courses are taught. During their college preparation and prior to entering the workforce, secondary education teachers study educational learning theories and teaching modalities. They are also required to continue to update their teaching credentials through continuing education courses and programs throughout their career. This being the case, there are many educational learning theories that high-school students are exposed to, and adhere to, when teaching interior design-related courses.

One example of a popular learning theory that is often used by teachers in secondary education is known as "inquiry continuums." According to Charles Pearce, this approach allows students to "mess around" with real materials and problems that lead the student to the questions which are at the heart of the inquiry. Such an inquiry-based approach emphasizes two types of important questions: (1) those that demand research and (2) those that can be investigated (Pearce 1999).

Questions that demand research are the type of inquiries that occur the most frequently in high-school classrooms, and they require students to use sources of existing information to find answers. The opposite of research questions are those which require the learner to investigate a problem. In most high-school curricula, questions that require investigation are less frequent because they require students to seek answers through direct observation.

According to the literature, the inquiry-based approach can be seen as an inquiry continuum, which occurs during the process of inquiry, beginning when the learner receives the data and is told to analyze it and continuing through a process whereby the learner formulates explanations from the evidence (Lee 2011). An example of this learning approach in action can be seen in a high-school interior design class where, prior to making a design decision, students use an inquiry process to investigate solutions and find answers to their own questions through such tools as personal observations, surveys, and discussions with experts.

Another learning theory often used by secondary education teachers is referred to as "understanding by design" (UbD) (Wiggins and McTighe 2001; Williams and Williams 2009). This theory is based on the belief that teachers are "curriculum designers." That is to say, they design the curriculum and learning experiences to meet specific goals from the perspective of assessment, rather than from the perspective of course objectives. This means that a curriculum is designed in reverse, with the assessment of student learning considered first rather than last.

The literature suggests that UbD is a process that allows critical thinking to be easily integrated into a curriculum by placing the focus on the internalization of big ideas – rather than a process that reinforces the rote learning of facts and data that students then simply regurgitate. According to this theory, such a process increases student understanding by involving students in an active process of discovery and inquiry – providing students with several contexts to assist them in learning why they are learning what they are learning.

Another popular learning theory is the brain-based learning theory, sometimes called brain-based instruction. Based on the premise that memorizing isolated data to pass assessment exams is not ideal, this theory suggests that learning is interconnected and can be creative, social, analytical, and contemplative – all at different times during the learning process (Stevens and Goldberg 2001).

Advocates of the brain-based theory point to research that describes the human brain as a composition of billions of nerve cells called neurons. According to this research, each neuron makes between 5,000 and 50,000 contacts with other neurons, making 100 trillion connections in the brain. As learning takes place, neurons grow and connect with synapses (gaps between neurons), which act as invisible bridges that make connections between information coming into the brain. According to this theory, all primary learning occurs at the synapse. For example, when a message is transmitted repeatedly along a specific sequence of neurons, the sequence becomes easier to repeat, thus forming the basis for meaning and memory.

Summary of K-12 Interior Design Research

Interior design research into the K-12 arena began in the early 1990s. Publications documenting directives and research concerning the need for interior designers to be involved in elementary and secondary education began in 1992 with an article published in *Interior Design* by Joy Dohr (Dohr 1992). The focus of Dohr's article was six predictions concerning the future of interior design education. In this article, Dohr argued that interior designers needed to become actively involved in K-12 education to ensure the growth and future of the profession.

Shortly after, Tew and Portillo published their research, which suggested that interior design was not accurately represented in secondary education courses (Tew and Portillo 1993). According to their research, the emphasis of most courses was on issues related to architecture or housing, rather than interior design. Only a few examples of curricula that focused on such things as floor plans, circulation patterns, spatial relationships, and furniture arrangements were found to be offered in high-school curricula at that time.

Later research by Portillo and Rey-Barreau determined that advocates for architecture had spearheaded the majority of K-12 design initiatives, with advocates for interior design largely absent from the effort. They concluded that there was a need for the development of substantive programs and in K-12 curricula to promote a deeper understanding of the importance of interior design (Portillo and Rey-Barreau 1995).

In 1996 Clemons began to look at ways to introduce elementary students to the elements and principles of design and the design process. Her first publication discussed the development and outcomes of summer-based computer workshops for third through eighth graders. The objectives of the workshop focused on the exploration of design fundamentals through the creation of animated storybooks (Clemons 1998).

Next, Clemons developed an interactive compact disk (CD-ROM) to educate sixth- through eighth-grade students about the role an interior designer plays in the design of the built environment (Clemons 1999). Within the context of new construction of a residence, the CD-ROM was set up to be an interactive storybook to illustrate 30 representative careers. Marketed to career counselors, the CD-ROM allowed students to explore several different career paths related to interior design. Those career paths that were found to be of interest to the student could be accessed through a link which directed them to information about the education requirements, salary ranges, and importance of the career.

In 2002, Clemons published research funded by the International Interior Design Association (IIDA) Foundation. The study resulted in a proposal that outlined a cohesive approach to the integration of interior design into elementary and secondary curricula (Clemons 2002a). The integrative model that was proposed incorporated two national movements: the school-to-work and the national education reform. In addition, the proposal suggested the use of common interior design projects, and experiential, learning-based activities such as internships, field trips, and simulations for use in FCS curricula in high schools. Further, three levels of participation of interior design professionals were suggested and another call was issued to interior design professionals and students to become involved in educating youth about the career of interior design.

At the same time as this study was being conducted, Nussbaumer developed a two-week interior design curriculum that was taught at the secondary level under the auspices of FCS course standards (Nussbaumer 2001). The curriculum integrated introductory interior design concepts, utilizing an intergenerational approach. This was done by having the high-school students who were enrolled in the FCS class teach introductory interior design concepts to children in third through fifth grades.

The objectives for the curriculum lesson plans in Nussbaumer's study were based on the FCS comprehensive standard related to careers in housing, interiors, and furnishings, and the goal was to stimulate interest in interior design as a career option. A pre- and post-test research design was used to assess learning during the two-week unit. The findings revealed that the high-school students knew more about interior design as a career option (including the education and skills needed to be successful in the profession) than they did before taking the class.

Further research on K-12 education and interior design-related curricula was done in 2001 using three focus groups (Clemons 2002b). The objective of this study was to assess what the perceived issues were in the integration of interior design into K-12 grade levels. The three groups comprised: (1) interior design educators and practitioners; (2) elementary and secondary teachers; and (3) K-12 principals and curriculum specialists from across the nation. Findings from this qualitative study resulted in the following recommendations:

1　Critical content areas of interior design such as design criticism and thinking, visual literacy, elements and principles of design, three-dimensional exploration, cultural and international influences, psychology of space, life-cycle changes, and terminology of design should be taught in K-12 levels.
2　Appropriate tools such as model-making as part of a design thinking process, inquiry exercises, and use of contextual concrete examples that enhance student learning should be used to teach interior design in K-12.
3　Critical issues such as clearly defining how interior design content relates to national standards, use of grade-appropriate lesson plans, integrating technology, and topics that support identification of careers should be addressed when integrating interior design into K-12 courses.

All three focus groups overwhelmingly supported the integration of interior design content areas into K-12.

Continuing her research on K-12 and interior design-related content, in 2006 Clemons reported on a study which was conducted to ascertain the amount and type of interior design curriculum materials available to K-12 teachers, curriculum specialists, and students. Using content analysis as a qualitative methodology, database resources were extensively searched to assess the presence of interior design in curricula and textbook materials. These included Internet websites (n = 1,000+), the Education Resources Information Center (ERIC), professional organizations (n = 33), professional foundations (n = 27), museums (n = 75), and design institutes (n = 7). Findings indicated that interior design-related content continued to have little presence in K-12 curricula (Clemons 2006).

Suggestions for K-12 Interior Design Research

A review of the literature indicates that the interior design profession has responded slowly to the movement to integrate interior design-related content and courses into elementary and secondary education. However, informal research indicates that many educators and practitioners are often in the secondary FCS classroom discussing the career and serving as content experts in the development of state standards. It is suggested that a quantitative study is needed to determine where, and to what extent, these experts have been involved in K-12 classes, and to examine the impact they have had on students' understanding of the profession of interior design.

Both the American Society of Interior Designers and Interior Design Educators Council have developed strategic plans which include setting the involvement in

K-12 education as a priority. Both organizations have dedicated resources to the development of materials for high-school students to inform them about interior design as a career path. For example, ASID and other professional organizations have developed the careersininteriordesign.org website that shares career information, and an IDEC Special Projects Grant has been awarded to help FCS high-school teachers develop interior design curricula.

Although these initiatives represent positive movement toward better integration of interior design into K-12 curricula, informal discussions indicate that professional designers and design educators feel the K-12 arena is too vast, complex, and different from the continuum from college to warrant exploration. This being the case, these organizations are reluctant to allocate extensive resources which they feel may have only minimal impact. It is suggested that a study could be developed to assess ways to maximize resources through the use of existing membership networks as distribution channels.

Another area that is ripe for study is in the assessment of how high-school students perceive interior design. For example, do they see it as a potential career and profession or as a vocation? How might interior design be repositioned in K-12 programs to attract more gender diversity? How well do high-school students appreciate the breadth of the profession of interior design (e.g., commercial versus residential design)?

Where to Go from Here

Several ongoing initiatives are in place to help raise awareness and clarify what interior design offers as a profession. Globally, through the International Federation of Interior Architects/Designers (IFI), more students are becoming educated about interior design and, nationally, a policy is under development to turn the STEM program (science, technology, engineering, and mathematics) into STEAM by incorporating the arts and aesthetics into the national standards for K-12.

Yet another initiative, spearheaded by a K-12 coalition of design educators, administrators, and professional organization representatives, is the writing of the first national design education standards. With federal dollars that support the arts diminishing, this coalition has placed emphasis on design rather than art, feeling that design is more fundable because it is a necessary element in a wider range of careers and fields of study. This coalition argues that by learning design thinking at the elementary and secondary education levels students become better problem-solvers – a skill that is needed in many fields of study.

These ongoing initiatives focused on K-12 raise a question about what college and university faculty and administrators are doing to help increase awareness of interior design in their students. It has been documented that, between 2000 and 2008, high-school education interior design programs experienced record enrollments; yet since the recession and subsequent building bust all careers associated with the built environment have suffered. Low enrollment in college-level interior design programs has been the subject of formal discussions at IDEC annual conferences. Given this scenario, it is suggested that one strategy to raise post-secondary enrollment in interior design programs could be to strengthen the link between high school and college interior design programs.

Research indicates that youth learn about interior design from four major sources: design reality shows (Waxman and Clemons 2007), architecture education in high school, national 4HCC curriculum and programs, and Family and Consumer Science housing and interior design courses in high school. None of these four sources is endorsed by professional interior design organizations. Should they be?

There is evidence that large manufacturers of furniture (e.g., Steelcase, Inc.) are interested in high-school students and realize the importance of shaping curricula before students enter the collegiate level. Could such manufacturers serve as new partners with interior design university faculty and administrators to prepare students to enter the workforce?

Lastly, national interior design career predictions indicate an upswing in enrollments and individuals entering the profession in the next few years. Are our colleges and the profession ready? Students who will be entering the profession of interior design are in high-school classes now. In order to ensure that the limited funds available that support interior design education through national, state, and local avenues are used wisely, continued research is necessary.

References

AAFCS (American Association of Family and Consumer Science). 2012a. *Pre-Professional Assessment and Certification (Pre-PAC) Program.* http://www.aafcs.org/prepac/. Accessed May 11, 2014.

AAFCS (American Association of Family and Consumer Science). 2012b. *PRE-PAC.* http://www.aafcs.org/credentialingcenter/test.asp. Accessed May 20, 2014.

ASID (American Society of Interior Designers). n.d. *ASID Strategic Plan FY 2012–2013.* http://www.asid.org/sites/default/files/ASID_Strategic_Plan_FY2013.pdf. Accessed May 20, 2014.

Bloom, B. S. 1956. *Taxonomy of Educational Objectives, Handbook I: The Cognitive Domain.* New York: David McKay.

CIDA (Council for Interior Design Accreditation). 2011. *CIDA Professional Standards.* http://accredit-id.org/professional-standards. Accessed December 31, 2012.

Clemons, S. 1998. "Computer animation: a tool for teaching design fundamentals to elementary school students," *Journal of Interior Design* 24: 40–47.

Clemons, S. 1999. "Development of interior design career information for dissemination to students in grades six through eight," *Journal of Interior Design* 25(2): 45–51.

Clemons, S. 2001. "Interior design K-12 curriculum in the United States [abstract]," *Proceedings of the International Interior Design Educators Council Annual Conference*, Chicago, pp. 20–22.

Clemons, S. 2002a. "Collaborative links with K-12: a proposed model integrating interior design with national education standards," *Journal of Interior Design* 28(1): 40–48.

Clemons, S. 2002b, July/August. "Interior design in K-12: let's ask the experts!" *Interiors & Sources*, pp. 72–75.

Clemons, S. A. 2006, "The presence of interior design content in K-12 curriculum materials," *Journal of Interior Design* 32: 17–27.

Clemons, S. 2010, March. "Junior certificate in interior design: rationale, development, status. [abstract + paper]," *Proceedings of the Interior Design Educators Council Annual Conference*, Atlanta, GA, pp. 68–73.

Dohr, J. 1992, October. "Six predictions: the future of design education," *Interior Design*, 63(14): 131.

FCCLA. 2012. *Star Event*. http://www.fcclainc.org/content/star-events/. Accessed January 23, 2013.

IDEC (Interior Design Educators Council). 2012. *Strategic Plan*. http://www.idec.org/documents/IDEC_Strategic_Chart_0209.pdf. Accessed December 30, 2012.

Lee, V. S. 2011, June. "The power of inquiry as a way of learning," *Innovative Higher Education* 36(3): 149–160.

NASASFACS (National Association of State Administrators of Family and Consumer Sciences). 2010. *National Standards for Family and Consumer Sciences*. Area of Study 11.0: Housing and Interior Design. http://www.nasafacs.org/national-standards–competencies.html.

NASDCTEc (National Association of State Directors of Career Technical Education Consortium). n.d. *CTE: The 16 Career Clusters: Pathways to College and Career Readiness*. http://www.careertech.org/career-clusters/glance/programs-study.html. Accessed May 11, 2014.

National Center for Education Statistics. 2011. *Digest of Education Statistics: 2011*. http://nces.ed.gov/programs/digest/d11/tables/dt11_349.asp. Accessed May 20, 2014.

National Governors Association Center for Best Practices, Council of Chief State School Officers, 2010. *Common Core State Standards*. National Governors Association Center for Best Practices, Council of Chief State School Officers, Washington DC. http://www.careertech.org/career-technical-education/cctc/info.html. Accessed May 11, 2014.

Nussbaumer, L. 2001. 'Theoretical framework for instruction that accommodates all learning styles,' *Journal of Interior Design* 27(2) 35–45.

Nussbaumer, L. L. 2002. "Interior design – an exciting career choice: a curriculum for high school students with an intergenerational approach," *Proceedings of the Interior Design Educators Council Conference*, Santa Fe, NM, pp. 56–57.

OWP/P Architects + VS Furniture + Bruce Mau Design. 2010. *The Third Teacher: 79 Ways You Can Use Design to Transform Teaching & Learning*. New York: Abrams.

Partnership for 21st Century Skills. 2011, March. *Framework for 21st Century Learning*. Washington DC. http://www.P21.org. Accessed May 11, 2014.

Pearce, C. 1999. *Nurturing Inquiry: Real Science for the Elementary Classroom*. Portsmouth, NH: Heinemann.

Portillo, M. and Rey-Barreau, J. 1995. "The place of interior design in K-12 education and the built environment education movement," *Journal of Interior Design* 21(1): 39–43.

Stevens, J. and Goldberg, D. 2001. *For the Learners' Sake: A Practical Guide to Transform Your Classroom and School*. Tucson: Zephyr Press.

Tew, S. and Portillo, M. 1993. "Increasing interior design recognition: the potential of built environment education," *Proceeding of the Interior Design Educators Council Conference*, Coeur D'Alene, ID, p. 43.

US Department of Education. 2005. *10 Facts About K-12 Education Funding*. Washington DC.

US Department of Education. 2010, February 1. *President's Education Budget Signals Bold Changes for ESEA*. http://www2.ed.gov/news/pressreleases/2010/02/02012010.html. Accessed May 11, 2014.

US Department of Education, OPEPD (Office of Planning, Evaluation and Policy Development). 2010. *ESEA Blueprint for Reform*, Washington DC.

US Department of Education, OVAE (Office of Vocational and Adult Education). 2012. *Investing in America's Future: A Blueprint for Transforming Career and Technical Education*, Washington DC.

Waxman, L. K. and Clemons, S. 2007, "Student perceptions: debunking television's portrayal of interior design," *Journal of Interior Design* 32: v–xi.

Wiggins, G. and McTighe, J. 2001. *Understanding by Design*. Upper Saddle River, NJ: Merrill/Prentice-Hall.

Williams, D. and Williams, M. 2009, Fall. "Learning experiences to develop critical thinking through understanding by design," *Understanding Our Gifted* 22(1): 19–23.

30

Community-Building through Interior Design Education

Patrick Lucas

Introduction

Design speaks to the value of healthy spaces, buildings, neighborhoods, and cities and supports decision-making that is connected to the human experience. Such a philosophy embraces a spirit of collaboration and represents connectivity that is manifested in tangible forms. Community engagement projects give credence to the idea that design does not happen in a vacuum and serves to inspire all collaborators. Through engaged scholarship students are given a sense of empowerment as interior designers and able to see themselves as agents of positive change.

Community engagement, as used here, means going beyond the common practice of simply situating an interior design studio in the community. The differentiation is that a truly engaged community project is reciprocal. That is to say, reciprocity occurs when there is engagement from the community to the university and back again to the community. While one-way service learning projects are commonplace in many interior design programs, projects with true reciprocity are rare.

By tethering what is taught to the local community students gain the ability to see that the world begins from a very personal place that is connected deeply with the universe beyond (Bachelard 1994). Through community engaged projects students learn to appreciate design as transformative and a means of responsibly allocating resources for the benefit of humanity – while at the same time teaching students the realities of design problem-solving (Architecture for Humanity 2006; Bell 2004; Bell and Wakeford 2008; Fuad-Luke 2009).

Although community engagement projects require doggedness and resiliency on the part of faculty, students, and community partners, they are more meaningful

The Handbook of Interior Design, First Edition. Edited by Jo Ann Asher Thompson and Nancy H. Blossom.
© 2015 John Wiley & Sons, Ltd. Published 2015 by John Wiley & Sons, Ltd.

and have a longer-lasting impact than other projects which are not engaged. Further, through engaged scholarship laypeople come to appreciate the value of interior design as a means of improving the quality of life.

Through a philosophy of community engagement in educational programs, interior design can reaffirm its social compact and embrace its multiple birthrights in home economics, art, architecture, and industrial design (Anderson, Honey, and Dudek 2007). In other words, interior design can be understood as one of the many scales of design that impacts humans in their everyday environments.

Literature Review

According to the literature, engaged scholarship stands at the forefront of current and future thinking about higher education (Hatcher and Bringle 2011). In a White Paper written at the Columbia University School of Law's Center for Institutional and Social Change community-based teaching and learning is cited as a high-impact educational practice (Kuh 2008; Sturm, Eatman, Saltmarsh, et al. 2011). Engaged scholarship requires understanding of how practices and programs relate to a larger system in communities both local and global (Driscoll and Sandman 2011; Saltmarsh 2010; Saltmarsh, Hartley, and Clayton 2009; Sturm et al. 2011).

Goldbard maintains that because there is no central body which awards credentials or dictates standards for the integration of community engagement in educational programs, such learning activities remain free from restrictions – offering fertile ground for reciprocity to occur between institutions of higher education and communities. Further, Goldbard suggests that students benefit from pre-community experiences that are embedded in curricula. Such experiences prepare them for community-based work and serve to create bridges among multiple departments, thereby establishing deep and sustained partnerships that take advantage of hybrid pedagogies (Goldbard 2008).

In keeping with this, Kecskes advocates for engaged departments, colleges, and universities. According to Kecskes, these are exemplified by a focus on common values and approaches and are composed of a transformative collection of faculty and students with diverse interests (Kecskes 2006). In these situations, structural and tactical issues that might impact community-engaged learning are readily recognized and discussed within the academy, creating a supportive environment for the development of a community engagement philosophy (Jordan, Wong, and Jungnickel 2009; Zlotkowski and Saltmarsh 2006).

Corser proposes a design engagement model rather than a design assistance model for faculty, students, and community partners – noting that the very terminology of design services perpetuates a hierarchy between the design professional and the client to be served (Corser 2008). Citing difficulties in gathering, quantifying, and assessing data, he indicates that many community-based projects struggle to truly engage their clients as real collaborators, and rarely include adequate post-project analysis or reflection, thereby resulting in projects that lack true depth and reciprocity in service (Corser 2008).

Calling for a fresh approach to design in the pursuit of greater social good – emphasizing process over product – Corser suggests that longstanding notions of professional status, privilege, and social responsibility, while useful in maintaining minimum standards and keeping the risk of public harm at bay, do not adequately serve the intense need in our societies for greater inclusion, participation, and collaboration in working toward social justice and the public good (Corser 2008). To counter this, Corser suggests five principles and practices as important to a successful design engagement approach: (1) acknowledging mutual value and values; (2) redefining problems and opportunities; (3) mutually defining success, failure, and risk; (4) creating and renewing structures for communication; and (5) getting serious about feedback, evaluation, and reflection (Corser 2008).

Case-Study Examples of Community Engagement Projects

Two case-study examples of community engagement projects are offered here. Although the specific attributes of the local community cannot be generalized broadly, each provides a model for reciprocity that is transferable and easy to translate to other circumstances. Through the documentation of the "ins and outs" of the two case studies, a worthwhile illustration of the evolution of the connections between the local community and design is provided. Also, familiar to each case study is a commonly accepted design process that moves from idea to development toward resolution.

Although the two projects are quite different in nature, each offers an engaged model that exemplifies Corser's five principles for engaged scholarship. The strong connections forged among the interior design students, the interior design faculty, and the local community leaders stand as testament to the importance of these principles when crafting a community engagement project. Also important to note, particularly in the second case-study example, is the role that participating community leaders can assume as co-educators with the faculty, rather than simply as tangential clients.

The focus of the first case study was social justice and serves to highlight how students became sensitized to social justice issues after participating in a community engagement project. Underpinning this project were Corser's three principles of (1) mutual value, (2) the creation of communication structures, and (3) reflection. The second case study offers a more fully engaged community project and exemplifies all five of Corser's principles.

Case Study #1. Shelter project: An example of social justice engagement

A fundamental goal behind grounding the design studio in the realities of the local community in the Shelter Project was to introduce students to the idea that design has the power to be an agent of change. The students were told the semester's focus was on public transportation (i.e., a bus/bus shelter). A one-week-long warm-up assignment was given for the student to read *The Image of the City* by Kevin Lynch. To complete the assignment, students were instructed to utilize the vocabulary from their readings (path, node, landmark, district, and edge) and explore the community, making connections through the description of a path from their own residence to an assigned point in town. Students took to their cars, navigated the landscape, and recorded their impressions, preparing both a digital and physical record of their recordings, musings, and discoveries. On review day, faculty dispatched students again to experience public transportation, noting the differences between the solo automobile drive and the crowded group experience of bus travel.

For many students this was their first foray into public transportation. Through this experience they discovered the inequities of the local bus system. To deepen the experience the design criteria were expanded to include the idea that, in the event of an emergency such as a hurricane, the shell of the bus could be used as one of several types of mobile relief structures – for housing, for dispensing supplies, and for service activities for relief workers temporarily relocated to the site.

The bus and bus shelter assignments, when linked together, allowed the students to work locally with a fixed structure and also regionally with a mobile structure. In this way, students were sensitized to significant social justice issues that included racism, disparities in class, disaster relief, team dynamics, and communication.

To optimize the learning experience, several diverse teaching strategies were implemented, including assigned readings, writings, sketches, diagrams, designs, research, analysis, interviews, blogs, and pin-ups of work for review. From these various exercises, students were able to amass information about all aspects of the design problem – which they were able to then incorporate into their design process. This led to a series of charrettes over a two-week period where their ideas were discussed and their designs were refined.

The design charrettes (i.e., collaborative sessions in which a group of designers draft solutions) served as a catalyst for the quick formation and execution of ideas in the studio (Lucas and Charest 2008). In keeping with Corser's principles of value, communication, and reflection, the charrettes also served to highlight how, through engagement with the community, students became more sensitized to important social justice issues and were able to express this new awareness in their design solutions.

Over the course of seven consecutive class sessions, charrettes were used as vehicles for exploration. These provided opportunities to draw the students' attention to the central design issue associated with the project, i.e., how to define the essence (value) of shelter. During the charrettes students distilled a broad range of information into cogent, well-crafted models, drawings, reports, and presentations for dissemination in the studio and community – relying heavily on basic data-collection methods and responses from people in the community who regularly used public transportation.

The charrettes were followed by a two-week design-intensive session called "experience: research." The resulting matrix from the "experience: research" segment of the project served as an organizing system for students at the individual, small group, large group, and class scale. Open communication among the members of each student team and each team's interaction with community participants were key to the production of a series of seamless digital presentations highlighting their individual and group research.

In addition to applying Corser's principles for successful design engagement in the design studio, faculty introduced the students to the notions of order, enrichment, and expression as proposed by Robert Rengel in his book, *Shaping Interior Space*. This resource, in combination with the continued use of Lynch's *Image of the City*, helped to frame the studio experience. Lastly, through the completion of a full-scale mock-up of their designs, it became evident that the students' empathy for, and understanding of, the essence of shelter (as a social justice issue) had been deepened.

Case #2. Identity by design: An example of community engagement

In this case study, students were given the task of examining the identity of three local institutions – an art museum, a historical museum, and the building occupied by the Industries of the Blind (IOB). The explicit objective of the project was to redesign the entry spaces and sequences of the entries of these institutions to enhance their coherence. In order to do this, students first had to determine and acknowledge the value structure of the IOB and to then redefine the problem (Corser 2008). A series of exercises in wayfinding and circulation, lighting and sound, and materials, colors, and textures was assigned to assist the students in the completion of these tasks.

The students worked both individually and as teams, collaborating with each other, community partners, guest critics, and faculty. An essential component of this process was the mutual agreement among the team members on their definition of success, failure, and risk. Equally important to the success of the project was the creation of communication structures, both within each team and with community partners (Corser 2008). These communication structures served as a framework for dialogue, not only within their teams and with community partners, but also with local museum professionals and museum designers to whom they were given access. This combination of communication venues provided the students with a deeper understanding of the place of cultural institutions in the world and the importance of design within and near such places.

As a result of the positive experience the IOB management had through their engagement with the interior design students, the project objectives were expanded by asking the students to create a design that would help inform visitors about the work of the IOB (i.e., its history and accomplishments). Once again applying Corser's principles of value and redefinition of the problem, students were encouraged to interview management and employees throughout the design process in order to deepen their understanding of the organization.

As a way to establish relevancy in their designs, the students studied Braille and made sketch models of Braille textures in different scales – often literally translating Braille while trying to continue to maintain fluidity in form and materials. As they moved through the textural studies, the communication structures established earlier were essential as ideas were abstracted and various ways of repeating geometric shapes in buildable form were explored. Working with a local lighting designer, the students examined lighting techniques and applications for experiencing light, texture, and color.

In keeping with Corser's principle of mutual agreement in the definition of success, failure, and risk, the students settled on a final graphic treatment (hexagon tessellations). After the graphic treatment was mutually determined, the students worked together to establish a central theme (symbol of value) to underpin the project. As a result, the white oak, a local tree, was chosen to symbolize the closeness and family-like work environment of the IOB.

Working at full scale with texture, pattern, color, and light, students designed three studio wall installations. A series of reviews was scheduled and attended by the IOB leaders, employees from the IOB, and university officials. The wall installations traced the engaged journey the students had experienced from their initial design explorations to their final concepts, providing a venue for them to reflect on the overall learning experience.

This project was viewed as exemplary engaged scholarship by both university officials and local community partners. As a result, additional opportunities for independent study and exploration continued to open up for students in subsequent semesters.

Conclusion

In the first case study, the focus was on issues of social justice, opening the eyes of students to the positive impact design can have on major societal issues. In the second case study, the students were closely aligned and engaged with community leaders, thereby creating more meaning to their design solutions. Further, these projects resulted in a noticeable and more positive shift in the philosophy and mindset of the design faculty and their approach to design studio and community engagement. These two projects demonstrate the possibilities of simple, yet engaged, work that emanates from design studios in a university setting.

By living in a place, one begins to know it more deeply and thus comprehend the needs of its constituents and organizations. Community-based work calls for faculty and students to leave their offices, classrooms, and studios, and be in the city – on its streets, patronizing its retail establishments and services, letting its culture seep into university life. By listening closely and examining where the community does not quite come together, or where there might be friction, or where a need exists to be met – these cracks and fissures provide golden opportunities for faculty, students, and universities to make a difference.

As noted in the literature, community engagement emphasizes the need for reciprocity among faculty, students, and community partners. In this way community partners are seen as co-educators and bear equal responsibility for the creation and dissemination of knowledge and discovery. This shifting landscape brings a different sensibility to academic design work – with community-engaged activities representing more than a one-way street where students drop in and out. Instead, community-engaged studios offer a reciprocal feeling of accomplishment among all the partners involved – faculty, students, and community groups alike.

References

Anderson, B., Honey, P., and Dudek, M. 2007. "Interior design's social compact: key to the quest for professional status," *Journal of Interior Design* 33(2): v–xii.

Architecture for Humanity, ed. 2006. *Design Like You Give a Damn: Architectural Responses to Humanitarian Crises*. New York: Metropolis Books.

Bachelard, G. 1994. *The Poetics of Space*. Boston, MA: Beacon Press.

Bell, B., ed. 2004. *Good Deeds, Good Design: Community Service through Architecture*. New York: Princeton Architectural Press.

Bell, B. and Wakeford, K., eds. 2008. *Expanding Architecture: Design as Activism*. New York: Metropolis Books.

Corser, R. 2008. *Design in the Public Interest: The Dilemma of Professionalism*. Imagining America: A Consortium of Universities and Organizations Dedicated to Advancing the Public and Civic Purposes of Humanities, Art, and Design. Syracuse University, Syracuse, New York.

Driscoll, A. and Sandman, L. 2011. *Evaluation Criteria for the Scholarship of Engagement*. http://www.scholarshipofengagement.org/evaluation/evaluation_criteria.html. Accessed January 18, 2013.

Fuad-Luke, A. 2009 . *Design Activism: Beautiful Strangeness for a Sustainable World*. New York: Earthscan.

Goldbard, A. 2008. *Culture and Community Development in Higher Education*. Imagining America. A Consortium of Universities and Organizations Dedicated to Advancing the Public and Civic Purposes of Humanities, Art, and Design. Syracuse University, Syracuse, New York.

Hatcher, J. A. and Bringle, B., eds. 2011. *Understanding Service Learning and Community Engagement: Crossing Boundaries through Research*. Campus Compact: International Association for Research on Service-Learning and Community Engagement.

Jordan, C. M., Wong, L. A., and Jungnickel, P. W. 2009. "The community engaged scholarship review promotion and tenure guide for faculty and committee members," *Metropolitan Universities Journal* 20(2): 66–86.

Kecskes, K., ed. 2006. *Engaging Departments: Moving Faculty Culture from Private to Public, Individual to Collective Focus for the Common Good*. San Francisco: Jossey-Bass.

Kuh, George D. 2008. *High-Impact Educational Practices: What They Are, Who Has Access to Them, and Why They Matter*. American Association of Colleges and Universities.

Lucas, P. and Charest, R. 2008. "Charrette: a high performance vehicle for the design studio," National Council on the Beginning Design Student Conference Proceedings, in *Batture: The Louisiana State University School of Architecture Journal*.

Lynch, K. 1960. *The Image of the City*. Cambridge, MA: MIT Press.

Rengel, R. J. 2007. *Shaping Interior Space* (2nd ed.). New York: Fairchild Publications.

Saltmarsh, J. 2010 "Changing pedagogies," in H. Fitzgerald, C. Burack, and S. Seifer (eds.), *Handbook of Engaged Scholarship: Contemporary Landscape, Future Directions*. East Lansing: Michigan State University Press, vol. 1, pp. 331–352.

Saltmarsh, J., Hartley, M., and Clayton, P. 2009. *Democratic Engagement White Paper*. Boston: New England Resource Center for Higher Education.

Sturm, S., Eatman, T., Saltmarsh, J., et al. 2011. *Full Participation: Building the Architecture for Diversity and Public Engagement in Higher Education*. White Paper. Columbia University Law School: Center for Institutional and Social Change.

Zlotkowski, E. and Saltmarsh, J. 2006. "The engaged department in the context of academic change," in K. Kecskes (ed.), *Engaging Departments: Moving Faculty Culture from Private to Public, Individual to Collective Focus for the Common Good*. San Francisco: Anker.

31

A Reflective Journey in Teaching Interior Design: The Virtual Studio

Kathleen Gibson

Introduction

My first introduction to the virtual interior began in 1989 as a graduate student at Ohio State University. As an undergraduate in 1983, I completed a weekend intensive computer-aided design and drafting – emphasis on drafting – course, but it was not until I modeled a three-dimensional digital interior that I fully understood the implications of the computer for design. At OSU, I grimaced my way through the entire semester, manually inputting XYZ coordinates into this black box while contemplating how I could complete the task much faster using foam core and balsa wood to build the model. My "ah-ha" moment arrived during finals week – in less than 20 minutes I was able to output five detailed perspectives from very diverse points in space. It was this revelation that guided the next 20 years of my academic career exploring the virtual interior.

Defining the virtual interior varies greatly among authors, academics, practitioners, and students. I take the broadest point of view and adhere to the idea that any design task which engages a computer is in effect initiating a virtual interior component. Therefore, everything from employing Photoshop to render a sketch to constructing a study model with SketchUp or composing a flyaround using 3D Studio Design are all justifiable activities in shaping and giving identity to the virtual interior.

As someone trained as an interior designer and not as a computer programmer, my interest was not in writing new code or developing new software. Instead my interest was to be inventive and explorative with existing software applications commonly used in the fields of architecture and interior design. I taught numerous

The Handbook of Interior Design, First Edition. Edited by Jo Ann Asher Thompson and Nancy H. Blossom.

requisite AutoCAD and digital media courses in multiple universities and found my greatest pleasure in authoring new ways to teach and conceptualize the virtual interior. I never used textbooks in my classes because they were too rote and prescriptive, giving the impression that computer-aided design was only technical and could not be used as an artistic medium. I credit the writings of Mumford with inculcating this belief in me when he made the distinction that a "machine lends itself to automation and routine actions, whereas the tool lends itself to manipulation and use as an extension of the user" (Mumford 1934; Muffoletto 1993).

In contrast to many interior design departments in the early 1990s, I taught digital skills alongside manual skills in one required introductory graphics course – I wanted my students to experience and envision digital software applications on par with traditional tools and without any preconceived identity when choosing an appropriate tool for the task at hand (Gibson 1994; Gibson and Sipes 1993, 1995).

Experimentation in the classroom revealed a unique design pedagogy when marrying the computer with creative activity. Empirical evidence showed an increase in speed and precision of basic hand drafting if entry-level students learned AutoCAD prior to manual drafting instruction. Testing my hypothesis over a three-year period (1995–1997) revealed that knowledge of CAD increased manual drafting speed by 25% and produced architectural hand drawings with superior drafting conventions. These results came through the evaluation of student work. When I taught manual drafting first using traditional tools and methods, scores followed a standard bell curve. When AutoCAD was taught first, the scores for manual drafting exercises were significantly skewed higher. The first year, I hypothesized the better scores were an anomaly, but the same outcome happened in subsequent years. The explanation centered on the fact that students expected their manual drawings to match the precision they experienced with AutoCAD. Assessment of speed was based on when students submitted their work for evaluation.

Beyond speed and precision, students demonstrated a difference in project knowledge and level of detail when using AutoCAD versus traditional drafting tools. For example, after using AutoCAD, students could quickly recite dimensions of walls and column spacing from memory, which was not the case when I queried students after completing a manual drafting exercise. It seemed typing actual dimensions into the computer versus using an architectural scale achieved a level of resonance for the students. These differences were unanticipated by me, and yet the student evidence was so overwhelming that it encouraged me to experiment more with digital media in my course instruction (Gibson 1996, 1999).

Benefits were also revealed with three-dimensional design tasks. Modeling software, e.g., 3D Max Designs and SketchUp, encouraged students to apply design decisions volumetrically and strengthened mental visualization abilities. For example, students would routinely tell me that the software forced them to immediately consider implications for walls and ceilings as they manipulated the design of their floor plan. Software applications also provided features rarely available with manual tools, such as shadow-casting, interior illumination, and walk-through animations. My pioneer work, along with that of my graduate students, included morphing as a new method for schematic design, morphing as a means for team-building, lighting simulation and user preference, and evaluating wayfinding cues during emergency situations (Chayutsahakij 1998; Gibson 2000, 2001, 2003a, 2003b, 2007; Gibson and Sipes 1995; Jung and Gibson 2006). These projects will be discussed in greater detail in the following section.

For several years I experimented with gaming software applications to explore whether they could provide meaningful advances for the virtual interior. During this period in my career I expended a lot of energy learning new software and developing engaging project scenarios for class instruction with very little tangible return. I witnessed the volatility of software development – as quickly as programs arrived, they disappeared. I was frustrated, having expended significant time and energy with minimal benefit. Thus, I refocused exclusively on proven industry-standard software applications for future pursuits.

In 2006 I taught an advanced digital media course, and for the first time used AutoDesk's Revit software, a building information modeling (BIM) package. Revit was unlike any CAD application I had ever experienced. Its supremacy over other three-dimensional programs revealed itself in the depth of data linked to each modeled object. Walls were no longer simple rectangles or vacant boxes but were populated with information about material, mass, and weight. Libraries of doors, windows, and furniture inherently contained accurate manufacturers' product information. At the end of the project, my students and I witnessed how effortlessly Revit accurately tabulated a window schedule and reported the total square footage of carpet to purchase. I marveled at the reality of BIM – a remarkable software that seized the long-held promise of computer-aided design as a truly revolutionary design tool – had finally arrived on my desktop computer. In that moment I envisioned a different future on the horizon for my students. BIM was a sea change – it was time to revise not just my digital media courses, but the way in which we imagine interior design education.

Instruction

"Cyber-ideation"

As a personal challenge from a colleague who insisted that computers were only useful in the final documentation stage of the design process, I began to explore if computers could, in fact, aid the creative design process. A friend gave me a copy of *Digital Dreams*, which I read many times over (Spiller 1998). The concepts were foreign to me and I struggled to digest what it might mean for my teaching and the field of interior design. I turned to books by Nicolas Negroponte and *Silicon Mirage* by Aukstakalnis and Blatner. Subsequently, the exhibit *Folds, Blobs + Boxes: Architecture in the Digital Era* advanced my resolve about the virtual interior (Rosa 2001).

In 1998, my discovery of *Would-Be Worlds* by John Casti became the catalyst for a series of experiments with digital morphing (Casti 1997). I investigated two-dimensional software programs popular for morphing two incongruent images together, but opted for a three-dimensional application to produce more tangible volumetric results. Through trial and error, I taught myself how to use the morphing features of 3D Studio, and I began to postulate how the automated traits of the computer could be creatively employed during the schematic design phase.

In his article "Creativity as a Mechanical Process," Schank compared human thinking to artificial intelligence (AI) algorithms, postulating that both subscribe to a set of rules for creativity to take place. He suggested that computer usage may amplify experience patterns (XPs) which would in turn encourage more abundant cognitive associations through the exploration of what-if scenarios (Schank 1988). I began to hypothesize, and asked myself: What if computers could perform mathematical operations on form, such as combining a percentage of several building facades into a single visual composite? Or what if the computer could combine two interior spaces – one that is more efficient with one that is more aesthetic – into one hybrid solution? If computer use can amplify experience patterns and encourage more abundant cognitive associations through the exploration of these what-if scenarios, I surmised they may have a positive impact on creative thinking for interior design.

Utilizing what I had learned from reading Casti's book on artificial worlds, I tailored my knowledge of morphing processes to the design disciplines, which I named "Cyber-Ideation" (Gibson 2000, 2007). In 1998 I introduced the concept into my junior interior design studio as a method to stimulate schematic ideation. Working in teams, students were asked to model an interior object, such as a chair, table, or lamp, and also a portion of a favorite modern building. These two disparate models were akin to two parents. The parents were then morphed together to produce hundreds of hybrid images (aka children).

Students assessed the hybrid images and selected one that would serve as the origin for their schematic ideation. Students morphed the origin two more times (grandchildren, great-grandchildren), once using traditional manual sketching techniques to incrementally transform the origin into iterative impressions and the other time using the computer to once again morph two dissimilar models together. We asked the student teams to create a family genealogy chart to document four generations of image occurrences that developed from the two-parent "seed" models.

At the conclusion of each morphing sequence, students would evaluate the numerous hybrid images and select one to move forward in the ideation process. The sheer quantity of images produced using "cyber-ideation" was unusual for the students and at times overwhelming for evaluation. After the experiment, students noted that they were generating more unexpected and unique ideas to explore when compared to their traditional method of ideation sketching. They acknowledged that use of "cyber-ideation" produced innovative form and surface color and texture that would not have been realized through traditional conceptual ideation techniques. Team dynamics improved in that all members contributed equally, and the computer process was viewed as an objective and unbiased regulator.

After completion, assessing the "cyber-ideation" process and debriefing with student participants revealed both expected and unexpected results. First, "cyber-ideation" was successful at breaking habitual thought patterns. Students who routinely struggled with idea generation swiftly realized the potential of this mechanized process. Feelings of impotence and lack of creativity were replaced with authority and control. The process formally encouraged a level of serendipity resulting in unplanned outcomes.

Students wanting a more conventional ideation procedure found the open-endedness of "cyber-ideation" disconcerting. The vastness of hybrid output was initially overwhelming for students to evaluate. Quantity, however, quickly became a benefit – the realization that an infinite number of alternatives could be generated made students less married to their first and second choices. Within this procedure, students also became adept at appraising small details – selections based on minute variations that appeared in neighboring iterations.

Personal style was minimized with this ideation method. One explanation may be attributed to the repeated merging of images, blending together several voices as in a choir. Students professed that this exercise produced work that was unexpected and more diverse than if they had been left to their own traditional work patterns. Substantial differences in computerized morphing and manual sketching ideation techniques were observed. Whereas the computer required a closed process – two seeds – to successfully accomplish the morphing process, hand sketches were open-ended.

Comparing their experiences, students believed the manual iterative process to be more difficult and time-consuming. In fact, most students underestimated the time it would take to generate 14 iterations by hand even though they were more experienced with manual sketching methods from previous studio classes. Another noted difference was that students did not choose to specify materials or color in their hand sketches, whereas these were major elements in the digital models. One explanation may be the seductiveness of the software's digital library to raise students' curiosity with surface characteristics. Another rationale may be that conventional thumbnail sketches are typically intended to study form and usually do not possess information about materials until further into the design process.

One unanticipated outcome was in the area of team dynamics. Ineffectual students who routinely had their ideas discounted in traditional teaming processes felt "cyber-ideation" neutralized the playing field. The mechanized process gave every team member an equal opportunity to contribute hybrid forms to the discussion. Another unforeseen result was that several students experimented with "cyber-ideation" in subsequent studios for idea generation. Individual examples included the mixing together of disparate cultural artifacts to find hybrids that contained a percentage of African and North American roots. Another example combined 18th- and 20th-century furniture into a composite piece. Value was realized by students or they would not have chosen to utilize this technique later in their own individual work.

For design education and practice, "cyber-ideation" is another tool to stimulate creative thinking and discovery. It utilizes the computer's strengths – of rapid calculation – in an innovative way. It also challenges one's perception of using the computer solely for documentation purposes at the end of the design process. "Cyber-ideation" may, in fact, increase experience patterns with the computer, which may augment the way in which computers are conceived of and utilized for interior design. It may lead interior designers out of their habitual mode of practice and toward more novel and suitable design solutions.

Online retailing

My next experimentation with the virtual interior came in 1999 with my assignment to teach a retail studio. As a frequent online shopper, I wanted to compare and contrast traditional bricks-and-mortar stores with e-retailing. According to a Pew Internet report (Horrigan 2008), more than 93% of American Internet users participate in e-commerce activity. This purchasing behavior translates into 875 million global consumers with a penchant for convenience and breadth of choice (Nielson Online 2008). Marketing researchers Davis, Wang, and Lindridge found differences between Chinese and American online shopping behaviors and the physical cues, or atmospherics, which impact consumer decision-making (Davis et al. 2008). What I discovered, however, was that no architect, interior or Web designer had made a connection between virtual and physical shopping environments with atmospherics and behavior.

An extensive design literature identified a relationship between people and their physical environment, and yet a similar empirical focus for the human-online design experience was indiscernible. For example, research found that people prefer physical landmarks to signage as a method to navigate the built environment (Passini 1984). I wondered if this same knowledge could be applied to the navigational system for online websites, or were the two "environments" different? What is known is that e-retailers can lose potential sales because of convoluted websites (Hausman and Siekpe 2009).

The method I chose for this case study paralleled that utilized by Lynch in *The Image of the City*. Like Lynch, my goal in this project was to investigate the idea of structure and imageability in the environment (Lynch 1960). While Lynch centered on the physical city, this exercise concentrated on the World Wide Web with a purpose to better understand consumer behavior and usage of e-retailing sites. Both studies focused on place-oriented environments on a grand scale – the urban landscape and the virtual landscape. Both used field reconnaissance as an instrument for data collection. From website analysis, students documented paths, districts, nodes, edges, and landmarks in 16 e-retailing sites. Wayfinding errors, facilitators, and obstructers were duly noted (Gibson 2003a, 2003b).

The site www.puma.com, for example, had six districts under the Sport heading. Some of Puma's districts were bilingual, others were geographically defined. Merchandise offered for sale was specific to each of Puma's districts: for example, different merchandise was sold on non-English districts within the Puma website. "Paths" were the most common element and were identified as either lineal, radial, networked, meandering, or a composite (Ching 2007). Students classified online examples as "dead end" when the path terminated at a destination and one had to retrace through use of the back button, or "cul-de-sac" when the path motion did not end but looped so that travel continued, but in the opposite direction.

The most identifiable online "edge" is the requirement of a plug-in, such as Micromedia Flash. Without the required plug-in, the site is like a gated community, impenetrable without permission. Log-ins, memberships, and registration requirements function as physical boundaries, monitoring entry and exit. Dead-end conditions and language also serve as edges, interrupting continuity of motion.

Strategic points of entry characterize the "node." In e-retailing sites, the shopping cart is a node, a junction of special prominence. At online auction sites PayPal[*] and Bidpoint become nodes in the e-retail landscape.

The most prominent "landmark" in e-retailing environments is the company's logo. It is generally visible from many locations, no matter where one navigates throughout the site. Landmarks that occur at intersections or decision points along a path enhance their prominence in the environment. A sequential series of landmarks aids consumers, first by triggering action cues and then by reassuring and confirming that past decisions were accurate. On the www.donnakaran.com website, a student noted that changes in color occurred when actions were taken as a method to encourage consumers that site tools were used correctly.

In addition to the five primary categories noted above, Lynch also identified three additional incidences: element interrelations, image quality, and shifting images (Lynch 1960). Images that differ in scale, viewpoint, time of day, season, and/or weather conditions are classified as shifting images. While external conditions such as changes in weather and time of day are absent in e-retailing sites, alterations still occurred. Most notable was how frequently websites are modified and transformed, how they evolve and then expire. Whether offline or online, retailing is constantly in flux given new products and seasonal merchandise. Constant change leaves little opportunity for the retention of path traces and other cognitive mapping cues.

The blurring between online and offline, physical and virtual atmospherics is yet another interesting outcome from this project. Even when consumers prefer making a physical store purchase, 70% had researched products online prior to buying, which strengthens the argument that the Web experience is part of a broader cross-channel branding and selling strategy (Underhill 2010). As retailers see online and offline sites as similar branding entities with common goals and complementary design requirements, both retailing venues merge into a single unified concept and solution. According to Lynch, "[t]he final objective of such a plan is not the physical shape itself, but the quality of an image in the mind" (Lynch 1960).

To fulfill the studio component of the course, students utilized their navigational and wayfinding knowledge of a particular e-retailing website in the design of its physical retail establishment. Relying on the website analysis from the first project phase, students explored schematic ideas for an offline, physical archetype of the online store. Appraisal of Web real estate for the e-retailers was collected by students and informed the allotment of physical area for merchandise and services in the bricks-and-mortar store design.

Issues of hierarchy on the e-retailer website also informed students' decision-making. Websites with an active introductory Flash page challenged students to create a similar experiential entry in the physical store. All students labored to bring characteristics of Web interactivity into their offline store designs. Solutions included ways for consumers to access additional information and receive similar product suggestions by touching a flat panel screen. One student utilized a hand-held scanner to replicate the placing of items into a virtual cart. At checkout, all items scanned would be pre-packaged and waiting for the shopper to take away. Another student retained the hologram changing-room feature from her e-retailer and highlighted this element in her bricks-and-mortar store design.

In all student work, landmarks, nodes, and districts were well demarcated to support a customer's retailing experience. Final design solutions were digitally constructed using AutoCAD and 3D Studio VIZ software, and an animation sequence was rendered. Students presented their projects to a jury of student peers and faculty, who noted the strength of wayfinding attributes throughout the student work and the branding parallels between the online and offline shopping experiences (Gibson 2003a, 2003b).

This case study suggests that the field of interior design is broader than just the physical space – that virtual environments are also within the realm of interior design expertise. Knowledge of human behavior coupled with design expertise in four dimensions gives interior designers an exceptional perspective in evaluating atmospherics in both offline and online environments which are experiential, manageable, and imageable.

Research

Lighting simulation and user preference

A broad literature exists in defining the relationship between store environment and consumer behavior. Bitner suggested that store atmosphere alone can amplify a business's success or failure (Bitner 1992). Among numerous factors that influence consumer patronage, Baker noted that design cues had a greater impact on store choice than other ambient characteristics, and Keller found the interior environment had a more immediate effect on decision-making than other forms of advertising (Baker 2002; Keller 1987).

Between 1996 and 1998, I supervised graduate student Praima Chayutsahakij with her research project, which investigated the impact of artificial lighting design on visual preference in a retail interior (Chayutsahakij 1998). Based on theories from social and environmental psychology as well as research on lighting design, a virtual model was constructed in 3D Studio for the experimental setting. Simulation was chosen over an actual setting to gain control over multiple variables, cost, and time. Lighting options were identified through a visual analysis of interior design trade publications and were codified into six different categories of illumination: direct illumination from the ceiling, indirect illumination from the ceiling, direct spotlight, indirect spotlight, direct radiant forest lighting, and indirect radiant forest lighting. Individual lighting schemes were simulated and calculated using Lightscape software.

Based on the six lighting categories, combinations resulted in the production of 60 unique images, which met the reliability criteria for Q-sorting. Images were created on film via the use of a film recorder and then printed via a color lab, paying close attention to color accuracy. Throughout this process, experts were consulted to evaluate all images and ensure they represented typical retail interiors and intended lighting effects. Subjects (n = 200) ranked the images using a one-way structured Q-sort along four dimensions (preference, mystery, complexity, image) and three levels (low, medium, high).

Subjects preferred interiors with direct illumination, while environments with indirect and radiant forest lighting were less preferred. Preference was related to complexity and mystery; however, mystery was found to be a negative predictor of preference for lighting design in this retail interior (Chayutsahakij 1998).

As evidenced in this experiment, virtual interiors have broader implications than just realistic representations of design ideas. Computer simulation can be a valuable tool to propose questions and research interior design hypotheses. In this case, it was a successful tool in assessing shoppers' preferences for retail lighting solutions.

Emergency exiting and wayfinding cues

Beginning in 2000, I supervised graduate student Jin Woo Jung on his research project, which focused on improving wayfinding and exiting during emergency situations (Jung 2002). Chertkoff and Kushigian noted that in the Beverly Hills Supper Club fire, human behavior was a contributing factor in loss of life. Because it is too difficult and dangerous to examine human behavior in actual emergencies, computer simulations have become an effective tool endorsed by many researchers (Chertkoff and Kushigian 1999).

Preparing the virtual reality (VR) simulation tools for this experiment involved building a three-dimensional model in AutoCAD, exporting the wireframe into 3D Studio Max to add surface materials and texture, exporting the 3D Studio Max file into World Up 4 software to define illumination and smoke properties within the virtual environment (VE). Avatars were developed in World Up 4 to enable participants to move through virtual space, and scripts were written to record subjects' behavior at choice points and to measure time. Fifty-two sub-areas were defined in the VE test site to evaluate where subjects would travel. Simulations for this experiment were similar to computer games in which users move themselves through space using a keyboard or mouse.

Samples of landmarks were gathered from various interior design magazines. They were sorted and classified, and finally they were analyzed to ascertain notable characteristics and identify alternative characteristics not previously reported in the literature. In analyzing the variety of landmarks, it was discovered that describability was a potentially important characteristic that prior work had not thoroughly examined. For example, nearly all potential landmarks have distinctiveness, such as unique shape, pattern, color, or history; however, if landmarks cannot be easily explained by words, people will not be willing to verbally use them in route communication.

Independent variables for this experiment were gender, smoke, and landmarks. Subjects (n = 69) were given five minutes to read and memorize a route description to a designated exit. After memorizing the route, subjects were asked to find the exit in the VE by using their memory. Arrow keys were used to move ahead and change direction; mouse clicks opened doors and enabled subjects to exit the building, which ended the experiment. After 15 minutes, if subjects had not yet found the exit, they were allowed to re-read the route description. The entire process was video-taped. Five standardized tests were then administered to ascertain mental cognition, attention fatigue, and mood. Demographic data were also collected with a questionnaire that identified gender and inquired (self-report) about wayfinding experience.

Results suggest that the describability of landmarks was a positive influence to route communication and increased participants' route recall. Individual factors, such as gender and travel experience, were also found to have a positive influence on participants' wayfinding abilities. Findings from this study, however, indicate that smoke condition did not significantly affect participants' wayfinding performance. Researchers hypothesized that while simulation was useful, in its present form it was impossible to replicate the same level of realism (sound, smell) found during an actual fire emergency (Jung and Gibson 2006).

While simulation is known as an ideal method for observing and measuring human interactions, this research project was unable to accurately replicate the totality of an emergency experience. As VR applications become more cost-efficient and less time-consuming to master, they will provide greater opportunities for designers and planners of behavioral research to study interior environments.

Millennials and communication

As of 2007, I found a different group of students enrolled in my studios – there was a sea change on my doorstep. Born after 1982, millennials are characterized by a lifestyle immersed in technology. At 27%, they compose the largest generational population in the United States, exceeding the baby boomers by 4% (Tapscott 2009). The numbers are more significant in other countries. This group of young adults is more digitally connected than previous generations. Seventy-six percent of students use instant messaging (IM) and spend on average 35 hours per week messaging (Junco and Mastrodicasa 2007). Sixty-nine percent have a FaceBook account; 62% rely on mobile phones for video, music, and entertainment (Schiller 2007: 267). Both genders spend nearly eight hours gaming per week (Winslow 2007).

In 2009 I conducted a small pilot study to investigate the ways in which the millennials are impacting interior design education and practice (Gibson 2012). Using the Boyer Report and Tapscott's *Grown Up Digital* to guide my methodology, an open-ended survey was created and administered to nine design educators and practitioners of varying age, gender, culture, and geographic location (Asia, North America) (Boyer and Mitgang 1996; Tapscott 2009).

If Kevin Carey is correct that the printed page is the canary in the coalmine and all traditional methods of information delivery – including current instructional methods used in design education – are at risk of becoming inconvenient or irrelevant, then educators and administrators must begin thinking aggressively about the future (Carey 2009). Reflection caused me to contemplate Tapscott's eight norms. Some may contest this assessment of the academy, but I propose that universities currently excel in the following millennial norms: "scrutiny," "integrity," "collaboration," "innovation" and "speed." Areas in which they are significantly lacking are "freedom," "customization/personalization," and "entertainment/fun." These three norms may provide a path for design education in the future.

Freedom equals choice. Further development of distance learning technologies may enable greater flexibility for the design student. Course selections may no longer be geographically limited to a single physical campus. MIT is advancing this concept; however, operationalizing this worldwide will be more complex to navigate than the elective offerings of one university. In 20 years, I anticipate students will be admitted into a global university and select classes and teaching methods pertaining to personal preference as well as tailoring instruction to individual learning style. Maximum freedom will engage the millennials and post-millennials in customizing their path for learning, which may or may not be a serial endeavor.

Personalization is about taking ownership and controlling one's environment. Today millennials use the Internet to customize their news, shopping venues, and social activity. In two decades, design students will create their own class assignments and learning objectives. Professors will operate more as advisors or personal coaches, offering guidance, encouragement, and evaluation when needed. Students will take more responsibility for learning through personalized instruction.

Entertainment is about stimulation and pleasure. For the post-millennials, digital technology will be more interactive and employed at the beginning of the design process instead of at the end for documentation. Curriculum sequences used today will be flipped in the future. BIM is the start of this trajectory – of flattening and reorienting the design process. Reduction in duplication and cumbersome translation between two- and three-dimensional records will result in additional time for exploration and design development (i.e., fun). Time seized in the past decade to learn computer applications will evolve into mastering one comprehensive and universal software package during the first year. Moreover, design educators in 20 years' time will be millennials. Methods of working and living will ultimately change to conform to their understanding of the world.

The three future scenarios presented above seem to parallel the "design synthesizer" and "design accelerator" provocations as outlined by *The Future Designer ThinkTank* (Victoria and Albert Museum 2008). Design synthesizers assemble what they need into a broad-based collaborative structure for problem-solving. Inherent in the synthesizer's repertoire is the sense of customization and freedom – the ability to shape a design team according to specific talents, viewpoints, experiences. Similarly, the millennials will shape their education team by taking courses at different universities, with different faculty members, and within a desired time frame. Design accelerators are known to challenge existing paradigms and traditional methods of practice. Like millennials, accelerators would advocate play and experimentation in their work processes, in search of discovering/reinterpreting new design models, services, and design processes for creating the virtual interior (Gibson 2012).

Conclusion

My 20-year academic journey with computers and virtual interiors encompasses a full range of instructional exploration and innovation along with empirical and epistemological research in search of progressing the field of interior design. Some inquiries began with a question based on the writings of diverse authors, other investigations reacted to intolerant viewpoints about computers and creativity. "Cyber-ideation" responded to widely held beliefs that computers were isolating and prescriptive. My findings demonstrated that variation exists in computer use, and methods can be authored to benefit teaming dynamics and creative exploration. The online-offline retail project used the computer to draw comparisons between mental cognition and virtual and physical wayfinding.

Empirical findings suggest that a connection exists that interior designers need to exploit in their business service model. The lighting and emergency simulations were constructive collaborations between me and two talented graduate students. At the time, we were pushing the boundaries of what virtual environments were and how they could contribute to building a scholarly knowledge base for the discipline of interior design. My most recent investigation – the millennial study – brings my academic journey full circle by asking how to best respond to the challenges of teaching creatively with technology. The question this time is driven less by new software applications and hardware availability than by managing social networking. I remain passionate about what can be learned through the examination of virtual interiors and I look forward to reimagining interior design pedagogy with a studio filled with millennial students.

References

Baker J. 2002. "The influence of multiple store environment cues on perceived merchandise value and patronage intentions," *Journal of Marketing* 66: 120–141.

Bitner, M. J. 1992. "Servicescapes: the impact of physical surroundings on customers and employees," *Journal of Marketing* 56: 57–71.

Boyer, E. and Mitgang, L. 1996. *Building Community: A New Venture for Architecture Education and Practice.* Princeton, NJ: Carnegie Foundation for the Advancement of Learning.

Carey, K. 2009. "What colleges should learn from newspapers' decline," *The Chronicle of Higher Education* 55(30): A21.

Casti, J. 1997. *Would-Be Worlds.* New York: John Wiley & Sons.

Chayutsahakij, P. 1998. "The Effects of Lighting Design on Preference in the Retail Interior Environment." Master's thesis, Cornell University.

Chertkoff, M. and Kushigian, H. 1999. *Don't Panic: The Psychology of Emergency Egress and Ingress.* New York: Praeger.

Ching, F. 2007. *Form, Space and Order* (3rd ed.). New York: John Wiley & Sons.

Davis, L. M., Wang, S., and Lindridge, A. M. 2008. "Cultural influences on emotional responses to on-line store atmospheric cues," *Journal of Business Research* 61(8): 806–812.

Gibson, K. 1994. "Color theory: a new educational approach using electronic media," in L. Nissen (ed.), *Design: A Multi-Cultural Experience.* Interior Design Educators Council Conference Proceedings, San Antonio, TX.

Gibson, K. 1996. "Learning from industry: the social and psychological aspects of CAD," in P. Hildebrand (ed.), *Horizons and Frontiers: New Challenges for Design Educators.* Interior Design Educators Council Conference Proceedings, Denver, CO.

Gibson, K. 1999. "Studio @ Cornell," *ACADIA Quarterly* 18(2): 18–21.

Gibson, K. 2000. "Cyber-ideation and its application for creative problem solving," *Symposium on Systems Research in the Arts Proceedings.* 12th International Conference on Systems Research, Informatics, and Cybernetics, Baden-Baden, Germany.

Gibson, K. 2001. "Byte-minded," *Interiors and Sources* (November).

Gibson, K. 2003a. "Designing offline space using online wayfinding data," *Interior Design Educators Council Conference Proceedings*, San Diego, CA.

Gibson, K. 2003b. "Spatial mapping: connections between virtual and physical navigation," *eCAADe Conference Proceedings*, Graz, Austria.

Gibson, K. 2007. "Automated creativity: digital morphology and the design process," *Journal of Interior Design* 32(3): 41–47.

Gibson, K. 2012. "Building community 2.0: millennials and the changing face of design education," *Interior Designers Educators Conference Proceedings*, Baltimore, MD.

Gibson, K. and Sipes, J. 1993. "Computers in the classroom: implications for design education and research," in L. Nissen (ed.), *Design Dialogues: Conversations with the Future.* Interior Design Educators Council Conference Proceedings, Couer d'Alene, ID.

Gibson, K., and Sipes, J. 1995. "Understanding the dynamics of lighting design through computer simulation," in L. Nissen (ed.), *Point and CounterPoint: Synergy throughout Design*. Interior Design Educators Council Conference Proceedings, Nashville, TN.

Hausman, A. and Siekpe, J. 2009. "The effect of web interface features on consumer online purchase intentions," *Journal of Business Research* 62(1): 5–13.

Horrigan, J. 2008. "Online shopping," *Pew Internet and American Life Project*. http://www.pewinternet.org/~/media//Files/Reports/2008/PIP_Online%20Shopping.pdf .pdf. Accessed March 30, 2012.

Junco, R. and Mastrodicasa, J. 2007. *Connecting to the Net.Generation: What Higher Education Professionals Need to Know about Today's Students*. National Association of Student Personnel Administrators.

Jung, J. W. 2002. "Wayfinding and Landmarks: A Study of Human Behavior in Interior Environments and Emergency Situations Using Virtual Reality." Master's thesis, Cornell University.

Jung, J. W. and Gibson, K. 2006. "The use of landmarks in fire emergencies: a study of gender and the descriptive quality of landmarks on successful wayfinding," *Journal of Interior Design* 32(2): 45–57.

Keller, K. 1987. "Memory factors in advertising: the effect of advertising retrieval cues on brand evaluations," *Journal of Consumer Research* 14(3): 316–333.

Lynch, K. 1960. *The Image of the City*. Cambridge, MA: MIT Press.

Muffoletto, R., ed. 1993. "The expert teaching machine: unpacking the mask," in *Computers in Education: Social Political and Historical Perspectives*. Cresswell, NJ: Hampton Press, p. 93.

Mumford, L. 1934. *Technics and Civilization*. New York: Harcourt, Brace & World.

Nielson Online. 2008. *875mm Consumers Have Shopped Online – Up 40 Percent in Two Years*. http://www.marketingcharts.com/direct/875mm-consumers-have-shopped-online-up-40-in-two-years-3225/. Accessed February 12, 2012.

Passini, R. 1984. *Wayfinding in Architecture*. New York: Van Nostrand Reinhold.

Rosa, J. 2001. *Folds, Blobs + Boxes: Architecture in the Digital Era*. The Heinz Architectural Center, Carnegie Museum of Art, Pittsburgh, Pennsylvania (February 3–May 7).

Schank, R. 1988. "Creativity as a mechanical process," in R. Sternberg (ed.), *Nature of Creativity*. New York: Cambridge University Press.

Schiller, D. 2007. *How to Think About Information*. Urbana-Champagne: University of Illinois Press.

Spiller, N. 1998. *Digital Dreams*. New York: Whitney Library of Design.

Tapscott, D. 2009. *Grown Up Digital*. New York: McGraw-Hill.

Underhill, P. 2010. *Respect the Shopper: Harmonizing the Cross-Channel Experience*. White Paper. RichRelevance, Inc. and Envirosell, Inc.

Victoria and Albert Museum. 2008. *The Future Designer ThinkTank*. http://www.vam.ac.uk/content/articles/t/think-tank-future-museum/. Accessed May 12, 2014.

Winslow, G. 2007. "Digital masters: Gen Y's ranks, influence continue to swell," *Multichannel News*. Reed Elsevier.

Index

AAFCS, *see* American Association of Family and Consumer Sciences
Aanstoos, C., 251
Abbuhl, M., 51–52
Abu-Ghazzah, T. M., 349
accessibility, 4–5, 6, 148–168, 188, 205–207, 218–220, 227–228, 327–344, 426–427, 465–475
Acheson, Donald, 318
action research, 467–471, 473
Active Aging Initiative (WHO), 228
ADA, *see* Americans With Disabilities Act
adaptability, and creativity, 115–116
Addams, Jane, 76–77, 78, 81, 82, 83, 84–85, 88
Adorno, T. W., 102, 479
aesthetics, 15–19, 22–23, 97–110, 399–400, 478–493
definition, 482
Afacan, Y., 214, 215, 216, 221
African Americans, discrimination against, 71–73
African culture, 433–437
agency, 161–162, 201, 203
Aggebo, M., 108–110
aging, 6, 136–138, 186–207, 212–223, 226–244
definition, 187–188, 207n, 216–217
independent living, 227, 235–244, 327–344
Agouridas, V., 449

AIA, *see* American Institute of Architects
Akalin, A., 451
Akao, Y., 221
Akin, O., 212, 220
Al-Qawasmi, J., 451
Alberti, L. B., 483
Albolafia, M., 132
Alexander, C., 151, 254, 294, 354, 358–361, 428
Algonquin culture, 441, 442t, 443t
Allen, S., 207, 487
Allison, E. W., 399
Allison, M. A., 399
Altmaier, E., 228
Altman, I., 153–154, 261, 348, 351, 367
Amabile, T., 118, 120, 128, 275, 276, 279–280, 400, 401
ambience, 98–110, 420–428
Ambrose, D., 115
American Association of Family and Consumer Sciences (AAFCS), 504–506
American Institute of Architects (AIA), 394
American Office, The (Schulze), 60
American Pneumatic Service Company, 62
American Society of Interior Design (ASID), 47, 511–512
Americans With Disabilities Act (ADA; 1990), 165–167, 329
Amiry, S., 266
Analytic Hierarch Process (AHP), 220–221

The Handbook of Interior Design, First Edition. Edited by Jo Ann Asher Thompson and Nancy H. Blossom.
© 2015 John Wiley & Sons, Ltd. Published 2015 by John Wiley & Sons, Ltd.

Anderson, B. G., 246, 448, 516
Anderson, K., 17–18, 369
Anderson, S. C., 331
Ang, S., 150
Ankerson, K., 48
Anstead, K., 312
Anthony, K. H., 489
Anthony, L., 448
Antonucci, T., 229
Anzul, M., 467
Apple, R. W., Jr., 278
Aquino, J., 228
Arapahoe culture, 441, 442t, 443t
Archer, B., 454
Archetypes in Architecture (Thiis-Evensen), 427–428
Architects Small House Service Bureau (ASHSB), 390–391
Architectural Forum, 85–86
architectural sustenance, definition, 427–428
architecture, and aesthetic theory, 481–493
Architecture for Humanity, 516
Architecture of Good Intentions, The (Rowe), 486
Architecture of Humanism, The (Scott), 483
Argyris, C., 172
Arkkelin, D., 234
Aron, L., 247
Artifacts and Organizations:Beyond Mere Symbolism (Rafaeli and Pratt), 131–132
ASHSB, *see* Architects Small House Service Bureau
ASID, *see* American Society of Interior Design
Asojo, A., 5, 432, 433, 434, 435
assembly lines, 62
Atkinson, R., 135
Attwell, Graham, 372
Auer, M., 384
authenticity, 128–145
autophotography, 154–156
Avolio, B. J., 132–133
Axtell, C., 366, 369
Azar, J., 221

Bachelard, G., 14, 47, 516
Baer, J., 274, 276, 286
Baird, J. C., 150, 154
Baker, J., 531
Baker, L., 368
Baker, N., 332, 333

Baldoni, J., 273
Ballantyne, A., 484
Ballard, R., 78, 81, 84, 86
Ballon, P., 466
Balogun, O., 434
Baltes, P. B., 186, 187
Balzer, W. K., 120
Barab, S., 455
Baritz, L., 34, 42n
Barnard, S. S., 275, 286
Barnes, J., 6, 173
Barnouw, J., 25n
Barrett, A., 230
Barthes, R., 150
Basadur, M., 116
bathrooms, 148, 167
Baudrillard, J., 99
Bauhaus, 486
Baumgarten, A. G., 12, 25n, 484
Be Your Own Decorator (Burbank), 34
beauty, definition, 483–485
    see also aesthetics
Beck, K., 221
Becker, F., 372
Beckstead, J., 314
bedrooms, 36f, 37
Beecher, M. A., 6, 405, 479, 480
Begemann, S. H. A., 314
being-in-the-world, 12–13, 15–16, 418, 419–420
Beld, G. J. van den, *see* van den Beld, G. J.
Belenky, M. F., 467
Bell, B., 516
Bell, C., 490
Bell, G., 17–18
Bell, R., 227
Benassi, V. A., 404
Bender, D., 249, 451
Bennett, C., 378n
Benton, C. C., 320
Berander, P., 220
Berger, P. L., 469
Bianca, S., 261
Bianchin, M., 166
Bierman, A., 315
Biggs, S., 187
Bilda, Z., 223, 451
Bindl, U. K., 131
Binford, J., 81
Bitner, M. J., 531
Bix, A., 51

Bjork, E., 165–166
Black, M., 351
Blakemore, R., 400
Bledstein, Burton J., 37
Bligh, T., 215
Block, J., 229
Bloom, B. S., 505
Bloomer, C. M., 152, 153, 156
Blossom, N., 29, 447, 448
Blueprint for Reform Act (2010), 499t, 500
Bluestone, D., 74
Blumenson, J., 400
Böhme, G., 99, 100
Boje, D., 134
Bolan, R. S., 172, 173, 177, 180
Boles, D., 23–24
Bommel, W. J. M. van, *see* van Bommel,
    W. J. M.
Book of a Hundred Houses, The (Dow), 34
Bose, M., 451
Boubekri, M., 315, 318, 319
Bouchey, L. M., 320
Bourdieu, P., 181, 208n
Boyce, P. R., 310–311, 313, 314, 320, 332
Boyer, E., 394, 446, 448, 534
Boyer, L. L., 319
brain-based instruction, 509
Brandeis, L., 66
branding, 530–531
Brandt, B., 38, 405
Brandt, T., 335
Brannigan, A., 319
Braverman, H., 59
Brent, R., 406
Brewer, G., 186
Brief, A. P., 131
Brill, M., 314
Bringle, B., 517
Brissett, D., 348, 353, 378n
Brosseau, T. L., 387
Brotheridge, C. M., 131
Brown, B., 352, 369
Brown, D. Scott, *see* Scott Brown, D.
Brown, T. J., 293–294
Brown, Z., 26n
Bruce, M., 181
Bruijn, J. C. M. de, *see* de Bruijn, J. C. M.
Bubner, R., 103
Bubolz, M. M., 189–193, 207n
Buchanan, P., 42n
Buchanan, R., 207, 274, 474

Buckley, C., 48
Buckner, J., 247
Bugental, J., 251
built environment
    accessibility issues, 4–5, 6, 148–168, 188,
        205–207, 218–220, 227–228, 327–344,
        426–427, 465–475
    aesthetics, 22–23, 97–110, 399–400,
        478–493
    cave dwellings, 18–19
    changing rooms and restrooms, 39–41,
        148, 167
    community engagement projects,
        516–522
    domestic interiors, *see* domestic interiors
    elderly users, 6, 186–207, 212–223,
        226–244, 327–344
    emergency exits, 532–533
    emotional connections to, 23–24, 38–41,
        43n, 74–89, 128–145, 159–166, 226–227,
        230–244, 248–249, 253–257, 293–307,
        347–348, 401–408, 420–428
    grassroots design, 50–56
    and health, 228–230
    heating systems, 219
    historic restorations, 5, 70–89, 382–391,
        393–410
    homeless shelters, 253–257
    lighting, 5–6, 14, 83, 84f, 85f, 219,
        310–321, 330, 331, 332–333, 335–336,
        337, 339, 341–342, 357, 358, 361, 532
    mirrors, 40–41, 340, 342
    movement of people, 62, 158, 240, 361,
        519–522, 532–533
    museums, 520–521
    outdoor spaces, 236, 262, 354, 358–360
    and power relationships, 6, 46–56, 65–66,
        87–88, 106–108, 114, 116–125, 195,
        435
    privacy issues, 39–41, 148, 240–241, 265,
        269, 374
    public transportation, 518–520
    regional styles, 15–17
    sacred spaces, 13–14, 20–21
    smart buildings, 23, 26n
    and social exclusion, 151–153, 158,
        161–162, 165–168, 193–199, 228,
        246–258, 465–475
    social spaces, *see* social spaces
    sustainable designs, 5–6, 24, 188, 382–391,
        395, 435–436

third places, 227, 231, 234–244, 347–362
virtual–physical continuum, 366–377, 530–531
water features, 293–307
workplaces, *see* workplaces
Bullough, J., 315
Burbank, E., 34
Burge, S., 230
Burnside, R., 120
Burt, M., 247
bus shelters, 518–520
Bush, George W., 500
Business Administration: The Principles of Business Organization and System (Parsons), 60
Butler, J., 470

Caan, B., 319
Cadw, 384
cafés, 226, 353–354, 355–356, 361, 366–377
Cakir, A., 319
Cakir, A. C., 319
Cameron, K. S., 131
Campbell, C. S., 296, 305
Campbell, D., 41
Campbell, L., 106–108
Campbell, N., 2
Canadian Human Rights Commission, 220
Cannuscio, C., 229
Canter, D., 366
Capra, F., 118
Caravella, P., 318
Career Clusters Framework, 507
Carey, K., 534
Carl D. Perkins Career and Technical Education Act (Perkins Act, 2006), 501, 503
Carlson, A., 482
Carmel-Gilfinen, C., 401
Carr, S., 234, 240
Casakin, H., 286
case study methodology, 74–76, 90n, 134–136, 235–239, 253–257, 436–444, 449–457, 532–533
Casey, E., 420, 423
Casti, J., 527
cave dwellings, 18–19
Cawthorne, D., 314
Caza, A., 131
Census Bureau (United States), 327, 329
Center for Universal Design, 220

Chair, The (Cranz), 427
chairs, 64, 114, 427
Chakrabarti, A. A., 215
Chan Kim, W., 122
Chandler, A. D., 67n
changing rooms, 39–41
character-defining features, historic buildings, 397, 400, 409
Charest, R., 519
Charmaz, K., 468
Chavis, D. M., 348, 350, 351, 352
Chayutsahakij, P., 526, 532
Chen, C., 275
Cheong, A. M. Y., 333, 335
Chermers, M., 153–154
Chertkoff, M., 532
Cheyenne culture, 441, 442t, 443t
Chicago (IL), 74–89
Chidster, M., 348
Chinese culture, 18–19, 275
Ching, F., 400, 530
Ching, F. D. K., 435
Chiras, D. A., 188, 208n
Chittipeddi, K., 132
Cho, J. Y., 2–3, 482, 487, 488, 489, 490, 491
Cho, M., 275
Cho, S., 228
Christiaans, H., 275, 286
churches, 13–14, 20–21
CIDA, *see* Council for Interior Design Accreditation
CIE, *see* Commission Internationale de l'Éclairage
circadian system, 314–317
City of Bolivar, 409
City of Portland Bureau of Planning, 399
City of Tampa, 399
Clarke, P., 188, 200
class (social class), 4, 29–42, 43n, 50–51, 149–153
Clayton, P., 517
Clayton, S., 403
Clemons, S., 500, 501, 507, 510–511, 513
clients, communication with, 13–14, 17–18, 31–32, 49, 56, 164–168, 177–179, 285, 288, 333–336, 405, 407, 519–521
Clinchy, B. M., 467
Clinton, Bill, 498
CMC (computer-mediated communication), definition, 377n
Cochrane, R., 315

Codman, O., 34

coffee shops, 226, 353–354, 355–356, 361, 366–377

Cogan, D. G., 335

cognitive mapping, 153–154, 156, 157–158, 372, 373, 375

Cohen, D., 24

Cohen, L., 77, 115

Cohen, M., 332

Cole, J., 426

Cole, R. J., 26n

Colloca, P., 406

Colonial Revival architecture, 395

color, 100–101, 104–108, 121, 329–330, 337–338, 339, 341–342

Commission Internationale de l'Éclairage (CIE), 314

Common Core Standards (United States), 506–507

communal spaces, *see* social spaces

community engagement, 23–24, 516–522

compatibility, and adaptation of historic buildings, 396–410

Competence-Press Model (CPM), 199–201

Complexity and Contradiction in Architecture (Venturi and Brown), 487

computer-aided design (CAD), 22–23, 26n, 524–536

computer-mediated communication (CMC), definition, 377n

connectedness, 401–408, 410

Connelly, S., 130

Conniff, R., 296

consciousness, 16–17

Consensual Assessment Technique (CAT), 276–280

conservation techniques, historic buildings, 383–391

consumerism, 29–42

content analysis, 174–184

context models, 188–193, 195–199, 204–205t, 207n

continuing care retirement communities (CCRCs), 226–244

Contract Magazine, 175–177, 179

Conway, S., 320

Cooper Marcus, C., 13, 15, 88, 240, 354, 358–361

Copenhagen, 108–110

Corbin, J., 488

Cordes, D., 221

corporate identity, 114, 128–145

corporate phenomenology, 16–19

Corry Hernandez, S., 4–5

Corser, R., 517–518, 519, 520–521

Cortina, K., 229

Coser, R. L., 298

Costarelli, S., 406

Council for Interior Design Accreditation (CIDA), 47, 247, 249, 449, 480, 481, 507

courtyards, 262

Cox, H., 263

Cranz, G., 427

creativity, 6, 19–20, 112–125, 128–129, 142, 273–289, 400–401
    definition, 114, 285, 286, 288–289

Cresswell, J., 468, 473

Cresswell, T., 366

Critique of Judgment, The (Kant), 484–485

cross-cultural studies, 150–151, 273–289, 293–307, 432–444

Cross, N., 19, 212, 215, 249, 253, 274, 286, 454

Csikszentmihalyi, M., 115, 117, 276, 286, 401

cultural capital, 180

culture, 15–21, 29–42, 43n, 50–51, 150–151, 216–218, 273–289, 293–307, 348, 362, 432–444, 516–522
    African culture, 433–437
    Chinese culture, 18–19, 275
    corporate identity, 114, 118, 119–120, 121–122, 128–145
    and gender differences, 48–49, 216–217, 295, 297–305
    Italian culture, 17–18
    Korean culture, 293–294
    Palestinian culture, 5, 260–272
    and phenomenology, 16–19, 22–23
    and social stratification, 149–153, 435
    Taiwanese culture, 295, 298–305
    Thai culture, 276–289

culture-based design pedagogy, 432–444

Cunningham, E., 5

Cutrona, C., 228

Cuttle, C., 314

Cvengros, J. A., 315

cyber-ideation, 526–529

cyberspace, definition, 377n

Czeisler, C. A., 314, 315

D-Tower (Doetinchem, NL), 23

Dahlback, A., 319

Dahlgren, G., 187

daily life, 265–266, 269–270

Daley, L. O., 319

Daniel, R., 6–7

Danish Ministry of Culture, 106–108

Danko, S., 5, 71, 73, 165, 448, 450

Danley, M., 406

Darbee, J., 398

data analysis, 156–164, 237–239, 279–285, 301–305, 372–376

Davis, B. L., 25n

Davis, C., 34

Davis, G. A., 115

Davis, L. M., 529

Day, J., 228

Day, J. C., 186

daylight, 5–6, 310–321, 332–333, 335–336

De Architectura (Vitruvius), 482–483

de Bruijn, J. C. M., 333

De Graaf, E., 469

de la Harpe, B., 451

de Medeiros, K., 186, 200

De Wolfe, Elsie, 30, 31, 32

Decorating Is Fun! (Draper), 32, 34, 35–38

Decoration of Houses, The (Wharton and Codman), 34

Decoratively Speaking (Miller), 34

Deetz, S., 143

Delgado, R., 71–72, 76

Demirbas, O. O., 214, 489

Demirbilek, O., 217, 222

Demirkan, H., 6, 212, 213, 214, 215, 216, 217, 220, 221–222, 223, 275, 451, 489

Denmark, Ministry of Culture, 106–108

Department of Education (United States), 498, 500–501

department stores, 39–41, 148

depth perception, loss of, 337–338

Descartes, R., 12, 25n

design awards, 171, 179–181

design ethnography, 17–18, 455

"design for all," 221–222

design press, 175–177

design process, 13–21, 48–49, 140–145, 212–223, 519–522

  communication with clients, 13–14, 17–18, 31–32, 49, 56, 164–168, 177–179, 285, 288, 333–336, 405, 407, 519–521

computer-aided design (CAD), 22–23, 26n, 524–536

conceptual phase, 213–223, 474–475

creativity, 273–289, 400–401

cultural context, 216–218, 432–444

evaluation and assessment of, 449–453, 474–475, 488–489

graphic design, 454–457

grassroots design, 50–56

participatory design, 23, 123

person-centric design, 246–258

portfolios, 273–289, 454–457

post-occupancy evaluation (POE), 328–343, 389

preservation of historic buildings, 383–391, 393–410

prioritization of requirements, 220–222, 229, 333–336

requests for proposals (RFPs), 177–179

universal design principles, 150–151, 164–168, 221–222, 228, 434–435, 482

Design Thinking for Interiors (Dohr and Portillo), 73

designers

  assessment of, 171, 179–181, 276–289, 503–508

  cognitive strategies, 214–216

  creativity, 112–125, 273–289, 400–401

  history of, 29–42, 43n, 46–56

  online communities, 17

  portfolio design, 273–289, 454–457

  professional development, 171–184, 288

Desjardins, M., 472

desks, 62–64, 67n–68n

Devine-Wright, P., 403

Devlin, A. S., 349, 351

Dick, B., 156

Dickinson, J. I., 448

Digital Dreams (Spiller), 526

digital morphing, 526–529

Dilnot, C., 405

dining rooms, 36f, 37, 82

disability, 4–5, 6, 148–168, 188, 205–207, 218–220, 426–427, 465–475

  definition, 188, 207n

  hearing impairment, 218

  mobility issues, 148, 161–162, 218–219

  visual impairment, 218, 327–344, 520–521

disciplinary society, 65–66

Disney, W., 38–39

dissipative structures, definition, 117

diversity, 116–117

Diversity in Design: Perspectives from the Non-Western World (Jani), 444

Dixon, J. M., 85

Dixon, L., 398, 410

Dobbins, K. W., 369

Dodge, T., 455

Dohr, J., 71, 73, 76, 90n, 116, 117, 121–122, 399, 400, 401, 405, 408, 509

Dollinger, S. J., 154, 276

Dollinger, S. M. C., 154

domestic interiors
  accessibility issues, 160–161, 218–220, 327–344
  and class values, 4, 29–42, 43n
  and cultural values, 5, 17–18, 22, 216–218, 260–272, 433
  and elderly people, 216–219, 327–343
  and emotional connection, 13, 38–41, 160–161
  historic buildings, 82–84, 85f
  lighting, 330, 331, 332–333, 335–336, 337, 339, 341–342
  mirrors, 340, 342
  post-occupancy evaluation (POE), 328–343
  and power relationships, 6, 37–38, 46–56
  use of color, 337–338, 339, 341–342

Dooley, K., 142

Dorst, K., 215, 253, 286

Douglas, M., 294

Douglas, T., 247

Dow, J. Wheeler, 34

Dowdy, J. C., 318

Downing, M., 467

Doyle, M. R., 370, 376–377

Drab, T., 176

Draper, D., 3–4, 29–42, 43n

DreamWorks, 121–122

drinking fountains, siting of, 62

Driscoll, A., 517

D'Souza, N., 2

Ducheneaut, N., 354

Duckitt, J., 404

Duckworth, S., 314

Dudek, M. T., 246, 516

Dudek, S. Z., 288

dynamic tectonics, 22–23

Eagle, P., 173

Ebersole, P., 188

Edelber, H. K., 336

education, 4
  and aesthetic theory, 478–493
  awards and qualifications, 174, 504–506
  computer-aided design (CAD), 524–536
  culture-based design, 432–444
  funding, 501
  history of, 50–56
  learning outcomes, 473–474, 481
  learning theories, 508–509
  legislation, 498–500, 501
  and the millennial generation, 533–536
  national and local standards, 506–508
  phenomenological approach, 417–428
  problem-based learning, 436–444, 465–475
  project-based learning, 405–407, 469–475, 516–522
  scholarship of teaching and learning, 446–461
  in schools (K-12), 497–513
  studio discussions, 450–457, 472–473, 487–493
  teacher training, 503

Edwards, L., 314, 337

Eicher, J. B., 189–193

Eisner, E. W., 467

Eklund, N. H., 314

El Nasser, H., 328

elderly people, 6, 136–138, 186–207, 212–223, 226–244
  definition, 187–188, 207n, 216–217
  independent living, 227, 235–244, 327–344

Elementary and Secondary Education Act (ESEA; 1965), 499t

elementary education, United States, 497–501, 506–513

Elephante, C., 383

Elfenbein, H. A., 131

Eliade, M., 21

Elkins, D., 251–252

Elleh, N., 434

Elsbach, K. D., 131

Eltinge, J. L., 297

Ely, M., 467, 468, 473

Embryological House, 22

emergency exits, 532–533

emotions, 5, 19, 23, 38–41, 43n, 74–89, 118, 119–120, 122, 128–145, 160–161, 226–227, 230–244, 248–249, 253–257, 293–307, 401–408, 410, 420–428

definition, 130
Seasonal Affective Disorder (SAD), 315–316
and "third places," 227, 231, 234–244, 347–362
Engholm, I., 104
English Heritage, 384
English, J. F., 180
Enlightenment, 12, 25n
environmental attributes, taxonomy of, 156
environmental embodiment, 423–427
epistemology, 172–173, 181–184, 212–223
Epps, Mrs., 51, 52–53, 56
Epstein, K., 320
escapism, 38–41, 43n
ESEA, *see* Elementary and Secondary Education Act
Essential Schools, 470
Estep, H. L., 64
Eubank, W., 406
Evans, G., 351, 362, 378n
Ewen, R., 252
Ewenstein, B., 187
Experiencing Architecture (Rasmussen), 14
extension programs, 50–56
eye, physical structure of, 329–330, 331–332
Eyes of the Skin: Architecture and the Senses (Pallasmaa), 14

Family and Consumer Science curriculum, 502–503
Family, Career and Community Leaders of America (FCCLA), 504
family homes, 5, 17–18, 35–38, 260–272, 433
Fänge, A., 201
fantasy, 38–41, 43n
Farbstein, J., 253
Farsoun, S., 262
FCCLA, *see* Family, Career and Community Leaders of America
Feldstein, L. M., 24
feminist theory, 48–49
feng shui, 306
Fernando, N. A., 451
Ferry, L., 484
Field, A., 280
Figueiro, M., 315
film, *see* movies
Fineman, S., 130
Fink, F., 469
Fink, S., 101

Finlay, L., 417, 418, 419, 423
Fiori, K., 229
Fischer, B. E. S., 38
Fisher, C., 384
Fisher, C. D., 131
Fisher, D., 22–23
Fitzsimmons, S. J., 294
Flagg, F., 226
Fleming, H., 80
Flischel, R., 395
flow, definition, 401
Flynn, C. E., 90n
Flynn, J. E., 316–317
Folds, Blobs + Boxes: Architecture in the Digital Era (exhibit, Rosa 2001), 526
Folkmann, M. N., 3, 99, 106
Follett, J., 25n
food outlets, 226, 353–354, 355–356, 361, 366–377
Foran, A., 423
Ford, H., 62
Ford, R. C., 119
Forlano, L., 370, 376
Forrester, J. W., 188
Forsyth, D. R., 407
Foucault, M., 59, 65, 66
Fountain, M., 320
fountains (water features), 293–307
framework, definition, 2
Frampton, K., 15
Francis, C., 240, 354, 358–361
Francis, M., 234
Frankham, N., 451
Franta, G., 312
Frantz, C., 399, 402–403, 404, 406, 407
Frazier, Raferty, Orr, and Fairbank, 82
Frijda, N., 130
Frisvad, J. R., 335
Fuad-Luke, A., 516
Fuchs, R., 262
functionalism, 66
furniture
  bedrooms, 36f, 37
  in historic buildings, 82–84, 85f
  kitchen cabinets and fittings, 51, 52–53, 56
  office furniture, 62–64, 67n–68n, 114
  in social spaces, 357–358, 361, 373, 427
Futurevisions, 394

Gabb, B., 48
Gadamer, H., 102

Gaddis, B., 275
Gage, F. M., 487, 493
Galle, P., 1
Galloway, L., 60
Gamez, J., 246
Ganoe, C., 71, 73, 165
Gapp, Paul, 91n
García Márquez, Gabriel, 424–426
Gardner, H., 114
Gardner, W. L., 132–133
Gatter, L. S., 61
Gemser, G., 180
gender, 48–49, 216–217, 295, 297–305
Gero, J. S., 215–216
Gibson, J., 249
Gibson, K., 4, 525, 526, 527, 529, 531, 533, 534
Giedion, S., 68n
Gifford, J. A., 316
Gifford, R., 117, 316
Gilmore, J. H., 100
Gilmore, T., 467
Gioia, D. A., 132
Giorgi, A., 252
Gisin, B., 316
Gitlin, L. N., 201
Glaser, B. G., 156, 488
Glasser, W., 327
Glăveanu, V. P., 273
Glenn, P., 182
Glerup, H., 318
Glover, T. D., 354
Goffman, E., 297
Goldbard, A., 517
Goldberg, D., 509
Goldberger, N. R., 467
Goldblatt, H., 318
Goldsmith, J., 5
Goodman, J., 72–73, 76, 89n
Google, 114–115
Gooty, J., 130
Gordon, B., 48
Gordon, G., 337
Gosling, E., 404
Graabæk, H., 109
Gracia, E., 351, 354
Graham, C., 406
Graham, S., 376
granny flats, definition, 328
graphic design, 454–457
Graumann, C. F., 418

Graves, A., 228
Graw, P., 316
Green Architecture Research Center (Xi'an), 18–19
Green, D., 182
Green, H., 74
Greene, J. C., 135
Greening, T., 251
Greeno, J. G., 249
Griffith, J., 130
Grimmer, A., 384
Groat, L., 13, 25n, 253
grounded theory, 156, 488
Grown Up Digital (Tapscott), 534
Grusky, D. B., 149
Gryskiewicz, S., 120
Guardia, J., 351
Guba, E. G., 175, 466
Guerin, D. A., 189, 193, 446, 447, 448
Guest, R. C., 288
Gulwadi, G. B., 354
Gupta, A., 130
Gupta, N., 354, 369
Gustafson, P., 351
Gutkowski, J. M., 316
Guzowski, M., 313

Haar, S., 90n
HABS, *see* Historic American Building Survey
Hackos, J. T., 334
Hadley, A., 30
Haley, W., 228
Hall, C., 251, 252
Hall of Fame Award, 179–180
Hall, W. B., 288
Hallett, M., 335
Hampton, K. N., 354
Hanisch, C., 48
Hanne, R., 351
happiness, 19, 38–41, 195, 199, 203, 208n, 248–249
Harbinson, D., 80, 81
Hargreaves, J. A., 332
Harpe, B. de la, *see* de la Harpe, B.
Harries, K., 484
Harrington, A., 482, 484
Harris, B., 335
Harris, C., 354
Harrison-Halstead neighborhood (Chicago), 74–89, 90n–91n
Hart, C. W. M., 319

Harter, J. K., 133
Hartkopf, V., 314
Hartley, M., 517
Harwood, B., 479
Hasirci, D., 275
Hatcher, J. A., 517
Hathaway, W. E., 315, 318, 332
Hausa culture, 435, 438t, 439t
Hausdorff, J. M., 336
Hausman, A., 529
Havenhand, L., 48, 49
Havens, C., 79
Hawver, T., 133
Hayes, C. E., 318
Hayles, Katherine N., 367
Head, M., 116
Healey, M., 457
health
    aging, 6, 218–219, 228–230, 327–344
    and daylight, 5–6, 310–321
    mental health, 228–230, 315–316
    mobility issues, 148, 218–219
    office workers, 64
    sensory impairments, 218, 327–344
hearing impairment, 218
heating systems, 219
Hedge, A., 313
Heerwagen, D. R., 311, 314
Heerwagen, J. H., 311, 314
Hegel, G. W. F., 16, 26n
Heidegger, M., 12–13, 15–16, 25n, 367, 418,
    419–420
Hein, K., 320
Hennessey, B. A., 128, 400, 401
Henriksen, J., 108–110
Henry Street Settlement (New York City), 74,
    75, 89n, 90n
heritage, *see* historic buildings
Herman, J., 188, 208n
hermeneutics, 101–103
Heron, J., 467
Herrero, J., 351, 354
Herrmann, N., 116
Heschong, L., 320
Hess, P. A., 188
Heumann, L. F., 186, 198, 199
Heylighen, A., 166
Hierarchy of Needs, 233, 252
Hierarchy of Purpose Model (HOP), 189,
    190f, 195–199, 204–205t
higher education extension programs, 50–56

Hildebrandt, H. P., 480
Hill, G., 67n
Hill, J. L., 351, 362
Hill, R., 485
Hillier, B., 181, 183, 184, 481
Himsel, A. J., 275
Hinds, J., 406
Hislop, D., 366, 369
Historic American Building Survey (HABS),
    386
historic buildings, 5, 70–89, 382–391,
    393–410
    legal status of, 73–74, 78–89
history, methodology, 72–73
Hitch, D., 150, 151
Hofland, B. F., 194, 198
Hogge, J. H., 350
Hohlbein, J., 25n
Hokanson, B., 274
Holden, K., 470
Holden, P., 384
Holick, M. F., 318, 319
Holl, S., 14
Holmes, C. A., 263
Holtzblatt, K., 472
homeless, 247, 252, 253–257
Honey, P. L., 246, 516
Höpfl, H., 143
Horan, T., 423
Hörisch, J., 102
Hornbrook, M. C., 336
Horrigan, J., 529
Hosey, L., 246
House, Form, and Culture (Rapoport),
    152–153
housing, sustainable designs for, 390–391
Howlett, O., 310–311, 320
Huber, M. T., 448, 457, 459
Hughes, Thomas Parke, 59, 60
Huitt, W., 253
Hull House Settlement (Chicago), 74–89,
    90n–91n
Hull, R., 435
Hull, R. B., 319
Human Ecology Model (HEM), 189–193,
    196–197t, 204–205t, 207n
humanistic psychology, 251–253
Hume, D., 484, 490
Humphrey, R. H., 133
Hunt, M., 229, 230
Hunter, C., 310–311, 320

Hussenot, A., 132
Husserl, E., 12, 98, 418
Hutchings, P., 448, 449, 457, 459
Hutter, C. D., 318

I-House, 390
IDEC, *see* Interior Design Educators Council
identity, 5, 37–38, 154, 260–272, 432–444
    corporate identity, 114
    and gender, 48–49
IDEO, 113
IES, *see* Illuminating Engineering Society
IFI, *see* International Federation of Interior
        Architects/Designers
Igbo culture, 435, 438t, 439t
Ihrke, M., 335
Illuminating Engineering Society (IES),
        320–321
Image of the City, The (Lynch), 519, 529, 530
Imel, S., 213
independent living, 227, 235–244, 327–343
Industries of the Blind (IOB), 520–521
inquiry-based learning, 508
intelligent buildings, 23, 26n
interdisciplinarity, 249, 479
interior design, 482
    awards, 171, 179–181, 503–504
    community engagement projects, 516–522
    computer-aided design (CAD), 22–23,
        26n, 524–536
    and cultural values, 5, 15–21, 29–42, 43n,
        150–151, 260–272, 273–289, 293–307,
        362, 432–444, 516–522
    definition, 480–481
    design press, 175–177
    grassroots design, 50–56
    in historic buildings, 383–391, 393–410
    history of, 11–24, 29–42, 43n, 46–56,
        58–69, 262
    interdisciplinarity, 249, 251–253, 479,
        482
    key terms, 2–3, 343–344, 408–410, 454
    practice-based research, 181–184
    regional styles, 15–17
    scholarship of teaching and learning,
        446–461
    teaching methods, *see* education
    theory–practice relationship, 1–2, 13–24,
        46–56, 97–110, 171–184, 212–223,
        242–244, 246–258, 405–407, 417–428,
        432–436, 447–449, 459–460, 478–493

universal design principles, 150–151,
        164–168, 221–222, 228, 286–288,
        434–435, 482
    use of color, 100–101, 104–108, 121,
        337–338, 339, 341–342
    see also design process
Interior Design Educators Council (IDEC),
        502, 511–512
Interior Design Magazine, 175–177,
        179–180
Interior Ecosystem Model, 193, 196–197t,
        204–205t
Interiors Handbook for Historic Buildings
        (Fisher et al.), 383–384
International Federation of Interior
        Architects/Designers (IFI), 512
Internet cafes, *see* wireless coffee shops
interviews, 120–121, 155, 279, 284–285,
        333–334, 372, 487, 488
*Introduction to Maurice Merleau-Ponty's
        Phenomenology of Perception*, 14
Ishikawa, S., 151, 254
Italian culture, 17–18
Ito, M., 369
Iwarsson, S., 201

Jacobs, J., 348
Janda, K., 26n
Jandl, W. H., 385, 397
Jang, S., 228
Jang, Y., 228
Jani, V., 432, 444
Janowitz, M., 350
Janz, B., 420
Japan, 150
Jarmusch, A., 328
Jarrett, C., 347
Jeanneret, C.-É. (Le Corbusier), 66
Jette, A. M., 188
Jochum, A., 316
Johansson, U., 182
John Muir College, 398
Johnson, P.-A., 489
Johnston, R., 253
Johnston, R. D., 37
Jones, F., 14
Joplin, A., 6
Jordan, C. M., 517
Jørgensen, M. B., 106
Junco, R., 534
Jung, J. W., 526, 532, 533

Jung, S., 273
Jungnickel, P. W., 517

K-12 education, 497–513
Kahn, P. H., Jr., 297
Kakihara, M., 376–377
Kampman, E., 319
Kanski, J. J., 331
Kant, I., 16, 484–485, 490
Kantrowitz, M., 253
Kaplan, R., 232
Kaplan, S., 232
Kardon, R. H., 331
Karlsson, J., 220
Karlsson, L., 220
Kasard, J., 350
Kasof, J., 275
Kaufman, J. C., 274, 276
Kaufman, N., 74, 76
Kauppinen, M., 220, 221
Kawachi, I., 229
Kawasaki, A., 331
Kecskes, K., 517
Keen, J., 19–20
Keep, J. P., 314
Kehayia, E., 472
Keller, K., 531
Kendall, L., 368
Kern, H., 315–316
Kerr's Department Store (Oklahoma City),
    39–41
Kesteren, I. E. H. van, *see* Van Kesteren,
    I. E. H.
Khari, M., 220
Khazian, A. M., 405
Kierkegaard, S., 252
Kim, K. H., 274
Kim, S., 227
Kinayoglu, G., 26n
Kinsella, K., 187, 188
Kirkham, P., 48
kitchens, 17–18, 51, 52–53, 56
Klassen, F., 447, 451
Kleusner, G., 182
Knecht, B., 166
knowledge, *see* epistemology
Knox, S., 472
Kobnithikulwong, S., 2
Koetter, F., 68n
Kolding School of Design, 101
Kolmos, A., 469

Koncelik, J. A., 187, 207n
Koon, S. G., 64
Kopec, D., 6, 329, 331
Korean culture, 293–294
Krantz, J., 467
Krauchi, K., 316
Krause, N., 230
Kreitler, S., 286
Kroelinger, M., 5–6, 311, 312
Krogh, L., 469
Kucho, J., 446
Kuh, George D., 517
Kujala, S., 220
Kumar, N., 220
Kupritz, V. W., 349
Kushigan, H., 532
Kvale, S., 155
Kvan, T., 451
Kyndrup, M., 100

Lagueux, M., 481
Laing, P., 318
land, and identity, 262, 266–267, 271
land-grant universities, extension programs,
    50–56
Landorf, C., 186
Lang, F. R., 199, 201–203, 208n
Lang, J., 241, 482
LaPlante, M. P., 152
Larkin, H., 150
Lauer, Q., 12
Lawrence, D., 261
Lawrence, M., 333
Lawrence, T. B., 132
Lawson, B., 212, 273, 446
Lawson, K., 354
Lawton, M. P., 187, 199–201, 203, 228
Le Corbusier, 66
Leach, W., 39, 41
leadership styles, 128–145
learned helplessness, 335–336
    definition, 327
learning environments, 372, 375
Learning from Las Vegas (Venturi and
    Brown), 487
learning outcomes, 473–474, 481
learning theories, 508–509
Lee, H., 228
Lee, J., 227, 276
Lee, R. T., 131
Lee, S., 228, 276

Lee, V. S., 508
Leffingwell, W. H., 60, 61, 62, 64
legal studies, methodology, 71–72
Legge, G., 333
legislation
    accessibility, 150, 165–167, 329
    education, 498–500, 501
    historic buildings, 73–74, 78–89, 91n,
        386–387, 389, 394–395, 399
Lehtola, L., 220, 221
Leonard-Barton, D., 141, 142
Leonard, D., 116
Levins, K. E., 275
Lewis, A., 30
Lewy, A., 315–316
Liberman, J., 315, 318
Libeskind, D., 21
Lichtman, S., 405
Lidwell, W., 470
Lieblich, A., 135
lifeworld, definition, 419–420
    see also being-in-the-world
lighting, 5–6, 14, 83, 84, 85f, 219, 310–321,
        330, 331, 332–333, 335–336, 337, 339,
        341–342, 357, 358, 361, 532
Liikkanen, L. A., 215, 222
Likert scales, 279
Lin, G. F., 2, 295, 305
Lin, Y. F., 2
Lincoln, Y. S., 175, 466
Lindridge, A. M., 529
Lindzey, G., 251, 252
Linstead, S., 143
Litwak, E., 186
Liu, Y. C., 215
Living Lab (research project), 465–475
Llewellyn, Mark, 76
Locke, J., 12
Lockheed, 319–320
Loftness, V., 314
Longino, C. F., 186
Longstreth, R., 400
Lorber, J., 297–298
Loversidge, R., Jr., 398
Low, D. R., 274
low-income housing, 247–248
Low, S., 348, 351
Low, S. M., 261
Lu, D., 486
Lucas, P., 2, 519
Luckmann, T., 469

Luggen, A. S., 188
Lund, H., 362
Lundén, O., 297
Luthans, F., 132
Lynch, K., 156, 157–158, 519, 529, 530
Lynn, G., 22

Mabley, J., 79
Macarthur, J., 487
Mackinnon, D., 115
MacKinnon, D. W., 288
MacNeill, R., 228
macular degeneration, 328–343
Mahdavi, A., 26n
Mahdjoubi, D., 181, 183
Maitlis, S., 132
Major, C. H., 469, 470
Malnar, J. M., 398, 423
Malpas, J. E., 420
management theory, and workplace design,
        58–67, 68n
Manen, M. van, *see* van Manen, M.
Maniccia, D., 314
Manzo, L., 263, 420
Marchand, R., 42n
Marcus, C. C., *see* Cooper Marcus, C.
Margolin, V., 474
Marian, K., 176, 179–180
marketing, 32–34, 39–41
Márquez, Gabriel García, *see* García Márquez,
        Gabriel
Marsden, J., 232, 234, 240–241
Marsden, J. P., 448
Marsh, M., 425
Marshall-Baker, A., 446, 450
Martin, C. S., 446
Martinez, M. L., 351
Martyniuk, O., 316
Marvin, S., 376
Maslow, A., 233, 252, 253–254
Mastrodicasa, J., 534
Mathematics of the Ideal Villa, The (Rowe),
        68n
Mauborgne, R., 122
May, D., 132
Mayer, F. S., 399, 402, 404
Mayo, E., 319
Mazrui, A., 434
McCann, R., 423
McCoy, M., 378n
McDonough, W., 24

McKinney, K., 448, 449, 457

McLaughlin, F., 119

McLeod, M., 65

McMillan, D., 348, 350, 351, 352

McNeill, T., 215–216

McQuarrie, F., 319

McTighe, J., 508

Meadows, D. H., 188–189, 190–192, 193, 195–198

meaning-making, 70–74, 81–82, 86–89, 98–110, 131–132, 149–153, 158–160, 162–164, 266, 270–271, 294, 296–297

Meaning of Water, The (Strang), 294

Means-End Theory (MET), 32–34

Medeiros, K. de, *see* de Medeiros, K.

Meek, J., 384

Mehta, B. K., 318

Meneely, J., 6, 71, 73, 115, 124

mental health, 228–230, 315–316

Merleau-Ponty, M., 14, 98, 418, 424

metaphysics, 20–21

methodology, 2–3
   action research, 467–471, 473
   autophotography, 154–156
   case studies, 74–76, 90n, 134–136, 235–239, 253–257, 436–444, 449–457, 518–522, 532–533
   cognitive mapping, 153–154, 156, 157–158, 372, 373, 375
   computer-aided design (CAD), 22–23, 26n, 524–536
   Connectedness-to-Nature scale (CNT), 402–404
   Consensual Assessment Technique (CAT), 276–280
   content analysis, 174–184
   control of variables, 235, 237, 239, 280, 295, 304–306, 320, 351, 370–371
   data analysis, 156–164, 237–239, 279–285, 301–305, 372–376
   design ethnography, 17–18, 455
   focus groups, 510–511
   grounded theory methods, 156, 488
   image preference task, 299–301
   interviews, 120–121, 155, 279, 284–285, 333–334, 372, 487, 488
   Likert scales, 279
   narrative inquiry, 5, 70–89, 90n, 134–136, 399
   person-centric design, 252–258
   practice-based research, 181–184
   quantitative methods, 120
   questionnaires, 237, 371–372, 378n
   site observation, 120–121, 295, 355–361, 468, 473, 487–488
   validity, 135–136, 156–157, 454–455

Meyer, H., 122

Michael, V., 90n

middle-class, 4, 29, 32, 34–42, 43n

Mikels, J. A., 187

Mikkelsen, K., 318

Milfont, T. L., 404

millennial generation, 533–536

Miller, A. M., 119–121, 122

Miller, G., 34

Miller, M., 328

Milne, A. J., 372

Ministry of Culture (Denmark), 106–108

Mirror Room (Kerr's Department Store), 39–41

Misselhorn, C., 108

Missonier, S., 132

Mitchell, D. R., 341

Mitchell, T. C., 479

Mitgang, L., 394, 446, 534

Mitrovic, B., 484

Moan, J., 319

mobile technology, 376–377

mobility issues, 148, 218–219

Modal Patterns for the Treatment of the Aged (MPTA), 193–199, 204–205t

modernism, 66, 486

Mokhtarian, P. L., 376

Møller, A. F., 106

Monaghan, P., 166

Montgomery, R., 248

Moody, H. R., 193–198, 203, 206

Mooney, R. L., 274

Moore, A. J., 423

Moore, C., 13, 23, 293, 294, 296, 305

Moore, E. O., 314

Moore, H. L., 150

Moore, R., 335

Moore, R. J., 354

Moores, S., 367, 423

Moran, D., 418, 419, 420

Morgan, G., 141, 143

Morgan, J., 384

morphing (digital morphing), 526–529

Morrow, W., 314

Mortimer, J., 228

movies, 38–39
Muffoletto, R., 525
Mumford, M. D., 275, 525
Murphy, C. D., 62
Murphy, S. A., 403–404
Murphy, Steve, 426
Murtagh, W., 396
museums, 520–521
Musgrove, J., 181, 183, 184
mydriasis, 335–337

NAACP, *see* National Association for the
    Advancement of Colored People
Nabet, B., 341
Nagel, E., 172, 175
Nagel, T., 249
Nahemow, L., 187, 199–201, 203
Nakamura, J., 401
Nancarrow, B. E., 294
narrative inquiry, 5, 70–89, 90n, 134–136,
    399
NASAFACS Housing and Interior Design
    Standards, 506, 507
National Alliance of Preservation
    Commissions, 400
National Association for the Advancement of
    Colored People (NAACP), 72
National Association of State Administrators
    of Family and Consumer Sciences
    (NASAFACS), 506, 507
National Career Clusters Framework, 507
National Council for Interior Design
    Qualification (NCIDQ), 393, 480, 506
National Eye Institute, 329
National Landmark Designation, 73–74, 86,
    89n, 91n, 385–386
National Park Service (NPS), 387, 394, 396,
    397, 410
National Trust for Historic Preservation
    (United States), 395, 399
Native American culture, 437, 441, 442–443t
Nayyar, K., 315
NCIDIQ, *see* National Council for Interior
    Design Qualification
NCLB, *see* No Child Left Behind Act
Nelson, L. H., 397
net zero housing, 390–391
Netsch, W., 82
New York City, 74, 75, 89n, 90n
New York State Federation of Home Bureaus
    Records, 53

Newbrough, J. R., 348
Newell, P., 163
Newell, P. B., 217
Newman, O., 241
Newstrom, J., 119
Nicolis, G., 118
Nielson Online, 529
Nieuwenhuijsen, E. R., 188, 200
Nigerian culture, 435, 436–437, 438t
Nimon, S., 369
Nisbet, E. K., 403–404
Niu, W., 275
No Child Left Behind Act (NCLB; 2001),
    499t, 500
Norberg-Schulz, C., 15–16, 25n
Noreika, J., 229
Norris-Baker, C., 199
Northwest Style, 15
Norton, C., 399, 402
Novitsky, D., 318, 332
NPS, *see* National Park Service
NTP, *see* National Trust for Historic
    Preservation
Nussbaumer, L., 510

Oakwood Village Retirement Community
    (WI), 234–243
Obama, Barack, 500
objectivity, critiques of, 71–73
Oblinger, D., 366, 368
Oblinger, J., 366, 368
O'Brien, R., 467
observational studies, 120–121, 295, 355–361,
    468, 473, 487–488
Office Management (Galloway), 60
offices, *see* workplaces
O'Hara, K., 369
Ojibwe culture, 437, 442t, 443t
Okabe, D., 369
Okura, S., 320
Oldenburg, R., 231, 234, 241, 348, 349, 350,
    353, 354, 356, 359–361, 362, 369, 378n,
    423
Olgunturk, N., 222
Oliver, C., 273
Olson, J., 4, 29, 32–33, 41
Olson, M., 423
On Architecture (Vitruvius), 482–483
One Hundred Years of Solitude (García
    Márquez), 424–426
online communities, 17, 366–377

online retailing, 529–531
  see also virtual–physical continuum
Onwueguzie, A., 253
Orthel, B. D., 4, 447
Ortner, S. B., 298
Ortony, A., 141, 143
O'Sullivan, P., 181, 183, 184
Oswald, F., 201, 203
Oswald, L. N., 199
outdoor spaces, 236, 262, 354, 358–360,
  518–520
Owen, C., 214
OWP/P Architects, 497
Oygur, I., 4, 447, 448
Ozenfant, A., 66
Ozguc, B., 213
Ozkaya, I., 220
Ozturk, M. N., 451

Pable, J., 4, 446, 450
Palestinian homes, 5, 260–272
palimpsest approach, historic restoration,
  383–391
Pallasmaa, J., 14, 423, 482
Panero, J., 465
Panton, V., 98, 104–106
Park, E., 228
Parker, S. K., 131
parlors, 83–84, 85f
Parry, D. C., 354
Parsons, C. C., 60–61
Parsons, F. A., 50
participatory design, 23, 123
Passini, R., 529
Pattern Language, A (Alexander), 151,
  428
Patterson, M., 296
Patterson, M. E., 420
Patton, M. Q., 155
Payne-Tofte, E., 447, 448
Pearce, C., 508
Pell, H. C., 40
Pennypacker, E., 451
Pequot culture, 437, 441, 442t, 443t
Percival, C. M., 51
Percival, J., 231
performance art, definition, 434
Perkins Act (2006), 501, 503
Perkins, D., 352
Perrin, J. L., 404
person-centric design, 246–258

person–environment interaction models,
  199–205, 208n, 232–233, 350–355,
  366–377, 378n, 404–408, 423–428
personal learning environments (PLEs), 372,
  375
Personality of a House, The (Post), 35
Perttula, M., 215, 222
Peter Fish Studios, 77
Peterson, J. F., 451
Peterson, L. C., 366, 370, 376
Peterson, S. J., 133
Pevsner, N., 67n
phanesthai, definition, 12
Pheasant, S., 465
phenomenology, 3, 11–24, 25n–26n, 97–110,
  367–368, 417–428, 468, 473
Phillipson, C., 198
philosophy, 12–13, 15–17, 246–253, 482,
  483–485
  see also phenomenology
physicality, definition, 367
Pierson, J., 320
Pine, B. J., 100
Pinter, R. B., 341
Pinto, C., 181
Pisano, G. P., 17
place attachment, definition, 348, 351–352
place attributes, definition, 369–370,
  377n–378n
place descriptions, 420–423
Place Matters, 399, 401
Plater-Zyberk, E., 23–24
Pleitez, M., 335
PLEs, *see* personal learning environments
Plucker, J. A., 276
Plympton, P., 320
Poetics of Space, The (Bachelard), 14
Poldma, T., 3, 446, 447, 448, 467, 468, 472,
  473, 474
politics, 6, 46–56, 106–108, 195
  and social justice, 518–520
Polkinghorne, D. E., 75
Pollack, J. M., 133
Pond & Pond, 77
Popper, K., 173, 183
popular culture, 38–41
portfolios, 273–289, 454–457
Portillo, M., 6, 70, 71, 73, 76, 90n, 116, 117,
  119, 121–122, 399, 400, 401, 405, 408,
  509–510
Post, E., 35

post-occupancy evaluation (POE), 328–343, 389

postmodernism, 486–487

Potter, J. D., 319

Potter, S., 181

Poulet, G., 201, 208n

Poutsen, R., 318

Powell, J. L., 198

power relationships, 6, 37–38, 46–56, 65–66, 87–88, 106–108, 114, 116–125, 195, 435

practice-based research, 181–184

practitioners, *see* designers

Pratt, M. G., 131–132

Preservation Brief 18 (Jandl), 383, 385–386

preservation techniques, historic buildings, 383–391, 393–410

Presier, W., 165

Pressman, A., 13

Preston, J., 479, 480, 481

Price, J., 468, 473

Prigogine, I., 118

Principles of Scientific Management, The (Taylor), 60, 68n

priority, definition, 220

privacy, 39–41, 148, 240–241, 265, 269, 374

problem-based learning, 436–444, 465–475

project-based learning, 469–475, 516–522

Pruitt Igoe (St. Louis), 247–248

public spaces, 149–153, 435, 516–522

  cafés, 226, 353–354, 355–356, 366–377

  emotional connections to, 23–24, 74–89, 118, 119–120, 122, 159–166, 226–227, 230–244, 248–249, 253–257, 293–307, 347–362

  and exclusion, 151–153, 158, 161–162, 165–168, 193–199, 228, 246–258, 465–475

  family homes, 5, 17–18, 35–38, 260–272, 433

  and gender, 295, 297–305

  lighting, 310–314, 357, 358, 361, 532

  museums, 520–521

  online retailing, 529–531

  outdoor spaces, 236, 262, 354, 358–360, 518–520

  privacy issues, 39–41, 148, 240–241, 265, 269, 374

  public interior plaza, 349

  retirement communities, 226–244

  seating arrangements, 357–358, 361, 373, 427

sense of community, 350–351

technology and Internet access, 356, 357, 360, 362, 366–377

"third places," 227, 231, 234–244, 347–362

water features, 293–307

in the workplace, 116–117

public transportation, 518–520

Puddifoot, J. E., 351

Pultar, M., 213

PUSH (agency), 119–121

Putnam, R., 23, 24, 195, 362

Putnam, R. D., 348

Quadagno, J., 230

Quality Function Deployment (QFD), 221, 222

quality of life, 160–161, 202–203, 228–230

quantitative methodology, 120

questionnaires, 237, 371–372, 378n

Quick, J. C., 131

Quick, J. D., 131

Race, P., 449

Rafaeli, A., 131–132

Ragan, J. W., 116

Ragette, F., 262

Ramirez, R., 467

Rapoport, A., 149, 152–153, 163, 261, 298

Rash, C., 335

Rasmussen, S. E., 14

Rea, M. S., 314, 315

Reason, P., 467

Rechie, N., 398

Redish, J. C., 334

regional design styles, 15–17

Regnell, B., 220

Rehabilitation Living Lab (research project), 465–475

Reisner, Y., 486

religion, *see* metaphysics

Relph, E., 367, 421–423

requests for proposals (RFPs), 177–179

Rescher, N., 258

research, definition, 1–2

restrooms, 148, 167

retirement communities, 137–138, 205–207, 226–244

Rey-Barreau, J., 509–510

Reynolds, T., 4, 29, 32–33, 41

RFPs, *see* requests for proposals

Rickey, B., 398

Riley, R. B., 348
Rios, D. A., 336
Ritschel, T., 335
Rivlin, L., 234
Roberts, L. M., 131
Robertson, E. R., 187
Robsahm, R. E., 319
Rock, M., 399, 402
Rocker, I. M., 22
Rog, D., 247
Rogers, S., 246
Rogoff, B., 367
Rohan, M. J., 130
Romagnoli, E., 318
Rosa, J., 526
Rose, G., 468
Rosenbaum, M., 230
Rosenfield, D., 335
Rosenthal, N., 315–316
Rowe, C., 68n, 486, 489
Rowe, P., 19, 446
Roy, R., 181
Rubin, H. J., 468, 473
Rubin, I. R., 468, 473
Rubinstein, R. L., 186, 200
Rudner, S. M., 479
Runco, M. A., 128–129
Russell, D., 228
Rutledge, B., 314
Ruys, T., 314
Ryan, R. L., 351
Rylander, A., 182–183

sacred spaces, 13–14, 20–21
Sadler, E., 187
sadness, 19
Safadi, S., 262, 265
Sagun, A., 216
St. Ignatius Chapel (Seattle), 14, 20–21
St. Matthew's Church (Los Angeles), 13–14
Saito, Y., 150
Salama, O., 294
Salamon, S., 351
Salny, S., 30
Saltmarsh, J., 517
Salvador, T., 17–18
Samanez-Larkin, G. R., 187
Sandberg, W. R., 116
Sandman, L., 517
Savin-Baden, M., 469, 470
Sayers, J. G., 130

Sayrafi, M., 5
Sayre, R. M., 318
Scala, F., 80, 87–88
Scarce, J., 262, 265
Scarnechia, L., 318
Schank, R., 527
Scheidt, R. J., 156, 199
schema, definition, 2–3
Schiller, D., 534
Schnetzler, N., 117
scholarship of teaching and learning,
    446–461
Schon, D., 172
Schon, D. A., 212–213, 489
School-to-Work Opportunities Act (STW;
    1994), 498, 499t
schools, 497–513
Schriver, C., 405
Schultz, P. W., 405
Schulz, H., 264, 267
Schulze, G., 100
Schulze, J. W., 60, 61, 62, 63, 64, 65, 68n
Schuster, H. G., 319
Schwartz, S., 331, 335
Schwarz, B., 2–3
Schweiger, D. M., 116
scientific method, definition, 25n
Scientific Office Management (Leffingwell), 60
Scott Brown, D., 487
Scott, G., 483, 489
Scott, G. M., 275
Scott, S., 232, 234
Scottsboro (AL), 72
Scruton, R., 26n, 103
Seamon, D., 369, 417, 418, 419, 422, 424
Seasonal Affective Disorder (SAD), 315–316
seating, 64, 357–358, 361, 373, 427
secondary education, United States, 497–513
Seel, M., 101, 102–103
Seidman, I., 90n
self-actualization, 195, 199, 203, 208n, 252,
    253–257
Sense and Place: The Perspective of Experience
    (Tuan), 14
sense of community, definition, 350–351
    see also social spaces
Sense of Purpose, A (narrative), 136–145
sensegiving, definition, 132
Serlin, I., 251
settlement houses, 70–89
Sewell, M., 155

Sezal, I., 451
Shafran, M., 276
Shapiro, L., 54
Shaw, D., 30
Shelter Project, 518–520
Shepherd, G. M., 331
Sheppard, L., 186
Sherwell, T., 263
Shirazi, M. R., 389
SHPO, *see* State Historic Preservation Office
Siekpe, J., 529
Silverstein, M., 151, 254
Simms, E. M., 426
Simon, H. A., 189, 212, 286
Simon, M., 486
Simonton, D. K., 275
Simpson, E., 335
Simpson, J. L., 143
Sims, W., 372
Sinclair, C., 246
single-pile plan type (housing), 390
Sipes, J., 525, 526
site observation, 120–121, 295, 355–361, 468, 473, 487–488
Skilton, P., 142
Skinner, J., 166
Slattery, M. L., 319
smart buildings, 23, 26n
Smith, R. K., 221
Smollan, R. K., 130
Snowdon, D., 198
Soames, K. N., 318
social capital, 23–24
social class, 4, 29–42, 43n, 50–51, 149–153
Social Construction of Reality, The (Berger and Luckmann), 469
social dynamics, definition, 433
social justice, 518–520
social networks, 23–24, 230–231, 264, 268–269
Social-Physical Places Over Time Model (SPOT), 201–205
social services, 195, 198
social spaces, 149–153, 435, 516–522
    cafés, 226, 353–354, 355–356, 366–377
    emotional connections to, 23–24, 74–89, 118, 119–120, 122, 159–166, 226–227, 230–244, 248–249, 253–257, 293–307, 347–362
    and exclusion, 151–153, 158, 161–162, 165–168, 193–199, 228, 246–258, 465–475

family homes, 5, 17–18, 35–38, 260–272, 433
    and gender, 295, 297–305
    lighting, 310–314, 357, 358, 361, 532
    museums, 520–521
    online retailing, 529–531
    outdoor spaces, 236, 262, 354, 358–360, 518–520
    privacy issues, 39–41, 148, 240–241, 265, 269, 374
    public interior plaza, 349
    retirement communities, 226–244
    seating arrangements, 357–358, 361, 373, 427
    sense of community, 350–351
    technology and Internet access, 356, 357, 360, 362, 366–377
    "third places," 227, 231, 234–244, 347–362
    water features, 293–307
    in the workplace, 116–117
Sontag, M. S., 189–193, 207n
Soukup, C., 354
South African culture, 435, 437, 438t, 439t, 440t
Space, Text, and Gender (Moore), 150
Spain, D., 469
Sparke, P., 30, 31, 39, 47, 58
Sparks, P., 406
Speaks, M., 22
Spencer, T. J., 316
Spiller, N., 526
spirit of the times, 16–17, 22
Stanger, W. A., 62
Stappers, P. J., 333
STAR event (national competition), 504
Starr, R. H., 351
State Historic Preservation Office (United States), 386–387
Stead, N., 487
Steemers, K., 332, 333
Steinbrenner, J., 100
Stellman, J. M., 340
Sternberg, E. M., 310, 321
Sternberg, R. J., 275
Stevens, J., 509
Stevens, V. J., 336
Stipe, R., 396
Stone, A., 234
Stone, P. T., 315–316
Stories of Scottsboro (Goodman), 72–73
Story, M. F., 218–219

Story, P. A., 407
Strang, Veronica, 294
Strange, J. M., 275
Strauss, A. L., 156, 488
Strauss, K., 131
Strauss, S., 116
Street, D., 230
Strobel, R. W., 314
Sturm, S., 517
STW, *see* School-to-Work Opportunities Act
subjectivity, 13–14, 250–251
Successful Social Space Attribute Model
    (SSSAM), 232–233
Suddaby, R., 488
Suger, Abbot, 21
Sugihara, S., 351, 362
sunlight, 5–6, 310–321, 332–333, 335–336
sustainability, 5–6, 24, 208n, 382–391, 395,
    435–436
    definition, 188
Suwa, M., 223
Svengren, L., 182
Swaine, B., 472
Swap, W. C., 141, 142
Swazi culture, 436, 438t, 439t
symbolism, 70–74, 81–82, 86–89, 98–110,
    131–132, 149–153, 158–160, 162–164,
    266, 270–271, 294, 296–297
Syme, G. J., 294

Tabanico, J. J., 405
Taiwanese culture, 295, 298–305
Tajfel, H., 403
Tapscott, D., 534
Tartaglia, S., 354
Tarule, J. M., 467
Tate, S., 398, 410
Taylor, F. W., 59–61, 67n, 68n
teacher training, 503
teaching methods, *see* education
Teague, M., 228
team work, 116–117, 121–122
Tenner, A. D., 314
Terkel, S., 87
Terman, J., 315
Terman, M., 315
Tetlow, K., 296
Tew, S., 509
texture, 104–110
Thai culture, 276–289
Thelin, T., 220

theory, 186–207
    context models, 189–193, 195–199,
        204t–205t, 207n
    creative ecology model, 119–125
    definition, 3
    feminist theory, 48–49
    grounded theory, 156, 488
    Hierarchy of Needs, 233, 252
    humanistic psychology, 251–253
    leadership theory, 132–134
    learning theories, 508–509
    Map of Phenomenology, 19–22
    Means-End Theory (MET), 32–34
    Modal Patterns for the Treatment of the
        Aged (MPTA), 193–199, 204t–205t
    person-centric design, 246–258
    person–environment interaction models,
        199–205, 208n, 232–233, 350–355,
        366–377, 378n, 404–408, 423–428
    third places, 227, 231, 234–244
    virtual–physical continuum, 366–377
theory–practice relationship, 1–2, 13–24,
    46–56, 97–110, 171–184, 212–223,
    242–244, 246–258, 405–407, 417–428,
    432–436, 447–449, 459–460, 478–493
    see also scholarship of teaching and
        learning
Thiis-Evensen, T., 427–428
third places, 227, 231, 234–244, 347–362
    definition, 348–349, 353–355
Thomas, M., 455
Thompson, G. W., 318, 332
Thompson, J. A. A., 447, 448
Thorncrown Chapel (AR), 14, 21
Thoutenhoofd, E., 154
Tiemann, T. K., 354
Tietgen Dormitory (Copenhagen), 108–110
Tilly and Henry Dreyfuss Associates,
    329–330
Tintner, R., 335
Tkaczyk, C., 114
Tofle, R., 378n
Tonello, G., 316
Toombs, S. K., 426
Torcellini, P., 314, 337
Toy, E. C., 335
Tracy, S. J., 143
Tretli, S., 319
Truex, Van Day, 30
Tuan, Yi-fu, 14
Tucker, L., 5

Tucker, L. M., 390, 391
Turkkan, E. E., 451
Turkle, S., 367
Turner, J. C., 403
Turpin, J. C., 3–4, 29, 31, 32, 48, 446
Tuval-Mashiach, R., 135
Tversky, B., 223
Twombly, R., 481

UbD, *see* understanding by design theory
Ulrich, R. S., 187, 203, 297, 314
Underhill, P., 530
understanding by design theory (UbD),
    508–509
Unger, D. G., 351
United States
    accessibility legislation, 150, 165–167
    community-building, 347–362
    higher education extension programs,
        50–56
    historic buildings, 74–89, 91n, 383–391,
        393–410
    K-12 education, 497–513
    values, 29–42, 43n, 50–51, 275–289, 295,
        298–305, 348, 354
universal design principles, 150–151, 164–168,
    221–222, 228, 286–288, 434–435, 482
universities
    extension programs, 50–56
    and the millennial generation, 533–536
    relationship with local communities,
        77–89, 90n–91n
    social spaces, 355–362, 370–377
University of Florida, 409–410
University of Illinois, 77–89, 90n–91n
upper-class values, 29–30
US Census Bureau, *see* Census Bureau
    (United States)
US Department of Education, *see* Department
    of Education (United States)
US State Historic Preservation Office (SHPO),
    see State Historic Preservation Office
    (United States)
User Analysis Questionnaire, 372, 378n

Vaikla-Poldma, T., 469
Valens Senior Living, 136–145
Valente, J., 247
Valera, S., 351
validity, research methods, 135–136,
    156–157, 454–455

Value Oriented Prioritization process, 221
values
    consumer values, 32–34, 37–38
    corporate identity, 114, 128–145
    cross-cultural studies, 273–289, 293–307,
        432–444
    and cultural identity, 5, 260–272, 432–444
    and emotional connection, 23, 87–88,
        128–145, 162–164, 347–362
    person-centric design, 246–258
    power relationships, 6, 37–38, 46–56,
        65–66, 106–108, 114, 116–125
    settlement houses, 70–89
    social class, 4, 29–42, 43n, 50–51
    treatment of the aged, 193–199
van Bommel, W. J. M., 314
van den Beld, G. J., 314
Van Deventer, J. H., 62
Van Kesteren, I. E. H., 333
van Manen, M., 417, 419
Van Meel, J., 113, 114
Van Rensselaer, M., 51–52
variables, control of, 235, 237, 239, 280, 295,
    304–306, 320, 351, 370–371
Varney, C., 30, 32, 42n
Vaux, D., 3
Veitch, J. A., 310, 315, 316
Veitch, R., 234
Velkoff, V. A., 186, 187, 188
Venturi, R., 487
Verbeek, P., 98–99
Verbrugge, L. M., 188
Verderber, R., 314
Verganti, R., 17
versioning, 22, 26n
    see also computer-aided design (CAD)
Vial, Stéphane, 99
Victoria and Albert Museum, 535
Vilnai-Yavetz, I., 131
Vincent, G. K., 186
Vinz, R., 467
virtual–physical continuum, 366–377,
    530–531
    see also online retailing
virtuality, definition, 367, 377n
Vischer, J., 447
Visiona II (exhibition project, 1970), 104–106
Visser, Willemien, 212
visual art, definition, 434
visual impairment, 218, 327–344, 520–521
Vitruvius, 482–483

Vodvarka, F., 398, 423
voice-situated studio learning, 472–473
Vorkinn, M., 351
Vos, P., 113, 114
Vredevoogd, J. D., 451

Wagner, S., 19
Wahl, H.-W., 199, 201–203, 208n
Wakeford, K., 516
Walsh, V., 181
Walumbwa, F., 132–133
Wandersman, A., 350, 351
Wang, D., 3, 13, 19, 20, 25n, 253
Wang, N., 319
Wang, S., 529
Wartenberg, T. E., 482
Watchorn, V., 150
water features, 293–307
Waxman, L., 350, 353–354, 362, 513
wayfinding cues, 532–533
Wazen, J. J., 341
Weaver, C. D., 480
Wedner, D., 328
Wehr, T., 315–316
Weigand, J., 479
Weimer, M., 448, 449, 457, 458
Weis, H. M., 131
Weisman, G., 366, 369, 376, 377n
Weisman, L. K., 149, 151, 298, 306
welfare services, 195, 198
Welsh Government Historic Environment
    Service (Cadw), 384
Wencel, E., 421
Werner, C. M., 352
Wernsing, T. S., 133
West African culture, 433, 435, 438t, 439t,
    440t
West, C., 298
Westwood, R., 274
Wharton, E., 34
What Things Do (Verbeek), 98–99
Wheatley, M. J., 128, 142
Wheeler, J., *see* Dow, J. Wheeler
White, A. C., 446
Whitehead, M., 187
Whitmarsh, L., 406
Whittaker, S., 366
WHO, *see* World Health Organization
Whyte, J. K., 187
Whyte, W., 227, 236, 237, 240, 354, 358–361
Wiegers, K., 220–221

Wiggins, G., 508
Wijnberg, N. M., 180
Williams, D., 508
Williams, D. R., 420
Williams, J., 398
Williams, J. H., 404
Williams, M., 508
Wilson, S. M., 366, 370, 376
Windley, P. G., 156
Wingfield, D. J., 336
Winslow, G., 534
wireless coffee shops, 366–377
Wirz-Justice, A., 316
Wixon, D., 472
Wohlin, C., 220
Wohlwill, J. F., 261
Wolcott, H. F., 135
Wolfe, Elsie de, *see* De Wolfe, Elsie
Wolfflin, H., 16–17
women
    design preferences, 48–49, 216–217, 295,
        297–305
    as designers, 29–42, 43n, 48, 50–56
Wong, L. A., 517
Wood, G., 72
Wooley, E. M., 63
Wooton Desk, 67n
workplaces
    and corporate culture, 114, 118, 119–120,
        121–122, 128–145
    creativity, 6, 112–125, 128–129, 142,
        273–289
    emotional connections to, 118, 119–120,
        122, 128–145
    lighting, 312–313, 314, 319–320
    office furniture, 62–64, 67n–68n, 114
    and power relationships, 65–66, 106–108
    symbolic artifacts, 134–145
    Taylorization of, 6–7, 58–69
    team work, 116–117, 121–122
World 3 knowledge, 173, 183
World Health Organization (WHO), 188, 228
Would-Be Worlds (Casti), 527
Wright, L., 327
Wright, R. L., 320
Wright, T. A., 131
Wurtman, R. J., 318
Wyatt, J. K., 315

Yahner, T., 451
Yang, B.-E., 293–294

yaodong (cave dwellings), 18–19
Ybor City (CA), 399
Yoon, P., 25n
Yoruba culture, 435, 436–437, 438t, 439t, 440t
Yukl, G. A., 133, 134, 142
Yunyan, J., 451

Zaff, J., 349, 351
Zeisel, J., 154
zeitgeist (spirit of the times), 16–17, 22

Zelenski, J. M., 403–404
Zelnik, M., 465
Zhu, Y., 448
Zilber, T., 135
Ziller, R. C., 154
Zimmerman, D., 298
Zlotkowski, E., 517
Zulu culture, 435, 437, 438t, 439t, 440t
Zumthor, P., 382
Zwerman, W., 319

CPSIA information can be obtained
at www.ICGtesting.com
Printed in the USA
BVHW012059160919
558587BV00025B/121/P